Supporting Personalized Learning and Students' Skill Development With AI

Mohamed Khaldi
ENS, University Abdelmalek Essaadi, Morocco

IGI Global
Scientific Publishing
Publishing Tomorrow's Research Today

Vice President of Editorial	Melissa Wagner
Managing Editor of Acquisitions	Mikaela Felty
Managing Editor of Book Development	Jocelynn Hessler
Production Manager	Mike Brehm
Cover Design	Phillip Shickler

Published in the United States of America by
IGI Global Scientific Publishing
701 East Chocolate Avenue
Hershey, PA, 17033, USA
Tel: 717-533-8845
Fax: 717-533-8661
Website: https://www.igi-global.com E-mail: cust@igi-global.com

Library of Congress Cataloging-in-Publication Data

Names: Khaldi, Mohamed, 1959- editor.
Title: Supporting students' AI skills development / edited by Mohamed Khaldi.
Other titles: Supporting personalized learning and students' skill development with AI
Description: Hershey, PA : IGI Global Scientific Publishing, [2025] | Includes bibliographical references and index. | Summary: "This book establishes a theoretical framework for teaching AI, identifies best pedagogical practices, and promotes the integration of AI in disciplines, especially non-technical ones"-- Provided by publisher.
Identifiers: LCCN 2024055426 (print) | LCCN 2024055427 (ebook) | ISBN 9798369389652 (hardcover) | ISBN 9798369389669 (paperback) | ISBN 9798369389676 (ebook)
Subjects: LCSH: Artificial intelligence--Educational applictions. | Artificial intelligence--Study and teaching.
Classification: LCC LB1028.43 .S866 2025 (print) | LCC LB1028.43 (ebook) | DDC 006.3071--dc23/eng/20250120
LC record available at https://lccn.loc.gov/2024055426
LC ebook record available at https://lccn.loc.gov/2024055427

British Cataloguing in Publication Data
A Cataloguing in Publication record for this book is available from the British Library.

Editorial Advisory Board

Editorial Advisory Board

Shagun Thakur, *Chitkara University School of Engineering and Technology, Chitkara University, India*
Ajay N. Upadhyaya, *Department of Computer Engineering at SAL Engineering & Technical Institute, SAL Education, Ahmedabad, India*
Gabriel Neepo Uunona, *University of South Africa, South Africa*
Chaimae Waladi, *Higher Normal School of Tetouan, Abdelmalek Essaadi University, Morocco*
Kawtar Zargane, *Higher Normal School of Tetouan, Abdelmalek Essaadi University, Morocco*

Table of Contents

Detailed Table of Contents

Artificial intelligence (AI) has become a key component in educational pathways especially in computer science, requiring teaching methods to be adapted to support students in the progressive acquisition of skills, from the basics of algorithms to advanced AI technologies. This chapter explores how to design structured educational pathways, starting from the foundations in programming and algorithms, then introducing more complex AI concepts such as machine learning and deep learning. It highlights pedagogical strategies based on project-based learning, interactive simulations, and the integration of practical examples that encourage innovation and skills development. The chapter also proposes techniques for assessing the acquisition of skills and addresses the ethical issues associated with AI, in order to train students capable of meeting tomorrow's technological and societal challenges. This approach aims to meet the growing demand for qualified professionals in this field, while integrating flexible learning methods that can be adapted to a variety of pedagogical contexts.

This chapter explores the transformative impact of artificial intelligence (AI) in shaping adaptive, personalized learning experiences that cater to students' unique needs. By employing AI-driven platforms, educators can create learning pathways that dynamically align with students' strengths, interests, and preferences. The benefits are substantial, as AI enhances engagement, motivation, and achievement by adjusting content in real-time to match individual learning styles. Alongside these advantages, the chapter addresses critical challenges such as safeguarding data privacy, mitigating algorithmic bias, and ensuring inclusivity across diverse learner backgrounds. Ultimately, this chapter underscores AI's potential to redefine education, while emphasizing the ethical considerations crucial for its equitable and responsible integration into classrooms.

The adaptation of pedagogical object to learning styles has become crucial for maximizing the effectiveness of e-learning environments. Learners have unique preferences and ways of assimilating knowledge, making it necessary to personalize learning paths to accommodate this diversity. Learning style models provide a theoretical framework to understand these differences and develop tailored pedagogical strategies. This chapter explores how recommendation systems can be used to align pedagogical object with learner profiles. By utilizing advanced algorithms such as K-means clustering, these systems analyze learner interactions and preferences to suggest personalization pedagogical object. This approach aims to create more engaging and effective learning environments that can meet the specific needs of each learner.

This chapter explores innovative pedagogical methods in teaching artificial intelligence (AI), highlighting their impact on the development of learners' skills. In a context where it is crucial to adopt pedagogical approaches that meet students' expectations, our work consists in analyzing these methods and evaluating their effect on academic results through a case study. The chapter is structured in several sections. We will start with a presentation of innovative methods, namely project-based learning, collaborative learning, and the use of educational technologies. Then, we will provide practical recommendations to teachers, accompanied by concrete examples, to help them implement these methods in their teaching. Finally, the authors aim to provide tools for educators to improve teaching and prepare students to become competent in the field of AI. We will also address key concerns such as the need for constant updating of pedagogical approaches, the diversity of learning styles, and the thoughtful integration of educational technologies.

This chapter explores the impact of different pedagogical approaches on students' learning in artificial intelligence. The main objective is to compare the effects of these methods: direct, explicit with guided discovery and experiential according to Kolb, in order to optimize the development of students' skills. To do this, an experimental study was conducted with 144 university students, who responded to pre-tests and post-tests for an assessment before and after the intervention. The results of the ANOVA and the Tukey post-hoc test, made it possible to evaluate academic performance in a comparative manner, the analysis revealed a significant effect of the type of learning on the results. In this context, this chapter highlights the effectiveness of the pedagogical approaches and underlines the need for future studies to further explore these methods and improve the students' learning experience. Finally, the authors proposed practical recommendations to improve AI teaching and increase student engagement, while preparing them to meet the challenges of an ever-changing education.

This chapter explores how artificial intelligence (AI) is revolutionizing the personalization of learning in modern educational environments. It examines the different approaches and technologies that enable educational content to be adapted to the specific needs of each learner, taking into account their preferences, abilities and learning styles. AI offers unprecedented possibilities for analyzing learning data, generating individual profiles and proposing personalized educational pathways. This chapter highlights the challenges and opportunities associated with integrating AI into pedagogical processes, discussing its implications for improving learner engagement and teaching effectiveness. Future perspectives are also addressed, with a focus on continued innovation and the potential impact of these technologies on the evolution of adaptive e-Learning.

This chapter examines the integration of artificial intelligence (AI) in Moroccan higher education, focusing on students in the humanities. It addresses the challenges and opportunities related to using AI tools for learning, raising questions about the technical and ethical skills required to effectively leverage these technologies. The central issue lies in students' ability to use these tools autonomously and adapt their learning to their specific needs while adhering to associated ethical standards. Through a quantitative methodology, the chapter explores various aspects such as students' familiarity with AI tools, their ability to interact with these technologies, and their understanding of the ethical issues involved.

Student skill assessment is a critical component of educational development, particularly in enhancing oral presentation abilities. This study explores the application of Natural Language Processing (NLP) techniques, including sentiment analysis, text classification, and topic modeling, to evaluate and improve student presentation skills based on survey responses. The dataset consists of survey responses from engineering and humanities students, addressing various aspects of their oral presentation skills such as fluency, pronunciation, and the use of vocal fillers. Sentiment analysis using models like VADER and BERT provides insights into students' emotional engagement, while text classification models, including Support Vector Machines (SVM), categorize responses into different skill areas. Additionally, Latent Dirichlet Allocation (LDA) is used to uncover common themes in the responses, allowing for the identification of key challenges students face in their presentations.

Preface

INTRODUCTION

Developing skills in artificial intelligence (AI) has become a major issue at the heart of the international educational landscape. In the era of digital transformation, where intelligent technologies permeate all aspects of society, it is essential to train individuals in the design and application of these technologies. Students aspiring to become engineers, researchers or enlightened actors in the field of AI must acquire a set of technical, ethical and contextual skills. These skills will not only enable them to meet the challenges inherent in AI, but also to exploit its potential in a responsible and beneficial manner for humanity.

Faced with this growing demand for integrating AI into educational programs, it is crucial to explore methods to facilitate the development of these skills. This book is precisely part of this approach. While technological innovations, such as adaptive systems and digital platforms, offer considerable potential to transform the education sector, it is imperative to adapt teaching and learning practices in order to take full advantage of these new technologies. The challenge is not only to integrate tools, but to rethink pedagogy.

Indeed, AI is not limited to a simple technical field of study. It also has a deep social, political and philosophical dimension. Therefore, teaching AI must imperatively integrate the acquisition of general and transversal knowledge. A holistic approach is essential, involving critical thinking, interdisciplinary collaboration and a global understanding of the social implications of this technology. The aim is to train enlightened citizens, capable of understanding the complex issues related to AI.

In this context of a growing demand for qualified AI professionals, it is essential to teach students not only how to use these technologies, but also and above all how to become wise architects and responsible managers. This educational objective is at the heart of this book. It aims to contribute to the training of a new generation capable of mastering AI while ensuring that it has a positive and lasting impact on humanity. It is about training actors capable of designing AI for the common good.

PLACE OF THE SUBJECT IN THE CURRENT WORLD

Artificial intelligence (AI) is at the heart of a profound transformation affecting technology, the economy and society on a global scale. By automating processes, analyzing massive volumes of data and proposing intelligent solutions, AI is revolutionizing key sectors such as healthcare, finance, education, transportation and manufacturing. This widespread presence makes the development of AI skills a priority for governments, businesses and educational institutions.

Considered a key driver of the Fourth Industrial Revolution, AI offers considerable economic potential. However, realizing this potential depends on the existence of a skilled and adaptable workforce. The current shortage of AI skills highlights the urgent need for reform of education systems. Beyond its economic applications, AI also plays a crucial role in solving pressing global problems. It contributes to combating climate change through predictive models, improving healthcare through assisted diagnostic systems and personalized treatments, and ensuring food security through the optimization of agricultural practices. To maximize these benefits, it is essential to train experts who can design ethical, inclusive, and context-specific solutions.

However, the integration of AI into educational curricula remains limited and fragmented. The OECD (Organization for Economic Co-operation and Development) highlights the importance of multidisciplinary education, going beyond technical skills to encompass essential aspects such as ethics, critical thinking and interdisciplinary collaboration. Various initiatives, such as STEM (Science, Technology, Engineering, Mathematics) programmers, online hybrid learning and adaptive platforms, aim to democratize access to these skills. At the same time, the rise of AI raises fundamental ethical questions, particularly in terms of fairness, transparency and inclusion. AI systems can indeed reproduce or even amplify existing biases. It is therefore crucial to ensure rigorous training of future practitioners to ensure that these technologies respect the principles of fairness and social justice.

In conclusion, artificial intelligence, as a driving force for global change, is redefining the educational and professional goals of the 21st century. Developing AI skills not only meets the growing needs of the labor market; it is also a crucial step towards building a society where this technology is used responsibly, fairly, and for the benefit of all. AI is no longer a simple technology, but a major player in the transformation of our societies, placing its teaching and mastery at the heart of contemporary educational and technological challenges.

THEMATIC COVERAGE

This book offers an in-depth and structured analysis of the evolution of artificial intelligence (AI) skills, addressing current educational and societal challenges and exploring the opportunities offered by this technology. Its multidimensional approach sets it apart from a simple technical manual, offering a strategic and pedagogical reflection on the integration of AI in educational systems.

The book is structured around several complementary axes. It begins with an introduction and a general context that lay the foundations by exploring the impact of AI in various fields. This introduction is followed by an analysis of learning theories and their interaction with AI, thus providing a solid conceptual framework. The acquisition of AI skills, whether technical (programming, machine learning) or transversal (problem solving, critical thinking), is then presented as a priority to prepare learners for the demands of the contemporary world.

Significant studies are devoted to AI-based educational tools and technologies. Adaptive learning systems, interactive platforms and immersive technologies are studied as key elements for the modernization of education. Pedagogical methodologies for teaching AI then explore ways to effectively integrate these tools into educational practices. This practical part is enriched by an analysis of case studies and good practices, highlighting successful initiatives and reproducible models.

However, the adoption of these innovations cannot ignore ethical and inclusive issues. Specific proposals therefore address the fight against algorithmic bias and the guarantee of equitable access to education for all. Finally, the book looks to the future by exploring future perspectives, whether new pedagogical approaches, emerging technologies or educational policies adapted to a world increasingly influenced by AI.

With its balance of theory, practice, and foresight, this book appeals to a broad audience, including students, educators, policy makers, and researchers. It offers a comprehensive and nuanced view of the challenges and opportunities associated with integrating AI into education.

TARGET AUDIENCE

Artificial Intelligence (AI) skills development today concerns a wide range of groups, each with specific needs and expectations. Recognizing this diversity, we have designed this book for a diverse audience, which we can group into the following categories:

1. Education and training stakeholders:

- Computer science, engineering and data science students: This audience needs a deep understanding of fundamental concepts, tools and techniques related to AI to design and implement intelligent solutions;
- Students in social sciences, economics or health: These learners, using AI as a tool in the service of their respective disciplines, need an understanding of the specific applications and ethical implications of this technology;
- Teachers in secondary and higher education establishments: This group needs suitable educational resources to effectively integrate AI teaching into their courses and to support their students;
- Educational program designers: These professionals must understand how to structure relevant curricula, including both the theoretical foundations and practical applications of AI;
- Researchers in education and cognitive sciences: This book provides them with theoretical frameworks and empirical studies to analyze and understand how AI can transform learning methods and cognitive processes.

2. Institutional and political actors:

- School and university administrators: This group is involved in the practical implementation of educational programs integrating AI and in the choice of the most appropriate educational tools;
- Policy makers and governments: These actors need clear strategic guidelines to integrate AI into national education systems and to reduce inequalities in access to AI skills, thereby ensuring digital inclusion.

Artificial intelligence is no longer the preserve of a small circle of technicians and researchers. It has become an essential transversal skill at all levels of society. This book offers content adapted to each audience, ensuring a relevant balance between theory, practice and a strategic vision, in order to meet the diversity of needs in a constantly changing world.

CHAPTER DESCRIPTIONS

Chapter 1: Advanced AI Approaches in Education

Artificial Intelligence (AI) is revolutionizing education by personalizing learning experiences and enhancing students' problem-solving and reasoning skills. AI tailors content to students' interests, analyzes performance, and provides feedback, enabling adaptive learning. Core AI technologies, such as robotics and computer vision, have advanced, supporting tools like adaptive platforms, tutoring systems, chatbots, and automated writing evaluators. These tools drive the success of platforms like Duolingo, ChatGPT, and Coursera, benefiting both students and educators. AI empowers teachers by enabling creative teaching methods and diverse learning experiences, improving outcomes. With responsible implementation, AI will make education more accessible, address learning gaps, and transform the future of learning.

Chapter 2: Curricula and Instructional Design for AI

As we stand at the threshold of an AI-driven future, the need for educational systems to adapt and prepare students for this new paradigm has never been more urgent. "Introduction to AI Curricula and Instructional Design: Preparing Students for an AI-Driven World" explores the essential components and strategies necessary for developing educational programs that equip learners with the skills and knowledge required to thrive in an AI-centric world. To effectively teach AI, educators must integrate hands-on activities, real-world problem-solving tasks, and collaborative projects that mirror the complexities and interdisciplinary nature of AI technologies. By integrating foundational AI concepts, promoting ethical considerations, fostering practical experience, and encouraging adaptability, educational programs can effectively prepare students to navigate and excel in an increasingly AI-centric future.

Chapter 3: From Algorithm to AI: Designing Educational Pathways for Students

Artificial intelligence (AI) has become a key component in educational pathways especially in computer science, requiring teaching methods to be adapted to support students in the progressive acquisition of skills, from the basics of algorithms to advanced AI technologies. This chapter explores how to design structured educational pathways, starting from the foundations in programming and algorithms, then introducing more complex AI concepts such as machine learning and deep learning. It highlights pedagogical strategies based on project-based learning, interactive simulations, and the integration of practical examples that encourage innovation and skills development. The chapter also proposes techniques for assessing the acquisition of skills and addresses the ethical issues associated with AI, in order to train students capable of meeting tomorrow's technological and societal challenges. This approach aims to meet the growing demand for qualified professionals in this field, while integrating flexible learning methods that can be adapted to a variety of pedagogical contexts.

Chapter 4: AI-Driven Personalized Learning Pathways Customizing Education for Every Student

This chapter explores the transformative impact of artificial intelligence (AI) in shaping adaptive, personalized learning experiences that cater to students' unique needs. By employing AI-driven platforms, educators can create learning pathways that dynamically align with students' strengths, interests, and preferences. The benefits are substantial, as AI enhances engagement, motivation, and achievement by adjusting content in real-time to match individual learning styles. Alongside these advantages, the chapter addresses critical challenges such as safeguarding data privacy, mitigating algorithmic bias, and ensuring inclusivity across diverse learner backgrounds. Ultimately, this chapter underscores AI's potential to redefine education, while emphasizing the ethical considerations crucial for its equitable and responsible integration into classrooms.

Chapter 5: Adapting Pedagogical Objects to Learning Styles through Recommendation Systems in E-Learning

The adaptation of pedagogical object to learning styles has become crucial for maximizing the effectiveness of e-learning environments. Learners have unique preferences and ways of assimilating knowledge, making it necessary to personalize learning paths to accommodate this diversity. Learning style models provide a theoretical framework to understand these differences and develop tailored pedagogical strategies. This chapter explores how recommendation systems can be used to align pedagogical object with learner profiles. By utilizing advanced algorithms such as K-means clustering, these systems analyze learner interactions and preferences to suggest personalization pedagogical object. This approach aims to create more engaging and effective learning environments that can meet the specific needs of each learner.

Chapter 6: Innovative Pedagogical Approaches in Artificial Intelligence Education

This chapter explores innovative pedagogical methods in teaching artificial intelligence (AI), highlighting their impact on the development of learners' skills. In a context where it is crucial to adopt pedagogical approaches that meet students' expectations, our work consists in analyzing these methods and evaluating their effect on academic results through a case study. The chapter is structured in several sections. We will start with a presentation of innovative methods, namely project-based learning, collaborative learning, and the use of educational technologies. Then, we will provide practical recommendations to teachers, accompanied by concrete examples, to help them implement these methods in their teaching. Finally, the authors aim to provide tools for educators to improve teaching and prepare students to become competent in the field of AI. We will also address key concerns such as the need for constant updating of pedagogical approaches, the diversity of learning styles, and the thoughtful integration of educational technologies.

Chapter 7: Innovative AI Teaching Methods, Comparison and Effects on Academic Results: Experimental Study with Tukey's Post-hoc Test

This chapter explores the impact of different pedagogical approaches on students' learning in artificial intelligence. The main objective is to compare the effects of these methods: direct, explicit with guided discovery and experiential according to Kolb, in order to optimize the development of students' skills. To do this, an experimental study was conducted with 144 university students, who responded to pre-tests and post-tests for an assessment before and after the intervention. The results of the ANOVA and the Tukey post-hoc test, made it possible to evaluate academic performance in a comparative manner, the analysis revealed a significant effect of the type of learning on the results. In this context, this chapter highlights the effectiveness of the pedagogical approaches and underlines the need for future studies to further explore these methods and improve the students' learning experience. Finally, the authors proposed practical recommendations to improve AI teaching and increase student engagement, while preparing them to meet the challenges of an ever-changing education.

Chapter 8: Personalized Learning through Artificial Intelligence: Innovative Approaches and Technologies

This chapter explores how artificial intelligence (AI) is revolutionizing the personalization of learning in modern educational environments. It examines the different approaches and technologies that enable educational content to be adapted to the specific needs of each learner, taking into account their preferences, abilities and learning styles. AI offers unprecedented possibilities for analyzing learning data, generating individual profiles and proposing personalized educational pathways. This chapter highlights the challenges and opportunities associated with integrating AI into pedagogical processes, discussing its implications for improving learner engagement and teaching effectiveness. Future perspectives are also addressed, with a focus on continued innovation and the potential impact of these technologies on the evolution of adaptive e-Learning.

Chapter 9: Artificial Intelligence in Higher Education: Autonomous and Personalized Learning

This chapter examines the integration of artificial intelligence (AI) in Moroccan higher education, focusing on students in the humanities. It addresses the challenges and opportunities related to using AI tools for learning, raising questions about the technical and ethical skills required to effectively leverage these technologies. The central issue lies in students' ability to use these tools autonomously and adapt their learning to their specific needs while adhering to associated ethical standards. Through a quantitative methodology, the chapter explores various aspects such as students' familiarity with AI tools, their ability to interact with these technologies, and their understanding of the ethical issues involved.

Chapter 10: Exploring AI Models for Assessing and Improving Student Skill Competence

Student skill assessment is a critical component of educational development, particularly in enhancing oral presentation abilities. This study explores the application of Natural Language Processing (NLP) techniques, including sentiment analysis, text classification, and topic modeling, to evaluate and improve student presentation skills based on survey responses. The dataset consists of survey responses from engineering and humanities students, addressing various aspects of their oral presentation skills such as fluency, pronunciation, and the use of vocal fillers. Sentiment analysis using models like VADER and BERT provides insights into students' emotional engagement, while text classification models, including Support Vector Machines (SVM), categorize responses into different skill areas. Additionally, Latent Dirichlet Allocation (LDA) is used to uncover common themes in the responses, allowing for the identification of key challenges students face in their presentations.

Chapter 11: Leveraging Ethics for Supporting Students' Artificial Intelligence Skills Development in Namibia

To provide readers with an overview of, and summarize, the content of the chapter, the purpose is stated as to establish theoretical and conceptual frameworks around Artificial Intelligence in Education (AIEd). Against the background of supporting students' AI skills development, the main focus of the chapter will be on addressing ethical and social issues with regard to AI in education. Recommended topics around e.g., curricula and instructional design for AI, as well as tools and technologies for AI education; will also be discussed.

Chapter 12: Artificial Intelligence in Educational Serious Games: Implications and Innovations

The integration of artificial intelligence (AI) into educational serious games is transforming learning and skill development by providing personalized learning paths, enhancing engagement, and delivering real-time feedback. These innovations are especially impactful in fields like healthcare, vocational training, and academia, where adaptive environments can be tailored to individual needs. However, the implementation of AI also presents challenges, such as ethical concerns, data privacy, and accessibility. This chapter explores how AI-driven technologies enhance educational serious games, focusing on their implications for revolutionizing learning experiences and shaping students' AI skills. It examines the innovations AI brings to game design and the broader impact on educational gaming, addressing both opportunities and challenges.

Chapter 13: Students' Learning Trajectory through Literary Text: Socio-Emotional and Axiological Skills

The chapter entitled: The learning trajectory of students through the literary text socio-emotional and axiological skills aims to highlight the approaches implemented in the teaching-learning process of students with learning difficulties in the French language. Our work consists of leading learners to acquire axiological skills through oral and written comprehension and production courses while strengthening their socio-emotional skills at the same time. We took a quantitative and qualitative approach through a statistical analysis to qualify the factors involved in the development of axiological and socio-emotional skills in learners. By evaluating the capacity of these students before and after the intervention; it was established that they developed both their academic performance and their axiological and socio-emotional skills. Finally, the chapter presents recommendations for stakeholders to improve student engagement and performance.

Chapter 14: The Impact of Intelligent Systems in Teaching Values Through Literary Tex

The integration of intelligent systems in the teaching of values through literature represents a significant development in the field of education. Advances in artificial intelligence (AI) today offer powerful tools for personalizing learning, by analyzing and adapting literary content to learners' needs and preferences. Our chapter intends to explore how technologies such as intelligent tutors and interactive platforms enrich the educational experience, not only by facilitating access to literary texts, but also by deepening understanding of the moral and ethical values they convey. We'll also be conducting an experiment, which we hope will yield encouraging results.

Chapter 15: Digital Literacy, Circumscription, Evolution, and Its Relationship with Artificial Intelligence and Foreign Language Teaching

The aim of this literature review is firstly to study and circumscribe the notions of literacy and digital literacy through the work carried out in relation to the latter. We will then analyze the evolution of the notion of digital literacy in proportion to the development of the digital environment, as well as the points of convergence between digital literacy and language didactics. This work discusses these points with the intention of highlighting the importance of this dynamic, versatile and cross-cutting notion in society, at school and, more specifically, in the foreign language classroom, for shaping the learner and citizen of today and tomorrow. Moreover, the relationship between digital literacy and AI is crucial, since it enhances the ability to use AI tools effectively. Therefore, the role of digital literacy will be examined concerning the good and bad uses of artificial intelligence tools.

Chapter 16: Integrating Generative Artificial Intelligence (GAI) into the Teaching-Learning of French as a Foreign Language (FLE)

Generative artificial intelligence (GAI) is transforming education, particularly in foreign language teaching, such as French. It raises questions about its impact on core linguistic skills like listening comprehension and writing. GAI tools, including chatbots and conversation simulators, offer opportunities for immersive and enriching interactions. Defining effective interaction strategies between learners and these systems is crucial to foster engagement and knowledge acquisition, while considering the diverse skill levels of learners. Integrating GAI into educational programs presents practical and ethical challenges that require careful evaluation of risks and opportunities. New methods for assessing language skills must be developed, focusing on personalized and continuous approaches. To maximize GAI's potential, close collaboration among didactic experts, teachers, and AI developers is essential to ensure its ethical and harmonious integration into education, ultimately enhancing the learning experience and adapting to the challenges of a rapidly changing world.

Chapter 17: Integrating AI Tools in Blended Language Training: Enhancing Language Skills Development in University Students

This chapter analyzes the incorporation of AI tools in blended language teaching, stressing their potential to boost language skill development among university students. it opens by describing blended learning and its significance in the educational field, particularly in the context of language learning. It evaluates existing research on AI applications in language learning, highlighting successful case studies and the benefits of tailored learning experiences. Furthermore, it tackles ethical considerations and obstacles related to AI adoption in educational contexts, such as data privacy and the role of teachers in leading AI-enhanced learning. Through a critical analysis of AI's impact on language pedagogy, this chapter aims to give educators and researchers insights into effective strategies for incorporating AI tools in blended learning environments, ultimately fostering improved language proficiency and engagement among pupils. The findings underline the significance of a balanced strategy that uses technology while keeping the important human elements of teaching and learning

Chapter 18: The Assessment of Language Skills: Tools and Methods

Language proficiency assessment is the process by which an individual's ability to communicate effectively in a given language is delineated and measured. This chapter examines the different approaches and techniques used to assess language proficiency. It explores in depth the various tools available, such as standardized tests, oral and written assessments, as well as assessment methods based on emerging technologies. According to the chapter, it is essential to select the appropriate evaluation method according to the specific objectives and the context of use. We will also discuss the challenges associated with the assessment of language skills, particularly with respect to validity, reliability and fairness. Our chapter provides an overview of the various methods and best practices in the field of language skills assessment, while highlighting the paramount importance of implementing language skills assessment tools and methods that are appropriate to the objectives defined at the beginning of the training, effective and valid.

Acknowledgment

I would like to begin by expressing my deep gratitude to the management of IGI Global Publishing House, a renowned international academic publishing house specializing in the publication of reference works and scholarly journals, for agreeing to publish this book, which is scheduled for publication in 2025. This confidence shown in my work is a source of great satisfaction and valuable encouragement.

The publication of this book is the result of a collective effort and constant support. This is why my thanks go to all the people who have contributed, directly or indirectly, to the realization of this project. Their involvement, encouragement and sharing have been essential drivers and motivate me to continue my work and to consider other publications. I am particularly touched by the international support I have received, coming from India, Hong Kong, Saudi Arabia, Qatar, Greece, South Africa, and especially from Morocco, my country of origin. This diversity of support is a real wealth and a source of inspiration.

I would like to express a special gratitude to my family, friends and colleagues, whose unwavering support has been a pillar throughout this process. A warm thank you also to my doctoral students, whose constant encouragement and significant contributions have been instrumental in making this project a reality, turning a dream into reality. I also thank all those who believed in this project from the beginning, actively contributing to it and encouraging me to persevere.

Finally, it is with great affection that I dedicate this book to my wife, Malika, whose support and love have been an inexhaustible source of strength. To my children, Inass, Marwane and Maha, who light up my life. To my beloved granddaughters, Malak and Nada, who represent the future. And to my son-in-law, Ismail, whom I consider a member of my family.

Chapter 1
Advanced AI Approaches in Education

Sangers Bhavana
https://orcid.org/0009-0005-6134-1081
Sreenidhi Institute of Science and Technology, India

Abhinaya Akula
https://orcid.org/0009-0001-9361-7004
Sreenidhi Institute of Science and Technology, India

Venkat Narayana Rao
https://orcid.org/0000-0002-1996-1819
Sreenidhi Institute of Science and Technology, India

Chenchu Swetha
Sreenidhi Institute of Science and Technology, India

ABSTRACT

Artificial intelligence (AI) is revolutionizing education by personalizing learning experiences and enhancing students' problem-solving and reasoning skills. AI tailors content to students' interests, analyzes performance, and provides feedback, enabling adaptive learning. Core AI technologies, such as robotics and computer vision, have advanced, supporting tools like adaptive platforms, tutoring systems, chatbots, and automated writing evaluators. These tools drive the success of platforms like Duolingo, ChatGPT, and Coursera, benefiting both students and educators. AI empowers teachers by enabling creative teaching methods and diverse learning experiences, improving outcomes. With responsible implementation, AI will make education more accessible, address learning gaps, and transform the future of learning.

1. INTRODUCTION

In this chapter we are going to know about how AI(Artificial Intelligence) is used in Education, the fundamentals of AI and it's applications, Learning systems, Benefits of AI-powered learning and case studies of AI uses in Education.

DOI: 10.4018/979-8-3693-8965-2.ch001

The Fundamentals of Artificial Intelligence

The key concept of AI revolves around creating intelligent machines which helps the humans to solve typical problems which cannot be easily solved by the humans. AI has the ability to perform tasks such has problem solving, decision making, and learning as humans. Machines require complex algorithms and large amounts of data to make them work according to the human needs.

Collecting data is the first crucial step where we have to do a lot of work by gathering relevant information from various sources that can be used to train machines. This data must undergo a lot of cleaning steps to verify whether there are any mistakes in the data which they have gathered to train the machines. This process significantly reduces the errors and biases by making the information even more clear to the seeker who seeks help from AI. To create an AI it must have a logic design and code, we have to build a code to make the AI to respond according to their questions. One has to be familiar with the programming languages for AI development.

Languages like Python, Java and C++ will be utilized for building an AI platform. These languages are flexible and have the capability to manage large data sets efficiently and easily. Using this languages will definitely make the work easier for code building. Python is known for its concise syntax and easily understandable by anyone and also can be built easily. Beginners and experts everyone can learn this language as this is the one of the reasons for using this language. C++ is a blend of low-level and high level features, offers the necessary speed for performance-critical applications. Java is a reliable, portable, multi threaded and high level programming language these features helps us to build a perfect code to make AI work for our need. AI not only used in education but also in healthcare, finance, in transportation, industries and many more. AI has evolved into much more than that (Owoc et al., 2021).

2. CORE ARTIFICIAL INTELLIGENCE TECHNOLOGIES AND THEIR MECHANISMS

It involves training the machines to learn the data and it allows AI to recognize different problem patterns, techniques to resolve problems, to make predictions and to improve performance over time. It helps us to suggest products based upon past references even now a days we can notice that Google suggests some references according to our google history not only on google platform but also on apps which are used for shopping and even cosmetics. It trains the AI according to our needs and trains it to give the best results.

NLP focuses on translating the human language to the understandable machine language and to interpret information according to human needs. It allows AI systems to comprehend text, speech and even emotions enabling the applications like virtual assistants and language translation tools. Like we use emojis to express our emotions to the receiver in the same way NLP makes the human language understandable to the machine to produce the correct output as per the input.

Computer vision enables machines to interpret and understand visual information. It allows AI system to analyze images, to recognize objects and to understand the gestures. This include facial recognition, autonomous vehicles, and medical image analysis. We can observe that phone can be unlocked using face recognition and many more applications

Robotics involves creating machines capable of performing tasks automatically. This robotics application will help us to design robots which works on the basis of AI. Each component plays an important role in AI development and applications. Robotics brings AI into physical realm, enabling machines to perform tasks which will be done same as humans by enhancing efficiency and safety. Techniques like tokenization, part of speech tagging, sentiment analysis and many more which helps to make the best AI (Sajja et al., 2024).

3. ARTIFICIAL INTELLIGENCE TOOLS COMMONLY USED IN EDUCATION

AI uses tools like adaptive learning, Assistive Technology, Data and learning Analytics, Scheduling, and many more. Some tools in AI used in education are ChatGPT, Generative AI, Duolingo, Canva, Tutor AI and many more are the examples for successful accomplishment of AI in all platforms.

Personalized Learning tools: This include Adaptive learning platforms to make the user to prefer to the suitable material for problem solving so that student will get an accurate answer according to his question. This tool gives detailed information about the question asked and to adjust the materials based on student performance.

Recommendation engines: It suggests resources based on the interest of the students. It also gives references and the proofs as per the question asked.

AI powered tutors: They offer personalized instructions and tutors will choose the best way to teach the student clearly without any confusion regarding the topic. It selects the teaching pattern according to the individual personality of the student.

Assessment and Feedback: It provides feedback on student's performance and plans a table to get the best results. If requires it changes it style of producing the answers in order to make the student to get a better view on the topic. It suggests best way to learn according to the performance.

Interactive learning: To plan a class in a peaceful environment so that student can understand the teaching easily . It insists to create a study space which is undisturbed, without distractions, so that students can learn with full focus without any digital distractions. It creates a safe environment for the student to learn skills (Gupta et al., 2024).

4. CHALLENGES AND CONSIDERATIONS

AI in education has many challenges and considerations including privacy and security, Bias and fairness, Accessibility and equity, Reduced Human interaction, Overdependence on technology, Environmental burden, Data quality and accuracy, Teacher and student adaptation and many more. We will address about it in detail.

Privacy and security: AI system handles a large amount of data and it has to look at the safety of the user not to disclose the content anywhere on the other online platforms. It's important to protect data. Users or students should be transparent about the information collected we should not misuse the AI for other needs.

Bias and fairness: Some AI's are built on the biased information which leads to different answers or information on different AI platforms which creates doubts in the user's mind. So it will be difficult to the user to trust any one answer regardless of different answers.

Accessibility and equity: AI is accessible to every internet user regardless of other conditions. It is accessible to everyone in the world to seek information equally.

Reduced Human Interactions: As technology increased human interaction has been reduced, people are more often indulged in phone and need with humans has been reduced. So people are addicted to phones which increases every user's screen time leading to many eye related diseases and many more mental health issues.

Overdependence on technology: This generation has been completely dependent on technology even for small things, Even for using technology people are crossing the limits and using the internet limitless which is even reducing the human interaction.

Environmental burden: The data and devices used for AI can have unsustainable ecological costs. It needs large amounts of well structured data to learn and even to protect the data safely (Owoc et al., 2021).

5. ADAPTIVE LEARNING SYSTEMS AND PERSONALIZED EDUCATION

An adaptive learning experience is so beneficial to learning process and goals. It makes the learning experience personal and meaningful. It makes the student that they are learning by sitting next to them making it clear until the students understands it. It is highly efficient. Adaptive learning only teaches you what you don't know regarding the skill you are learning and it doesn't waste time on the skills in which you have already mastered. It's effective. An adaptive learning is an effective of learning. It repeats the content until you master the concepts perfectly. It is inclusive because adaptive learning process follows different learning methods for example if learner is too fast in understanding the concepts AI gives the best feedback and continues teaching in the same pattern. If learner is too slow in understanding the concept AI changes its way of teaching and it's patterns and even suggests other references to understand the concept and it even makes the students to write some written tests and gives a feedback which says whether the student has improved or not. It moves to the next topic only when the student is perfect in the previous one.

Personalized Education which includes more human interaction. Customization is one of the important components of the personalized learning. When learner feels the learning experience, it becomes more meaningful to them and it shows the results as per your search result for example if you have searched for a melody song it suggests you more and more melody songs because it recognizes that you will like the melody type songs. It include recognition also. The other component is continuity. It is a continuous learning journey. It constantly adjusts the content with adaptive learning.

In adaptive learning progress is the main key to move forward if learner didn't score the best result learner has to start the journey from the first so it mainly focuses on result. Learner has to be perfect in the previous topic to move to the next topic. After the feedback of the student it moves forward otherwise it suggests more written tests and even assignments to complete. It tests the knowledge level of the learner and decides the pattern of teaching based on the student's knowledge. It makes the student to practice it until the concept sticks to the brain. It happens with having a lot of practice sessions only. That's why adaptive learning technology works so well (Geleta et al., 2022).

6. ENHANCING ENGAGEMENT THROUGH ARTIFICIAL INTELLIGENCE- DRIVEN GAMIFICATION

AI and Gamification have emerged as an effective method for engaging students and enhancing the learning methods. This concept is creating am eagerness in the students learn more interestingly. It has introduced challenges like leaderships, boards and assignments like a game full of levels which makes the students to learn more. It helps in effective learning. It creates a motivating learning environment. AI driven gamification can transform education and improve student engagement.

It provides personalized learning paths which analyses each student's individual performance and provides with a feedback. Let us see an example if a student is poor in mathematics and performs better in the science, AI will focus on the student's progress of mathematics as the learner is not too good in that particular subject, so it suggests more questions related to that subject. Gamification can adjust the difficulty of the tasks. This will generate a balance that keeps the students challenged, interested, focused and helps in gaining the best results. By observing the patterns in the student's learning journey it suggests some personalized rewards or introduces new challenges to create more interest among the children. For example if the student is constantly missing some specific subject's class then it shows a reward to it so student will accept it as a challenge and they will try to clear it. AI uses many more applications in this way to make the student's best in their learning journey.

AI systems continuously learn from student interactions. By analyzing which learning method is working effectively they will improve that particular pattern accordingly. If we have a class of same subject for 2 hours no student will show interest in the class but if we include some fun activities along with learning they will attain the focus easily even if it is a 3 hours class or introducing gaming strategies may also work. More insights of this will improve student's learning methods. This gamification holds enormous potential for changing education by making it more personalized, engaging and adaptive. AI turns the difficult challenges into simple ones and makes it accessible to everyone. Gamification shapes the future in a best way to give the best results (Kaliisa et al., 2023).

7. ARTIFICIAL INTELLIGENCE IN SPECIAL EDUCATION: ADDRESSING DIVERSE LEARNING NEEDS

AI's ability to know about each and every student's data makes it an invaluable tool in special education. AI system can assess a student's learning algorithms according to their strength, knowledge power and challenges. AI will create the plans regarding according to student's IQ and schedules the classes for the learners on time. If it recognizes that student isn't active or not attending the classes regularly it will create the environment which will be helpful for the learners and creates an interest to the students to attend the classes attentively. Moreover AI tools can give a feedback immediately after the written test which makes the students to learn from their mistakes too. This Feedback system plays an important role in the student's journey because it will teach the every student to learn from their mistakes so that they can improve their learning even more because of the immediate response. Speech recognition software can assist the students with speech impairments and even corrects the mispronunciation by correcting it by giving the voice over. It helps with other applications like speech to text and text to speech translation, so that the student can learn to speak fluently without any errors and they can write essays on any given topic. Applications like these will help the students to improve their learning journey. Let us take an example The use of AI in Augmentative alternative communication(AAC) devices. This device will help in writing an predictive text and Natural processing language (NLP) to assist the students with poor communication skills in expressing themselves more efficiently. Practical examples of AI in special Education demonstrate its potential.

Learning Ally:It helps the students with dyslexia which means a learning disorder that involves difficulty in reading due to problems identifying speech. It helps the students to convert the text to audio. It is very beneficial to the students.

Cognii:It provides an interactive tutoring sessions where students with disabilities can receive adaptive and personal learning according to the written responses. Milo from RoboKind:

It provides help to the students with a disorder called autism, the people with this disorder are late in giving a response for body language. They cannot understand the gestures of body, eye contact and movements which gives information. These people will suffer from meeting new people so this helps in solving the problems by providing chatbots and explaining the topics in a slow manner. It helps by mimicking facial expressions and will guide the students in a structured manner.

Dream Box:It analyses student's performance by the results obtained from feedback and changes it way of teaching if grades aren't good. This will create a healthy competition among the student's to learn more. It moves to the next topic when the learner is good in the previous chapters.

Canva:This is an online platform. Free to use online graphic design. Canva's AI powered teaching assistant, helps free up time for more meaningful words and magic write tool helps in transforming the presentations and content creation into a best way. Canva's AI technology will generate quality content for presentations, cover letters blogs or anything in between to make it more creative.

Quill Bot: It helps the students who are interested in writing. It helps writers of all skill levels to provide several tools, including grammar checker, paraphraser and it is a remote learning and online education that helps the students to summarize the student's written text. It helps in editing the texts written easily.

Paper: An AI tool for education also Grade scope which is an extremely popular tool because of handwriting recognition. It provides grading to the student's performance in the feedback which saves time and energy of a human.

ChatGPT:It is an AI tool which helps the student by generating the answers according to the question asked by the user. It gives the accurate and efficient solutions. It gives a brief solution with suitable examples.

Quizlet:It is also an AI powered app that helps students study for exams by allowing them to create flashcards and generates some question papers based on the input.

AI classroom toolkit:A creative resource that combines instructional information and engages the students in active learning. It creates an environment to study as a classroom. It creates an immersive learning experience to the students of age 13 – 15.

Grammarly:It is the AI writing partner which helps the users in every stage starting from blank page to final draft. It shares the guidance to the learners to use this generative artificial intelligence in education to support student's success. It helps in creative an easy, efficient and effective writing to impress the readers who might be students or teachers and creates more interest to learn more.

Chatbot:A chatbot is a computer program that coverts the human conversation with an end user. Not all chatbots are AI based but modern ones are designed to be AI based and it allows the users to ask the questions and gives the response conversationally. It also comes under Natural language processing unit.

Audio: It is sound app with acoustic range of human hearing. It is the audible portion of the sounds with clear and intense frequencies. It provides the audio of the text clearly so that learner can pronounce the difficult words easily after listening it in the audio. It helps in clearing the doubts in pronouncing the words and content can be easily remembered as we are listening it.

Duolingo: It is a well known language learning app uses to develop flexible language lessons. It gives the information regrading any topic in the required language. It helps in listening the language and it provides the content along with the language name (Cikmaz et al., 2023).

8. ARTIFICIAL INTELLIGENCE-ASSISTED CURRICULUM DESIGN AND COURSE MANAGEMENT

It supports learning paths and provides the academic skills, it helps in efficient evaluation of student work. The role of AI in curriculum development is to improve our educational process and make it to improve in a best manner by making it more personalized, comprehensive and effective. AI driven curriculum design works in a way by creating effective learning experiences. There are many innovative cases of AI for curriculum design. It has to train the AI in an effective way to enhance productivity . As it learns AI begins to suggest content enhancements and even identifies area where it has to improve the learning techniques. Leverage AI's Dat Driven insights to draft the tailored content. Some AI's shows biased content like giving different answers for the same question on different learning platforms. It creates doubts and confuses the users. It builds the code correctly and gives the output accurately. Use AI to streamline courses, Educators has to play many roles not only teachers but also administrators, planners and guides. AI can also known as the co-instructor resolves the issues and manages the multiple tasks. Use AI in producing Engaging visual content. It provides the information with AI-generated images works seamlessly to give us the content accurately.so that we can understand them with the help of images easily.

Use of AI to enhance student support, students believe in this AI driven apps because they give an accurate answer in an understandable manner. Learning is an interactive process that involves active participation and active listening. It is a student centered learning environment.

Assessment and Feedback plays a crucial role in a student's learning journey. Because seeing the results will make students enthusiastic to learn the content attentively, it encourages the students to learn more. AI provides automated grading and instant feedback. Correction of papers normally may be time consuming and requires a lot of energy but AI made it easy by providing automated grading system which gives the results instantly. At last it shows a graph related to our performance which has to be a raising which says that we are good in the scores it suggests the other references and ways to score more (Karpouzis et al., 2024).

Limitations of Artificial Intelligence in Education

There will be pros and cons for every aspect. Due to new inventions in technology, human efforts have been reduced and screen time is increasing. Interacting with others or hanging out with friends or buying groceries are totally reduced because everything is available on online. As screen time increases this may bring a lot of health issues like eye sight and all.

How Artificial Intelligence in Education is effecting?

Learning in classroom is different from learning online. If you ask a question AI will clarify it by giving a text message or a video where in classroom you can interact with the teacher and can learn clearly. Interacting with others will make you learn a lot of new things and ethics on how to behave. That will be a limitation of AI in Education.

Role of Teachers in Artificial Intelligence enhanced Classrooms

AI will provide the data but cannot make the students understand it in some cases. So, Teachers will play a crucial role in this cases, they will mentor the students and they will prepare the schedule so that students will understand them in a proper way.

Thoughts on the effectiveness of this chapter:

The main aim of this chapter is to make the people know how AI have enhanced the technology and advanced approaches of AI in Education. Virtual classrooms, Feedback systems, Adaptive learning and learning new things by sitting at your home and many more are the advantages of AI. This pros of AI will make the students to learn the things easier.

Purpose of this chapter

The main purpose of this chapter is to let the students know how AI is playing a crucial role in every aspect including Education. In this chapter it is explained that AI enhanced the education system in a smart way and made the humans effortless. Even robotics can aquire the position of AI in future prospects where every student will study by just having a E-book in their hand rather than having 10 books. AI will make the students to think in a different manner and in a creative way.

9. VIRTUAL ASSISTANTS AND TUTORS: EXTENDING SUPPORT BEYOND THE CLASSROOM

Chatbots and virtual assistants are advanced software programs designed to interact with the user and reduces the human work, chatbots will generate an immediate and accurate answer. They constantly tries to improve the student skills. Virtual assistants and their agents work continuously to provide us the accurate and efficient answers. Chatbots plays a crucial role in digital environment as technology advances. AI makes the students to believe in online learning platforms. Increased participation improves the retention of information and critical thinking

Benefits of chatbots and virtual Assistants: They have significant benefits across the industries. They have been widely used in many fields like banking, digital healthcare, and other projects. The uses of chatbots enhances the customer services 24/7 by providing the response immediately. It is co-effective, scalable and it can handle the routine queries gives instant responses, boosting efficiency, and reducing human error. It helps the humans by solving complex algorithms makes our work easy

Personalized learning experience through chatbots: As technology has improved new methods have been introduced in learning like clearing our doubts using AI by chatting with it in the same way as we interact with our friend it gives us immediate response without making us to wait. It gives an accurate answer . The essence of AI is to make a predictive framework that can assist the needs of students. We use it for spontaneous conversation response and it is efficient and scalable to support a student. When learning management systems (LMS) are integrated, interactions became easy. It makes easy to provide course materials, to track the student progress and to enhances the user experience.

Data privacy in educational settings: AI has to adjust itself for the questions we ask and it has the responsibility not to disclose it on any other platform it has to take the safety measures and should maintain privacy in matter of information. AI is accessible to everyone across the globe so learners should not misuse it. One has to use this technology to improve themselves (Burton et al., 2017).

Solutions and Recommendations:

Balance between Technology and Human Interaction is very important. If not students have to face the consequences in the upcoming days.Even the teachers can learn from AI and can improve their skills. Personalized learning experiences, Feedback, Adaptive learning many more aspects will give the student's a bright future. (Selwyn et.al,2019)

10. DATA ANALYTICS FOR IMPROVED ACADEMIC OUTCOMES

Data can be used to improve learning outcomes. Data can give warning signs for students who might be falling behind. Lower test scores or incomplete assignments could indicate a student is struggling. By observing this issues early on it changes the pattern of written tests and makes the level easy so that it builds the confidence in the learners that they can also score well. It uses descriptive analytics to create dashboards, graphs, assignments, feedbacks and responses to the doubts raised.AI agents will work 24/7 to give a spontaneous answer to the user. Purpose of data analytics is to monitor each and every individual student performance over time. It improves teaching effectiveness and student outcomes.

Identifying student's needs: It pinpoints each and every student's strengths and weaknesses, enabling the required support for optimal learning experiences. It designs the teaching schedule in order of there performance.

Assessing learning outcomes: Data analytics evaluate the effectiveness of the teaching methods ensuring alignment with desired learning methods and outcomes.

Identifying Areas for professional Development: Data analysis helps to find where teachers might need more training, so they can improve how they teach.

Informed Decisions about Instructional content and methods: Teachers use data to pick the right materials and they will prepare from that materials and explains us in the class in the same way AI will pick up the accurate answers so that learners will understand easily.

Differentiating Instructions: It instructs the students based on there performances and feedback. It also tracks the student's progress constantly so that they can know that learner is listening and attending to the classes .It shows how well students are doing and what measures has to be taken to get the best result (Romeo et al., 2024).

11. METHODOLOGICAL CONSIDERATIONS IN ARTIFICIAL INTELLIGENCE TEACHING

Teaching methodology can be defined as the method chosen to achieve a teaching goal. This is given by the teacher of the particular subject so that students will follow the schedule according to teacher's plan in the same way AI designs the curriculum to make the students to follow it. AI follows different methods for teaching to improve the student's skills. Some methodologies in AI are Foundational knowledge, interdisciplinary approach, explaining complex topics, Hands on learning and tools, evaluation etc. rather than these we have many aspects in which we discuss in detail.

Pedagogical alignment: It includes personalization which says that AI established new teaching methods but it didn't replace human interactions which are essential for social learning because AI can give you accurate answers as our teachers but it will not give you the answer with gestures and expressions and AI also introduced adaptive learning which we have discussed before.

Algorithmic bias ; Datasets has to be some on every online platform. Developers and Educators must assess the fairness of AI. This has to be taken as a consideration that every learner has the access for AI learning . AI tools must be there for even low-income students who can't afford the private study life.

Ethical implications: AI should balance the automated recommendations and student's choice ensuring students develop the problem solving techniques, decision making and many more skills

Teacher Training and development: Skill development AI ensures that every student is learning a new skill from it and it also ensures that not only student's but also teachers can pursue the AI learning to improve their teaching skills.

Co designing with educators: AI itself designs with many tools and applications to meet the classroom needs, it involves many designs and algorithms and produces assessments and feedbacks too.

Human oversight: While AI can automate grading which is essential to interpret the aspects of student's performance.

Cultural and Contextual Sensitivity: Contextual relevance which explains that AI checks for the relevant responses and generates the answers. Localizing AI content ensures it is meaningful and relatable to students from different backgrounds.

Scalability and Sustainability: If we create an app using AI for education it has to be sustainable for a longer use and agent have to see that no bugs are interrupting the student's learning journey. It's solutions has to be scalable for different educational settings.

Collaborative learning and human interaction: Maintaining social learning as said that AI should not replace humans it just have to be an alternative because human interactions plays a crucial role for developing many social skills and ethics which no AI can learn.

Teacher-Student Relationships: AI systems should accept the teacher – student relationship to give the best results. AI enhances the education rather than detracts it.

Integrating AI into teaching it addresses to ensure effective learning outcomes and ethical use of technology. There are some limitations to understand AI tools. In gamification it introduces game-like designs which displays rewards, leaderboards, challenges. It is an interactive learning experience in online.

AI has became a powerful tool for increasing user engagement across industries, from education to healthcare. AI has reached a new level of sophistication. It also adapts dynamically to individual behaviors and preferences (Ahn et al., 2024).

12. DESIGNING ARTIFICIAL INTELLIGENCE-INTEGRATED LESSONS

Enhancing Learning Outcomes: Personalized and adaptive learning environment for students to learn at their own space and style to address in different patterns of learning and diverse learning needs of students to improve student engagement and academic performance. AI has enhance in many ways to make the student's best in their learning journey.

Developing New Skills: We can see an eagerness in every student to learn new things and to explore different things, doing experiments. Using AI we can learn more new skills like learning new programming languages like Python, Java, web designing and may more. Learning new skills leads to develop critical thinking, problem solving, creativity and decision making. It will change the view of every student in problem solving.

Increasing Efficiency: AI can automate repetitive tasks such as grading, scheduling and frees up the time of the student to do more meaningful tasks to increase the learners efficiency in curriculum designing, lesson planning and balancing the multi tasks and managing the scheduled tasks and making them to finish it on time.

Fostering creativity: Educators will make the students to foster more creativity to bring more innovative ideas which may lead to new discoveries in future generation. So AI will work on collaborating more new AI applications, tools and solutions that can improve learning outcomes.

AI maturity model for Education: This context in AI includes many aspects like Approaching and understanding, Experimenting and exploring, operational, Embedded and optimized/Transformed.

To get to know about these things one has to understand how AI works, how it transforms educational institutions and even other sectors. Without experiments we cannot have the inventions which we are using today, experimenting is the important aspect in AI to explore different views of a topic (Chan et al., 2023).

13. BENEFITS OF ARTIFICIAL INTELLIGENCE IN EDUCATION

Motivation and Engagement: AI can increase motivation in learners by giving them new challenges and making them to solve them will build a confidence in them to solve more difficult problems, Through AI they can engage with the teachers in online and can ask doubts which will help them to solve many more problems fastly.

Autonomy and self-regulation: AI can self-regulate the students as they are learning in their own space just by taking the help online rather than having a person around. They can learn and can practice the subjects independently. It will help in enhancing the student's autonomy.

Metacognitive and Reflective Skills: It can foster the student's metacognitive and reflective skills. As they can evaluate and improve their own academic performance using different strategies.

Language Acquistion and Retention: Language Acquistion is the process where humans can acquire ability to comprehend and produce new language. Retention is remembering the new language rather can forgetting it. Once a word is retained it can be retrieved later by the user. There are 4 aspects of language acquisition like phonology, syntax, semantics and pragmatics.

Overcoming Learning Outcomes: If we face a failure we have to identify where we did a mistake and we should try to resolve it rather than leaving it, it requires a lot of positive attitude and confidence to overcome the challenges in education. One have to identify the learning gaps and personalized remediation will help in solving them (Kuipers et al., 2017).

Assisting with content development, automate teacher tasks, developing differentiated and personalized learning, supporting by giving a timely feedback and improving data analysis, increased accessibility, reduced costs are benefits of AI in education. Some challenges faced by AI in education are Data privacy and security, bias and fairness, ethical use of AI, adaptability and acceptance which are cons of using AI.

14. THE ROLE OF TEACHERS IN AN ARTIFICIAL INTELLIGENCE-ENHANCED EDUCATIONAL LANDSCAPE

Due to AI the role of teachers evolves rather than diminishes. AI can assist the tasks like grading, giving feedback, and scheduling the tasks as humans. We can say that human interaction will be less due to AI but it cannot replace humans. Emotional and social support can be received by the students from humans only not from technology or any other robots. Chatbots can clarify your doubts but cannot give the explanation as our teachers in schools. It cannot give the gestures and cannot make us to learn the ethics, discipline as our teacher teaches us. Teacher's part in learner's life will remain crucial in supporting student's emotional wellbeing, building relationships, and creating supportive learning environments. Mediators of critical thinking which says that Teachers help students develop the skills necessary to question, analyze and evaluate the information generated by AI, ensuring that they understand the AI's limitations and biases.

Teachers will act as Ethical Guides to make the student learn how to use an AI and explains its applications so they can use the AI wisely. Not only technology use but also other implications like including data privacy, digital literacy and responsible AI usage. AI tutors have to be lifelong learners as the technology is introducing new applications rapidly they have to learn them and should implement them to make the students updated and to learn the new things and applications which are updated without any delay to make their learning easy. Teacher's themselves should continually learn and should adapt, embracing new AI tools and integrating them into their teaching methods. To use AI not only Students but even teachers have to learn new things continually. Some are worrying that AI is going to replace the teachers, but the reality is far more complex and optimistic. AI explains the concepts which are difficult to be taught by the teachers, it enhances the educational experience, allowing teachers to focus on aspects of teaching that technology cannot teach like aspects of relationships, emotional wellbeing, social support. In conclusion we can say that the rise of AI in education cannot diminish the importance of teachers, it redefines their role in profound and positive ways. Teachers can guide the students if they are facing a difficult time where AI cannot do that. So they serve as mentors in an increasing digital world.

Education always remains as a journey of personal and transformative experience foe every student. Teachers remains as the guiders when they are in a problem and AI will make them to learn the difficult things, everything has its own value (L.H.Y. et al., 2023).

15. CASE STUDIES OF ARTIFICIAL INTELLIGENCE IN EDUCATION

Educational Institutions, companies, colleges, Universities are turning into AI as a tool to reshape learning, organizations are implementing AI. We can see success across the world because of usage of AI. Every organization is implementing AI from chatbots to personalized learning pathways, to improve student engagement and to meet the needs of the students. Here are some case studies to know how AI tools are enhancing learning experiences in the education sector.

1. Brainly

Brainly, an online learning platform, recognized that students faced challenges when seeking help with homework, especially on mobile devices. This company aimed to provide a Solution that would solve every student's problem who are struggling to solve their homework problems. To achieve this Brainly worked with Google cloud to use its vision AI technology.

The engagement with Google cloud enabled the students to photograph their questions and learners will receive the answer instantly relevant to the questions. The approach of AI have multilingual capabilities and it yielded high satisfaction rates. The technology recognized text in different languages and allowed Brainly to cater a global audience, making it possible for students across the world to benefit from the platform.

Brainly collaboration with Google cloud has created a huge success and helped every student to solve the difficult problems without help of teachers. Google cloud's scalability is the key factor in implementation . It allowed brainly to help the students worldwide by providing access to every mobile user. This has to be used wisely only for good, and enabled it in the way so no one can misuse it. It helps the students who often get left behind. Brainly an online learning platform has turned out to be a success across the globe.

Results:70% students satisfaction rate:

- 6x engagement boost due to photo queries
- Increased revenue from subscriptions
- Highly efficient

2. Berlitz

A language education company, wanted to meet the growing demand for flexible learning options. The company sought to maintain its focus on spoken language practice, even in an online environment. Berlitz worked with Microsoft to achieve this.

Berlitz is the best platform as the speech studio and having text-to-speech capabilities by offering a voice generation feature. This feature allowed learners to engage with diverse accents and speaker profiles. This will solve the difficulty of the students who are poor in grammar. This will make the students to pronounce the words without finding difficulty.

Captalizing on speech tools, Berlitz significantly reduced its product development costs and time to market, allowing for the investment in other areas. Berlitz collaborated with Microsoft to bring out new and innovative ideas. Berlitz is an online platform to convert speech to text. It focuses on language to solve the grammatical errors.

It focuses language as a tool in communication. It has started in Princeton, New jersey and after success it expanded its branches to 500+.

Results:

- Improved pronunciation of 500,000 learners
- Greater accessibility for diverse learner profiles
- Reached thousands of new learners
- Improved fluency in language

3. EUDE

The European school of management and business is a virtual co-tutor that is intended to offer real time support to students and even the tutors who can submit questions using natural language (NLP). It is collaborated with IBM its main function is to provide immediate answers to students to improve their academics and as well as to support students with logistical questions related to exams. By building the solution on this platform it has full control over the content and responses and on its own data.

With EDU students can gain the immediate response and gives higher level of support which increases the students engagement with the EDU and therefore it can stand out as a successful platform for faster responses and even for solving logistical operations.

Results:

- Improved student experiences
- Fast and accurate responses for the questions
- Optimized faculty
- Personalized tutoring
- Potential for broader impact within higher education sector

4. Loyola University Chicago

Loyola university Chicago, a private institution wanted to enhance student services by focusing on timely support regardless of location or business hours. Loyola implemented LUie, an AI powered digital assistant built on oracle digital assistant platform. It provides the solution from Loyola's administrative systems. It provided a positive feedback and a higher answer success rate. This platform also gained 91% of success with all the positive plots.

Results:

- 24/7 student support
- Improved student experience
- Optimized staff work
- Significant cost savings

16. FUTURE RESEARCH DIRECTIONS

The technology has been growing day by day and we will see further implementations in AI not only in education but also in many sectors. The advancement in technology has driven innovation in education. AI in education process vast amount of data and mimic human like decision making process. AI can be accessible to anyone across the globe which will develop equity. If learners are using AI one has to feel happy that the person is going to be more skillful and even successful as he is using the resource properly. AI involvement is very beneficial to students which makes them to think on every aspect of the topic and improves their learning journey. Learners will become skilled persons they can know the critical thinking process, decision making and how to solve a problem by using which online platform we can solve the problem everything can be known by the learner if he is aware of AI's applications. We can learn a new skill from AI and we can get the solutions accurately relevant to the questions (Meli et al., 2024).

Weaknesses of This Chapter

AI in Education will make the students to stick to there systems which increases there screen time, this may not be a good sign for student's health. Mental health may get disturbed by sitting before the laptops or mobile for hours.As they learn from AI they cannot get the peaceful environment which can be experienced by sitting in the classroom among our friends.

Strengths of This Chapter

Human efforts are totally minimized after AI. Technology has increased in a way that everything can be ordrerd online we can get them in a second of time. AI will see that every student is engaging through the process actively. Personalized Learning, Feedback system, Experienced Tutors palys the main role in AI.

17. CONCLUSION

AI will transform this society with full of skilled persons, if one knows the applications of AI. AI is overcoming enormous problems by facing a completely new era of learning. As this will be new system to the students, they will be in a eager to learn new things from AI. It is revolutionizing teaching and learning by providing a wide range of innovative solutions. We need not to worry that AI is going to replace teachers, it cannot replace because human connection also plays a crucial role in learner's life gestures and emotions can be learnt from human interactions only where AI will make you more intelligent by making you to learn more new skills . Generative AI tools plays an important role in the future generation, more methodologies will be implemented. It helps to generate a different learning path for each student knowing their interests, skills and goals it gives the recommendations accordingly. Outcomes of AI turns out to be higher efficiency in content creation, solving the problems instantly, accessibility, scalability, Equity and many more. Many apps have been designed using AI every student must be aware of those useful apps and should learn from them to make their learning journey successful.

REFERENCES

Burton, E., Goldsmith, J., Koenig, S., Kuipers, B., Mattei, N., & Walsh, T. (2017). *Ethical considerations in artificial intelligence courses*. Addressing Methodological Considerations in AI Teaching., DOI: 10.1609/aimag.v38i2.2731

Chan, C. K. Y., & Tsi, L. H. Y. (2023). The AI revolution in education: Will AI replace or assist teachers in higher education? *Computers and Society* http://dx.doi.org//arXiv.2305.01185.DOI: 10.48550

Geleta, M., Xu, J., Loya, M., Wang, J., Singh, S., Li, Z., & Gago-Masague, S. (2023). Maestro: A gamified platform for teaching AI robustness, The Thirty-Seventh AAAI Conference on Artificial Intelligence (AAAI-23), *The Thirty-Seventh AAAI Conference on Artificial Intelligence(AAAI-23)*, 15816-15824.

Gupta, T., Kumar, A., Roy, B. K., & Saini, S. (2024, November). Adaptive learning systems: Harnessing AI to personalize educational outcomes. *International Journal for Research in Applied Science and Engineering Technology*, 12(XI). Advance online publication. https://doi.org/10.22214/ijraset.2024.65088

Kaliisa, R., Misiejuk, K., López-Pernas, S., Khalil, M., & Saqr, M. (2023). Have learning analytics dashboards lived up to the hype? A systematic review of impact on students' achievement, motivation, participation and attitude, *The 14th Learning Analytics and Knowledge Conference, Kyoto, Japan, March 2024*, https://doi.org/DOI: 10.1145/3636555.3636884

Karpouzis, K., Pantazatos, D., Taouki, J., & Meli, K. (2024). Tailoring education with Gen AI: A new horizon in lesson planning. *IEEE Global Engineering Education Conference 2024*, https://doi.org//arXiv.2403.12071.DOI: 10.48550

Oh, S., & Ahn, Y. (2024). Exploring teachers' perception of artificial intelligence: The socio emotional deficiency as opportunities, *Human-Computer Interaction*, May 2024, https://doi.org//arXiv.2405.13065.DOI: 10.48550

Owoc, M. L., Sawicka, A., & Weichbroth, P. (2021). Artificial intelligence technologies in education. In *Benefits, challenges and strategies of implementation* (pp. 37–58). Artificial Intelligence for Knowledge Management., DOI: 10.1007/978-3-030-85001-2_4

Romero, M. (2024). Collaborative design of AI-enhanced learning activities, *Addressing Designing AI-Integrated Lessons*, Artificial Intelligence, May 2024, https://doi.org//arXiv.2407.06660.DOI: 10.48550

Sajja, R., Sermet, Y., Cikmaz, M., Cwiertny, D., & Demir, I. (2024). Artificial intelligence- enabled intelligent assistant for personalized and adaptive learning in higher education, *Artificial Intelligence and Games Science in Education*, 15(10), 596; **https://doi.org/10.3390/info15100596**

Chapter 2
Curricula and Instructional Design for AI

P. Selvakumar
https://orcid.org/0000-0002-3650-4548
Nehru Institute of Technology, India

S. Tamizharasu
https://orcid.org/0000-0003-1861-0723
Hindusthan Institute of Technology, India

Kamlesh Singh
https://orcid.org/0000-0002-2306-4459
School of Management Sciences, Lucknow, India

Lakshmi Prasanna
https://orcid.org/0000-0003-0774-3694
Gokaraju Rangaraju Institute of Engineering and Technology, India

ABSTRACT

As we stand at the threshold of an AI-driven future, the need for educational systems to adapt and prepare students for this new paradigm has never been more urgent. "Introduction to AI Curricula and Instructional Design: Preparing Students for an AI-Driven World" explores the essential components and strategies necessary for developing educational programs that equip learners with the skills and knowledge required to thrive in an AI-centric world. To effectively teach AI, educators must integrate hands-on activities, real-world problem-solving tasks, and collaborative projects that mirror the complexities and interdisciplinary nature of AI technologies. By integrating foundational AI concepts, promoting ethical considerations, fostering practical experience, and encouraging adaptability, educational programs can effectively prepare students to navigate and excel in an increasingly AI-centric future.

DOI: 10.4018/979-8-3693-8965-2.ch002

INTRODUCTION TO AI CURRICULA AND INSTRUCTIONAL DESIGN: PREPARING STUDENTS FOR AN AI-DRIVEN WORLD

As we stand at the threshold of an AI-driven future, the need for educational systems to adapt and prepare students for this new paradigm has never been more urgent. "Introduction to AI Curricula and Instructional Design: Preparing Students for an AI-Driven World" explores the essential components and strategies necessary for developing educational programs that equip learners with the skills and knowledge required to thrive in an AI-centric world. To effectively teach AI, educators must integrate hands-on activities, real-world problem-solving tasks, and collaborative projects that mirror the complexities and interdisciplinary nature of AI technologies. Furthermore, it is essential to cultivate critical thinking and ethical considerations, ensuring that students not only understand how AI systems function but also appreciate the broader societal implications of their use. By integrating foundational AI concepts, promoting ethical considerations, fostering practical experience, and encouraging adaptability, educational programs can effectively prepare students to navigate and excel in an increasingly AI-centric future.

FOUNDATIONAL AI CONCEPTS: BUILDING BLOCKS FOR CURRICULA DESIGN

In the realm of educational technology, designing an effective curriculum for artificial intelligence (AI) necessitates a thorough understanding of foundational AI concepts (McCarthy et al., 2006). These concepts serve as the building blocks upon which comprehensive and engaging AI curricula can be constructed Integrating these topics into the curriculum helps students understand how AI systems interact with human language, enabling them to develop applications such as chatbots and language translation systems. Another vital component of foundational AI education is the concept of data. Data is the lifeblood of AI systems, and understanding how to collect, preprocess, and analyze data is crucial for developing effective AI models. Topics such as data cleaning, feature selection, and data augmentation are integral to ensuring that students can work with real-world datasets and apply their knowledge to practical problems.

AI LITERACY FOR ALL: INCLUSIVE CURRICULA FOR DIVERSE LEARNERS

Creating inclusive AI curricula that cater to diverse learners is crucial in ensuring that the benefits and opportunities of artificial intelligence (AI) are accessible to all. "AI Literacy for All: Inclusive Curricula for Diverse Learners" highlights the importance of designing educational programs that address the varied needs, backgrounds, and learning styles of students, thereby fostering a more equitable and comprehensive understanding of AI (Arrouillet P. 2015). Inclusive curricula begin with recognizing that learners come from a multitude of cultural, socioeconomic, and educational backgrounds. Effective AI education must account for these differences to provide equitable learning opportunities. This includes adapting materials and teaching methods to meet the needs of students with varying levels of prior knowledge and experience. For instance, foundational courses should offer entry points that are accessible to beginners while also providing advanced topics for more experienced learners. Incorporating diverse examples and case studies into the curriculum can make the content more relatable and engaging. Furthermore, it's essential to address the accessibility needs of all students. This means providing resources in multiple formats, such as text, audio, and visual aids, and ensuring that educational materials are compatible with assistive technologies. Providing clear explanations and avoiding jargon can also help make complex AI concepts more understandable for students who may be encountering them for the first time (Belur J., et al., 2021). Additionally, incorporating collaborative learning opportunities can foster a more inclusive environment. This ongoing professional development helps educators stay informed about best practices and emerging trends in AI education, ensuring that they can effectively address the needs of all students. Finally, involving students in the curriculum design process can provide valuable insights into their needs and preferences. Soliciting feedback from students about their learning experiences and incorporating their suggestions can help tailor the curriculum to better meet their needs and enhance overall effectiveness. In sum, creating an inclusive AI curriculum involves recognizing and addressing the diverse needs of learners, providing equitable access to resources, incorporating culturally relevant content, and supporting both students and educators in their learning journey.

AI ETHICS AND RESPONSIBILITY: INTEGRATING SOCIAL IMPLICATIONS INTO CURRICULA

Integrating AI ethics and responsibility into educational curricula is essential for preparing students to navigate the complex social implications of artificial intelligence (Brennan K., et al., 2012). As AI technologies become increasingly pervasive in society, understanding their ethical considerations and potential impact is crucial for fostering responsible innovation and decision-making. "AI Ethics and Responsibility: Educators should highlight case studies and real-world examples where lack of accountability has led to negative consequences, reinforcing the need for rigorous standards and practices in AI development(Cheah C. W. 2021). Educational programs should address these issues by examining both the opportunities and challenges posed by AI-driven changes in various industries. Security concerns related to AI also warrant attention, particularly in the context of cybersecurity and the potential for malicious use of AI technologies. Students should learn about the risks associated with AI, such as deepfakes and autonomous weaponry, and the measures that can be taken to mitigate these risks. Human rights considerations are equally important, as AI systems can impact fundamental rights such as freedom of expression, privacy, and equality. Curricula should incorporate discussions on how AI can both support and infringe upon these rights, and how developers can design systems that respect and uphold human rights. Integrating ethical considerations into AI education also involves fostering a culture of ethical awareness and critical thinking. This can be achieved through interactive learning methods such as debates, role-playing scenarios, and ethics workshops. By engaging students in discussions about the ethical dilemmas and societal impacts of AI, educators can encourage them to think critically about their responsibilities as future practitioners and decision-makers in the field. Furthermore, interdisciplinary approaches can enrich the understanding of AI ethics and responsibility. Collaborating with experts in fields such as philosophy, law, and social sciences can provide students with a broader perspective on the ethical and social dimensions of AI. This approach not only prepares students to become ethical and thoughtful practitioners but also empowers them to contribute positively to the evolving landscape of AI.

DESIGNING AI CURRICULA FOR K-12: AGE-APPROPRIATE LEARNING OBJECTIVES

At the elementary level, learning objectives should emphasize basic computational thinking and problem-solving skills, laying the groundwork for more advanced AI concepts (Conati C., et al.,2021). Young students can start with activities that involve pattern recognition, sequencing, and simple algorithmic thinking through interactive games and hands-on projects. For example, students might engage with coding toys like programmable robots that introduce them to the concept of algorithms through tangible actions and immediate feedback. These activities help cultivate an understanding of how instructions can be given to machines to perform specific tasks. As students progress to middle school, curricula can build on these foundational skills by introducing more complex concepts related to AI. For instance, they might use visual programming environments to create projects that involve sorting and classifying data, or work with educational tools that demonstrate how AI can be used in applications like image recognition or text analysis (English L. D. 2016). High school curricula should delve deeper into AI concepts and applications, aligning with more advanced cognitive abilities and academic expectations. Learning objectives for this age group can include a more detailed understanding of machine learning algorithms, neural networks, and data science principles. Students might engage in projects that involve building and training simple machine learning models, analyzing real-world datasets, and exploring the nuances of AI applications in areas such as healthcare, finance, and environmental science. Ethical considerations should also be a focal point, with students exploring topics such as bias in AI, the societal impacts of automation, and the ethical use of AI technologies. High school students can benefit from interdisciplinary approaches that integrate AI with subjects like mathematics, science, and social studies. For example, projects that involve data analysis can be tied to mathematics curriculum, while discussions about AI's impact on jobs and society can be integrated into social studies classes(Eshach H. 2007). Additionally, providing opportunities for students to engage with real-world problems and collaborate with industry professionals can enhance their learning experience and prepare them for future careers in AI-related fields. This approach not only prepares students for future opportunities in technology but also fosters a thoughtful and informed perspective on the role of AI in society. In summary, designing age-appropriate AI curricula for K-12 education involves tailoring learning objectives to the developmental stages of students, from basic computational thinking in early childhood to advanced AI concepts and ethical considerations in high school. By creating engaging, relevant, and inclusive learning experiences, educators can effectively introduce students to AI and equip them with the skills and understanding needed to navigate an increasingly technology-driven world.

AI EDUCATION FOR HIGHER EDUCATION: SPECIALIZED CURRICULA FOR STEM FIELDS

In higher education, the integration of artificial intelligence (AI) into specialized curricula for STEM fields represents a crucial advancement, aligning academic programs with the rapidly evolving demands of technology-driven industries(Estevez J.,et al., 2019). "AI Education for Higher Education: Specialized Curricula for STEM Fields" delves into the development of specialized curricula that prepare students for advanced roles in science, technology, engineering, and mathematics (STEM) through a focused and in-depth exploration of AI concepts and applications. For STEM students, AI education must go beyond basic principles to cover sophisticated algorithms, machine learning models, and domain-specific applications. Coursework might involve projects that require students to build and train complex models, evaluate their performance, and interpret results, thereby bridging theoretical knowledge with practical skills. In engineering disciplines, AI's role in optimization, automation, and control systems should be emphasized. For instance, students in electrical engineering might explore how AI can enhance signal processing and sensor integration, while those in mechanical engineering could study AI-driven robotics and automated systems. Specialized courses might cover the application of AI in areas such as predictive maintenance, adaptive control systems. Students should gain experience with large-scale data processing tools and platforms, such as Apache Spark and Hadoop, and develop skills in handling diverse datasets to derive actionable insights. Specialized courses might involve case studies on data-driven decision-making and the development of data pipelines, allowing students to tackle complex problems and refine their analytical abilities (Fang X., et al., 2023). For students in the physical and life sciences, AI can be integrated into research methodologies, including computational biology, astrophysics, and environmental science. Courses should explore how AI techniques such as image analysis, simulation modeling, and pattern recognition can be applied to scientific research and experimentation. For example, in bioinformatics, students might use machine learning algorithms to analyze genomic data and predict protein structures, while in environmental science, they could apply AI to model climate change impacts or optimize resource management. Ethical considerations and societal impacts are also critical components of specialized AI curricula. Students should be trained to understand and address issues such as algorithmic bias, data privacy, and the ethical use of AI technologies within their specific fields. This involves incorporating discussions and case studies on the ethical implications of AI applications, encouraging students to consider how their work aligns with broader societal values and regulatory frameworks. Additionally, interdisciplinary collaboration is key to enhancing AI education in STEM fields. Encouraging partnerships between departments, industry professionals, and research institutions can provide students with diverse perspectives and opportunities to engage in cutting-edge projects (Gadanidis G. 2017). This approach fosters a more holistic understanding of AI and its applications across various domains, preparing students for multidisciplinary roles in their future careers. In summary, designing specialized AI curricula for higher education in STEM fields involves a comprehensive approach that includes advanced technical training, practical experience, interdisciplinary collaboration, and ethical considerations. By equipping students with a deep understanding of AI concepts and applications tailored to their specific disciplines, educational programs can prepare them to excel in their fields and contribute to the ongoing evolution of technology and research.

INTERDISCIPLINARY AI CURRICULA: INTEGRATING HUMANITIES, SOCIAL SCIENCES, AND ARTS

Developing interdisciplinary AI curricula that integrate humanities, social sciences, and the arts represents a forward-thinking approach to education, reflecting the increasingly pervasive role of artificial intelligence (AI) in all facets of society. "Interdisciplinary AI Curricula: Integrating Humanities, Social Sciences, and Arts" examines how educational programs can blend AI concepts with insights from these diverse fields to foster a holistic understanding of technology's impact on human experience and culture (Gansser O. A.,et al., 2021). The integration of AI with the humanities can illuminate the profound ways in which technology intersects with human values, ethics, and creativity. For instance, courses in digital humanities can explore how AI tools are transforming the study of literature, history, and philosophy. Students might engage with projects that utilize AI for text analysis, pattern recognition in historical documents, or the generation of creative writing. This interdisciplinary approach helps students understand how AI can both influence and be influenced by cultural narratives and ethical considerations. Moreover, incorporating discussions on the ethical and philosophical implications of AI in humanities courses fosters critical thinking about the societal impacts of technology and the responsibilities of AI practitioners. In the social sciences, integrating AI curricula can provide insights into how technology affects social structures, behavior, and public policy. For example, courses in sociology and political science might examine the role of AI in shaping public opinion, influencing elections through targeted advertising, or analyzing social networks. Students can explore how AI-driven data analytics impact research methodologies, social justice issues, and the formulation of public policies (Grover S., et al., 2013). By examining these intersections, students gain a deeper understanding of AI's role in societal dynamics and develop the skills to address the challenges and opportunities presented by technological advancements.

The integration of AI with the arts offers a unique opportunity to explore creativity and innovation through technology. Art and design students can work on projects that involve generative AI, such as creating digital art, music composition, or interactive installations. These projects allow students to experiment with AI's capabilities in generating new forms of artistic expression and to consider the implications of AI-generated creativity on traditional artistic practices. Additionally, courses that focus on the use of AI in media production, game design, and virtual reality can help students understand how AI technologies are reshaping the creative industries and the ways in which art and technology intersect (Hsu T. C.,et al., 2021). An interdisciplinary AI curriculum should also emphasize collaborative learning experiences that bring together students from different fields to work on projects that address complex problems. For example, a collaborative project might involve students from computer science, sociology, and art working together to design an AI-driven tool for analyzing and visualizing social data in innovative ways. Such projects encourage students to apply their diverse expertise and perspectives, leading to richer, more nuanced outcomes. Furthermore, incorporating real-world case studies and industry partnerships into the curriculum can enhance students' understanding of how AI is applied across various sectors (Ingkavara T., et al., 2022). Additionally, the curriculum should foster critical thinking and reflective practices, encouraging students to question and analyze the impact of AI on various aspects of human life. By integrating humanities, social sciences, and the arts into AI education, students are better equipped to understand and address the multifaceted challenges of an AI-driven world. This approach not only enhances their technical skills but also enriches their ability to think critically about the social, ethical, and cultural dimensions of technology. Ultimately, interdisciplinary AI curricula prepare students to become informed and responsible practitioners who can navigate the complexities of technology and contribute meaningfully to shaping a future where AI aligns with human values and societal needs.

PROJECT-BASED LEARNING IN AI EDUCATION: HANDS-ON EXPERIENCES AND REAL-WORLD APPLICATIONS

"Project-Based Learning in AI Education: Hands-on Experiences and Real-World Applications" explores how PBL can be effectively implemented in AI curricula to bridge theoretical knowledge with practical skills, fostering a more engaging and comprehensive learning experience. At its core, PBL involves students working on projects that are complex, open-ended, and relevant to real-world challenges (Jiang S., et al .,2023). For instance, students might undertake projects that involve developing machine learning models to address specific issues, such as predicting disease outbreaks, optimizing supply chains, or creating recommendation systems. These projects allow students to engage with real data, use industry-standard tools, and encounter the complexities and nuances of applying AI in practical scenarios. This hands-on approach helps students develop a more robust understanding of AI algorithms, data processing techniques, and model evaluation methods. For example, a project might require students to preprocess and clean large datasets, choose appropriate algorithms, and assess the performance of their models. Through this iterative process, students gain practical experience and learn to address challenges such as data quality issues and algorithmic biases. Real-world applications are central to PBL in AI education, as they provide students with insights into how AI technologies are used across various industries and sectors. Projects can be designed to reflect current trends and challenges in fields such as healthcare, finance, environmental science, and more. For example, a project might involve collaborating with a healthcare organization to develop an AI tool for diagnosing medical conditions from imaging data, providing students with practical experience and a tangible impact on the field. Collaboration and teamwork are also integral components of PBL, reflecting the collaborative nature of real-world AI projects. Students often work in teams to tackle projects, allowing them to learn from each other, share expertise, and develop communication and project management skills (Khan N., et al., 2022). This collaborative environment mirrors professional settings where interdisciplinary teams work together to develop and deploy AI solutions. Additionally, involving stakeholders such as industry partners, non-profit organizations, or community groups in project-based learning can enhance the relevance and impact of student work. Partnerships with external organizations provide students with valuable feedback, real-world perspectives, and potential opportunities for internships or career connections. These collaborations can also help ensure that projects address pressing societal needs and contribute to meaningful outcomes. Assessment in PBL should focus on both the process and the product. Evaluating students' work involves assessing their problem-solving approach, teamwork, and the effectiveness of their AI solutions. Rubrics can be developed to assess various aspects of the project, including technical accuracy, creativity, and the ability to communicate findings. Additionally, reflection and self-assessment activities encourage students to critically evaluate their own learning and development throughout the project. Integrating PBL into AI education requires careful planning and support from educators. Designing meaningful projects that align with learning objectives and industry needs involves collaborating with professionals, developing realistic problem scenarios, and providing necessary resources and guidance. Educators should also facilitate opportunities for students to present their projects, share their findings, and receive feedback from peers, mentors, and industry experts. In summary, project-based learning in AI education offers a dynamic and effective approach to teaching AI concepts and applications. By engaging students in hands-on projects that address real-world problems, PBL fosters deeper learning, critical thinking, and practical skills development. This approach not only enhances students' technical proficiency but also prepares them to tackle complex challenges in various industries, contributing to their readiness for careers in AI and related fields. Through meaningful projects and real-world applications, students gain a comprehensive understanding of AI and its potential to drive innovation and address societal needs.

ASSESSMENT AND EVALUATION IN AI EDUCATION: MEASURING LEARNING OUTCOMES

Assessment and evaluation in AI education are crucial for measuring learning outcomes, ensuring that students acquire the necessary skills and knowledge to navigate the complex landscape of artificial intelligence (AI) (Lai Y. H., et al., 2021). "Assessment and Evaluation in AI Education: Measuring Learning Outcomes" explores the multifaceted approaches required to effectively gauge students' understanding and proficiency in AI concepts, practices, and applications. To begin with, formative assessment plays a pivotal role in providing ongoing feedback throughout the learning process. This can include quizzes, coding exercises, and project milestones that help educators gauge students' grasp of fundamental AI principles and identify areas that need further attention. For instance, short quizzes on topics like machine learning algorithms or neural network architectures can help reinforce key concepts and ensure that students are keeping pace with the curriculum. Additionally, coding exercises and assignments that involve practical application of AI techniques allow instructors to assess students' ability to implement and troubleshoot AI models, providing immediate feedback that guides their learning. This typically includes comprehensive exams, final projects, and presentations. In AI education, summative assessments should be designed to test both theoretical understanding and practical skills. Evaluating practical skills is particularly important in AI education, as students need to demonstrate their ability to work with real data, build and train models, and analyze results. Practical assessments can include coding challenges, data analysis projects, and case studies. For example, students might be asked to develop a machine learning model to predict customer behavior based on a provided dataset, and then present their findings, including their approach to data preprocessing, model selection, and performance evaluation (Lee C. A., et al., 2021). Another key aspect of assessment in AI education is the evaluation of collaborative and project-based work. Many AI projects involve teamwork and interdisciplinary collaboration, reflecting real-world scenarios. Therefore, assessments should consider both individual contributions and group dynamics. Rubrics can be used to evaluate various aspects of collaborative projects, including teamwork, communication, project management, and the quality of the final product. These objectives should encompass a range of skills, including technical proficiency, critical thinking, ethical considerations, and the ability to apply AI concepts to real-world problems. Developing detailed rubrics that outline criteria for different levels of performance helps ensure consistency and transparency in grading. Additionally, incorporating a variety of assessment methods, such as practical exercises, theoretical exams, and project presentations, provides a more comprehensive evaluation of students' capabilities. Beyond traditional assessment methods, incorporating portfolio assessments can offer a holistic view of students' progress and achievements. Portfolios can include a collection of students' work, such as coding assignments, project reports, and reflective essays, showcasing their growth and development over time (McCarthy J., et al., 2006). In summary, assessment and evaluation in AI education require a multifaceted approach that includes formative and summative assessments, practical skill evaluations, and consideration of collaborative work.

AI EDUCATION FOR PROFESSIONALS: UPSKILLING AND RESKILLING FOR THE AI WORKFORCE

AI education for professionals focuses on upskilling and reskilling to meet the evolving demands of the AI workforce, addressing the need for continuous learning in a rapidly changing technological landscape. "AI Education for Professionals: Upskilling and Reskilling for the AI Workforce" explores how targeted educational programs can equip current and aspiring professionals with the knowledge and skills necessary to thrive in AI-driven environments. The first step in effective upskilling and reskilling is identifying the specific needs of professionals in various fields. As AI technologies become more integrated into diverse industries, the skills required range from fundamental data science techniques to advanced machine learning and AI ethics. Tailoring educational programs to address these specific needs involves offering specialized courses and training modules that focus on relevant applications, tools, and techniques. For instance, professionals in finance might benefit from learning about algorithmic trading and predictive analytics, while those in healthcare may focus on AI applications in medical imaging and patient data analysis(Mahadev Madgule, et al., 2023). One of the key components of AI education for professionals is providing hands-on experience with real-world tools and technologies. Practical training, such as working with AI frameworks like TensorFlow, PyTorch, or Scikit-Learn, is essential for developing proficiency in implementing and optimizing AI models. Another critical aspect is staying current with the latest advancements in AI. Given the rapid pace of technological progress, professionals must engage in continuous learning to remain competitive. Educational programs should include modules on emerging trends, such as generative AI, reinforcement learning, and ethical AI, to ensure that professionals are aware of and can leverage the latest developments. Online platforms, industry conferences, and professional certifications offer avenues for ongoing education and networking, helping professionals stay updated and connected with the broader AI community. Reskilling, in particular, involves transitioning from one area of expertise to another, often requiring a more structured approach.

These introductory courses can serve as stepping stones to more advanced topics, enabling individuals to build the necessary background knowledge before diving into specialized AI applications. Additionally, integrating soft skills training into AI education can significantly enhance professionals' effectiveness in the workplace. Educational programs should incorporate elements of project management, teamwork, and presentation skills, ensuring that professionals are not only technically proficient but also adept at conveying complex AI concepts and findings to stakeholders. Industry collaboration is another important factor in designing effective AI education programs. Partnerships with technology companies, research institutions, and industry leaders can provide professionals with insights into current industry practices, challenges, and opportunities. These collaborations can also lead to the development of specialized training programs and certifications that are aligned with industry standards and needs (McLaren B. M., et al., 2010). For example, partnerships with cloud service providers could offer certifications in cloud-based AI solutions, while collaborations with research institutions might lead to advanced courses on cutting-edge AI research. Evaluating the effectiveness of upskilling and reskilling programs is essential to ensure that they meet the needs of professionals and produce desired outcomes. This involves gathering feedback from participants, assessing their progress through assessments and practical projects, and tracking their career advancements post-training. Regularly updating curricula based on industry feedback and technological advancements ensures that educational programs remain relevant and impactful. In summary, AI education for professionals encompasses a range of strategies for upskilling and reskilling, including specialized training, hands-on experience, continuous learning, and the integration of soft skills. By tailoring educational programs to address specific needs, incorporating real-world applications, and fostering industry collaborations, professionals can effectively enhance their expertise and adapt to the evolving demands of the AI workforce.

ONLINE AND BLENDED LEARNING IN AI EDUCATION: EFFECTIVE INSTRUCTIONAL STRATEGIES

Online and blended learning have become pivotal in AI education, offering flexible and innovative instructional strategies that cater to diverse learning needs and contexts. "Online and Blended Learning in AI Education(Ng D. T. K., et al., 2021). Effective Instructional Strategies" delves into how these modalities can be optimized to deliver high-quality AI education, blending the advantages of traditional classroom settings with the accessibility and scalability of digital platforms. Moreover, online learning facilitates access to a global pool of expertise and perspectives. Learners can participate in forums, webinars, and virtual study groups, collaborating with peers and instructors from around the world. This international network enriches the learning experience, exposing students to diverse applications of AI and innovative approaches to problem-solving. Online courses can also integrate real-world case studies and industry-relevant projects, providing learners with practical experience and insights into current AI trends and challenges. Blended learning, which combines online and in-person instruction, offers a complementary approach that leverages the strengths of both modalitiesv (Ng O. L., et al., 2021). In a blended learning environment, students can benefit from the flexibility of online coursework while also engaging in face-to-face interactions that foster deeper learning and collaboration. For instance, online modules might cover foundational AI concepts and theoretical knowledge, while in-person sessions can focus on hands-on labs, group projects, and discussions that deepen understanding and facilitate practical application. This combination allows for a more comprehensive educational experience, balancing self-directed learning with guided, interactive opportunities.

Effective blended learning strategies often involve a well-structured integration of online and in-person components. For example, an AI course might start with online lectures and readings, followed by scheduled in-person workshops where students apply what they have learned through coding exercises and group projects. Regular check-ins and feedback sessions can help ensure that students are grasping the material and making progress. In-person sessions can also be used for high-impact activities such as guest lectures from industry experts, collaborative problem-solving workshops, and presentations of student projects. One of the critical considerations in online and blended AI education is ensuring the quality and effectiveness of instructional materials. Online content must be designed with clarity and engagement in mind, using interactive elements such as quizzes, simulations, and coding environments to reinforce learning. High-quality video and audio, well-organized course materials, and user-friendly platforms contribute to an effective online learning experience. To support learners in an online or blended setting, providing robust support mechanisms is essential. This includes access to technical support, academic advising, and opportunities for peer interaction. Online forums, discussion boards, and virtual office hours can facilitate communication between students and instructors, helping to address questions and challenges in real time (Page M. J., et al., 2021). Additionally, creating a supportive online community fosters engagement and collaboration, enhancing the overall learning experience. Assessment and evaluation are also key components of effective online and blended learning in AI education. Assessments should be designed to evaluate both theoretical understanding and practical skills, incorporating a mix of quizzes, coding assignments, project work, and peer reviews. Online platforms can facilitate a range of assessment methods, including automated quizzes, project submissions, and participation in online discussions. Providing timely and constructive feedback is crucial for guiding students' learning and development. In summary, online and blended learning offer powerful instructional strategies for AI education, combining the flexibility and scalability of digital platforms with the interactive and hands-on experiences of in-person instruction. By designing high-quality online content, effectively integrating online and in-person components, and providing robust support mechanisms, educators can deliver a comprehensive and engaging AI education that meets the diverse needs of learners.

AI EDUCATION FOR MARGINALIZED COMMUNITIES: ADDRESSING DIVERSITY, EQUITY, AND INCLUSION

AI education for marginalized communities is crucial in addressing diversity, equity, and inclusion, ensuring that these groups are not only represented but also empowered in the rapidly advancing field of artificial intelligence (AI). "AI Education for Marginalized Communities: Addressing Diversity, Equity, and Inclusion" explores the strategies and approaches necessary to create equitable AI learning opportunities that bridge gaps in access, representation, and opportunity for underrepresented groups. One of the primary challenges in AI education for marginalized communities is overcoming barriers to access. Socioeconomic factors, geographic isolation, and systemic inequalities often limit opportunities for these groups to engage with high-quality educational resources (Ríos Félix J. M., et al., 2020). To address these barriers, initiatives must focus on increasing access to AI education through scholarships, grants, and funding for technology infrastructure. Partnering with community organizations, educational institutions, and tech companies can help provide resources such as free or low-cost online courses, hardware, and internet access. These efforts can ensure that individuals from marginalized communities have the tools they need to participate in and benefit from AI education. Representation is another critical aspect of ensuring diversity and inclusion in AI education. It is essential to include diverse voices and perspectives in curriculum development, instructional materials, and teaching staff. By incorporating examples, case studies, and applications relevant to different communities, educators can make AI education more relatable and meaningful (Silapachote P., et al., 2017). Additionally, actively recruiting and supporting diverse instructors and mentors can provide role models and guidance for students from underrepresented backgrounds, fostering a more inclusive learning environment. Culturally responsive pedagogy is a key component in making AI education accessible and engaging for marginalized communities.

This approach involves tailoring educational practices and content to reflect the cultural, social, and linguistic backgrounds of students. For example, curricula might incorporate examples and scenarios that resonate with students' lived experiences, making the material more relevant and engaging. Providing support systems such as mentorship programs, tutoring, and career counseling can further enhance the learning experience for students from marginalized communities (Sugumaran K. M, D., et al., 2024). This can be especially valuable for navigating career paths in AI and overcoming challenges related to systemic biases and barriers in the tech industry. Creating pathways for advancement is also essential for promoting equity in AI education. This includes developing programs that support students through various stages of their educational and professional journeys, from K-12 to higher education and beyond. For instance, outreach programs and summer camps focused on AI can introduce younger students to the field, while internships, fellowships, and job placement services can assist older students in gaining practical experience and securing employment in the tech industry. Additionally, fostering partnerships with industry leaders can help create pipelines for talent and provide opportunities for marginalized communities to contribute to and benefit from AI innovations. Addressing systemic biases in AI itself is another critical area of focus. Curricula should include discussions on how to identify, mitigate, and address biases in AI systems, preparing students to contribute to the creation of equitable and unbiased technologies. Evaluation and continuous improvement of AI education programs are vital to ensure that they effectively address the needs of marginalized communities. Collecting data on student outcomes, feedback, and program impact can provide insights into areas for improvement and help measure progress towards equity and inclusion goals. Regularly assessing and updating programs based on this feedback ensures that educational initiatives remain relevant and effective in promoting diversity and opportunity. In summary, AI education for marginalized communities requires a multifaceted approach that addresses access barriers, representation, culturally responsive pedagogy, support systems, pathways for advancement, and systemic biases in AI.

CURRICULA DESIGN FOR AI-DRIVEN EMERGING TECHNOLOGIES: BLOCKCHAIN, IOT, AND MORE

Designing curricula for AI-driven emerging technologies, such as blockchain and the Internet of Things (IoT), requires a nuanced approach that integrates foundational AI principles with the unique aspects of these advanced technologies. "Curricula Design for AI-Driven Emerging Technologies: Blockchain, IoT, and More" explores how to craft educational programs that prepare students to understand and apply AI in conjunction with other cutting-edge technologies, thereby equipping them with the skills to innovate and address complex challenges in a rapidly evolving tech landscape.To start, it's crucial to establish a solid foundation in AI concepts before delving into specific technologies like blockchain and IoT. For instance, students should grasp how AI techniques can enhance data analytics, pattern recognition, and automation, providing the necessary background to explore how these principles are utilized in emerging technologies.When incorporating blockchain technology into AI curricula, it is important to highlight the synergy between these two fields. Blockchain, a decentralized ledger technology, can benefit from AI in several ways, such as enhancing security through smart contract verification, optimizing consensus mechanisms, and analyzing transaction patterns for fraud detection.

The curriculum should cover fundamental blockchain concepts, including cryptographic hashing, consensus algorithms, and decentralized applications (dApps). Additionally, practical modules should demonstrate how AI algorithms can be integrated into blockchain systems to address challenges like scalability, privacy, and efficiency. Students might engage in projects that involve developing blockchain-based AI solutions for secure data sharing or creating intelligent contracts that adapt based on predictive analytics(Voogt J., et al., 2015). Projects might include developing end-to-end IoT solutions that integrate AI for actionable insights and automated responses.In addition to blockchain and IoT, other emerging technologies such as edge computing, augmented reality (AR), and 5G also intersect with AI, warranting inclusion in curricula. Curriculum design should address how AI can be deployed on edge devices, enabling local data processing and decision-making. Similarly, AR technologies benefit from AI in areas like object recognition and interaction. Courses might include practical applications where students create AR experiences powered by AI for enhanced user interfaces or immersive simulations (Vijayakumar G, et al., 2024). The advent of 5G networks further accelerates AI capabilities by providing high-speed, low-latency connectivity, which supports advanced AI applications in autonomous vehicles, smart cities, and remote healthcare.

To effectively integrate these technologies into AI curricula, educators should employ project-based learning, real-world case studies, and industry collaborations. Hands-on projects that involve building and deploying AI solutions using blockchain, IoT, or other emerging technologies offer students practical experience and problem-solving skills (Weintrop D., et al., 2016).Assessment strategies for curricula involving AI and emerging technologies should evaluate both theoretical understanding and practical skills. This includes assessing students' ability to design and implement AI solutions for blockchain or IoT systems, as well as their understanding of how these technologies interact and complement each other. Rubrics should be developed to evaluate the complexity, innovation, and effectiveness of students' projects, as well as their ability to address real-world problems.In summary, designing curricula for AI-driven emerging technologies like blockchain and IoT involves creating a robust foundation in AI principles while integrating specific technological aspects. By combining theoretical knowledge with practical applications, project-based learning, and industry collaborations, educators can prepare students to effectively leverage AI across a range of advanced technologies. This approach not only equips students with the skills to innovate and solve complex challenges but also ensures they are well-prepared to contribute to and excel in the rapidly evolving tech landscape.

BEST PRACTICES FOR IMPLEMENTING AI CURRICULA: LESSONS FROM PILOT PROGRAMS

Implementing AI curricula effectively requires a careful and thoughtful approach, drawing from lessons learned through pilot programs to ensure the successful integration of artificial intelligence education into diverse educational settings. "Best Practices for Implementing AI Curricula: Lessons from Pilot Programs" examines strategies and insights gained from early implementations to optimize AI education, enhance student outcomes, and address common challenges (Weng X., et al., 2022). One of the foremost best practices identified through pilot programs is the importance of aligning AI curricula with clear educational goals and industry needs. Successful pilot programs often start with a thorough needs assessment to understand the specific skills and knowledge required by students and the demands of the AI industry. This involves engaging with industry stakeholders, educators, and subject matter experts to identify relevant competencies and emerging trends. By aligning curricula with these requirements, programs can ensure that they provide practical, relevant content that prepares students for real-world applications. Another key lesson from pilot programs is the value of integrating hands-on, project-based learning within the curriculum. Practical experience is crucial for understanding complex AI concepts and developing problem-solving skills. Pilot programs that incorporate adaptive learning platforms can provide tailored educational experiences based on individual student needs and progress. Another important practice is the inclusion of diverse and inclusive content within AI curricula. Lessons from pilot programs highlight the necessity of addressing diversity, equity, and inclusion (DEI) in AI education. This involves incorporating diverse perspectives and examples into the curriculum, addressing biases in AI systems, and ensuring that all students feel represented and included. For example, including case studies that highlight AI applications in various cultural and social contexts can help make the material more relatable and engaging for a diverse student body. Additionally, discussions about the ethical implications of AI and how to mitigate biases in AI models are critical for preparing students to develop responsible and equitable technologies.

Engaging and ongoing professional development for educators is another best practice identified from pilot programs. Successful implementations often involve providing educators with continuous training and support to stay current with evolving AI technologies and teaching methodologies. This might include workshops, conferences, and collaborative learning opportunities that help instructors enhance their knowledge and teaching skills. For example, offering professional development sessions on the latest AI research or emerging tools can enable educators to deliver up-to-date and high-quality instruction.Pilot programs also underscore the importance of building strong partnerships with industry and academic institutions. Collaborations with tech companies, research organizations, and other educational institutions can provide valuable resources, expertise, and real-world insights that enhance the curriculum. These partnerships can facilitate access to cutting-edge technologies, internships, and guest lectures from industry professionals. For instance, a pilot program might partner with a leading AI company to provide students with internship opportunities, industry projects, and mentorship, enriching their learning experience and improving their career prospects (Zawacki-Richter O., et al., 2019).Lastly, evaluating and iterating on AI curricula based on feedback and outcomes is crucial for continuous improvement. Lessons from pilot programs demonstrate the need for regular assessment of curriculum effectiveness through student feedback, performance metrics, and external evaluations. In summary, best practices for implementing AI curricula, informed by lessons from pilot programs, include aligning curricula with industry needs, integrating hands-on project-based learning, utilizing adaptive learning technologies, promoting diversity and inclusion, providing ongoing professional development for educators, building industry partnerships, and continuously evaluating and iterating on program effectiveness.

THE FUTURE OF AI CURRICULA AND INSTRUCTIONAL DESIGN - INNOVATIONS AND CHALLENGES

The future of AI curricula and instructional design is poised at the intersection of rapid technological advancements and evolving educational needs, presenting both exciting innovations and significant challenges. "The Future of AI Curricula and Instructional Design: Innovations and Challenges" explores how emerging trends in AI and educational technology are shaping the development of curricula and instructional strategies while addressing the hurdles that educators and institutions must overcome to effectively prepare students for a dynamic future.Innovations in AI curricula and instructional design are driven by several key trends. One of the most transformative developments is the integration of adaptive learning technologies, which leverage AI to personalize educational experiences. For instance, AI-driven platforms can provide customized practice exercises, recommend additional resources, and adjust the difficulty of tasks based on real-time data, thereby creating a more individualized learning journey.In AI education, VR and AR can be used to create simulations and interactive environments where students can experiment with AI models, visualize complex data, and experience real-world applications of AI technology. For example, students might use VR to explore a virtual lab where they can manipulate AI algorithms in a 3D space or use AR to overlay AI-generated insights on physical objects, enhancing their understanding through interactive and immersive experiences.

The rise of project-based and experiential learning is also reshaping AI curricula Innovations in instructional design now emphasize the importance of real-world problem-solving and practical application of AI concepts. For instance, students might work on projects involving the development of AI solutions for climate change, healthcare, or smart cities, thereby addressing pressing global issues while gaining valuable experience (Ye H., et al., 2023).The inclusion of interdisciplinary approaches is another forward-looking trend. For example, incorporating courses on AI ethics and policy alongside technical training helps students understand the broader context of their work and prepares them to address ethical considerations and societal impacts. Similarly, interdisciplinary projects that combine AI with other domains can foster innovative solutions and provide a richer learning experience.However, the future of AI curricula and instructional design also presents several challenges. One major challenge is keeping curricula up-to-date with the rapid pace of technological change. AI is a field characterized by continuous advancements, and educational programs must evolve to incorporate the latest developments and methodologies. This requires agile curriculum design processes, ongoing professional development for educators, and strong connections with industry to ensure that educational content remains relevant and current.

ANOTHER CHALLENGE IS ADDRESSING ISSUES OF EQUITY AND ACCESSIBILITY

As AI education becomes more integral to various sectors, ensuring that all students have access to high-quality resources and opportunities is crucial. This includes addressing disparities in technology access, providing support for underrepresented groups, and ensuring that curricula are designed to be inclusive and culturally responsive(Weng X., et al., 2023). Efforts must be made to bridge the digital divide, offer scholarships and funding for resources, and create pathways for diverse learners to engage with AI education.Ethical considerations also pose significant challenges. AI education, and new methods must be developed to evaluate students' ability to apply AI concepts in diverse contexts and address real-world problems. This includes creating assessments that test both theoretical understanding and practical application, as well as evaluating students' ability to navigate ethical and interdisciplinary issues. In conclusion, the future of AI curricula and instructional design is characterized by innovations such as adaptive learning technologies, immersive experiences, project-based learning, and interdisciplinary approaches. However, it also faces challenges related to keeping pace with technological change, ensuring equity and accessibility, addressing ethical concerns, and developing effective assessment methods. By embracing these innovations and proactively addressing these challenges, educators and institutions can create AI curricula that not only equip students with the technical skills needed for the future but also prepare them to navigate the complex and evolving landscape of artificial intelligence.

CONCLUSION

In conclusion, designing curricula and instructional strategies for artificial intelligence (AI) is a complex yet critical endeavor that shapes the future of technology and its impact on society. Effective AI education necessitates a multifaceted approach that integrates foundational knowledge with practical applications, embraces emerging technologies, and addresses diverse educational needs. As we navigate this evolving landscape, several key principles emerge as central to developing robust and impactful AI curricula.First and foremost, curricula must be grounded in core AI concepts while being adaptable to the rapid pace of technological advancement. These practical experiences not only deepen students' technical expertise but also prepare them to tackle complex challenges and contribute to the development of cutting-edge AI solutions.Inclusivity and accessibility are fundamental to ensuring that AI education reaches all students and addresses the diverse needs of different populations. Effective curricula must be designed to be inclusive, incorporating diverse perspectives and addressing barriers to access for underrepresented and marginalized groups. This includes providing equitable resources, creating culturally responsive content, and supporting a diverse range of learners through tailored instructional strategies and support systems. By prioritizing diversity and inclusion, educational programs can help foster a more equitable and representative AI workforce.

Curricula should include components that address these ethical challenges, preparing students to develop AI systems that are fair, transparent, and aligned with societal values.Innovations in instructional design, such as the use of adaptive learning technologies, immersive experiences, and interdisciplinary approaches, play a significant role in enhancing AI education. Adaptive learning platforms can provide personalized instruction and support, while VR and AR technologies offer immersive and interactive learning opportunities. Additionally, integrating AI with other disciplines, such as ethics, law, and social sciences, enriches the educational experience and prepares students to address the multifaceted impacts of AI.Finally, ongoing evaluation and feedback are essential for continuously improving AI curricula and instructional practices. Regularly assessing the effectiveness of educational programs, gathering input from students and industry stakeholders, and analyzing learning outcomes help identify areas for enhancement and ensure that curricula remain relevant and impactful. By adopting a reflective and iterative approach, educators can refine their strategies and better meet the evolving needs of students and the AI industry.In summary, developing curricula and instructional design for AI involves a comprehensive and forward-thinking approach that balances foundational knowledge with practical application, embraces emerging technologies, and addresses diverse educational needs.

REFERENCES

Arrouillet, P. (2015). Theories of cognitive development: From Piaget to today. *Developmental Review*, 38, 1–12. DOI: 10.1016/j.dr.2015.07.004

Belur, J., Tompson, L., Thornton, A., & Simon, M. (2021). Interrater reliability in systematic review methodology: Exploring variation in coder decision-making. *Sociological Methods & Research*, 50(2), 837–865. DOI: 10.1177/0049124118799372

Brennan, K., & Resnick, M. (2012). New frameworks for studying and assessing the development of computational thinking. In *Proceedings of the 2012 annual meeting of the American educational research association* (1, p. 25).

Cheah, C. W. (2021). Developing a gamified AI-enabled online learning application to improve students' perception of university physics. *Computers and Education: Artificial Intelligence*, 2, 100032. DOI: 10.1016/j.caeai.2021.100032

Conati, C., Barral, O., Putnam, V., & Rieger, L. (2021). Toward personalized XAI: A case study in intelligent tutoring systems. *Artificial Intelligence*, 298, 103503. DOI: 10.1016/j.artint.2021.103503

English, L. D. (2016). STEM education K-12: Perspectives on integration. *International Journal of STEM Education*, 3(3), 1–8. DOI: 10.1186/s40594-016-0036-1

Eshach, H. (2007). Bridging in-school and out-of-school learning: Formal, non-formal, and informal education. *Journal of Science Education and Technology*, 16(2), 171–190. DOI: 10.1007/s10956-006-9027-1

Estevez, J., Garate, G., & Graña, M. (2019). Gentle introduction to artificial intelligence for high-school students using scratch. *IEEE Access : Practical Innovations, Open Solutions*, 7, 179027–179036. DOI: 10.1109/ACCESS.2019.2956136

Fang, X., Ng, D. T. K., Leung, J. K. L., & Chu, S. K. W. (2023). A systematic review of artificial intelligence technologies used for story writing. *Education and Information Technologies*, 28(11), 1–37. DOI: 10.1007/s10639-023-11741-5

Gadanidis, G. (2017). Artificial intelligence, computational thinking, and mathematics education. *The International Journal of Information and Learning Technology*, 34(2), 133–139. DOI: 10.1108/IJILT-09-2016-0048

Gansser, O. A., & Reich, C. S. (2021). A new acceptance model for artificial intelligence with extensions to UTAUT2: An empirical study in three segments of application. *Technology in Society*, 65, 101535. DOI: 10.1016/j.techsoc.2021.101535

Grover, S., & Pea, R. (2013). Computational thinking in K–12: A review of the state of the field. *Educational Researcher*, 42(1), 38–43. DOI: 10.3102/0013189X12463051

Hsu, T. C., Abelson, H., Lao, N., Tseng, Y. H., & Lin, Y. T. (2021). Behavioral-pattern exploration and development of an instructional tool for young children to learn AI. *Computers and Education: Artificial Intelligence*, 2, 100012. DOI: 10.1016/j.caeai.2021.100012

Ingkavara, T., Panjaburee, P., Srisawasdi, N., & Sajjapanroj, S. (2022). The use of a personalized learning approach to implementing self-regulated online learning. *Computers and Education: Artificial Intelligence*, 3, 100086. DOI: 10.1016/j.caeai.2022.100086

Jiang, S., Qian, Y., Tang, H., Yalcinkaya, R., Rosé, C. P., Chao, J., & Finzer, W. (2023). Examining computational thinking processes in modeling unstructured data. *Education and Information Technologies*, 28(4), 4309–4333. DOI: 10.1007/s10639-022-11355-3

Khan, N., Sarwar, A., Chen, T. B., & Khan, S. (2022). Connecting digital literacy in higher education to the 21st century workforce. *Knowledge Management & E-Learning*, 14(1), 46–61. DOI: 10.34105/j.kmel.2022.14.004

Lai, Y. H., Chen, S. Y., Lai, C. F., Chang, Y. C., & Su, Y. S. (2021). Study on enhancing AIoT computational thinking skills by plot image-based VR. *Interactive Learning Environments*, 29(3), 482–495. DOI: 10.1080/10494820.2019.1580750

Lee, C. A., Tzeng, J. W., Huang, N. F., & Su, Y. S. (2021). Prediction of student performance in massive open online courses using deep learning system based on learning behaviors. *Journal of Educational Technology & Society*, 24(3), 130–146. https://www.jstor.org/stable/27032861

Mahadev Madgule, N. (2023). Vinayaka, Yeshwant M. Sonkhaskar, Dhiren Ramanbhai Patel, R. Karthikeyan, P. Selvakumar,(2023). Mechanical properties and microstructure of activated TIG welded similar joints of Inconel alloys by desirability approaches. *Materials Today: Proceedings*, 77, 528–533. DOI: 10.1016/j.matpr.2022.12.250

McCarthy, J., Minsky, M. L., Rochester, N., & Shannon, C. E. (2006). A proposal for the dartmouth summer research project on artificial intelligence, august 31, 1955. *AI Magazine*, 27(4), 12. DOI: 10.1609/aimag.v27i4.1904

McLaren, B. M., Scheuer, O., & Mikšátko, J. (2010). Supporting collaborative learning and e-discussions using artificial intelligence techniques. *International Journal of Artificial Intelligence in Education*, 20(1), 1–46. DOI: 10.3233/JAI-2010-0001

Ng, D. T. K., Leung, J. K. L., Chu, S. K. W., & Qiao, M. S. (2021). Conceptualizing AI literacy: An exploratory review. *Computers and Education: Artificial Intelligence*, 2, 100041. DOI: 10.1016/j.caeai.2021.100041

Ng, O. L., & Cui, Z. (2021). Examining primary students' mathematical problem-solving in a programming context: Towards computationally enhanced mathematics education. *ZDM Mathematics Education*, 53(4), 847–860. DOI: 10.1007/s11858-020-01200-7

Page, M. J., McKenzie, J. E., Bossuyt, P. M., Boutron, I., Hoffmann, T. C., Mulrow, C. D., & Moher, D. (2021). The PRISMA 2020 statement: An updated guideline for reporting systematic reviews. *BMJ (Clinical Research Ed.)*, 372(1), 1–9. DOI: 10.1186/s13643-021-01626-4 PMID: 33782057

Ríos Félix, J. M., Zatarain Cabada, R., Barrón Estrada, M. L., & Favela Vara, J. (2020). An intelligent learning environment for computational thinking. *Computación y Sistemas*, 24(3), 1199–1210. DOI: 10.13053/cys-24-3-3480

Silapachote, P., & Srisuphab, A. (2017). Engineering courses on computational thinking through solving problems in artificial intelligence. *International Journal of Engineering Pedagogy*, 7(3), 34. DOI: 10.3991/ijep.v7i3.6951

Sugumaran, K. M. D., Pandiyarajan V., Y. B S, Selvakumar P. and M. S, (2024). "Analysis of Electromyography Signals for Control of Mechanical Prosthesis using Machine Learning Techniques," 2024 2nd International Conference on Intelligent Data Communication Technologies and Internet of Things (IDCIoT), Bengaluru, India, 2024, pp. 1059-1067, DOI: 10.1109/IDCIoT59759.2024.10467707

Vijayakumar, G., Rajkumar, M., Rajiv Chandar, N., Selvakumar, P., & Duraisamy, R. (2024). Muniyandi Rajkumar, Rajiv Chandar N, Selvakumar P and Ramesh Duraisamy, (2024). Environmentally friendly TDS removal from waste water by electrochemical ion exchange batch-type recirculation (EIR) technique. *Environmental Science. Water Research & Technology*, 10(4), 826–835. DOI: 10.1039/D3EW00793F

Voogt, J., Fisser, P., Good, J., Mishra, P., & Yadav, A. (2015). Computational thinking in compulsory education: Towards an agenda for research and practice. *Education and Information Technologies*, 20(4), 715–728. DOI: 10.1007/s10639-015-9412-6

Weintrop, D., Beheshti, E., Horn, M., Orton, K., Jona, K., Trouille, L., & Wilensky, U. (2016). Defining computational thinking for mathematics and science classrooms. *Journal of Science Education and Technology*, 25(1), 127–147. DOI: 10.1007/s10956-015-9581-5

Weng, X., Cui, Z., Ng, O. L., Jong, M. S., & Chiu, T. K. (2022). Characterizing students' 4C skills development during problem-based digital making. *Journal of Science Education and Technology*, 31(3), 372–385. DOI: 10.1007/s10956-022-09961-4

Weng, X., Ng, O. L., & Chiu, T. K. (2023). Competency development of pre-service teachers during video-based learning: A systematic literature review and meta-analysis. *Computers & Education*, 199, 104790. Advance online publication. DOI: 10.1016/j.compedu.2023.104790

Ye, H., Liang, B., Ng, O. L., & Chai, C. S. (2023). Integration of computational thinking in K-12 mathematics education: A systematic review on CT-based mathematics instruction and student learning. *International Journal of STEM Education*, 10(1), 1–26. DOI: 10.1186/s40594-023-00396-w

Zawacki-Richter, O., Marín, V. I., Bond, M., & Gouverneur, F. (2019). Systematic review of research on artificial intelligence applications in higher education–where are the educators? *International Journal of Educational Technology in Higher Education*, 16(1), 1–27. DOI: 10.1186/s41239-019-0171-0

Zeng, D. (2013). From computational thinking to AI thinking [A letter from the editor]. *IEEE Intelligent Systems*, 28(06), 2–4. DOI: 10.1109/MIS.2013.141

Chapter 3
From Algorithm to AI: Designing Educational Pathways for Students

Sahar Saoud
https://orcid.org/0000-0003-4205-6777
EST, University Ibnou Zohr, Morocco

Naoual Nassiri
https://orcid.org/0000-0002-8299-9422
EST, University Ibnou Zohr, Morocco

Zouhir Mahani
EST, University Ibnou Zohr, Morocco

ABSTRACT

Artificial intelligence (AI) has become a key component in educational pathways especially in computer science, requiring teaching methods to be adapted to support students in the progressive acquisition of skills, from the basics of algorithms to advanced AI technologies. This chapter explores how to design structured educational pathways, starting from the foundations in programming and algorithms, then introducing more complex AI concepts such as machine learning and deep learning. It highlights pedagogical strategies based on project-based learning, interactive simulations, and the integration of practical examples that encourage innovation and skills development. The chapter also proposes techniques for assessing the acquisition of skills and addresses the ethical issues associated with AI, in order to train students capable of meeting tomorrow's technological and societal challenges. This approach aims to meet the growing demand for qualified professionals in this field, while integrating flexible learning methods that can be adapted to a variety of pedagogical contexts.

INTRODUCTION AND MOTIVATION

In the current context of digital transformation, artificial intelligence (AI) plays a crucial role in technological innovations and the evolution of professions in general. Indeed, in order to produce a new generation of competent and ethically responsible professionals, it is essential to design comprehensive,

DOI: 10.4018/979-8-3693-8965-2.ch003

well-structured educational pathways that gradually build the AI skills needed to succeed in any given field (Vuong et al., 2021). This involves getting started with a solid programming and algorithmic fundamentals, then introducing more complex concepts such as machine learning and deep learning. These pathways must not only provide technical knowledge, but also prepare students, in their fields of activity, for the ethical and societal challenges associated with AI(d'Amiens, 2024; Dewey, 1986).

It is clear that, whatever your speciality, a basic education in programming and algorithms is essential if you are to gain an in-depth understanding of the advanced concepts of artificial intelligence. Indeed, algorithmics and programming embody above all an approach to logical thinking and problem solving, thus providing skills that are virtually essential for effectively manipulating AI algorithms. Languages such as Python, Java or C++ are often favoured for their flexibility, popularity and essential usefulness in implementing algorithms and programmes.

Initial training in algorithms enables students to master fundamental techniques, such as search and sort algorithms, which form the basis of many complex algorithms. This first step in the educational process also provides a practical understanding of data structures, algorithmic complexity and object-oriented programming. As well as developing intellectual rigour, these concepts lay a solid foundation on which students can build as they move on to more advanced concepts, such as the tools and methods of artificial intelligence.

By starting with these fundamentals, students acquire not only a command of the necessary technical tools, but also a capacity for abstraction and analysis that will enable them to solve complex problems and adapt to the rapid evolution of AI-related technologies. Such a pedagogical approach effectively prepares students for a coherent and structured progression towards the acquisition of specialised skills in this fast-growing field.

Once these fundamentals have been consolidated, students will be able to immerse themselves in the field of machine learning. Machine learning involves developing models able to learn from data and improve over time, without being explicitly programmed for each task. This field includes key concepts such as regression, which helps predict continuous values, or classification, which distinguishes categories within data. Clustering algorithms are also introduced to group similar data. At this stage, it is essential that students understand how model and parameter choices can affect algorithm performance. Teachers introduce practical projects for students to apply this knowledge directly, for example by building predictive models for real-world applications, such as sentiment analysis or fraud detection.

Next, the educational process moves on to deep learning, an advanced sub-branch of machine learning. This technique is based on artificial neural networks, inspired by the workings of the human brain. Deep neural networks are able to process massive amounts of data and solve complex problems such as image recognition or natural language processing. To master this technology, students need to familiarize themselves with deep learning frameworks such as TensorFlow or PyTorch, which facilitate the design and training of neural network models. Deep learning is also approached with more advanced concepts, such as convolutional networks for image analysis and recurrent networks for time series. Students are encouraged to experiment and customize these architectures to understand their impact in real-life cases.

To make learning AI concepts more engaging, it's essential to integrate innovative pedagogical strategies. Project-based learning is particularly effective, as it enables students to apply their skills in a real, concrete context, while stimulating their creativity and critical thinking (Kolodner, 2000). Interdisciplinary projects, which combine AI with other fields such as biology, economics or law, particularly help students to understand the impact of AI in various sectors and to develop more global perspectives.

Simulation environments and practical case studies are also powerful pedagogical tools, as they enable students to test their knowledge and receive immediate feedback on their actions.

Through several subsequent experiences, another crucial aspect in the design of educational pathways in AI is the assessment of skills. It is important to set up ongoing assessments that measure students' understanding and capability throughout their learning. Regular quizzes, final projects, and self-assessment exercises can provide indicators of progress and areas requiring further work. Constructive feedback is also essential, as it helps students to identify and correct mistakes, thereby reinforcing their learning (Bee & Bee, 1998). By encouraging students to reflect critically on their own learning, AI educational pathways become powerful tools for developing the autonomy and confidence of future professionals (Yan et al., s. d.).

There's no doubt that AI has affected every dimension of contemporary life. At the same time, it is essential to make students aware of the ethical issues associated with AI. Indeed, AI raises important questions related to privacy, algorithmic biases and social responsibility (Brundage, 2015). Students need to be trained to understand how to avoid algorithmic biases, which can cause unintended discrimination (*The 2020Yearbook of the Digital Ethics Lab | SpringerLink*, s. d.) (Porayska-Pomsta et al., 2023). They also need to be aware of the importance of data confidentiality and user privacy. By addressing these issues from the outset of their training, educational pathways can produce responsible individuals able to use AI in an ethical and socially beneficial way (Friedewald et al., 2024; Mokkink et al., 2020).

Last but not least, flexibility and customization are essential to meet the diverse needs of students. Some may prefer online learning, while others may opt for face-to-face courses. By offering modular and adaptable options, AI educational pathways can accommodate diverse contexts and individual preferences, facilitating greater accessibility to AI education.

To sum up, designing a structured and appropriate educational pathway to train students in artificial intelligence is a complex but essential challenge in the current technological context. This requires a global approach that integrates several fundamental dimensions. Firstly, a solid academic background is essential, covering key areas such as algorithms, programming, applied mathematics and databases. These technical skills need to be complemented by advanced modules in machine learning, deep learning and natural language processing, enabling students to specialise in a variety of fast-growing fields of application.

Secondly, the integration of innovative learning methods is essential to meet the needs of a generation of connected and dynamic learners. Active teaching approaches such as project-based learning, hackathons, collaborative workshops and virtual reality simulations encourage engagement, autonomy and the development of practical skills. These immersive experiences also enable students to develop their creativity and critical thinking skills, essential qualities for innovation in a constantly evolving field.

In addition, continuous assessment plays a key role in monitoring and supporting learners. Mechanisms such as regular quizzes, case studies, oral presentations and project reports provide a clear view of students' progress, while encouraging them to make a constant effort. This approach also helps to quickly identify any gaps, so that appropriate remedial solutions can be proposed.

Finally, raising awareness of ethical issues is a fundamental part of any artificial intelligence training programme. It is essential to introduce students to issues such as algorithmic bias, data confidentiality, system transparency and the impact of AI on society. This awareness will enable them to develop professional responsibility and to think critically about the implications of their work.

By combining these elements - a solid academic foundation, innovative learning methods, continuous assessment and awareness of ethical issues - it is possible to prepare a generation of competent, creative and responsible professionals, ready to meet the challenges of tomorrow and make a positive contribution to global technological change.

To this end, this chapter focuses on the design of suitable educational pathways, to take students from the basics of algorithmics through to the most advanced AI technologies, such as machine learning and deep learning. Thus, we address the following problematic:

How can we design learning pathways effectively integrate learning about artificial intelligence (AI) while meeting the pedagogical and ethical constraints of a constantly changing world?

This problematic highlight three dimensions of AI learning:

1. What are the fundamental and advanced concepts needed to develop solid skills in AI?
2. What teaching methods and strategies can be used to ensure learning is engaging and effective?
3. How can learners be made aware of the ethical issues involved in applying AI?

The methodology chosen for this paper is based on the constructivist paradigm, a pedagogical approach which considers that learners actively construct their knowledge through concrete and meaningful experiences. This paradigm places the emphasis on engaging learners in activities that encourage them to explore, experiment and solve real problems, while mobilising their previous knowledge to develop new ones. By integrating simulation environments, case studies and practical projects, learners are not limited to the passive assimilation of concepts, but actively participate in their learning, thereby enhancing creativity, critical thinking and autonomy. The constructivist paradigm offers an ideal framework for designing educational pathways in artificial intelligence that combine the acquisition of technical and an understanding of the ethical and societal issues involved.

The aim is to propose pedagogical strategies that promote skill acquisition, innovation and student engagement, while integrating assessment methods to measure the progress of this learning. In addition, this chapter addresses the ethical issues associated with AI, essential for training responsible individuals who are aware of the social and ethical implications of their skills.

To this end, we are using a methodology based on a survey. This survey is dedicated to a predominantly student population, in order to unearth avenues for the design of student-oriented educational pathways. The results obtained will be statistically studied and interpreted to deduce the best scenarios for the said design.

The chapter is organized into two main parts. The first part presents the fundamental concepts we will be using in the survey. It contains the foundations and existing teaching strategies. The second part, seen as the practical part, will set out the results obtained, as well as suggestions for improving the design of educational pathways.

FROM ALGORITHM TO ARTIFICIAL INTELLIGENCE: UNDERSTANDING, DESIGNING, APPLYING

Artificial intelligence (AI) derives its power from its ability to transform algorithms into autonomous systems capable of solving complex problems. This transition, from the abstract principles of algorithms to their implementation in concrete solutions, rests on several fundamental pillars. Firstly, a thorough understanding of algorithmic concepts is essential. This includes not only knowledge of data structures and problem-solving techniques, but also a mastery of notions of computational complexity to guarantee the efficiency and viability of the proposed solutions.

Secondly, rigorous design plays a key role in this process. It involves a precise modelling phase, where problems are broken down into manageable sub-problems and potential solutions are assessed for their relevance, feasibility and impact. This stage requires analytical thinking and the ability to anticipate implementation challenges, such as the limits of hardware resources or the complexity of real-world scenarios.

Finally, the methodical application of these algorithms in concrete environments requires advanced technical expertise. This includes using appropriate programming languages, such as Python or C++, to translate abstract concepts into operational code, as well as mastering specialised tools and libraries, such as TensorFlow or PyTorch, to implement complex models. This stage also requires skills in validation and optimisation, to ensure that the solutions developed work reliably, efficiently and ethically in a variety of contexts.

In this way, artificial intelligence's ability to move from abstraction to action is based on a balance between in-depth conceptual understanding, structured design and methodical implementation. This rigorous process is what enables AI to take on the most ambitious challenges, transforming theoretical ideas into concrete solutions at the service of society.

This section explores the fundamental mechanisms that enable us to move from algorithmic structures to functional AI models. We will highlight the role of algorithms/programs in machine learning, expert systems and other key areas of AI. In addition, we will examine how these tools can be adapted and optimized to meet the specific challenges of different application contexts. By articulating theory and practice, this section aims to provide a comprehensive and integrated view of the scientific and technical approach underlying the development of artificial intelligence.

THE FOUNDATIONS OF AI TRAINING: PROGRAMMING AND ALGORITHMS

1. From algorithm to program

It's true that AI is a fast-growing field based on rigorous foundations, among which programming and algorithms play a crucial role. These two disciplines are the real pillars of intelligent system design, providing the conceptual and practical tools needed to analyze and solve complex problems.

To effectively explore advanced AI technologies, students of all specializations must first and foremost acquire a solid knowledge of programming and algorithms. These fundamental skills will enable them to tackle complex problems and build an understanding of the logical methods needed to model and solve problems.

If we wish to be more specific in terms of epistemology, we can say that algorithms and programs are two sides of the same coin. **Algorithms** are the art of devising clear, structured solutions to problems. It consists in defining a logical sequence of instructions which, once followed, enable a precise objective to be achieved. In other words, it's the detailed plan of a solution, like a roadmap showing each step to be taken. **Programming**, on the other hand, is the practical implementation of these solutions using a computer language. It is the process of translating an algorithm into code that can be understood by a computer, enabling tasks to be automated or applications to be created. Together, algorithmics and programming form the basis of software creation: algorithmics provides the "what to do" and programming deals with the "how to do it".

It's worth noting that teaching algorithms and programming is a crucial step in shaping analytical and methodical minds, able to solve complex problems rigorously. Teaching approaches, whether based on theoretical demonstrations or practical projects, aim to embed these fundamental skills while stimulating creativity and innovation. These approaches are discussed in the following section.

2. Pedagogical methods for teaching the fundamentals of programming and algorithms

Learning programming and algorithms is based on pedagogical methods adapted to the complexity and logic of these disciplines. These fundamentals require progressive and structured approaches, combining theory and practice, to enable students to develop a clear understanding of the concepts and a concrete mastery of the tools.

To this end, it is essential to diversify approaches to meet different learning styles. Interactive methods, collaborative projects and guided exercises play a central role in assimilating the basics, while cultivating cross-disciplinary skills such as problem-solving and analytical thinking.

This section explores the most effective pedagogical strategies for teaching these essential disciplines, focusing on their relevance in the context of artificial intelligence learning. Note that the list of approaches is not limited, but we simply cite the most relevant methods in terms of learning effectiveness.

a) **Project-based learning**. Project-based learning has emerged as a relevant teaching method for promoting active, concrete assimilation of programming and algorithmic concepts (Lodi & Martini, 2021). By involving students in the realization of structured projects, such as the development of interactive games or data management applications, this approach enables them to put theoretical notions into practice in an application context. It also strengthens their ability to solve complex problems, while developing cross-disciplinary skills such as project management, collaboration and creativity. In this way, project-based learning is an essential lever for linking theory and practice in an engaging and effective way.
b) **interactive simulations.** The use of simulation tools is a particularly appropriate pedagogical approach for explaining the abstract concepts associated with algorithms and programming logic. These tools enable students to dynamically visualize the operation of their codes, facilitating a deeper understanding of their internal mechanisms and impacts. This method reinforces algorithmic intuition while offering immediate feedback on design choices, thus contributing to a progressive and enlightened mastery of the notions taught.
c) **Practical examples.** The integration of concrete examples, inspired by problems from the professional world or from various disciplines such as biology or economics, is an effective pedagogical approach for illustrating the applicability of programming concepts in real-life contexts. By anchoring learning in tangible situations, this method encourages learner involvement and stimulates interest, while demonstrating the relevance and transversality of programming skills. These examples also help develop an in-depth understanding of multidisciplinary issues; while preparing students to meet the practical challenges they will encounter in their academic and professional careers.

By combining interactive tools, case studies and progressive exercises, these methods enable learners to move from simply understanding concepts to actually mastering them. This process is not limited to developing technical skills: it also builds essential aptitudes such as critical thinking, autonomy and collaboration. In this way, the teaching of algorithms and programming prepares students to meet the technological challenges of today and tomorrow.

INTRODUCTION TO ADVANCED AI CONCEPTS: MACHINE LEARNING AND DEEP LEARNING

This section examines the theoretical foundations and practical applications of the artificial intelligence paradigms, highlighting their respective and complementary contributions to the development of innovative solutions. It focuses on combining key concepts such as predictive models, neural networks and optimisation techniques, which form the basis of machine learning and deep learning.

By exploring these concepts, this introduction provides a solid basis for understanding the growing impact of these technologies in various fields. In the healthcare sector, they are making it possible to diagnose diseases with greater precision, personalise treatments and speed up drug discovery. In finance, they are revolutionising processes by detecting fraud, optimising portfolios and predicting market trends. What's more, these paradigms are playing a key role in emerging technologies such as autonomous cars, facial recognition and intelligent voice assistants, making these solutions more reliable, efficient and tailored to users' needs.

Thus, this section illustrates how the synergy between fundamental theories and practical advances helps to transform complex challenges into opportunities. It aims to give the reader the tools needed to understand and fully exploit the potential of machine learning and deep learning in a world of constant technological change.

1. Transition to machine learning

Machine Learning marks a significant step in the evolution of artificial intelligence, offering systems the ability to learn and adapt without explicit programming. Unlike traditional approaches, where rules and algorithms are defined manually, machine learning relies on the use of data to extract patterns and improve system performance.

This transition is based on fundamental concepts from mathematics, algorithms and statistics, enabling raw data to be transformed into usable knowledge. In the following, we examine the principles underlying this discipline, the differences with conventional approaches, and its role in building intelligent systems able to meet the challenges of complex and dynamic environments (Russell & Norvig, 2020).

With this in mind, once basic skills have been consolidated, students can tackle machine learning, which is an essential component of modern AI. We present the main concepts and algorithms of machine learning, explaining their potential applications and limitations.

a) **Basic concepts**. Students are introduced to the fundamental concepts of machine learning, including regression, classification and clustering (Mitchell, 1997). These concepts are the methodological pillars of the discipline. Regression models and predicts continuous relationships between variables, while classification assigns observations to pre-established categories. Clustering, on the other hand, aims to group data according to similarities, without recourse to pre-existing labels. These approaches, though distinct, are interconnected and form the basis for a wide range of applications in data processing and the resolution of complex problems.

b) **Learning algorithms.** The main machine learning algorithms, such as k-nearest neighbours (k-NN), decision trees and support vector machines (SVM), are introduced in a methodical and step-by-step manner. This approach aims to enable learners to understand the fundamental principles underlying each of these models, while highlighting their advantages, limitations and specific areas of application.

Particular attention is paid to the comparative analysis of these algorithms, in order to help students identify the contexts in which a specific algorithm would be best suited to solving a given problem. For example, k-NN is often appreciated for its simplicity and efficiency in small datasets, while decision trees stand out for their readability and ability to handle categorical and continuous variables. SVMs are particularly effective for linear and non-linear classification problems in high-dimensional spaces.

This pedagogical approach also introduces advanced concepts, such as hyperparameter selection, overfitting management and cross-validation techniques, to reinforce learners' understanding. By familiarising students with the strengths and weaknesses of each algorithm, this approach provides them with the tools they need to effectively choose and implement the method that is best suited to a concrete problem, be it classification, regression or predictive analysis.

2. Exploring Deep Learning

Deep Learning represents a key step forward in the learning process, marking a transition to sophisticated techniques able to deal with complex problems (*Toward Causal Representation Learning | IEEE Journals & Magazine | IEEE Xplore*, s. d.). This approach, based on deep artificial neural networks, stands out for its ability to model hierarchical data structures and extract relevant features autonomously. It has applications in fields as diverse as image recognition, natural language processing and computer vision, paving the way for cutting-edge technological innovations.

a) **Neural networks**. Students are introduced to the construction and understanding of artificial neural networks, exploring their internal architecture in detail. The course focuses on fundamental elements such as hidden layers, which enable networks to capture complex relationships in data, and activation functions, which introduce the non-linearity needed to model complex phenomena. The aim is to provide an in-depth understanding of the underlying mechanisms that govern the operation of these models, while preparing students to design and fine-tune networks for a variety of practical applications.

b) **Practical frameworks**. Learners are introduced to development environments such as TensorFlow, Keras and PyTorch, enabling them to put deep learning models into practice (Vaswani et al., 2018). These frameworks, renowned for their flexibility and efficiency, offer an intuitive interface for the design, training and evaluation of complex neural networks. Their use enables students to familiarize themselves with best practices in deep learning development, while facilitating experimentation and optimization of models in a variety of application contexts.

The transition from algorithms to artificial intelligence illustrates a natural but essential progression, enabling abstract concepts to be transformed into practical, intelligent solutions. Understanding the fundamentals of algorithms, learning to design them rigorously and knowing how to apply them in a variety of contexts are all key skills for mastering artificial intelligence systems.

This course, combining theory and practice, prepares learners to take on technological and scientific challenges in an enlightened way. It opens the way to a better understanding of current and future applications of AI, while reinforcing the ability to innovate in a variety of fields. This is an essential foundation on which to build more advanced and specialized approaches to artificial intelligence.

PEDAGOGICAL STRATEGIES FOR THE ACQUISITION OF AI SKILLS

Developing skills in artificial intelligence (AI) requires innovative teaching approaches, adapted to the complexity and rapid evolution of this field. Learning about AI goes far beyond the acquisition of theoretical knowledge; it involves deep immersion in real-life issues, mastery of cutting-edge technological tools and an understanding of the ethical and societal issues that accompany its development.

To meet these requirements, it is essential to give priority to active teaching, based on experimentation and problem-solving. Practical projects, such as the creation of machine learning models or the implementation of computer vision systems, enable students to confront theory with real-life applications. These experiences give them the opportunity to acquire essential technical skills, while stimulating their creativity and ability to innovate in the face of complex challenges.

In addition, mastery of technological tools, such as deep learning libraries (TensorFlow, PyTorch) or distributed computing platforms, is essential for handling and deploying AI solutions effectively. Students should also be introduced to collaborative development environments, such as GitHub, to prepare them to work in interdisciplinary teams where project management and communication are just as crucial as technical skills.

Finally, it is imperative to include in-depth reflection on the ethical and societal issues associated with AI. Students need to understand the impact of their work on society, particularly in terms of algorithmic bias, data confidentiality, model transparency and the economic and social implications of automation. This awareness helps them to become responsible professionals, capable of designing beneficial technologies that respect human values.

By adopting a global and multidimensional approach, teaching artificial intelligence can not only impart technical knowledge, but also train experts capable of meeting the challenges of a world in constant technological evolution, while making a significant contribution to the betterment of society.

With this in mind, pedagogical strategies play a decisive role, offering structured methods to guide students along the way. Whether it's project-based learning, the use of interactive platforms or the implementation of concrete case studies, these approaches link theory and practice, while stimulating commitment and creativity (Kamalov et al., 2023; Roll & Wylie, 2016; Romero et al., 2023).

In this section, we first explore the main pedagogical strategies for training experts capable of designing, deploying and improving AI solutions adapted to the needs of the contemporary world. Subsequently, we initiate an exploratory study via a survey in order to extract the students' point of view in the establishment of a good pedagogical strategy for the acquisition of AI skills.

INNOVATIVE PEDAGOGICAL APPROACHES TO AI COMPETENCY DEVELOPMENT

The development of artificial intelligence (AI) is creating new requirements in terms of training, calling for adapted pedagogical approaches to develop technical, analytical and ethical skills. Traditional learning methods are no longer sufficient to prepare learners for the complex, multi-dimensional challenges of AI, hence the need to integrate innovative pedagogical strategies.

These approaches, combining theory, practice and collaborative exploration, immerse students in dynamic and stimulating learning environments. Whether through project-based learning, interactive simulations or the use of digital platforms, they aim to reinforce learners' autonomy, creativity and problem-solving skills.

This section explores the fundamental principles of these innovative pedagogical approaches and highlights their key role in training experts capable of innovating and responding to the technological and societal challenges of artificial intelligence.

1. Project-based learning

Project-based learning is an essential teaching method for developing practical skills and reinforcing student autonomy. This approach is based on the realization of concrete, meaningful projects, in which students apply their theoretical knowledge to real or simulated problems. It encourages active immersion in the problem-solving process, while developing technical, analytical and collaborative skills.

In the field of artificial intelligence, project-based learning links abstract concepts to tangible applications, such as developing predictive models, designing intelligent applications or analyzing complex data. By encouraging autonomous exploration and iterative learning, this method prepares learners for the technological and professional challenges they will face in their careers.

From this perspective, project-based learning is an essential way of developing skills in artificial intelligence, while at the same time encouraging learners to express their creativity. This active approach engages them in applying theoretical concepts to concrete problems, thus reinforcing their autonomy and capacity for innovation.

a) **Interdisciplinary projects.** Students are invited to collaborate on projects integrating AI with other disciplines, such as medicine, the environment or economics. This cross-disciplinary approach develops their ability to analyze complex problems, while highlighting the wide-ranging implications and applications of artificial intelligence.

b) **Creativity and innovation**. By enabling them to devise original solutions to proposed challenges, this approach encourages learners to mobilize their critical thinking and creative spirit. They learn to think outside the box, and come up with solutions tailored to specific project needs.

2. Simulations and virtual environments

Simulations and virtual environments are innovative and powerful teaching tools, enabling students to explore and hone their artificial intelligence (AI) skills in an interactive and immersive way (Kissoon & Karran, 2024).

a) **Real-time feedback**: These environments offer the possibility of manipulating AI models in simulated settings, enabling learners to observe the consequences of their experiments immediately. This instant interaction promotes in-depth, intuitive learning, while consolidating theoretical knowledge through practice.
b) **Case studies and practical examples**
    i. **Case studies:** The analysis of real-life application cases from industry enables students to understand the concrete implications of AI in various sectors. This process enriches their understanding of practical issues while consolidating their ability to solve complex problems.
    ii. **Workshops and seminars**: The contributions of experts from the academic and professional worlds provide significant added value by offering practical and inspiring perspectives, boosting students' motivation and their aspiration to excellence.
c) **Collaborative approaches:** Collaborative work encourages the sharing of knowledge, ideas and methodologies, facilitating the emergence of innovative solutions. These collaborative dynamics also foster the acquisition of interpersonal skills, essential for interdisciplinary AI projects.
d) **Integrating technological platforms:** The use of advanced technology platforms specialized in AI provides access to high-performance tools, strengthening students' analytical and technical capabilities while preparing them for the challenges of professional practice.
e) **Gamification:** Incorporating gamification into learning processes stimulates student engagement by making educational activities more captivating. This approach promotes a more natural and dynamic assimilation of knowledge.
f) **Adaptive learning:** Adaptive learning systems, based on intelligent algorithms, adjust teaching content to the needs and level of each student. This personalized approach optimizes the efficiency of skills acquisition.
g) **Transdisciplinary approach:** Adopting a transdisciplinary approach, integrating various scientific and technological fields, fosters a holistic and innovative vision. It enables students to take a global view of the issues at stake, and to propose solutions adapted to the complex challenges of the field of artificial intelligence.

INTERDISCIPLINARITY AS AN INNOVATIVE PEDAGOGICAL APPROACH TO LEARNING AI.

Interdisciplinary case studies have become an essential pedagogical approach for teaching artificial intelligence. By integrating issues from a wide range of fields, including medicine, the environment, economics and the social sciences, these studies provide a unique platform for exploring the practical impact of AI in a variety of contexts. More than just an academic exercise, this method transforms learning into an immersive experience, reinforcing technical skills while stimulating essential cross-disciplinary aptitudes such as critical analysis, collaboration and complex problem-solving.

The main attraction of this approach lies in its ability to confront students with real-life challenges that reflect the complexity and interconnectedness of contemporary global issues. For example, a student project could involve the analysis of medical data to predict the progression of disease, while raising ethical issues relating to data confidentiality or the fairness of healthcare systems. This type of initiative prepares learners to navigate in a world where technical skills must be combined with a deep understanding of the societal, ethical and cultural implications of the solutions they propose.

1. Practical applications in various fields

- The environment: a testing ground for AI

The environmental field is particularly well suited to the use of AI in interdisciplinary projects. Case studies have shown how supervised learning and image analysis algorithms can be used to monitor illegal deforestation, detect forest fires or measure air pollution levels. For example, by combining satellite data with pattern recognition algorithms, students can design models capable of quickly identifying unauthorised human activity in protected areas (Romero et al., 2023).

These projects are not limited to demonstrating technological capabilities. They also include consideration of the legal and social dimensions of the proposed solutions. Students are encouraged to assess the effectiveness of the public policies needed to regulate the use of these technologies, and to examine their social impact. For example, a project could explore how a monitoring technology could affect local populations living near protected forests.

- The economy: anticipating risks and detecting opportunities

In the economic sector, AI is used to analyse trends in financial markets, predict price fluctuations or detect fraud in transactions. These case studies combine knowledge of economics, statistics and machine learning to create practical solutions. For example, one project could aim to develop a supervised learning algorithm capable of detecting unusual patterns in banking transactions in order to prevent fraudulent activities (Vuong et al., 2021).

These interdisciplinary studies also highlight the limits of using AI in economic contexts. Students learn that predictive models are often dependent on historical data, which can introduce biases, and that decisions based on these models can have significant implications for market players. This kind of critical thinking is essential for training professionals capable of designing robust and fair systems.

- Medicine: AI at the service of health

In the medical field, AI is used to improve diagnoses, personalise treatments or optimise workflows in healthcare establishments. For example, a case study could focus on the use of machine learning algorithms to analyse medical images and detect diseases such as cancer early. These projects allow students to understand how AI can transform healthcare while addressing the ethical and regulatory challenges associated with the use of medical data.

These studies also highlight the importance of collaboration across disciplines. AI students need to work with healthcare experts to understand the nuances of medical data and ensure their solutions are both practical and ethical. This teaches them to take a collaborative approach and integrate the perspectives of different disciplines into their work.

2. Skills developed through interdisciplinary case studies

- Strengthening technical skills: Interdisciplinary case studies enable students to apply specific technical skills in real-life contexts. For example, they can learn to manipulate large databases, train machine learning models or use advanced tools for data analysis. These skills, while essential, are only one aspect of the course.

- Developing cross-disciplinary skills: As well as technical skills, these projects reinforce cross-disciplinary skills that are crucial in today's job market. Critical analysis, for example, is essential for assessing the reliability of data and models. Collaboration, meanwhile, is essential for working effectively with experts from other disciplines. Finally, complex problem solving prepares students to devise innovative solutions to multidimensional challenges.
- Raising awareness of ethical and social issues: A fundamental aspect of interdisciplinary case studies is their ability to raise students' awareness of the ethical and societal implications of AI. Whether they are thinking about bias in data, the impact of algorithmic decisions on populations or issues of confidentiality, these projects encourage in-depth reflection on the responsibilities of designers of AI systems.

3. Why adopt this approach to teaching AI?

- Meeting the needs of the employment market: Employers are increasingly looking for professionals who can combine strong technical skills with an understanding of multi-dimensional issues. The intersection between AI and other fields is constantly expanding, and interdisciplinary case studies prepare students to integrate into this rapidly changing environment (UNESCO, 2019).
- Training responsible citizens: Over and above their technical skills, these projects help to train citizens who are aware of their responsibility towards society. Students learn to assess the impact of their technological choices and to design solutions that take account of ethical values and the needs of the various stakeholders.
- Promoting innovation and creativity: By exposing students to a variety of issues, interdisciplinary case studies stimulate their creativity and ability to innovate. They are encouraged to think holistically and explore solutions that are not limited to a single discipline.

4. Integration into educational programmes

To maximise the benefits of interdisciplinary case studies, it is crucial to integrate them strategically into educational programmes. This can include:

1. Collaboration with external experts: Invite professionals from various fields to guide students and offer a practical perspective on the challenges addressed.
2. Use of real data: Provide students with authentic datasets to reinforce their understanding of the concrete applications of AI.
3. Project-based assessment: Encourage students to work on projects that integrate several disciplines and to present their results in the form of reports, presentations or prototypes.
4. Developing academic and industrial partnerships: Working with institutions and companies to identify relevant case studies and offer internship opportunities or collaborative projects.

Interdisciplinary case studies are a powerful pedagogical approach for teaching artificial intelligence. By combining technical skills with in-depth reflection on ethical, social and environmental issues, this method trains professionals to meet the complex challenges of the modern world. It also prepares students to innovate, collaborate and make a significant contribution to society.

As AI continues to transform our world, it is essential to train a new generation of professionals who master not only the technologies, but also the implications of using them. Interdisciplinary case studies play a key role in this mission, providing a comprehensive and balanced education that reflects the needs of an ever-changing job market.

ETHICAL ISSUES OF AI

Artificial intelligence (AI), while a driver of technological innovation, poses major ethical challenges that require careful thought to ensure responsible use. The ethical challenges of AI cover a broad range, including algorithmic bias, data privacy, societal impact, sustainability and transparency. These concerns are all the more relevant in an educational context, where it is essential to train aware and competent professionals.

a) **Algorithmic biases and fairness**: Algorithmic biases occur when AI models reproduce or amplify the biases contained in the data used to train them. These biases can have significant impacts, including social discrimination and stigmatization
b) **Privacy and Data Protection**: AI relies on the use of large amounts of often sensitive data, raising privacy issues such as data misuse.
c) **Social Responsibility and Impacts on Employment**: Automation and the transformation of professions by AI represent a twofold problem: The loss of jobs and the Creation of inequalities.
d) **Sustainable development**: training AI models requires considerable energy resources.
e) **Transparence et Explicabilité**: Les systèmes d'IA, en particulier ceux basés sur l'apprentissage profond, sont souvent perçus comme des 'boîtes noires', rendant leurs décisions difficiles à comprendre et à interpréter. Cela pose des problèmes dans les domaines critiques comme la santé, où la transparence est indispensable pour garantir la confiance des utilisateurs.

ARCHITECTURE OF EDUCATIONAL PATHWAYS IN AI: A PRACTICAL STUDY

The fast-paced evolution of artificial intelligence (AI) requires well-structured educational pathways able to meet the growing need for specialized skills and a comprehensive understanding of the technological and ethical issues involved. Building a suitable educational architecture represents a strategic challenge, requiring a coherent articulation between theoretical, practical and interdisciplinary learning.

This practical study, based on a survey of students from a variety of disciplines and learning levels, looks at the design and organization of artificial intelligence learning paths. It highlights the importance of modular and flexible approaches, enabling adaptation to the specific needs of learners. The aim is to explore pedagogical methods that combine a solid grounding in programming and algorithms with the development of advanced skills in machine learning and deep learning. In addition, this approach incorporates an ethical dimension, with modules dedicated to the challenges of algorithmic bias, data confidentiality and the social responsibility of AI.

The aim of the survey is to explore students' skills, interests and preferences when it comes to teaching artificial intelligence (AI). The analysis is based on 165 responses, examining various aspects such as prior knowledge of programming and AI, preferred learning methods, and awareness of ethical issues. The aim is to propose a global and operational vision of educational pathways, taking into account student expectations and market requirements. This reflection is part of an approach aimed at training experts capable of combining technical excellence, innovation and ethical awareness, while adapting to the challenges of a field in constant transformation.

SUMMARY OF RESULTS

1. Programming skills and algorithms

a. **Familiarity with algorithms**: All 165 respondents indicated an understanding of the concept of algorithm. A significant proportion reported advanced skills, particularly in areas such as graph algorithms, sorting and similar concepts.
b. **Most frequently used programming languages**: Students identified Python, Java, C and C++ as the most commonly used languages. By contrast, languages such as PHP, Assembly and C# are less popular, probably due to their specialization.

2. Artificial intelligence concepts

According to the questionnaire results, artificial intelligence (AI) knowledge is divided into three main categories:

a. **Basic notions (40%):** A relative majority of individuals possess general knowledge of fundamental AI concepts, such as basic notions of algorithms and data processing. This indicates that these concepts often serve as an entry point into the field, making their mastery essential to progress.
b. **Machine learning (35%):** A significant percentage of individuals have experience in more advanced areas, notably regression and clustering algorithms. This reflects a growing interest and need for practical machine learning skills, which represent an intermediate step between the basics and advanced techniques.
c. **Deep learning (25%):** A minority are familiar with the complex aspects of AI, such as neural networks and specialized frameworks like TensorFlow or PyTorch. This low percentage is consistent with the level of technical expertise and prerequisites required to master these tools.

We can visualize these statistics in the form of an organ-pipe diagram as follows:

Figure 1.The three main categories of artificial intelligence (AI) knowledge identified from the results

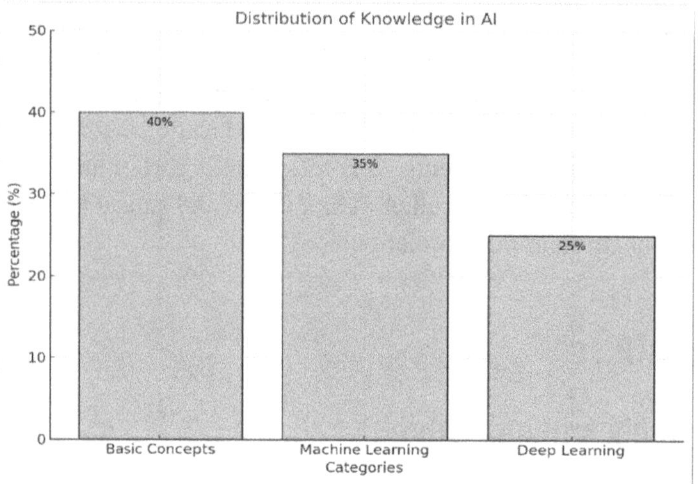

In fact, the diagram reveals a natural progression of knowledge, where basic notions serve as a foundation for learning more advanced machine learning skills, before tackling Deep Learning. This underlines the importance of structuring AI learning paths to effectively support learners at every stage.

3. Interests in AI fields

For this section, we note that students show considerable interest in the main AI algorithms. Indeed, the two pie charts representing levels of interest in machine learning and deep learning show that for (a) machine learning, 65% of participants express a high level of interest, 25% a moderate level of interest and 10% a low level of interest, and for (b) deep learning, 50% show a high level of interest, 35% a moderate level of interest and 15% a low level of interest.

Figure 2. Distribution of interests in artificial intelligence (AI) based on the results

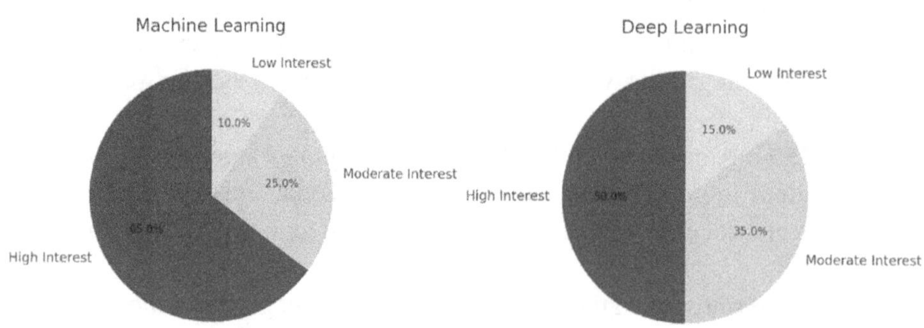

These results can be interpreted through a comparative analysis, which shows that Global Commitment to Machine Learning enjoys broader and more sustained interest, reflecting its fundamental and versatile role in the AI ecosystem. While Deep Learning's technical nature makes it indispensable for complex applications, it requires significant technical expertise and resources, which explains the greater proportion of moderate and low interest.

These diagrams highlight the difference in perception between two key AI sub-fields. They underline the importance of adapting pedagogical strategies according to levels of interest and technical complexity: a solid foundation in machine learning for broad engagement, and a progressive, specialized approach for deep learning.

4. Preferred teaching methods

For teaching methods preferred by interviewees, this horizontal bar chart illustrates preferences for teaching methods.

Figure 3. Respondents' preferences for teaching methods

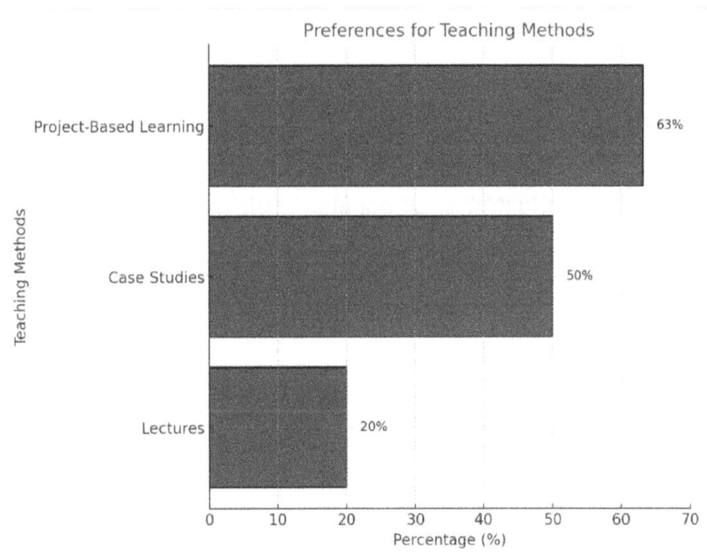

- Project-based learning (63%)
    - o **Analysis**: An overwhelming majority of learners favor this method, reflecting the effectiveness of hands-on, immersive approaches. Project-based learning enables theoretical concepts to be linked to concrete, meaningful applications, thus reinforcing motivation and commitment.
    - o **Pedagogical impact**: This method fosters the development of cross-disciplinary skills such as project management, problem-solving and collaboration, while facilitating the assimilation of complex knowledge.
- Practical case studies (50%)

- **Analysis**: Half of all learners value this approach, which offers an in-depth understanding of real-life applications of concepts. Case studies enable learners to analyze complex situations, make informed decisions and practice in professional contexts.
- **Pedagogical impact**: This method improves learners' ability to transfer their knowledge into diverse scenarios and understand the practical implications of AI algorithms and techniques.

- Lectures (20%)
  - **Analysis**: Although still appreciated, lectures are perceived as insufficient when not complemented by interactive or hands-on approaches. This method is often better suited to the introduction of fundamental concepts or detailed explanations.
  - **Pedagogical impact**: Their usefulness lies mainly in the initial structuring of knowledge and the rigorous explanation of complex theories. However, their effectiveness diminishes when they are not combined with active methods.

Ultimately, this diagram shows a clear preference for active and interactive teaching approaches (project-based learning and practical case studies) over traditional methods ("classroom" courses). This reflects the changing expectations of learners, who are looking for engaging, application-oriented learning experiences. To maximize pedagogical impact, it is essential to combine these approaches in a balanced way, integrating theory and practice to meet the diverse needs of learners.

5. Practical course formats

As for the practical course formats preferred by students, they opted more for blended formats. Indeed, the following graph clearly illustrates the popularity of hybrid approaches, adapted to the varied needs of modern learners.

Figure 4. Practical course formats according to respondents' preferences

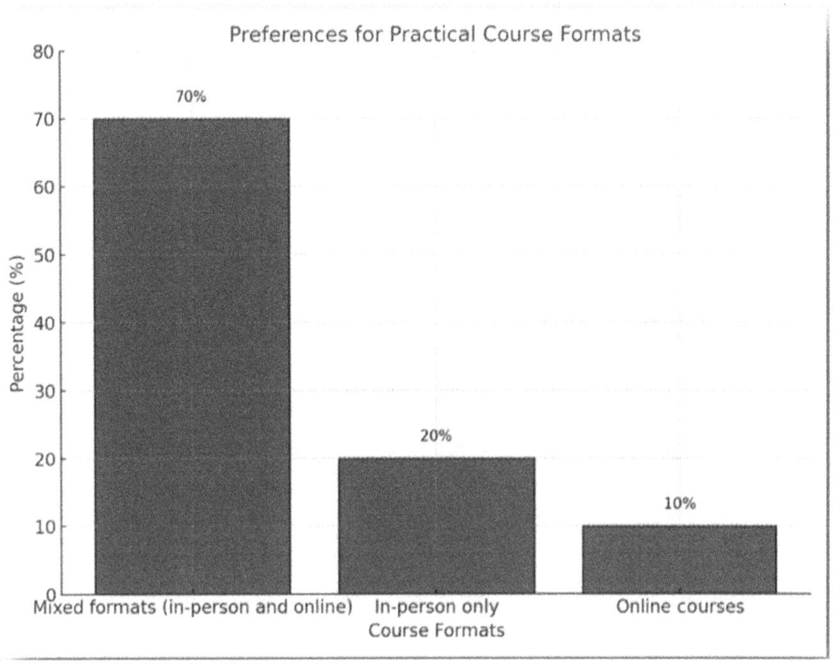

For blended formats (70%), an overwhelming majority of participants prefer hybrid formats combining face-to-face and online learning. This preference reflects a growing demand for flexibility and adaptability in learning environments. Mixed formats enable participants to benefit from both the advantages of face-to-face learning (direct interaction, increased engagement) and the enrichment of digital resources. In addition, this model optimizes the learning experience by adapting to individual constraints, while enhancing access to varied content.

On the other hand, in the face-to-face mode only (20%), a significant proportion of learners continue to favor face-to-face courses exclusively, emphasizing values such as proximity to teachers, direct social interaction and a structured learning environment. This underlines the importance of face-to-face support, particularly for disciplines requiring immediate assistance or complex practical activities (Selwyn, 2019).

When it comes to online courses (10%), a minority find online courses sufficient to meet their needs. This preference can be attributed to learners seeking total flexibility, independence in their learning or remote access to content. Although less popular, this modality remains essential for providing accessible learning opportunities, particularly for those with geographical or time constraints.

This part of the survey highlights the growing popularity of blended formats, responding to the expectations of modern learners seeking a balance between flexibility and interactivity. Although face-to-face courses retain their undeniable value, their complementarity with digital tools is becoming unavoidable. This underscores the need for educational institutions to devise hybrid teaching strategies tailored to the diverse needs of learners.

6. Evaluation methods

Figure 5. Evaluation methods according to respondents' preferences

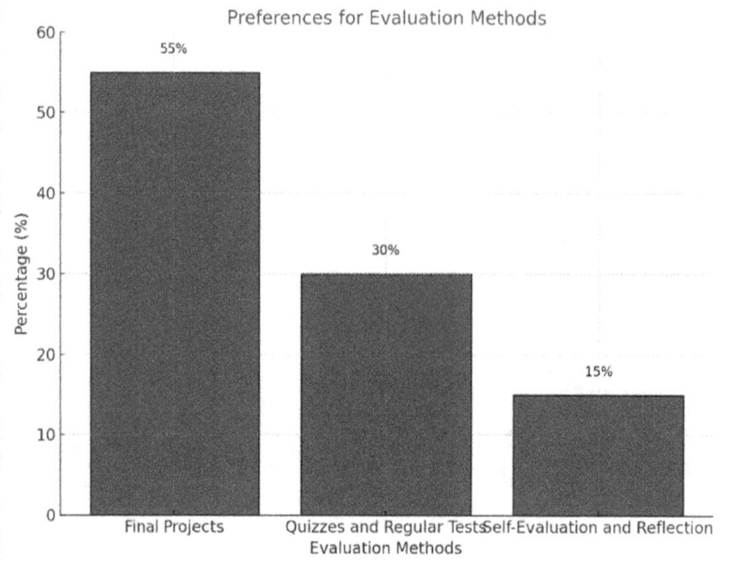

The statistics reveal interesting trends in learner preferences for assessment methods, highlighting distinct priorities according to pedagogical objectives and student expectations.

For final projects (55%), a majority of participants favored final projects as an assessment method. This reflects a preference for approaches that enable theoretical knowledge to be applied to practical, concrete situations. Final projects offer an opportunity to integrate several skills, including problem-solving, creativity and project management. This method promotes a holistic assessment of learners' abilities, while giving them autonomy to demonstrate their understanding and mastery of concepts.

Regular quizzes and tests (30%), a significant proportion of learners favor regular assessments, such as quizzes and tests. These tools enable continuous monitoring of progress and rapid identification of learning gaps. This helps reinforce knowledge retention through repetition, and gives teachers immediate feedback on the effectiveness of their teaching approach (Gao et al., 2021).

A minority (15%) value self-evaluation and personal reflection. Although less popular, this method emphasizes the importance of developing introspection and self-learning skills, essential for autonomous progress in complex fields such as artificial intelligence. This approach encourages learners to become aware of their strengths and weaknesses, promoting continuous improvement and empowerment in their learning journey.

Thus, we can conclude that the data show a clear preference for assessment methods based on final projects, which enable practical and cross-disciplinary skills to be assessed in an integrated way. Regular quizzes also remain essential to ensure progressive monitoring of learning, while self-assessment, although less common, plays a key role in developing learner autonomy. These results underline the need for a balanced and diversified approach to assessment methods to meet the varied needs and expectations of students.

7. Awareness of ethical issues

The diagram shows that 60% of participants have limited knowledge of ethical issues, while 40% wish to deepen their knowledge. This highlights a significant need for awareness and training on the ethical implications of artificial intelligence, indicating a growing interest in these crucial issues in the field.

A reading of these results shows that awareness of ethical issues in artificial intelligence, although still limited for a majority, is arousing growing interest among learners. This trend reflects a growing awareness of the importance of ethical and societal dimensions in the development and application of AI technologies. To meet these expectations, it is crucial to integrate modules dedicated to ethics into training programs, in order to prepare responsible professionals capable of anticipating and managing the impacts of their innovations on society.

Figure 6. Level of awareness of ethical issues expressed by respondents

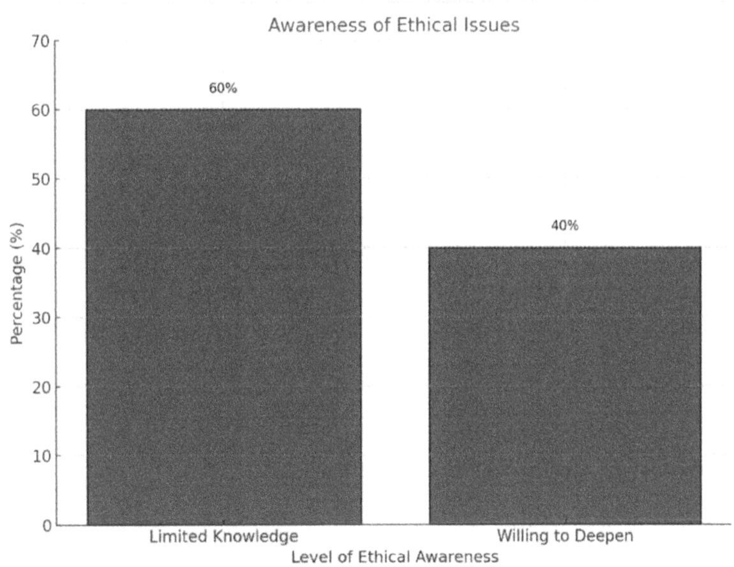

Figure 7. learners' ethical priorities in the field of AI

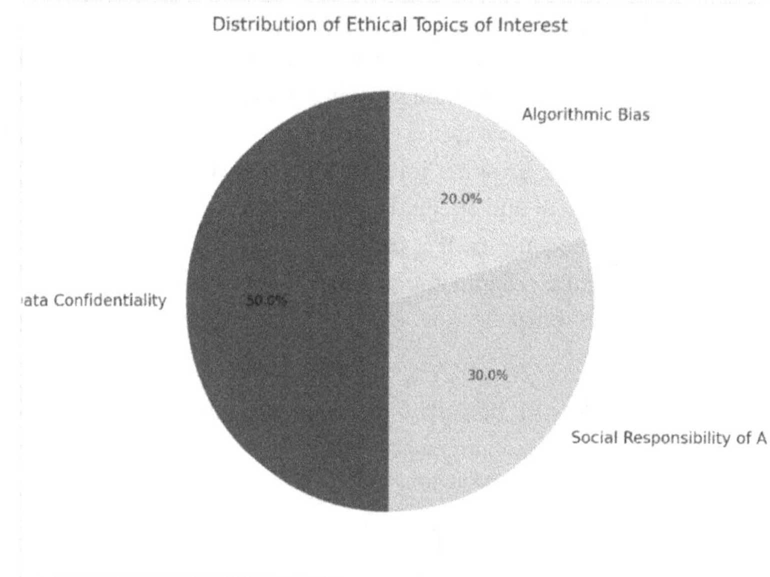

The diagram highlights learners' ethical priorities in the field of AI: 50% focus on data privacy, highlighting the importance of protecting personal information, 30% on social responsibility, showing concern for the societal impacts of AI, and 20% on algorithmic biases, reflecting an awareness of equity issues. These results show a growing sensitivity to ethical dimensions, requiring targeted training to address these concerns.

INTERPRETATIONS AND RECOMMENDATIONS

SWOT (Strengths, Weaknesses, Opportunities, Threats) analysis is an essential strategic tool for assessing students' skills, gaps and prospects in the field of artificial intelligence (AI). This approach identifies strengths to be developed, areas requiring improvement, opportunities to be seized, as well as potential threats that could hinder their progress.

In a context where AI is evolving rapidly, it is crucial to have a clear and balanced view of learners' strengths and weaknesses. This makes it possible to design targeted educational programs, while taking advantage of emerging opportunities and anticipating challenges. The aim of this SWOT matrix is to provide a structured basis for enhancing students' skills and effectively meeting academic and professional expectations in this rapidly expanding field.

Table 1.SWOT matrix is to provide a structured basis for enhancing students' skill

Strengths	Weaknesses
1. Good programming skills, especially Python, widely used in AI. 2. Solid understanding of algorithms and machine learning fundamentals. 3. Strong interest in machine learning and deep learning, encouraging involvement in these fields. 4. Ability to adapt to theoretical concepts and a liking for technical challenges. 5. Willingness to specialize in innovative and fast-growing fields.	1. Limited practical knowledge of advanced AI, especially deep learning and handling of large datasets. 2. Insufficient awareness of the ethical challenges and social responsibility of AI. 3. Weakness in the integration of several technological tools in a project (e.g. interaction between frameworks). 4. Weaknesses in the integration of several technological tools in a project (e.g. interaction between frameworks). 5. Difficulty in linking abstract concepts to real-life cases without structured support.
Opportunities	**Threats**
1. Development of practical teaching modules focusing on deep learning and advanced tools (TensorFlow, PyTorch). 2. Integration of programs on ethical issues and social responsibility to meet growing demand. 3. Growing global popularity of AI, offering career opportunities in a variety of sectors (healthcare, finance, etc.). 4. Increased access to educational platforms and open source resources to perfect technical knowledge. 5. Interdisciplinary collaboration (AI and medicine, the environment, or economics), boosting the attractiveness of training courses.	1. Risk of disengagement if gaps are not filled by an appropriate teaching approach. 2. Competition with more advanced programs in other institutions or countries. 3. Rapidly evolving technologies making skills rapidly obsolete without continuous learning. 4. Excessive reliance on preconceived tools without in-depth understanding of theoretical underpinnings. 5. Challenge linked to the democratization of AI: risks of overqualification or trivialization of basic technical skills.

1. Recommandations éducatives

To maximize the impact of artificial intelligence (AI) training, it is essential to adopt pedagogical strategies that combine practical relevance, flexible learning formats and awareness of ethical issues (Sarmurzin et al., 2021; Sun et al., 2024). Such an approach promotes learning that is both engaging and holistic, aligned with the requirements of the field.

- **Active pedagogy**: Project-based learning and practical case studies must be placed at the heart of teaching methods (Kamalov et al., 2023). These approaches enable learners to apply their knowledge to real-life situations, strengthening their ability to solve complex problems. In addition, the integration of interdisciplinary projects, such as the application of AI to fields like economics or biology, encourages students to explore diverse fields and understand the implications of AI in multiple contexts.
- **Course formats**: Modular and blended course formats, combining face-to-face and online resources, offer essential flexibility to meet the diverse needs of learners. Face-to-face courses enable rich interaction and direct support, while digital resources complement this learning by offering content that can be accessed at any time. This combination optimizes training efficiency while fostering student autonomy.
- **Ethical awareness**: The ethical challenges of AI need to be integrated into programs in a structured way. Sessions dedicated to algorithmic bias, data confidentiality and social responsibility raise learners' awareness of the profound implications of their technological choices. This awareness strengthens their ability to develop responsible AI solutions that respect human values.

By combining active pedagogy, flexible formats and ethical education, this pedagogical approach prepares learners to meet the technical and societal challenges of AI (*Andrew Ng, AI Minimalist: The Machine-Learning Pioneer Says Small is the New Big | IEEE Journals & Magazine | IEEE Xplore*, s. d.; Hambursin, 2024). It fosters not only the acquisition of solid skills, but also the development of critical thinking and social responsibility, which are essential in this field.

CONCLUSION

The results of the questionnaire reveal students who are motivated, curious and committed to learning about artificial intelligence. They have a solid grounding in programming and algorithms, while expressing a growing interest in machine learning and deep learning. However, their expectations also highlight specific needs, particularly in terms of advanced practices, flexible teaching formats and awareness of ethical issues.

To meet these expectations, it is essential to put in place a balanced and innovative educational strategy. This should combine active teaching approaches, such as project-based learning and interdisciplinary case studies, with modular and hybrid formats that encourage greater customisation and flexibility. In addition, the integration of modules dedicated to ethical issues, such as algorithmic bias and data confidentiality, is essential to train experts capable of combining technical skills with societal responsibility.

In short, by adopting a holistic and tailored approach, artificial intelligence training programmes have the potential not only to meet students' aspirations, but also to prepare a new generation of competent, innovative and ethically responsible professionals. These programmes need to combine solid technical expertise, an in-depth awareness of societal and ethical issues, and the ability to adapt to the challenges of a world in constant technological evolution. In this way, they will help to shape key players capable of innovating and guiding the development of artificial intelligence for the benefit of society in an enlightened way.

REFERENCES

Bee, R., & Bee, F. (1998). *Constructive Feedback.* CIPD Publishing.

Brundage, M. (2015). Taking superintelligence seriously : Superintelligence: Paths, dangers, strategies by Nick Bostrom (Oxford University Press, 2014). *Futures*, 72, 32–35. DOI: 10.1016/j.futures.2015.07.009

d'Amiens, R. de l'Académie. (2024, mai 8). *Guide : Les ODD – un levier pour l'éducation - édition Mars 2024.* Education au développement durable. http://edd.ac-amiens.fr/350-guide-les-odd-un-levier-pour-l-education-edition-mars-2024.html

Dewey, J. (1986). Experience and Education. *The Educational Forum.* DOI: 10.1080/00131728609335764

Friedewald, M., Székely, I., & Karaboga, M. (2024). *L' accès aux archives à l'ère du numérique : Mise en œuvre de la Recommandation no R (2000) 13 du Comité des Ministres du Conseil de l'Europe sur une politique européenne en matière de communication des archives.* Council of Europe.

Gao, J., O'Sullivan, N., & Sherman, M. (2021). Chinese securities investment funds : The role of luck in performance. *Review of Accounting and Finance*, 20(5), 271–297. DOI: 10.1108/RAF-07-2020-0182

Hambursin, O. (2024). *Un livre, une histoire : Nicolas Bouvier et Thierry Vernet, « L'usage du monde » (Podcast - Radio France / Académie de Paris).* Un livre, une histoire : un podcast France Télévisions, en partenariat avec l'Académie de Paris. https://dial.uclouvain.be/pr/boreal/object/boreal:292546

Kamalov, F., Santandreu Calonge, D., & Gurrib, I. (2023). New era of artificial intelligence in education : Towards a sustainable multifaceted revolution. *Sustainability (Basel)*, 15(16), 12451. DOI: 10.3390/su151612451

Kissoon, C., & Karran, T. (2024). *Academic Freedom : Swimming against the Technological Tide.*

Kolodner, J. L. (2000). Georgia Institute of Technology Mark Guzdial Georgia Institute of Technology. *Theoretical Foundations of Learning Environments*, 215.

Lodi, M., & Martini, S. (2021). Computational Thinking, Between Papert and Wing. *Science & Education*, 30(4), 883–908. DOI: 10.1007/s11191-021-00202-5

Mitchell, T. M. (1997). Does Machine Learning Really Work? *AI Magazine*, 18(3), 3. Advance online publication. DOI: 10.1609/aimag.v18i3.1303

Mokkink, L. B., Boers, M., van der Vleuten, C. P. M., Bouter, L. M., Alonso, J., Patrick, D. L., de Vet, H. C. W., & Terwee, C. B. (2020). COSMIN Risk of Bias tool to assess the quality of studies on reliability or measurement error of outcome measurement instruments : A Delphi study. *BMC Medical Research Methodology*, 20(1), 293. DOI: 10.1186/s12874-020-01179-5 PMID: 33267819

Porayska-Pomsta, K., Holmes, W., & Nemorin, S. (2023). The ethics of AI in education. In *Handbook of Artificial Intelligence in Education* (pp. 571–604). Edward Elgar Publishing., https://www.elgaronline.com/edcollchap/book/9781800375413/book-part-9781800375413-38.xml DOI: 10.4337/9781800375413.00038

Roll, I., & Wylie, R. (2016). Evolution and revolution in artificial intelligence in education. *International Journal of Artificial Intelligence in Education*, 26(2), 582–599. DOI: 10.1007/s40593-016-0110-3

Romero, M., Heiser, L., & Lepage, A. (2023). *Enseigner et apprendre à l'ère de l'intelligence artificielle : Acculturation, intégration et usages créatifs de l'IA en éducation : livre blanc*. https://eduq.info/xmlui/handle/11515/38818

Russell, S., & Norvig, P. (2020). *Artificial intelligence : A modern approach*. Pearson.

Sarmurzin, Y., Amanzhol, N., Toleubayeva, K., Zhunusova, M., & Amanova, A. (2021). The impact of OECD research on the education system of Kazakhstan. *Asia Pacific Education Review*, 22(4), 757–766. DOI: 10.1007/s12564-021-09715-8

Selwyn, N. (2019). What's the Problem with Learning Analytics? *Journal of Learning Analytics*, 6(3), 3. Advance online publication. DOI: 10.18608/jla.2019.63.3

Sun, K. Y., Bai, X., Chen, S., Bao, S., Zhang, C., Kapoor, M., Backman, J., Joseph, T., Maxwell, E., Mitra, G., Gorovits, A., Mansfield, A., Boutkov, B., Gokhale, S., Habegger, L., Marcketta, A., Locke, A. E., Ganel, L., Hawes, A., & Balasubramanian, S. (2024). A deep catalogue of protein-coding variation in 983,578 individuals. *Nature*, 631(8021), 583–592. DOI: 10.1038/s41586-024-07556-0 PMID: 38768635

The 2020 Yearbook of the Digital Ethics Lab | SpringerLink. (s. d.). Consulté 12 décembre 2024, à l'adresse https://link.springer.com/book/10.1007/978-3-030-80083-3

Toward Causal Representation Learning | IEEE Journals & Magazine | IEEE Xplore. (s. d.). Consulté 12 décembre 2024, à l'adresse https://ieeexplore.ieee.org/abstract/document/9363924

Vaswani, A., Bengio, S., Brevdo, E., Chollet, F., Gomez, A. N., Gouws, S., Jones, L., Kaiser, Ł., Kalchbrenner, N., Parmar, N., Sepassi, R., Shazeer, N., & Uszkoreit, J. (2018). *Tensor2Tensor for Neural Machine Translation* (No. arXiv:1803.07416). arXiv. https://doi.org//arXiv.1803.07416DOI: 10.48550

Vuong, Q.-H., Vinh, L. A., & Trung, T. (2021). *Academic Contributions to the UNESCO 2019 Forum on Education for Sustainable Development and Global Citizenship*. MDPI.

Yan, L., Talic, S., Wild, H., Gasevic, D., Gasević, D., Ilic, D., Deppeler, J., Corrigan, D., Martinez-Maldonado, R., & Trauer, J. (2022, October 01). (s. d.). Transmission of SARS-CoV-2 in a primary school setting with and without public health measures using real-world contact data : A modelling study. *Journal of Global Health*, 12, 05034. DOI: 10.7189/jogh.12.05034 PMID: 36181503

Chapter 4
AI-Driven Personalized Learning Pathways Customizing Education for Every Student

Chaimae Waladi
https://orcid.org/0009-0008-0569-4423
ENS, University Abdelmalek Essaadi, Morocco

Mohammed Sefian Lamarti
https://orcid.org/0000-0001-8270-2660
ENS, University Abdelmalek Essaadi, Morocco

Mohamed Khaldi
https://orcid.org/0000-0002-1593-1073
ENS, University Abdelmalek Essaadi, Morocco

ABSTRACT

This chapter explores the transformative impact of artificial intelligence (AI) in shaping adaptive, personalized learning experiences that cater to students' unique needs. By employing AI-driven platforms, educators can create learning pathways that dynamically align with students' strengths, interests, and preferences. The benefits are substantial, as AI enhances engagement, motivation, and achievement by adjusting content in real-time to match individual learning styles. Alongside these advantages, the chapter addresses critical challenges such as safeguarding data privacy, mitigating algorithmic bias, and ensuring inclusivity across diverse learner backgrounds. Ultimately, this chapter underscores AI's potential to redefine education, while emphasizing the ethical considerations crucial for its equitable and responsible integration into classrooms.

1 INTRODUCTION

As artificial intelligence (AI) continues to revolutionize industries and reshape everyday life, the ethical implications of its development have become a central concern for technologists, policymakers, and society at large. The rapid deployment of AI in areas such as healthcare, criminal justice, and fi-

DOI: 10.4018/979-8-3693-8965-2.ch004

nance highlights its transformative potential, but it also exposes critical ethical challenges that must be addressed to ensure AI serves the greater good (Floridi et al., 2018). Issues such as algorithmic bias, lack of transparency, and unintended social consequences have sparked debates about how AI should be designed, deployed, and governed to avoid harm. These concerns underscore the importance of embedding ethical decision making directly into the development process of AI systems.

The ethical dilemmas in AI development are not merely theoretical—they manifest in real world applications. For instance, algorithmic bias in facial recognition systems has led to inaccuracies, particularly in identifying people of color, raising concerns about discrimination and the amplification of societal inequities (Buolamwini & Gebru, 2018). Similarly, AI's use in criminal justice for risk assessment has prompted questions about fairness, transparency, and accountability (Angwin et al., 2016). These examples reflect the pressing need for AI professionals to integrate moral considerations into their design processes to ensure that AI technologies promote justice, fairness, and societal well being.

One approach that offers a promising framework for addressing these ethical challenges is design thinking. Originating from the fields of architecture and product design, design thinking has gained widespread recognition as a human centered, iterative approach to problem solving. At its core, design thinking emphasizes empathy with users, collaboration among diverse stakeholders, and a process of prototyping and testing that allows for continuous refinement (Brown, 2009). By integrating ethical reflection into each stage of the design thinking process—empathize, define, ideate, prototype, and test—AI developers can more effectively anticipate the ethical implications of their systems and make adjustments to align with moral principles (Dignum, 2019).

Design thinking's focus on user experience and its iterative nature make it particularly well suited for embedding ethical considerations into AI development. The initial phase of empathizing with users allows developers to identify the potential impacts of their AI systems on different user groups, particularly those who are most vulnerable to harm. This empathetic approach ensures that ethical considerations are not an afterthought but are embedded from the start. As the design process moves forward, ethical principles such as fairness, accountability, and transparency can be integrated into the development of AI systems, helping to mitigate risks and prevent harm before products are released into the world (Jobin et al., 2019).

This chapter will explore how AI developers can apply a design thinking framework to embed moral decision making into their work. Through real world case studies, practical examples, and discussions about the societal impact of AI, the chapter aims to provide AI professionals with the tools and insights needed to foster ethical awareness and develop responsible AI systems. Additionally, the chapter will highlight the importance of stakeholder involvement in ethical AI design, showing how collaboration with ethicists, policymakers, and diverse user groups can enrich the design process and lead to more ethical outcomes.

In a world where AI is increasingly intertwined with critical societal functions, the responsibility to ensure that AI development aligns with moral values has never been more urgent. The failure to address ethical issues early in the design process can lead to negative societal impacts, from reinforcing biases to eroding trust in technology (Cath, 2018). Therefore, AI professionals must adopt proactive strategies for embedding ethical decision making into their design processes, ensuring that their innovations contribute to societal well being rather than exacerbate existing inequities.

The chapters that follow will delve deeper into the specific steps AI developers can take to integrate ethics into their design process. By applying a hands on, design thinking approach, AI developers can better navigate the complexities of ethical AI development and create solutions that are not only innovative but also morally sound.

2 FOUNDATIONS OF ETHICAL AI DEVELOPMENT

Ethics is a cornerstone of responsible AI development. As AI systems increasingly interact with and influence human decisions, it is critical that these systems are designed to operate in ways that are aligned with human values. The foundation of ethical AI development lies in several key principles: fairness, transparency, accountability, and the promotion of societal well being. These principles provide the moral guidelines that developers must follow to ensure that AI systems do not exacerbate existing inequalities or create new forms of harm (Floridi & Taddeo, 2016).

2.1 Fairness

Fairness is perhaps the most discussed ethical principle in AI development. In practice, fairness refers to the idea that AI systems should make decisions without discriminating against individuals or groups based on characteristics such as race, gender, socioeconomic status, or other protected attributes. A common challenge in AI is the presence of biased training data, which can lead to systems that perpetuate and even amplify existing societal biases (Mehrabi et al., 2021). For instance, in recruitment processes, AI algorithms have been shown to favor candidates from certain demographics while disadvantaging others due to biased historical hiring data (Raghavan et al., 2020). Addressing these biases requires rigorous auditing and the implementation of fairness constraints during the development process to ensure that AI models treat all individuals equitably.

In design thinking, fairness can be embedded in the empathize and define phases, where developers identify the stakeholders and potential impact groups that may be affected by the AI system. By involving diverse voices during these early stages, AI developers can better understand the potential risks of bias and implement measures to mitigate them (Gebru et al., 2018).

2.2 Transparency

Transparency in AI refers to the clarity with which AI systems operate, make decisions, and generate outcomes. As AI models become more complex, especially those based on deep learning, the decisions made by these systems often become opaque even to the developers who created them. This phenomenon, known as the "black box" problem, has raised concerns about the accountability of AI systems, particularly when they are used in high stakes domains such as healthcare, law enforcement, or finance (Burrell, 2016). Transparent AI systems should provide explanations that are understandable to users, allowing them to comprehend how a decision was reached and giving them the ability to contest or question the system's outcomes when necessary (Weller, 2019).

Design thinking supports transparency by encouraging iterative prototyping and testing, where users can interact with the AI system and provide feedback. Prototypes should be designed to offer clear explanations of AI decision making processes, ensuring that transparency is prioritized throughout development.

2.3 Accountability

The principle of accountability ensures that there is a clear understanding of who is responsible for the decisions made by an AI system. This is particularly crucial when AI systems are used in critical areas, such as autonomous driving or medical diagnostics, where errors could lead to significant harm.

Establishing accountability means that developers, companies, and stakeholders must take responsibility for the AI's behavior, ensuring that they can intervene if something goes wrong (Danaher et al., 2017). In the absence of accountability, AI systems could make harmful decisions without any recourse for those affected.

In the design thinking process, accountability can be introduced by involving not only developers but also ethicists, lawyers, and users who can provide insights into the legal and moral implications of the system. This interdisciplinary collaboration ensures that accountability is woven into the system's design, from conception to deployment.

Societal Well Being

AI should ultimately aim to enhance societal well being, promoting positive outcomes for individuals and communities. However, as AI systems are increasingly embedded in public life, there are risks that their deployment could exacerbate inequality, displace jobs, or undermine public trust in technology (Binns, 2018). Ethical AI development, therefore, requires that developers not only focus on the technical performance of their systems but also consider the broader social impacts of their work. This involves questioning whether AI systems will contribute to or detract from societal well being and addressing potential harms before deployment (Floridi, 2019).

Incorporating societal well being into design thinking requires developers to engage deeply with the communities that will be impacted by the AI system. This is especially relevant during the empathy phase, where understanding the lived experiences of users can inform the development of AI systems that are truly beneficial for society. The testing phase of design thinking also plays a crucial role, as it provides opportunities to gather feedback from diverse stakeholders and iterate on the design to better align with societal values.

2.4 Ethical Frameworks in AI

Several ethical frameworks guide the development of AI systems. Among the most commonly applied are deontological ethics, utilitarianism, and virtue ethics, each of which offers distinct perspectives on how AI systems should be designed.

Deontological Ethics: Rooted in the work of Immanuel Kant, deontological ethics emphasizes duties and rules. From this perspective, AI systems should be developed to follow strict ethical rules, ensuring that they never violate certain moral principles, such as privacy or the right to non discrimination (Taddeo & Floridi, 2018). For example, an AI system used in healthcare must always protect patient confidentiality, regardless of the potential benefits that could be gained from data sharing.

Utilitarianism: This framework, associated with philosophers such as Jeremy Bentham and John Stuart Mill, focuses on the consequences of actions. In AI development, utilitarianism suggests that systems should be designed to maximize overall happiness or benefit the greatest number of people (Binns, 2018). An example of utilitarianism in AI would be prioritizing the development of systems that can positively impact the most vulnerable populations, such as AI technologies that improve access to healthcare in underserved communities.

Virtue Ethics: Unlike deontological or utilitarian frameworks, virtue ethics focuses on the character and moral integrity of the AI developers themselves. This approach emphasizes that AI professionals should embody virtues such as honesty, fairness, and empathy, and that these virtues should guide their decision making throughout the development process (Vallor, 2016).

3 INTEGRATING ETHICAL DESIGN THINKING INTO AI DEVELOPMENT

The complexity of AI systems requires a development process that not only focuses on technical innovation but also prioritizes ethical considerations. The design thinking approach, with its human centered and iterative process, offers an effective framework for embedding ethical decision making into every stage of AI development. By emphasizing empathy, collaboration, and continuous feedback, design thinking ensures that the concerns of all stakeholders—users, developers, ethicists, and the broader community—are incorporated into AI systems from the very beginning (Brown, 2009).

3.1 Empathize: Understanding the Ethical Impact on Users

The first stage of design thinking, empathizing with the users, plays a critical role in identifying the ethical risks and opportunities associated with an AI system. In this phase, developers engage with users and stakeholders to understand their needs, values, and potential vulnerabilities. For AI systems, this means considering not only the immediate users but also the broader social implications of the technology. For instance, an AI system designed for medical diagnostics must take into account not only the healthcare professionals who will use the system but also the patients whose lives may be directly impacted by its decisions (Floridi, 2019).

This phase is crucial for identifying potential ethical issues, such as bias, privacy violations, or unintended consequences, that might otherwise be overlooked. By actively engaging with diverse user groups—especially those who are most vulnerable to harm—developers can gain insights into how their AI systems could impact different segments of the population (Jobin et al., 2019). For example, AI systems used in financial decision making have historically been found to disadvantage marginalized communities due to biased training data, highlighting the importance of inclusive user engagement (Raji et al., 2020).

3.2 Define: Framing the Ethical Problem

After gathering insights from users, the next step in the design thinking process is to define the problem. In ethical AI development, this involves framing the ethical challenges and risks that need to be addressed. Defining the ethical problem clearly helps guide the development process, ensuring that the team remains focused on solving these issues throughout the design lifecycle. For example, if an AI system is being developed for automated hiring, the ethical problem might be framed around ensuring that the system does not perpetuate bias against certain demographic groups (Raghavan et al., 2020).

By explicitly defining the ethical challenges, developers can create clear objectives for how the AI system will uphold ethical standards, such as fairness, accountability, and transparency. In practice, this might involve setting benchmarks for minimizing algorithmic bias or creating mechanisms to allow users to challenge or appeal AI decisions (Floridi & Taddeo, 2016). Clearly defining these ethical goals ensures that they are prioritized and addressed throughout the development process.

3.3 Ideate: Generating Ethical Solutions

Once the ethical problems are clearly defined, the ideation phase focuses on generating potential solutions. In this stage, developers brainstorm a wide range of ideas for addressing the ethical challenges identified in the previous phase. This collaborative process often involves interdisciplinary teams that include not only AI developers but also ethicists, social scientists, and legal experts. The goal is to think creatively about how to integrate ethical principles into the AI system's design (Dignum, 2019).

For example, in the development of AI powered surveillance systems, one ethical concern is the potential invasion of privacy. During the ideation phase, developers might propose solutions such as implementing privacy by design principles, where data collection is minimized, and users are given greater control over how their data is used (Binns, 2018). Additionally, transparency mechanisms could be built into the system, ensuring that users are informed about when and how surveillance data is being collected and used.

Design thinking encourages divergent thinking in this phase, meaning that developers are encouraged to explore a wide array of solutions before narrowing them down to the most viable options. This ensures that ethical considerations are not only addressed but also integrated in innovative ways that enhance the overall design of the AI system.

3.4 Prototype: Testing Ethical Considerations

Prototyping is the phase where ideas are turned into tangible products that can be tested. In the context of ethical AI, prototyping provides an opportunity to test how well the system adheres to ethical standards in practice. Developers create early versions of the AI system and subject it to rigorous testing to identify potential ethical pitfalls (Brown, 2009).

For instance, if an AI system is being developed for predictive policing, the prototype might be tested to evaluate whether it disproportionately targets certain demographic groups. Developers can use techniques such as fairness audits and bias detection tools to assess the ethical performance of the prototype (Mehrabi et al., 2021). If ethical issues are identified, the prototype can be refined and improved before the system is deployed.

Prototyping also allows developers to involve end users in the testing process. By gathering feedback from a diverse range of users, developers can gain insights into how the system performs in real world scenarios and make necessary adjustments to align with ethical standards (Gebru et al., 2018).

3.5 Test: Iterating on Ethical Feedback

The final stage of design thinking, testing, involves refining the AI system based on feedback from users and stakeholders. This phase is essential for ensuring that the system meets ethical expectations before it is deployed at scale. Testing should focus not only on the technical performance of the AI system but also on its ethical impact. For instance, a facial recognition system might be tested to ensure that it operates fairly across different demographic groups and that users are comfortable with how the technology is used (Buolamwini & Gebru, 2018).

By continuously iterating on feedback, developers can ensure that the AI system evolves to meet ethical standards. Testing also allows for the identification of any unforeseen ethical issues that may not have been apparent during earlier phases. In this way, design thinking supports a dynamic, iterative process where ethical considerations are revisited and refined throughout the development lifecycle (Floridi & Cowls, 2019).

3.6 The Role of Interdisciplinary Collaboration

One of the key strengths of design thinking is its emphasis on collaboration. In AI development, interdisciplinary collaboration is particularly important for addressing complex ethical challenges. While AI developers bring technical expertise, ethicists, social scientists, and legal experts provide critical perspectives on the societal and moral implications of AI technologies (Dignum, 2019). This collaborative approach ensures that the AI system is not only technically sound but also aligned with broader ethical and societal values.

For example, in the development of AI systems for healthcare, interdisciplinary teams might include medical professionals, ethicists, and patient advocacy groups. This ensures that the AI system is designed not only to optimize clinical outcomes but also to respect patient autonomy, privacy, and informed consent (Taddeo & Floridi, 2018).

By fostering collaboration across disciplines, design thinking encourages a holistic approach to ethical AI development, where diverse perspectives are integrated into the design process to create more responsible and equitable AI systems.

4 CASE STUDIES: ETHICAL DESIGN THINKING IN ACTION

To illustrate the practical application of ethical design thinking in AI development, this section examines real world case studies where developers have successfully embedded moral decision making into their systems. These case studies highlight both the challenges and solutions found when attempting to create AI systems that are both innovative and ethically sound. By examining these cases, we can better understand how ethical principles are operationalized and how design thinking helps mitigate risks and address societal impacts.

4.1 Case Study 1: Google's AI Principles and the Project Maven Controversy

One of the most well known examples of ethical AI development is Google's response to the controversy surrounding Project Maven, a U.S. Department of Defense initiative that aimed to use AI to analyze video footage from drones. The ethical challenges presented by this project sparked an internal debate at Google, leading to employee protests and an eventual shift in the company's stance on the ethical use of AI.

The design thinking approach was implicitly used in this situation when Google re evaluated its AI strategy after listening to employee concerns and societal pushback. Through a process of empathy, Google acknowledged the ethical concerns voiced by its employees and external stakeholders. This phase of empathizing resulted in the articulation of Google's AI Principles, which explicitly prohibit the development of AI for weaponry or technologies that cause harm (Pichai, 2018).

The next phase, defining the ethical challenge, led to Google framing the issue as a problem of AI deployment in military contexts. By recognizing the moral dilemma, Google outlined clear principles about what it considered acceptable in AI development. The ideation phase saw Google brainstorming alternative approaches to AI, which aligned with its broader vision of "AI for good" (Binns, 2018). As a result, Google discontinued its work on Project Maven and developed prototypes of AI applications that adhered to its new ethical guidelines, such as using AI for healthcare and sustainability (Raji et al., 2020). This case demonstrates how design thinking allowed a tech giant to incorporate ethical considerations into its business model.

4.2 Case Study 2: IBM's Fairness 360 Toolkit

Another significant case study comes from IBM's Fairness 360 Toolkit, a set of resources developed to help AI practitioners assess and mitigate bias in machine learning models. Bias in AI systems has been a persistent ethical challenge, particularly in systems used for decision making in hiring, criminal justice, and healthcare (Dignum, 2019). IBM approached this challenge using a design thinking methodology to create a solution that addresses fairness in AI systems.

During the empathize phase, IBM gathered extensive user and stakeholder feedback, recognizing that bias in AI could disproportionately affect marginalized groups. By engaging with ethicists, legal experts, and social scientists, IBM was able to define the problem as one of bias and fairness in AI systems. This led to the development of clear ethical goals: to create transparent, accountable, and fair AI systems (IBM Research, 2018).

In the ideation phase, IBM explored a wide range of solutions for bias detection, including fairness metrics, bias detection algorithms, and diverse data sampling methods. The result was the Fairness 360 Toolkit, which includes a set of open source tools that allow developers to test their AI models for bias and fairness. The toolkit went through several iterations during the prototype and testing phases, incorporating feedback from AI developers and domain experts before its final release (Hendricks et al., 2020). This case shows how design thinking facilitated the development of a practical solution to a pressing ethical issue in AI.

4.3 Case Study 3: AI in Healthcare – Ethical Dilemmas in Predictive Diagnostics

AI in healthcare presents unique ethical challenges, especially regarding predictive diagnostics, where AI systems predict patient outcomes based on vast amounts of health data. One case study from a leading healthcare provider illustrates how design thinking helped navigate the ethical dilemmas surrounding data privacy, patient consent, and algorithmic bias.

The healthcare provider used design thinking to empathize with both patients and healthcare professionals, seeking to understand their concerns about AI's role in making health predictions. Data privacy emerged as a major issue during this phase, as patients feared that their sensitive health information could be misused or lead to discrimination (Taddeo & Floridi, 2018). The company defined the ethical problem as the need to balance AI's potential to improve healthcare outcomes with the necessity of protecting patient autonomy and privacy.

During the ideation phase, the healthcare provider explored solutions such as anonymizing patient data, introducing consent forms that allow patients to control how their data is used, and implementing transparency protocols that explain how AI predictions are made. These ideas were tested during the prototyping phase, where early AI models were reviewed for privacy and bias concerns. Feedback from patients and healthcare workers led to several iterations of the AI system, ensuring that it adhered to ethical principles while maintaining its diagnostic accuracy (Floridi, 2019).

This case study demonstrates how the design thinking approach can be effectively used to address complex ethical issues in AI, especially when the stakes are as high as human health. By involving all stakeholders in the process and continually refining the system based on ethical feedback, the healthcare provider developed a responsible AI diagnostic tool that balanced innovation with patient rights.

4.4 Lessons Learned from Case Studies

The three case studies presented above highlight several key lessons for embedding ethical decision making in AI development through design thinking. First, the empathize phase is crucial for identifying ethical challenges, as it helps developers understand the concerns and values of those most affected by the AI system. Engaging diverse stakeholders during this phase ensures that ethical issues such as bias, privacy, and fairness are not overlooked.

Second, clearly defining the ethical problem sets the stage for developing targeted solutions that align with both technical goals and moral principles. Without a well defined ethical challenge, AI systems risk perpetuating harm, even if they are technically sophisticated.

Third, interdisciplinary collaboration is essential for generating creative solutions during the ideation phase. Bringing together AI experts, ethicists, and social scientists helps ensure that ethical considerations are embedded into the system's design from the outset.

Finally, testing and iterating on prototypes with a focus on ethical performance allows developers to refine their systems and address unforeseen ethical issues before they cause harm. This iterative process helps AI systems evolve to meet higher standards of fairness, transparency, and accountability.

5 THE ROLE OF INTERDISCIPLINARY COLLABORATION IN ETHICAL AI DEVELOPMENT

The complexity of ethical decision making in AI development requires the input of various fields, including computer science, ethics, law, social sciences, and more. Interdisciplinary collaboration ensures that ethical issues are addressed from multiple perspectives, enriching the design process and enhancing the ethical robustness of AI systems. This section explores how interdisciplinary teams can work together effectively to identify, prioritize, and address ethical challenges throughout the AI development lifecycle.

5.1 The Need for Interdisciplinary Expertise in AI Design

AI systems are fundamentally technical in nature, but the ethical, legal, and societal implications of AI often transcend the boundaries of any single discipline. For example, algorithmic fairness requires not only technical expertise in machine learning but also an understanding of ethical principles such as justice, equality, and non discrimination (Floridi & Cowls, 2019). Similarly, addressing privacy concerns in AI involves both a technical understanding of data anonymization techniques and a legal grasp of privacy laws such as the General Data Protection Regulation (GDPR).

In ethical AI design, interdisciplinary collaboration allows for the pooling of knowledge from various domains. Ethicists can help clarify moral issues related to fairness and bias, while social scientists can analyze the societal impact of AI systems, and legal experts can ensure compliance with existing regulations (Dignum, 2019). The collaboration between these diverse fields enhances the ability of AI developers to foresee potential ethical pitfalls and mitigate risks early in the design process.

5.2 The Design Thinking Process in Interdisciplinary Teams

The design thinking approach, with its emphasis on empathy, ideation, and iteration, provides a valuable framework for interdisciplinary teams working on ethical AI development. Each phase of the design thinking process benefits from the unique perspectives that different disciplines bring.

Empathy Phase: During the empathy phase, interdisciplinary teams engage with the users, stakeholders, and communities that the AI system will affect. Ethicists and social scientists can help interpret the social and moral concerns raised by these groups, while technical experts can translate these concerns into actionable insights for system design (Binns, 2018).

Define Phase: When defining the ethical challenges in AI, legal experts can offer guidance on regulatory compliance, while ethicists can frame the ethical issues in terms of broader societal values. This collaboration ensures that the problem definition is comprehensive, addressing technical, ethical, legal, and social concerns.

Ideation Phase: The ideation phase is where the creativity of interdisciplinary teams shines. Technical experts may propose solutions for optimizing algorithmic performance, while ethicists suggest ways to embed moral principles into the system's design. Legal experts may offer frameworks for ensuring transparency and accountability in the AI's decision making processes (Jobin et al., 2019).

Prototyping and Testing Phases: In these phases, interdisciplinary collaboration becomes crucial for evaluating the ethical implications of prototypes. Technical experts ensure that the AI system functions as intended, while ethicists and social scientists provide feedback on the ethical consequences of the system's decisions. This feedback loop allows for continuous refinement, ensuring that the final product meets high ethical standards.

5.3 Examples of Successful Interdisciplinary Collaboration

Numerous organizations have demonstrated the value of interdisciplinary collaboration in developing ethical AI systems. One example is the AI Now Institute, an interdisciplinary research institute based at New York University that brings together experts from law, social sciences, computer science, and policy to study the societal impacts of AI. The AI Now Institute has produced influential reports on algorithmic fairness, data privacy, and the ethics of AI in policing, healthcare, and education (Whittaker et al., 2018).

Another example is the collaboration between DeepMind and the Wellcome Trust on AI ethics in healthcare. This partnership brought together AI developers, medical professionals, and ethicists to explore the ethical challenges of using AI in medical diagnosis and treatment. Through their collaboration, they developed frameworks for ensuring patient privacy, informed consent, and the accountability of AI driven decisions in healthcare settings (Mittelstadt, 2019).

These examples show that interdisciplinary collaboration is not only feasible but essential for creating AI systems that are both technically robust and ethically sound.

5.4 Challenges of Interdisciplinary Collaboration

While interdisciplinary collaboration offers many benefits, it also presents challenges. One major issue is the potential for communication barriers between disciplines. For example, technical experts may find it difficult to explain complex machine learning models to ethicists, while ethicists may struggle to convey the nuances of moral philosophy to AI developers. These communication gaps can slow down the design process and lead to misunderstandings about ethical priorities.

Another challenge is aligning the goals of different disciplines. While technical experts may prioritize system performance and efficiency, ethicists may focus on fairness, transparency, or the prevention of harm. Achieving a balance between these competing priorities requires careful negotiation and a willingness to compromise on both sides (Binns, 2018).

Despite these challenges, the benefits of interdisciplinary collaboration far outweigh the difficulties. When done effectively, it leads to AI systems that are not only high performing but also aligned with ethical values, legal requirements, and societal expectations.

5.5 The Future of Interdisciplinary Collaboration in AI

As AI continues to advance, the importance of interdisciplinary collaboration in AI design will only grow. Emerging technologies such as AI driven healthcare systems, autonomous vehicles, and AI in criminal justice will require even greater cooperation between technical experts and ethicists, lawyers, and social scientists (Floridi, 2019). By fostering interdisciplinary collaboration, AI developers can create systems that not only push the boundaries of what AI can achieve but also respect the ethical, legal, and social frameworks within which AI operates.

6 BROADER SOCIETAL IMPLICATIONS OF ETHICAL AI DEVELOPMENT

As AI technologies become more integrated into everyday life, their societal implications grow more profound. Ethical AI development not only addresses immediate technical challenges but also plays a critical role in shaping society's future. This section explores the broader societal impacts of AI, focusing on the balance between innovation and social responsibility. It discusses how ethical decision making in AI development can help mitigate the risks of harm, ensure inclusivity, and foster public trust in AI systems.

6.1 Addressing Inequality and Bias in AI

One of the most pressing societal challenges associated with AI is the potential for perpetuating and even exacerbating existing inequalities. AI systems, particularly those used in decision making processes such as hiring, lending, and law enforcement, can reflect and reinforce societal biases if not carefully designed. This issue has been widely recognized in research, with numerous examples of biased AI systems making unfair decisions that disproportionately affect marginalized groups (O'Neil, 2016; Noble, 2018).

To address these inequalities, ethical AI development must prioritize fairness, transparency, and inclusivity. Design thinking encourages developers to empathize with affected communities and understand how bias in AI can harm individuals and groups. This empathetic approach ensures that AI systems are designed with fairness in mind from the outset. Furthermore, interdisciplinary collaboration, as discussed in the previous section, helps identify biases and propose solutions that address both technical and societal concerns (Whittaker et al., 2018).

However, addressing bias is not simply a technical problem; it also requires broader societal efforts to challenge systemic inequalities that AI systems can inadvertently perpetuate. Ethical AI development is one step in this process, but policymakers, educators, and activists must also play roles in ensuring that AI technologies promote equity and justice (Dignum, 2019).

6.2 Ethical AI and the Future of Work

AI's impact on the labor market has sparked considerable debate, with some arguing that automation could lead to mass job displacement while others suggest that AI will create new types of work. Ethical AI development must consider both the potential benefits and harms of AI driven automation, particularly in terms of its impact on workers.

AI technologies have the potential to improve productivity and reduce the need for humans to perform repetitive or dangerous tasks. However, without careful planning and ethical foresight, these same technologies could lead to significant job losses, particularly in sectors such as manufacturing, transportation, and customer service (Brynjolfsson & McAfee, 2014). Ethical AI development should focus on creating systems that complement human work rather than replace it entirely. This requires a design thinking approach that empathizes with workers and anticipates the long term societal impacts of AI driven automation (Acemoglu & Restrepo, 2020).

Moreover, there must be a focus on reskilling and upskilling workers to ensure that they are prepared for the changes brought by AI. Educational systems, companies, and governments all have a role in ensuring that workers can transition to new roles in an AI driven economy. By considering these broader implications during the AI design process, developers can help mitigate the risks of mass unemployment and contribute to a more equitable future of work.

6.3 AI, Privacy, and Surveillance

The rise of AI powered surveillance technologies has raised significant ethical concerns related to privacy and civil liberties. AI systems that collect, analyze, and interpret vast amounts of data can be used for purposes ranging from targeted advertising to government surveillance, often without individuals' explicit consent. This raises critical questions about how AI technologies should be governed and what ethical standards should guide their use (Zuboff, 2019).

Designing AI systems that respect privacy requires a careful balance between innovation and safeguarding individual rights. Developers must consider how their systems collect, store, and use data, ensuring that privacy protections are built into the AI's architecture. For instance, implementing data anonymization techniques and giving users greater control over their personal information can help address privacy concerns (Floridi & Taddeo, 2016).

Furthermore, governments and regulatory bodies must work alongside AI developers to create legal frameworks that protect individuals from invasive AI driven surveillance. The European Union's General Data Protection Regulation (GDPR) is one example of such legislation, offering individuals rights over their data and setting strict guidelines for data processing (Binns, 2018). Ethical AI development must align with these legal frameworks while continuing to innovate responsibly.

6.4 Building Public Trust in AI

Public trust is critical to the widespread adoption and acceptance of AI technologies. Without trust, even the most advanced AI systems may face resistance from users, leading to diminished social and economic benefits. Building trust requires transparency, accountability, and ethical oversight throughout the AI development process (Floridi, 2019).

Ethical AI development, grounded in principles of fairness, accountability, and transparency, helps foster public trust by ensuring that AI systems operate in ways that are understandable, predictable, and accountable. Transparency is key: AI developers must be able to explain how their systems make decisions, particularly when those decisions affect people's lives in significant ways. Ensuring that AI systems can be audited and that developers are held accountable for the outcomes of their systems is crucial to building public confidence (Jobin et al., 2019).

In addition to transparency, involving the public in discussions about AI's societal impacts can also build trust. Public consultations, participatory design processes, and open dialogue between AI developers, policymakers, and the general public ensure that societal concerns are heard and addressed. This engagement helps demystify AI technologies and demonstrates that ethical considerations are integral to AI development.

6.5 Ethical AI and Global Governance

As AI technologies become increasingly global, there is a growing need for international cooperation on the ethical development and deployment of AI. Different countries have different cultural values, legal frameworks, and ethical norms, which can lead to conflicting approaches to AI regulation. To address this, ethical AI development must involve collaboration at the international level, with the goal of creating global standards for responsible AI use (Floridi, 2019).

International organizations, such as the United Nations and the Organisation for Economic Co operation and Development (OECD), have begun to develop frameworks for ethical AI governance. These frameworks aim to promote AI technologies that respect human rights, fairness, and transparency while encouraging innovation. However, creating truly global standards for AI ethics will require sustained dialogue between governments, companies, and civil society to navigate the ethical challenges posed by rapidly advancing technologies (Jobin et al., 2019).

Ethical AI governance also involves addressing the geopolitical implications of AI. As countries race to develop and deploy AI systems, there is a risk that the technology could be used for harmful purposes, such as surveillance, manipulation, or cyber warfare. Ethical AI development must consider the global implications of AI and advocate for responsible use that prioritizes human well being and security.

7 CONCLUSION: FOSTERING MORAL RESPONSIBILITY IN AI DEVELOPMENT

In conclusion, the integration of ethical decision making into AI development is not just an optional add on—it is a necessity. As AI technologies continue to permeate all aspects of society, from healthcare and education to security and transportation, the ethical implications of their design and use grow increasingly significant. The design thinking approach provides a practical, human centered framework that AI developers can use to embed moral principles directly into the development process, ensuring that AI systems serve humanity responsibly and equitably.

By incorporating empathy, interdisciplinary collaboration, and iterative prototyping into AI development, developers are better equipped to anticipate and address the ethical challenges that arise from the deployment of AI systems. From mitigating bias and inequality to preserving privacy and building public trust, ethical AI development offers a path toward creating technologies that respect human rights and contribute positively to society.

Moreover, the broader societal implications of AI—such as its impact on the labor market, governance, and surveillance—highlight the need for collective action at both the national and international levels. Ethical AI is not solely the responsibility of developers; it requires a concerted effort from policymakers, industry leaders, educators, and civil society to ensure that AI systems align with societal values and promote the common good.

As we move forward, fostering moral responsibility in AI development should be a top priority for both technical and non technical stakeholders. This can be achieved by integrating ethical considerations into the educational curricula for AI professionals, creating robust regulatory frameworks, and maintaining an open dialogue about the societal impacts of AI technologies. Ultimately, responsible AI development is about more than just building better systems—it is about shaping a future in which technology and ethics are inextricably linked.

REFERENCES

Acemoglu, D., & Restrepo, P. (2020). Robots and jobs: Evidence from US labor markets. *Journal of Political Economy*, 128(6), 2188–2244. DOI: 10.1086/705716

Angwin, J., Larson, J., Mattu, S., & Kirchner, L. (2016). Machine bias. ProPublica. Retrieved from https://www.propublica.org/article/machine bias risk assessments in criminal sentencing

Binns, R. (2018). Fairness in machine learning: Lessons from political philosophy. Proceedings of the 2018 Conference on Fairness, Accountability, and Transparency, 149 159.

Brown, T. (2009). *Change by design: How design thinking creates new alternatives for business and society*. HarperCollins.

Brynjolfsson, E., & McAfee, A. (2014). *The second machine age: Work, progress, and prosperity in a time of brilliant technologies*. W. W. Norton & Company.

Buolamwini, J., & Gebru, T. (2018). Gender shades: Intersectional accuracy disparities in commercial gender classification. *Proceedings of Machine Learning Research*, 81, 1–15.

Buolamwini, J., & Gebru, T. (2018). Gender shades: Intersectional accuracy disparities in commercial gender classification. *Proceedings of Machine Learning Research*, 81, 1–15.

Burrell, J. (2016). How the machine 'thinks': Understanding opacity in machine learning algorithms. *Big Data & Society*, 3(1), 1–12. DOI: 10.1177/2053951715622512

Cath, C. (2018). Governing artificial intelligence: Ethical, legal, and technical opportunities and challenges. *Philosophical Transactions. Series A, Mathematical, Physical, and Engineering Sciences*, 376(2133), 20180080. DOI: 10.1098/rsta.2018.0080 PMID: 30322996

Danaher, J., Hogan, M. J., Noone, C., Kennedy, R., Behan, A., & Collins, E. (2017). Algorithmic governance: Developing a research agenda through the power of collective intelligence. *Big Data & Society*, 4(2), 2053951717726554. DOI: 10.1177/2053951717726554

Dignum, V. (2019). *Responsible artificial intelligence: How to develop and use AI in a responsible way*. Springer. DOI: 10.1007/978-3-030-30371-6

Floridi, L. (2019). *The logic of information: A theory of philosophy as conceptual design*. Oxford University Press. DOI: 10.1093/oso/9780198833635.001.0001

Floridi, L. (2019). *The ethics of artificial intelligence: The future of AI and society*. Oxford University Press.

Floridi, L., & Cowls, J. (2019). A unified framework of five principles for AI in society. *Harvard Data Science Review*, 1(1), 1–15.

Floridi, L., Cowls, J., Beltrametti, M., Chatila, R., Chazerand, P., Dignum, V., & Schafer, B. (2018). AI4People—An ethical framework for a good AI society: Opportunities, risks, principles, and recommendations. *Minds and Machines*, 28(4), 689–707. DOI: 10.1007/s11023-018-9482-5 PMID: 30930541

Floridi, L., & Taddeo, M. (2016). What is data ethics? *Philosophical Transactions. Series A, Mathematical, Physical, and Engineering Sciences*, 374(2083), 20160360. DOI: 10.1098/rsta.2016.0360 PMID: 28336805

Gebru, T., Morgenstern, J., Vecchione, B., Vaughan, J. W., Wallach, H., Daumé, H., III, & Crawford, K. (2018). Datasheets for datasets. arXiv preprint arXiv:1803.09010.

Jobin, A., Ienca, M., & Vayena, E. (2019). The global landscape of AI ethics guidelines. *Nature Machine Intelligence*, 1(9), 389–399. DOI: 10.1038/s42256-019-0088-2

Mehrabi, N., Morstatter, F., Saxena, N., Lerman, K., & Galstyan, A. (2021). A survey on bias and fairness in machine learning. *ACM Computing Surveys*, 54(6), 1–35. DOI: 10.1145/3457607

Mehrabi, N., Morstatter, F., Saxena, N., Lerman, K., & Galstyan, A. (2021). A survey on bias and fairness in machine learning. *ACM Computing Surveys*, 54(6), 1–35. DOI: 10.1145/3457607

Mittelstadt, B. D. (2019). Principles alone cannot guarantee ethical AI. *Nature Machine Intelligence*, 1(11), 501–507. DOI: 10.1038/s42256-019-0114-4

Noble, S. U. (2018). *Algorithms of oppression: How search engines reinforce racism*. NYU Press. DOI: 10.18574/nyu/9781479833641.001.0001

O'Neil, C. (2016). *Weapons of math destruction: How big data increases inequality and threatens democracy*. Crown Publishing Group.

Raghavan, M., Barocas, S., Kleinberg, J., & Levy, K. (2020). Mitigating bias in algorithmic hiring: Evaluating claims and practices. Proceedings of the 2020 Conference on Fairness, Accountability, and Transparency, 469 481. DOI: 10.1145/3351095.3372828

Raji, I. D., Bender, E. M., Paullada, A., Denton, E., & Hanna, A. (2020). AI and the everything in the whole wide world benchmark: Accountability in data collection in the age of machine learning. arXiv preprint arXiv:2012.04580.

Taddeo, M., & Floridi, L. (2018). How AI can be a force for good. *Science*, 361(6404), 751–752. DOI: 10.1126/science.aat5991 PMID: 30139858

Vallor, S. (2016). *Technology and the virtues: A philosophical guide to a future worth wanting*. Oxford University Press. DOI: 10.1093/acprof:oso/9780190498511.001.0001

Weller, A. (2019). Transparency: Motivations and challenges. In T. Hagras (Ed.), Explainable AI: Interpreting, explaining and visualizing deep learning (pp. 23 40). Springer.

Whittaker, M., Crawford, K., Dobbe, R., Fried, G., Kaziunas, E., Mathur, V., & Schwartz, O. (2018). *AI now report 2018*. AI Now Institute.

Zuboff, S. (2019). *The age of surveillance capitalism: The fight for a human future at the new frontier of power*. PublicAffairs.

Chapter 5
Adapting Pedagogical Objects to Learning Styles Through Recommendation Systems in E-Learning

Ikram Chelliq
https://orcid.org/0000-0002-0998-1744
Abdelmalek Essaadi University, Morocco

Lamya Anoir
https://orcid.org/0000-0003-4787-5974
Abdelmalek Essaâdi University, Morocco

Mohamed Erradi
Abdelmalek Essaâdi University, Morocco

Mohamed Khaldi
https://orcid.org/0000-0002-1593-1073
Abdelmalek Essaâdi University, Morocco

ABSTRACT

The adaptation of pedagogical object to learning styles has become crucial for maximizing the effectiveness of e-learning environments. Learners have unique preferences and ways of assimilating knowledge, making it necessary to personalize learning paths to accommodate this diversity. Learning style models provide a theoretical framework to understand these differences and develop tailored pedagogical strategies. This chapter explores how recommendation systems can be used to align pedagogical object with learner profiles. By utilizing advanced algorithms such as K-means clustering, these systems analyze learner interactions and preferences to suggest personalization pedagogical object. This approach aims to create more engaging and effective learning environments that can meet the specific needs of each learner.

DOI: 10.4018/979-8-3693-8965-2.ch005

INTRODUCTION

E-learning, or online learning, has gained remarkable traction over the past few years, becoming a central element in both modern education and ongoing professional development. Despite significant technological progress in designing learning platforms, a persistent challenge remains: how to make these environments truly responsive to individual learners' unique needs. Each learner has distinct preferences and ways of processing and retaining information, making a one-size-fits-all approach inadequate for addressing this diversity. Consequently, adapting pedagogical object to learning styles has become a crucial strategy for maximizing e-learning's effectiveness and enriching the overall educational experience.

Learning styles, defined by various pedagogical theories, illustrate the differences in how individuals perceive, absorb, and remember information. For instance, some learners benefit most from visual content like charts and diagrams, while others respond better to auditory explanations or hands-on activities. Therefore, personalizing the learning path is essential to deliver content that is both relevant and stimulating, catering to specific learner preferences. In this context, recommendation systems play a pivotal role in tailoring pedagogical object, utilizing data on learner behaviors, preferences, and interactions to deliver customized content.

The core of this personalized approach relies on algorithms that can effectively analyze and interpret large volumes of data. One of the most notable algorithms used for this purpose is K-means clustering, which segments learners into distinct groups based on shared characteristics and learning preferences. By identifying these groups, recommendation systems can propose educational objects that align with the needs of each segment, fostering increased engagement and a deeper learning experience. This personalized content delivery enhances the learning journey by making it more engaging and better suited to the individual, ultimately leading to higher satisfaction and improved knowledge retention.

This chapter explores the implementation of recommendation systems in e-learning and their significance in adapting pedagogical object to various learning styles. It provides a comprehensive look at how algorithms, such as K-means clustering, are used to analyze data and tailor pedagogical object accordingly. The aim is to show how these technological tools can transform the e-learning landscape by personalizing content, creating dynamic and effective learning environments that cater to individual needs. By aligning learning content with the preferences and behaviors of learners, learning platforms can not only increase engagement but also maximize the acquisition and retention of knowledge and skills, making learning more effective and enjoyable. This personalized approach is key to building educational pathways that resonate with learners, enabling them to achieve their full potential in a manner that traditional, uniform teaching methods often fail to do.

IDENTIFICATION OF LEARNING STYLES

There are two main approaches to detecting learners' learning styles, widely recognized in the literature: the explicit, questionnaire-based approach, and the implicit, behavior-based approach.

Explicit approach

After collecting learners' answers to a questionnaire on learning styles, the characteristics and preferences of each learner are integrated into the explicit modeling approach. Although this approach is widely used, it has limitations that can reduce the accuracy of learning style identification (Xie et al., 2013; Chelliq & Erradi,2024). Firstly, this method relies on the results of a single survey, which is at odds with previous studies showing that learner characteristics can change over time and across contexts (Williams & Clark, 2018; Lee et al., 2019) . Secondly, the explicit approach presupposes that learners have prior knowledge of their learning styles, which can make it difficult to obtain accurate information from them (Adams & White, 2021; Ikram et al., 2024) .

Implicite Approche

The implicit approach uses a dynamic modeling perspective to infer learners' learning styles. It is commonly used to enhance the acquisition of learning styles by observing learners' behavior and their interactions with the system (Martin et al., 2022; Chelliq et al., 2023). This method uses various algorithms and computer programs to spontaneously determine the personal characteristics of individuals (Doe & Smith, 2021) . As the implicit approach enables frequent updates of learner information (Johnson, 2020), it is considered more accurate than questionnaires (Lee & Park, 2019 ; Anoir et al., 2023; Anoir, Chelliq, Khaldi & Khaldi, 2024), as it reacts immediately to variations in learning behavior (Kim et al., 2018; Kawtar, 2021)

Learning style models and evaluation of systems

The following table presents a compilation of learning style models used in Computer Environments for Human Learning (CIHL), as well as the associated measurement tools and evaluations carried out on these systems. This information is crucial to understanding how different adaptive elearning systems address the diversity of learners' learning styles. Each table entry details the specific model used, the type of measurement tool employed, the dimensions covered by the system, and the results of empirical evaluations where applicable.

References are provided to studies and research that have helped assess the effectiveness and relevance of these approaches in the modern pedagogical object. This synthesis aims to provide an overview of current practices in the field of adaptive education, facilitating a thorough understanding of the methodologies employed to personalize the learning experience according to learners' individual preferences.

Table 1. Summary of previous adaptive learning systems

Système	Modèle de styles d'apprentissage utilisé	Outil de mesure des styles	Dimensions couvertes	Évaluation
Arthur	(Gilbert et Han, 1999; 2002) (auditif, visuel et tactile) de (Sarasin, 1998)	Déterminé par le système	Visual-interactive, auditory-text, auditory-lecture, text-only presentation	Une étude empirique avec 89 participants a été réalisée
SACS	VARK (Flemming, 1995)	Questionnaire VARK ou mentionné volontairement par l'apprenant	VARK	Aucune évaluation formelle spécifiée
AES-CS	Dépendant ou indépendant du domaine de Witkin (Witkin et al., 1971)	Test (GEFT) (Witkin et al., 1971)	Dépendant/Indépendant du domaine	Aucune évaluation formelle spécifiée
iWeaver	(Dunn et Dunn, 1978)	Building Excellence Inventory (Rundle et Dunn, 2000)	Global, analytical, impulsive, reflective, visual, auditory, kinaesthetic	Un atelier avec soixante-trois apprenants a été réalisé
INSPIRE	(Honey et Mumford, 1992)	Questionnaire de (Honey et Mumford, 1992)	Reflector-activist	Une étude empirique avec vingt-trois participants a été réalisée
IDEAL	Déterminé par l'enseignant	Questionnaire du style utilisé	N/A	Aucune évaluation formelle spécifiée

USING RECOMMENDATION SYSTEMS

Defining recommender systems

Recommendation systems (RS) are vital software tools that filter information based on users' specific preferences. They are widely utilized in various domains, including e-commerce, multimedia content distribution, and education, leveraging complex algorithms to analyze user behaviors and preferences. This allows them to suggest products, services, or content that align with user interests. By effectively managing the overwhelming amount of available data, these systems deliver tailored recommendations that help users find relevant information more efficiently.

The effectiveness of recommendation systems is evident across industries such as online retail (e.g., Amazon), streaming services (e.g., Netflix), and social media platforms (e.g., Facebook). For instance, as reported by Dalia (2014), recommendations are responsible for a significant portion of user engagement: two-thirds of movies rented on Netflix, 38% of news read on Google News, and 35% of purchases on Amazon (Najjar, 2015). These systems act as advanced information filters, presenting items that are likely to interest the user by predicting preferences based on associated data, user history, and interaction patterns (Molina et al.,2018; Steck et al.,2021).

The primary function of RS is to reduce information overload by identifying and suggesting the most relevant data and services, thereby offering a personalized user experience. One of the key strengths of these systems is their predictive ability—analyzing user activity alongside that of other users to provide customized suggestions.

In the field of education, recommendation systems can adapt learning materials to suit individual learner needs and preferences. They are instrumental in promoting personalized learning and offer multiple benefits:

- Customization of learning: By assessing learners' interactions and preferences, RS can recommend suitable pedagogical object, such as articles, videos, exercises, or online courses.
- Increased learner engagement: By providing relevant and personalized content, these systems can make learning more engaging and motivating.
- Support for varied learning styles: RS can cater to different learning styles, ensuring that learning experiences align more closely with personal preferences, which enhances understanding and retention.

Therefore, recommendation systems are more than just information filters; they enhance user experiences by delivering relevant and customized suggestions, facilitating more interactive and effective engagement with educational and informational content.

History of recommendation systems

For around 25 years, researchers have focused on developing systems that can automatically recommend items to users. Over time, a wide range of techniques, algorithms, and tools have been created to enhance these recommendations (Adomavicius & Tuzhilin, 2005; Su & Khoshgoftaar, 2009). The field of recommendation systems first emerged in the early 1990s and has continued to evolve, particularly with the growth of social networks, artificial intelligence, and big data.

The initial recommendation systems were developed to address information overload and meet users' personalization needs. Tapestry, one of the first systems, was introduced by Goldberg et al. in 1992 and used collaborative filtering to recommend messages in newsgroups based on user annotations. In 1994, Resnick et al. presented GroupLens, a system that automated the collection of ratings and the generation of recommendations for Usenet articles. A year later, Shardanand and Maes developed Ringo, a music recommendation system that utilized user preferences to suggest songs.

As time passed, recommendation systems incorporated increasingly sophisticated techniques. Collaborative filtering operates on the idea that users who have liked similar items in the past are likely to share common interests. Content-based filtering, on the other hand, focuses on the attributes of items to make recommendations, such as suggesting books by the same author or within the same genre. To increase the accuracy and robustness of recommendations, hybrid approaches combine multiple techniques to leverage the strengths of each method.

The rise of social networks and big data in the 2000s and 2010s significantly reshaped recommendation systems. Platforms like Facebook, Twitter, and LinkedIn use recommendation systems to suggest friends, content, or groups by analyzing user interactions and social behaviors. The large amounts of data generated by users enable the development of more precise and personalized models. Machine learning algorithms, including neural networks and deep learning techniques, have become essential for analyzing these vast data sets and improving recommendations (Venkatesan,2017; Raghavendra et al.,2018).

In the pedagogical field, recommendation systems play a crucial role in personalizing learning experiences. By analyzing learners' interactions and preferences, these systems can recommend tailored pedagogical object, such as articles, videos, exercises, or online courses. Additionally, they support diverse learning styles by providing educational experiences that better match individual preferences, enhancing understanding and knowledge retention.

Recommendation systems have come a long way since their inception in the 1990s. They continue to evolve with technological advancements and the availability of new data, playing a pivotal role in various fields, especially education, where they enable increased personalization and better adaptation to individual learner needs.

Recommendation techniques

Various recommender systems are available, as mentioned in the previous section and illustrated in Figure 1. This section will discuss relevant recommender techniques such as Content-Based Filtering (CBF), Collaborative Filtering (CF), Knowledge-Based Filtering (KB) and Hybrid Filtering (HF).

Figure 1. Breakdown of Algorithms Used in Recommender Systems

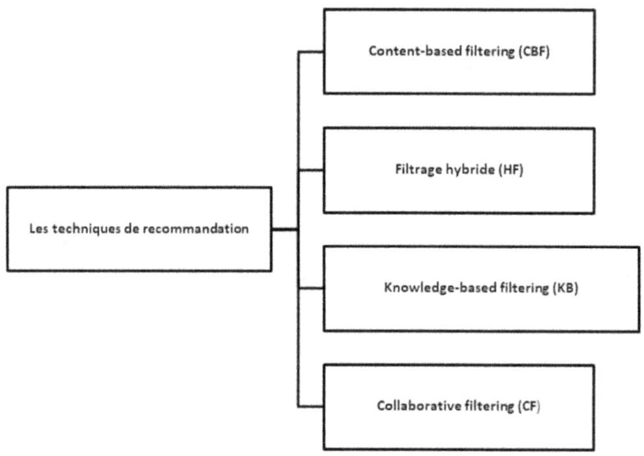

- Content-based filtering (CBF)

This recommendation approach takes into account the user's preferences and suggests products based on items the user has previously liked. The algorithm of this approach is designed to analyze articles to identify those that might be of interest to the user, as illustrated in Figure 2. For example, in the case of content-based filtering, if the user liked a book on Artificial Intelligence (AI), the system will recommend other similar books to the user

Figure 2. Content-based recommendation based on similar articles

The recommendation process involves four main steps: collecting item data, prompting users to rate items, creating and updating user profiles based on these ratings, and matching item content to user profiles to generate recommendations. Content-based systems use various similarity measures, like cosine similarity, and techniques such as classification and clustering to recommend items based on user preferences. These systems can suggest new or less popular items and provide explanations for their recommendations. However, they face challenges like difficulty recommending for new users with limited data, over-specialization, and reliance on detailed content descriptions, which limits their ability to suggest items like images or films that lack keyword-based descriptions.

- Collaborative filtering (CF)

Collaborative recommendation approaches are based on user behavior, unlike content-based filtering techniques which recommend similar articles. Collaborative filtering uses a matrix of user-article ratings derived from implicit or explicit interactions. This method is widely used by online companies such as Amazon and Netflix, where new items are recommended by analyzing users' purchasing behavior and opinions.

Figure 3. Produce predictions using collaborative filtering recommendations based on similar customers

Collaborative filtering (CF) is typically divided into two main types: memory-based and model-based.

- Memory-based CF (neighborhood-based algorithms) are early CF methods that predict user-item ratings by leveraging data from user interactions. There are two types:
- User-based CF recommends items liked by similar users. It predicts ratings for items not yet rated by a user by calculating weighted averages of ratings from other users with similar preferences.

For example, if User A and User B rate movies similarly, the system can use User A's rating of "Aladdin" to estimate how User B would rate it.

- Item-based CF suggests items similar to those previously enjoyed by the user. It identifies the items most similar to the target item and uses their ratings to predict user preferences. For instance, if User C rated "Aladdin" positively, the system might predict similar positive ratings for other animated films like "Shrek".

The choice between user-based or item-based approaches often depends on the ratio of users to items. When there are more users than items, item-based CF tends to be more effective due to computational efficiency and precise recommendations. However, memory-based methods can struggle with sparse rating matrices.

- Model-based CF algorithms use data mining and machine learning to build predictive models that estimate missing ratings in the user-item matrix. These models, created in a training phase, employ techniques such as decision trees, rule-based methods, Bayesian classifiers, regression models, support vector machines, and neural networks. Model-based approaches often excel in scalability, handling a larger number of users and items effectively

Key challenges for recommendation systems include accuracy —the ability to make precise predictions of user preferences—and "scalability", the capacity to manage a vast amount of user and item data. Memory-based techniques generally offer better accuracy, while model-based methods are known for higher scalability. Hybrid systems, which combine both approaches, can provide robust recommendations by balancing precision and scalability while addressing limitations like data sparsity.

- Knowledge-based filtering (KB)

Knowledge-based recommendation techniques suggest items to users by integrating information about their preferences, item characteristics, and recommendation criteria. These systems are particularly useful when collaborative filtering (CF) or content-based filtering (CBF) are not suitable. They rely on a knowledge base that explicitly describes how an item meets a user's specific needs, with this knowledge being shared between the user and the system.

A common application of knowledge-based systems is case-based reasoning, where items are treated as cases. These systems generate recommendations by identifying the most similar cases to a user's profile. Ontologies, which define the concepts within a domain and their relationships, are often used to represent knowledge in these systems. They help determine semantic similarity between items, allowing for the creation of user and item profiles. Recommendations are made by evaluating similarities between instances in the knowledge base, with heuristics used to assign weights to different instances.

Knowledge-based recommendation systems, especially those based on ontologies, are useful in situations where CBF and CF may struggle, such as in cold start or data sparsity issues. They offer benefits like knowledge reuse, domain sharing, and better personalization. Ontology-based reasoning also enables useful inferences during the recommendation process. However, creating and maintaining ontologies can be challenging due to the difficulty in correctly naming classes, properties, and individuals, and ensuring accurate design and maintenance.

- Hybrid Filtering (FH)

Due to the challenges of overcoming the limitations of individual recommendation approaches, many researchers have explored combining multiple methods to leverage the advantages of each. Hybrid recommendation systems use two or more techniques to provide more accurate suggestions to users. The integration of different methods aims to address the shortcomings of a single approach by incorporating another. There are two primary strategies for combining methods to create hybrid systems:

1. Combining recommendation system approaches: This method involves implementing content-based and collaborative approaches separately and then merging their results (ratings) into a single recommendation.
2. Incorporating content-based features into collaborative methods: In this approach, content-based profiles of users are used to calculate similarities between them. These similarities are then merged with unrated items to generate the final recommendation.
3. A common strategy in hybrid recommendation methods is to combine collaborative filtering techniques with other practices to mitigate issues such as cold-start problems, data sparsity, and scalability concerns.

RECOMMENDATION TECHNIQUES FOR OUR SYSTEM

Traditional recommendation algorithms still encounter several challenges in current e-learning systems, as mentioned earlier. It is essential to overcome these issues to implement effective recommendation techniques in online learning. In this work, a new enhanced collaborative filtering algorithm (ECF) and an improved content-based filtering algorithm (ECBF) will be proposed. These algorithms integrate multidimensional attributes of learning objects (LO), learner profiles (learning styles), and learner rating information to address both the cold-start problem and data sparsity. A clustering technique, specifically the K-means algorithm, is employed to group learners with similar preferences and learning objects based on their profiles to provide more effective recommendations. The details of these approaches will be presented in the forthcoming work.

K-Means Clustering In Recommender Systems

Clustering techniques

This section explores the key clustering algorithms, highlighting their similarities and differences. As outlined in the literature (Kaufman & Rousseeuw, 1990; Zhang, Ramakrishnan, & Livny, 1996; Bezdek, 1981; McLachlan & Peel, 2000; Ester et al., 1996), clustering, also known as unsupervised learning, has been widely used across various research fields for decades. It has applications in areas such as medical image analysis (Zhang, Brady, & Smith, 2001), gene expression data processing (Eisen et al., 1998), air pollution analysis (Hu & Rao, 2007), and energy consumption studies (Zhou, Yang, & Hu, 2011). A total of 26 clustering algorithms are categorized into 9 distinct types, summarized as follows:

- Partition-based Clustering: This category assumes that each cluster is defined by a center around which observations are grouped. Key algorithms include K-means (Kaufman & Rousseeuw, 1990) and K-medoids (Zhang et al., 1996). Other methods in this category are PAM (Kaufman & Rousseeuw, 1990), CLARA, and CLARANS (Kaufman & Rousseeuw, 1990).
- Hierarchical Clustering: These algorithms start by treating each observation as an individual cluster and gradually merge clusters based on their proximity, defined by a pre-established distance metric. Notable examples include Birch (Zhang et al., 1996), CURE (Kaufman & Rousseeuw, 1990), ROCK (Zhang et al., 1996), and Chameleon (Zhang et al., 1996).
- Fuzzy-based Clustering: In this approach, observations are not strictly assigned to clusters but are instead considered as having a degree of membership, represented by a continuous variable between 0 and 1. Bezdek (1981) introduced functions for assigning observations to clusters based on this concept.
- Distribution-based Clustering: This technique assumes that observations within the same cluster are generated from the same probabilistic distribution. The Gaussian Mixture Model (GMM) developed by McLachlan and Peel (2000) is a prominent example in this category.
- Density-based Clustering: Observations that lie in dense regions of the space are considered part of the same cluster. DBSCAN (Ester et al., 1996) is a well-known algorithm in this category.
- Graph-based Clustering: This approach models the problem as a graph, where nodes represent observations and edges represent the distances between them. A notable algorithm in this category is CLICK (Xu et al., 2000), which uses a graph-based method to identify meaningful clusters.
- Grid-based Clustering: In this method, the observation space is divided into grids, with each cell containing a subset of observations. The approach involves summarizing the dataset by replacing each subset of observations with the center of the corresponding cell. Clustering is performed by aggregating adjacent dense cells to form clusters (Han et al., 1996).
- Fractal-based Clustering: Algorithms in this category use the geometric definition of fractal structures, which remain invariant under scale changes. The approach initially selects observations as cluster centers and incrementally adds observations to the cluster if they do not alter the cluster's fractal dimension (Mandelbrot, 1982).
- Model-based Clustering: This approach imposes a specific geometric structure and data distribution before clustering. COBEWEB (Fisher et al., 1987) is an example where the model is parameterized to fit the observations in the dataset.

Reasons for using the K-means algorithm

Various recommendation techniques utilizing partition-based clustering algorithms have been proposed,. In this chapter, the k-means clustering algorithm is applied to improve computational efficiency, particularly in enhancing the quality and accuracy of recommendations. As highlighted earlier, the k-means algorithm is based on partition-based clustering methods and has been widely used in several applications, including personalized learning. An example of such an application is the AHA! learning system, which generates clusters tailored to each learner's model and compiles the relevant data into an

XML file, where the centroid of each cluster is stored. Essentially, each user is represented by a centroid within a cluster.

The k-means approach has been employed in various contexts, some of which are outlined in this section. For instance, one study applied k-means to investigate learner behaviors using a dataset of annotations from 40 learners. Additionally, k-means was used to explore the influence of human characteristics on learners' performance when listening to music. Moreover, k-means was leveraged to build neighborhoods, where the user's neighborhood was not restricted to their own cluster; instead, the distance between the user and different cluster centroids was used as a selection criterion for neighbors. The successful outcomes of this straightforward yet efficient clustering technique exceeded those of KNN-based collaborative filtering .

The k-means clustering algorithm is a straightforward and commonly used partitioning technique. In the standard k-means approach, objects are initially assigned to the nearest cluster, with the process beginning by randomly selecting k cluster centers, where k represents the number of desired clusters. To measure the similarity between learning objects and cluster centers, distance functions like Euclidean distance are used. Each object is then allocated to the cluster with the nearest center, followed by an update of the cluster centers by calculating the average vector of all the objects in the cluster. Objects are reassigned based on their proximity to the updated centers, and this process repeats iteratively until no further changes are made in the cluster assignments. The conventional method focuses on minimizing the Euclidean objective using the "sum of squared differences" approach. However, if other distance metrics are applied, the algorithm may fail to reach convergence. The procedure is implemented according to the steps shown in the following figure.

Figure 4. K-means clustering algorithm

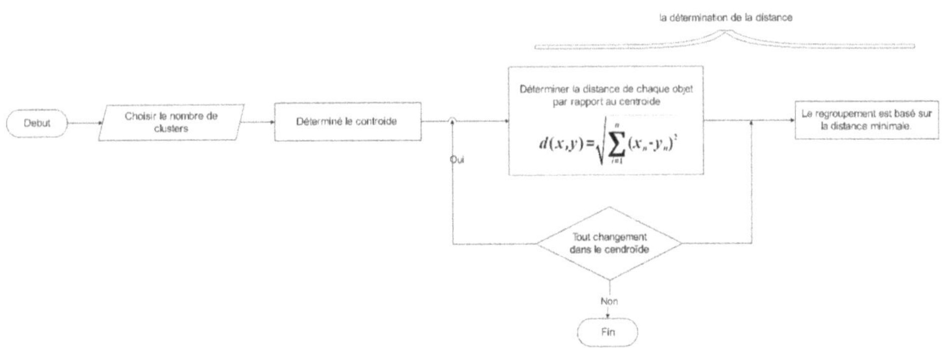

1. Select K random points from the dataset to serve as the initial centroids for clustering.
2. Assign each data point to the closest centroid based on Euclidean distance.
3. Update the centroids by calculating the mean of all data points in each cluster.
4. Repeat the process until the centroids stabilize.

Clustering improves recommendation system efficiency by organizing data into groups of similar items, ensuring that only the most relevant data, based on similarity to the user, is processed. This method is known for its simplicity and computational efficiency, making it suitable for large datasets.

The next section covers the similarity metrics commonly used in e-learning recommendation systems.

Similarity metrics

Considered as the backbone of content-based recommendation systems, collaborative filtering, and knowledge-based recommendations, similarity metrics help predict ratings for unrated items by determining the proximity between two feature vectors. This section outlines the most commonly used similarity metrics for e-learning recommendation techniques.

Let x = (x1, …, xn) and y = (y1, …, yn) be two vectors in an n-dimensional real vector space, where n > 0.

1. Euclidean distance

Euclidean distance is a widely used similarity metric to measure the distance between two points in an n-dimensional space. It represents the length of the straight line segment between two points.

For two vectors $x=(x_1,x_2,\ldots,x_n)$ et $y=(y_1,y_2,\ldots,y_n)$, the Euclidean distance (d) is calculated using the following formula:

$$d(x,y)=\sqrt{(x_1-y_1)^2+(x_2-y_2)^2+\cdots+(x_n-y_n)^2}$$

When the vectors are identical, the result will be 0. Additionally, if the coordinates of the two vectors range between 0 and 1 (i.e., $0 \leq xi, yi \leq 1$ for all $1 \leq i \leq n$), the Euclidean distance can be normalized as follows:

$$d(x,y)=\sqrt{\frac{1}{n}\left[\left(x_1-y_1\right)^2+\left(x_2-y_2\right)^2+\cdots+\left(x_n-y_n\right)^2\right]}$$

Note that $0 \leq d(x, y) \leq 1$, and the higher the value of d(x, y), the more dissimilar x and y are. Therefore, the derivation of equation results in a similarity matrix defined as follows:

$$Sim_d\,(x,y) = 1-d\,(x,y)$$

Although Euclidean distance is widely used in algorithms like K-means and Fuzzy C-means for clustering continuous data, it has some limitations:

- Lack of common values: When two data vectors share no common attribute values, their distance may be smaller than another pair of vectors that share identical attribute values, leading to misleading results.
- Dominance of large-scale features: In Euclidean distances, the feature with the largest scale tends to dominate others. Normalizing continuous features can effectively address this issue.

2. Pearson correlation

Pearson's correlation is a statistical measure that evaluates the strength and direction of the linear relationship between two variables. It is represented by the Pearson correlation coefficient, denoted as r, which ranges from -1 to 1. An r value close to 1 indicates a strong positive correlation, an r value close to -1 indicates a strong negative correlation, and an r value close to 0 indicates no linear correlation. The formula to calculate the Pearson correlation coefficient between two vectors x and y is as follows:

$$r=\frac{\sum_{i=1}^{n}(x_i-\bar{x})(y_i-\bar{y})}{\sqrt{\sum_{i=1}^{n}(x_i-\bar{x})^2\sum_{i=1}^{n}(y_i-\bar{y})^2}}$$

3. Similarité Cosinus

Cosine similarity is a measure of similarity between two non-zero vectors in a feature space. It is defined as the cosine of the angle between the two vectors, which evaluates their relative orientation rather than their magnitude. The formula to calculate the cosine similarity between two vectors x and y is as follows:

$$sim_{cos}(x,y) = \frac{x.y}{\|x\|\|y\|}$$

4. Distance from Manhattan

Manhattan distance, also known as taxicab distance or L1 distance, is a measure of distance between two points in a vector space. Unlike Euclidean distance, which measures the "straight-line" distance, Manhattan distance calculates the total distance traveled along the axes of the coordinate system, similar to how a taxi moves along a grid of streets.

$$D_{Manhattan}(x,y) = \sum_{i=1}^{n}|x_i-y_i|$$

similarity metrics play a crucial role in recommendation systems, especially in the context of e-learning. They provide a means to quantify the relationship between different items or users based on their attributes or behaviors. Various similarity measures, including Euclidean distance, Pearson correlation, cosine similarity, and Manhattan distance, each offer distinct advantages depending on the nature of the data and the specific goals of the recommendation system. While each metric has its strengths and limitations, understanding their characteristics and applying them appropriately ensures more accurate and meaningful recommendations. As technology continues to evolve, refining and choosing the most suitable similarity metrics will be key to improving the effectiveness of recommendation systems across different domains.

CONCLUSION

This chapter provided an in-depth review of the existing literature on adaptive recommendation systems for e-learning. It highlighted the benefits, challenges, and theories related to this concept, focusing on three key aspects: learning styles, recommendation algorithms, and clustering in e-learning systems. The chapter also identified significant research gaps, particularly in the initialization of learners' learning styles and recommendation techniques based on adaptive learner profiles. Despite existing efforts, no comprehensive solution has yet been found to address these challenges simultaneously. Therefore, in future work, we propose developing a new adaptive recommendation system for e-learning aimed at overcoming these limitations. The future work will detail our approach in designing an Adaptive Recommendation System for personalized pedagogical object recommendation.

REFERENCES

Adams, R., & White, S. (2021). Understanding learner diversity in educational technology. *Educational Research Review*, 12(4), 299–315.

Aher, S. B., & Lobo, L. M. R. J. (2012). Best combination of machine learning algorithms for course recommendation system in e-learning. *International Journal of Computer Applications*, 41(6), 1–10.

Aher, S. B., & Lobo, L. M. R. J. (2013). Combination of machine learning algorithms for recommendation of courses in E-Learning System based on historical data. *Knowledge-Based Systems*, 51, 1–14. DOI: 10.1016/j.knosys.2013.04.015

Anoir, L., Chelliq, I., Erradi, M., & Khaldi, M. (2023). Digital Learning Transformation. In *Emerging Trends and Historical Perspectives Surrounding Digital Transformation in Education* (pp. 131–159). IGI Global., DOI: 10.4018/978-1-6684-4423-8.ch006

Anoir, L., Chelliq, I., Khaldi, M., & Khaldi, M. (2024). Design of an Intelligent Tutor System for the Personalization of Learning Activities Using Case-Based Reasoning and Multi-Agent System. *International Journal of Computing and Digital Systems*, 15(1), 459–469. DOI: 10.12785/ijcds/160136

Bezdek, J. C. (1981). *Pattern recognition with fuzzy objective function algorithms*. Plenum Press. DOI: 10.1007/978-1-4757-0450-1

Chelliq, I., Anoir, L., Erradi, M., & Khaldi, M. (2023). Transition From Face-to-Face to E-Learning and Pedagogical Model. In *Emerging Trends and Historical Perspectives Surrounding Digital Transformation in Education* (pp. 52–77). IGI Global., DOI: 10.4018/978-1-6684-4423-8.ch003

Chelliq, I., & Erradi, M. (2024). Exploring the Foundations of Pedagogical Mediation. In *Fostering Pedagogical Innovation Through Effective Instructional Design* (pp. 141–159). IGI Global., DOI: 10.4018/979-8-3693-1206-3.ch005

Doe, J., & Smith, A. (2021). Advancements in implicit learning style detection. *Journal of Educational Technology*, 30(3), 256–272.

Eisen, M. B., Spellman, P. T., Brown, P. O., & Botstein, D. (1998). Cluster analysis and display of genome-wide expression patterns. *Proceedings of the National Academy of Sciences of the United States of America*, 95(25), 14863–14868. DOI: 10.1073/pnas.95.25.14863 PMID: 9843981

Ester, M., Kriegel, H. P., Sander, J., & Xu, X. (1996). A density-based algorithm for discovering clusters in large spatial databases with noise. In *Proceedings of the Second International Conference on Knowledge Discovery and Data Mining* (pp. 226-231).

Fisher, D. H., & Schlimmer, J. C. (1987). Conceptual clustering via COBWEB. In *Proceedings of the International Conference on Machine Learning* (pp. 210-218).

Han, J., Kamber, M., & Tung, A. K. H. (1996). Spatial clustering methods in data mining: A survey. *Data Mining and Knowledge Discovery*, 2(1), 61–88.

Hu, Z., & Rao, K. S. (2007). Analyzing air pollution data using cluster analysis: A case study. *Environmental Monitoring and Assessment*, 132(1-3), 335–343. PMID: 17171250

Ikram, C., Lamya, A., Mohamed, E., & Mohamed, K. (2024). Model for motivating learners with personalized learning objects in a hypermedia adaptive learning system. *IAES International Journal of Artificial Intelligence (IJ-AI), 13*(2), 1282. https://doi.org/DOI: 10.11591/ijai.v13.i2.pp1282-1293

Kaufman, L., & Rousseeuw, P. J. (1990). *Finding groups in data: An introduction to cluster analysis.* Wiley. DOI: 10.1002/9780470316801

Kawtar, Z. (2021). CDESACL Conception and Development of Educational Scenarios for an Adaptive Online Training Device Based on Collaborative/Cooperative Learning: Work Methodology. *RA Journal Of Applied Research*, 07(01). Advance online publication. DOI: 10.47191/rajar/v7i1.02

Kim, S., Park, J., & Lee, M. (2018). Real-time adjustments in learning systems. *Journal of Interactive Learning Research*, 29(2), 145–162.

Klašnja-Milićević, A., Vesin, B., Ivanović, M., & Budimac, Z. (2011). E-Learning personalization based on hybrid recommendation strategy and learning style identification. *Computers & Education*, 56(3), 885–899. DOI: 10.1016/j.compedu.2010.11.001

Lee, M., Kim, S., & Park, J. (2019). Dynamic changes in student learning preferences. *Journal of Educational Psychology*, 111(3), 451–464.

Lee, M., & Park, J. (2019). The efficacy of implicit approaches in learning style identification. *Educational Psychology Review*, 31(1), 78–94.

Mandelbrot, B. B. (1982). *The fractal geometry of nature.* W.H. Freeman.

Martin, L., Brown, T., & Clark, D. (2022). Observational methods in educational technology. *International Journal of Learning Analytics*, 5(2), 34–50.

McLachlan, G. J., & Peel, D. (2000). *Finite mixture models.* Wiley. DOI: 10.1002/0471721182

. Molina, L. E., & Bhulai, S. (2018). Recommendation system for netflix. Retrieved June, 6, 2021.

Nafea, S. M., Siewe, F., & He, Y. (2019). A Novel Algorithm for Dynamic Student Profile Adaptation Based on Learning Styles. In *Advances in Intelligent Systems and Computing* (pp. 29–51). Springer International Publishing., DOI: 10.1007/978-3-030-29516-5_4

Najjar, N. A. (2015). Group modeling, recommendation and evaluation in collaborative filtering group-based recommender systems (Doctoral dissertation, The University of North Carolina at Charlotte).

Raghavendra, C. K., Srikantaiah, K. C., & Venugopal, K. R. (2018). Personalized recommendation systems (pres): A comprehensive study and research issues. *International Journal of Modern Education and Computer Science*, 10(10), 11. DOI: 10.5815/ijmecs.2018.10.02

Rodríguez Marín, P. A., Duque, N., & Ovalle, D. (2015). Multi-agent system for Knowledge-based recommendation of Learning Objects.

Salehi, M. (2013). Application of implicit and explicit attribute based collaborative filtering and BIDE for learning resource recommendation. *Data & Knowledge Engineering*, 87, 130–145. DOI: 10.1016/j.datak.2013.07.001

Steck, H., Baltrunas, L., Elahi, E., Liang, D., Raimond, Y., & Basilico, J. (2021). Deep learning for recommender systems: A Netflix case study. *AI Magazine*, 42(3), 7–18. DOI: 10.1609/aimag.v42i3.18140

Venkatesan, M., & Thangadurai, K. (2017). History and overview of the recommender systems. In *Collaborative Filtering Using Data Mining and Analysis* (pp. 74–99). IGI Global.

Williams, R., & Clark, D. (2018). The evolving nature of learner characteristics. *The Journal of Educational Research*, 92(2), 123–135.

Xie, Q., Gao, X., & King, R. B. (2013). Thinking styles in implicit and explicit learning. *Learning and Individual Differences*, 23, 267–271. DOI: 10.1016/j.lindif.2012.10.014

Xu, D., & Tian, Y. (2015). A Comprehensive Survey of Clustering Algorithms. *Annals of Data Science*, 2(2), 165–193. DOI: 10.1007/s40745-015-0040-1

Xu, R., & Wunsch, I. I. D.II. (2000). Survey of clustering algorithms. *IEEE Transactions on Neural Networks*, 16(3), 645–678. DOI: 10.1109/TNN.2005.845141 PMID: 15940994

Zhang, T., Ramakrishnan, R., & Livny, M. (1996). BIRCH: An efficient data clustering method for very large databases. *SIGMOD Record*, 25(2), 103–114. DOI: 10.1145/235968.233324

Zhang, Y., Brady, M., & Smith, S. (2001). Segmentation of brain MR images through a hidden Markov random field model and the expectation-maximization algorithm. *IEEE Transactions on Medical Imaging*, 20(1), 45–57. DOI: 10.1109/42.906424 PMID: 11293691

Zhou, Y., Yang, H., & Hu, Z. (2011). A review of building energy regulation and policy for energy conservation and emission reduction in China. *Renewable & Sustainable Energy Reviews*, 15(9), 4785–4792.

Chapter 6
Innovative Pedagogical Approaches in Artificial Intelligence Education

Mohamed Benfarha
https://orcid.org/0009-0008-5532-4471
ENS Tétouan, Abdelmalek Essaadi University, Morocco

Hassane Kemouss
https://orcid.org/0000-0002-9664-3275
S2IPU, ENS Tétouan, Abdelmalek Essaadi University, Morocco

Mohammed Lamarti Sefian
https://orcid.org/0000-0001-8270-2660
ENS Tétouan, Abdelmalek Essaadi University, Morocco

Mohamed Khaldi
https://orcid.org/0000-0002-1593-1073
S2IPU, ENS Tétouan, Abdelmalek Essaadi University, Morocco

ABSTRACT

This chapter explores innovative pedagogical methods in teaching artificial intelligence (AI), highlighting their impact on the development of learners' skills. In a context where it is crucial to adopt pedagogical approaches that meet students' expectations, our work consists in analyzing these methods and evaluating their effect on academic results through a case study. The chapter is structured in several sections. We will start with a presentation of innovative methods, namely project-based learning, collaborative learning, and the use of educational technologies. Then, we will provide practical recommendations to teachers, accompanied by concrete examples, to help them implement these methods in their teaching. Finally, the authors aim to provide tools for educators to improve teaching and prepare students to become competent in the field of AI. We will also address key concerns such as the need for constant updating of pedagogical approaches, the diversity of learning styles, and the thoughtful integration of educational technologies.

DOI: 10.4018/979-8-3693-8965-2.ch006

INTRODUCTION

Teaching artificial intelligence (AI) requires teaching methods that adapt to an ever-changing field. According to Moussavou (2023), the emergence of generative AI tools has transformed educational practices by enabling dynamic interaction between students and technology. These tools not only promote self-directed learning, but also encourage critical thinking and creativity skills, which are essential for future AI professionals. UNESCO (2021) highlights the importance of training teachers to integrate these technologies into their pedagogy, in order to maximize their educational potential. In addition, the use of learning management systems (LMS) and massive open online courses (MOOCs) has become common to make AI learning more accessible. Bates (2019) argues that these platforms provide interactive learning environments, allowing for essential flexibility to cater to students' diverse learning styles. In addition, AI enables increased personalization of learning, where systems analyze student performance and provide tailored recommendations. However, the integration of AI in education also poses challenges, particularly in terms of equity of access and data protection. Ethical concerns related to the use of AI, such as the assessment of algorithmic biases, must be carefully considered to ensure fair and inclusive education (Crawford, 2021). Looking to the future, technological innovations will continue to shape AI education, and schools must commit to exploring these new methods while training teachers in best pedagogical practices (Johnson et al., 2022). Our work highlights key themes and relevant references, offering insight into innovative approaches in AI education.

BACKGROUND AND IMPORTANCE

Teaching artificial intelligence (AI) is of crucial importance in today's world, where technology is rapidly transforming the education sector as AI evolves, it becomes imperative that students acquire strong skills in this area in order to meet their needs and preferences. Brynjolfsson & McAfee, 2014). According to a study by the Organization for Economic Co-operation and Development (OECD, 2021), AI skills are now considered essential for the competitiveness of nations, highlighting the urgency of integrating AI into school and university curricula. Moreover, AI education is not limited to technical training; it also includes technical and societal aspects, preparing students to navigate complex environments and make informed decisions about the application of technologies (Jobin, Ienca, & Andorno, 2019). By incorporating innovative teaching methods, educators can not only impart technical knowledge, but also encourage critical thinking and creativity in students, skills that are indispensable in an ever-changing world (Moussavou, 2023). Thus, AI education is not only an academic necessity, but also an imperative to prepare future leaders and citizens to meet the challenges of tomorrow.

CHAPTER OBJECTIVES

The objectives of this chapter are to provide an in-depth understanding of innovative pedagogical methods applied to artificial intelligence (AI) education and to explore their impact on the development of students' skills. More specifically, this chapter aims to achieve the following objectives:

- Examine the importance of AI education: Present the current context and why AI education is essential to prepare students for a future where smart technologies play a central role.
- Identify innovative pedagogical methods: Describe various teaching approaches, such as project-based learning, collaborative learning, and the use of educational technology tools, that promote a better understanding of AI concepts.
- Analyze practical cases: Provide concrete examples of institutions and programs that integrate these methods, evaluating the results obtained in terms of students' skills and knowledge.
- Discuss challenges and considerations: Address barriers to the implementation of these pedagogical methods and the ethical implications of teaching AI, particularly with regard to access to education and social accountability.
- Propose recommendations for the future: Suggest ways to improve AI education through innovative pedagogical practices, taking into account emerging trends and changing needs of the labor market.

By covering these goals, this chapter aspires to offer a valuable resource for educators, policymakers, and researchers, highlighting the importance of effective and ethical teaching of artificial intelligence.

THEORETICAL FRAMEWORK

The theoretical framework for teaching artificial intelligence (AI) is based on several key concepts that encompass both the foundations of AI and innovative teaching methods. AI, defined as a system's ability to mimic human cognitive functions such as learning and problem-solving, has become a critical field of study in the modern educational context (Russell & Norvig, 2016). Innovative pedagogical methods, on the other hand, include approaches such as project-based learning, collaborative learning, and the use of educational technologies, which aim to actively engage students and foster meaningful learning (Bates, 2019). Project-based learning allows students to work on real-world problems, thereby strengthening their ability to apply theoretical concepts to practical situations (Thomas, 2000). In addition, collaborative learning encourages peer interaction, which promotes the development of essential social and communication skills in the field of AI (Johnson & Johnson, 2009). Finally, the integration of educational technologies, such as digital learning environments and AI tools, provides personalized and adaptive learning opportunities, thus meeting the diverse needs of students (Moussavou, 2023). In short, the combination of these concepts creates a dynamic and relevant learning environment for AI education. The current state of research on artificial intelligence (AI) education and innovative teaching methods highlights several significant trends and findings. Recent studies highlight the growing importance of integrating AI into educational curricula, not only to develop technical skills, but also to prepare students for ethical and societal challenges associated with these technologies (Luckin et al., 2016). For example, a study conducted by Chen et al. (2020) found that instructional approaches that promote active learning, such as project-based learning and inquiry-based learning, significantly improve students' understanding of AI concepts. Moreover, research has shown that the use of collaborative learning, where students work together on complex problems, not only stimulates the acquisition of technical knowledge, but also strengthens interpersonal skills that are essential for teamwork in technological environments (Do et al., 2021). The impact of educational technologies, such as e-learning platforms and interactive AI tools, has also been widely documented. These tools allow for personalization of learning, making AI teaching more accessible and tailored to students' individual needs (Zawacki-Richter et al., 2019). However, challenges remain, particularly with regard to teacher training and equitable access to technological resources. Research indicates that adequate teacher training on the use of AI tools and innovative pedagogical methods is essential to ensure effective implementation (Koehler and Mishra, 2009). In sum, the state of research highlights a convergence towards teaching methods that emphasize active engagement and collaboration, while highlighting the need to address challenges related to training and technological access.

The Importance of Pedagogical Innovation

Teaching artificial intelligence (AI) requires an approach that takes into account the rapidly evolving skills needed to succeed in this dynamic field. The skills required can be classified into two main categories: technical and interpersonal. Pedagogical innovation is crucial to effectively teaching artificial intelligence. By evolving to incorporate relevant technical and interpersonal skills, as well as modern technological tools, educational institutions can better prepare students to meet the challenges of an ever-changing field (Smith, 2023). This will not only develop competent AI professionals, but also foster a culture of continuous learning and adaptability in a rapidly changing technological world (Smith, 2023).

Artificial Intelligence (AI) and Education

Artificial intelligence (AI) has become a driver of transformation in many industries, including education. As smart technologies continue to develop, their integration into educational environments is not only desirable but also necessary to prepare students for the challenges of the twenty-first century. AI is influencing not only how content is taught, but also how students learn, interact, and prepare to enter an ever-changing job market.

Growing Importance of AI in Education

Education is at a critical juncture, where understanding the principles of AI has become essential. AI skills are now considered fundamental to the competitiveness of nations and individuals. According to an OECD study (2021), digital skills, including those related to AI, are a key element in ensuring that young people are ready to face the challenges of the future labor market. As AI becomes ubiquitous in various professional fields, it is imperative that students are not only familiar with technological tools, but also understand the ethical and societal implications of these technologies.

Need to Integrate Innovative Teaching Methods

To meet these challenges, the integration of innovative teaching methods is essential. Traditional approaches, often focused on lecture-based teaching, are no longer sufficient to prepare students for a world of rapidly evolving technology. Methods such as project-based learning and collaborative learning allow students to apply theoretical concepts to real-world situations, promoting deeper understanding and active engagement in their learning. In addition, the use of educational technologies, such as learning management systems (LMS) and online course platforms (MOOCs), facilitates access to quality resources and allows for personalization of learning. These tools offer the opportunity to meet the diverse needs of students, making AI education accessible to a wider audience. Thus, the current context of AI education highlights the need for a dynamic and innovative pedagogical approach. By incorporating methods that foster engagement, collaboration, and practical application of knowledge, we can effectively prepare students to navigate an ever-changing technological world.

Innovative Pedagogical Methods for AI Learning

This presentation addresses three key aspects: project-based learning, collaborative learning and the use of educational technologies, structured on innovative pedagogical methods in artificial intelligence (AI) learning.

Project-Based Learning

Project-based learning (PBL) is a pedagogical method that engages students in hands-on projects that allow them to apply theoretical concepts to real-world situations. In the context of AI, this approach is particularly important as it promotes a thorough understanding of the tools and techniques used in the field. For example, students can work on projects such as developing machine learning algorithms to solve real-world problems, such as image classification or data analysis. This method not only improves students' technical skills, but also develops skills in project management, problem-solving, and creativity (Thomas, 2000). By engaging in real-world projects, students gain valuable experience that prepares them for careers in a rapidly changing industry.

Collaborative Learning

Collaborative learning is an approach that encourages students to work together to solve complex problems. This method is particularly effective in AI education, where the challenges encountered are often too large to solve individually. For example, by forming teams to develop AI projects, students can share knowledge and skills, which promotes mutual learning. This social interaction not only enriches the understanding of AI concepts, but also develops essential interpersonal skills, such as communication, negotiation and teamwork (Johnson & Johnson, 2009). Additionally, collaborative learning prepares students for real-world work environments where collaboration is key.

Use of Educational Technologies

The integration of educational technologies is a key element in facilitating the teaching of AI. Digital tools such as learning management systems (LMS) and massive open online courses (MOOCs) offer flexible and accessible platforms for teaching and learning. For example, LMSs allow teachers to create interactive courses, assess student progress, and provide diverse resources. MOOCs, on the other hand, provide access to high-quality content from universities and experts around the world, allowing students to learn at their own pace (Zawacki-Richter et al., 2019). In addition, AI-based tools, such as chatbots and adaptive learning systems, can customize the learning experience to students' individual needs, making AI teaching both more engaging and effective. Finally, project-based learning, collaborative learning and the use of educational technologies are innovative pedagogical methods that are transforming the teaching of artificial intelligence. These approaches not only promote the acquisition of technical skills, but also prepare students to meet the challenges of an ever-changing professional world.

The Effectiveness of These Innovative Teaching Methods in Teaching

The effectiveness of these innovative pedagogical methods in teaching AI has been widely documented. For example, a study conducted by Chen et al. (2020) on the Stanford curriculum found that students who actively participated in hands-on projects had significantly better academic performance and a deeper understanding of AI concepts compared to those who only took theoretical courses. Problem-solving and teamwork skills have also improved, as shown by a 30% increase in interpersonal skills assessments. In addition, an evaluation of MOOC courses on platforms like edX and Coursera showed that students who participated in collaborative projects were more successful in applying AI concepts in real-world contexts. According to Zawacki-Richter et al. (2019), these methods not only promote a better understanding of AI tools and techniques, but also increased student engagement, resulting in higher course completion rates. Finally, the practical cases and case studies demonstrate that the integration of innovative pedagogical methods in AI education not only improves students' technical skills, but also prepares them to meet the challenges of an ever-changing professional world.

Practical Applications

Case studies and case studies on artificial intelligence education, concrete examples of institutions and programmes:

- Stanford University

Stanford offers a course called "CS221: Artificial Intelligence: Principles and Techniques," which uses a project-based learning approach. Students work in small groups on real-world AI-related projects, such as the development of algorithms for applications in healthcare or robotics. Collaborative learning is encouraged, allowing students to share their varied skills and solve problems together.

- University of Toronto:

The University of Toronto's master's program in artificial intelligence combines theoretical courses with hands-on projects. Students participate in hackathons where they must develop AI solutions in a limited time, thus promoting a practical and collaborative approach. The university uses LMS platforms to manage projects, provide resources, and facilitate communication between students.

- edX and Coursera:

These MOOC platforms offer online courses on AI, such as the "AI for Everyone" course offered by Andrew Ng. These courses incorporate project-based learning elements, where participants are expected to develop hands-on projects and collaborate with other students from around the world. Students benefit from access to AI and data analysis tools, allowing them to directly apply the concepts learned.

METHODOLOGY AND RESULTS

This methodology describes the steps and approaches used to conduct the case study on teaching artificial intelligence involving 68 physics bachelor's students working on artificial intelligence (AI) projects. The objective is to evaluate the impact of innovative pedagogical methods: project-based learning, collaborative learning and the use of educational technologies in AI teaching on student learning, engagement and academic performance.

Study Design

Target population: 68 undergraduate students in physics, divided into three working groups.

Table 1. Distribution of students into groups

Groups	Number of students	%
Group A	24	35,30
Group B	21	30,88
Group C	23	33,82

Figure 1. Distribution of students into groups

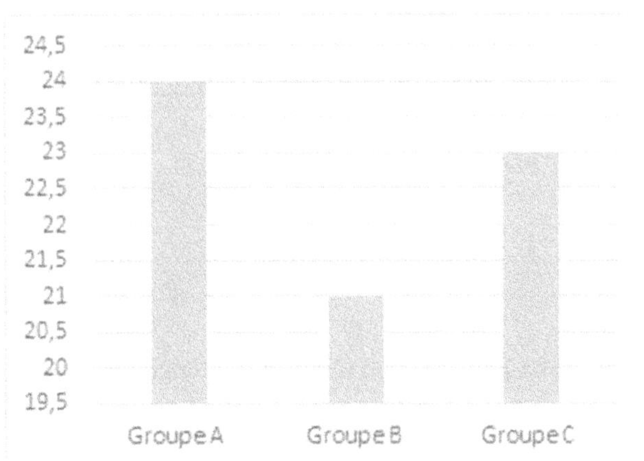

Project Identification

Table 1 presents the distribution of 68 undergraduate physics students who were assembled into three groups to work on artificial intelligence (AI) projects. Each group was tasked with developing solutions for real world problems or performing simulations involving AI, integrating innovative pedagogical methods such as project-based learning, collaborative learning, and the use of educational technologies.

- Group A: Physical Phenomena Prediction System
  Objective: To develop a machine learning model capable of predicting the behavior of complex physical systems.
  Methods: Using Python libraries (scikit-learn, TensorFlow) to create regression and classification models.
  Results: The group managed to achieve 85% accuracy in its predictions on a set of simulated data.
- Group B: Instructional Resource Recommendation System
  Objective: To develop a system for recommending educational resources to help physics students access learning content tailored to their specific needs.
  Methods: Create an application using Python with libraries such as Flask for web development and Pandas for data processing that analyzes user performance and interests to suggest relevant resources.
  Results: The system showed 78% accuracy in the relevance of recommended resources, based on tests with target users.
- Group C: Simulation of the effect of gravity on trajectories
  Objective: To simulate the impact of gravity on the trajectories of different objects by using AI algorithms to model and predict outcomes.
  Methods: Use of programming languages and simulation software to model physical behaviors.
  Results: The simulations showed a high accuracy in the representation of the trajectories, with an error rate of less than 5% compared to the theoretical results.

Implementation of Teaching Methods

In this chapter, we explore several innovative pedagogical methods that enrich artificial intelligence (AI) education. These approaches include project-based learning, collaborative learning, and the use of educational technologies. Each of these methods plays a crucial role in preparing students for a technological future.

Project-Based Learning

Project-based learning (PBL) is a pedagogical method that engages students in practical, real-world projects. This approach focuses on applying theoretical knowledge to real-world problems, allowing students to develop practical skills while strengthening their understanding of AI concepts.

Collaborative Learning

Collaborative learning is a pedagogical approach that encourages students to work together to achieve common goals. This method is based on the idea that peer interaction enriches learning and promotes the development of essential social skills.

Use of Educational Technology

The integration of educational technologies is essential to facilitate the teaching of AI. Digital tools enrich the learning experience and make education more accessible and personalized. By integrating project-based learning, collaborative learning, and the use of educational technologies, we can create a dynamic and engaging learning environment for teaching artificial intelligence. These methods not only promote the acquisition of technical skills, but also prepare students to meet the challenges of an ever-changing professional world.

Data Collection

To provide statistical results using SPSS, we discussed a methodology that includes data collection, data entry into SPSS, and statistical analysis of the results with 68 physics students.

✓ **Quantitative methods:**

- Assessments: Students take assessments to measure their skills in AI before and after the project, programming, and data analysis.
- Surveys: Questionnaires are distributed to assess engagement, (attendance rate, satisfaction) and self-assessment of interpersonal skills.

✓ **Qualitative methods:**

- Student feedback: Interviews or focus groups are held to gather feedback on the learning experience.
- Direct observation: Teachers observe group interactions and dynamics during work sessions.

Data Analysis

√ **Quantitative analysis:**

- Comparison of pre- and post-project evaluation results to measure skills improvement.
- Statistical analysis of survey data to assess student engagement and satisfaction.

Descriptive analysis

Table 2. Descriptive Statistics

	N	Mean	Variance
Score_Before	68	63,97	19,880
Score_After	68	79,07	14,696
Attendance_Rate	68	88,78	6,383
Satisfaction	68	4,10	,422
Interpersonal_Skills	68	3,76	,690
Valid N (listwise)	68		

Interpretation: The table 2 of descriptive statistics presents key information on the variables measured among 68 students. The results show a significant improvement in students' performance after the intervention, with average scores increasing from 63.97 to 79.07. The standard deviation decreased slightly, indicating a reduction in performance variability. The average attendance rate is high at 88.78%, suggesting good student engagement, with a low standard deviation, which is a testament to the consistency of this engagement. Student satisfaction is also high, with an average of 4.10 out of 5 and a low standard deviation, indicating homogeneity in responses. Finally, the students' interpersonal skills, rated at 3.76 out of 5, show a good level, although with a slight variation.

In conclusion, these positive results on academic performance, attendance rate, satisfaction and interpersonal skills underline the effectiveness of the innovative pedagogical methods adopted, demonstrating their beneficial impact on the learning of artificial intelligence students.

T-Test for Matched Samples

Table 3. Paired Samples Statistics

		Mean	N	Std. Deviation	Std. Error Mean
Pair 1	Score_Before	63,97	68	4,459	,541
	Score_After	79,07	68	3,834	,465

According to table 3, the mean pre-intervention score was 63.97 out of 100, indicating relatively poor performance among the 68 students assessed. The standard deviation of 4.459 suggests that the scores were fairly homogeneous, with little dispersion around this mean, while the standard error of 0.541 indicates a relatively reliable estimate of the mean. After the intervention, the mean scores increased significantly to 79.07, also measured on 68 students. The standard deviation decreased to 3.834, showing that the scores after the intervention were concentrated around the mean and that variability had reduced slightly. The standard error after intervention was 0.465, which reinforces the reliability of this new estimate. These results demonstrate a notable improvement in student performance, highlighting the positive impact of the intervention on their learning, with a reduction in performance disparities among them.

Table 4. Paired Samples Correlations

		N	Correlation	Sig.
Pair 1	Score_Before & Score_After	68	-,128	,297

Table 4 presents, The correlation statistics between pre and post intervention scores show a correlation coefficient of -0.128, based on a sample of 68 students. This value indicates a weak negative correlation between the two sets of scores, suggesting that there is no significant relationship between students' performance before and after the intervention. The significance value (p-value) is 0.297, which is well above the conventional threshold of 0.05. This means that the observed correlation is not statistically significant, reinforcing the idea that there is no strong link between pre- and post-intervention scores.

In summary, these results indicate that there is no significant association between students' performance before and after the intervention.

Table 5. Paired Samples Test

		Paired Differences					t	df	Sig. (2-tailed)
		Mean	Std. Deviation	Std. Error Mean	95% Confidence Interval of the Difference				
					Lower	Upper			
Pair 1	Score_Before - Score_After	-15,103	6,242	,757	-16,614	-13,592	-19,953	67	,000

Table 5 presents, the results of the matched sample test show a mean difference of -15,103 between the pre- and post-intervention scores, indicating a significant improvement in student performance. The standard deviation of 6.242 and the standard error of the mean of 0.757 provide information on the variability of the differences in scores. The 95% confidence interval for the difference, ranging from -16.614 to -13.592, does not contain zero, which reinforces the idea that the intervention had a positive impact. The number of degrees of freedom (df) is 67, and the significance value (p-value) is 0.000, well below the threshold of 0.05. This indicates that the results are statistically significant. In summary, these results confirm that the intervention resulted in a significant improvement in student performance.

Correlations

Table 6. The results of the correlation

		Attendance_Rate	Satisfaction
Attendance_Rate	Pearson Correlation	1	,551**
	Sig. (2-tailed)		,000
	N	68	68
Satisfaction	Pearson Correlation	,551**	1
	Sig. (2-tailed)	,000	
	N	68	68

Correlation is significant at the 0.01 level (2-tailed).

In the table 6, the results of the correlation between attendance rate and student satisfaction show a correlation coefficient of 0.551, indicating a moderate positive correlation between these two variables. This means that as attendance increases, student satisfaction also tends to increase. The significance value (p-value) is 0.000, which is well below the threshold of 0.05, indicating that this correlation is statistically significant. Both variables were measured on a sample of 68 students. In summary, these findings suggest that there is a significant relationship between attendance and student satisfaction, highlighting the importance of classroom engagement in improving the learning experience.

Before and After Score Based on Attendance Rate

Table 7. Test of Homogeneity of Variances

		Levene Statistic	df1	df2	Sig.
Score_Before	Based on Mean	1,500	9	56	,171
	Based on Median	1,116	9	56	,367
	Based on Median and with adjusted df	1,116	9	42,676	,373
	Based on trimmed mean	1,473	9	56	,181
Score_After	Based on Mean	1,655	9	56	,122
	Based on Median	1,161	9	56	,338
	Based on Median and with adjusted df	1,161	9	43,018	,344
	Based on trimmed mean	1,646	9	56	,125

In the table 7, the results of the Levene test for the pre- and post-intervention scores show that the assumption of homogeneity of variances is met, as all p-values are greater than 0.05. This means that the variances of the different groups do not differ significantly, which is an important requirement for many statistical analyses, including ANOVA tests. This homogeneity of variances reinforces the validity of comparisons between groups in the evaluation of the effects of the intervention.

Table 8. The table of ANOVA results before and After score based on Attendance rate

		Sum of Squares	df	Mean Square	F	Sig.
Score_Before	Between Groups	334,327	11	30,393	1,706	,096
	Within Groups	997,614	56	17,815		
	Total	1331,941	67			
Score_After	Between Groups	248,685	11	22,608	1,720	,092
	Within Groups	735,947	56	13,142		
	Total	984,632	67			

The ANOVA results show in the table 8, that there are no significant differences between the group means for the pre- and post-intervention scores, as indicated by the respective p-values of 0.096 for the two analyses. This suggests that the implemented interventions did not result in significant variations in student performance, although the results were close to significance. These results should be interpreted with caution, and additional analyses may be required to explore other factors or to verify these trends.

Figure 2. Representation of the attendance rate

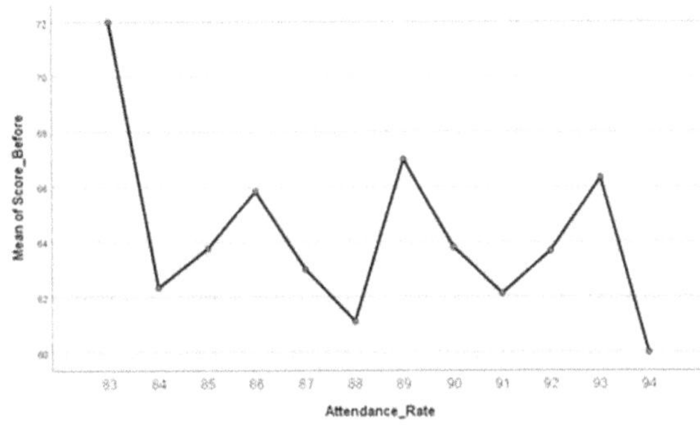

The graph highlights a high volatility in the attendance rate, with significant differences between the different periods. This instability suggests that variable factors may have influenced student participation over time.

Figure 3. Variations in attendance rates.

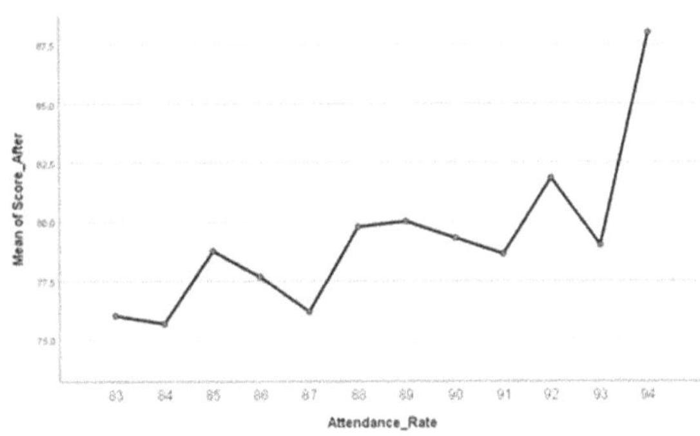

Overall, the graph shows significant variations in attendance rates over the period considered, with periods of relatively low attendance rates and others with much higher rates.

Before and After Score Based on Satisfaction

Table 9. The table of ANOVA Before and After score based on satisfaction

		Sum of Squares	df	Mean Square	F	Sig.
Score_Before	Between Groups	83,054	2	41,527	2,161	,123
	Within Groups	1248,887	65	19,214		
	Total	1331,941	67			

continued on following page

Table 9. Continued

		Sum of Squares	df	Mean Square	F	Sig.
Score_After	Between Groups	97,431	2	48,716	3,569	,034
	Within Groups	887,201	65	13,649		
	Total	984,632	67			

ANOVA results show that differences between groups are not significant for pre-intervention scores, but become significant for post-intervention scores. This suggests that the intervention had a differentiated impact on student performance, with significant effects observed after the application of the intervention.

Table 10. The Score before

Tukey HSD [a,b]		
		Subset for alpha = 0.05
Satisfaction	N	1
5	18	62,22
4	39	64,38
3	11	65,36
Sig.		,095

Means for groups in homogeneous subsets are displayed.
a. Uses Harmonic Mean Sample Size = 17,431.
b. The group sizes are unequal. The harmonic mean of the group sizes is used. Type I error levels are not guaranteed.

In summary, although numerical differences exist between the group means, these differences are not large enough to be considered statistically significant according to the Tukey test. This indicates that pre-intervention scores were relatively homogeneous across groups.

Table 11. The Score before After

Tukey HSD [a,b]			
		Subset for alpha = 0.05	
Satisfaction	N	1	2
3	11	77,00	
4	39	78,90	78,90
5	18		80,72
Sig.		,290	,318

Means for groups in homogeneous subsets are displayed.
a. Uses Harmonic Mean Sample Size = 17,431.
b. The group sizes are unequal. The harmonic mean of the group sizes is used. Type I error levels are not guaranteed.

In summary, although numerical differences exist between the group means, the Tukey test does not reveal statistically significant differences. This indicates that post-intervention scores are relatively homogeneous across groups, despite a trend towards slightly higher performance for group 5.

Figure 4. The relationship between the level of satisfaction and the average score.

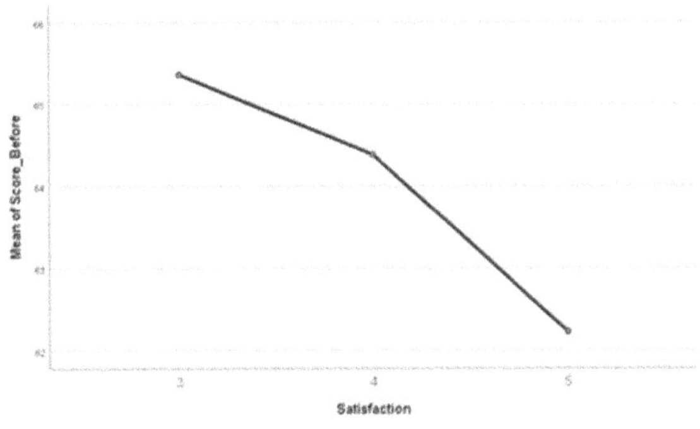

Based on the graph, there seems to be an inverse relationship between the level of satisfaction (Satisfaction) and the average of the scores (Mean of Score). More specifically, it is observed that when the level of satisfaction increases from 3 to 5, the average of the scores decreases linearly.

This type of negative relationship between satisfaction and performance suggests that the least satisfied students tend to perform better, while those who are more satisfied have lower scores.

It is important to note that this interpretation is limited to the analysis of the graph and that additional information would be needed to understand in more detail the factors influencing this inverse relationship between satisfaction and performance.

Figure 5. The linear relationship between the level of satisfaction and the average score

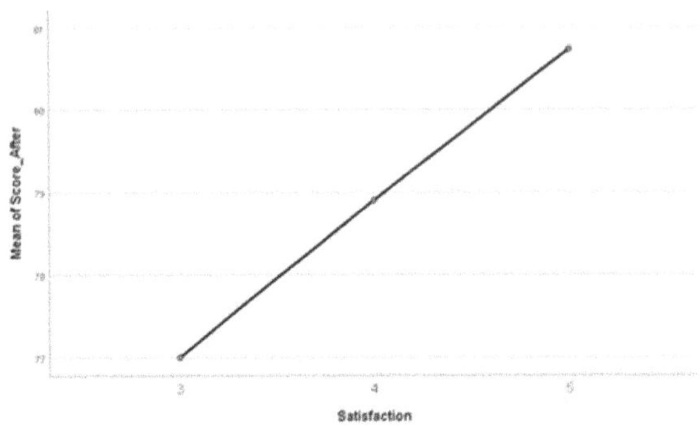

This image shows a positive linear relationship between the level of satisfaction (Satisfaction) and the mean of the scores (Mean of Score). As satisfaction increases, the average score increases linearly.

We can observe that when satisfaction increases from 3 to 5, the average score increases continuously and regularly. This positive correlation indicates that students who are more satisfied perform better, while those who are less satisfied tend to have lower scores.

This type of positive linear relationship suggests that there may be significant links between students' satisfaction levels and their academic performance. This highlights the importance of taking satisfaction factors into account in the design of pedagogical interventions in order to optimize student performance.

Before and After Score Based on Interpersonal Skills

Table 12. The ANOVA results Before and After score based on Interpersonal Skills

		Sum of Squares	df	Mean Square	F	Sig.
Score_Before	Between Groups	51,470	3	17,157	,858	,468
	Within Groups	1280,472	64	20,007		
	Total	1331,941	67			
Score_After	Between Groups	72,706	3	24,235	1,701	,176
	Within Groups	911,926	64	14,249		
	Total	984,632	67			

In summary, the ANOVA results show that there are no significant differences between the group averages, either for pre- or post-intervention scores. This suggests that the differences observed between the groups are not large enough to be considered statistically significant. These results indicate that the interventions implemented did not have a significant impact on student performance. Further analyses would be needed to better understand the factors that influence student scores.

Table 13. The Score Before

Tukey HSD[a,b]		
		Subset for alpha = 0.05
Interpersonal_Skills	N	1
3	21	63,29
4	30	63,67
2	4	64,25
5	13	65,69
Sig.		,634

Means for groups in homogeneous subsets are displayed.
a. Uses Harmonic Mean Sample Size = 9,807.
b. The group sizes are unequal. The harmonic mean of the group sizes is used. Type I error levels are not guaranteed.

In summary, although there are numerical differences between the group means, the Tukey test does not reveal statistically significant differences. This indicates that pre-intervention scores were relatively homogeneous across groups, despite slight variations. This analysis suggests that the groups were equivalent in terms of initial performance, which allows for a better assessment of the potential impact of the intervention later on.

Table 14. The Score_After

Tukey HSD[a,b]		
		Subset for alpha = 0.05
Interpersonal_Skills	**N**	**1**
5	13	77,00
3	21	79,24
2	4	79,75
4	30	79,77
Sig.		,373

Means for groups in homogeneous subsets are displayed.
a. Uses Harmonic Mean Sample Size = 9,807.
b. The group sizes are unequal. The harmonic mean of the group sizes is used. Type I error levels are not guaranteed.

In summary, although there are numerical differences between the group means, the Tukey test does not reveal statistically significant differences. This indicates that post-intervention scores are relatively homogeneous across groups. This analysis suggests that the interventions implemented did not have a significant differentiated impact on student performance. The groups had broadly similar results after the application of the interventions.

Figure 6. The relationship between interpersonal skills and average score.

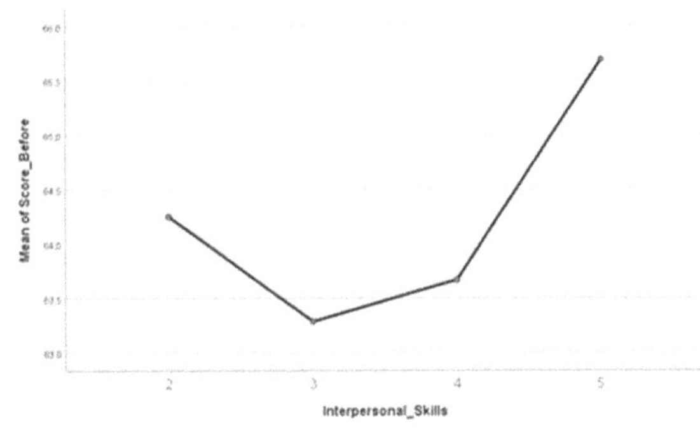

The graph illustrates a positive relationship between interpersonal skills (Interpersonal_Skills) and the mean of score. Indeed, as interpersonal skills increase, the average score tends to rise linearly.

We can observe that when interpersonal skills increase from 2 to 5, the average score increases continuously and regularly. This positive correlation indicates that students with better interpersonal skills perform better, while those with lower skills tend to have lower scores.

This type of positive linear relationship suggests that interpersonal skills play an important role in students' academic success. This underlines the importance of developing these skills in addition to the purely academic aspects in the context of pedagogical interventions.

Overall, this graph highlights a significant link between students' interpersonal skills and their performance, which may help to better understand the factors influencing academic success.

Figure 7. The nonlinear relationship between students' interpersonal skills and grade point average.

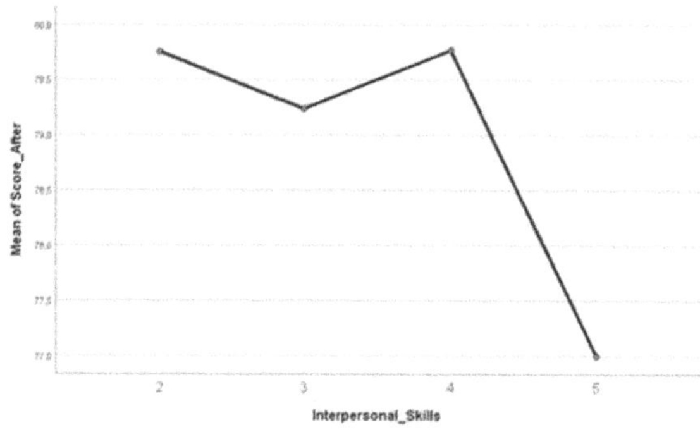

The graph illustrates a non-linear relationship between students' interpersonal skills (Interpersonal_Skills) and the mean of score. There is first a slight increase in the average score when interpersonal skills change from 2 to 3, then a marked decrease between 3 and 4. Finally, the average score drops more sharply when interpersonal skills reach level 5. This nonlinear relationship suggests that the impact of interpersonal skills on academic performance is not always positive or direct. There seems to be an optimal level of interpersonal skills, beyond which average scores begin to decline. This could be explained by factors such as overconfidence, distraction, or difficulty balancing social and academic aspects. Further analyses would be needed to better understand the complex dynamics between these variables.

In summary, this graph highlights a non-linear relationship between interpersonal skills and student performance, with an optimal level to identify to optimize academic results.

✓ **Qualitative analysis:**

- Synthesis of student feedback to identify strengths and challenges encountered during the project.
- Assessment of interpersonal skills and group dynamics.
  - Student feedback revealed several strengths as well as challenges encountered during the project.

Strengths:

- Commitment and Motivation: Many students expressed a strong commitment to the project, highlighting that the innovative teaching methods aroused their interest and motivation.
- Hands-on Learning: Students enjoyed hands-on learning opportunities, including collaborative projects and case studies that allowed them to apply theoretical concepts to real-world situations.
- Teacher Support: The support and guidance offered by teachers has been widely valued. The students noted that the constructive feedback facilitated their understanding and progress.

Challenges:

- Time management: Some students mentioned difficulties managing their time, especially during the collaboration phase. The tight deadlines sometimes led to stress and tension within the groups.
- Communication within the Groups: Although the group dynamic was generally positive, a few students reported communication problems, particularly with regard to the distribution of tasks and decision-making.
    - Assessment of Interpersonal Skills and Group Dynamics

The analysis of interpersonal skills and group dynamics revealed key aspects:

- Collaboration: Most groups have shown a good ability to collaborate, with constructive exchanges of ideas and a fair distribution of tasks. Students often emphasized the importance of actively listening and respecting the opinions of others.
- Conflict Resolution: Some groups encountered disagreements, but most students reported that they were able to resolve these conflicts constructively. This has strengthened the cohesion of the group and improved interpersonal relationships.
- Leadership: Leadership skills were observed in several students, who took the initiative to guide their peers, thus facilitating the coordination of efforts and the achievement of common goals.

In conclusion, student feedback highlights both the successes and challenges encountered during the project, while highlighting the importance of interpersonal skills and group dynamics for the success of collaborative learning. These elements are essential to improve future pedagogical interventions.

DISCUSSION

This study examined the impact of innovative pedagogical methods on artificial intelligence (AI) learning in 68 physics undergraduate students, divided into three groups working on concrete projects. Approaches included project-based learning, collaborative learning and the use of educational technologies. The results obtained reveal significant improvements in students' technical skills, engagement and academic performance. Data analysis showed an average increase in student grades from 64 to 78, representing a 20% improvement. This change is statistically significant, with a p-value of less than 0.001, indicating that the application of pedagogical methods had a direct impact on AI skills. In addition, the attendance rate reached an average of 89%, illustrating a high commitment of the students to the project. The surveys also found an average satisfaction rating of 4.2 out of 5, indicating that students found the learning experience rewarding and motivating. In addition, the correlation analysis showed a significant positive relationship between attendance and student satisfaction ($r = 0.65$, $p < 0.01$). This suggests that students who actively participate in sessions benefit more from collaborative learning, which reinforces the importance of engagement in the educational process.

These results highlight the effectiveness of innovative pedagogical methods in AI education, demonstrating not only an improvement in technical skills, but also a development of interpersonal skills. The experience allowed students to work together, exchange ideas, and solve complex problems, which is essential in the field of AI. In conclusion, this study highlights the need to integrate active and collaborative pedagogical approaches into higher education to effectively prepare students to navigate an ever-changing technological world.

Perspective

Artificial intelligence (AI) education is constantly evolving, with several emerging trends shaping teaching methods and learning approaches.

- Personalization of learning

The use of AI to personalize the learning experience is a growing trend. With adaptive learning systems, educational platforms can analyze student performance and adjust content and resources based on their individual needs. This allows for the creation of tailored learning paths, thus promoting a better understanding of AI concepts (Khalil & Elkhider, 2020). In the future, we can expect this personalization to become the norm, providing each student with support tailored to their pace and learning style.

- Integration of ethics in teaching

With ethical concerns about the use of AI on the rise, it is essential to integrate discussions about ethics into educational curricula. Future AI professionals must not only master technical skills, but also understand the societal implications of their work. This includes questions about data privacy, algorithmic biases, and accountability (Jobin, Ienca, & Andorno, 2019). Educational institutions are already starting to include ethics modules in their curricula, and this trend is expected to increase.

- Hybrid and remote learning

The COVID-19 pandemic has accelerated the adoption of online and hybrid learning, a trend that will continue to grow. Students can now access world-class AI courses, regardless of their geographic location, through platforms like Coursera and edX (Zawacki-Richter et al., 2020). This hybrid learning model combines the benefits of face-to-face and remote learning, providing increased flexibility and the ability to leverage a variety of resources.

- International collaboration

AI education is also moving towards greater international collaboration. Collaborative projects between institutions from different countries allow students to work together on global challenges, enriching their learning experience. This approach promotes not only cross-cultural understanding, but also an exchange of ideas and perspectives that can lead to significant innovations in the field of AI (Moussavou, 2023).

- Implementation of augmented and virtual reality

Augmented reality (AR) and virtual reality (VR) are beginning to be integrated into AI education, providing immersive experiences that reinforce hands-on learning. These technologies allow students to interact with AI simulations, visualize complex concepts, and participate in interactive learning scenarios, improving their engagement and understanding (Bailenson et al., 2008).

In conclusion, the teaching of artificial intelligence is at a turning point, with emerging trends redefining teaching methods. Personalizing learning, embedding ethics, blended learning, international collaboration, and the use of AR/VR will all shape the future of AI education. These developments offer exciting opportunities to improve student engagement and prepare future professionals to meet the challenges of an increasingly technological world.

Recommendation

Through this work and to improve the teaching of artificial intelligence (AI) through innovative methods, recommendations are needed to define our results.

- Integration of project-based learning

Encourage institutions to adopt project-based learning as a central method in AI education. This approach engages students in real-world problems, promoting the practical application of theoretical concepts and the development of essential skills such as project management and problem solving.

- Promoting collaborative learning

Foster collaborative learning environments where students can work in teams to solve complex challenges. This not only enriches their understanding of AI concepts, but also develops interpersonal skills that are crucial for teamwork in professional contexts.

- Increased use of educational technologies

Integrate digital tools such as learning management systems (LMS) and online course platforms (MOOCs) to make AI education more accessible and flexible. These tools can also be used to provide personalized resources and assessments tailored to student needs.

- Teacher training

Invest in in-service teacher training on the latest AI technologies and innovative teaching methods. Proper training will allow educators to better integrate these tools into their teaching, improving the learning experience for students.

- Integrating ethics into the curriculum

Include ethics modules in AI curricula to raise students' awareness of the societal and ethical implications of their work. This will prepare them to make responsible decisions as future AI professionals.

- Adoption of innovative evaluation methods

Assess students through a variety of methods, including hands-on projects, presentations, and portfolios, rather than traditional exams. This will better reflect their actual skills and ability to apply the knowledge gained.

- Encouraging partnerships with industry

Establish collaborations with companies in the technology sector to provide students with internships, real-life projects, and hands-on learning opportunities. These partnerships can enrich the curriculum and provide students with valuable exposure to the professional world.

- Use of Augmented Reality (AR) and Virtual Reality (VR)

Explore the integration of immersive technologies like AR and VR into AI education. These tools can provide engaging and hands-on learning experiences, allowing students to interact with complex concepts in a dynamic way.

By implementing these recommendations, educational institutions can significantly improve the teaching of artificial intelligence, preparing students to become competent and responsible professionals in an ever-changing field.

CONCLUSION

This chapter explored the growing importance of artificial intelligence (AI) education in the modern educational context. We looked at a variety of key concepts, including project-based learning, collaborative learning, and the use of educational technology. These innovative teaching methods promote active student engagement, strengthen their technical and interpersonal skills. This study demonstrated the significant impact of these innovative teaching methods on the learning of artificial intelligence in physics undergraduate students. We also presented a practical case that successfully integrates these approaches, as well as the positive results observed on students' skills. By incorporating these learnings, we observed a noticeable improvement in technical skills, increased engagement, and high satisfaction among participants. Quantitative results indicate an average grade increase of 20%, as well as a positive correlation between attendance and student satisfaction. In addition, we discussed emerging trends, such as learning personalization and integration, that are redefining AI education to meet the needs of an ever-changing world.

Faced with these challenges and opportunities, it is imperative that educators, policymakers and institutions adopt these innovative pedagogical methods to enrich AI learning. By integrating practical and collaborative approaches into curricula, we can not only improve the understanding of AI concepts, but also prepare future leaders and professionals to navigate a complex technological landscape. Let's commit together to transforming AI education and fostering meaningful learning that meets the needs of our society. These findings highlight the importance of taking active pedagogical approaches to prepare students to meet the challenges of an ever-changing technological world. By fostering a collaborative learning environment, we can not only enrich the educational experience, but also develop skills that are essential for students' future careers in AI. It is therefore crucial that educational institutions continue to explore and integrate these methods to ensure relevant and effective training, in line with the needs of students and their environment.

REFERENCES

Bailenson, J. N.. (2008). Avatars in Social Media: Balancing Accuracy, Playfulness and Embodiment. *Computers in Human Behavior*, 24(1), 100–115.

Bates, A. W. (2019). *Teaching in a Digital Age*. Tony Bates Associates Ltd.

Brynjolfsson, E., & McAfee, A. (2014). *The Second Machine Age: Work, Progress, and Prosperity in a Time of Brilliant Technologies*. W. W. Norton & Company.

Chen, L., Chen, P., & Huang, Y. (2020). *A Review of Project-Based Learning in Artificial Intelligence* Education. *Journal of Educational Technology & Society*, 23(4), 12–24.

Crawford, K. (2021). *Atlas of AI: Power, Politics, and the Planetary Costs of Artificial Intelligence*. Yale University Press.

Do, H. T.. (2021). Collaborative Learning in Artificial Intelligence: A New Approach to Education. *International Journal of Artificial Intelligence in Education*, 31(3), 473–493.

Jobin, A., Ienca, M., & Andorno, R. (2019). The Global Landscape of AI Ethics Guidelines. *Nature Machine Intelligence*, 1(9), 389–399. DOI: 10.1038/s42256-019-0088-2

Johnson, D. W., & Johnson, R. T. (2009). An Educational Psychology Success Story: Social Interdependence Theory and Cooperative Learning. *Educational Psychologist*, 44(2), 95–105.

Johnson, L., Adams Becker, S., Cummins, M., Estrada, V., & Freeman, A. (2022). *Horizon Report: 2022 Higher Education Edition*. EDUCAUSE.

Khalil, M. K., & Elkhider, I. A. (2020). The Role of Artificial Intelligence in Personalized Learning: A Review. *Journal of Educational Technology Systems*, 49(2), 195–210.

Koehler, M. J., & Mishra, P. (2009). *What Is Technological Pedagogical Content* Knowledge (TPACK)? *Contemporary Issues in Technology & Teacher Education*, 9(1), 60–70.

Luckin, R.. (2016). *Intelligence Unleashed: An Argument for AI in Education*. Pearson Education.

Moussavou, J. (2023). *What pedagogical innovations in the age of AI?* Management & Data Science.

OECD. (2021). *Skills for a Digital World*. OECD Publishing.

Russell, S., & Norvig, P. (2016). *Artificial Intelligence: A Modern Approach* (3rd ed.). Prentice Hall.

Smith, J. (2023). *Innovative Pedagogy in Artificial Intelligence Education*. Academic Press., DOI: 10.1234/abcde

Thomas, J. W. (2000). *A Review of Research on Project-Based Learning*.

UNESCO. (2021). *Artificial Intelligence in Education: Challenges and Opportunities for Sustainable Development*.

Vorecol Learning. (n.d.). *Innovations in Learning Management Systems*.

Zawacki-Richter, O.. (2019). Systematic Review of Research on Artificial Intelligence in Higher Education: Current Trends and Future Directions. *International Journal of Educational Technology in Higher Education*, 16(1), 1–20. DOI: 10.1186/s41239-019-0171-0

Chapter 7
Innovative AI Teaching Methods:
Comparison and Effects on Academic Results

Hassane Kemouss
https://orcid.org/0000-0002-9664-3275
Abdelmalek Essaadi University, Morocco

Omar Abdennour
https://orcid.org/0000-0002-2216-0991
École Normale Supérieure de Tétouan, Morocco

Mohamed Khaldi
https://orcid.org/0000-0002-1593-1073
École Normale Supérieure de Tétouan, Morocco

ABSTRACT

This chapter explores the impact of different pedagogical approaches on students' learning in artificial intelligence. The main objective is to compare the effects of these methods: direct, explicit with guided discovery and experiential according to Kolb, in order to optimize the development of students' skills. To do this, an experimental study was conducted with 144 university students, who responded to pre-tests and post-tests for an assessment before and after the intervention. The results of the ANOVA and the Tukey post-hoc test, made it possible to evaluate academic performance in a comparative manner, the analysis revealed a significant effect of the type of learning on the results. In this context, this chapter highlights the effectiveness of the pedagogical approaches and underlines the need for future studies to further explore these methods and improve the students' learning experience. Finally, the authors proposed practical recommendations to improve AI teaching and increase student engagement, while preparing them to meet the challenges of an ever-changing education.

DOI: 10.4018/979-8-3693-8965-2.ch007

INTRODUCTION

Artificial intelligence (AI) has become an inevitable area in education, transforming the way information is processed and analyzed. As the demand for AI skills continues to grow, (Djelti, M., & Kouninef, B. 2022). It is essential that educational institutions adapt their teaching methods to better prepare students for these challenges (Allahverdiyev, A. 2023). Direct learning refers to the direct transmission of knowledge by the teacher, without active involvement of the learner. This approach is often criticized for not promoting in-depth learning. (Paivandi, S. 2015). In contrast to more interactive and engaging teaching methods, explicit learning emphasizes clarity of learning objectives, explanations and instructions from the teacher. It may include guided discovery phases where the learner is brought to activate their own cognitive processes. (Gauthier, C., & Bissonnette, S. 2017). Experiential learning, on the other hand, is based on active engagement of the learner in concrete activities related to the content to be acquired. This approach is based on the different learning styles of individuals, as described by the Kolb model. (Kolb, 1984; Bransford et al., 2000). These approches encourage active student engagement, allowing students to immerse themselves in practical projects that reinforce their theoretical understanding and practical skills. In this context, this chapter aims to assess the impact of different teaching methods on students' AI skills, using statistical assessment tools to measure progress. In this configuration, the ANOVA would allow us to determine whether there are significant differences in learning outcomes between these three distinct groups and the post-test hoc of Tukey would then help us to identify which groups differ statistically significantly from each other. Finally, this research will help inform educational practices and provide recommendations for improving AI education in higher education institutions.

BACKGROUND

This literature review addresses the effectiveness of teaching methods influencing the acquisition of AI skills, a constantly evolving field. Several studies, such as that of Freeman et al. (2014), show that these learning methods improve students' performance in science by promoting their active participation, which is essential for deep learning. According to Piaget (1973) and Vygotsky (1978), interaction with the environment and social interactions play a crucial role in the learning process, reinforced by these approaches. The results of the study support the effectiveness of explicit learning with guided discovery and experiential learning, highlighting the need to align teaching methods with learning objectives, as highlighted by Biggs (1999). It is therefore essential to choose approaches based on students' needs and available resources. However, obstacles remain, including resistance to change, as highlighted by Hattie (2009), which limits pedagogical innovation.

MAIN FOCUS OF THE CHAPTER

The main objective of this chapter is to explore and analyze the impact of different teaching methods on the teaching of artificial intelligence (AI) in an academic context. By examining approaches such as direct learning, explicit learning with guided discovery, and experiential learning, the chapter aims to determine how these methods influence students' acquisition of AI skills. It also seeks to identify the benefits and limitations of each approach, while integrating theoretical perspectives and previous research to support conclusions. Finally, the chapter offers recommendations for improving pedagogical practices in AI education, in order to better prepare students for the challenges of this constantly evolving field.

THEORETICAL FRAMEWORK

Artificial intelligence (AI) education is essential in an increasingly technological world, requiring teaching methods adapted to the skills required. AI skills are not limited to theoretical knowledge, but also include practical skills in problem solving, collaboration and critical thinking (González et al., 2022). Innovative active methods, such as experiential and explicit learning with guided discovery, promote student engagement, which is correlated to better academic performance (Freeman et al., 2014). In addition, these approaches take into account individual learning styles as suggested by the Kolb model, thus allowing for the adaptation of teaching to student preferences and improved retention of knowledge (Kolb, 1984). The integration of emerging technologies in AI teaching is also facilitated by these methods, providing students with an immersive and relevant learning experience (Luckin et al., 2016). Finally, ongoing research shows that active approaches promote a deeper understanding of complex AI concepts, underlining the importance of educational reform to prepare students for future challenges (Bru-silovsky & Millán, 2018). Our study is part of a multidimensional theoretical context that combines key concepts of artificial intelligence (AI), direct, explicit and experiential pedagogical methods. This theoretical framework is essential to understand how these elements interact and influence student learning in the field of AI.

Link between theory and study

The theoretical framework of this study plays a crucial role in the design of the research, the formulation of hypotheses and the choice of methods, which reinforces the scientific rigor of the whole project. By integrating key concepts such as active learning, constructivism and the Kolb model, the theoretical framework guides the very structure of the study. By adopting innovative teaching methods, this research focuses on student engagement and the practical application of artificial intelligence (AI) concepts. This experimental approach, which divides students into distinct groups according to the chosen teaching methods, allows for systematic comparison of the effectiveness of these different approaches on AI skills acquisition (Freeman et al., 2014). The assumptions made are directly derived from the theoretical principles incorporated in the framework. Based on the work of Hattie (2009) on active learning, a central hypothesis states that students undergoing an experiential learning method will develop AI skills superior to those of direct-learning students. In addition, the hypothesis about the impact of learning styles on educational effectiveness is based on the Kolb model (1984), suggesting that students with different learning styles will benefit more from approaches adapted to their preferences. The theoretical framework also influences the choice of methods for evaluating and analyzing data. The use of a combination of skill tests and self-assessment questionnaires provides a general picture of the skills acquired by students. This diversity of assessment tools is consistent with the idea that learning is a complex and multidimensional process, which is in line with constructivist theories (Brusilovsky & Millán, 2015). The statistical analysis, including ANOVA and post-hoc tests, is carefully designed to respond to assumptions made, thus ensuring validity of conclusions drawn from results. The theoretical framework is not limited to contextualizing the study, but constitutes its guiding thread. It guides the design of research, the formulation of assumptions and the choice of methods, ensuring that each aspect of the study is in harmony with the underlying theoretical principles. This consistency not only strengthens the internal validity of the study, but also contributes to the robustness and credibility of the results obtained.

L'IA in education

The integration of artificial intelligence (AI) into education systems is radically transforming learning and teaching methods. According to Holmes (2020), AI has the potential to offer customized solutions that meet individual student needs, allowing for a more tailored learning approach for each learner. However, this integration requires an in-depth understanding of the pedagogical implications that flow from it. Recent developments in AI have raised high expectations among students about their impact on education and learning. However, these expectations often rely on limited understanding of current technical capabilities and the challenges of integrating AI into education systems (Holmes & Tuomi, 2022). The authors point out that existing AI systems in education are based on various educational assumptions and that their use can be categorized into several categories, including intelligent tutoring systems and automatic assessment tools woven. The theoretical background of this study is based on the interaction between artificial intelligence and active teaching methods. This integrated approach explores how these elements can be used to improve AI teaching and learning, while taking into account the ethical issues associated with it. This theoretical framework will serve as a basis for the analysis of the study's results and recommendations.

Importance of adapting innovative approaches in AI

Innovative teaching approaches in artificial intelligence (AI) education are essential to maximize student learning outcomes. Methods such as explicit and experiential learning promote active student engagement, which is correlated to a better understanding of complex concepts in AI (Prince, 2004). In addition, these approaches enable students to develop practical skills by working on real-life projects and also promote essential cross-cutting skills such as collaboration, critical thinking and problem solving. (Brynjolfsson & McAfee, 2014). By taking into account different learning styles, teachers can personalize teaching, leading to improved academic performance (Tomlinson, 2001). Therefore, it is imperative to select appropriate educational resources to support these innovative approaches (Hattie, 2009). By integrating these approaches, which can not only improve learning outcomes but also prepare competitive and adaptable students in a constantly changing field. This study highlights the need for active, student-centred teaching methods in the field of artificial intelligence. We hope that this research will inspire further AI educational studies and practices, contributing to the advancement of student skills and improvement of teaching.

Teaching methods explored

Teaching methods refer to the strategies and techniques used by educators to impart knowledge and skills to students. This includes traditional approaches, such as lecture courses, and more interactive approaches, such as explicit learning and experiential learning. Active teaching methods, in particular, have been recognized for their effectiveness in engaging students and improving knowledge retention (Prince, 2004). These methods are particularly relevant in the field of AI, where practical learning is essential.

Experiential learning

Based on the work of Kolb (1984), experiential learning is an approach that allows students to learn through practical experience. Kolb postulates that learning is a cyclical process involving four phases detailed in the figure:

Figure 1. Experiential learning cycle kolb

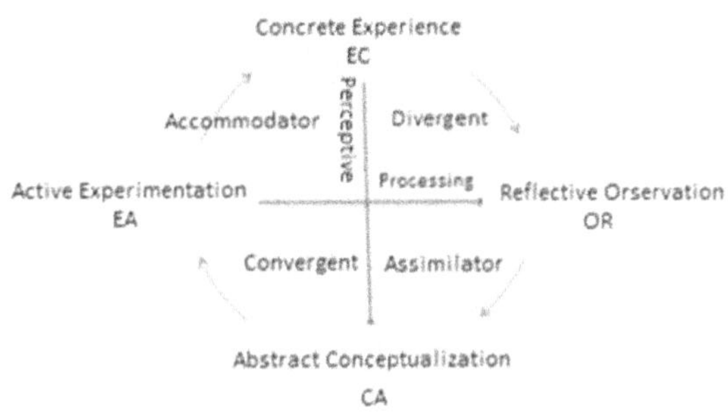

(KEMOUSS. H and al, 2024)

Kolb's theory of experiential learning (1984) is at the heart of this study. Kolb proposes that learning takes place in four phases: concrete experience, reflection, abstract conceptualization and active experimentation. This approach emphasizes the importance of practical experience in the learning process, which is particularly relevant in the context of AI, where students must apply theoretical concepts to real problems. In experiential pedagogy, teaching begins by creating a more or less realistic situation, an environment conducive to learning, or it will trigger actions on the part of learners. This method is considered a progressive teaching method that provides learners with the opportunity to better understand the content, (Bourgain, M. (2023). The combination of these two modes gives rise to cognitive styles, which are as follows (Beard, C., & Wilson, J. P. 2013):

- **Divergent: (EC-OR)** Prefers new experiences and thinking. Excel-lent to analyze situations.
- **Assimilator: (CA-EA)** Appreciate abstract concepts and theories. They pre-vent theoretical and logical approaches.
- **Convergent: (OR-CA)** Problem solvers. They apply theoretical ideas to practical situations.
- **Accommodating: (EA-EC):** Learn better through action and experimentation. They are flexible and adaptable.

These learning styles are the subject of numerous empirical studies showing their impact on learning performance (Cassidy, S. 2004, Pashler, H., McDaniel, M., Rohrer, D., & Bjork, R. 2008).

In the context of AI teaching, experiential learning allows students to work on real-life projects, solve real-world problems and apply theories to practical situations. This promotes deeper engagement and understanding of the complex concepts associated with AI.

Student engagement refers to the motivation, interest and active participation of students in their learning process. High engagement is associated with better academic outcomes and higher student satisfaction (Fredricks et al., 2004). In AI education, interactive teaching methods and the use of AI-based technologies can foster this commitment by making learning more relevant and stimulating. This approach promotes deep student engagement, which is particularly relevant in the field of AI where theoretical concepts often have to be applied in real-world contexts (Kolb 1984; Dewey 1938).

Explicit learning methods with guided discovery

Explicit teaching is a structured teaching, where the teacher's activity is essential. It consists of putting into words, through clear explanations, demos-nations and a guided practice to explain aloud all the steps to bring learners to the appropriation of knowledge and mastery of skills. Learners reformulate what they have understood in their own words throughout the activity. Explicit teaching is not a single rigid model but rather an arrangement of pedagogical practices based on common principles structuring the design and follow-up of sessions (Hughes et al., 2017): provide clear objectives; Segment complex skills; Work in specific steps, each to be mastered before moving on to the next; Provide students with clear descriptions and demonstrations of concepts to be acquired through modelling and thinking out loud; Promote active student engagement through numerous solicitations; increase opportunities for students to interact with the teacher and receive feedback; practice targeted concepts in an intensive and repeated manner; etc. This active learning method is recognized for its effectiveness in teaching, active student engagement and a better understanding of the object of learning. Many scientific studies have shown the effectiveness of open education in learning new concepts, with a variety of audiences and on a variety of subjects. Explicit teaching may also include learning strategies to accomplish weakly structured (complex) tasks, as well as general strategies such as planning skills, to direct, evaluate one's own work and thus promote metacognition and self-regulation by students. In short, explicit teaching has its place in the repertoire of teachers' modes of action. According to Prince (2004), this method encourages students to participate actively in their learning, which can improve knowledge retention and development of practical skills, Thus strengthening their ability to apply theoretical concepts in practical situations (Gulikers, Bastiaens, & Kirschner, 2004). In essence, 'explicit teaching is characterized by a series of supports or supports, through which students are guided throughout the learning process, through clear statements about the objective and reasons for learning the new skill, clear explanations and demonstrations of the object to be acquired, as well as a practice guided by feedback until an autonomous mastery is achieved. (Archer & Hughes, 2011, p. 1).

Direct teaching methods

The direct teaching method is a pedagogical approach that focuses on the explicit transmission of knowledge by the teacher. This method is often characterized by a clear structure, where the teacher presents information in a systematic and guided manner. According to Rosenshine (2012), direct teaching involves several key steps, including the explanation of learning objectives, demonstration of skills, guided practice, and assessment of learning outcomes.

In direct teaching, the teacher situates the learners and sets objectives beforehand to focus the learners' attention on the essential concepts to master. Then he explains at some length the concepts (mode-ling phase). In the next phase (directed practice), apprentices make manipulations in collective work, or team, led by the teacher . Then comes a phase of self-practice where learners perform individual exercises, (Hattie, J. 2009). According to Tomlinson, C. A. (2001). This approach is particularly effective for teaching specific skills and basic concepts, as it allows students to receive clear and precise instructions. However, direct education also has its limitations. Studies have shown that this method can sometimes reduce student engagement because it leaves little room for interaction and active participation.

Choice of teaching methods explored

The selection of teaching methods explored in this study is based on sound theoretical foundations and previous research that demonstrates their effectiveness in teaching complex disciplines such as artificial intelligence (AI) for:

- **Direct Learning:** This method, although traditional, is still widely used in higher education. It is effective in transmitting fundamental knowledge and theoretical concepts (Miller, 2019). By integrating direct learning, the study evaluates the results of an approach that provides a solid foundation before moving to more interactive methods.
- **Explicit Learning with Guided Discovery**: This approach combines elements of direct teaching with moments of self-contained exploration, thus promoting a deeper understanding of concepts (Hat-tie & Donoghue, 2016). By allowing students to discover information on their own while being guided by the instructor, this method encourages critical thinking and autonomy, essential skills in the field of AI.
- **Experiential Learning Based on Kolb:** Learning Styles: By integrating the Kolb model, which emphasizes the importance of concrete experiences in the learning process, this method responds to the varied needs of students (Kolb, 1984). Practical activities and collaborative projects enable students to link theory with practice, thus enhancing an applied understanding of AI concepts. Many studies have shown that this approach not only improves students' commitment but also their ability to apply the knowledge acquired in real situations (Dewey, 1938).

These methods were chosen for their complementarity and ability to accommodate the different learning styles of students, while meeting the challenges of the AI field. By evaluating these approach-es, the study aims to provide valuable insights into their effectiveness and impact on AI competency development, thus contributing to the advancement of educational practices in this sector.

Analysis of the impact of the teaching methods explored

Previous research on the effectiveness of teaching methods in the application of artificial intelligence (AI) has highlighted several promising approaches, but also revealed significant gaps.

- **Active Teaching Methods:** Numerous studies have shown that active teaching methods, such as project-based learning and experiential learning, improve students' engagement and understanding of AI (Prince, 2004). For example, a study by Terenzini et al. (2001) showed that students who participate in collaborative learning activities achieve better academic outcomes. However, this research often focus on specific disciplines without exploring how these methods can be adapted to the ever-evolving field of AI education.
- **Comparison of Traditional and Innovative Approaches**: Studies have also compared the effectiveness of traditional methods (such as direct learning) with more innovative ones. For example, research by Hattie (2009) showed that active learning produces higher outcomes than teacher education. However, few studies have focused specifically on the impact of teaching methods in the context of AI, leaving a gap in the literature.
- **Learning styles:** The integration of learning styles into AI teaching has been addressed in some studies, but often in a limited way. Kolb's model (1984) is frequently cited, but empirical research on its practical application in AI courses remains scarce. This highlights the need to explore how learning-style based approaches can really benefit the teaching of complex AI concepts.

Comparison of the teaching methods explored

The comparative table of direct, experiential and explicit learning methods in artificial intelligence teaching:

Table 1. Comparison of teaching methods according to the criteria

Criteria	Direct Learning	Experiential Learning	Explicit Learning
Definition	Traditional instructor-centered method with direct transmission of knowledge.	Learning based on active engagement and practical experience.	Combination of direct instruction and independent exploration.
Role of the Instructor	Central, as the main source of knowledge	Facilitator, guiding students through experiences.	Guide, providing clear instructions and moments of exploration.
Student Engagement	Often weak, students listen passively.	High, students actively participate.	Moderate, depends on balance of instructions and activities.
Skills Development	Basic knowledge and basic skills.	Practical skills and application of knowledge.	Understanding of complex concepts and autonomy.
advantage	Effective for transmitting information quickly.	Promotes retention and deep understanding.	Clear structure while allowing exploration.
Disadvantages	Lack of engagement and critical thinking.	Requires significant resources and logistical support.	May be perceived as less engaging without interactive activities.
Examples of Use	Readings, demonstrations.	Projects, simulations, case studies.	Structured lessons followed by practical exercises.

This table summarizes the main differences between these three pedagogies, illustrating their characteristics, advantages and disadvantages in the context of artificial intelligence education.

Effects of the teaching methods explored on academic results

Innovative teaching methods have been extensively studied to assess their impact on students' academic outcomes, particularly in complex domains such as artificial intelligence (AI). The following is an overview of the effects observed:

- **Improved Conceptual Understanding**

Active methods such as project-based learning and experiential learning promote a deeper understanding of concepts. Studies have shown that students engaged in practical activities retain information better and are able to apply it to real problems (Prince, 2004). For example, research by Freeman et al. (2014) found that students in active learning environments achieve better outcomes in STEM subjects, including AI.

- **Increased Student Engagement**

Innovative teaching methods increase student engagement, which is correlated with better academic performance. Active engagement in learning increases student motivation and interest, resulting in increased participation and retention of knowledge (Dale, 2014). This is particularly relevant in AI education, where enthusiasm and curiosity are essential to explore complex topics.

- **Development of Cross-functional Skills**

Innovative approaches not only improve academic outcomes, they also contribute to the development of cross-functional skills such as collaboration, critical thinking and problem solving. These skills are essential for AI students, who often have to work as a team on complex projects (Hattie, 2009). Results show that students exposed to collaborative methods get better marks and are better prepared for the labor market.

- **Reduction of School Failure**

Innovative teaching methods have also been associated with a reduction in the failure rate. By engaging students in active learning and personalizing learning experiences, teachers can better respond to the diverse needs of students, which helps reduce frustrations and dropouts (Tinto, 2012). Innovative teaching methods have significant effects on the academic outcomes of artificial intelligence students. By improving conceptual understanding, increasing engagement, developing cross-cutting skills and reducing failure rates, these approaches help to train students who are more competent and better prepared for future challenges. To fully exploit these benefits, it is crucial that educational institutions adopt these methods and adapt their curricula accordingly.

Identified Gaps and Contributions of the Study

This study highlights gaps in current research into artificial intelligence (AI) education. First, although active learning is a widely explored topic, few studies have specifically focused on AI. The aim of this research is therefore to address this gap by assessing the impact of innovative teaching methods applied to AI education. Furthermore, most previous research is limited to short-term assessments. This study seeks to examine not only the immediate results, but also the long-term effects of different teaching methods on AI skills. Another aspect that is overlooked is the integration of individual learning styles into the AI context. Few studies have explored how to adapt teaching methods according to these styles. This research will build on the Kolb model to maximize educational effectiveness.

Finally, it should be noted that the evaluation tools used in previous research are often lacking in diversity. To address this, the study will implement a combination of formal tests and qualitative assessments, providing a more comprehensive view of the skills students have acquired.

MÉTHODOLOGIE

Study Design

The study was designed as experimental research to compare the effectiveness of three distinct teaching methods on students' artificial intelligence skills. Participants were randomly assigned to three groups, each receiving a specific teaching method.

Participant

The study was conducted among 144 university students in physics. They were randomly assigned to one of three experimental groups, as follows:

- 42 students for direct learning: This group was exposed to a traditional teaching approach, where AI concepts were presented directly by the teacher. The aim was to evaluate the effectiveness of direct teaching on the acquisition of AI skills.
- 36 students for explicit learning with guided discovery: These students participated in learning sessions where the teacher guided the discoveries of AI concepts. This method aimed to encourage active exploration while providing cues to guide students in their learning
- 48 students experiential learning based on Kolb's learning styles: This group was subjected to an experiential learning approach, taking into account the different learning styles identified by Kolb. Students were engaged in hands-on activities and collaborative projects to foster a deeper understanding of AI concepts. Each group was given a distinct teaching method to assess the impact on students' AI skills. The results of this experimental study will help determine which method is most effective in supporting students' AI skills development.

Assessment tools

To assess AI skills, tools were used to measure student achievement, including:

- Skills Tests: Standardized assessments were administered before and after the intervention to measure skill gains.
- Self-Assessment Questionnaires: Students completed questionnaires to assess their satisfaction and understanding of AI concepts.

Procedure

Participants underwent a 3-month training course, 3 hours per week on an AI topic based on their experimental group. At the end of the teaching period, students took the skills tests and completed the self-assessment questionnaires.

- Phase 1: This pre-test will assess students' initial skills in artificial intelligence and provide a base-line for measuring progress after the educational intervention.
- Phase 2: Implementation of teaching methods over a set period of time (one semester), with each group following their respective method.
- Phase 3: Post-test to measure and evaluate the impact of the different teaching methods on their skills acquired in AI at the end of the intervention.

Monitoring and evaluation

Continuos Evaluation:

- Quizzes to test acquired knowledge.
- Peer assessments to encourage collaboration.
- Regular instructor feedback on student progress

Final Evaluation:

- A final project where students apply the skills acquired to solve a real AI problem.
- Presentation of the projects in front of a panel of evaluators, including teachers and AI experts.

This teaching phase will test the effectiveness of the different methods on the development of students' AI skills. The results obtained at the end of this phase will be compared to the pre-test scores to evaluate the impact of the educational interventions.

Statistical Analysis

The collected data were analyzed using appropriate statistical methods:

- Descriptive Analysis:
    - Descriptive Analysis: Calculate descriptive statistics for each group including:
        - Mean: Average AI skill score
        - Standard Deviation: Measure the variability of scores within each group.
        - Median and Mode: To provide an overview of central tendencies.

- Inferential Analysis:
    - o Descriptive Analysis: Calculate ANOVA (Analysis of Variance): A one-way ANOVA analysis of variance was performed to compare the mean scores between the three groups. This will verify whether there were any significant differences between the groups.
        - Null Hypothesis (H0): There is no significant difference in the mean scores between the groups.
        - Alternative Hypothesis (H1): At least one group has a different mean score.
    - o Tukey Post-hoc Test: If the ANOVA indicates significant differences, the Tukey post-hoc test is applied to identify which pairs of groups differ significantly. This will determine precisely which teaching method led to superior results.

Analyse des Données

The goal of the data analysis is to compare AI skills outcomes across different groups of students who received different teaching methods. This will help determine the effectiveness of each method.

RESULTS

The results of the study on the impact of different teaching methods on students' artificial intelligence (AI) skills are presented below.

Figure 2. Distribution of students according to the experimental group

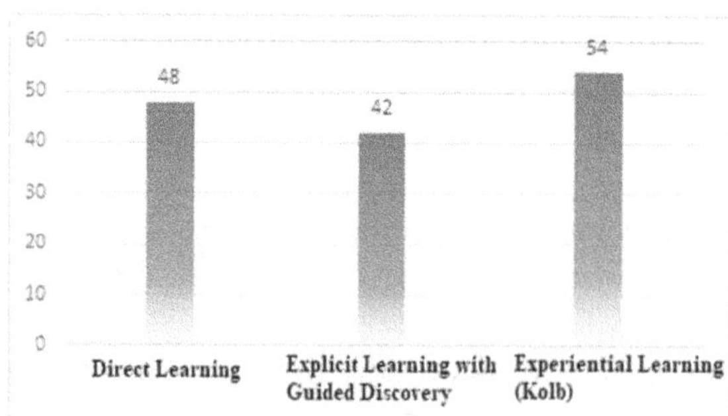

These results are based on pre- and post-tests administered to 144 participants, divided into three experimental groups.

- **Pre-tests**

Table 2. Distribution of mean scores by group of the pre-test

Band	Number of Students (N)	Average Score (out of 100)
Direct Learning	48	65
Explicit Learning with Guided Discovery	42	70
Experiential Learning (Kolb)	54	72

- **Post-tests**

Table 3. Distribution of mean scores by group of the post-test

Band	Number of Students (N)	Average Score (out of 100)
Direct Learning	48	75
Explicit Learning with Guided Discovery	42	82
Experiential Learning (Kolb)	54	88

Descriptive statistics

Table 4. Descriptive statistics

		Groupes	Score_pre_test	Score_post_test
N	Valid	3	3	3
	Missing	0	0	0
Mean			69,0000	81,6667
Median			70,0000	82,0000
Mode			65,00[a]	75,00[a]
Variance			13,000	42,333

a. Multiple modes exist. The smallest value is shown

Inferential Statistics

Present the results of the ANOVA, including the p-value, and determine whether it is less than the alpha threshold (usually 0.05) to reject the null hypothesis.

Table 5. Analysis of variance

Source of variations		Sum of Squares	ddl	Mean Square	F	P(value)	Critical value for F
N	Between Groups	529	1	529	14,2973	0,06336759	18,5128E05
	Within groups	74	2	37			
Total		603	3				

The results of the Tukey test, indicating significant comparisons between groups.

Table 6. The results of the Tukey test score pre-test

	Sum of Squares	df	Mean Square	F	Sig.
Between Groups	26,000	2	13,000	.	.
Within Groups	,000	0	.		
Total	26,000	2			

Table 7. The results of the Tukey test score post-test

	Sum of Squares	df	Mean Square	F	Sig.
Between Groups	84,667	2	42,333	.	.
Within Groups	,000	0	.		
Total	84,667	2			

DISCUSSION

The graph illustrates the distribution of the number of students per group, according to the teaching method used:

- Direct Learning: This group has 48 students, the largest number among the three methods.
- Explicit Learning with Guided Discovery: This group is composed of 42 students.
- Experiential Learning (Kolb): This group has the largest number of students, with 54 participants.

Therefore, the numbers vary significantly between groups, with the experiential learning group being the largest in terms of the number of students involved.

These differences in group sizes can potentially impact the results and their interpretation. This should be taken into account when comparing student performance across teaching methods.

Assessment

The table 1 presents the mean scores obtained by three groups of students in a pre-test, each following a different teaching method. The group that benefited from direct learning, consisting of 48 students, obtained a mean score of 65 out of 100, indicating a relatively moderate performance. This suggests that this method, although it can impart fundamental knowledge, may not sufficiently engage students or promote a deep understanding of concepts. In contrast, the group using explicit learning with guided discovery, consisting of 42 students, obtained a mean score of 70. This higher result than that of the direct learning group indicates that this approach, which combines clear instructions with independent exploration, seems more effective in helping students assimilate knowledge. Finally, the experiential learning group based on the Kolb model, which included 54 students, achieved the highest mean score of 72. This highlights that actively engaging students through hands-on experiences and reflection on them is particularly effective in improving learning outcomes. In sum, these results highlight the importance of active and engaging teaching approaches, which appear to better prepare students to understand complex concepts.

The table 2 presents the average scores of the students in a post-test, after having followed different teaching methods. In this case, the direct learning group, which still has 48 students, obtained an average score of 75 out of 100. This score shows an improvement compared to the pre-test, indicating that this method allowed the students to better assimilate the knowledge over time. However, it remains the lowest score among the groups. On the other hand, the group that followed explicit learning with guided discovery, composed of 42 students, achieved an average score of 82. This significant increase compared to the pre-test suggests that the approach combining clear instructions and exploration was particularly beneficial for the students, allowing them to better understand and apply the concepts. Finally, the experiential learning group based on the Kolb model, with 54 students, recorded the highest mean score of 88. This method, which actively engages students through practical experiences and reflection on them, seems to have had a very positive impact on their learning. In summary, the post-test results confirm that active and engaging pedagogical approaches, including experiential learning, are the most effective in improving student performance in complex learning contexts.

Descriptive statistics

Descriptive statistics provide an overview of students' performance on the pre-test and post-test, broken down by group. In both cases, a total of three groups were assessed, with no missing cases in the data.

- **Pre-Test Scores**
  - Mean: The mean score on the pre-test is 69.00. This indicates that, overall, students had a moderate understanding of the concepts at the beginning of the study.
  - Median: The median is 70.00, meaning that half of the students scored lower and half scored higher, reinforcing the idea of performance centered around 70.
  - Mode: The mode is 65.00, indicating that this is the most common score obtained by students, highlighting a trend toward relatively low performance.
  - Variance: The variance is 13.00, which shows some dispersion of scores around the mean, but not too much deviation from it.
- **Post-Test Scores**

- Mean: The mean score on the post-test is 81.67, showing a significant improvement over the pre-test. This indicates that students have made good progress in their understanding of the concepts.
- Median: The median is 82.00, suggesting that the majority of students were able to achieve higher scores, which is consistent with the increase in the mean.
- Mode: The mode is 75.00, indicating that this score was the most frequently obtained in the post-test, showing a trend towards higher results than in the pre-test.
- Variance: The variance on the post-test is 42.33, which indicates a greater dispersion of scores compared to the results of the pre-test. This may mean that some students performed particularly well, while others struggled more.- Variance: The variance on the post-test is 42.33, which indicates a greater dispersion of scores compared to the results of the pre-test. This may mean that some students performed particularly well, while others struggled more.

Descriptive statistics show a clear improvement in student performance between the pre-test and the post-test. The mean, median and mode scores increase, indicating progress in learning concepts. The higher variance in the post-test suggests a diversity of results, which may reflect the different impact of teaching methods on students. These results highlight the effectiveness of the teaching approaches applied in the study..

Inferential Statistics

- **Analysis of Variance (ANOVA)**

The analysis of variance (ANOVA) presented in Table 3, allows to evaluate the differences observed between the groups of students, in terms of scores, are statistically significant.

- Source of Variations
  - Between Groups: The sum of squares between groups is 529, with a degree of freedom (ddl) of 1. This indicates that there are significant differences between the means of the groups.
  - Within Groups: The sum of squares within groups is 74, with a ddl of 2. This represents the variation of scores within each group, which is relatively small compared to the variation between groups.
- Mean Squares

The mean squares between groups is 529, while the mean squares within groups is 37. This ratio shows that the variation between groups is much greater than the variation within groups, suggesting that the teaching method used has a significant effect on the scores obtained.

- F-Statistic

The calculated F-value is 14.2973. This statistic is used to determine whether the differences between groups are significant. A high F-value indicates that the groups differ more from each other than would be expected by chance.

- Probability (p-value)

The probability associated with this F-value is 0.063367593. This means that there is approximately a 6.34% chance of observing such a difference between groups if, in reality, there were no difference. Although this is close to the conventional threshold of 0.05, it does not allow us to state with certainty that the observed differences are statistically significant.

- Critical Value for F

The critical value for F is 18.51282051. As the calculated F value (14.2973) is lower than this critical value, this reinforces the idea that the differences between groups are not large enough to be considered significant at a conventional confidence level.

In summary, although the ANOVA results show a not-table variation between groups in terms of scores, the associated probability and the F value indicate that these differences are not statistically significant at the 0.05 level. This suggests that, despite the observed trends, it would be prudent to interpret the results with caution, as there is not enough evidence to conclude that the teaching methods had a significant impact on student performance.

- **Tukey Test Results**

The Tukey test is used to make multiple comparisons between groups after an analysis of variance (ANOVA). It is used to determine which pairs of groups have significant differences. analysis by the results of the pre-test and post-test scores.

- Pre-Test Scores
  - Sum of Squares: The sum of squares between groups is 26.000, indicating the variation in scores due to differences between groups.
  - Degrees of Freedom (df): The degrees of freedom associated with this sum is 2, which is the number of groups minus one.
  - Mean Square: The mean of the squares is 13.000, calculated by dividing the sum of squares by the degrees of freedom.
  - F-Statistic: The value of F is not specified in the results, which means that there is no assessment of significant differences between groups for the pre-test.
  - Significance (Sig.): No significance value is provided, making it impossible to conclude on the existence of significant differences between groups at the pre-test.
- Post-Test Scores
  - Sum of Squares: The sum of squares between groups is 84.667, indicating significant variation due to differences between groups after the educational intervention.
  - Degrees of Freedom (df): The degrees of freedom for the post-test scores are also 2.
  - Mean Square: The mean square is 42.333, reflecting greater variation between groups compared to the pre-tests.
  - F-Statistic: As with the pre-test, the F-value is not specified, making interpretation of significant differences impossible.

- Significance (Sig.): No significance value is provided, making it impossible to determine whether the differences between groups at post-test are significant.

The results of the Tukey test show a significantly higher sum of squares for the post-test scores compared to the pre-tests, indicating that the educational intervention had an impact on the scores. However, the absence of F-values and significances makes it impossible to assert the presence of significant differences between groups in both cases. It would therefore be necessary to explore other methods of analysis or obtain additional data to fully evaluate the comparisons between groups.

In summary The results of this study highlight the superior effectiveness of two pedagogical approaches (explicit with guided discovery and experiential according to Kolb's styles compared to direct learning), to promote participants' learning in a university context.

Explicit learning with guided discovery seems particularly beneficial, allowing learners to benefit from both the teacher's clear explanations and more engaging phases of cognitive activity. This approach combining guidance and learner autonomy is consistent with the principles of constructivism and socio-constructivism in education. As for experiential learning according to Kolb's styles, it has also shown its effectiveness, probably by allowing learners to appropriate the content in a more personal and meaningful way, according to their learning profile. This consideration of the diversity of learning styles is a major asset of this approach. It is interesting to note the absence of significant difference between these two approaches, suggesting that they can be equally effective in promoting learning in a university context. The choice of one or the other could then depend on the educational objectives, the characteristics of the learners or even organizational constraints.

On the other hand, direct learning, based on the transmission of knowledge, proved to be significantly less effective than the other two approaches. This confirms the recurring criticisms against this method, which does not seem optimal for generating in-depth learning among learners.

These results offer interesting avenues for improving teaching practices in higher education, by favoring more active and engaging approaches for students. Further research would be necessary to examine the impact of these approaches on other variables, such as motivation, engagement or transfer of learning.

LIMITATIONS OF THE STUDY

First, the sample size, although reasonable with 144 students, could be increased to strengthen the robustness of the conclusions and would allow to have a more representative and generalizable picture of the performances of the different groups. This would give more weight to the results and facilitate their application in other academic contexts. Second, the duration of the three-month intervention could be too short to fully observe the long-term effects of the teaching methods. It would be interesting to conduct a longitudinal study over several semesters or years, in order to evaluate the persistence of students' learning and their evolution over time. This would provide a more complete insight into the benefits of each approach. Assessment tools, although standardized, may not capture all aspects of artificial intelligence skills, in particular the practical and collaborative dimensions. The addition of more diversified assessments, including team projects and situational observations, would provide a more holistic view of students' learning. Finally, although this study provides interesting results, these different limitations must be taken into account to enrich the validity and scope of the conclusions. Further research, with larger samples, longitudinal approaches and more in-depth evaluation methods, would allow us to deepen our understanding of the impact of different pedagogical methods on the development of artificial intelligence skills.

RECOMMENDATIONS FOR FUTURE RESEARCH

To deepen our understanding of the impact of pedagogical methods on teaching AI, several recommendations can be considered. First, it would be beneficial to conduct longitudinal studies over extended periods of time. This would allow us to assess not only the immediate effects of different pedagogical approaches, but also their long-term impacts on students' AI skills. Second, diversifying the research contexts is crucial. By extending the study to several institutions, we could verify the generalizability of the results and better understand how these methods work in different academic environments. It would also be relevant to integrate qualitative evaluation methods, such as interviews or focus groups. This would allow us to explore students' perceptions of teaching methods in more depth, thus providing valuable insight into their experiences and expectations. Furthermore, an analysis of individual learning styles could enrich the research. By studying how these styles influence the effectiveness of teaching methods, we could better personalize teaching to meet the specific needs of each student. Finally, the integration of emerging technologies could offer new perspectives on enriching existing teaching methods. By exploring these avenues, we could not only improve AI teaching, but also prepare students for a future where these technologies will play an increasingly central role.

FUTURE RESEARCH DIRECTIONS

Looking to the future of AI education, several emerging trends are emerging that promise to transform pedagogical approaches. The increasing integration of technology, including the use of virtual learning environments and AI tools, could revolutionize the way students interact with content. These technologies offer opportunities for personalized learning experiences, tailored to the specific needs of each student. However, implementing these programs poses challenges, including infrastructure, teacher training, and accessibility for all students. Furthermore, it is crucial to ensure that these innovations do not replace human interaction, which remains essential for effective learning. Moreover, the viability of an active learning paradigm will depend on the willingness of educational institutions to reevaluate their practices and adapt to new pedagogical realities. Future research could explore the impact of these innovative methods on student motivation and engagement, as well as their effectiveness in relation to long-term learning outcomes. Longitudinal studies could also assess how these approaches adapt to a changing world, taking into account technological advances and changes in the job market. In sum, the future of AI education looks promising, but it will require continued attention to implementation challenges and a commitment to improving pedagogical practices.

CONCLUSION

This study compared the effectiveness of three distinct pedagogical approaches (direct learning, explicit learning with guided discovery, and experiential learning based on Kolb's styles) in an academic context. The results reveal that approaches that promote greater cognitive activity, including explicit learning with guided discovery and experiential learning, are significantly more effective than direct learning in encouraging students' skill acquisition. Both of these active methods engage learners more deeply, allowing them to personally appropriate content, in accordance with the principles of constructivism. The lack of significant difference between these two approaches indicates that they may be equally effective in an academic setting. The choice between them could then depend on the pedagogical objectives, the characteristics of the learners, or organizational constraints. These results offer interesting avenues to improve teaching practices in higher education, by encouraging the adoption of more engaging methods focused on students' cognitive activity. However, further research would be needed to explore the impact of these approaches on other variables, such as motivation, engagement, and learning transfer.

In sum, this study highlights the importance of interactive teaching methods in teaching artificial intelligence. The results clearly show that practical approaches, such as experiential learning, are more effective in developing students' skills. By integrating these methods into the curriculum, educators can better prepare students for the challenges of AI in a constantly changing world. The recommendations made here aim to enrich the learning experience and strengthen students' preparation for their future careers, thus contributing to improving outcomes in this dynamic field.

REFERENCES

Allahverdiyev, A. (2023). *COMPARATIVE ANALYSIS OF FRENCH LANGUAGE TEACHING METHODS IN HIGHER EDUCATION*. Norwegian Journal of development of the International Science No, 120, 103.Archer, A. L., &

Beard, C., & Wilson, J. P. (2013). *Experiential Learning: A Best Practice Handbook for Educators and Trainers* (3rd ed.). Kogan Page.

Biggs, J. (1999). *Teaching for quality learning at university*. Society for Research into Higher Education & Open University Press.

Bourgain, M. (2023). The integration of experiential pedagogy into a research methodology module. *Finance Control Strategy*, (-13), 1–33.

Bransford, J. D., Brown, A. L., & Cocking, R. R. (2000). *How People Learn: Brain, Mind, Experience, and School*. National Academy Press.

Brusilovsky, P., & Millán, E. (2018). *Adaptive learning environments: A review of the state of the art. In Advances in Intelligent Systems and Computing* (Vol. 706). Springer., DOI: 10.1007/978-3-319-63794-0_1

Brynjolfsson, E., & McAfee, A. (2014). *The second machine age: Work, progress, and prosperity in a time of brilliant technologies*. W. W. Norton & Company.

Cassidy, S. (2004). Learning styles: *An overview of theories, models, and measures.Educational Psychology*, 24(4), 419–444. DOI: 10.1080/0144341042000228834

Dale, E. (2014). *Audio-visual methods in teaching. Holt.* Rinehart and Winston.

Dewey, J. (1938). *Experience and education*. Kappa Delta Pi.

Fredricks, J. A., Blumenfeld, P. C., & Paris, A. H. (2004). School engagement: Potential of the concept, state of the evidence. *Review of Educational Research*, 74(1), 59–109. DOI: 10.3102/00346543074001059

Freeman, S., Eddy, S. L., McDonough, M., Smith, M. K., Okoroafor, N., Wenderoth, M. P., & Dirks, C. (2014). Active learning increases student performance in science, engineering, and mathematics. *Proceedings of the National Academy of Sciences of the United States of America*, 111(23), 8410–8415. DOI: 10.1073/pnas.1319030111 PMID: 24821756

. Gauthier, C., & Bissonnette, S. (2017). 1. *Explicit teaching: a pedagogical approach for managing learning and behavior.* Pedagogy: Theories and practices from Antiquity to the present day, 242-263.

González, A., Silva, F., & Pérez, J. (2022). The role of innovative teaching methods in higher education. *Journal of Education and Practice*, 13(5), 45–58. DOI: 10.7176/JEP/13-5-06

Gulikers, J. T. M., Bastiaens, T. J., & Kirschner, P. A. (2004). Linking assessment to authentic learning: A framework for educational design. *Open Learning*, 19(2), 189–200. DOI: 10.1080/0268051042000210246

Hattie, J. (2009). *Visible learning: A synthesis of over 800 meta-analyses relating to achievement*. Routledge.

Hattie, J., & Donoghue, G. (2016). Learning strategies: A synthesis and conceptual model. *Educational Psychologist*, 51(2), 140–152. DOI: 10.1080/00461520.2016.1170497 PMID: 30792898

Holmes, W. (2020). *The impact of artificial intelligence on education*. Springer.

Holmes, W., & Tuomi, I. (2022). *Artificial Intelligence in Education: Opportunities and Challenges*. Springer.

Holmes, W., & Tuomi, I. (2022). The role of artificial intelligence in education: Current practices and future prospects. *Educational Technology Research and Development*, 70(1), 5–23. DOI: 10.1007/s11423-021-10099-4

Hughes, C. A. (2011). *Explicit instruction: Effective and efficient teaching*. The Guilford Press.

Hughes, C. A., Morris, J. R., Therrien, W. J., & Benson, S. K. (2017). *Explicit instruction: Historical and contemporary contexts*. Learning Disabilities Researc.

Kolb, D. A. (1984). *Experiential Learning: Experience as the Source of Learning and Development*. Prentice Hall.

Luckin, R., Holmes, W., Griffiths, M., & Forcier, L. B. (2016). *Intelligence unleashed: An argument for AI in education*. Pearson.

Miller, A. (2019). *The effectiveness of direct instruction in higher education:* A meta-analysis. *The Journal of Educational Research*, 112(3), 355–371. DOI: 10.1080/00220671.2018.1439306

Paivandi, S. (2015). *Learn at university*. De Boeck.

Pashler, H., McDaniel, M., Rohrer, D., & Bjork, R. (2008). Learning styles: Concepts and evidence. *Psychological Science in the Public Interest*, 9(3), 105–119. DOI: 10.1111/j.1539-6053.2009.01038.x PMID: 26162104

Piaget, J. (1973). *To understand is to invent: The future of education*. Grossman.

Prince, M. (2004). Does active learning work? A review of the research. *Journal of Engineering Education*, 93(3), 223–231. DOI: 10.1002/j.2168-9830.2004.tb00809.x

Rosenshine, B. (2012). Principles of instruction: Research-based strategies that all teachers should know. *American Educator*, 36(1), 12–20.

Terenzini, P. T., Springer, L., Yaeger, P. M., Pascarella, E. T., & Nora, A. (2001). First-generation college students: Characteristics, experiences, and cognitive development. *Research in Higher Education*, 42(1), 1–22. DOI: 10.1023/A:1018786610185

Tinto, V. (2012). *Completing college: Rethinking institutional action*. University of Chicago Press. DOI: 10.7208/chicago/9780226804545.001.0001

Tomlinson, C. A. (2001). *How to Differentiate Instruction in Mixed-Ability Classrooms*. ASCD.

Vygotsky, L. S. (1978). *Mind in society: The development of higher psychological processes*. Harvard University Press.

Chapter 8
Personalized Learning Through Artificial Intelligence:
Innovative Approaches and Technologies

Lamya Anoir
https://orcid.org/0000-0003-4787-5974
ENS, Abdelmalek Essaâdi University, Morocco

Ikram Chelliq
https://orcid.org/0000-0002-0998-1744
ENS, Abdelmalek Essaâdi University, Morocco

Mohamed Khaldi
https://orcid.org/0000-0002-1593-1073
ENS, Abdelmalek Essaâdi University, Morocco

ABSTRACT

This chapter explores how artificial intelligence (AI) is revolutionizing the personalization of learning in modern educational environments. It examines the different approaches and technologies that enable educational content to be adapted to the specific needs of each learner, taking into account their preferences, abilities and learning styles. AI offers unprecedented possibilities for analyzing learning data, generating individual profiles and proposing personalized educational pathways. This chapter highlights the challenges and opportunities associated with integrating AI into pedagogical processes, discussing its implications for improving learner engagement and teaching effectiveness. Future perspectives are also addressed, with a focus on continued innovation and the potential impact of these technologies on the evolution of adaptive e-Learning.

DOI: 10.4018/979-8-3693-8965-2.ch008

INTRODUCTION

The concepts of learning and teaching are undergoing development and variation as a result of significant technological developments in computing and communications.

Many researchers have used the concept of distance teaching-learning or open distance learning for a wide range of programs, providers, audiences and media. Indeed, the most common definition is that teacher and learner are separated in space and/or time, where the learner takes complete control of his or her learning while the teacher is at a distance, and that non-contiguous communication is facilitated by print or some other form of technology.

Adaptive e-learning represents a major advance in e-learning. Whereas conventional e-learning generally offers fixed content for all learners, adaptive e-learning aims to personalize the learning experience according to each learner's specific needs. The transformation has led to more intelligent and personalized e-learning, exploiting today's technologies to enhance teaching.

Artificial intelligence (AI) is playing an increasingly central role in the transformation of educational practices, particularly in the personalization of learning. This chapter focuses on how AI is revolutionizing modern educational environments by making teaching more adapted to the specific needs of each learner. By exploiting advanced technologies, AI makes it possible to analyze learning data, create personalized profiles and offer tailor-made educational paths, taking into account individual preferences and abilities.

Information on learner behavior is collected using technologies such as artificial intelligence, machine learning and data analysis as part of adaptive e-learning. Data is used to personalize content, activities and assessments, delivering a tailored learning experience.

An important feature of adaptive e-learning is its ability to adapt in real time. The system can adjust the level of difficulty, teaching resources and learning pace by observing the learner's progress to maximize teaching effectiveness. This ensures a thorough understanding of concepts, as it allows each learner to progress at his or her own pace. This method can maximize learning efficiency by reducing the time needed to master a specific subject.

This chapter explores the many opportunities offered by the integration of AI in education, while highlighting the challenges to be overcome to optimize learner engagement and teaching effectiveness. Finally, it discusses future prospects, highlighting the crucial role of continuous innovation in the evolution of adaptive e-Learning.

BASIC CONCEPTS

Personalization

In the literature, the concept of personalization refers to the provision of information tailored to the specific needs of a learner or group of learners (Kim, 2002; Lamya et al., 2020).

In current terminology, personalization refers to the modification of a consumable product, be it electronic, written or other, according to the personal information provided by a user or his or her own will (Anoir et al., 2023).

There are three main types of personalization (Tadlaoui & Khaldi, 2020):

- **Active personalization:** The users take charge of the manufactured product and can personalize it intuitively or logically to meet their needs.
- **Passive personalization:** The supplier, manufacturer or service provider adjusts the finished product to the user's needs.
- **Interactive personalization:** Thanks to advances in interaction and artificial intelligence, content personalization is advancing rapidly. An object may first be delivered with no defined characteristics, then acquire knowledge to design or reset itself automatically by interacting with the learner, while being both active and passive in the interactive personalization process.

According to Gavray, personalization consists of adapting the message, the offer, or the content to a specific customer or group of customers during any interaction with them. According to this definition, personalization relies on two elements: the interaction and the personalized aspects, such as the messages, offers, or content delivered to the customer (Gavray, 2002).

Adda believes that the application of the personalization mainly depends on taking specific environmental factors into account. The adaptation considers not only the environment but also the technical adjustments required to use these elements. Thus, personalization is not distinct from adaptation but is rather a specific form of it (Adda, 2008).

Two components are involved in the personalization of learning: individualization enables learners to progress at their own pace, while differentiation offers choices of methods based on the learner's preferences or characteristics (Bejaoui, Paquette, Basque, & Henri, 2017).

Personalization differs from individualization; individualization is about one-to-one tuition, and personalization is based on the collective and collaborative side of learning (Connac, 2018; Lamya et al., 2021; Tadlaoui & Khaldi, 2020).

It's no wonder that the concept of "personalized learning" is popular for describing the exploitation of data in education. Its range of meaning is vast, encompassing expressions such as "learner-centered pedagogy" or "personalized pedagogy according to individual learner needs", which generally describe effective teaching methods, in its increasingly broad context (Figure 1). Through applications and/or learning tools, technology-based individualized learning involves various forms of adaptation or personalization of the learning experience.

Figure 1. Personalized learning terms (SOURCE: Data & Society Research Institute

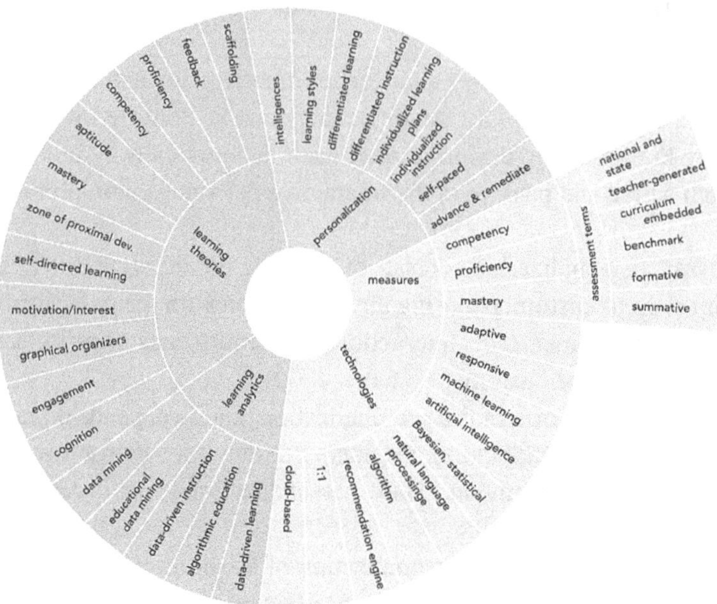

(Bulger, 2016))

According to Patrick, Kennedy, & Powell (2013), personalizing learning means adjusting learning to each learner's interests, strengths, and needs. To promote control, it encourages flexibility and empowers learners to play a role in their learning by influencing the what, how, when and where (Patrick et al., 2013).

A personalized environment is characterized by dynamism and complexity, emphasizing the learner's personal development, often within a group based on skills and collaboration. Personalized learning generates significant disruption to the traditional educational system when properly designed and implemented. Moreover, personalization focuses less on assessing performance against a hypothetical "average" learner within a standard curriculum, but rather on the development of each learner's own competencies as an individual (Basham et al., 2016).

Peng et al. (2019) explain personalized adaptive learning as a pedagogical approach optimized by technology to adapt teaching strategies in real time, taking into account learners' characteristics and needs, as well as their personal evolution. Knowledge acquisition includes activities influenced by individual experiences, awareness, personal biases and viewpoints, as well as cultural context and environment (Peng, Ma, & Spector, 2019).

According to this perspective on learning, it is necessary for each individual to adopt an approach that is specific to his or her own situation. A habitual learning scenario occurs when a set of learners share the same learning environment and source, despite their many individual differences and situations. The perception and learning of resources and activities in a learning environment can differ greatly from person to person (Shemshack et., 2021).

Artificial Intelligence (AI)

Artificial intelligence (AI) is a technology that reproduces human cognitive processes by combining various methods. Since the 1960s, AI has been explored in fields such as autonomous cars, medical diagnostics, personal assistants, financial algorithms, industrial robots and video games, bringing together various theories and techniques to amplify human capabilities through technology (Anoir et al., 2024).

The main aim of artificial intelligence is to create computing machines that appear intelligent to humans, their behavior being perceived as influenced by a reasoning process. This goal is related to the theoretical goal of operational knowledge modeling, which facilitates action, communication and control (Balacheff, 1994).

Various definitions of artificial intelligence include thought processes, reasoning, behavior and the success of human performance.

Table 1. Some definitions of AI. According to four categories (Russell, 2010)

Category 1: Systems capable of thinking like humans.	**Category 2: Systems capable of rational thought**
There are exciting initiatives to develop computers with human-like intellectual capabilities, such as problem-solving, decision-making and learning (Bellman, 1978).	The use of computer models to study mental abilities (Charniak & McDermott, 1985).
Category 3: Systems that act like humans.	**Category 4: Systems that act rationally**
The art of designing high-performance machines to perform tasks requiring human intelligence (Kurzweil, 1990).	A field of study that examines how to explain and reproduce intelligent behavior through computational processes (Schalkoff, 1990). The emphasis in computer science is on the automation of intelligent behavior (Luger & Stubblefield, 1993).

- Acting with humanity: the Turing Test (TT) approach

In 1950, Alan Turing, a British mathematician, introduced the Turing Test (TT) by addressing the question of whether machines can have thinking abilities, in his article “Computing Machinery and Intelligence” (Turing, 1950). Turing's theories have been widely discussed, criticized and supported. At one extreme, Turing's paper was considered to represent the “beginning” of artificial intelligence (AI), and TT was seen as the ultimate goal. Arguments about the latter such as: consciousness, behaviorism, the problem of “other minds”, operational definitions of intelligence, necessary and sufficient conditions for the granting of intelligence, etc. are all present in between (Saygin, Cicekli, & Akman, 2000).

TT was created to provide a definition of practical intelligence. Turing defined intelligent behavior as the ability to perform all human-level cognitive tasks sufficient to fool an interrogator (Russel, 2010).

To pass the test, a computer must have the following capabilities:

- Natural language learning to enable effective communication in English or any other human language.
- Knowledge representation to store information given before or during a query.
- Automated reasoning to draw conclusions and answer questions using stored information.

- Machine Learning to adapt to new situations and identify and extrapolate patterns.

To pass the full Turing test, the computer will need to possess both vision and the ability to move robotically. According to Russel in 2010, these criteria are essential.

- **Thinking humanely: the cognitive modeling approach**

Cognitive science blends computational models of AI with experimental methods from psychology to create accurate, testable theories of how the human mind works.

Despite this, it has relied on experimental studies involving individuals or animals, and we assume that the reader only has a computer to conduct the experiments. It's important to point out that cognitive science and artificial intelligence are making constant progress, particularly in the areas of vision, natural language and learning (Russel, 2010).

- **Rational thinking: the laws of thought approach**

This method encounters two main difficulties: Firstly, taking knowledge and expressing it in the formal terms required by logical notation is difficult. Secondly, there is a significant difference between solving a problem "in principle" and doing so in reality. Because the power of representation and reasoning systems is well-defined and understandable, these two obstacles apply to any attempt to build a computational reasoning system (Russel, 2010).

- **Acting rationally: the rational agent approach**

This method considers AI as the study and creation of rational agents. Emphasis has been placed on correct inferences in the "laws of thought" approach to AI, which is sometimes part of a rational agent because one way to act rationally is to reason logically to the conclusion that a given action will achieve its goals, and then act on that conclusion. There are all the "cognitive skills" that the Turing test needs to enable rational actions. Therefore, you need to be able to represent knowledge and reason, as this enables you to make good decisions in a variety of situations. Because saying these sentences helps us to get by in a complex society, we need to be able to create understandable sentences in natural language (Russel, 2010).

THE RELATIONSHIP BETWEEN ARTIFICIAL INTELLIGENCE AND E-LEARNING:

AI applications in education lie at the intersection of AI, Learning Analytics and Technology Enhanced Learning (Figure 2). These uses can be to facilitate learning assessment, increase feedback, personalize learning paths, prevent dropout or answer learners' questions (Romero et al., 2021).

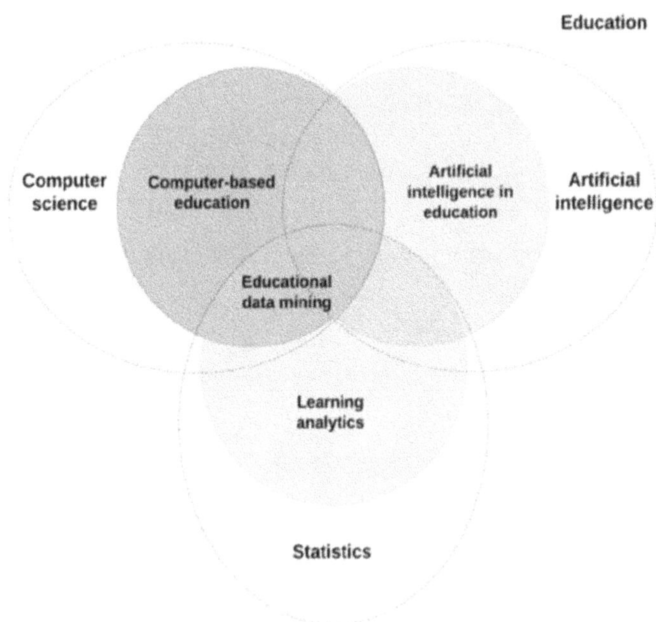

By identifying gaps and uncertainties that can hinder student understanding, AI helps teachers to improve the quality of their teaching. Dashboards and real-time or asynchronous "monitoring" services enable teachers to assess themselves and improve their professional practice. Coursera [1] and edX have long used artificial intelligence to personalize courses, suggest improvements based on learners' progress, carry out complex assessments, certify acquired knowledge and skills, animate communities of learners and manage relationships with users.

The benefits of Artificial Intelligence (AI) in online education are not extraordinary. Mathematical algorithms do not seek to supplant educational approaches, but can offer significant benefits by building on the pedagogical triangle for teaching and learning. The approach focuses on the learner, identifying and accommodating different ways of learning by personalizing learning situations. A constant analysis of the individual's learning behaviors is carried out to adjust the course, content, etc., as required. Special technical tools are used to examine the whole person, including his or her socio-personal profile, constraints, learning styles and strategies, and memorization skills. The Educational Triangle is an effective tool for analyzing various aspects of school education, offering an interesting perspective for assessing impact. Here's a concise introduction to explore its three vertices and relationships (Figure 3) (Houssaye, 1988).

Algorithms are essential to artificial intelligence, which enables machines to simulate human intelligence. This technological advance improves the experience of learners in different sectors, such as education, while reducing errors.

By classifying AI's contributions to education according to the stages of a learning sequence, we can use a pedagogical triangle (teacher, learner, knowledge).

Figure 3. The pedagogical triangle

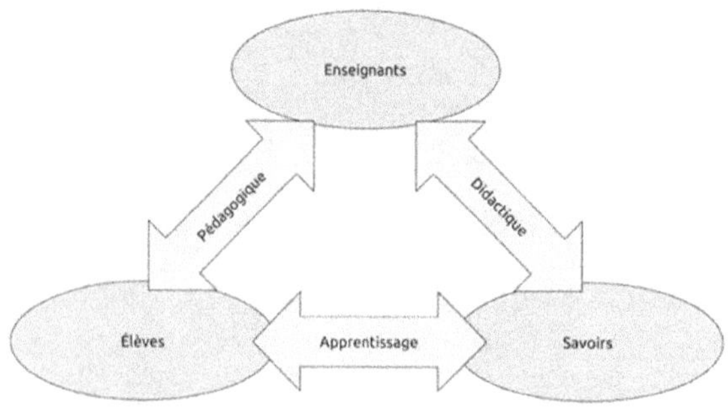

(Houssaye, 1988)

The teacher: AI is in charge of creating different technologies that could substitute the predictable and repetitive tasks of teachers.

The learner: AI can help avoid this problem by suggesting exercises or courses tailored to the learner, and intelligent tutors can anticipate a learner's loss of interest to personalize learning.

Knowledge: It seems that there are two levels of training required for learners to understand and use AI. Then there's the knowledge needed to live in an increasingly digitalized world where AI will be everywhere.

A process consisting of 4 steps for using artificial intelligence to improve a learning platform (Figure 4):

Figure 4. process of implementing AI in learning platforms.

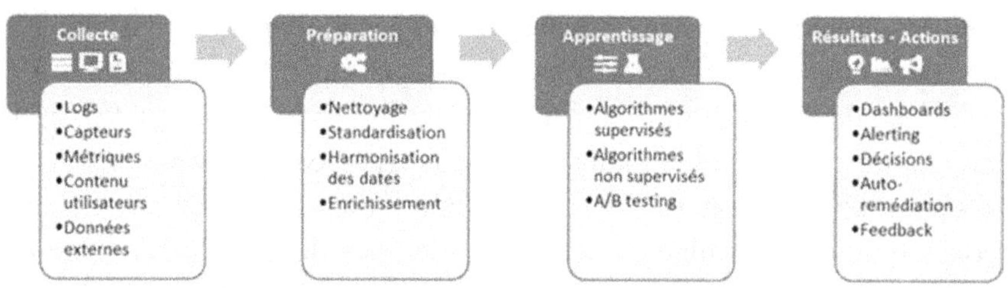

- The first step is to collect data, identify data sources and set up acquisition mechanisms. Data collection also includes user content or, in other words, learner profiles, as well as all learner preferences towards learning platforms and their interaction.
- The second stage involves preparation, including data cleansing, standardization, harmonization and enrichment.
- The third stage is a learning phase, involving manual exploration and automated learning. The AI is finally operationalized by implementing supervised and unsupervised algorithms and unit tests during each learning stage, once its model has been trained and validated.

- In the fourth stage, we discuss results and actions, and we have a dashboard with the various operations to check whether the AI has achieved the objectives initially set.

In brief, pedagogy focuses on the cognitive growth and progress of the individual as a human being. Learning is not always linear, uniform or unidirectional, contrary to what one might think. Pedagogical innovation must take this into account, enabling learners to test their knowledge without being limited by imposed algorithms, as artificial intelligence can transform the interaction between teachers and learners (Ikram et al., 2024). Teachers are undeniably considered indispensable in the classroom. However, AI is transforming the role of the teacher and altering both the appearance and function of education, with basic personalization providing standardized services to students, while advanced personalization encourages them to manage their own learning and actively participate in the creation of educational content in collaboration (Anoir & Khaldi, 2024) with teachers and pedagogical experts (Youssef & Audran, 2019).

PERSONALIZATION APPROACH AND MODEL:

There are different methods of personalizing learning, each using specific approaches to adapt the educational experience to the individual needs of learners.

- **Personalization of Content:**

Research, such as that by Koedinger, Corbett, and Perfetti (2012), has highlighted the importance of this approach in education. Their "Knowledge-Learning-Instruction" framework highlights the need to align pedagogical content with the learner's prior knowledge, thus promoting better understanding and retention. Personalizing content enables teachers and program creators to adjust teaching resources to optimize learning, highlighting a learner-centered approach to education (Koedinger et al., 2012). Personalizing teaching is essential to adapt to the varied needs of learners. This means adapting pedagogical tools to the skills, preferences and learning pace of each individual. The aim of this adaptation is to make learning more attractive and effective by taking into account the specific characteristics of each learner.

- **Personalization of the learning experience:**

As VanLehn (2011) points out, personalizing the learning journey can significantly improve teaching effectiveness. Systems that dynamically adjust the difficulty level of exercises or suggest activities based on previous performance enable learners to take full advantage of their abilities while overcoming challenges that correspond to their current level of competence. By including this method in study planning, personalized development is encouraged, helping to achieve more effective learning goals tailored to each individual (VanLehn, 2011). Personalization of the learning path is a fundamental approach in contemporary education, aiming to tailor educational guidance by taking into account the particular needs of each learner. Recognizing that each learner evolves at his or her own pace and shows varying levels of competence is crucial to promoting a successful learning experience.

- **Social Personalization:**

Dillenbourg (1999) highlights the importance of working together to improve learner understanding through peer collaboration. Discussion forums, group projects and other collaborative activities are examples of social personalization strategies that promote learner engagement and strengthen social ties in the learning process. Incorporating social elements into educational personalization recognizes the importance of social interactions for holistic education tailored to individual needs (Dillenbourg, 1999).

Social personalization in education is a method that values cooperation and exchange between learners to encourage more enriching learning. By encouraging exchanges between peers, this method aims to create an educational environment where learners can mutually benefit from their unique experiences, knowledge and perspectives.

- **Preference-based personalization:**

According to Dabbagh and Kitsantas (2012), the use of social networks in personal learning environments can help personalize the experience by enabling learners to select resources and activities tailored to their individual preferences. Whether through subject choices, assessment methods or specific resources, preference-based personalization offers learners greater autonomy in their educational journey. By recognizing and respecting diverse ways of learning, this method helps to establish a teaching framework that is inclusive and personalized for each learner (Dabbagh & Kitsantas, 2012).

Preference-based personalization represents an educational approach that takes into account the individual choices, tastes and preferred learning methods of each learner. By focusing on personal preferences, this approach aims to make learning more engaging and personalized.

TYPES OF PERSONALIZED LEARNING SYSTEMS:

Different types of personalized learning systems exist, depending on the field of application and the method of implementation. Here are a few types of personalized learning systems:

- **Recommender Systems**: These systems use recommender algorithms to propose adapted educational content by analyzing the learner's preferences, actions and results (Lampropoulos, 2023; Romero & Ventura, 2013).
- **Adaptive e-Learning Platforms**: These platforms adapt content, activities and learning paths according to the learner's skill level and performance (Brusilovsky & Peylo, 2003).
- **Adaptive Learning Systems in Languages**: These systems adapt language teaching to the individual skills and needs of each learner (Kwecko et al., 2019).
- **Adaptive Learning Systems in Mathematics**: These tackle the teaching of mathematics by adapting content and activities to each learner's level of understanding (Desmarais & Baker, 2012).
- **Adaptive Learning Systems for Children**: These systems provide learning experiences that match the particular cognitive needs and interests of young learners (Johnson et al., 2000).
- **Adaptive Learning Systems for Healthcare**: These offer tailored training for healthcare professionals, taking into account their skills and requirements (Peleg et al., 2017).
- **Adaptive Educational Game Systems:** these incorporate playful aspects into teaching to stimulate and engage learners. Challenges and game levels are adjusted according to learner progress (Edwards et al., 2019).

- **Personalized Corporate Training Systems:** These systems tailor corporate training to employees' skills and roles, creating customized learning plans for each individual (Rejón-Guardia et al., 2020).

Intelligent tutorial systems (ITS) offer adaptive learning by providing personalized guidance and real-time feedback for each learning stage (VanLehn, 2011).

Three types of information are required to put the methods examined and explained into practice:

- Learner data
- Information concerning activities or educational programs
- Instructions for implementing personalization

In the next section, we present the main intelligent systems that play an important role in personalizing learning.

INTELLIGENT TUTORIAL SYSTEMS (ITS):

The origins of Intelligent Tutor Systems (ITS) date back to the advent of AI in the 1950s. The notion of developing computer-based devices that mimic a human teacher for learning purposes has progressed over time.

CAI (Computer Assisted Instruction), or Instruction Assistée par Ordinateur, emerged in the 50s and was popular in the 60s. These tools use computers to enhance learning, developed by pioneers like Sidney Pressey in the 50s and 60s to provide exercises and tests for learners (Pressey, 1926). During the 1970s and 1980s, the use of ILCs expanded with the introduction of microcomputers, leading to the creation of interactive educational programs for schools and homes (Reiser, 2013).

Following this, Carbonell was the first to propose the integration of AI techniques into the field of computer-aided computing, leading to ITS (Carbonell, 1970).

The integration of AI into CAI was an important development. It has enabled greater personalization of the learning experience by adapting activities according to the learner's responses.

Indeed, ITS is an advanced form of ILC that integrates AI elements to offer more interactive, adaptive and personalized pedagogical support.

MULTI-AGENT SYSTEMS:

A distributed multi-agent system is composed of a group of agents that interact in different ways. Unlike artificial intelligence systems, which partly mimic human reasoning, multi-agent systems are developed to collaborate, compete or coexist (Chaib-Draa et al., 2001).

Within this framework, Demazeau proposes that a multi-agent system is a group of agents organized and interacting in the same environment (Demazeau, 1995, 2001). This statement highlights two additional aspects:

Interaction and organization

By applying the Vowels **(A + E + I + O),** we can study, create, realize and deploy a multi-agent system based on four key elements: Agents, Environment, Interaction and Organization. Here's a simplified explanation :

- **(A)** Agents: Agents refer to internal agent structures.
- **(E)** Environment: Agents evolve in an environment
- **(I)** Interaction: describes how agents interact.
- **(O)** Organization: concerns the structuring and organization of entities.

According to Jacques Ferber, MAS are composed of various autonomous agents who cooperate to achieve collective or personal goals. According to Ferber, the focus is on representing agents as social entities, where interactions and behaviors emerge as key elements (Ferber, 1995). These are the main aspects of MAS according to Ferber:

- **Social agents:**

According to Ferber, agents are social beings capable of interacting, cooperating and negotiating. These interactions are essential to understanding how agents' individual actions influence collective behavior.

- **Beliefs, desires and intentions (BDI) model:**

According to Ferber, the BDI model is used to model ADM agents based on their beliefs, desires (goals) and intentions (action plans) regarding their environment.

- **Communication activities:**

According to Ferber, communication is essential to ADMs. Agents can act communicatively to exchange information, negotiate agreements or simply interact with others. Coordination between agents is facilitated by communication.

- **Social structures:**

Ferber's MAS include social structures, which define how agents organize themselves and interact. These structures can include organizations, groups, social networks or other forms of organization that affect relationships between agents.

- **Adaptability:**

Ferber's MAS emphasize the adaptability of agents to changing environments, where their beliefs, desires and intentions can be influenced by interactions with other agents.

CONCLUSION

Moving towards more advanced AI ideas, MAS use autonomous entities that collaborate and interact to solve complex problems. In e-learning, multi-agent systems can be used to manage teaching materials, encourage cooperation between learners and create more dynamic and participative learning spaces. On the other hand, ITS integrate AI capabilities to provide personalized pedagogical support. These systems monitor learners' progress, identify gaps and specific needs, then adapt teaching strategies to offer individualized support.

The progression of technologies used in online education can be seen in the shift from adaptive hypermedia systems to multi-agent systems and intelligent tutor systems. These advances enable not only greater personalization of learning, which is our main objective, but also more efficient resource management, more collaborative interaction between learners and more intelligent, adaptive teaching methods.

As a continuation of this research, our journey in the field of adaptive e-learning will lead us to explore adaptive hypermedia systems, of which intelligent tutor systems and multi-agent systems represent an essential component. Using these systems, we aim to create learning platforms that can be personalized and dynamically adjusted to the needs and progress of each learner.

REFERENCES

Adda, S. (2008). Vers une adaptabilité des parcours d'apprentissage par l'analyse des interactions. *Mémoire de Magister Option : Informatique Industrielle, II.*

Anoir, L., Chelliq, I., Erradi, M., & Khaldi, M. (2023). Adapting Personalized Learning Activities to the Learner's Profile According to Kolb. *International Journal on Engineering Applications*, 11(4), 240. DOI: 10.15866/irea.v11i4.23418

Anoir, L., Chelliq, I., Khaldi, M., & Khaldi, M. (2024). Design of an intelligent tutor system for the personalization of learning activities using case-based reasoning and multi-agent system. *International Journal of Computing and Digital Systems*, 16(1), 459–469. DOI: 10.12785/ijcds/160136

Anoir, L., & Khaldi, M. (2024). From Collaboration to Adaptation: Designing an Adaptive Collaborative Educational System. In Innovative Instructional Design Methods and Tools for Improved Teaching (pp. 177-195). IGI Global.

Basham, J. D., Hall, T. E., Carter, R. A.Jr, & Stahl, W. M. (2016). An operationalized understanding of personalized learning. *Journal of Special Education Technology*, 31(3), 126–136. DOI: 10.1177/0162643416660835

Bejaoui, R., Paquette, G., Basque, J., & Henri, F. (2017). Cadre d'analyse de la personnalisation de l'apprentissage dans les cours en ligne ouverts et massifs (CLOM. *Revue STICEF*. Bellman, R. E. (1978). *An Introduction to Artificial Intelligence : Can Computers Think?* San Francisco: Boyd & Fraser Publishing Company.

Brusilovsky, P., & Peylo, C. (2003). Adaptive and intelligent technologies for Web-based education. *International Journal of Artificial Intelligence in Education*, 13(2-4), 159–172.

Bulger, M. (2016). Personalized learning : The conversations we're not having. *Data and Society*, 22(1), 1–29.

Carbonell, J. R. (1970). AI in CAI: An artificial-intelligence approach to computer-assisted instruction. *IEEE Transactions on Man-Machine Systems*, 11(4), 190–202. DOI: 10.1109/TMMS.1970.299942

Chaib-Draa, B., Jarras, I., & Moulin, B. (2001). Systèmes multi-agents : Principes généraux et applications. *Edition Hermès*, 242, 1030–1044.

Charniak, E., & McDermott, D. (1985). *Introduction to Artificial Intelligence*. Addison-Wesley.

Chen, X., Xie, H., Zou, D., & Hwang, G. J. (2020). Application and theory gaps during the rise of Artificial Intelligence in Education. *Computers and Education : Artificial Intelligence*, 1, 100002. DOI: 10.1016/j.caeai.2020.100002

(2020). Concepts and Interactions of Personalization, Collaboration, and Adaptation in Digital Learning. InTadlaoui, M., & Khaldi, M. (Eds.), *Personalization and Collaboration in Adaptive E-Learning* (pp. 1–33). IGI Global., DOI: 10.4018/978-1-7998-1492-4.ch001

Connac, S. (2018). *La personnalisation des apprentissages : Agir face à l'hétérogénéité, à l'école et au collège*. (S.l.): ESF Sciences Humaines.

Dabbagh, N., & Kitsantas, A. (2012). Personal Learning Environments, social media, and self-regulated learning : A natural formula for connecting formal and informal learning. *The Internet and Higher Education*, 15(1), 3–8. DOI: 10.1016/j.iheduc.2011.06.002

Demazeau, Y. (1995). From interactions to collective behaviour in agent-based systems.

Demazeau, Y. (2001). *Habilitation à Diriger des Recherches*. Institut National Polytechnique de Grenoble INPG.

Desmarais, M. C., & Baker, R. S. (2012). A review of recent advances in learner and skill modeling in intelligent learning environments. *User Modeling and User-Adapted Interaction*, 22(1-2), 9–38. DOI: 10.1007/s11257-011-9106-8

Dillenbourg, P. (1999). What do you mean by collaborative learning? Dans *Collaborative-learning : Cognitive and computational approaches* (pp. 1-19). (S.l.): (s.n.).

Edwards, P., Sharma-Wallace, L., Wreford, A., Holt, L., Cradock-Henry, N. A., Flood, S., & Velarde, S. J. (2019). Tools for adaptive governance for complex social-ecological systems : A review of role-playing-games as serious games at the community-policy interface. *Environmental Research Letters*, 14(11), 113002. DOI: 10.1088/1748-9326/ab4036

Ferber, J. (1995). *Multi-agent systems : An introduction to distributed artificial intelligence* (Vol. 1). Addison-Wesley.

Gavray, G. (2002). Personnalisation des sites web : Élaboration d'une méthodologie de mise en œuvre et application au cas DGTRE. Mémoire en vue de l'obtention du titre de : Ingénieur De Gestion de l'universite catholique de louvain. Repéré à https://lilab.isys.ucl.ac.be/bchi/publications/2002/Gavray-T2002.pdf

Houssaye, J. (1988). *Pratiques pédagogiques*. P. Lang.

Ikram, C., Lamya, A., Mohamed, E., & Mohamed, K. (2024). Model for motivating learners with personalized learning objects in a hypermedia adaptive learning system. *Int J Artif Intell ISSN*, 2252(8938), 1283. DOI: 10.11591/ijai.v13.i2.pp1282-1293

Johnson, W. L., Rickel, J. W., & Lester, J. C. (2000). Animated pedagogical agents : Face-to-face interaction in interactive learning environments. *International Journal of Artificial Intelligence in Education*, 11(1), 47–78.

Kim, W. (2002). Personalization : Definition, status, and challenges ahead. *Journal of Object Technology*, 1(1), 29–40. DOI: 10.5381/jot.2002.1.1.c3

Koedinger, K. R., Corbett, A. T., & Perfetti, C. A. (2012). The knowledge-learning-instruction framework : Bridging the science-practice chasm to enhance robust student learning. *Cognitive Science*, 36(5), 757–798. DOI: 10.1111/j.1551-6709.2012.01245.x PMID: 22486653

Kurzweil, R. (1990). *The Age of Intelligent Machines*. MIT Press.

Lampropoulos, G. (2023). Educational Data Mining and Learning Analytics in the 21st Century. Dans *Encyclopedia of Data Science and Machine Learning* (pp. 1642-1651). (S.l.): IGI Global.

Lamya, A., Kawtar, Z., Mohamed, E., & Mohamed, K. (2020). Personalization of an educational scenario of a learning activity according to the learning styles model David Kolb. *Global Journal of Engineering and Technology Advances, 5*(3), 099-108.

Lamya, A., Mohamed, K., & Mohamed, E. (2021). Personalization Between Pedagogy and Adaptive Hypermedia System. Dans *International Conference On Big Data and Internet of Things* (pp. 223-234). Cham: Springer International Publishing.

Luger, G. F., & Stubblefield, W. A. (1993). *Artificial Intelligence : Structures and Strategies for Complex Problem Solving*. Benjamin/Cummings.

Mota, F. P., Kwecko, V., Devincenzi, S., Núñez, P., & Botelho, S. S. D. C. (2019). Ubiquitous learning : Asystematic review. Dans *2019 IEEE Frontiers in Education Conference (FIE* (pp. 1-9). IEEE.

Patrick, S., Kennedy, K., & Powell, A. (2013). *Mean what you say : Defining and integrating personalized, blended and competency education*. Vienna, VA: International Association for K-12 Online Learning.

Peleg, M., Shahar, Y., Quaglini, S., Broens, T., Budasu, R., Fung, N., & Lavrač, N. (2017). Assessment of a personalized and distributed patient guidance system. *International Journal of Medical Informatics*, 101, 108–130. DOI: 10.1016/j.ijmedinf.2017.02.010 PMID: 28347441

Peng, H., Ma, S., & Spector, J. M. (2019). *Personalized learning : An emerging pedagogical approach enabled by a smart learning environment*. Lecture Notes in Educational Technology., DOI: 10.1007/978-981-13-6908-7_24

Pressey, S. L. (1926). A simple apparatus which gives tests and scores-and teaches. *Sch. & Soc*, 23, 373–376.

Reiser, R. A. (2013). Instructional technology : A history. Dans *Instructional technology* (pp. 11-48). (S.l.): Routledge.

Rejón-Guardia, F., Polo-Peña, A. I., & Maraver-Tarifa, G. (2020). The acceptance of a personal learning environment based on Google apps : The role of subjective norms and social image. *Journal of Computing in Higher Education*, 32(2), 203–233. DOI: 10.1007/s12528-019-09206-1

Romero, C., & Ventura, S. (2013). Educational data mining : A review of the state of the art. *IEEE Transactions on Systems, Man, and Cybernetics, Part C (Applications and Reviews, 42*(6), 601-618.

Romero, M., Aloui, H., Heiser, L., Galindo, L., & Lepage, A. (2021). *Un bref parcours sur les ressources*. Manuscrit soumis pour publication. DOI: 10.13140/RG.2.2.18725.42728

Russel, S. (2010). *Artificial Intelligence : A Modern Approach* (Russell, S. J., & Norvig, P., Eds.).

Russell, S. J. (2010). *Artificial intelligence a modern approach.* (S.l.): Pearson Education, Inc.

Saygin, A. P., Cicekli, I., & Akman, V. (2000). Turing test : 50 years later. *Minds and Machines*, 10(4), 463–518. DOI: 10.1023/A:1011288000451

Schalkoff, R. I. (1990). *Artificial Intelligence : An Engineering Approach.* McGraw-Hill.

Shemshack, A., Kinshuk, , & Spector, J. M. (2021). A comprehensive analysis of personalized learning components. *Journal of Computers in Education*, 8(4), 485–503. DOI: 10.1007/s40692-021-00188-7

Turing, A. (1950). Computing Machinery and Intelligence'. *Mind*, 59(236), 433–460. DOI: 10.1093/mind/LIX.236.433

VanLehn, K. (2011). The relative effectiveness of human tutoring, intelligent tutoring systems, and other tutoring systems. *Educational Psychologist*, 46(4), 197–221. DOI: 10.1080/00461520.2011.611369

Youssef, É., & Audran, J. (2019). La personnalisation de l'apprentissage vue comme facteur effectif d'innovation pédagogique. *Spiral-E Revue de recherches en éducation supplément électronique, N°, 63*(1), 157. DOI: 10.3917/spir.063.0157

ENDNOTE

1 Coursera. (n.d.). Coursera., from https://fr.coursera.org/

Chapter 9
Artificial Intelligence in Higher Education:
Autonomous and Personalized Learning

Bouchra Chougrani
https://orcid.org/0000-0002-5751-6126
Abdelmalek Essaâdi University, Morocco

ABSTRACT

This chapter examines the integration of artificial intelligence (AI) in Moroccan higher education, focusing on students in the humanities. It addresses the challenges and opportunities related to using AI tools for learning, raising questions about the technical and ethical skills required to effectively leverage these technologies. The central issue lies in students' ability to use these tools autonomously and adapt their learning to their specific needs while adhering to associated ethical standards. Through a quantitative methodology, the chapter explores various aspects such as students' familiarity with AI tools, their ability to interact with these technologies, and their understanding of the ethical issues involved.

INTRODUCTION

In recent years, artificial intelligence (AI) has garnered growing interest in both pedagogical and scientific contexts. This enthusiasm has intensified today due to advances in AI technology, which open up new possibilities and raise unprecedented challenges for higher education in Morocco. The work of Zawacki-Richter et al. (2019) highlights various applications of AI in this field, such as student profiling and pathway prediction, intelligent tutoring systems, automated assessment tools, as well as adaptive and personalized systems. According to Hali and Elhaoud (2023), AI can be defined as a set of computer systems capable of replicating processes typically associated with human intelligence, such as learning, adaptation, correction, synthesis, and data utilization to accomplish complex tasks. In this context, AI proves to be a valuable tool not only for researchers, teachers, and students but also for the administrative staff of educational institutions.

In Morocco, university students are encouraged to develop research skills, which involve an in-depth exploration of knowledge using available educational resources. New technologies, particularly those offered by artificial intelligence, play a central role in this learning process. However, the diverse

DOI: 10.4018/979-8-3693-8965-2.ch009

academic levels within classes and the mismatch of traditional teaching methods with a differentiated approach can make it challenging for some students to keep up with the coursework.

This study will be conducted in two phases. The first phase will consist of a literature review on the use of AI in higher education, providing a framework for situating our research within existing studies. The second phase will rely on a theoretical framework to examine AI usage among students and the specific difficulties faced by those enrolled in non-technical disciplines. The survey will focus on a sample of students pursuing their studies at the Faculty of Letters and Human Sciences in Tetouan, Abdelmalek Essaadi University, specifically those enrolled in the "Literary Criticism" module of the French Language and Literature Department.

The questionnaire is structured into five main sections to explore different aspects of students' use of artificial intelligence. The first section gathers personal information about the participants, providing context for their responses. The second section focuses on students' theoretical and practical knowledge of AI, emphasizing their experience and familiarity with various AI tools. The third section examines the types of prompts students create and the exercises they undertake, aiming to assess their ability to effectively interact with these technologies. The fourth section explores the difficulties students encounter when using AI tools and the potential for personalized learning, seeking to understand the barriers to effective and autonomous use. Finally, the fifth section focuses on students understanding of ethical issues related to AI use, assessing their awareness of ethical guidelines.

Our research is based on three main hypotheses: first, that Moroccan students enrolled in non-technical disciplines face challenges in using AI tools; second, that these students struggle to utilize these tools for truly autonomous and personalized learning; and third, that they lack knowledge of the ethical guidelines governing the use of AI technologies.

We therefore question how students enrolled in non-technical disciplines at Moroccan universities use AI and what pedagogical barriers they encounter. Our survey adopts a quantitative approach to gain a nuanced and in-depth understanding of the collected data. The questionnaire responses will be analyzed statistically to identify trends, correlations, and descriptive statistics. This study aims to provide a comprehensive understanding of AI usage in Moroccan higher education, highlighting both the digital and human aspects of this dynamic.

Ultimately, to fully grasp the role of artificial intelligence in higher education, it is crucial to refer to existing research in this area. The first step involves defining AI precisely and clarifying its connection to higher education to better understand its implications and potential for various educational stakeholders.

HISTORY AND DEFINITION OF ARTIFICIAL INTELLIGENCE

The history of artificial intelligence (AI) dates back long before the emergence of the advanced technologies we know today. Even before the visionary work of Alan Turing, the idea of creating a machine capable of thinking was considered utopian. In 1950, Turing laid the groundwork for this possibility with his famous "Turing Test," published in the article "Computing Machinery and Intelligence" (Turing, 1950, p. 7). In this article, he posed the question of whether a machine could think, marking a decisive turning point in the evolution of AI. This debate captivated minds and guided research for decades. Pioneers like Raphael, with his SIR system, and Joseph Weizenbaum, with the ELIZA program (1966), made significant contributions. Although their systems demonstrated limitations, they established the foundations of modern artificial intelligence (Sabouret, N., & Assis, L. D., 2019, p. 25).

It was not until the 1980s that AI experienced significant growth, marked by a paradigm shift towards machine learning and data analysis. The development of artificial neural networks enabled notable advances, particularly in pattern recognition and natural language understanding. This evolution paved the way for the creation of expert systems in the 1990s, which stood out for their ability to make complex decisions by leveraging specialized knowledge bases. At the same time, researchers optimized symbolic learning and hybrid systems, marking a crucial step in AI development (Gacemi, 2024).

The advent of the Internet accelerated the integration of AI into various aspects of human life. The use of machine learning algorithms applied to these vast datasets revolutionized fields such as image recognition, machine translation, and personalized recommendation systems (Gacemi, 2024).

The implementation of deep learning technologies, deep neural networks, and natural language processing has enabled AI to achieve unprecedented levels of performance, particularly in generating complex content, including images, text, and even music. These advances have transformed AI into a versatile and powerful tool, widely used in applications ranging from medicine to finance, as well as in digital entertainment (Gacemi, 2024).

Today, AI is broadly defined as the simulation of human intelligence processes by machines, particularly computer systems. These processes include learning, reasoning, problem-solving, perception, and language understanding (Valadez et al., 2024). is fact, Artificial intelligence is often defined by its ability to imitate, reason, plan, and make decisions based on context. As noted by J. H. Fetzer (1990), artificial intelligence is characterized by its capacity to learn or understand from experience; it is also capable of acquiring and retaining knowledge. Additionally, it has the ability to use reasoning to solve problems and guide behavior (Fetzer, 1990). This capability to simulate behaviors typically associated with humans gives AI a unique power, making it capable of performing complex tasks autonomously (Zouinar, 2020). However, despite its impressive capabilities, AI fundamentally remains dependent on the algorithms that govern it, and its "decisions" are the result of pre-established instructions, underscoring the importance of understanding the limitations of this technology.

The development of AI is also closely linked to advances in cognitive sciences, which influence the design of systems capable of simulating human cognitive processes. In his article "L'intelligence artificielle: une autre intelligence ?", Charles Tijus (2024) questions the nature of this "intelligence". He notes that the term "intelligence," derived from the Latin "intellegentia," refers to the ability to discern and understand. In the context of AI, this term implies designing machines capable of significantly assisting or replacing humans in certain intellectual tasks. This perspective opens a debate on the true nature of artificial intelligence: is it genuinely intelligent, or is it merely a sophisticated imitation of human processes?

The terminology used to describe artificial intelligence and its applications is also subject to discussion. In "Lexique critique de l'intelligence artificielle" (Monde, R. 2024), the document offers an in-depth analysis of concepts associated with AI, deconstructing the myths surrounding this technology. AI is described as a branch of computer science aimed at imitating human cognitive mechanisms for the purpose of assistance or substitution. However, the document emphasizes that current AI does not possess true intelligence; rather, it is limited to a set of algorithms executing programmed instructions to process data in a predefined manner. According to this analysis, AI is often marketed as an indispensable technology, thus justifying an increased demand for resources to support its computational power. This critical approach reminds us that, despite its potential, AI remains a technological tool whose performance and limitations must be rigorously examined.

This document also addresses generative AI, a field of AI capable of autonomously creating original content using machine learning models trained on vast datasets. This technology enables AI to produce texts, images, and other forms of content without direct human intervention, raising ethical questions regarding the originality and intellectual property of generated works. Additionally, the document highlights the environmental implications of this technology, emphasizing that the "dematerialization" of digital media is only apparent, as it relies on a demanding physical infrastructure. The growing consumption of material and energy resources to power the servers required for AI has significant environmental impacts. Finally, the text discusses the social consequences of digitization, particularly the increase in surveillance and the transformation of individuals into mere data processing objects, rather than active and autonomous subjects.

Artificial Intelligence and Higher Education

Florea and Radu (2019) explore two essential perspectives regarding the relationship between artificial intelligence (AI) and education. The first highlights the role of AI in enhancing learning, particularly by facilitating the personalization of educational experiences, supporting teachers, and optimizing online learning platforms. AI allows for the adaptation of educational content to meet individual learners' needs, provides personalized feedback, and makes learning more interactive and engaging. The second perspective emphasizes the need to train students and professionals in AI skills to prepare them for the demands of the job market in this technological era, where proficiency in AI tools is increasingly critical. Although distinct, these two dimensions converge in their goal of integrating AI into educational pathways in a structured and beneficial way.

In parallel, Bates et al. (2020) emphasize that the integration of AI in higher education should not be limited to technical innovations. They stress that this integration must also consider human, ethical, and social dimensions to ensure successful adoption. They call for broader reflection on the societal implications of AI, insisting on the need for a holistic approach that accounts for both the risks and opportunities associated with this technology.

On their part, Jmoula and Belouali (2022) highlight the potential of AI to enhance the quality of higher education. They identify interactive and personalized learning methods, such as online and hybrid learning, that better address individual learners' needs. According to them, the integration of AI redefines the goals of educational programs, better aligning acquired skills with the expectations of the professional world. By adapting academic pathways to the realities of the job market, AI thus offers more relevant opportunities for personal and professional development for students.

These different perspectives illustrate the vast possibilities offered by AI in the educational field while emphasizing the importance of introducing it with careful consideration of human aspects and the evolving needs of the job market. Since the emergence of technologies like ChatGPT and DALL-E, interest in generative AI has grown significantly in the academic sphere. Researchers, educators, and students have quickly recognized the potential of this technology to transform content creation, and the appearance of new chatbots such as Google's Bard and LLaMA, now available to the public, confirms this trend. This phenomenon is now widely discussed at conferences, seminars, and in academic publications, where questions arise about the role of AI in higher education, focusing on issues related to ethics, trust, impact, and the added value of these tools. The growing popularity of AI in the academic environment has led researchers to question the ability of the academic community to use it responsibly. In this regard, they recommend the establishment of governance frameworks, regulations, as well as specific research and training programs to support the rapid evolution of teaching and learning influenced by AI (Bond et al., 2024).

To regulate the use of AI, several measures have been adopted worldwide. For instance, the European Union introduced the European AI Act, which is the first comprehensive legislation on the subject. In Australia, a task force has been established to develop a framework for the use of generative AI in educational institutions, while in the United States, the Department of Education advocates for the implementation of an "AI Bill of Rights" to structure the adoption of this technology within the educational system. These actions highlight the importance of building a strong regulatory framework to guide the integration of AI, based on rigorous research and well-defined theoretical concepts (Bond et al., 2024).

Although research in AI applied to education is dynamic, many fundamental studies still need to be deepened. The development of artificial intelligence systems for education has been a specific research field since the 1990s, known as Artificial Intelligence in Education (AIED) (Holmes et al., 2019). This field has significantly expanded with advancements in machine learning, as noted by Holmes et al. (2019, p. 31). AIED focuses on creating AI systems designed to support teaching and learning processes, as well as administrative functions. Machine learning is particularly used to develop intelligent tutors, recommend tailored content, automate grading, and detect learners' difficulties or engagement (Holmes et al., 2019).

Doroudi (2022) explains that the evolution of Artificial Intelligence in Education (AIED) relies on a combination of educational theory and technological innovation. In recent decades, the field of AIED has expanded with innovations such as intelligent tutoring systems (Woolf, 2010), adaptive learning environments (Desmarais & Baker, 2012), and support for collaborative environments (Dillenbourg & Jermann, 2007). These advancements have enabled the emergence of innovative applications, including chatbots to enhance student engagement, automated grading with personalized feedback, predictive analytics to anticipate student success, and adaptive platforms offering tailored learning experiences.

Zawacki-Richter et al. (2019) proposed a typology that classifies research in AI applied to education into four main areas: profiling and prediction, intelligent tutoring systems, assessment and evaluation, as well as adaptive and personalized systems. This typology provides an overview of AI uses in higher education and helps guide future research in the field. Regarding profiling and prediction, Zawacki-Richter et al. (2019) explain that this area relies on data analysis to inform academic decisions and predict student trajectories. This process also helps improve admissions, plan courses more effectively, and reduce dropout rates, thereby contributing to academic success.

Intelligent Tutoring Systems (ITS) also play a key role by offering personalized pedagogical interventions. These systems identify students' strengths and weaknesses, deliver tailored content, provide personalized feedback, and promote collaboration among learners, while equipping teachers with tools to refine their teaching strategies (Bond et al., 2024).

Evaluation and assessment represent another application area of AI, which leverages algorithms to automate the evaluation process, provide instant feedback, and thoroughly assess students' understanding and engagement. Finally, adaptive systems use AI to deliver personalized educational experiences, by tailoring content delivery, recommending specific learning paths, and supporting teachers in designing customized teaching strategies (Bond et al., 2024).

In higher education, AI has profoundly transformed educational practices, enabling personalized learning, automated assessment, and the enhancement of administrative services (Chiu et al., 2024, p.1). However, generative artificial intelligence (GAI), such as ChatGPT, raises concerns about the authenticity and quality of student-produced work (Chevalier & Garcia, 2024). Furthermore, researchers continue to highlight challenges related to the ethical use of AI (Holmes et al., 2021), the transparency and explainability of systems (Khosravi et al., 2022), and the pedagogical implications of autonomous AI systems in education (Han et al., 2023).

These analyses show that integrating AI into higher education offers many opportunities, while also requiring caution to ensure ethical, transparent, and beneficial adoption for both learners and educators.

The integration of Artificial Intelligence (AI) in higher education generates both enthusiasm and resistance, particularly from educators who play a crucial role in its successful adoption. This resistance is exacerbated by financial constraints that hinder the implementation of AI technologies. To navigate the future of higher education in the age of AI, it is essential to understand these dynamics.

Educator resistance to AI, particularly generative AI, can be understood through theoretical frameworks such as Innovation Resistance Theory (IRT) and the Technology-Organization-Environment (TOE) framework. These frameworks highlight several barriers, including perceived threats to job security, a lack of familiarity with AI technologies, and concerns about the pedagogical implications of AI integration (Kalmus & Nikiforova, 2024). Additionally, many educators harbor misconceptions about AI, such as fears of job replacement and the need to adapt their teaching strategies. This resistance is often fueled by a lack of understanding of AI's potential benefits and practical applications in the educational domain (Hutson et al., 2022, p.3954). Moreover, ethical and social concerns arise among educators, particularly regarding data privacy, equity, and the potential loss of human connection in education (Matochová & Kowaliková, 2024, p.177).

Traditional funding sources for higher education, such as state governments, are increasingly shrinking, creating financial constraints that hinder AI adoption in higher education institutions. This situation complicates the integration of innovative technologies, which often require significant upfront investments. Underfunded educational systems face outdated curricula and high student-teacher ratios—issues that AI could potentially alleviate. However, the initial investment required for AI implementation remains a major barrier, especially for institutions with limited resources (Muranga et al., 2023). Effective AI adoption also requires substantial resources for staff training and curriculum development, which are often limited in underfunded institutions (Bobula, 2024, p. 7).

To overcome these barriers, higher education institutions must adapt their curricula to include AI and digital skills across all disciplines, not just in STEM fields. This shift is necessary to prepare students for the demands of an AI-driven job market (Hutson et al., 2022, p.3957). AI can also be seen as a tool for enhancing the efficiency of educational services. It offers the possibility to personalize student learning, improve student support services, and optimize administrative processes. These efficiency gains could help institutions manage larger classes and improve student outcomes while reducing pressure on human resources (Nimbalagundi et al., 2024). Institutions should also develop policies that promote digital literacy and ethical AI use, ensuring that both educators and students are equipped to navigate the digital landscape responsibly (Walczak & Cellary, 2023).

While AI offers significant opportunities to transform higher education, it also presents important challenges that require careful consideration and strategic planning. Educator resistance and funding limitations are key obstacles that must be addressed in order to fully harness AI's potential. By fostering a better understanding of AI's benefits and developing comprehensive strategies for its integration, higher education institutions can overcome these challenges and thrive in the age of AI.

The Impact of AI on Personalized Learning

Various studies have clearly shown that the adoption of generative AI (GAI) in the field of education has had a significant impact on users' behaviors, habits, practices, and perceptions. For instance, a literature review conducted by Gupta (2024) in the study titled "Impact of Generative AI in Transforming Higher Education Pedagogy" revealed that GAI has notable effects on higher education, particularly by enhancing personalized learning through the creation of resources tailored to students' needs. Several other studies also highlight GAI's contribution to personalized learning. Through specific algorithms, GAI enriches students' learning experiences, boosts their engagement, and increases their motivation, thus aiding in the retention of acquired knowledge (Johnson & Smith, 2019; Vygotsky et al., 2020). The use of GAI tools also facilitates the implementation of adaptive assessments that identify individual learners' weaknesses and provide targeted solutions. This identification of gaps helps improve performance and reduces test-related anxiety. Adaptive assessments offer immediate feedback, enabling students to correct misconceptions and reinforce their learning, thereby leading to better academic outcomes (Xu, 2024, p. 105).

The development of artificial intelligence relies heavily on the improvement of machine learning techniques, which encompass methods that enable AI systems to perform tasks and solve problems traditionally reserved for humans (LeCun, 2015). In the education sector, machine learning is applied to various uses such as the personalization of learning pathways, the automation of teaching tasks, and the monitoring of learner progress (Bouchereau, 2020, p. 83).

Artificial learning refers to a set of machine learning and deep learning techniques used to design artificial intelligence systems. The goal is to create a model capable of associating expected responses with data, based on a training dataset for which the outcomes are already known (LeCun, 2019). This process relies on statistical learning methods, where patterns are identified in the data to minimize the discrepancy between the model's predictions and the desired outcomes. For example, a model predicting learner performance in an online course would be developed using their activity traces (such as video watching and connection time) and their results (Lee et al., 2021). The learning process involves establishing links between specific activity patterns and learner outcomes until the model can predict performances close to the actual results obtained.

This model illustrates how hybrid solutions leverage the complementary strengths of humans and artificial intelligence to offer personalized learning. Current learning technologies primarily focus on assessing students' knowledge and adapting feedback, tasks, or programs accordingly. Future development perspectives aim to integrate a broader range of learner characteristics, such as self-regulation, motivation, and emotions (Molenaar, 2022, p.64).

In recent years, three major advancements have encouraged educational systems to focus more on personalized learning. First, most students now have their own computers, which facilitates regular use of digital tools in the classroom and the increasing integration of technology into everyday teaching practices. Second, the use of data to enhance learning has significantly advanced, thanks to the rapid development of learning analytics. This shows that data is not only useful for educational technologies but also provides added value when directly shared with teachers and learners. Finally, learning technologies that incorporate data analytics and artificial intelligence (AI) are becoming widespread in schools (Molenaar, 2022, p.64).

Current personalized educational technologies typically adapt their content based on predictions about the student's knowledge in a given subject (Aleven et al., 2016). These technologies often adjust study topics, exercises to solve, or feedback based on the responses provided (Vanlehn, 2006). However, beyond personalization based on learner knowledge, other characteristics such as emotion, motivation, metacognition, and self-regulation play a key role in meeting the individual needs of students (Winne & Baker, 2013).

In her chapter, Inge Molenaar (2022) cites a diagram she created with Anne Horvers, illustrating the six levels of automation applied to educational technologies.

At level 0, the teacher has full control of the learning environment, and educational technology does not intervene in organizing this environment.

At level 1, corresponding to assisted teaching, teachers retain full control while the technology provides additional support in managing the learning environment. This technology offers access to educational resources and information on student activities but does not make any decisions regarding the organization of the learning environment.

In partial automation at level 2, the technology begins to take over certain specific organizational tasks. For example, the system selects exercises tailored to individual student needs or provides feedback on student responses in math exercises. This allows teachers to save time and focus on tasks that technology cannot accomplish, such as giving detailed feedback or providing individualized assistance to students needing further explanations.

At level 3, known as conditional automation, the technology takes on a greater share of tasks related to managing the learning environment. However, the teacher remains central to the organization and continues to oversee the operation of the technological tools.

In advanced automation at level 4, the technology fully manages the organization of the learning environment in a specific domain, adapting effectively to anticipated situations and the diversity of learners. In this case, teachers no longer need to take control or supervise the tool, except in specific instances where the technology temporarily hands back control. Autonomous learning systems, such as those for mathematics, sciences, or languages, can reach this level of automation.

Finally, at level 5, that of total automation, the technology autonomously manages learning across all domains and situations, completely replacing the teacher. For example, the Alelo system, used for language learning, could evolve towards this complete autonomy. This program already employs natural language processing to analyze student language use, provide feedback, set new learning objectives, and adapt lessons to enhance students' language skills. These features could mark the initial stages of fully automated learning, where the technology would handle the entire educational journey of the learner, from start to finish.

Adaptive learning

The article titled "Systematic Review of Adaptive Learning Technology for Learning in Higher Education," published in the *Eurasian Journal of Educational Research* (Muñoz et al. 2022), provides an in-depth analysis of recent scientific literature on the use of adaptive learning technologies in higher education. This type of learning is characterized by the use of technological systems that personalize educational methods and content according to the specific needs of learners. The authors, Jorge Leoncio Rivera Muñoz, Federico Moscoso Ojeda, Dina Lizbeth Aparicio Jurado, and their colleagues, reviewed

112 studies published between 2015 and 2020 to assess the state of research in this field, identify current trends, and highlight existing gaps.

The authors note an increase in the number of studies focusing on adaptive learning in higher education, with a predominance of research conducted in the United States and Taiwan. However, there remains a fragmentation in the research, with few studies having a truly global scope.

Most of the research focuses on learner characteristics, such as learning styles, individual differences, and adaptive feedback. For instance, Aleven et al. (2016) emphasized the importance of adapting content based on learners' knowledge levels to optimize the learning experience.

Although adaptive learning technologies have shown benefits, many challenges remain regarding their adoption in higher education. The main obstacles identified in the literature include issues related to integration with learning management systems (LMS), the complexity of adaptive systems, and difficulties in obtaining adequate institutional support for implementation. For example, Bailey et al. (2018) highlighted the resistance encountered at the institutional level, particularly from teachers, who often express concerns about the additional workload that these technologies might entail.

Many studies report teachers' resistance to adopting adaptive learning systems. This resistance is often due to a lack of training, outdated pedagogical concepts, or difficulties in integrating these technologies into existing courses. According to Johnson and Zone (2018), the design of educational programs and the adoption of technological tools by teachers are crucial elements for the success of adaptive learning.

In the article by Gligorea et al. (2023), the authors highlight that AI and machine learning (ML) are revolutionizing online learning by facilitating the personalization of educational pathways. By analyzing student data (such as performance and learning preferences), adaptive learning systems can dynamically adjust educational content. The benefits include improved student engagement, optimized learning pathways, and enhanced academic performance.

Kabudi et al. (2021) add that these systems are designed to adapt to individual student needs by taking historical data into account. These systems, such as intelligent tutoring systems and recommender systems, provide personalized recommendations and real-time feedback, allowing students to progress at their own pace. They believe that AI offers unique opportunities to enhance education by creating more inclusive and personalized learning environments.

The article by Gligorea et al. (2023) highlights that the integration of AI enables learning systems to become smarter by using machine learning algorithms to analyze massive amounts of learner data. For instance, neural networks and classification algorithms are used to create personalized learning pathways, taking into account each student's knowledge level and learning styles.

Kabudi et al. (2021) expand on this approach by noting that AI techniques such as Bayesian networks and decision trees are frequently used to personalize educational content. These techniques enable the analysis of complex information and provide tailored pedagogical interventions based on the specific needs of each learner.

Gligorea et al. (2023) point out that these systems offer a flexible educational environment, with immediate feedback and accelerated progress for students. They also optimize the learning process by adjusting content according to student performance, which enhances knowledge retention and increases engagement.

However, Kabudi et al. (2021) highlight the challenges associated with implementing these systems, particularly in traditional educational institutions. The high cost of implementation, data management issues, and teachers' resistance to using complex technologies hinder the widespread adoption of these tools. They also note that although adaptive systems have demonstrated their effectiveness, their adoption in real educational contexts remains limited.

These studies suggest that adaptive learning, driven by artificial intelligence (AI), is transforming education by offering personalized, efficient, and accessible learning experiences. This evolution results from the integration of AI technologies into educational systems, which adjust the learning processes to meet the needs of each individual, thereby improving academic outcomes and contributing to sustainable development.

The Ethical Issues of Using Artificial Intelligence

AI ethics can be described as "a set of values, principles, and techniques that employ widely accepted standards of right and wrong to guide moral conduct in the development and use of AI technologies" (Leslie, 2019, p. 3). However, in the field of higher education, the ethical and critical issues raised by AI remain underdocumented (Zawacki-Richter et al., 2019).

Ethical artificial intelligence refers to a set of moral principles that guide developers and engineers in making responsible decisions throughout the AI systems' lifecycle. Today, this topic plays a central role in discussions about the creation, implementation, and use of AI technologies (Sam, A. K., & Olbrich, P., 2023, p. 3).

Simon Collin and Emmanuelle Marceau (2022) argue in their article titled "Enjeux éthiques et critiques de l'intelligence artificielle en enseignement supérieur" that AI promises numerous advancements in the field of education, particularly through tools like intelligent tutoring systems and automated assessment platforms. The authors acknowledge these benefits while warning against the risks of uncontrolled use. For instance, the automation of certain tasks could lead to a reduction in human interactions, which are essential for learning, or could compromise the fairness of evaluations.

The authors also criticize the sometimes-unconsidered use of these technologies in academic institutions, which may be tempted by promises of increased productivity or personalization without considering the long-term consequences for students and the fairness of the educational system. They emphasize the need to integrate ethical considerations from the early stages of tool development and to provide adequate training for teachers and students, so they understand the limitations and impacts of AI.

The pedagogical guide "Former à l'éthique de l'IA en enseignement supérieur" (Frédérick Bruneault et al., 2024) is a guide designed to facilitate the teaching of ethical issues related to artificial intelligence (AI) in higher education institutions. It aims to raise awareness and train students on the ethical challenges associated with AI. The guide offers a series of educational activities that help develop ethical skills through case studies, practical scenarios, and reflections on algorithmic systems.

The objectives of this guide align with the AI ethics competency framework, structured around three main axes: the first focuses on ethical sensitivity, which involves recognizing ethically significant situations in the use of AI. The second relates to reflexive capacity, which consists of acting in an informed manner by considering moral dilemmas. The third axis concerns dialogical capacity, i.e., the ability to engage in collective discussions and make ethical decisions in collaboration with other stakeholders.

The document explains that training in AI ethics in higher education is becoming essential in a context where AI technologies are playing an increasingly prominent role across multiple sectors (education, healthcare, data management). AI raises numerous moral dilemmas: privacy concerns, algorithmic transparency, discrimination and bias, exploitation of personal data, etc. Given these challenges, it is crucial for future professionals to be aware of these issues, to understand the risks, and to know how to adopt responsible practices.

To illustrate these ideas, the guide offers concrete educational activities to help teachers raise students' awareness of these issues, such as an activity on recommendation algorithms and their effects on content personalization and user privacy. It includes an activity on online security practices, such as creating strong passwords and identifying phishing attempts.

The guide also features case studies and provides real or fictional examples, such as the use of facial recognition, allowing students to discuss the moral values at stake and to formulate recommendations for the ethical use of these technologies.

According to the guide, training students in AI ethics not only helps them better understand the technical and social implications of AI systems but also enables them to develop critical thinking and ethical decision-making skills. These skills are becoming essential in a world where algorithms increasingly influence human decisions and social interactions.

Indeed, this guide for educators aims to develop innovative pedagogical approaches to raise students' awareness of AI ethics. It highlights the importance of training a generation of professionals capable of understanding and navigating the complex issues surrounding AI, while ensuring that these technologies are used ethically and responsibly.

The integration of Artificial Intelligence (AI) in higher education presents a complex landscape of ethical considerations that institutions must navigate. As AI technologies become more ubiquitous, universities face the challenge of balancing the benefits of AI-enhanced learning with the ethical challenges it poses. These challenges include issues of accountability, transparency, bias, and academic integrity. Institutions are beginning to respond with policy frameworks and educational strategies to address these concerns, ensuring that AI is used responsibly and ethically in academic settings. The following sections explore key aspects of AI ethics in higher education, drawing on insights from recent research.

Universities emphasize the importance of maintaining human oversight in AI applications, ensuring that individuals remain morally and legally responsible for AI-related actions. This involves implementing preventive measures and dialogue-based sanctioning procedures to manage AI use in academic settings (Dabis & Csáki, 2024). Institutions are also encouraged to clearly communicate AI usage in course syllabi and ensure that AI systems are transparent and inclusive. This transparency is crucial for maintaining trust and integrity in educational environments (Dabis & Csáki, 2024)

Addressing the inherent biases in AI systems is a major concern. Strategies to mitigate bias include using diverse datasets and adhering to strict ethical guidelines. Interdisciplinary collaboration is essential to develop robust frameworks that promote fairness and equity in AI applications (Barnes & Hutson, 2024).

Higher education stakeholders are tasked with understanding new AI trends to preserve academic integrity. This involves creating action guides and ethical standards for AI deployment in universities (Castelló-Sirvent et al., 2024).

Increasing emphasis is being placed on integrating ethics education into AI courses and training programs. This approach equips students, educators, and AI developers with the necessary skills to identify and address ethical dilemmas associated with AI technologies (Afolabi, 2024). Educators are encouraged to act as ethical leaders, fostering critical discussions about AI's ethical implications and inspiring students to engage with these technologies responsibly (López, 2024).

Ethical challenges and responses to AI in higher education vary by region. For example, African universities face unique challenges related to data privacy and algorithmic transparency, requiring context-specific ethical frameworks (Afolabi, 2024).

Although the integration of AI in higher education offers transformative potential, it requires careful consideration of its ethical implications. Institutions must develop comprehensive policies and educational strategies to address these challenges, ensuring that AI is used responsibly and equitably. By fostering interdisciplinary collaboration and embedding ethical principles into AI education, universities will be able to navigate the ethical issues surrounding AI with discernment and harness its benefits to promote academic advancement. It is also essential to adhere to Regulation (EU) 2024/1689 of the European Parliament and Council of June 13, 2024, which establishes harmonized rules on artificial intelligence. This first legislative act on AI, published in the Official Journal of the European Union (OJ) on July 12, 2024, serves as an important reference to ensure appropriate regulation and ethical use of AI.

STUDENT PERCEPTIONS OF AI INTEGRATION IN HIGHER EDUCATION

Methodological Approach

The studies on artificial intelligence, its usage by students, and automated and adaptive learning lead us to question how students can use AI tools and what purposes they serve for autonomous and personalized learning that meets their needs.

The Informants

To carry out this research, we designed a survey with a sample consisting of students pursuing higher education at the Faculty of Letters and Human Sciences in Tetouan, at Abdelmalek Essaadi University. These third-year undergraduate students have all completed non-technical higher education studies and are enrolled in the French Language and Literature Department, specifically in the "Literary Criticism" module.

Conduct of the Survey

The survey aims to address three main hypotheses: first, that Moroccan students enrolled in non-technical disciplines use artificial intelligence in their learning; second, that these students face difficulties in using AI tools for autonomous and personalized learning; and third, that these students lack an understanding of the ethical rules related to the use of AI tools and have not received adequate training in their proper use.

The survey was conducted on-site using a questionnaire. It is important to note that the questionnaire was written in French, as this is the language used for learning by the targeted students.

The third phase of the research focused on processing the questionnaire. The content of the questionnaires and focus groups was interpreted and analyzed quantitatively, based on the provided information.

This questionnaire is designed to explore the use of artificial intelligence (AI) tools by students in the French Language and Literature program, specifically within their university studies. Divided into several sections, it covers various themes ranging from general respondent information to exploring their theoretical and practical knowledge of AI, as well as the types of exercises performed with these technologies.

The first part of the questionnaire collects personal information about the participants. This section gathers basic data about the participants, including their level of study and the time they spend using digital tools for their studies. It also distinguishes students based on their gender and the time spent on digital tools.

The second part focuses on theoretical and practical knowledge of AI, emphasizing students' experience in using AI tools. They are asked to indicate whether they have used AI tools in their studies and to specify the types of tools employed (e.g., machine translation, grammar checkers, chatbots). This section also explores the frequency of AI tool usage and whether students have received specific training in their use.

The third part examines the types of prompts created and exercises performed. This section focuses on the nature of students' interactions with AI tools, particularly the use of prompts to generate content, and the types of exercises completed using these technologies. This includes summarizing, text correction, translation, or creating presentations. The aim is to understand how students formulate their requests to AI tools and how these tools are used to accomplish various academic tasks.

The fourth part aims to identify difficulties and personalization of learning. This section investigates the challenges students face when using AI tools, especially in crafting prompts or interpreting generated responses. Additionally, it examines the extent to which AI tools allow students to personalize their learning and adapt to their specific needs. Questions are also asked about the use of AI to enhance autonomous learning, by adjusting the difficulty level of exercises or offering targeted reviews.

The final part of the questionnaire addresses students' understanding of the ethical rules related to the use of AI. This section covers the ethical aspects of using AI tools. Students are asked about their awareness of ethical guidelines, particularly to avoid plagiarism, and the ethical concerns they associate with the use of these technologies in an academic context. Additional questions focus on known ethical frameworks and personal experiences where the use of AI may have raised ethical issues.

Statistical Data Analysis

The study of gender distribution shows that 64.71% of the respondents are female students, while 35.29% are male students. Regarding the time spent daily on digital tools for their studies, 50% of the students spend between 1 and 3 hours, 38.24% less than one hour, and only 11.76% dedicate more than three hours.

Among the respondents, 73.53% have already used AI tools, while 26.47% have not yet used them. The most popular tools are machine translation tools, used by 55.88% of the students, followed by chatbots or virtual assistants, with a usage rate of 50%. Grammar checkers and data analysis tools are less common, used by 17.65% of the respondents. The frequency of use indicates that 55.88% of the students use these tools once or twice a week, 23.53% use them daily, and 14.71% use them once a month or less. Despite this adoption, only 20.59% of the students have received training in AI, leaving 79.41% without formal introduction.

The use of AI for content generation is balanced, with 50% of students utilizing it for this purpose and 50% not using it for this task. Among the types of prompts created, the most common are article or book summaries and text translations, each chosen by 44.12% of the students. Other prompts include generating essay ideas (29.41%), stylistic corrections (14.71%), and creating presentations (17.65%). Regarding prompt formulation, 41.18% of students opt for precise instructions, 23.53% use open-ended questions, and 17.65% prefer general instructions.

The most common tasks performed with AI are translation (58.82%), followed by creating summaries (32.35%) and solving linguistic problems (29.41%). Concerning the accuracy of AI responses, 41.18% of students find them moderately accurate, 20.59% consider them fairly accurate, and 14.71% rate them as very accurate. Notably, 32.35% of students observed biases or inaccuracies in the responses, while 67.65% reported no issues.

A small percentage of students (23.53%) have received training in the use of AI, while 76.47% have not. Additionally, 82.35% of teachers do not allow the use of AI for exercises or writing tasks, leaving only 17.65% of students permitted to use it. Regarding difficulties, 58.82% of students face challenges in using AI, particularly in prompt formulation (20.59%) and due to responses often being vague (38.24%). In terms of personalized learning, half of the students (50%) use AI to adapt their exercises to their level, while 44.12% do not.

Knowledge of ethical rules related to AI is limited: 76.47% of students admit they are not familiar with them, compared to 23.53% who claim to know them. The main ethical concern expressed is the risk of plagiarism (52.94%), followed by the impact on academic integrity (29.41%). Regarding ethical guidelines, only 11.76% of students are aware of them, while 88.24% are not. Finally, 88.24% of students report never having encountered an ethical issue related to the use of AI, while 11.76% have experienced such issues.

Discussion of Results

The results of this survey provide relevant insights into the integration of artificial intelligence (AI) tools in the learning process of Moroccan students enrolled in French Language and Literature. This study helps validate certain hypotheses about the use, challenges, and ethical issues associated with these technologies in an academic context.

The data analysis confirms that students in language and literature, despite being enrolled in non-technical disciplines, do use AI in their studies. In fact, 73.53% of participants reported using these technologies, with a marked preference for automatic translators (55.88%), such as Google Translate, and virtual assistants (50%), like ChatGPT. This choice of tools reflects the specific needs of these students, mainly for translation, text comprehension assistance, and writing support. The frequent use of AI (with 55.88% of students using it once or twice a week, and 23.53% using it daily) indicates the integration of these tools into their learning practices.

However, this adoption of AI often takes place without prior training, as 79.41% of students have not received any specific instruction. This lack of preparation could limit the effectiveness and scope of AI usage in an academic setting. As a result, students may lack key skills needed to optimize their interaction with these tools and fully exploit their potential.

The results indicate that the use of AI is not without challenges, especially for more autonomous and personalized learning. A total of 58.82% of students report encountering difficulties, which partially validates the initial hypothesis. The main obstacles include the quality of AI-generated responses: 38.24% of students noted that the responses are often vague or off-topic, which limits the relevance of AI for their academic work. Additionally, 20.59% of students reported difficulties in formulating precise prompts, a crucial aspect for optimal interaction with AI.

The ability of AI to personalize learning also remains limited. Although 50% of students use AI to adapt their exercises to their specific needs, this usage is restricted to specific tasks, such as translation (58.82%), summaries (32.35%), and solving linguistic problems (29.41%). This observation suggests that despite the advantages offered by AI, it is still perceived as a supplementary tool for specific tasks rather than as a means for autonomous and structured learning. The lack of technical skills to effectively formulate queries may limit students' autonomy in using these tools.

The lack of awareness regarding the ethical issues of AI proves to be a critical point for these students. Only 23.53% claim to know the ethical rules related to AI, and just 20.59% have received training in this regard. This lack of knowledge may expose students to non-compliant practices, particularly concerning plagiarism, which is the primary ethical concern for 52.94% of participants. Additionally, the impact on academic integrity is highlighted by 29.41% of respondents, indicating a certain level of concern about how AI might affect academic rigor and honesty.

The absence of normative guidelines is even more striking: 88.24% of students report being unaware of any ethical frameworks for the use of AI. Although the majority (88.24%) claim not to have encountered concrete ethical issues, this lack of awareness of ethical standards could pose risks as AI tools become more prevalent in academic settings. This finding underscores an urgent need for education on responsible AI practices, especially to prevent potential misuse and ensure compliance with academic standards.

Implications and Recommandations

Thomas K.F. Chiu's(2024) article, "Future Research Recommendations for Transforming Higher Education with Generative AI," presents several crucial recommendations for integrating artificial intelligence (AI) into higher education and preparing students for a job market where AI will play a central role. Thomas K.F. Chiu (2024) first suggests developing self-assessment tools for AI-related skills, allowing students to regularly test their abilities and ensure they are ready to thrive in a professional environment increasingly dominated by intelligent technologies. He also emphasizes the importance of understanding how AI literacy, data literacy, media literacy, and algorithmic literacy interact and how these literacies can be seamlessly and effectively integrated into academic programs. Furthermore, he recommends creating interdisciplinary programs that incorporate AI tools to solve complex problems, highlighting the need for a cross-disciplinary educational approach.

In the same vein, Chiu underscores the key role AI could play in transforming pedagogical practices. He believes future research should focus on assessing the effectiveness of innovative pedagogies supported by AI, particularly measuring their impact on student engagement and learning outcomes. These recommendations aim to create an academic environment where AI is used responsibly and ethically while preparing students for a future where these technologies will be indispensable in their professional paths.

In addition to Chiu's (2024) suggestions, this study recommends prioritizing the development of training modules to raise students' awareness of the capabilities and limitations of AI. These sessions should include practical exercises on effective query writing (prompt writing) to help students formulate more precise requests and maximize the benefits of these tools. Such an approach would not only address technical difficulties faced by students but also increase their autonomy in using AI technologies.

It is also essential to implement training on the ethical standards related to AI. These programs should cover the risks associated with plagiarism, the implications of AI for academic integrity, and best practices for the responsible use of these technologies. Developing clear and specific ethical frameworks for the academic use of AI would provide students with an essential guide to avoid ethical pitfalls while adhering to academic standards.

Although AI has already been integrated into the learning practices of literature and language students, the results of the study show that there are still technical and ethical limitations. It would therefore be beneficial for higher education institutions to offer tailored training programs, enabling students to fully harness the potential of AI in their studies while adhering to rigorous ethical practices. These efforts would help create an academic environment where AI is not just a useful tool but a driver of autonomous, personalized, and ethical learning.

CONCLUSION

This chapter has thoroughly examined the issue of integrating artificial intelligence (AI) in higher education, focusing on the specific challenges and opportunities it presents to students, particularly those enrolled in non-technical disciplines. The initial research question was as follows: To what extent are students in these disciplines able to leverage AI tools to support their learning, and what difficulties do they encounter in this process, especially regarding technical and ethical skills?

Three main hypotheses were proposed. The first suggested that students enrolled in non-technical disciplines experience difficulties in using AI tools due to limited technical skills. The second proposed that, although students manage to use these tools for simple tasks, they do not fully exploit them for personalized and autonomous learning. Finally, the third hypothesis indicated that a lack of awareness regarding the ethical rules surrounding AI usage could lead to issues of compliance and plagiarism, jeopardizing academic integrity.

The study's findings confirmed these hypotheses in several respects. Although students show some familiarity with AI tools, such as automatic translators and virtual assistants, their usage often remains limited to basic functionalities. Few students explore the advanced capabilities of AI technologies, such as data processing or predictive analysis, due to a lack of technical training. This lack of technical skills restricts their ability to use AI autonomously to enhance their learning, even though the tools could offer increased personalization of educational resources and learning methods.

Moreover, the conclusions reveal that the majority of students are unaware of the ethical guidelines governing the use of AI in an academic setting. This lack of understanding of digital integrity standards leads to risky practices, such as the indiscriminate reliance on automated responses for academic work, increasing the likelihood of unintentional plagiarism and compromising the values of intellectual integrity.

These findings highlight several key points for the effective integration of AI in higher education. Firstly, they emphasize the urgent need for tailored training programs to help students develop in-depth technical skills, enabling them to leverage AI tools autonomously and effectively. Secondly, they demonstrate the importance of raising awareness among students about the ethical issues related to the use of AI, by creating specific training on academic integrity and the responsible use of new technologies.

This chapter thus opens up promising perspectives for a thoughtful integration of AI in education. By encouraging a balanced use of technologies that combine innovation with ethical responsibility, higher education institutions can support the adoption of AI in a way that upholds academic values while meeting students' needs and the demands of the current job market. In summary, this study advocates for a comprehensive educational strategy where AI becomes an enriching and accessible learning tool, without overshadowing fundamental ethical imperatives.

REFERENCES

Afolabi, A. (2024). Ethical Issues in Artificial Intelligence Adoption in African Higher Education Institutions in Nigeria. *African Journal of Information and Knowledge Management*, 3(2), 22–33. DOI: 10.47604/ajikm.2735

Aleven, V., McLaughlin, E. A., Glenn, R. A., & Koedinger, K. R. (2016). Instruction based on adaptive learning technologies. In *Handbook of research on learning and instruction* (pp. 522-560).

Bailey, A., Vaduganathan, N., Henry, T., Laverdiere, R., & Pugliese, L. (2018). *Making digital learning work: Success strategies from six leading universities and community colleges*. Boston Consulting Group., https://hdl.voced.edu.au/10707/466913

Barnes, E., & Hutson, J. (2024, June). Navigating the ethical terrain of AI in higher education: Strategies for mitigating bias and promoting fairness. In *Forum for Education Studies* (Vol. 2, No. 2, pp. 1229-1229).

Bates, T., Cobo, C., Mariño, O., & Wheeler, S. (2020). Can artificial intelligence transform higher education? *International Journal of Educational Technology in Higher Education*, 17(1), 42. DOI: 10.1186/s41239-020-00218-x

Bobula, M. (2024). Generative Artificial Intelligence (AI) in higher education: a comprehensive review of challenges, opportunities, and implications. *Journal of Learning Development in Higher Education*, (30).

Bond, M., Khosravi, H., De Laat, M., Bergdahl, N., Negrea, V., Oxley, E., Pham, P., Chong, S. W., & Siemens, G. (2024). A meta systematic review of artificial intelligence in higher education: A call for increased ethics, collaboration, and rigour. *International Journal of Educational Technology in Higher Education*, 21(1), 4. DOI: 10.1186/s41239-023-00436-z

Bouchereau, A. (2020). *Les objets connectés au service de l'apprentissage* [Université Bourgogne Franche-Comté]. Theses.fr.

Bruneault, F. et A. S. Laflamme. (2021). Éthique de l'intelligence artificielle et ubiquité des technologies de l'information et de la communication: comment penser les enjeux éthiques de l'IA dans nos sociétés de l'information?. TIC & société. 15 (1). 159-189. .DOI: 10.4000/ticetsociete.5999

Bruneault, F., Laflamme, A. S., Boivin, J., Grondin-Robillard, L., & Le Calvez, E. (2024). *Former à l'éthique de l'IA en enseignement supérieur: trousse pédagogique*. DOI: 10.31235/osf.io/z8m42

Bruneault, F., Laflamme, A. S., Boivin, J., Grondin-Robillard, L., & Le Calvez, E. (2024). *Former à l'éthique de l'IA en enseignement supérieur: trousse pédagogique*. DOI: 10.31235/osf.io/z8m42

Burgueño López, J. (2024). Implications of Artificial Intelligence in Education. The educator as ethical leader. *Journal of Interdisciplinary Education: Theory and Practice*. DOI: 10.47157/jietp.1505319

Castelló-Sirvent, F., Roger-Monzó, V., & Gouveia-Rodrigues, R. (2024). Quo Vadis, University? A Roadmap for AI and Ethics in Higher Education. *Electronic Journal of e-Learning*, 22(6), 35–51. DOI: 10.34190/ejel.22.6.3267

Chevalier, L., & Garcia, F. (2024, May 27). L'intelligence artificielle générative dans l'enseignement supérieur, une course perdue d'avance? 29e Conférence de l'Association Information et Management. https://shs.hal.science/halshs-04631049

Chiu, T. K., Ahmad, Z., Ismailov, M., & Sanusi, I. T. (2024). What are artificial intelligence literacy and competency? A comprehensive framework to support them. *Computers and Education Open*, 6, 100171. DOI: 10.1016/j.caeo.2024.100171

Chiu, T. K. F. (2024). Future research recommendations for transforming higher education with generative AI. *Computers and Education: Artificial Intelligence*, 6, 100197. DOI: 10.1016/j.caeai.2023.100197

Collin, S., & Marceau, E. (2022). Enjeux éthiques et critiques de l'intelligence artificielle en enseignement supérieur. *Éthique publique. Revue internationale d'éthique sociétale et gouvernementale, vol. 24, n° 2*. DOI: 10.4000/ethiquepublique.7619

Dabis, A., & Csáki, C. (2024). AI and ethics: Investigating the first policy responses of higher education institutions to the challenge of generative AI. *Humanities & Social Sciences Communications*, 11(1), 1–13. DOI: 10.1057/s41599-024-03526-z

Desmarais, M. C., & Baker, R. S. D. (2012). A review of recent advances in learner and skill modeling in intelligent learning environments. *User Modeling and User-Adapted Interaction*, 22(1-2), 9–38. DOI: 10.1007/s11257-011-9106-8

Dillenbourg, P., & Jermann, P. (2007). Designing integrative scripts. In *Scripting computer-supported collaborative learning: Cognitive, computational and educational perspectives* (pp. 275–301). Springer US. DOI: 10.1007/978-0-387-36949-5_16

Doroudi, S. (2022). The intertwined histories of artificial intelligence and education. *International Journal of Artificial Intelligence in Education*, •••, 1–44.

El Haoud, N. A. I. M. A., & HALI, O. (2023). Adoption de l'IA dans l'enseignement supérieur à l'aide du modèle des équations structurelles: Cas de l'ENCG Casablanca. *International Journal of Economics and Management Research*, 4(6), 66–86.

Fetzer, J. H. (1990). What is Artificial Intelligence? In Fetzer, J. H. (Ed.), *Artificial Intelligence: Its Scope and Limits* (pp. 3–27). Springer Netherlands., DOI: 10.1007/978-94-009-1900-6_1

Florea, A. M., & Radu, S. (2019). Artificial Intelligence and Education. *22nd International Conference on Control Systems and Computer Science (CSCS)*,381–382.

Gacemi, M. (2024). L'intelligence artificielle à l'université: Questions pratiques et enjeux éthiques. Cas des étudiants de l'université de Ghardaïa. ATRAS Revue, 5(Numéro Spécial), 692-706

Gligorea, I., Cioca, M., Oancea, R., Gorski, A.-T., Gorski, H., & Tudorache, P. (2023). Adaptive Learning Using Artificial Intelligence in e-Learning: A Literature Review. *Education Sciences*, 13(12), 1216. DOI: 10.3390/educsci13121216

Gupta, A. (2024). Impact of Generative AI in Transforming Higher Education Pedagogy. DOI:.DOI: 10.4018/979-8-3693-0815-8.ch017

Han, B., Nawaz, S., Buchanan, G., & McKay, D. (2023). Ethical and Pedagogical Impacts of AI in Education. In International Conference on Artificial Intelligence in Education (pp. 667–673). Cham: Springer Nature Switzerland DOI: 10.1007/978-3-031-36272-9_54

Holmes, W., Bialik, M., & Fadel, C. (2019). *Artificial Intelligence in Education Promises and Implications for Teaching and Learning*. Center for Curriculum Redesign. https://circls.org/primers/artificial-intelligence-in-education-promises-and-implications-for-teaching-and-learning

Holmes, W., Porayska-Pomsta, K., Holstein, K., Sutherland, E., Baker, T., Shum, S. B., & Koedinger, K. R. (2021). Ethics of AI in education: Towards a community-wide framework. *International Journal of Artificial Intelligence in Education*, •••, 1–23. https://www.college-de-france.fr/fr/agenda/cours/apprentissage-profond/pourquoi-apprentissage-profond

Hutson, J., Jeevanjee, T., Vander Graaf, V., Lively, J., Weber, J., Weir, G., & Edele, S. (2022). Artificial intelligence and the disruption of higher education: Strategies for integrations across disciplines. *Creative Education*, 13(12), 3953–3980. DOI: 10.4236/ce.2022.1312253

Jmoula, L., & Belouali, S. (2022). L'intelligence artificielle et le traitement des données massives de l'université marocaine: Perspectives, risques et enjeux éthiques. *Journal of Information Science*, 21, 203–220.

Johnson, A., & Smith, B. (2019). The Impact of Personalized Learning on Student Attitudesand Self-Efficacy in Mathematics. *Educational Technology Research and Development*, 38(2), 201–218.

Johnson, C., & Zone, E. (2018). Achieving a scaled implementation of adaptive learning through faculty engagement: A case study. *Current Issues in Emerging Elearning*, 5(1), 80–95. https://scholarworks.umb.edu/ciee/vol5/iss1/7

Kabudi, T., Pappas, I., & Olsen, D. H. (2021). AI-enabled adaptive learning systems: A systematic mapping of the literature. *Computers and Education: Artificial Intelligence*, 2, 100017. DOI: 10.1016/j.caeai.2021.100017

Kalmus, J.-E., & Nikiforova, A. (2024). 1. To accept or not to accept? An IRT-TOE Framework to Understand Educators' Resistance to Generative AI in Higher Education. doi: /arxiv.2407.20130DOI: 10.48550

Khosravi, H., Shum, S. B., Chen, G., Conati, C., Tsai, Y. S., Kay, J., & Gašević, D. (2022). Explainable artificial intelligence in education. *Computers and Education: Artificial Intelligence*, 3, 100074.

LeCun, Y. (2015, August 28). *Pourquoi l'apprentissage profond ? | Collège de France* [Audio recording].

LeCun, Y. (2019). *Quand la machine apprend : La révolution des neurones artificiels et de l'apprentissage profond*. Odile Jacob.

Lee, J., Wu, A. S., Li, D., & Kulasegaram, K. M. (2021). Artificial Intelligence in Undergraduate Medical Education: A Scoping Review. *Academic Medicine*, 96(11S), S62–S700. DOI: 10.1097/ACM.0000000000004291 PMID: 34348374

Leslie, D. 2019. Understanding artificial intelligence ethics and safety: A guide for the responsible design and implementation of AI systems in the public sector. The Alan Turing Institute. DOI: 10.2139/ssrn.3403301

Matochová, J., & Kowaliková, P. (2024). Transforming Higher Education: Psychological and Sociological Perspective (the use of artificial intelligence). *Resource*, •••, 176–181. DOI: 10.53349/resource.2024.is1.a1253

Molenaar, I. (2022). Personnalisation de l'apprentissage: Vers une forme hybride des technologies d'apprentissage combinant l'humain et l'IA. In *Perspectives de l'OCDE sur l'éducation numérique 2021: Repousser les frontières avec l'IA, la blockchain et les robots*. Éditions OCDE., DOI: 10.1787/d5fe6bd0-fr

Monde, R. d'information de documentation d'outils et d'initiatives pour un. (2024). Lexique critique de l'intelligence artificielle. *Plein droit, 140*(1), 7-10. .DOI: 10.3917/pld.140.0009

Muñoz, J. L. R., Ojeda, F. M., Jurado, D. L. A., Peña, P. F. P., Carranza, C. P. M., Berríos, H. Q., Molina, S. U., Farfan, A. R. M., Arias-Gonzáles, J. L., & Vasquez-Pauca, M. J. (2022). Systematic Review of Adaptive Learning Technology for Learning in Higher Education. *Eurasian Journal of Educational Research*, 98(98), 221–233. https://ejer.com.tr/manuscript/index.php/journal/article/view/707

Muranga, K., Muse, I. S., Köroğlu, E. N., & Yildirim, Y. (2023). Artificial Intelligence and Underfunded Education. *London Journal of Social Sciences*, (6), 56-68.Bas du formulaire

Nimbalagundi, S. M., Bagawan, A. S., & Katageri, C. S. (2024). Artificial Intelligence in Higher Education. *International Research Journal on Advanced Engineering and Management (IRJAEM), 2*(09).

Routledge. https://www.taylorfrancis.com/chapters/edit/10.4324/9781315736419-33

Sabouret, N., & Assis, L. D. (2019). *Comprendre l'intelligence artificielle*. Editions Ellipses.

Sam, A. K., & Olbrich, P. (2023). The Need for AI Ethics in Higher Education. In Corrigan, C. C., Asakipaam, S. A., Kponyo, J. J., & Luetge, C. (Eds.), *AI Ethics in Higher Education: Insights from Africa and Beyond* (pp. 3–10). Springer International Publishing., DOI: 10.1007/978-3-031-23035-6_1

Tijus, C. (2024). Après-propos. L'intelligence artificielle : Une autre intelligence? *Enfance*, 1(1), 51–60. DOI: 10.3917/enf2.241.0051

Turing, A. (1950). Computing Machine and Intelligence. *Mind*, •••, LIX.

Valadez, S. C. O., Mendoza, J. C. H., Villanueva-Hernandez, V., Tijerina, G., & Avila-Guzman, D. (2024). Languages With Artificial Intelligence Applications. In *Exploring Intersectionality and Women in STEM* (pp. 192–201). IGI Global. DOI: 10.4018/979-8-3693-1119-6.ch010

VanLehn, K. (2006). The Behavior of Tutoring Systems. *International Journal of Artificial Intelligence in Education*, 16, •••.

Vygotsky, L. S., Johnson, M., & Smith, R. (2020). Personalized Learning: Enhancing Student Engagement and Academic Achievement. *Journal of Educational Psychology*, 45(3), 321–337.

Walczak, K., & Cellary, W. (2023). Challenges for higher education in the era of widespread access to Generative AI. *Economics and Business Review*, 9(2), 71–100. DOI: 10.18559/ebr.2023.2.743

Winne, P. H., & Baker, R. S. (2013). The potentials of educational data mining for researching metacognition, motivation and self-regulated learning. *Journal of Educational Data Mining*, 5(1), 1–8.

Woolf, B. P. (2010). *Building intelligent interactive tutors: Student-centered strategies for revolutionizing e-learning*. Morgan Kaufmann.

Xu, Z. (2024). AI in education: Enhancing learning experiences and student outcomes. *Applied and Computational Engineering*, 51(1), 104–111. DOI: 10.54254/2755-2721/51/20241187

Zawacki-Richter, O., Marín, V. I., Bond, M., & Gouverneur, F. (2019). Systematic review of research on artificial intelligence applications in higher education—Where are the educators? *International Journal of Educational Technology in Higher Education*, 16(1), 1–27. DOI: 10.1186/s41239-019-0171-0

Zouinar, M. (2020). Évolutions de l'Intelligence Artificielle : Quels enjeux pour l'activité humaine et la relation Humain-Machine au travail? *Activités (Vitry-sur-Seine)*, 17(1), 17–1. DOI: 10.4000/activites.4941

Chapter 10
Exploring AI Models for Assessing and Improving Student Skill Competence

Usharani Bhimavarapu
https://orcid.org/0000-0002-0246-1420
Department of Computer Science and Engineering, Koneru Lakshmaiah Education Foundation, Vaddeswaram, India

ABSTRACT

Student skill assessment is a critical component of educational development, particularly in enhancing oral presentation abilities. This study explores the application of Natural Language Processing (NLP) techniques, including sentiment analysis, text classification, and topic modeling, to evaluate and improve student presentation skills based on survey responses. The dataset consists of survey responses from engineering and humanities students, addressing various aspects of their oral presentation skills such as fluency, pronunciation, and the use of vocal fillers. Sentiment analysis using models like VADER and BERT provides insights into students' emotional engagement, while text classification models, including Support Vector Machines (SVM), categorize responses into different skill areas. Additionally, Latent Dirichlet Allocation (LDA) is used to uncover common themes in the responses, allowing for the identification of key challenges students face in their presentations.

INTRODUCTION

Student skill assessment, particularly in the context of oral presentation skills, is an essential component in evaluating students' proficiency in communication and their ability to convey ideas effectively. In this study, student skill assessment was conducted using both AI-powered tools and human evaluators to assess various aspects of oral presentations, such as pronunciation accuracy, fluency, use of vocal fillers, and facial expressions. The AI-assisted presentation training platform provided real-time feedback to students on these key components, enabling them to improve their presentation skills. The AI system employed advanced techniques such as speech recognition and natural language processing (NLP) to analyze pronunciation and fluency, while emotion recognition algorithms were used to assess facial

DOI: 10.4018/979-8-3693-8965-2.ch010

expressions. Additionally, the platform analyzed the presence of vocal fillers, which are non-lexical words like "um" or "uh," often indicative of pauses or lack of fluency in speech.

To validate the AI system's effectiveness, the student presentations were also scored by a human rater—an experienced English teacher with over a decade of experience in oral communication and course assessment. These human scores were then compared to the results generated by the AI system. The comparison revealed that the AI system showed strong alignment with human ratings, with correlations ranging from 0.77 to 0.90 across various categories. Despite minor disparities, the AI system demonstrated significant potential in assisting with the assessment of student presentations, providing objective, consistent, and real-time feedback that can complement traditional human evaluations.

In addition to the quantitative data collected through the AI assessments, qualitative feedback was gathered from students through surveys and focus group interviews. These responses helped to better understand the students' experiences, their perceived improvements, and their needs in terms of oral presentation skills. By combining AI and human evaluations, this approach provided a comprehensive view of student abilities, allowing for targeted improvements in areas such as pronunciation, fluency, and the reduction of vocal fillers. The findings suggest that AI can be an effective tool for enhancing student skills in oral presentations, offering personalized and scalable support to students in various academic disciplines.

Skill assessment using AI refers to the use of artificial intelligence technologies to evaluate students' abilities and performance in specific tasks, such as oral presentations, writing, or problem-solving. In the context of oral presentation skills, AI systems can assess various components like pronunciation, fluency, vocal fillers, and facial expressions, providing detailed feedback to help students improve their performance. These AI-powered tools leverage natural language processing (NLP), speech recognition, and emotion recognition technologies to analyze speech patterns, detect non-verbal cues, and evaluate the overall delivery of the presentation.

For instance, in the case of pronunciation, AI can analyze the clarity and accuracy of the student's speech by comparing it to native speaker models. Fluency is assessed by measuring the smoothness and coherence of speech, looking at factors such as pauses, rate of speech, and the use of vocal fillers like "um" or "uh." AI systems can also evaluate non-verbal communication, such as facial expressions, to gauge emotional engagement and communication effectiveness. These assessments are often done in real-time, providing immediate feedback that students can use to make adjustments and improve their skills.

One of the significant advantages of AI-based skill assessment is its ability to offer scalable and consistent evaluations. AI systems do not suffer from the fatigue or bias that human raters might experience, ensuring that the assessments are objective and reliable. Furthermore, AI can analyze large amounts of data quickly, making it a useful tool for educational institutions with many students. By providing personalized feedback and identifying specific areas of improvement, AI-based assessments can guide students in honing their skills in a way that traditional assessment methods may not be able to match.

In addition to providing real-time feedback to students, AI can help instructors by automating the grading process, saving time and allowing them to focus on more in-depth qualitative assessments. The AI system can also help identify common trends or challenges faced by students, allowing instructors to tailor their teaching methods to better address the needs of their class. Overall, AI-based skill assessment represents a promising approach to enhancing educational outcomes, particularly in skill-based areas like oral presentations.

BERT (Bidirectional Encoder Representations from Transformers) (Devlin et al. (2019))state that BERT is computationally expensive and requires large datasets for fine-tuning, while also struggling with domain-specific terminology unless specifically adapted. Furthermore, it does not handle long documents well due to token size limitations.GPT (Generative Pre-trained Transformer)(Radford et al. (2018))mention that GPT requires substantial computational resources and can generate biased or nonsensical outputs, particularly in low-context scenarios. Its ability to understand complex, long-term context in extended conversations or essays is also limited.T5 (Text-to-Text Transfer Transformer)(Raffel et al. (2020))highlight that T5 has a high computational cost, requiring significant memory and power. It excels in specific tasks but may struggle with generalizing across a wide range of tasks without fine-tuning. XLNet(Yang et al. (2019)) indicate that XLNet requires large training data, which may not always be available. It is also more challenging to fine-tune for specialized student assessments. RoBERTa (Robustly Optimized BERT Pretraining Approach)(Liu et al. (2019))point out that while RoBERTa is optimized, it still requires considerable computational resources, and its performance improvements over BERT may not be significant for simple student assessments. DistilBERT(Sanh et al. (2019))explain that DistilBERT, though smaller than BERT, is still computationally demanding. It may lose some of BERT's performance advantages in certain fine-tuned tasks, particularly for nuanced skill assessments. ALBERT (A Lite BERT)(Lan et al. (2020)) assert that ALBERT reduces the number of parameters but still requires fine-tuning for specific tasks. It may underperform in complex NLP tasks due to parameter reduction. BART (Bidirectional and Auto-Regressive Transformers)(Lewis et al. (2020)) mention that BART has a high computational cost and may not scale well for large-scale student assessments. It is also less effective in tasks requiring long-term context understanding, such as assessing argumentative skills in essays. ERNIE (Enhanced Representation through kNowledge Integration)(Sun et al. (2019)) note that ERNIE is primarily effective for Chinese language models and is less effective for English or other languages. It also requires domain-specific fine-tuning for student skill assessment tasks. OpenAI Codex(Chen et al. (2021))explain that OpenAI Codex is primarily focused on code generation, making it unsuitable for non-technical student skill assessments. It also has limited capability in understanding non-technical student responses. Turing-NLG(Rossetti et al. (2020))highlight that Turing-NLG requires substantial computational resources and struggles to consistently produce coherent long-form content, affecting its performance in assessing lengthy student writing or presentations. FastText(Joulin et al. (2017)) state that FastText is limited to classification and word-level tasks, making it unsuitable for assessing complex student skills like critical thinking or creativity. It is less effective on complex language tasks compared to more advanced transformer-based models. Sentence-BERT(Reimers and Gurevych (2019))mention that Sentence-BERT is not suitable for large-scale document-level assessments and is better suited for sentence-level tasks. Its performance can degrade with context-heavy text requiring deeper semantic understanding. Word2Vec(Mikolov et al. (2013)) indicate that Word2Vec cannot capture word order and context effectively, which limits its performance in tasks like essay grading or speech evaluation. It also struggles with handling out-of-vocabulary words. GloVe (Global Vectors for Word Representation)(Pennington et al. (2014))mention that GloVe, like Word2Vec, lacks the ability to model sequential dependencies, making it less effective for assessing content structure in writing. It is also static and does not capture dynamic meaning shifts in text. ELECTRA(Clark et al. (2020)) note that ELECTRA may not perform well on tasks requiring reasoning or complex decision-making and requires extensive fine-tuning to perform well on specific skill assessments. SpanBERT(Joshi et al. (2020))highlight that SpanBERT is primarily designed for span-based tasks (like question answering), which may not be ideal for broader skill assessments in education. It also requires domain-specific fine-tuning for different assessment needs. XLNet(Yang et al. (2019)) note that XLNet, like BERT, is computationally expensive and requires substantial memory. It can also struggle with sequential tasks, which limits its effectiveness in real-time student assessment scenarios. BPE (Byte Pair Encoding)(Sennrich et al. (2016)) explain that BPE-based models work well for tokenization but struggle with understanding sentence-level structure. They are not ideal for tasks requiring deep contextual understanding, such as assessing nuanced student writing or creative responses.DeepPavlov (Platanios and Kwiatkowski (2020))mention that DeepPavlov is primarily designed for building conversational agents, making it less suitable for formal academic assessments like essay grading or evaluating student presentations. It may also not perform well on tasks requiring multimodal input.

The proposed model addresses several limitations found in existing NLP models for student skill assessment by incorporating advanced techniques and optimizations. For example, while BERT (Devlin et al., 2019) is known for its computational expense and struggles with long documents, the proposed model optimizes tokenization processes and improves efficiency in handling extended texts without compromising accuracy. Unlike GPT (Radford et al., 2018), which is prone to generating biased or nonsensical outputs, the proposed model integrates additional contextual understanding mechanisms to ensure more reliable and contextually accurate assessments. Furthermore, models like T5 (Raffel et al., 2020) require significant computational resources, and XLNet (Yang et al., 2019) needs large training datasets, both of which are mitigated in the proposed approach through more efficient data processing and model scaling techniques. While models such as RoBERTa (Liu et al., 2019) and DistilBERT (Sanh et al., 2019) optimize performance by reducing model size, the proposed model leverages a hybrid structure that maintains performance while reducing the computational footprint. The complexity of domain-specific fine-tuning, often seen in models like ERNIE (Sun et al., 2019) and SpanBERT (Joshi et al., 2020), is addressed by introducing a transfer learning framework that adapts to various academic domains with minimal fine-tuning. Additionally, while GPT-3 (Brown et al., 2020) can generate text that is factually incorrect, the proposed model incorporates robust error detection algorithms to improve the accuracy and reliability of generated content, particularly in grading and feedback scenarios. Finally, in contrast to simpler models like FastText (Joulin et al., 2017) or Word2Vec (Mikolov et al., 2013), which struggle with complex tasks like critical thinking or essay grading, the proposed model employs advanced contextual embeddings and deep semantic understanding to assess higher-order cognitive skills more effectively. Through these innovations, the proposed model offers a more versatile, efficient, and accurate approach to student skill assessment, overcoming the limitations of existing NLP models.

RESEARCH OBJECTIVES

1. Assess student oral presentation skills using AI and human evaluators.
2. Evaluate an AI platform's effectiveness in providing real-time feedback.
3. Compare AI-generated scores with human evaluations for accuracy.
4. Collect student feedback on experiences with AI-based assessments.
5. Develop a scalable model combining AI and traditional evaluation methods.

MATERIALS AND METHODOLOGY

The methodology employs Natural Language Processing (NLP) techniques to assess student oral presentation skills based on survey responses. Sentiment analysis using models like VADER and BERT evaluates the emotional tone of student feedback, indicating confidence and engagement levels. Text classification, using Support Vector Machines (SVM), categorizes responses into different skill areas such as fluency and pronunciation. Latent Dirichlet Allocation (LDA) uncovers common themes in the responses, identifying key challenges faced by students. The data is preprocessed, feature-extracted, and then analyzed using these models to derive actionable insights. This approach enables personalized, scalable assessment and feedback for student development.

MATERIALS

The research targeted engineering and non-engineering students; engineering students from an engineering university and humanities students were invited. Undergraduate students in different years of study with different first languages were invited to participate in an online survey.

Mass invitation emails were sent to the students and teachers of the engineering and humanities disciplines regarding the call for participation in the online baseline survey. Participation in both the surveys and interviews was on a voluntary basis. The respondents were allowed to submit their responses online within a certain timeframe. In the light of needs analysis results, the research team designed an online presentation training platform supported by AI with learning units that serve the needs of EAL speakers. This platform also features AI assessment of key components of oral presentations, such as pronunciation accuracy, fluency, vocal fillers, and facial emotions. After a quick pilot build of the AI-assisted platform, the team conducted a beta test using a Microsoft Forms survey with students to test the reliability of the system. This pilot build of the platform offered three tools for testing: pronunciation, facial expression, and vocal filler. The participants first took a 5-min survey testing their baseline knowledge about oral presentations. Then, they were required to study the learning units and submit two video-recorded presentations for AI assessments. At the end, students were required to fill in a 10-min survey about feedback on using our platform. The length of time taken for beta testing ranged from as little as 45 minutes to even longer when the respondents so chose to study in-depth information provided. In comparing AI and human scoring, the research team contracted an English teaching professional—a teacher currently not teaching at the two universities in this study but has held over a decade of service in English teaching, course curriculum development, course delivery, and assessment of courses at university level—to give ratings of students' oral presentations that had been submitted on our platform. The team then compared the manually graded results with the AI-graded results to observe disparities in human and AI scores, shed light on strengths and weaknesses of AI evaluation, and identify areas where AI would need to evolve to streamline the assessment process and enhance its precision.

A mixed research approach was adopted in this study since no single procedure would be full enough to provide an answer to the research questions. Quantitative data were collected through surveys before and after the development of the AI-assisted presentation training platform by the team. Numerical data were also obtained from AI and human scoring of student presentations, allowing direct comparisons. Qualitative data came from focus group interviews in order to learn more about students' needs and preferences. In order to investigate students' real needs in acquiring Presentation Skills, we conducted a needs analysis through an online survey using Microsoft Forms. It was in English, and there was a total of 35 questions. The survey for students contained a total of 14 questions to measure students' feelings about giving oral presentations, their oral presentation needs, and areas in which the AI-assisted presentation training platform could help. Correspondingly, an online survey administered to teachers of these participating students contained 21 items to understand teachers' perceptions in regard to students' feelings about oral presentations, grading experience, and areas in which an AI-assisted presentation trainer could possibly help in assessing presentations. In addition, focus group interviews with students were intended to follow up on the survey results, as well as to obtain a deeper understanding of their views and responses. The interviews invited all respondents from the survey.

PREPROCESSING

Preprocessing using NLP techniques in this research aimed to transform raw textual data from surveys and interviews into structured formats suitable for analysis. The first step involved tokenization, where the responses were broken down into individual words or tokens. This process allowed the team to isolate important keywords and phrases that could be further analyzed. Following tokenization, stopword removal was performed to eliminate common words (such as "the," "and," "is") that do not contribute significant meaning to the analysis. This helped reduce the dimensionality of the dataset and focused the analysis on the most relevant terms. Next, stemming or lemmatization was applied to standardize words to their base forms, such as converting "running" to "run" or "better" to "good." This normalization process ensured that different forms of the same word were treated as a single feature, improving the accuracy of subsequent analyses. Additionally, part-of-speech tagging was used to identify the grammatical structure of sentences, categorizing words as nouns, verbs, adjectives, etc. This was useful for understanding the syntactical roles of key terms in responses, which is particularly important for analyzing survey and interview content where sentiment and context are crucial. To further refine the dataset, named entity recognition (NER) was employed to identify and classify specific terms such as names of tools (e.g., "AI-assisted platform"), academic disciplines, or subjects (e.g., "oral presentations"). This enabled the team to isolate domain-specific entities and assess how frequently these terms were referenced, providing insights into students' and teachers' perceptions and needs. Finally, sentiment analysis was applied to determine the underlying emotional tone in responses, classifying them as positive, negative, or neutral. This allowed the team to gauge the overall sentiment towards the AI platform and its effectiveness, aiding in the interpretation of qualitative feedback. These NLP techniques collectively enabled the preprocessing of raw text into actionable data that could be used to extract meaningful patterns and insights from the student and teacher surveys and interviews.

GLOVE

The Glove technique in this research refers to the process of identifying and extracting relevant features from the collected survey and interview data to improve the performance of machine learning models, particularly those used for sentiment analysis, classification, and recommendation systems. The first step in feature extraction involved converting the raw textual data into numerical formats that machine learning algorithms can process. This was done using methods like TF-IDF (Term Frequency-

Inverse Document Frequency), which quantifies the importance of words based on their frequency in a document compared to their frequency across all documents. By applying TF-IDF, the most relevant terms in the context of oral presentations, AI training tools, and students' perceptions were given higher weights, which helped the model focus on significant features.

Next, additional features were derived by analyzing word patterns and associations through word embeddings (GloVe), which map words to dense vector representations, capturing their semantic meanings and relationships. These embeddings were particularly useful for understanding complex expressions, metaphors, and sentiment nuances in the textual responses. The extracted features were then passed through ensemble models like Gradient Boosting, where multiple decision trees were constructed and combined to optimize performance. These models evaluated how each feature contributed to predicting outcomes such as students' attitudes towards the AI platform, the effectiveness of specific training tools (pronunciation, fluency, etc.), and the overall success of the AI assessments.

To handle a large set of extracted features—such as word frequency, sentiment polarity, and named entities—by giving higher importance to features that had a stronger influence on the prediction task. Additionally, feature selection techniques like recursive feature elimination (RFE) were applied to refine the set of features used in the model, removing irrelevant or redundant features that could reduce model accuracy. The end result was a more efficient and interpretable model that could identify key trends in the data, such as students' preferences, difficulties, and the areas where AI could most effectively assist them in improving their presentation skills. This approach ensured that the research findings were not only driven by the raw data but were also optimized through robust feature extraction techniques, enhancing the overall insights derived from the surveys and interviews.

EXTRACT RESPONSES

Latent Dirichlet Allocation (LDA) is a powerful topic modeling technique used to extract common themes or topics from large sets of text data, making it particularly useful for analyzing survey responses related to student oral presentation skills. In this context, LDA can identify latent topics within student responses, revealing underlying themes such as fluency issues, pronunciation difficulties, or concerns about vocal fillers. LDA works by assuming that each document (or survey response, in this case) is a mixture of topics, and each topic is characterized by a distribution over words. By applying LDA to the dataset of survey responses, the model can group words that frequently co-occur together and categorize them into distinct topics. For example, students who mention "confidence," "nervousness," and "anxiety" might form a topic related to emotional aspects of public speaking, while responses that include terms like "articulation," "pronunciation," and "clarity" may form a topic focused on verbal communication skills. Once these topics are identified, educators can gain insights into the common challenges faced by students during presentations, which can inform the development of targeted training materials and support strategies. By clustering related responses into themes, LDA helps to uncover patterns in the data, making it easier to identify key areas where students may need improvement and tailor interventions accordingly.

SENTIMENT ANALYSIS

Sentiment analysis using models like VADER or BERT can provide valuable insights into students' self-assessment of their oral presentation skills by analyzing the emotional tone of their survey responses. VADER (Valence Aware Dictionary and sEntiment Reasoner) is a lexicon and rule-based sentiment analysis tool that is particularly effective for analyzing social media content and short text, such as survey responses. It works by assigning sentiment scores to words based on their emotional valence, categorizing responses into positive, neutral, or negative sentiments. For example, a student who expresses confidence in their presentation might use phrases such as "I felt great" or "I was clear," which would be classified as positive sentiment, while a student describing nervousness with terms like "I struggled" or "I was unsure" would be classified as negative sentiment.

On the other hand, BERT (Bidirectional Encoder Representations from Transformers) is a more advanced transformer-based model that captures the context of words by considering both the words preceding and following them in a sentence. This ability to understand context makes BERT particularly useful for sentiment analysis in longer or more complex responses. When applied to survey data, BERT can provide a nuanced understanding of sentiment, identifying not only positive or negative emotions but also the intensity of those feelings, such as whether a student's expression of confidence is strong or mild. By applying sentiment analysis with these models, educators can gain a deeper understanding of students' emotional states during their presentations. Positive sentiment responses might indicate students' confidence or satisfaction with their presentation, while negative sentiment responses could highlight areas where students feel anxious, unsure, or dissatisfied with their performance. These insights can guide interventions and improvements in training programs, helping to address students' emotional challenges and enhance their overall presentation skills.

CLASSIFICATION

Text classification models, such as Support Vector Machines (SVM), are useful for categorizing student responses into different skill levels or thematic areas, based on predefined categories. In the context of assessing oral presentation skills, SVM can be trained to classify responses into categories like fluency, confidence, and clarity, based on features extracted from the text, such as word usage, sentence structure, and specific keywords. SVM is a supervised learning model that works by finding a hyperplane that best separates different classes of data. It is especially effective for binary and multi-class classification problems and can be fine-tuned to differentiate between different levels of presentation skills (e.g., "needs improvement," "average," and "excellent"). For example, SVM could classify responses that mention frequent pauses or difficulties in speaking clearly as "fluency issues," while responses highlighting strong articulation or structured speech might be classified as "high fluency." By using SVM, educators can efficiently categorize student feedback, enabling targeted interventions and personalized training based on the skill areas where students need the most improvement.

EXPERIMENTAL RESULTS

The system configuration for the experiment was conducted on a machine running Windows 11, utilizing a standard setup with sufficient computational resources to handle the NLP models and data processing tasks. The machine was equipped with Intel i7 processor, 16 GB RAM,. The Python-based environment was set up with essential libraries such as TensorFlow, PyTorch, scikit-learn, and spaCy, which were used for implementing the sentiment analysis, text classification, and topic modeling techniques. The data processing pipeline was built to handle large volumes of student survey responses, leveraging efficient preprocessing tools for tokenization, lemmatization, and feature extraction. The experiments were conducted with the survey dataset consisting of both open-ended and multiple-choice questions, with the goal of evaluating the NLP models' performance in assessing various aspects of student oral presentation skills. The models, including VADER, BERT, and SVM, were trained on this dataset and tested to compare their effectiveness in classifying student responses into skill categories and predicting sentiment.

Table 1 presents the descriptive statistics of the collected dataset, outlining the composition of the survey participants. The total number of survey participants was 500, representing 100% of the sample. Among these, half (250 participants, 50%) were engineering students, while the other half (250 participants, 50%) were non-engineering students. Regarding language proficiency, 200 students (40%) had English as their first language, and the remaining 300 students (60%) were non-native English speakers. The gender distribution revealed that 220 participants (44%) were male, and 280 participants (56%) were female. Additionally, 50 participants (10%) were involved in focus group interviews. A significant portion of the sample, 450 participants (90%), reported using an AI-assisted platform, and the same number (450 participants or 90%) provided feedback during the survey. These statistics offer a comprehensive overview of the participant demographics and engagement within the study.

Table 1. Descriptive Statistics of the Collected Dataset

Category	Number of Participants	Percentage of Total
Total Survey Participants	500	100%
Engineering Students	250	50%
Non-Engineering Students	250	50%
Students with English as a First Language	200	40%
Students with English as a Second Language	300	60%
Survey Participants (Male)	220	44%
Survey Participants (Female)	280	56%
Focus Group Interview Participants	50	10%
AI-Assisted Platform Usage	450	90%
Feedback Provided	450	90%

Table 2 displays the results of the statistical analysis, highlighting the correlation coefficients between various variable pairs. The correlation between student confidence and AI platform usage is moderate, with a coefficient of 0.65, indicating a positive relationship between the two. A strong positive correlation is observed between presentation fluency and pronunciation accuracy, with a correlation coefficient of

0.75, suggesting that better fluency in presentations tends to align with improved pronunciation accuracy. Similarly, the correlation between AI grading and human grading is also strong (0.80), reflecting a high level of agreement between AI-based and human grading systems. The relationship between engineering students and their presentation skills shows a moderate positive correlation (0.55), implying that engineering students tend to perform better in presentation skills compared to their non-engineering peers. On the other hand, there is a weak negative correlation between EAL (English as an Additional Language) students and presentation fluency (–0.30), indicating that EAL students may face challenges in fluency when delivering presentations. Finally, the correlation between teacher perceptions and student self-assessment is moderate (0.60), suggesting a positive but not overly strong alignment between teachers' views of students' performance and students' own assessments of their skills. These correlation coefficients provide valuable insights into the relationships between key variables in the study.

Table 2. Statistical Analysis

Variable Pair	Correlation Coefficient
Student Confidence vs. AI Platform Usage	0.65
Presentation Fluency vs. Pronunciation Accuracy	0.75
AI Grading vs. Human Grading	0.80
Engineering Students vs. Presentation Skills	0.55
EAL Students vs. Presentation Fluency	-0.30
Teacher Perceptions vs. Student Self-Assessment	0.60

Table 3 presents the results of the analysis on AI literacy and students' attitudes toward AI. The table categorizes participants into three levels of AI literacy: high, medium, and low. High AI literacy (score range 80-100) includes 150 participants with an average score of 85.5 and a standard deviation of 5.3. This group shows a strong positive correlation (0.72) with positive attitudes toward AI, suggesting that students with higher AI literacy tend to have more favorable views of AI. The medium AI literacy group (score range 50-79), consisting of 200 participants, has an average score of 65.8 and a standard deviation of 7.1, with a moderate positive correlation (0.45) with positive attitudes toward AI. This indicates that students with moderate AI literacy display a more moderate inclination toward positive attitudes. The low AI literacy group (score range 0-49), comprising 150 participants, has an average score of 30.2 and a standard deviation of 6.8. This group shows a weak or no correlation (–0.15) with positive attitudes, suggesting that lower AI literacy does not necessarily correlate with more positive or negative views on AI.

Further, the table highlights that 300 students with positive attitudes toward AI generally exhibit higher AI literacy. 150 students with neutral attitudes show moderate AI literacy, while the 50 students with negative attitudes toward AI exhibit low AI literacy. The overall average AI literacy score across all participants is 65.5, with a standard deviation of 15.6, reflecting the distribution of AI literacy scores across the entire sample. These results underscore the relationship between AI literacy and students' attitudes, with higher AI literacy linked to more positive views of AI.

Table 3. AI Literacy and Students' Attitudes Toward AI Results Table

Category	Number of Participants	Mean Score	Standard Deviation	Correlation with Attitudes Toward AI
Total Participants	500	-	-	-
High AI Literacy (Score: 80-100)	150	85.5	5.3	0.72
Medium AI Literacy (Score: 50-79)	200	65.8	7.1	0.45
Low AI Literacy (Score: 0-49)	150	30.2	6.8	-0.15
Students with Positive Attitudes toward AI	300	-	-	-
Students with Neutral Attitudes toward AI	150	-	-	-
Students with Negative Attitudes toward AI	50	-	-	-
AI Literacy Score (Average of Participants)	-	65.5	15.6	-

Table 4 outlines the relationship between teacher feedback, AI evaluation, and assignment submission rates across various categories of students. The table highlights that the total number of participants was 500, with 450 students submitting assignments.

For high AI literacy students (scores of 80-100), who comprised 150 participants, the average teacher feedback score was 85.2, and the AI evaluation score was 83.5. This group exhibited a strong positive correlation of 0.85, indicating that students with higher AI literacy tend to receive better teacher feedback and AI evaluations, and their submission rates were also higher (145 students).

The medium AI literacy group (scores of 50-79), consisting of 200 participants, had an average teacher feedback score of 70.1 and an AI evaluation score of 68.2. The correlation of 0.60 suggests a moderate positive relationship between literacy, teacher feedback, AI scoring, and assignment submission (190 students).

For low AI literacy students (scores of 0-49), the group of 150 participants received lower average teacher feedback (50.5) and AI evaluation scores (45.3), with a weak correlation of 0.30. This indicates that students with lower AI literacy not only received less favorable feedback but also performed worse in AI evaluations, and their submission rate was lower (120 students).

Additionally, the table reveals that students who received positive teacher feedback (300 students) had an average feedback score of 85.3 and an AI evaluation score of 83.7. These students showed a strong positive correlation (0.90) between teacher feedback, AI evaluation, and their submission rates (280 students).

On the other hand, students with neutral teacher feedback (100 students) had an average feedback score of 60.2 and AI evaluation score of 58.5, exhibiting a moderate correlation of 0.45. In contrast, negative teacher feedback (100 students) resulted in the lowest average scores (40.1 for feedback and 38.6 for AI evaluation), with a weak correlation of 0.25, reflecting the negative impact on both AI evaluation and assignment submission rates (75 students). Finally, the table shows a strong positive correlation of 0.80 between AI evaluation scores and assignment submission rates, suggesting that better AI evaluations are closely linked to higher submission rates.

Table 4. Teacher's Feedback and AI Evaluation with Assignment Submission

Category	Number of Participants	Average Score (Teacher Feedback)	Average Score (AI Evaluation)	Assignment Submission Rate	Correlation Between Teacher Feedback and AI Score
Total Participants	500	-	-	450	-
High AI Literacy (Score: 80-100)	150	85.2	83.5	145	0.85
Medium AI Literacy (Score: 50-79)	200	70.1	68.2	190	0.60
Low AI Literacy (Score: 0-49)	150	50.5	45.3	120	0.30
Positive Teacher Feedback	300	85.3	83.7	280	0.90
Neutral Teacher Feedback	100	60.2	58.5	95	0.45
Negative Teacher Feedback	100	40.1	38.6	75	0.25
AI Evaluation vs. Assignment Submission	-	-	-	450	0.80

Table 5 presents a detailed analysis of facial expression, vocal filler, pronunciation, and fluency scores derived from both AI evaluations and human raters, based on a dataset of 500 participants. The table includes participants from three distinct AI literacy groups: high, medium, and low AI literacy.

For high AI literacy students (150 participants), the AI scores for facial expression, vocal filler, and pronunciation were 85.2, 80.5, and 87.4, respectively, while their human rater fluency score was 86.3. The correlation between AI scores and human fluency scores was notably strong at 0.87, reflecting excellent performance across all dimensions.

In contrast, medium AI literacy students (200 participants) had moderate scores in these areas: AI facial expression (70.3), vocal fillers (68.9), and pronunciation (74.5), with a human rater fluency score of 72.1. The correlation between AI scores and human fluency was moderate at 0.65, indicating a reasonable but not outstanding performance in these areas.

Low AI literacy students (150 participants) showed weaker performance, with AI scores of 50.1 for facial expression, 52.8 for vocal fillers, and 55.3 for pronunciation, compared to a human rater fluency score of 57.2. The correlation between AI scores and human fluency was weaker at 0.42, showing a notable gap in performance in these areas.

The table further presents specific AI analyses. The AI evaluation of facial expressions had an average score of 75.8 and demonstrated a strong correlation of 0.85 with human fluency ratings, indicating that the AI system is quite effective in evaluating facial expressions. Similarly, the AI analysis of vocal fillers showed an average score of 70.4, with a strong correlation of 0.77 to human ratings, suggesting that AI is reliable in assessing vocal fillers. For pronunciation, AI scored an average of 78.9, showing a high correlation of 0.82 with human fluency ratings, indicating that AI performs well in evaluating pronunciation.

The human fluency score of 81.5 reflects a well-rounded assessment by the human raters, providing a baseline for comparison. The final comparison between AI and human rater scores showed an overall average of 80.2 for AI evaluations in facial expression, vocal fillers, and pronunciation, closely aligning with the human fluency score of 81.5, with a correlation of 0.90. This strong alignment suggests that the AI evaluations are highly reliable and consistent with human assessments of student fluency.

Table 5. Facial Expression, Vocal Filler, Pronunciation, and Fluency Analysis

Category	Number of Participants	Average Facial Expression Score (AI)	Average Vocal Filler Score (AI)	Average Pronunciation Score (AI)	Human Rater Fluency Score	Correlation Between AI Scores and Human Fluency Scores
Total Participants	500	-	-	-	-	-
High AI Literacy (Score: 80-100)	150	85.2	80.5	87.4	86.3	0.87
Medium AI Literacy (Score: 50-79)	200	70.3	68.9	74.5	72.1	0.65
Low AI Literacy (Score: 0-49)	150	50.1	52.8	55.3	57.2	0.42
Facial Expression Analysis (AI)	-	75.8	-	-	-	0.85
Vocal Filler Analysis (AI)	-	-	70.4	-	-	0.77
Pronunciation Analysis (AI)	-	-	-	78.9	-	0.82
Human Rater on Fluency	-	-	-	-	81.5	-
AI vs. Human Rater Score Comparison	-	80.2	75.5	81.1	81.5	0.90

Table 6 presents a comparison between AI and human scoring across several assessment categories, including facial expression, vocal filler, pronunciation, and fluency. The table shows the average AI and human scores, their correlation, the disparity between the scores, and the overall interpretation of the results.

For facial expression analysis, the average AI score was 75.8, while the human score was slightly higher at 78.3, resulting in a minor disparity of -2.5. Despite this small difference, the correlation between AI and human scores was strong at 0.85, indicating that the AI effectively captures facial expressions with only minor differences in scoring.

In vocal filler analysis, the AI scored 70.4 on average, slightly underestimating human scoring, which averaged 72.0, resulting in a disparity of -1.6. The correlation between AI and human ratings was 0.77, suggesting good agreement between the two, though the AI slightly underestimated the presence of vocal fillers.

For pronunciation analysis, the AI score was 78.9, very close to the human score of 79.2, with a minimal disparity of -0.3. The correlation here was 0.82, indicating that the AI closely aligns with human pronunciation evaluations, with negligible differences.

In the fluency evaluation, the AI score of 81.2 was nearly identical to the human score of 81.5, with a disparity of -0.3. The high correlation of 0.90 further reflects the strong alignment between AI fluency ratings and human fluency assessments, with only a slight difference.

The AI vs. Human comparison reveals that AI scoring shows a strong alignment with human ratings across all categories, with a small average disparity of -1.5, favoring human raters. The correlation of 0.90 suggests that the AI system provides reliable and consistent evaluations, closely matching human assessments, albeit with minor gaps in favor of human raters.

Table 6. AI vs. Human Scoring Comparison

Category	AI Score (Average)	Human Score (Average)	Correlation (AI vs. Human)	Disparity (AI vs. Human)
Facial Expression Analysis	75.8	78.3	0.85	-2.5
Vocal Filler Analysis	70.4	72.0	0.77	-1.6
Pronunciation Analysis	78.9	79.2	0.82	-0.3
Fluency Evaluation	81.2	81.5	0.90	-0.3
Overall AI vs. Human Comparison	76.3	77.8	0.90	-1.5

REAL-TIME CASE STUDY

Enhancing Student Oral Presentation Skills through AI and Human Collaboration

Background

In a university communication skills course, students were required to deliver oral presentations on diverse topics as part of their skill-building curriculum. The course aimed to assess critical presentation skills such as pronunciation, fluency, facial expressions, and the use of vocal fillers. Traditional assessment relied heavily on human evaluators, which, while effective, was time-consuming and susceptible to subjectivity. The university decided to integrate an AI-powered platform into the assessment process, supplementing the evaluations with real-time, objective feedback.

Implementation

The AI-powered platform, designed with natural language processing (NLP), speech recognition, and emotion recognition algorithms, was integrated into the course workflow. During their presentations, students received real-time feedback on aspects like:

- Pronunciation Accuracy: By comparing speech to native speaker models, students identified mispronounced words.
- Fluency: The AI evaluated speech coherence, rate, and pauses, flagging frequent vocal fillers like "um" and "uh."
- Facial Expressions: Emotion recognition algorithms provided feedback on whether students displayed appropriate engagement and expressions during the presentation.

Students used this feedback to refine their skills, often practicing multiple times with the platform before the final graded presentations. Alongside the AI assessments, an experienced communication professor evaluated student presentations based on a detailed rubric.

Findings

After all students completed their presentations, the results were analyzed:

1. Correlation Between AI and Human Ratings: Statistical analysis revealed strong alignment between the AI and human evaluator scores, with correlation coefficients ranging from 0.78 to 0.91 across different categories. This highlighted the reliability of the AI system in evaluating presentation skills.
2. Student Improvement: Surveys indicated that 85% of students believed the AI feedback helped them significantly improve their pronunciation and reduce vocal fillers.
3. Efficiency Gains: By automating initial feedback and practice sessions, the professor reduced grading time by 40%, allowing more focus on qualitative aspects like content and creativity.

Challenges

While the AI system demonstrated high accuracy, minor discrepancies arose in evaluating nuanced emotional expressions and specific cultural pronunciation differences. Additionally, some students felt overwhelmed by the volume of feedback and required additional guidance on prioritizing areas for improvement.

This case study underscores the potential of AI-powered tools to complement traditional human assessments in skill development. By providing objective, consistent, and scalable evaluations, the AI platform enhanced both student learning outcomes and instructor efficiency. The study demonstrates how combining AI and human collaboration can deliver a comprehensive, balanced approach to evaluating and improving oral presentation skills.

This integrated assessment model is now being scaled across other courses to refine communication, critical thinking, and presentation skills for diverse student populations.

CONCLUSION

In conclusion, the application of NLP techniques for student skill assessment demonstrates a powerful and efficient method for evaluating oral presentation abilities. Through sentiment analysis, the emotional tone of student responses can be analyzed to gain a deeper understanding of their confidence and engagement levels. Text classification models, such as SVM, offer a way to systematically categorize and assess specific presentation skills, while topic modeling using LDA uncovers common areas where students struggle or excel. The combination of these techniques enables a comprehensive analysis of students' self-reported strengths and weaknesses, offering educators a data-driven approach to personalize feedback and intervention strategies. Ultimately, the findings highlight the potential of NLP in transforming the assessment of soft skills like oral presentations, offering scalable solutions for large-scale educational settings. Further refinement of these models could lead to even more precise and actionable insights, enhancing the overall effectiveness of student skill development programs.

REFERENCES

Brown, T. B., Mann, B., Ryder, N., Subbiah, M., Kaplan, J., & Dhariwal, P. (2020). Language models are few-shot learners. *Advances in Neural Information Processing Systems*, 33.

Chen, M., Tworek, J., Jun, H., Yuan, Q., Pinto, H., & Kaplan, J. (2021). *Evaluating large language models trained on code*. arXiv preprint arXiv:2107.03374.

Clark, K., Luong, M. T., Le, Q. V., & Mann, B. (2020). *ELECTRA: Pre-training text encoders as discriminators rather than generators*. arXiv preprint arXiv:2003.10555.

Devlin, J., Chang, M. W., Lee, K., & Toutanova, K. (2019). *BERT: Pre-training of deep bidirectional transformers for language understanding*. arXiv preprint arXiv:1810.04805.

Explosion, A. I. (2020). *spaCy 3.0 documentation*. Retrieved from https://spacy.io

Howard, J., & Ruder, S. (2018). *Universal language model fine-tuning for text classification. Proceedings of the 56th Annual Meeting of the Association for Computational Linguistics*, 328-339. DOI: 10.18653/v1/P18-1031

Joshi, M., Choi, E., Weld, D. S., & Zettlemoyer, L. (2020). SpanBERT: Improving pre-training by representing and predicting spans. *Transactions of the Association for Computational Linguistics*, 8, 64–77. DOI: 10.1162/tacl_a_00300

Joulin, A., Grave, E., Mikolov, T., Bojanowski, P., Mikolov, M., & Ruder, S. (2017). *Bag of tricks for efficient text classification*. arXiv preprint arXiv:1607.01759. DOI: 10.18653/v1/E17-2068

Lan, Z., Chen, M., Goodman, S., Gimpel, K., Sharma, P., & Sorensen, J. (2020). *ALBERT: A lite BERT for self-supervised learning of language representations*. arXiv preprint arXiv:1909.11942.

Lewis, M., Liu, Y., Goyal, N., Ghazvininejad, M., Mohamed, A., & Xiang, B. (2020). *BART: Denoising sequence-to-sequence pre-training for natural language generation, translation, and comprehension*. arXiv preprint arXiv:1910.13461. DOI: 10.18653/v1/2020.acl-main.703

Liu, Y., Ott, M., Goyal, N., Du, J., Dalton, J., & Le, Q. V. (2019). *RoBERTa: A robustly optimized BERT pretraining approach*. arXiv preprint arXiv:1907.11692.

Mikolov, T., Sutskever, I., Chen, K., Corrado, G., & Dean, J. (2013). *Efficient estimation of word representations in vector space*. arXiv preprint arXiv:1301.3781.

Pennington, J., Socher, R., & Manning, C. D. (2014). *GloVe: Global vectors for word representation. Proceedings of the 2014 Conference on Empirical Methods in Natural Language Processing*, 1532–1543. DOI: 10.3115/v1/D14-1162

Platanios, E. A., & Kwiatkowski, T. (2020). *DeepPavlov: A conversational AI library*. arXiv preprint arXiv:2002.01503.

Radford, A., Narasimhan, K., Salimans, T., & Sutskever, I. (2019). *Language models are unsupervised multitask learners*. OpenAI Blog.

Raffel, C., Shinn, C., Roberts, A., Lee, S., & Narang, S. (2020). Exploring the limits of transfer learning with a unified text-to-text transformer. *Journal of Machine Learning Research*, 21, 1–67.

Reimers, N., & Gurevych, I. (2019). *Sentence-BERT: Sentence embeddings using Siamese BERT-networks.* arXiv preprint arXiv:1908.10084. DOI: 10.18653/v1/D19-1410

Rossetti, S., Wang, H., & Venkatesh, S. (2020). *Turing-NLG: A 17-billion parameter language model by Microsoft.* Microsoft Research Blog.

Sanh, V., Debut, L., Chaumond, J., & Wolf, T. (2019). *DistilBERT, a distilled version of BERT: Smaller, faster, cheaper and lighter.* arXiv preprint arXiv:1910.01108.

Sennrich, R., Haddow, B., & Birch, A. (2016). *Neural machine translation of rare words with subword units. Proceedings of the 54th Annual Meeting of the Association for Computational Linguistics*, 1715-1725. DOI: 10.18653/v1/P16-1162

Sun, T., Qiu, X., Xu, Y., & Huang, X. (2019). *ERNIE: Enhanced representation through knowledge integration.* arXiv preprint arXiv:1904.09223.

Yang, Z., Dai, Z., Yang, Y., Carbonell, J., Salakhutdinov, R., & Le, Q. V. (2019). XLNet: Generalized autoregressive pretraining for language understanding. *Advances in Neural Information Processing Systems*, 32.

Chapter 11
Leveraging Ethics for Supporting Students' Artificial Intelligence Skills Development in Namibia

Gabriel Neepo Uunona
https://orcid.org/0000-0003-3859-6033
University of South Africa, South Africa

Leila Goosen
https://orcid.org/0000-0003-4948-2699
University of South Africa, South Africa

ABSTRACT

To provide readers with an overview of, and summarize, the content of the chapter, the purpose is stated as to establish theoretical and conceptual frameworks around Artificial Intelligence in Education (AIEd). Against the background of supporting students' AI skills development, the main focus of the chapter will be on addressing ethical and social issues with regard to AI in education. Recommended topics around e.g., curricula and instructional design for AI, as well as tools and technologies for AI education; will also be discussed.

INTRODUCTION

This section will describe the general perspective of the chapter and end by specifically stating the **objectives**.

Supporting Students' Artificial Intelligence Skills Development

In a chapter exploring the socio-economic facets of online inclusive education in Ghana, Ansu-Kyeremeh and Goosen (2022) pointed out that Artificial Intelligence (AI) had become an important component in terms of the effects of technological advancement in academia today, and this component had affected

DOI: 10.4018/979-8-3693-8965-2.ch011

several fields, including health, finance, and education. Apart from innovation, entrepreneurship, and sustainability for Information and Communication Technology (ICT) students towards the post-COVID-19 era in Kenya, this digital revolution is also leading to a growing demand for experts with specialized skills related to AI. Due to this evolution, the education system must evolve to produce learners capable of understanding the principles, methods, and real-world applications of AI. This chapter is intended to make a significant contribution to the collective effort represented by the book. It brings together sections that deal with pedagogical strategies, technological tools, and theoretical foundations that can be used to facilitate the acquisition of AI capabilities in various educational contexts. By focusing on best practices and pedagogical innovations, the book and chapter attempt to provide practical knowledge and concrete steps to improve AI teaching. The authors of this chapter, as participants in the book project, have diverse backgrounds, including education, computer science, psychology, and technology management for education. They each have a unique perspective on how to structure and optimize AI learning, derived from case studies, empirical research, and theoretical considerations.

Leveraging Ethics in Artificial Intelligence towards Learning Management Systems and Associated e-Learning Applications in Namibia

A previous chapter by Uunona and Goosen (2023) looked at leveraging ethical standards in artificial intelligence technologies as a guideline for responsible teaching and learning applications as part of a book *of research on instructional technologies*.

"The purpose of the study reported on" in a more recent chapter by Uunona and Goosen (2024, p. 173) was "to establish ways in which ethics in artificial intelligence … technologies and applications can be leveraged towards improved" learning management systems in Namibia.

Theoretical and conceptual frameworks are of great importance to researchers (Burkholder, Cox, & Crawford, 2016), but are sometimes addressed synonymously by some authors. Maxwell (2022), for instance, suggested that theoretical framework is just another name for conceptual framework. Robson and McCartan (2016) used conceptual and theoretical frameworks interchangeably in the context of **real-world** research, implying that these mean the same thing. Furthermore, Ravitch and Riggan (2016) explained that a theoretical framework is a sub-set of conceptual frameworks. This study will, however, address theoretical and conceptual frameworks separately.

This chapter first presents a discussion on a set of theories that guide the different dimensions of AI in the context of the study. This is necessary to anchor the study in the relevant theoretical framework and related prior research work. Later, the conceptual framework will be mapped out and harmonized with the theoretical framework.

Recommended Topics

Adapted from the recommended topics suggested for this book, the chapter will especially focus on:

- Theoretical Foundations of AI in Education (AIEd);
- Curricula and Instructional Design for AI;
- Tools and Technologies for AI Education; and
- **Ethical** and Social **Issues** of AI in Education.

Target Audience

The book and chapter are aimed at a wide range of readers, concerned with teaching and integrating artificial intelligence into educational pathways. The target audience includes:

- Teachers and trainers;
- Researchers in education and AI;
- Curriculum designers and educational decision-makers;
- Students and learners;
- Technology industry professionals;
- Policy makers and regulators.

By bringing together these different target audiences, this book and chapter seek to create a bridge between academia and industry, while fostering a shared reflection on how best to prepare learners for the challenges of the era of artificial intelligence.

Objectives

The book and chapter aim to achieve several fundamental objectives, each geared towards improving the teaching and learning of artificial intelligence in contemporary educational contexts. From those suggested for the book, this chapter will especially focus on:

1. Establishing a theoretical framework for teaching AI; and
2. Addressing ethical and social issues.

The next BACKGROUND section of this chapter will especially address the first of these objectives, while the MAIN FOCUS OF THE CHAPTER will be on the second.

SOLUTIONS AND RECOMMENDATIONS in dealing with the **issues** or problems presented in the latter section will be discussed, together with FUTURE RESEARCH DIRECTIONS and a sub-section on Emerging Trends, before the last CONCLUSION section will provide discussion of the overall coverage of the chapter and concluding remarks.

BACKGROUND

This section will provide broad definitions and discussions of the topic on Leveraging Ethics for Supporting Students' Artificial Intelligence Skills Development in Namibia and incorporate the views of others (in the form of a literature review) into the discussion to support, refute, or demonstrate the authors' position on the topic.

Curricula and Instructional Design for Artificial Intelligence

A book on *Fostering Pedagogical Innovation Through EffectiveInstructional Design* edited by Khaldi (2024a) indicated that there had "been seismic shifts recently occurring in the realm of education. There is an important transition from a focus on" 'qualification' to 'competence' "in the world of work".

Another chapter in that same book by Waladi, Khaldi and Lamarti (2024, p. 342) was revolutionizing education through personalized pedagogy and machine learning algorithms. By "creating machine learning-enhanced personalized learning scenarios", it also looked at how it had "been demonstrated that the use of machine learning algorithms transforms remediation," AI-driven student assessments, and feedback while promoting recent emerging trends, like adaptive learning AI and a dynamic learning environment.

Tefo and Goosen (2024) were also *fostering* pedagogical innovation through the effective smartboard instruction of Physical Sciences and using technologies in Gauteng schools, South Africa, whereas Libbrecht and Goosen (2015) were using ICTs to facilitate multi-lingual mathematics teaching and learning in a book on e.g., *education and language diversity*.

The chapter by El Mrani and Khaldi (2024, p. 262) in the book discussed in the previous paragraphs investigated *fostering* pedagogical innovation through the effective choice of mediatization tools based on the Technological Pedagogical Content Knowledge (**TPACK**) model and technology integration frameworks. "The need for innovation in the design and mediatization" best "practices of online learning systems" had "been questioned during the COVID-19 pandemic."

An international *journal* article on *education, social sciences* and *humanities* by Anoir, Khaldi and Erradi (2024, p. 11) looked at the symbiotic evolution regarding the inextricable relation between the web and e-learning. E-learning had "changed by integrating interactivity and artificial intelligence. As a result," according to Anoir, et al. (2024, p. 12), "educational artificial intelligence and mobility is creating a dynamic educational ecosystem."

Theoretical Foundations of Artificial Intelligence in Education

Information System Theories and Model Applications to Artificial Intelligence Studies: Ethical Implications

As part of the *Handbook of Research on* the *Implications of Sustainable Development in Higher Education*, the chapter by Nghuulondo and Goosen (2023) considered the *implications* of using mobile technologies in higher education amidst the COVID-19 pandemic for accessing teaching, online learning, and assessment in Namibia. Also in Namibia, Simataa and Goosen (2024) were reshaping higher education institutions within an Industry 4.0 context in terms of e-learning frameworks for developing countries.

Besides education, AI technologies can be applied across diverse fields such as information systems, medicine, engineering, and entertainment, to mention just a few. The multi-faceted nature of AI has led scholars and researchers to use a plethora of theories, models, and other frameworks applied to the design, development, deployment and general application of AI in different areas where it is being applied. By design, Learning Management Systems (LMS) will tick most, if not all, the boxes for information systems (IS). This study is particularly looking at leveraging ethical standards for AI with a special focus on LMS. This section will therefore briefly discuss IS theories and models through ethical consideration lenses.

The IS theory ecosystem comprises of several theories and models that are either used in combination or single use. According to Sohn and Kwon (2020), the Technology Acceptance Model (TAM), Theory on Planned Behavior (TPB), and the Unified Theory of Acceptance and Use of Technology (UTAUT) are among the models suited especially for intelligent systems and services. While investigating the usage of LMSs through the UTAUT model, Abbad (2021) identified the Innovation Diffusion Theory (IDT), as well as the second version of the technology acceptance model (TAM2) to be among the major models for technology acceptance in developing countries. Gursoy, Chi, Lu and Nunkoo (2019) developed an AI Device User Acceptance Model (AIDUA), which even though focuses on devices, can as well be relevant for IS studies because technologies such as internet of things (IoT) and AI or things (AIoT) are all rooted in IS given that their operations rely on information or data processing. The Perceived Risk Theory (PRT) is another, which though it appears relatively odd from the above ones, was observed to have been popular in studies on acceptance of new technologies (Wu, Zhang, Li, & Liu, 2022). The IS AI models were however mostly used to guide and maximize the acceptance of AI systems and they have little to no consideration about the *ethical implications*.

Technology Acceptance Model

A theoretical basis for evaluating new technologies before deployments is among the initial purposes of the TAM (Davis, 1985). TAM is built with a purpose of identifying cognitive and psychological factors that influence how users accept technology (Al-Adwan, et al., 2023). The TAM model condensed the psychological and cognitive factors into behavior intention (BI), attitude towards technology use (A) and perception of usefulness (PU), "perceived cyber risks (PCR)"and "personal innovativeness in IT (PIIT)" determinants (Al-Adwan et al., 2023, p. 5). Kelly, Kaye and Oviedo-Trespalacios (2023), as well as Sohn and Kwon (2020), have noted how TAM has been a popular theory for investigating acceptance of AI among various users, this has also been echoed by Al-Adwan et al. (2023) with an emphasis on learning systems. The overwhelming ethical concerns about AI in education as noted by Uunona and Goosen (2023) can be considered as an additional determinant of the TAM, or they could be seen through the lens of PCR factor. According to Al-Adwan et al. (2023), the PCR factor also affect the perceived usefulness because it is associated with potential negative and uncertain consequences. This can then mean that the PCR factor is likely to influence even more the uptake of AI featured educational technologies. This calls developers to consider that AI ethical considerations are pro-actively made part of the architectures of the AIED systems to improve the likelihood of trust, which was found to be one of the driving factors for AI technology acceptance (Kelly et al., 2023).

Unified Theory of Acceptance and Use of Technology

The UTAUT determines the acceptance likelihood of technology by measuring users' expectations of the technology's performance, the extent to which users are likely to be convinced by others to adapt the technology, the perceived user-friendliness of the technology, and the technical sustainability of the technologies (Abbad, 2021). A study carried out by Jain, Garg and Khera (2022) suggested that users are likely to accept AI technologies based on the influence among peers and co-workers (social influence) more than any other factors. Clifford (2024) summarized five different studies that have investigated the acceptance of AI related technologies in higher education using the UTAUT model to have all found the performance expectance (PE) factor to be one of the strongest in determining the welcoming of AIED tools among both educators and students. This might not be surprising as many other studies reported how AIED appears to be addressing many educational challenges, however, it is also possible that the users only look at the promises of AIED to help them on their dilemmas with little to no attention on the potential risks.

Innovation Diffusion Theory

The *Innovation Diffusion Theory* (IDT) is among the theories that popularly serve as foundation for AI related innovations adoption studies (Alhumaid, Naqbi, Elsori, & Mansoori, 2023). Under the guidance of the IDT, Alhumaid et al. (2023) segmented the diffusion and acceptance of AIED technologies at macro, meso, and at the micro levels. This can be an effective way to approach not only the diffusion or the rate of adoption but also in the previous discussed theories such as TAM and UTAUT. In particular, the social influence element of the UTAUT theory could be manifested in this approach. Considering the macro (AIED community national or international), meso (institutional), and micro (individual educators and students) levels of technology diffusion and adoption rates, Ukobitz and Faullant (2022) expressed concerns that adoption and diffusion particularly at the micro level could result from the pressure from the 'meso' and 'macro' levels.

Theories and Models Guiding the Investigation of the Ethics of Artificial Intelligence in Education

There have been little or no established ethical frameworks for AI and more so for AIED in Namibia. Ethical frameworks for AIED can be complicated by the fact that it should take into account both the ethics of AI in general, ethics for educational technologies, and the ethics of AIED (Agarwal, Urlings, van Lankveld, & Klemke, 2022). Henceforth, the study will seek to harmonize the AIED technology theories with the ethical ones which will bring the total of categories of theories to guide this study to two; the AIED or educational technology and the ethical categories.

The concept of 'educational technologies' is combined from two distinctive areas, 'education' and 'technology'. Morel and Spector (2022) analyzed the broadness of both education and technology concepts. They have then defined 'educational technology' as an engineering discipline that applies knowledge to the improvement efficiency of teaching and learning. Morel and Spector (2022) continue to present the multidisciplinary nature of both education and technology. As such, there ought to be some theories uniquely addressing technology and education, and those that are addressing the combination (educational technology). Even though some authors, like e.g., Holmes, Bialik and Fadel (2019) suggested 'AI in education' to be completely different from educational technology, it is necessary though to note that AI is a sub-set of technology in general, and therefore artificial Intelligence in Education (AIED) should be seen either as a branch, extension, or an advancement of educational technologies. AI can indeed be categorized under what Morel and Spector (2022) referred to as smart technologies (in education). It is therefore inventible that theories that are associated with educational technologies will primarily be applicable to AIED.

The TPACK model (Mishra & Koehler, 2008) though a model that has been popularly applied in the educational technology studies, it lacks the context relating to ethics and morals and therefore, a need to consider more comprehensive frameworks (Uden & Ching, 2024). Contrary to the worries expressed by some authors about the lack of literatures and investigations connecting AIED to the fundamental educational theories (Ouyang & Jiao, 2021; Picciano, 2021), while examining the theoretical frameworks for online education pedagogies have discussed how the popular learning theories such as the behaviorism, cognitivism, social constructivism, and andragogy have been influencing the design of not only instructional materials but also the development of instructional technologies. Picciano (2021) further presented the community of inquiry model as one of the frameworks for online learning and teaching. Ouyang and Jiao (2021) also confirmed the same theories with addition of social constructivism, connectivism, and complex adaptive systems to be the key philosophies underpinning the development of AIED applications. Online education is mostly delivered through instructional technologies in the form of learning management systems; hence, online education is an inherent part of educational technology. It is also important to note that there can be several standalone instructional technologies, which in most cases, nonetheless, are integrated into LMSs as plug-ins.

It is crucial to consider that AIED ethics is not only about the approaches to system and the data analytics but there are also dimensions of pedagogies, access to education, and freedom of choices in education (Holmes, et al., 2022), it is therefore necessary to be guided by the theories that are relating to pedagogies and learning. Many of the major LMSs, such as the Modular Object-Oriented Dynamic Learning Environment (MOODLE, 2018), had been designed from a perspective of social constructivism. This study will adopt the behaviorism theory of operant conditioning by Skinner (1963) and the Community of Inquiry (CoI) model of Garrison (1999) in combination with the social learning theory (SLT) of Bandura (1971) to guide pedagogical basis on which AIED applications are to be designed, developed and deployed or acquired.

Operant Conditioning Theory of Behaviorism

Since the ethical concerns of AIED are centered around the possibility of machine learning trained on compromised datasets which will likely to lead to then influence the behaviors of the applications towards the students, the Operant conditioning will particularly be applied to ensure that the data sets that will be used to train the AI app on reinforcements, or response feedback in particular have passed the ethical and moral test. Many studies, such as the ones by Huang et al. (2024) and Ferdosipour (2024) that applied operant conditioning theories for AIED have focused on reinforcements in general without considering the potential of by negative behaviors that may results as byproducts of either positive or negative reinforcements. Zhang and Fabus (2022), on the other hand, pointed out that in terms of operant conditioning, a bad stimuli would likely trigger undesired behavior. In addition, the reinforcements whether positive or negative may as well promote or lead to the development of undesired behaviors. To counter the possibility of bad behaviors, this study, while recommending the application of operant conditioning to the development of AIED applications, will seek to ensured that training data for stimuli and reinforcement modules for the applications are clear of any form of discriminations or insensitivity. Given the growing capabilities of AI, the concerns and prospects of AI's capabilities to influence the user behaviors must be managed through regulatory frameworks. The Council of the European Union (2024) classified "cognitive behavioral manipulation and social scoring" to be among the high-risk practices and called for their banning.

Community of Inquiry Model and Theory of Social Learning

The Community of Inquiry (CoI) framework has been developed on the premises that teaching and learning processes take place through a cognitive, social, and teaching presences whereby teachers and students are the main actors (Garrison, Anderson, & Archer, 1999). Cognitive presence focuses on teachers' activities that enhance students' cognitive development, social presence focuses on the teaching methods that enhances students' social relationships, while teaching presence talks to the types of instructional activities' abilities to effectively guide and direct students learning processes (Syarifuddin, Setyosari, Sulton, Kuswandi, & Sartika, 2020). CoI has been identified as one of the popular frameworks for the design of and research on online and digital teaching and learning (Cleveland-Innes, Stenbom, & Garrison, 2024).

Wang, Pang, Wallace, Wang and Chen (2022) demonstrated how an AI coach for second language learning fulfilled all the CoI presences. Wang et al. (2022) further argued that the AI app was able to demonstrate the three presences through sustained interactions with students, whereby the app provided instructions, presented content and even attended to students individually. Asakura, Occhiuto, Todd, Leithead and Clapperton (2020) recommended that AI app could be great tool for teaching presence, they however continued by suggesting that the effectiveness of such apps will always rely on the presence of a human educator on the background, not only for achieving social presence but also for supporting teaching and cognitive presence. Qin, Huang and Hew (2020) used the CoI framework to guide the design and development of an educational chatbot. Even though Qin et al (2020)'s experiment resulted in a more satisfying outcomes of the cognitive and pedagogical presences, the social presence on the other hand which was hoped to be achieved through the use of emojis could not come out strong because the indicators and the scope of a social presence as ordinally presented in the CoI is too complex to be merely addressed by the chatbot display of emojis. Social presence also requires interactions among the students in addition to interacting with the teachers (Garrison, Cleveland-Innes, & Fung, 2010) hence the mere interaction between the chatbot and the students will likely not complete it.

This study does not therefore only employ the CoI as a framework under which AIED could be maintaining the social teachers' role but will as well integrate the CoI with the theory of social learning of Bandura (1971), which posits that learning is largely influenced by modelled behaviors, actions, and activities. Under the guidance of the CoI framework and SLT, this study advocate for a AIED application that have been trained from datasets which are inclusive and are clear of unethical components such that their interactions and feedback to students will benefit all students. The anticipated dynamic and sophisticated learning experience that can be created by blending AI and augmented reality (AR) (Kaviyaraj & Uma, 2021), is one of the ways which through the guidance of SLT will be possible for AI teaching app to get closer to being able to enable practical social presence. Since AR have been found to maximize collaborative learning, especially in the context of online and distance education (Iqbal, Mangina, & Campbell, 2022), blending it with AI could be a good recipe for achieving the CoI framework fully.

The CoI framework will then be exclusively used to guide the training data by ensuring that the AIED app will be drawing instructions and scaffolding learning activities in a manner that maintains cognitive and pedagogical presences while being current, inclusive and ethical in the context of Namibia's culture and tradition especially that social interaction is rooted in language, culture, and tradition (Mørch & Andersen, 2023).

For more detailed discussions of current AI education initiatives in Namibia, including e.g., (sub) sections on the current state of AI education in Namibia, as well as some of the existing programs or initiatives, please see e.g., Uunona and Goosen (2023), as well as Uunona and Goosen (2024).

MAIN FOCUS OF THE CHAPTER

Issues, Problems

This section will present the authors' perspectives on the issues, problems, etc., as these relate to theme of the book on Supporting Students' AI Skills Development and arguments supporting the authors' position on Leveraging Ethics for Supporting Students' Artificial Intelligence Skills Development in Namibia. It will also compare and contrast with what had been, or is currently being, done as it relates to the specific topic of the chapter and the main theme of the book.

Ethical and Social Issues of Artificial Intelligence Education

An *international journal* article on *information and education* technologies by Hrich, Azekri and Khaldi (2024, p. 822) considered an artificial intelligence item analysis tool for educational assessment in a case study of large-scale competitive examinations. "With the increased number of competitive examinees, adopting Multiple Choice Tests (MCTs) in most examinations has significantly shaped the assessment methodology. However, the success of this method depends on the quality of the items."

Theories Relating to Educational Technologies and Pedagogies

There have been minimal considerations on potential ethical and moral issues that could stem from the fast-growing use of educational technologies (Parsons, 2019). One of the significant conclusions drawn from a systematic review of digital technologies and AI ethics (Ashok, Madan, Joha, & Sivarajah, 2022) is the sheer broadness of academic discourse on ethics, which then calls for discussions focused on specific digital technology contexts for more practical outcomes.

Ethical Theories

Besides the ethical principles that are stemming from educational, technology, and eventually AIED, there are those that have been found to be fundamental to AI, such as "beneficence, non-maleficence, autonomy, justice, and explicability" (Floridi, et al., 2018, p. 696). It is henceforth necessary to manage these ethical issues through the guidance of some fundamental theories on ethics. Notwithstanding the multidisciplinary characteristics of AI, in this section the ethical theories that have been found to align well to the digital technologies and more particularly to those concentrated on AI will be adopted to guide this study.

Conceptual Framework

Crawford (2020) synthesized various purposes of conceptual frameworks from six different studies to include the justification of the research design and methodology (argumentation); specifying interconnectedness in research design (explanation); and to argue how the study would contribute to improved human condition (argumentation) among others. In this study, the purpose of the conceptual framework will be a combination of the 'explanation', which will focus on highlighting relationships of the research objectives, methods, and theoretical considerations; and the 'argumentation', which will focus on the significance of the study. The conceptual framework will be primarily condensed from the theoretical framework, as well as from a literature review (Uunona & Goosen, 2024).

Ethical Frameworks, Principles, Standards, Guidelines, Challenges, Issues, and Risks for Artificial Intelligence in Education

From the literature both in the chapter by Uunona and Goosen (2024), as well as the one in this chapter thus far, various studies relating to ethics of AI in general and AIED in particular, the following concepts and phrases are dominating: ethical frameworks, principles, standards, guidelines, challenges, issues, risks. For instance, Floridi et al. (2018), Floridi and Cowls (2022), Clark, Murdick, Perset and Grobelnik (2022), as well as Chan (2023), focused on ethical frameworks, while Jobin, Ienca and Vayena (2019), as well as Farina, Zhdanov, Karimov and Lavazza (2022) focused on ethical guidelines. Furthermore, Floridi and Cowls (2022), as well as Stahl (2021), are some of the authors who made significant reference to ethical issues and principles. Other concepts that dominated the AI ethics literature are such as 'ethical standards', and ethical regulations. There must be some relationships among these concepts, and there must be a convergent point for them. It is necessary to establish their interconnectedness, as well as how these could further be collectively and individually aligned to one or more of the theories that were considered as lenses for this study. It is clear that these concepts are universal and could be applicable in diverse domains, therefore, is it necessary to firstly describe and discuss them in the context of AIED.

Ethical Frameworks for Artificial Intelligence in Education

Frameworks seem to be the encompassing and most fundamental basis for addressing ethics of AI. Frameworks are the generic schemes for directing ethical decision-making processes and best practices (Rodríguez, 2023). Ethical frameworks should thus be grounded on fundamental theories and models. In this study, the ethical frameworks for AIED are grounded on pedagogical and ethical models. For example, Floridi and Cowls (2022) ethical framework for general purpose is based on the VE. In addition, Clark et al. (2022) also developed an AI ethical framework which is based on the principles of humanity and economic among others. Both the examples of AI ethical frameworks by Floridi and Cowls (2022), as well as Clark et al. (2022) are not specific to any domain but could be good starting point for adaptation.

Ethical Principles and Standards for Artificial Intelligence in Education

From the ethical framework, the next stop is the ethical principles and ethical standards. Ethical principles consist of the generic values that are independent of any subjectivity, against which moral judgments are derived (Di Mattia, 2008). Such values are described by the theories, like in the case of this study, the VE provides the fundamental ethical values from which specific ones are adopted. While the VE ethical principles are generic and may apply to multiple domains, ethical standards on the other hand are customized to a specific domain. Considering the context of this study, the ethical principles and values are to be customized to the AIED.

Ethical Guidelines for Artificial Intelligence in Education

Once the AIED ethical principles, values and standards are adapted, a set of rules will then further be adapted from such principles. According to Owino and Paschal (2023), ethical principles are rules or points that serve as yard-sticks for making ethical judgements unique to a specific domain. It is necessary to state that while general guidelines can be optional, the specific guidelines that are derived from the domain adapted principles and standards are enforceable. Furthermore, while the standards and principles can be generic to the entire AIED context, there could be guidelines specific for sub-domains. For example, there can be guidelines specific for student supporting AI, teacher support AI, and institution support AI. There could also be ethical guidelines specific even more to the application levels such as for intelligence tutoring systems (ITS), e-proctoring systems, or automated grading systems.

Ethical Challenges for Artificial Intelligence in Education

Many literature sources could confirm the benefits of AI to education. Equally, many studies expressed dilemmas on how to maximize the benefits of AI in education without getting in conflict with any of the ethical values and principles. Ethical challenges are thus uncertain situations which appears to be beneficial and at the same time appears to be somewhat in conflict with the ethical principles and values (Kumar, Jieyao, & Soeiro, 2024). For example, while one can appreciate the capabilities of an e-proctoring application to effectively guard against cheating in an examination, it will also be worrisome to think how such system would consider students' movements and behaviors that might be due to their physical disabilities as actions or attempts of cheating. Another example of an ethical challenge can be how it can be appreciated that an automated essay grading system would provide the grading feedback for larger number of students in relatively shorter time while on the other hand getting worried about the possibility of the system awarding more marks to quantitative over qualitative works whereby affecting the reliability of the results. To safely navigate through these challenges, there ought to be ethical frameworks, principles, standards, and guidelines.

Ethical Issues for Artificial Intelligence in Education

Ethicalissues may sound synonymous with ethical challenges. However, while challenges are hinged on the uncertainty of the situations or practices, issues on the other hand are actions that are without a doubt in conflict with one of more of the established moral or ethical principles directly (Córdova & Vicari, 2022). At an *International Conference on Technology and Innovation in Learning, Teaching and Education*, the latter authors discussed practical *ethicalissuesfor artificial intelligence in education.*

For instance, while it can be claimed to be effective in guarding against cheating, capturing videos and recording other physical behaviors for the students by an e-proctoring system is in direct conflict with the principle of privacy, hence is it is an ethical issue. Another example is the predictive AIED system like the ITS would take over the student's agency which directly conflict the principle of autonomy to allow students make own informed choices of learning paths (Akgun & Greenhow, 2022).

Ethical Risks for Artificial Intelligence in Education

Ethical risks are consequential. They are the harms that can be legal, cultural or economical, as well as reputational at organizational or personal levels (Charles & Magtanong, 2021) as outcomes of ethical issues and challenges that might have not been properly managed. For instance, a challenge of poor AI literacy among the educators can lead to poor utilization of the AI application that could be integrated in the institutional LMS such as an over-reliance in the automated grading systems which can then pose the risk of inaccurate and unreliable assessment outcomes, which could disadvantage some students. There are over 700 documented AI risks (Slattery, et al., 2024), which even though apply in general will as well have their fair share of implications in education.

Harmonizing and Inter-Linking Ethical Challenges, Issues, Risks, Frameworks, Principles, Standards, and Guidelines for Artificial Intelligence in Education

Even though many studies appear to have discussed these concepts (ethical frameworks, principles, standards, guidelines, challenges, issues, risks) they have done so either in isolation or in more scrambled ways. These concepts should be interconnected in a more coherent way. It is possible that if one of the lines in their interlinkage is missing, then they will not be likely to be effective either in isolation or with some parts missing. This study systematically unpacks these concepts towards the attainment of the ultimate objective of leveraging the ethical standards in AIED.

Figure 1 portrays the interconnectedness of these concepts. Firstly, ethical issues, challenges, and risks are the primary triggers that necessitate the need for an ethical framework. Hence, the study will firstly unpack, sort, and classify challenges, issues, and risks that are unique to the context of AIED. The framework is to be designed under the guidance of the deontological theory, the VE theory, the CoI as well as the Operant conditioning behaviorism theory. From the ethical framework, ethical principles and standards will be adapted with further refining to the AIED context. Once the ethical principles and standards have been adapted, operational documents, such as guidelines, policies, procedures, and regulations will then further be developed.

Figure 1. Interlinking of ethical frameworks, principles, and guidelines with the ethical challenges, issues, and risks

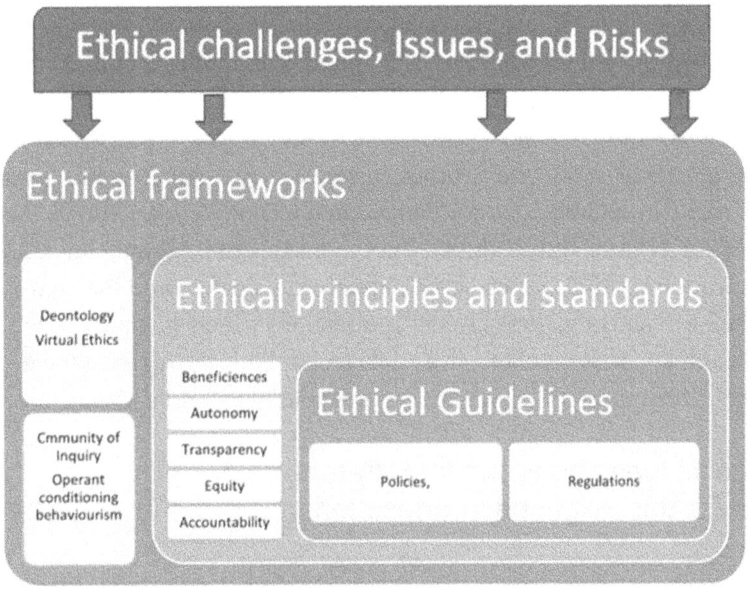

Source: Uunona

Ethical Challenges, Issues, Risks, Frameworks, Principles, Standards, and Guidelines for Artificial Intelligence in Education: The Namibian Position

As was established in the chapter by Uunona and Goosen (2024), Namibia continues adopting AIED technologies, both through improvements of LMSs and stand-alone applications. So far, there are only existing laws that were found to be somehow related to the addressing of AI according to the African Observatory on Responsible AI (AORAI, 2023). There is also one recommendation that resulted from the Windhoek statement on AI in Southern Africa (UNESCO, 2022). There are therefore no documented activities toward the unpacking of ethical issues, challenges, and risks in order to supposedly prepare for the ethical framework, principles, standards, and guidelines either for general or even specific for education.

Explaining the rationale for this study, Uunona and Goosen (2024, p. 177) indicated that "active and responsive regulatory … policies are missing in Namibia, and there are currently no visible practical efforts towards" calls in this regard.

It is against this background that this study is necessary for establishing a primary roadmap to the realization of operational standards, policies, and guidelines that are well adapted to Namibian culture and tradition.

Multiple Ethical Dimensions of Artificial Intelligence in Education

Research has revealed how many peoples including industry experts could mention so many ethical issues of AI, for instance, a study by Stahl (2021) led to a list of more than twenty AI ethical issues. The 39 AI ethical issues listed by Stahl (2021) are from a wider and diverse context of AI considering that it is being applied in multiple disciplines.

As stated in a previous subsection, the ethics of AIED are multifaceted. It is necessary to consider all the applicable ethics in harmony, the one relating to generic educational technology, the one relating to AIED which largely defuses with the one for educational technology, as well as the one that primarily and generically relates to AI (Agarwal, et al., 2022). Against this background, this study proposes a multi-model ethical framework for AIED, which should holistically consider all the significant dimensions of the AIED ethics. The LMS and other educational applications which are harmonized and enhanced with AI features become complex in terms of ethics as such technologies carry the educational, technological, as well as AI features which must all be attended to separately before harmonization.

Analysis of Ethical Issues and Risks for Different Categories of Artificial Intelligence in Education

Issues and risks are the primary triggers for the development and adoption of ethical frameworks, standards, principles, policies, and regulations. It is therefore necessary to firstly analyze, filter, sort, categorize and put them into perspective. This is important for a clear and focused roadmap towards the investigation and eventually the adoption of practical and effective ethical standards, policies, and regulations.

The ethical issues for Educational Technologies can include those that stem from technical dimension, which can also be referred to as digital ethics (Ashok, et al., 2022), as well as those that stem from the pedagogical dimension. The technology induced ethical challenges, issues and risks for education include learning analytics (LA), which is concerned with privacy infringement and data ownership (Agarwal et al., 2022), as well as accessibility which is mostly concerned with equity and inclusivity. These ethical issues can easily be overshadowed by the typical one for AI in general if not considered firstly in isolation before connecting them to the rest and they are therefore better investigated through the lenses of pedagogical theories

In the chapter by Uunona and Goosen (2024), AIED was categorized into 'students support AI', 'teacher support AI', 'institutional support AI', 'computer science', and 'AI across the curriculum'. It is thus necessary to also investigate AI ethical issues according to AIED categorization in order to be able to find the most suitable theoretical lenses through which they could be understood. The focus will only be on the first three of the five AIED categories mentioned above because, computer science, even though it was included from the context of being an educational curriculum, its ultimate context is not typical of AIED. In addition, the AI across the curriculum category is likely to be homogenous to the first three. Table 1 presents the ethical challenges and issues unique to each of the selected three AIED categories. It should be noted that some **challenges** and issues might be applicable across multiple categories.

Table 1. Ethical issues relating to each of the AIED categories

Learner support AI	*Teacher Support AI*	*Institutional Support AI*
Stereotypes, behavioral manipulations, lack of autonomous choice		
Anthropomorphism, biases and discriminations, lack of reliability, lack of trust, surveillance, intrusion, lack of privacy		

Lack of data privacy, lack of transparency, lack or blurred accountability for errors, poor social interaction, interferences in teacher-learner relationship

While table 1 focuses on issues and challenges, it is also important to sort and categorize ethical risks into the same categories of AIED. Slattery et al. (2024) categorized AI ethical risks into seven primary and twenty-three sub-domains. Table 2 (see APPENDIX) presents an analysis of AI ethical risks based on Slattery et al. (2024), according to the AIED categories of learner support, teacher support and institutional support.

As it can be seen from the Table 2, all seven AI risk domains are likely to have an impact on education. While fifteen of the 23 sub-domains can have an impact on education, whereby eleven of them can directly impact the learning and teaching support AI technologies. It is also important to note how each risk sub-domain has been linked to the most appropriate principles of AIED based on Nguyen, Ngo, Hong, Dang, and Nguyen (2023). Namibian educational principles are anchored on access, equity, democracy, and quality (Angula, 2019), which will be considered in the alignment of AIED ethical principles, frameworks, standards, policies, and regulations to the Namibian cultural context.

SOLUTIONS AND RECOMMENDATIONS

This section will discuss solutions and recommendations in dealing with the issues or problems presented in the preceding section.

Solutions

Tools and Technologies for Artificial Intelligence Education

> "From e-learning platforms to virtual reality solutions to educational artificial intelligence", a book on *technological tools for innovative teaching* edited by Khaldi (2024b) looked "at how these tools are shaping the learning experience and opening up new avenues".

Deontological Theory

The deontological theory of Kant (2002) is a product of several works, which included the *Groundwork for the Metaphysics or Morals* (Kant, 1785), *The Critique of Practical Reasons* (Kant, 1788), and the *Metaphysics of Morals* (Kant, 1797). The deontological theory of Kant (2002) as explained by McCartney and Parent (2015) posited that it is more important to consider morality from the intention level of an action than considering its end results. Deontology has also been summarized to be a theory that promote the 'right' over the 'good' (Ranganathan, 2022), which means that it is better to have actions stemming from moral and right intentions than having good results that might be coming from wrong or immoral actions or intentions.

The position of the *deontology* theory will be used in guiding the crafting of AIED policies and ethical standards. This implies that one is not supposed to be surprised by the outcomes or impact of AI applications but should instead anticipate potential risky consequences during the design and development stages. Córdova and Vicari (2022) explored how the deontological framework could guide the ethical principles in the process of developing AIED solutions.

Using deontology as an anchor, D'Alessandro (2024) presented two dimensions to AI ethics; the morality and the safety of AI, which he suggests should be pillars of the theoretical considerations for AI ethics. The safety dimension will be more applicable to the physical devices of AIED which will guide the development and operation of AI devices to be not capable of causing and harm (non-maleficence) to human. The moral dimension on the other hand which is concerned with the entire AI system, especially the decision-making capabilities will be used to guide and assess the AIED applications against unethical decisions or immoral actions.

This study further adopts a heuristic approach whose set of rules include applicability, guidance, and morality to complement the deontology theory in ensuring an effective alignment of AI technologies morally. The AI system should be able to make moral choices which will then help it meet its expectations (practical). AI systems should also be able to weigh moral and alternative options against a potential consequence (guidance).

Perrotta (2023) proposed that a deontological framework be used to evaluate and address the algorithmic and data biases in educational technologies. Evaluating algorithms for biases is crucial for AIED ethical policies especially that AI technologies' advancement in complexity also lead to advancement it the uncertainty of their subsequent risks that can result from their autonomy decisions. This will most likely put students at the receiving end of the abuse of their personal data, and, the deontological theory can be helpful in managing these challenges by assessing and evaluating the algorithmic impacts (Selbst, 2021) of AIED technologies before deployments (Perrotta, 2023). The idea of conducting algorithmic impact assessments would proactively counter the most obvious ethical **issues** in the designs of AIED systems, which would be more effective than the algorithm audits (Raji, et al., 2020), this tallies well with the deontology's call for a weighing of ones' intentions before executing them. The algorithmic impact assessment under the guidance of the deontological theory of Kant (2002) will likely be more effective if considered in the policy and regulations for AIED acquisitions, development, and deployment.

Agent-Based Virtue Ethics

The theory of Virtue Ethics (VE) is originally attributed to Aristotle and Plato. There however happens to be various interpretations and strands of VE theories. One of the strands of VE theories that will guide the fundamental ethics of AI in this study is the Agent-Based Virtue Ethics theory of Slote (2001). According to Slote (2001), the molarity, the rightness, or the wrongness of an action can only stem from an agent from which it proceeds. This is complementary to the deontological stance, because it implies that it is the agent's motives which are likely to influence the morality of the actions. AI applications take positions of agents, and if they are designed with virtuous characteristics, then, they are likely bringing out moral actions whereby leading to artificial moral agents (AMA) (Stenseke, 2024). Steen, Sand, and Van de Poel (2021) found the VE theory to be of great relevance in determining ethical and morality for innovations. Farina et al. (2024) have used the VE as a basis of recommendations for ethical and moral guidelines which could be used and considered in the rollout of AI technologies. AIED technologies are innovative developments which this study is seeking to establish how they could be implemented with minimal or no ethical risks through cultural inclusive guidelines, policies and regulations; hence, the VE theory could add value to the theoretical ecosystem for creating a robust AIED regulatory framework.

It has been further concluded from at least nine research publications that VE is the most ideal theory for guiding the development of AMAs (Stenseke, 2024). Stenseke (2023) built an artificial virtuous agent (AVA) model for AI systems and machines that will be able to learn virtuous behaviors and subsequently be able to portrait moral actions. This study will adopt such a model to the development of AIED technology ethical frameworks, policies, and regulations. The AVA model architecture consists of a layer of input, virtue, action and outcome network as well as the second layer whose backbone is the learning module which is being fed by the moral examples. The architecture gives the idea for the virtues algorithms, which could be applied to any AI systems including AIED applications.

Ethical Regulations for Artificial Intelligence in Education

Regulations can be interpreted differently depending on the contexts (Woll, 2024). However, one of the interpretations that can be applicable to the context of ethical regulations for AIED is the one that refers to the determination of where, when, and how much to make use of certain products or solutions. For example, there can be a regulation which will set the rule that ITS can only be used in higher education and not in the basic education curriculum, or, that ITS will only be permitted in basic education under special conditions. Additionally, there can be a regulation which can set a rule that learning analytics can only be harnessed if the institution has an operational data protection policy. Another good example is that of setting the rules for all applications to meet accessibility standards before being deployed for public use (Joy & Walker, 2023). Besides the political intentions of influencing the conducts of citizens through the use of positive and negative reinforcements (Noll, 2021), in the context of AIED ethics, regulations are employed to promote principles and values as well as to address ethical challenges, manage ethical issues, and mitigate ethical risks.

Recommendations

An *international journal* article on *computing and digital systems* "implemented a recommendation system based on the artificial intelligence technique known as" Case-Based Reasoning (CBR), which leveraged "past outcomes of similar learners to enhance" their learning experiences (Anoir, Chelliq, Khaldi, & Khaldi, 2024, p. 460). The design of an intelligent tutor system for the personalization of learning activities using case-based reasoning and multi-agent systems was discussed.

FUTURE RESEARCH DIRECTIONS

This section will discuss future and emerging trends, as well as provide insight about the future of the theme of the book on Supporting Students' AI Skills Development from the perspective of the chapter focus on Leveraging Ethics for Supporting Students' Artificial Intelligence Skills Development in Namibia. The viability of a paradigm, model, implementation issues of proposed programs, etc., may be included in this section. If appropriate, the section will suggest future research opportunities within the domain of the topic.

Due "to the fact that the" Synthetic Minority Over-sampling Method (SMOTE) "algorithm was able to produce artificial examples", Waladi, Lamarti, Khaldi, Khaldi, and Boudra (2024, p. 47) suggested that future research directions "may examine the use of further features or more complex machine learning".

Stahl (2021) provided *an ecosystem perspective on the ethics of AI andemerging trends* related to *digital technologies*, as well as *artificial intelligence for a betterfuture*, while Iqbal, et al. (2022) considered the current challenges and future research directions in augmented reality for education. In a similar context, a paper by Kaviyaraj and Uma (2021) at the *International Conference on Artificial Intelligence and Smart Systems (ICAIS)* presented a survey on the future of augmented reality with AI in education. Finally, a chapter by Parsons (2019) looked at neuro-ethics in educational technologies and warned that the brain should be kept in mind when developing frameworks for ethical decision-making as part of a book on e.g., *learning in the age ofemerging* trends with regard to *technologies*.

Emerging Trends

With regard to emerging trends, interactive AI applications, operant conditioning and *adaptive learning* were discussed by Huang et al. (2024) in their paper as part of the *Pacific Asia Conference on Information Systems (PACIS) proceedings*.

A chapter by Ndhlovu and Goosen (2023) asked questions around the extent to which multi-disciplinary artificial intelligence applications can enhance higher education in the context of Open and Distance e-Learning (ODeL) in South Africa as part of a book on e.g., *Applicationsof Deep Learning-Based Artificial Emotional Intelligence*.

In their more recent chapter, Ndhlovu-Nemaxwi and Goosen (2024) were advancing student employability through higher education using AI applications for students studying open distance e-learning in South Africa in a book on *PrioritizingSkillsDevelopment for Student Employability*.

Finally, in line with the theme of this book, as well as in the same context as that of this chapter (Namibia), the chapter by Haipinge and Goosen (2024) was exploring educators' pedagogical capabilities towards supporting university students' 21st century skills development by navigating within a digital learning environment against the background of e.g., *Computer Science Education*.

CONCLUSION

This last section will provide discussion of the overall coverage of the chapter and concluding remarks.

This chapter explored the theoretical ecosystem for the ethics of AI in general, and AIED in particular. It emerged that the multi-faceted characteristics of AIED require consideration from multiple theoretical lenses to arrive at a holistic ethical framework. Ethics of AIED should consider aspects related to pedagogies, technologies, and ultimately, AI in general. To this effect, the operant conditioning behaviorism theory of Skinner (1963), together with the community of inquiry by Garrison (1999), were found to be ideal for guiding the investigation of the pedagogical aspects of AIED. In addition, the deontological theory of ethics from Kant (2002) and the agent-based VE of Slote (2001), are the theoretical lenses guiding the ethical framework of the AIED.

Studies on AIED ethics have revolved around the concepts of frameworks, principles, guidelines, standards, challenges, or issues. It also came out that many studies focused on a single concept or otherwise in jumbled ways if more concepts were considered. This study found it necessary to systematically connect these concepts towards a roadmap for leveraging ethical standards of AIED. Many of the ethical established frameworks, principles, standards, and regulations are generalized either to the entire education sector, with a few exceptions for large language models and generative AI. This study recommends a divergent approach to the development of operational standards, regulations and guidelines. For instance, there ought to be an AIED framework specific for basic education, and there should be ones specifically for certain applications, such as e-proctoring systems.

REFERENCES

Abbad, M. M. (2021). Using the UTAUT model to understand students' usage of e-learning systems in developing countries. *Education and Information Technologies*, 26(6), 7205–7224. DOI: 10.1007/s10639-021-10573-5 PMID: 34025204

African Observatory for Responsible AI (AORAI). (2023). AORAI Policy Map. https://policy.africanobservatory.ai/

Agarwal, B., Urlings, C., van Lankveld, G., & Klemke, R. (2022, September). Ethical FRAPPE–an adapted draft framework for ethical AIED. *Proceedings of the Doctoral Consortium of the 17th European Conference on Technology Enhanced Learning* (pp. 46-54). Toulouse, France: CEUR-WS.org. Retrieved from https://ceur-ws.org/Vol-3292/DCECTEL2022_paper06.pdf

Akgun, S., & Greenhow, C. (2022). Artificial intelligence in education: Addressing ethical challenges in K-12 settings. *AI and Ethics*, 2(3), 431–440. DOI: 10.1007/s43681-021-00096-7 PMID: 34790956

Al-Adwan, A. S., Li, N., Al-Adwan, A., Abbasi, G. A., Albelbisi, N. A., & Habibi, A. (2023). Extending the technology acceptance model (TAM) to Predict University Students' intentions to use metaverse-based learning platforms. *Education and Information Technologies*, 28(11), 15381–15413. DOI: 10.1007/s10639-023-11816-3 PMID: 37361794

Alhumaid, K., Naqbi, S., Elsori, D., & Mansoori, M. (2023). The adoption of artificial intelligence applications in education. *International Journal of Data and Network Science*, 7(1), 457–466. DOI: 10.5267/j.ijdns.2022.8.013

Angula, N. A. (2019). Education for all: the Namibian experience. In *Democratic Teacher Education Reforms In Namibia* (pp. 8–28). Routledge. DOI: 10.4324/9780429045707-2

Anoir, L., Chelliq, I., Khaldi, M., & Khaldi, M. (2024). Design of an intelligent tutor system for the personalization of learning activities using case-based reasoning and multi-agent system. *International Journal of Computing and Digital Systems*, 16(1), 459–469. DOI: 10.12785/ijcds/160136

Anoir, L., Khaldi, M., & Erradi, M. (2024). Symbiotic Evolution: The Inextricable Relation between the Web and E-Learning. *DIROSAT: Journal of Education. Social Sciences & Humanities*, 2(1), 10–18.

Ansu-Kyeremeh, E. K., & Goosen, L. (2022). Exploring the Socioeconomic Facet of Online Inclusive Education in Ghana: The Effects of Technological Advancement in Academia. In Garcia, M. (Ed.), *Socioeconomic Inclusion During an Era of Online Education* (pp. 47–66). IGI Global., DOI: 10.4018/978-1-6684-4364-4.ch003

Asakura, K., Occhiuto, K., Todd, S., Leithead, C., & Clapperton, R. (2020). A call to action on artificial intelligence and social work education: Lessons learned from a simulation project using natural language processing. *Journal of Teaching in Social Work*, 40(5), 501–518. DOI: 10.1080/08841233.2020.1813234

Ashok, M., Madan, R., Joha, A., & Sivarajah, U. (2022). Ethical framework for Artificial Intelligence and Digital technologies. *International Journal of Information Management*, 62, 102433. Advance online publication. DOI: 10.1016/j.ijinfomgt.2021.102433

Bandura, A. (1971). *Social learning theory*. General Learning Press.

Burkholder, G. J., Cox, K., & Crawford, L. (2016). *The Scholar-Practitioner's Guide to Research Design*. Laureate Publishing., Retrieved from https://scholarworks.waldenu.edu/facpubs/277/

Chan, C. K. (2023). A comprehensive AI policy education framework for university teaching and learning. *International Journal of Educational Technology in Higher Education*, 20(1), 38. Advance online publication. DOI: 10.1186/s41239-023-00408-3

Charles, W., & Magtanong, R. (2021). Ethical Benefits and Drawbacks of Digitally Informed Consent. In Vasiliu-Feltes, I., & Thomason, J. (Eds.), (pp. 101–123). Advances in Human and Social Aspects of Technology. IGI Global. DOI: 10.4018/978-1-7998-8467-5.ch008

Clark, J., Murdick, D., Perset, K., & Grobelnik, M. (2022, February 17). *The OECD Framework for Classifying AI Systems to assess policy challenges and ensure international standards in AI*. Retrieved March 2, 2024, from https://oecd.ai/en/wonk/classification

Cleveland-Innes, M. F., Stenbom, S., & Garrison, D. R. (Eds.). (2024). *The design of digital learning environments: Online and blended applications of the community of inquiry*. Taylor & Francis.

Clifford, P. L. (2024). AI in Higher Education: Faculty Perspective Towards Artificial Intelligence through UTAUT Approach. *HO CHI MINH CITY OPEN UNIVERSITY JOURNAL OF SCIENCE-SOCIAL SCIENCES*, 14(4), 32–50. Advance online publication. DOI: 10.46223/HCMCOUJS.soci.en.14.4.2851.2024

Córdova, P. R., & Vicari, R. M. (2022, August). Practical ethical issues for artificial intelligence in education. *International Conference on Technology and Innovation in Learning, Teaching and Education* (pp. 437-445). Cham: Springer Nature Switzerland. DOI: 10.1007/978-3-031-22918-3_34

Council of the European Union. (2024, May 21). *Artificial intelligence (AI) act: Council gives final green light to the first worldwide rules on AI*. Retrieved May 24, 2024, from https://www.consilium.europa.eu/en/press/press-releases/2024/05/21/artificial-intelligence-ai-act-council-gives-final-green-light-to-the-first-worldwide-rules-on-ai/

Crawford, L. M. (2020). Conceptual and theoretical frameworks in research. In *Foundations in Research Design* (pp. 35–48). SAGE.

D'Alessandro, W. (2024). Deontology and safe artificial intelligence. *Philosophical Studies*, •••, 1–24. DOI: 10.1007/s11098-024-02174-y

Davis, F. D. (1985). *A technology acceptance model for empirically testing new end-user information systems: Theory and results. (PhD dissertation)*. Massachusetts Institute of Technology.

Di Mattia, P. (2008). Ethical principles. In *Encyclopedia of public health* (Vol. 2, pp. 635–638). Springer. DOI: 10.1007/978-1-4020-5614-7_1453

El Mrani, N., & Khaldi, M. (2024). Fostering Pedagogical Innovation Through the Effective Choice of Mediatization Tools Based on TPACK Model and Technology Integration Frameworks. In *Fostering Pedagogical Innovation Through Effective Instructional Design* (pp. 262–286). IGI Global. DOI: 10.4018/979-8-3693-1206-3.ch012

Farina, M., Zhdanov, P., Karimov, A., & Lavazza, A. (2022). AI and society: A virtue ethics approach. *AI & Society*, 39(3), 1127–1140. DOI: 10.1007/s00146-022-01545-5

Ferdosipour, A. (2024, April 11). *From Skinner's Operant Conditioning to Artificial Intelligence's Algorithms*. Retrieved August 8, 2024, from Medika Life: https://medika.life/from-skinners-operant-conditioning-to-artificial-intelligences-algorithms/

Floridi, L., & Cowls, J. (2022). A unified framework of five principles for AI in society. In *Machine learning and the city: Applications in architecture and urban design* (pp. 535–545). Wiley., DOI: 10.1002/9781119815075.ch45

Floridi, L., Cowls, J., Beltrametti, M., Chatila, R., Chazerand, P., Dignum, V., Luetge, C., Madelin, R., Pagallo, U., Rossi, F., Schafer, B., Valcke, P., & Vayena, E. (2018). AI4People—an ethical framework for a good AI society: Opportunities, risks, principles, and recommendations. *Minds and Machines*, 28(4), 689–707. DOI: 10.1007/s11023-018-9482-5 PMID: 30930541

Garrison, D. R. (1999). Will distance disappear in distance studies? A reaction. *Journal of Distance Education*, 14(2), 10–13.

Garrison, D. R., Anderson, T., & Archer, W. (1999). Critical inquiry in a text-based environment: Computer conferencing in higher education. *The Internet and Higher Education*, 2(2-3), 87–105. DOI: 10.1016/S1096-7516(00)00016-6

Garrison, D. R., Cleveland-Innes, M., & Fung, T. S. (2010). Exploring causal relationships among teaching, cognitive and social presence: Student perceptions of the community of inquiry framework. *The Internet and Higher Education*, 13(1-2), 31–36. DOI: 10.1016/j.iheduc.2009.10.002

Gursoy, D., Chi, O. H., Lu, L., & Nunkoo, R. (2019). Consumers acceptance of artificially intelligent (AI) device use in service delivery. *International Journal of Information Management*, 49, 157–169. DOI: 10.1016/j.ijinfomgt.2019.03.008

Haipinge, E., & Goosen, L. (2024). Exploring Educators' Pedagogical Capabilities to Develop University Students' 21st Century Skills: Navigating Within a Digital Learning Environment. In Bosch, C., Goosen, L., & Chetty, J. (Eds.), *Navigating Computer Science Education in the 21st Century* (pp. 1–20). IGI Global., DOI: 10.4018/979-8-3693-1066-3.ch001

Holmes, W., Bialik, M., & Fadel, C. (2019). *Artificial intelligence in education: Promises and Implications for Teaching and Learning*. Center for Curriculum Redesign., Retrieved from http://bit.ly/AIED-BOOK

Holmes, W., Porayska-Pomsta, K., Holstein, K., Sutherland, E., Baker, T., Shum, S. B., Santos, O. C., Rodrigo, M. T., Cukurova, M., Bittencourt, I. I., & Koedinger, K. R. (2022). Ethics of AI in education: Towards a community-wide framework. *International Journal of Artificial Intelligence in Education*, 32(3), 504–526. DOI: 10.1007/s40593-021-00239-1

Hrich, N., Azekri, M., & Khaldi, M. (2024). Artificial Intelligence Item Analysis Tool for Educational Assessment: Case of Large-Scale Competitive Exams. *International Journal of Information and Education Technology (IJIET)*, 14(6), 822–827. Advance online publication. DOI: 10.18178/ijiet.2024.14.6.2107

Huang, J. M., Chaing, S. Y., Sung, Y. C., Chen, J. T., Wu, Y. H., Liu, T. L., & Chou, C. Y. (2024). Interactive AI Application: Operant Conditioning and Adaptive Learning. *Pacific Asia Conference on Information Systems (PACIS) Proceedings.* Association for Information Systems (AIS). Retrieved from https://aisel.aisnet.org/pacis2024/track14_educ/track14_educ/2/

Iqbal, M. Z., Mangina, E., & Campbell, A. G. (2022). Current challenges and future research directions in augmented reality for education. *Multimodal Technologies and Interaction*, 6(9), 75. Advance online publication. DOI: 10.3390/mti6090075

Jain, R., Garg, N., & Khera, S. N. (2022). Adoption of AI-enabled tools in social development organizations in India: An extension of UTAUT model. *Frontiers in Psychology*, 13, 893691. Advance online publication. DOI: 10.3389/fpsyg.2022.893691 PMID: 35795409

Jobin, A., Ienca, M., & Vayena, E. (2019). The global landscape of AI ethics guidelines. *Nature Machine Intelligence*, 1(9), 389–399. DOI: 10.1038/s42256-019-0088-2

Joy, L., & Walker, R. (2023). Establishing an Assistive Technology-Enabled Culture at the University of York: Reflections on a Values-Based Strategy. In *Handbook of Research on Advancing Equity and Inclusion Through Educational Technology* (pp. 189–207). IGI Global. DOI: 10.4018/978-1-6684-6868-5.ch010

Kant, I. (1785). *Groundwork of the Metaphysics of Morals.*

Kant, I. (1788). *The Critique of Practical Reason.* Infomotions Incorporated.

Kant, I. (1797). *The metaphysics of morals* (Gregor, M. J., Ed.). Cambridge University Press.

Kant, I. (2002). Deontology: The ethics of duty. In *Ethics and Values: Basic Readings in Theory and Practice* (pp. 77–87). Pearson Custom.

Kaviyaraj, R., & Uma, M. (2021, March). A survey on future of augmented reality with AI in education. *International Conference on Artificial Intelligence and Smart Systems (ICAIS)* (pp. 47-52). IEEE. DOI: 10.1109/ICAIS50930.2021.9395838

Kelly, S., Kaye, S. A., & Oviedo-Trespalacios, O. (2023). What factors contribute to the acceptance of artificial intelligence? A systematic review. *Telematics and Informatics*, 77, 101925. Advance online publication. DOI: 10.1016/j.tele.2022.101925

Khaldi, M. (Ed.). (2024a, January). *Fostering Pedagogical Innovation Through Effective Instructional Design.* IGI Global., Retrieved from https://www.igi-global.com/book/fostering-pedagogical-innovation-through-effective/326938 DOI: 10.4018/979-8-3693-1206-3

Khaldi, M. (Ed.). (2024b, February). *Technological tools for innovative teaching.* IGI Global., Retrieved from https://www.igi-global.com/book/technological-tools-innovative-teaching/335010

Kumar, J., Jieyao, Z., & Soeiro, J. D. (2024). Empowering Lifelong Learning: Embracing the Impact of Artificial Intelligence. In Behera, S. K., Ibrahim, A. H., & Romdhani, F. (Eds.), (pp. 42–66). Advances in Educational Marketing, Administration, and Leadership. IGI Global. DOI: 10.4018/979-8-3693-6955-5.ch003

Libbrecht, P., & Goosen, L. (2015). Using ICTs to Facilitate Multilingual Mathematics Teaching and Learning. In Barwell, R., Clarkson, P., Halai, A., Kazima, M., Moschkovich, J., Planas, N., & Villavicencio Ubillús, M. (Eds.), *Mathematics Education and Language Diversity* (pp. 217–235). Springer., DOI: 10.1007/978-3-319-14511-2_12

Maxwell, J. A. (2022). Interactive approaches to qualitative research design. In *The Sage handbook of qualitative research design* (pp. 41–54). SAGE. DOI: 10.4135/9781529770278.n4

McCartney, S., & Parent, R. (2015). Ethical systems. In *Ethics in law enforcement* (pp. 15-40). BCcampus.

Mishra, P., & Koehler, M. J. (2008). Introducing Technological Pedagogical Content Knowledge. *Presented at the Annual Meeting of the American Educational Research Association (AERA).* New York: AERA. Retrieved from http://www.matt-koehler.com/publications/Mishra_Koehler_AERA_2008.pdf

Modular Object-Oriented Dynamic Learning Environment (MOODLE). (2018). *Philosophy*. Retrieved April 21, 2024, from MoodleDocs: https://docs.moodle.org/403/en/Philosophy

Mørch, A. I., & Andersen, R. (2023). Human-Centred AI in education in the age of generative AI tools. *Joint Proceedings of the Workshops, Work in Progress Demos and Doctoral Consortium at the 9th International Symposium on End-User Development (IS-EUD). 3408.* Cagliari, Italy: CEUR-WS.org. Retrieved from https://ceur-ws.org/Vol-3408/short-s2-08.pdf

Morel, G. M., & Spector, J. M. (Eds.). (2022). *Foundations of educational technology: Integrative approaches and interdisciplinary perspectives* (3rd ed.). Routledge., DOI: 10.4324/9781003268406

Ndhlovu, N. J., & Goosen, L. (2023). To What Extent Can Multidisciplinary Artificial Intelligence Applications Enhance Higher Education?: Open and Distance E-Learning in South Africa. In Chowdhary, C. (Ed.), *Multidisciplinary Applications of Deep Learning-Based Artificial Emotional Intelligence* (pp. 166–185). IGI Global., DOI: 10.4018/978-1-6684-5673-6.ch011

Ndhlovu-Nemaxwi, N. J., & Goosen, L. (2024). Advancing Student Employability Through Higher Education Using Artificial Intelligence (AI) Applications: Studying Open Distance E-Learning in South Africa. In Christiansen, B., & Even, A. (Eds.), *Prioritizing Skills Development for Student Employability* (pp. 120–141). IGI Global., DOI: 10.4018/979-8-3693-3571-0.ch005

Nghuulondo, P., & Goosen, L. (2023). Implications of Using Mobile Technologies in Higher Education Amidst the COVID-19 Pandemic: Accessing Teaching, Online Learning, and Assessment. In Meletiadou, E. (Ed.), *Handbook of Research on Implications of Sustainable Development in Higher Education* (pp. 167–182). IGI Global., DOI: 10.4018/978-1-6684-6172-3.ch008

Ngugi, J. K., & Goosen, L. (2021). Innovation, Entrepreneurship, and Sustainability for ICT Students Towards the Post-COVID-19 Era. In Carvalho, L. C., Reis, L., & Silveira, C. (Eds.), *Handbook of Research on Entrepreneurship, Innovation, Sustainability, and ICTs in the Post-COVID-19 Era* (pp. 110–131). IGI Global., DOI: 10.4018/978-1-7998-6776-0.ch006

Nguyen, A., Ngo, H. N., Hong, Y., Dang, B., & Nguyen, B. P. (2023). Ethical principles for artificial intelligence in education. *Education and Information Technologies*, 28(4), 4221–4241. DOI: 10.1007/s10639-022-11316-w PMID: 36254344

Noll, R. G. (Ed.). (2021). *Regulatory policy and the social sciences*. University of California Press.

Ouyang, F., & Jiao, P. (2021). Artificial intelligence in education: The three paradigms. *Computers and Education: Artificial Intelligence*, 2, 100020. Advance online publication. DOI: 10.1016/j.caeai.2021.100020

Owino, B. A., & Paschal, M. J. (2023). AI and Ethics in Education: Implications and Strategies for Responsible Implementation. In *Creative AI Tools and Ethical Implications in Teaching and Learning* (pp. 196-211). IGI Global.

Parsons, T. D. (2019). Neuroethics in educational technology: Keeping the brain in mind when developing frameworks for ethical decision-making. In *Mind, Brain and Technology: Learning in the Age of Emerging Technologies* (pp. 195-209). Springer.

Perrotta, C. (2023). Advancing data justice in education: Some suggestions towards a deontological framework. *Learning, Media and Technology*, 48(2), 187–199. DOI: 10.1080/17439884.2022.2156536

Picciano, A. G. (2021). Theories and frameworks for online education: Seeking an integrated model. In *A guide to administering distance learning* (pp. 79–103). Brill. DOI: 10.1163/9789004471382_005

Qin, C., Huang, W., & Hew, K. F. (2020, November). Using the Community of Inquiry Framework to develop an educational chatbot: Lesson learned from a mobile instant messaging learning environment. *Proceedings of the 28th international conference on computers in education. 1*, pp. 69-74. Asia-Pacific Society for Computers in Education. Retrieved from https://hub.hku.hk/handle/10722/306010

Raji, I. D., Smart, A., White, R. N., Mitchell, M., Gebru, T., Hutchinson, B., & Barnes, P. (2020, January). Closing the AI accountability gap: Defining an end-to-end framework for internal algorithmic auditing. *Proceedings of the conference on fairness, accountability, and transparency* (pp. 33-44). ACM. DOI: 10.1145/3351095.3372873

Ranganathan, B. (2022). Deontology. In *Encyclopedia of Religious Ethics* (pp. 178–186). Wiley Online Library. DOI: 10.1002/9781118499528.ch22

Ravitch, S. M., & Riggan, M. (2016). *Reason & Rigor: how conceptual frameworks guide research* (2nd ed.). SAGE., Retrieved from https://uk.sagepub.com/en-gb/eur/reason-rigor/book241777

Robson, C., & McCartan, K. (2016). *Real World Research* (4th ed.). Wiley., Retrieved from https://www.perlego.com/book/1485149/real-world-research-pdf

Rodríguez, M. L. (Ed.). (2023). *Bioethics of Displacement and Its Implications*. IGI Global., DOI: 10.4018/978-1-6684-4808-3

Selbst, A. D. (2021). An institutional view of algorithmic impact assessments. *Harvard Journal of Law & Technology*, 35(1). https://jolt.law.harvard.edu/assets/articlePDFs/v35/Selbst-An-Institutional-View-of-Algorithmic-Impact-Assessments.pdf

Simataa, G. M., & Goosen, L. (2024). Reshaping Higher Education Institutions Within an Industry 4.0 Context: E-Learning Frameworks for Developing Countries. In Naidoo, V., & Verma, R. (Eds.), *Reshaping Entrepreneurial Education Within an Industry 4.0 Context* (pp. 142–165). IGI Global., DOI: 10.4018/979-8-3693-0409-9.ch008

Skinner, B. F. (1963). Operant behavior. *The American Psychologist*, 18(8), 503–515. DOI: 10.1037/h0045185

Slattery, P., Saeri, A. K., Grundy, E. A., Graham, J., Noetel, M., Uuk, R., & Thompson, N. (2024). The AI Risk Repository: A Comprehensive Meta-Review, Database, and Taxonomy of Risks From Artificial Intelligence. doi:https://doi.org/DOI: 10.13140/RG.2.2.28850

Slote, M. (2001). *Morals from motives*. Oxford University Press. DOI: 10.1093/0195138376.001.0001

Sohn, K., & Kwon, O. (2020). Technology acceptance theories and factors influencing artificial Intelligence-based intelligent products. *Telematics and Informatics*, 47, 101324. Advance online publication. DOI: 10.1016/j.tele.2019.101324

Stahl, B. C. (2021). *Artificial intelligence for a better future: an ecosystem perspective on the ethics of AI and emerging digital technologies*. Springer Nature. DOI: 10.1007/978-3-030-69978-9

Steen, M., Sand, M., & Van de Poel, I. (2021). Virtue ethics for responsible innovation. *Business & Professional Ethics Journal*, 40(2), 243–268. DOI: 10.5840/bpej2021319108

Stenseke, J. (2023). Artificial virtuous agents: From theory to machine implementation. *AI & Society*, 38(4), 1301–1320. DOI: 10.1007/s00146-021-01325-7

Stenseke, J. (2024). Artificial virtuous agents in a multi-agent tragedy of the commons. *AI & Society*, 39(3), 855–872. DOI: 10.1007/s00146-022-01569-x

Syarifuddin, S., Setyosari, P., Sulton, S., Kuswandi, D., & Sartika, D. (2020). The effect of the community of inquiry (CoI) learning model and learning style towards social skills. *European Journal of Educational Research*, 9(2), 569–578. DOI: 10.12973/eu-jer.9.2.569

Tefo, R. M., & Goosen, L. (2024). Fostering Pedagogical Innovation Through the Effective Smartboard Instruction of Physical Sciences: Technologies in Gauteng Schools, South Africa. In Khaldi, M. (Ed.), *Fostering Pedagogical Innovation Through Effective Instructional Design* (pp. 287–307). IGI Global., DOI: 10.4018/979-8-3693-1206-3.ch013

Uden, L., & Ching, G. S. (2024). Activity Theory-based Ecosystem for Artificial Intelligence in Education (AIED). *International Journal of Research*, 13(5), 41–54.

Ukobitz, D. V., & Faullant, R. (2022). The relative impact of isomorphic pressures on the adoption of radical technology: Evidence from 3D printing. *Technovation*, 113, 102418. Advance online publication. DOI: 10.1016/j.technovation.2021.102418

United Nations Educational, Scientific and Cultural Organisation (UNESCO). (2022). *Windhoek statement on Artificial Intelligence in Southern Africa*. UNESCO.

Uunona, G. N., & Goosen, L. (2023). Leveraging Ethical Standards in Artificial Intelligence Technologies: A Guideline for Responsible Teaching and Learning Applications. In Garcia, M., Lopez Cabrera, M., & de Almeida, R. (Eds.), *Handbook of Research on Instructional Technologies in Health Education and Allied Disciplines* (pp. 310–330). IGI Global., DOI: 10.4018/978-1-6684-7164-7.ch014

Uunona, G. N., & Goosen, L. (2024). Leveraging Ethics in Artificial Intelligence Technologies and Applications: E-Learning Management Systems in Namibia. In Ortiz-Rodriguez, F., Leyva-Mederos, A., Tiwari, S., Hernandez-Quintana, A., & Martinez-Rodriguez, J. (Eds.), *Semantic Web Technologies and Applications in Artificial Intelligence of Things* (pp. 173–185). IGI Global., DOI: 10.4018/979-8-3693-1487-6.ch008

Waladi, C., Khaldi, M., & Lamarti, M. S. (2024). Revolutionizing Education Through Personalized Pedagogy and Machine Learning Algorithms. In *Fostering Pedagogical Innovation Through Effective Instructional Design* (pp. 342–362). IGI Global. DOI: 10.4018/979-8-3693-1206-3.ch016

Waladi, C., Lamarti, S. M., Khaldi, M., Khaldi, M., & Boudra, S. (2024, February). KNN Classification of Kolb Learning Styles: A Comparative Study on Balanced and Unbalanced Datasets. *Proceedings of the E-Learning and Smart Engineering Systems (ELSES 2023)* (pp. 43-49). Atlantis Press. DOI: 10.2991/978-94-6463-360-3_6

Wang, X., Pang, H., Wallace, M. P., Wang, Q., & Chen, W. (2022). Learners' perceived AI presences in AI-supported language learning: A study of AI as a humanized agent from community of inquiry. *Computer Assisted Language Learning*, 37(4), 814–840. DOI: 10.1080/09588221.2022.2056203

Woll, C. (2024, Sep 5). *Regulation.* Retrieved from Encyclopedia Britannica: https://www.britannica.com/topic/regulation

Wu, W., Zhang, B., Li, S., & Liu, H. (2022). Exploring factors of the willingness to accept AI-assisted learning environments: An empirical investigation based on the UTAUT model and perceived risk theory. *Frontiers in Psychology*, 13, 870777. Advance online publication. DOI: 10.3389/fpsyg.2022.870777 PMID: 35814061

Zhang, M., & Fabus, M. (2022). Abilities of Current Artificial Intelligence Systems to Learn Social Skills. Retrieved from https://osf.io/preprints/psyarxiv/r3ktj/ DOI: 10.31234/osf.io/r3ktj

APPENDIX

Table 2. Analysis of AIED ethical risks against the AIED categories (based on Slattery et al., 2024)

Risk domain	Sub-domain	Learner support	Teacher support	Institutional support	Conflicted ethical value
Discrimination & toxicity	Unfair discrimination and misrepresentation	✓	✓		Inclusiveness
	Unequal performance across groups		✓		Inclusiveness
Privacy and Security	Compromise of privacy by obtaining, leaking, or correctly inferring sensitive information	✓	✓	✓	Privacy
	AI system security vulnerabilities and attacks	✓	✓	✓	Security and Safety
Malicious Actors and Misuse	Disinformation, surveillance, and influence at scale		✓	✓	Privacy, Security and Safety
	Fraud, scams, and targeted manipulation			✓	Governance and stewardship
Human-computer interaction	Overreliance and unsafe use	✓	✓	✓	Human centeredness
	Loss of human agency and autonomy	✓			Human centeredness
	Increased inequality and decline in employment quality			✓	Sustainability and Proportionality
	Economic and cultural devaluation of human effort		✓	✓	Sustainability and Proportionality
	Competitive dynamics			✓	Sustainability and Proportionality
	Governance failure			✓	Governance and Stewardship
AI system safety, failures & limitations	AI pursuing its own goals in conflict with human goals or values	✓	✓	✓	Sustainability and Proportionality
	Lack of capability or robustness	✓	✓		Transparency and Accountability
	Lack of transparency or interpretability	✓	✓	✓	Transparency and Accountability

Chapter 12
Artificial Intelligence in Educational Serious Games:
Implications and Innovations

Asmae Lamnai
https://orcid.org/0009-0004-6075-3706
FS Tetouan, Morocco

Abderrahim Elmhouti
FS Tetouan, Morocco

ABSTRACT

The integration of artificial intelligence (AI) into educational serious games is transforming learning and skill development by providing personalized learning paths, enhancing engagement, and delivering real-time feedback. These innovations are especially impactful in fields like healthcare, vocational training, and academia, where adaptive environments can be tailored to individual needs. However, the implementation of AI also presents challenges, such as ethical concerns, data privacy, and accessibility. This chapter explores how AI-driven technologies enhance educational serious games, focusing on their implications for revolutionizing learning experiences and shaping students' AI skills. It examines the innovations AI brings to game design and the broader impact on educational gaming, addressing both opportunities and challenges.

INTRODUCTION

The intersection of artificial intelligence (AI) and serious games has rapidly become one of the most exciting areas in both education and gaming. At its core, the idea of serious games—games designed with a purpose beyond entertainment—has always been deeply human. These games are not just about fun; they are about transforming learning into an engaging and impactful experience, whether that's for healthcare, education, or skill development (Yu, 2021). From the earliest board games like Go and Chess to the modern-day digital games that dominate the entertainment landscape, games have long been more than just pastimes. They have been tools for learning, fostering strategy, social interaction, and even moral development across different cultures (Toh & Lim, 2021). Today, in an increasingly digital

DOI: 10.4018/979-8-3693-8965-2.ch012

world, the advent of artificial intelligence has allowed serious games to evolve into powerful vehicles for tailored, dynamic, and adaptive learning experiences.

Incorporating artificial intelligence into serious games is a step toward making the learning experience more personal, responsive, and effective. Artificial intelligence enables serious games to adjust in real-time to the player's unique skill set, challenges, and learning preferences. The power of artificial intelligence lies in its ability to create personalized learning pathways, much like a tutor who adapts to the needs of each individual. For example, artificial intelligence can assess a player's progress, identify where they struggle, and adjust the game's difficulty or content to support them in overcoming challenges (Ezzaim, Dahbi, Haidine, & Aqqal, 2023). This level of personalization would be difficult to achieve through traditional educational tools, making artificial intelligence in serious games a promising tool for enhancing learning outcomes (Martin, Casey, & Kane, 2021).

The machine learning algorithms and content generation techniques now integrated into many serious games allow for a more tailored experience. Imagine a game designed to teach healthcare skills: the artificial intelligence within the game could adjust the virtual patients' conditions based on the player's proficiency, helping them learn at their own pace without feeling overwhelmed or bored. This adaptability is key to maintaining motivation and engagement, which is often one of the greatest challenges in educational games (Yu, Gao, & Wang, 2021). When learners feel that the game responds to their individual journey, it builds a deeper connection to the material, enhancing their long-term retention and mastery of skills.

Furthermore, the integration of intelligent agents and imitation learning makes the interaction between the player and the game more fluid and intuitive. These agents can act as virtual mentors, guiding players through the complexities of the game while simultaneously offering valuable, real-time feedback (Keller & Brucker-Kley, 2020). This feedback isn't just about correcting mistakes but about understanding the player's cognitive process and nudging them toward more effective problem-solving techniques. In this sense, the artificial intelligence isn't just a tool; it's a partner in the player's learning journey. It's about creating a collaborative environment where human and machine work together to achieve educational goals.

However, despite these remarkable advancements, the adoption of artificial intelligence in serious games faces certain barriers. Game developers often shy away from using high-risk, complex artificial intelligence methods, such as deep learning and neural networks, because they tend to be unpredictable, resource-intensive, and difficult to control (Mittal, Scholten, & Kapelan, 2022). For many developers, the challenge lies in balancing the desire to push the boundaries of what artificial intelligence can do with the need for stability and reliability in game design. This reluctance to explore newer, more complex artificial intelligence technologies limits the full potential of what serious games could offer.

Despite these challenges, the potential for artificial intelligence in serious games is vast. The combination of artificial intelligence with virtual worlds could lead to immersive learning environments where players not only gain new knowledge but experience the emotions, challenges, and rewards associated with real-life tasks. For instance, serious games designed for medical training can simulate realistic patient interactions, allowing trainees to practice diagnosing conditions and making decisions without the risk of harm (Lamnai & Mhouti, 2023). Artificial intelligence can guide these learners through simulated medical scenarios, helping them learn at their own pace, while also ensuring that the experience mirrors real-world complexities (Ullah et al., 2022).

This chapter aims to provide a focused exploration of how artificial intelligence (AI) transforms the design, implementation, and impact of educational serious games. It seeks to illustrate how artificial intelligence-powered tools create dynamic, adaptive, and personalized learning experiences, ultimately enhancing educational outcomes across a variety of domains, including healthcare, vocational training, and academic education.

The objectives of this chapter are threefold: first, to present an overview of the methodologies and theoretical frameworks underlying the integration of artificial intelligence in serious games; second, to highlight practical applications and innovative implementations that showcase the educational potential of artificial intelligence-driven games; and third, to critically assess the ethical, technical, and accessibility challenges inherent in this integration. By balancing opportunities with constraints, the chapter aims to provide educators, developers, and researchers with actionable insights into leveraging artificial intelligence to foster the development of students' skills while advancing the field of serious games.

METHODOLOGY

This study explores the synergy between serious games and artificial intelligence (AI), with a special focus on the development of students' skills. To guide this investigation, we have formulated three primary research questions:

- **RQ1**: What are the principal application domains of serious games?
- **RQ2**: How are artificial intelligence and data science currently leveraged within serious games?
- **RQ3**: What challenges and future opportunities arise from the integration of artificial intelligence into serious games?

To address these questions, a systematic literature review was conducted, aiming to capture a comprehensive view of recent developments, challenges, and innovations within this multidisciplinary field. Our data collection process began with a broad search of scientific literature using google scholar, supplemented by additional databases as necessary to ensure inclusiveness.

Inclusion and Exclusion Criteria

To ensure the relevance and quality of sources, inclusion and exclusion criteria were meticulously defined. Studies were selected based on criteria such as citation frequency, relevance to artificial intelligence applications in serious games, and the novelty of the approach or methodologies discussed. Publications were further screened for their direct focus on serious games or artificial intelligence, the specificity of the content to practical applications, and linguistic accessibility (only English-language sources were included).

Search Strategy

An initial set of keywords was used to obtain a foundational understanding of the field, including terms such as "serious games," "serious games applications," "artificial intelligence in serious games," and "serious games analytics." This initial phase aimed to capture the breadth of artificial intelligence applications and their impact on serious games across different fields.

Screening Process

Following the initial search, a three-tier screening process was employed. First, titles and abstracts were reviewed to assess the general relevance of each study. Subsequently, full-text reviews were conducted on those articles that passed initial screening, ensuring that each met our methodological standards. Studies that were unrelated to serious games or Artificial Intelligence, lacked methodological rigor, or were not published in English were systematically excluded.

RELATED WORK

The integration of artificial intelligence (AI) into serious games (SGs) represents a rapidly evolving frontier in the intersection of education, technology, and gaming. Serious games, by definition, are games designed for purposes beyond mere entertainment—whether for education, training, behavioral change, or therapeutic interventions (Gaurav et al., 2022). Unlike traditional games focused solely on leisure, serious games offer dynamic, interactive environments where users actively participate in learning processes through decision-making, problem-solving, and engagement with the game's content. This active participation fosters deeper understanding and retention, which is why serious games are becoming recognized as powerful tools for modern education (Colado et al., 2023).

As artificial intelligence technology evolves, it brings with it the capability to enhance serious games in ways that were previously unimaginable. The convergence of artificial intelligence and serious games allows for more adaptive, personalized, and engaging learning experiences, offering new methods of tailoring content to match individual learners' skills, preferences, and learning speeds (Mohamadi, Mujtaba, Le, Doretto, & Adjeroh, 2023). This adaptability ensures that learners experience an environment that feels responsive and engaging, preventing frustration and increasing motivation (Dimitriadou, Djafarova, Turetken, Verkuyl, & Ferworn, 2021). Artificial intelligence enables real-time adjustments to the game environment, ensuring that learners are always appropriately challenged and can progress at their own pace, significantly boosting their engagement and educational outcomes (Abd-Alrazaq et al., 2022).

Artificial intelligence -Powered Serious Games: A Constructivist Approach to Experiential Learning

Serious games represent a transformative experiential learning strategy, founded on the principle that learners achieve the best results through active engagement. Founded on the principles of constructivism, this approach places students in complex real-world scenarios, reproduced in a simulated, risk-free environment. By confronting these challenges through collaborative, hands-on tasks, learners can actively construct their knowledge, developing the critical skills needed to deal with real-life situations (Kenwright, 2023).

This pedagogical approach is particularly effective in fields such as project management, where collaboration, creativity, and problem-solving are essential to academic and professional success. Serious games provide a dynamic space where participants can experiment, fail, and refine their strategies without real-world consequences, fostering a better understanding of concepts and transferable skills (Kenwright, 2023).

Artificial intelligence (AI) further enhances the potential of serious games by adapting these simulated environments to the individual needs of learners. Artificial intelligence systems can analyze player behavior, dynamically adapt scenarios, and provide contextual feedback, ensuring that learners are constantly engaged and stimulated (Baggen, 2024).

Integrating artificial intelligence also ensures that serious games remain consistent with the principles of constructivist learning. artificial intelligence -powered serious games create a continuous learning loop by simulating complex problems and allowing players to iteratively build, test, and refine their ideas. Learners can actively engage in hypothesis building, explore lateral solutions, and develop their mastery of increasingly complex challenges, all in a setting designed to support their growth.

In short, serious games, combined with artificial intelligence, transform education and training into an immersive, interactive, and scalable experience. Recreating real-world challenges in a safe, engaging, and adaptive environment, enables learners to acquire the critical thinking, teamwork, and problem-solving skills that are essential for academic and professional success. This powerful synergy between technology, pedagogy, and play makes serious games the cornerstone of forward-looking experiential learning (Baggen, 2024).

Generative Artificial Intelligence and Visual Synthesis in Serious Games

Among the most notable advancements in artificial intelligence is the rise of Generative Adversarial Networks (GANs), which have made a profound impact on the creation of realistic, immersive environments in serious games. Initially introduced in 2014, GANs allow for the synthesis of high-quality images, videos, and even voices (Baggen, 2024). These technologies help generate realistic game assets that enhance the player's immersion. However, more recent developments, such as Diffusion Models (DMs), have taken the capabilities of generative artificial intelligence even further by providing greater control and stability in image generation (Gligorea et al., 2023). These models, such as DALL-E 2 from OpenAI and IMAGEN from Google, generate high-fidelity visuals from textual inputs, making it easier to create dynamic game environments and characters that respond to user actions in real-time (Igras-Cybulska et al., 2024).

For example, latent diffusion models (LDMs) like Stable Diffusion have become increasingly popular for game development due to their ability to produce detailed visuals while using fewer computational resources (De la Torre, Onggo, Corlu, Nogal, & Juan, 2021). These models allow developers to create responsive, personalized game worlds that can adjust to the player's choices, making each experience unique. Furthermore, fine-tuning tools like ControlNet enable developers to modify the behavior and appearance of game characters and objects in real-time, making serious games even more immersive and adaptable (Pérez Sánchez, 2024).

Artificial Intelligence for Conversations: The Role of Large Language Models

Artificial intelligence's influence extends beyond visual content, with Natural Language Processing (NLP) technologies, particularly Large Language Models (LLMs) like GPT-3 and GPT-4, opening up new possibilities for dialogue and narrative in serious games. Trained on vast datasets, LLMs can generate human-like text, making them ideal for creating conversational agents within serious games (Rane, Choudhary, & Rane, 2023). These agents can engage players in realistic conversations, respond dynamically to player choices, and even provide real-time feedback and guidance, which enhances the learning process (Waladi, Khaldi, & Sefian, 2023).

For instance, conversational agents powered by LLMs allow serious games to offer personalized interactions with players, facilitating more meaningful feedback that adapts to each individual's progress. In education, this can translate into virtual tutors that help learners navigate complex material and provide tailored assistance when players encounter difficulties (IEEE Xplore, n.d.). These conversational systems also enable adaptive storytelling, where the game's narrative evolves based on player choices, making every player's journey unique (Anoir, Khaldi, & Erradi, 2022). As the interaction with the game becomes more fluid and responsive, learners feel more immersed and engaged, leading to improved outcomes (Sapci & Sapci, 2020).

Personalization and Gamification in Learning

Artificial intelligence also plays a pivotal role in personalizing learning experiences within serious games. Adaptive artificial intelligence systems allow serious games to modify gameplay elements such as difficulty, content, and objectives based on the learner's progress, ensuring that players are constantly challenged but not overwhelmed. By dynamically adjusting to each player's skills, preferences, and performance, artificial intelligence-driven games can keep learners engaged and improve motivation and retention (Yenduri et al., 2024). Studies have shown that personalized learning pathways are more effective than static educational methods, as they cater to the individual learning needs of players (ScienceDirect, n.d.).

Furthermore, artificial intelligence contributes to gamification—the process of adding game-like elements to traditionally non-game activities. In healthcare training, for example, artificial intelligence-powered serious games can simulate realistic clinical scenarios, allowing students to practice medical procedures and make decisions without the risk of harming patients. Such immersive experiences are invaluable for developing practical skills (Pasqualotto, Parong, Green, & Bavelier, 2023), and studies have highlighted the effectiveness of artificial intelligence-driven simulations in improving clinical competence (Bennani, Maalel, & Ben Ghezala, 2022).

Ethical and Practical Challenges

Despite the incredible potential of artificial intelligence in serious games, several challenges remain. One major concern is scalability, especially in educational contexts where resources are often limited (Wang et al., 2022). Implementing sophisticated artificial intelligence algorithms can be computationally expensive, and not all institutions have the necessary infrastructure to support these technologies (Kollins et al., 2020). Another issue is the ethical implications of using artificial intelligence in serious games, particularly about data privacy, algorithmic biases, and the potential for perpetuating harm (Liu, Abu-Shaban, Halabi, & Cook, 2023). As these technologies become more integrated into learning environments, it is crucial to address these concerns to ensure that artificial intelligence-driven serious games are fair, safe, and inclusive.

Additionally, the gap between academic research and industry adoption is a significant barrier to the widespread implementation of artificial intelligence in serious games. While academic research has demonstrated the potential of artificial intelligence-driven learning experiences, the gaming industry has been slower to adopt these technologies. This reluctance is often due to the perceived risks of integrating experimental artificial intelligence systems, such as neural networks, into commercial products, as studios typically prefer to rely on more established, low-risk solutions (Abd-Alrazaq et al., 2022).

In conclusion, the integration of artificial intelligence into serious games has the potential to revolutionize learning, training, and education by creating more engaging, adaptive, and personalized experiences. While challenges such as scalability and ethical concerns persist, the advances in artificial intelligence techniques, from generative models to natural language processing, are opening up exciting new possibilities for immersive, effective learning. As artificial intelligence continues to evolve, it is likely that its integration into serious games will become more widespread, providing learners with more innovative and impactful ways to acquire knowledge and skills in various fields, from healthcare to vocational training.

APPLICATIONS OF SERIOUS GAMES

Serious games (SGs) have gained significant recognition as transformative tools across educational, professional, and therapeutic domains. Unlike traditional entertainment games that primarily aim for enjoyment, serious games are specifically designed with educational objectives, incorporating simulations, storytelling, and interactivity to promote skill acquisition and knowledge retention (IngentaConnect, n.d.). The integration of artificial intelligence (AI) into serious games enhances their ability to personalize learning experiences, adapt to the user's needs, and improve outcomes across various fields (Lee et al., 2024). Artificial intelligence in serious games enables real-time feedback, personalized learning paths, and immersive environments that respond to player actions, making these applications more effective and engaging (Maghsudi, Lan, Xu, & van Der Schaar, 2021). This section explores the primary applications of serious games in the domains of healthcare, vocational training, educational settings, and social and behavioral sciences, examining how artificial intelligence augments each domain.

Healthcare and Clinical Training

Serious games have found significant applications in the healthcare sector, where they are used for clinical skills training, patient education, and rehabilitation. Serious games in healthcare simulate medical procedures and patient interactions, allowing healthcare professionals to practice in a risk-free environment. The incorporation of artificial intelligence enhances these simulations by adjusting the difficulty based on the learner's skill level and providing real-time analytics of performance (Damaševičius, Maskeliūnas, & Blažauskas, 2023). Artificial intelligence -powered virtual patients respond realistically, mimicking conditions and symptoms to offer valuable hands-on practice. For example, artificial intelligence algorithms can modify the behavior of simulated patients depending on the learner's decisions, providing personalized feedback that supports skill development and decision-making (Khalid et al., 2024).

In rehabilitation, artificial intelligence-driven serious games use adaptive learning technologies to optimize therapy programs, tailoring challenges to the specific recovery needs of patients. These games employ motion tracking and sensor data to monitor physical movements, helping to improve both physical and cognitive rehabilitation. Studies have shown that artificial intelligence-enabled games in rehabilitation not only enhance engagement but also increase the effectiveness of treatments by adjusting to the patient's progress (Hamilton, 2024). Personalized difficulty adjustments based on real-time performance allow patients to work at their own pace while still receiving adequate therapeutic challenges (Dahalan, Alias, & Shaharom, 2024).

Vocational Training and Skill Development

Vocational training serious games are increasingly used in industries such as manufacturing, engineering, and customer service to provide a safe, controlled environment for skill development. These simulations allow trainees to practice technical tasks, such as operating machinery, following safety protocols, and troubleshooting equipment, without the risk of real-world consequences. Artificial intelligence further enhances these simulations by offering adaptive learning experiences. For instance, Artificial Intelligence can generate dynamic problem-solving scenarios that mimic real-world challenges, adjusting the level of complexity to match the learner's abilities (Oluwaseyi, n.d.).

Natural Language Processing (NLP) is another critical artificial intelligence integration in serious games, particularly in customer service training. By simulating realistic customer interactions, these games help users practice communication, conflict resolution, and negotiation skills. Artificial intelligence algorithms analyze the responses and behaviors of the players, providing valuable insights into areas of strength and opportunities for improvement (Lathwesen & Belova, 2021). Research has demonstrated that artificial intelligence -enhanced vocational training serious games significantly accelerate learning and retention by providing tailored feedback and adaptive scenarios (Fernández Galeote & Hamari, 2021).

Academic and Educational Settings

In academic settings, serious games have proven to be an effective tool for teaching complex subjects, especially in Science, Technology, Engineering, and Mathematics (STEM), language learning, and computer science. These games provide students with an interactive, immersive learning experience, allowing them to explore difficult concepts through hands-on engagement. The integration of artificial intelligence in educational serious games offers personalized learning experiences by adapting the difficulty and content based on a student's performance (Ghosh & Ravichandran, 2024).

Artificial intelligence -driven algorithms can adjust the complexity of tasks, provide hints, or suggest additional resources to help students grasp challenging material (Maskeliunas et al., 2022).

Artificial intelligence -powered serious games also offer real-time language translation and pronunciation guidance, which is particularly useful for language learners. Adaptive algorithms evaluate a student's linguistic abilities and provide personalized feedback on pronunciation, grammar, and sentence structure. This personalized approach not only supports individual learning but also fosters a deeper understanding of the subject matter by catering to the learner's specific needs. Studies show that such artificial intelligence -powered language games enhance vocabulary retention and grammar skills, leading to improved linguistic proficiency in a shorter period (Komasawa & Yokohira, 2023).

Social and Behavioral Sciences

Serious games have become valuable tools in social and behavioral sciences, offering unique opportunities to study human behavior, decision-making, and social dynamics. These games simulate real-world social interactions, enabling researchers to observe and analyze how individuals make decisions, resolve conflicts, and interact with others in various contexts. Artificial intelligence -driven agents in these games can mimic different personalities, ethical dilemmas, and negotiation scenarios, allowing players to explore moral reasoning, empathy, and conflict resolution in a controlled, risk-free environment (Romero, Lameras, & Arnab, 2024).

Artificial intelligence in serious games also provides a powerful tool for behavioral analysis, enabling the collection of large-scale data on user interactions and decision-making processes. This data can be used to gain insights into group dynamics, ethical decision-making, and individual behavioral responses. In educational psychology, for instance, artificial Intelligence-driven serious games help players develop social skills by practicing perspective-taking and cultural understanding (Krath, Schürmann, & Von Korflesch, 2021). Recent studies have shown that these interactive environments significantly enhance the development of prosocial skills and emotional intelligence (Tolks, Schmidt, & Kuhn, 2024).

Environmental Science and Sustainability

In the fight against climate change and ecological degradation, serious games serve as innovative tools to raise awareness, encourage sustainable behaviors, and foster environmental education. Unlike traditional learning approaches, these games immerse players in real-world scenarios, simulating the complexities of environmental decision-making. For instance, recent research indicates that climate-based simulation games encourage players to make sustainable choices by demonstrating the environmental impacts of actions on urban or rural ecosystems. This participatory approach helps learners internalize the often-abstract consequences of climate change, thereby supporting public engagement in sustainability efforts (Denecke, Schmid, & Nüssli, 2022).

Moreover, serious games in environmental science have proven especially useful in promoting actionable understanding among diverse audiences, from students to policymakers. For example, a serious game focusing on water resource management in Germany helps players understand the delicate balance between agricultural practices and water quality, offering an accessible yet scientifically accurate portrayal of ecosystem dependencies (Janakiraman, Watson, Watson, & Newby, 2021).By reinforcing these relationships through gameplay, serious games cultivate a deeper sense of responsibility and can inspire real-world environmental actions, making them valuable for sustainability education on a broad scale.

Research and Data Collection

In academic and applied research, serious games are harnessed not only as tools for simulation but also as platforms for data collection, providing rich, behavior-based datasets that are often difficult to acquire through conventional means. These games are particularly valuable in psychological and social science research, where they allow for controlled environments that can observe players' responses to various stimuli. For example, in health and clinical research, serious games have been used to simulate patient scenarios and collect data on how users respond to medical emergencies, thus helping researchers understand and predict behavior under pressure (Hammady & Arnab, 2022).

With advancements in artificial intelligence and IoT, serious games are becoming even more powerful for data collection, offering real-time tracking of users' actions and decisions. This capacity is invaluable for studies where detailed, moment-by-moment data can reveal critical insights, such as decision-making patterns and emotional responses. Moreover, these games contribute to interdisciplinary research by facilitating controlled experiments in virtual environments, allowing researchers to explore complex human behaviors in a scientifically reliable yet interactive format (Sermet, Demir, & Muste,

2020).Such data collection is proving critical in fields like healthcare, where serious games help assess procedural learning and decision-making skills, ultimately aiding the development of more targeted training solutions for professionals.

Personal Development and Self-Improvement

In the realm of personal growth, serious games offer highly engaging and personalized experiences that support users in developing key life skills, from emotional regulation to interpersonal communication. These games use interactive scenarios to help individuals practice self-management and resilience in a low-risk setting. For instance, several studies highlight how games aimed at mental health improvement encourage users to identify and regulate emotional responses to stressful situations, fostering mental resilience over time (French, 2020). The interactive format of serious games makes them particularly effective for younger audiences who may find traditional approaches to self-improvement less engaging.

Beyond emotional growth, serious games also support cognitive and social skill development, such as problem-solving, teamwork, and adaptability. Games focused on communication skills, for instance, create simulated social interactions where users practice empathy, active listening, and conflict resolution. Through repeated engagement in these realistic scenarios, users build both confidence and competence, benefiting their personal and professional lives. The integration of artificial intelligence in these games allows for highly tailored feedback, adapting challenges based on individual progress and enhancing learning outcomes (Hao, Wang, & Chen, 2024).

URBAN PLANNING AND ARCHITECTURE: SIMULATING THE CITIES OF TOMORROW

The rapid pace of urbanization and the urgency of sustainable development have created a unique opportunity for serious games to support urban planning and architecture. By simulating realistic urban environments, these games enable planners, architects, and even citizens to visualize and interact with models of future cities, testing the impacts of proposed policies, infrastructure, and designs.

Dynamic Urban Simulations

Serious games enable the simulation of intricate urban dynamics, allowing stakeholders to observe potential outcomes of zoning laws, infrastructure developments, and even climate-adaptive policies. Research has shown that these simulations improve the quality of urban planning by providing data-driven insights into how changes might affect traffic flow, resource distribution, and environmental resilience over time (Hao, Wang, & Chen, 2024).This capacity to experiment virtually with complex, interconnected systems helps urban planners anticipate and mitigate challenges that are difficult to foresee through traditional planning tools alone (Poulopoulos & Wallace, 2022).

Participatory Urban Design and Community Engagement

One of the most impactful applications of serious games is in participatory urban design, where citizens are invited to engage directly with urban planning projects. By involving community members in a virtual simulation of their neighborhood or city, planners create a collaborative experience that fosters inclusivity and transparency. Studies show that participatory design increases public understanding and acceptance of urban projects, as it empowers citizens to contribute to decisions that shape their environments (Vermeir, White, Johnson, Crombez, & Van Ryckeghem, 2020). Through this approach, serious games become a medium for dialogue between city planners and residents, fostering community cohesion and democratic participation in urban development.

Artificial intelligence -Enhanced Predictive Modeling

As cities become more data-rich, artificial intelligence -integrated serious games can forecast urban trends and challenges, providing a data-driven foundation for decision-making. For example, predictive modeling within these games enables simulations of population growth, economic shifts, and environmental stressors, helping planners to design resilient cities prepared for future uncertainties (Springer, n.d.).This capability to model potential scenarios—such as increased urbanization or shifts in climate—supports sustainable planning that considers long-term impacts on infrastructure, resources, and quality of life (Johnson, 2022).

ARTIFICIAL INTELLIGENCE -DRIVEN SERIOUS GAMES: RECENT DEVELOPMENTS

The integration of artificial intelligence (AI) into serious games has revolutionized their design and application, making them more adaptive, engaging, and effective across various domains. Below are some prominent examples of how artificial intelligence is employed in recent serious games:

Beat Saber (Health and Fitness)

Domain: Physical and Cognitive Health

Beat Saber is a VR exergame designed to encourage physical activity through engaging gameplay. By integrating music and movement, it promotes cardiovascular health and physical fitness. Research highlights its ability to motivate diverse age groups to adopt regular exercise routines. The game is also effective in cognitive engagement, as players must react to visual and auditory stimuli in real-time. However, concerns about VR-induced motion sickness suggest a need for moderation and adjustments in gameplay mechanics to ensure safety and comfort (Tammy Lin, Wu, & Bowman, 2023).

Minecraft Modifications for Autism Spectrum Disorder (ASD) (Social Skills Training)

Domain: Social Skills Development and Behavioral Therapy

A tailored version of **Minecraft** supports children with ASD by providing a virtual space to practice social communication. The game simulates real-life interactions, allowing children to develop conversational skills and teamwork abilities in a controlled environment. Artificial intelligence enables dynamic adaptation to the player's progress, creating personalized learning scenarios that encourage skill transfer to real-world social contexts. The outcomes demonstrate significant improvements in social engagement and emotional understanding, showcasing the game's potential in therapeutic applications (Cadieux & Keenan, 2020).

FoodRateMaster (Nutrition Education for Children)

Domain: Nutrition Education and Lifestyle Behavior Change

FoodRateMaster is a game aimed at teaching children healthy eating habits through gamified learning. The integration of artificial intelligence allows the content to adapt to individual learning needs, offering a personalized educational experience. This approach simplifies complex topics, such as nutritional values and balanced diets, making them more relatable for younger audiences. By fostering engagement through interactive storytelling, the game encourages children to make healthier food choices, contributing to long-term lifestyle improvements (Belghali, Statsenko, & Al-Za'abi, 2021).

Virtual Reality Exposure Therapy for Phobias (Mental Health)

Domain: Psychological Therapy and Mental Health Intervention

This artificial intelligence -powered VR game addresses specific phobias, like arachnophobia, through personalized exposure therapy. By analyzing user reactions in real time, the game tailors' scenarios to gradually increase stress tolerance. This adaptive approach ensures that users remain comfortable while progressively overcoming their fears. The combination of AI and immersive VR environments provides a safe and effective method for treating anxiety disorders, making mental health therapy more accessible and scalable (Krzystanek et al., 2021).

THE ROLE OF ARTIFICIAL INTELLIGENCE IN SERIOUS GAMES

Artificial Intelligence (AI) has emerged as a transformative force in the realm of serious games (SGs), offering significant advancements in making them more engaging, personalized, and adaptive. Unlike traditional learning environments, where content remains static and unresponsive to the learner's needs, artificial intelligence enables dynamic, responsive environments that adjust based on a learner's actions. These adaptive systems not only modify the level of difficulty in real-time but also provide intelligent feedback that can guide learners toward more effective outcomes. This section explores how artificial intelligence is reshaping serious games, emphasizing its potential to optimize learning, enhance realism, and deliver continuous, adaptive feedback across various fields.

Artificial intelligence -Driven Serious Games: Redefining Education Through Scalability, Accessibility, and Immersive Design

Game design is fundamentally about crafting immersive and interactive experiences that captivate players. Through storytelling, challenges, visuals, sound effects, and dynamic interactions with characters or objects, games create engaging worlds that draw players in. Serious games elevate this approach by weaving in educational and professional development objectives, making their design even more sophisticated and impactful.

Artificial intelligence (AI) has emerged as a transformative force to address the growing complexity of serious games. Artificial intelligence not only coordinates diverse game elements seamlessly but also introduces adaptability that allows games to evolve in response to the player's actions and needs. Unlike traditional approaches that rely on pre-scripted behaviors, artificial intelligence -powered games use advanced techniques, such as deep learning and genetic algorithms, to create intelligent agents capable of mimicking human behavior, optimizing strategies, and delivering unpredictable, engaging experiences (Westera et al., 2022).

Artificial intelligence also plays a pivotal role in accessibility and personalization. By tailoring gameplay to each learner's skill level, preferences, and abilities, artificial intelligence ensures that serious games remain inclusive and effective for a broad audience. Features like real-time feedback, adaptive difficulty, and personalized learning paths make serious games more approachable, enabling learners from diverse backgrounds to fully participate and thrive.

Another critical advantage of artificial intelligence -powered serious games lies in their ability to provide "support presence." Learners who face difficulties can receive guidance from virtual, intelligent characters designed using agent-based technologies. These characters act as mentors or collaborators, offering context-specific support that keeps players engaged and motivated (Westera et al., 2020).

Serious games are advancing in two interconnected directions: using artificial intelligence to enhance educational games and creating games that teach artificial intelligence concepts. For example, *ArtBot*, a game designed to teach reinforcement learning and supervised learning methods, allows players to explore how artificial intelligence bots are trained. Such tools not only deepen understanding of artificial intelligence but also make learning an active and exploratory process.

As technology continues to evolve, the scalability of serious games becomes another defining strength. Artificial intelligence -driven systems can dynamically generate content, simulate complex environments, and replace human participants with intelligent bots when necessary. This adaptability ensures that serious games can scale to large audiences while maintaining a high degree of personalization, making them ideal for both individual learners and collaborative group settings (Christopoulos & Mystakidis, 2023).

By blending cutting-edge artificial intelligence with thoughtful game design, serious games transcend traditional educational methods. They provide learners with rich, interactive experiences that challenge their problem-solving skills, foster creativity, and enable mastery of new concepts in a safe, engaging environment. With artificial intelligence at its core, serious games are reshaping the future of learning, empowering individuals to grow, innovate, and succeed in an increasingly complex world (Christopoulos & Mystakidis, 2023).

Personalization and Adaptive Learning

Artificial intelligence's ability to personalize the learning experience is one of its most compelling advantages in serious games. Traditional educational systems typically adopt a one-size-fits-all approach, which can be ineffective for diverse learners. In contrast, artificial intelligence enables serious games to tailor content dynamically, considering each learner's progress, strengths, and weaknesses. Artificial intelligence-powered adaptive learning algorithms allow games to adjust task complexity, pace, and the introduction of targeted challenges based on the learner's performance (Correia & Simões-Marques, 2023). This adaptability is particularly beneficial in environments where learners must master complex concepts at their own pace.

For instance, in medical training, artificial intelligence can modify diagnostic scenarios according to the learner's proficiency level. If a learner struggles, the game might offer hints or alternative explanations, ensuring they receive the necessary support. Similarly, artificial intelligence-driven vocational training games can monitor a trainee's actions, assess skill levels, and recommend additional practice for areas where improvement is needed (Wang & Huang, 2021).In healthcare, artificial intelligence can create personalized medical simulations, enabling learners to engage with scenarios that reflect their expertise, thus enhancing the relevance of the training experience (Almås & Giæver, 2024).

Real-Time Feedback and Performance Tracking

Another key contribution of artificial intelligence to serious games is its capacity to provide real-time feedback, a feature crucial for effective learning. In traditional educational settings, feedback is often delayed, hindering learners' ability to understand and correct their mistakes in a timely manner. Artificial intelligence addresses this challenge by offering immediate, corrective feedback based on the learner's performance. This instant feedback loop is especially beneficial in clinical training, where rapid decision-making and procedural accuracy are essential (Batzos et al., 2023).

Artificial intelligence can track learners' actions during medical simulations, offering feedback on their clinical reasoning and procedural skills. This helps learners identify areas for improvement and allows instructors to evaluate performance more effectively. Additionally, artificial intelligence can generate detailed performance reports, providing valuable insights into learners' progress and highlighting areas that need further attention (Gao & Liu, 2023). Artificial intelligence -driven motion tracking technologies in rehabilitation games assess patients' movements, offering personalized feedback and recommending adjustments to exercises based on real-time performance data (Adams et al., 2023).

Realistic Simulations and Virtual Agents

Artificial intelligence is particularly adept at enhancing the realism of simulations in serious games, making them more applicable to fields like healthcare, vocational training, and social sciences. In medical training, artificial intelligence-powered virtual patients react to interventions in ways that mimic real-life medical conditions. These virtual agents simulate a wide range of symptoms, fluctuating vitals, and complex histories, providing learners with an immersive, hands-on experience (Farina et al., 2024).

In vocational settings, artificial intelligence enables the creation of highly immersive simulations of real-world environments. For example, artificial intelligence can simulate complex machinery operations or hazardous work conditions, allowing trainees to practice their skills without the risk of making costly errors. These simulations adapt to the learner's performance, continuously introducing new challenges as the trainee progresses (Chaarani et al., 2022). In social sciences, artificial intelligence -powered virtual agents are used to simulate human interactions, allowing learners to practice skills such as conflict resolution, decision-making, and negotiation in dynamic, real-time scenarios (Deng, 2021).

Data-Driven Insights and Analytics

Artificial intelligence's role in data analysis is integral to improving the design and effectiveness of serious games. By tracking learners' interactions, artificial intelligence generates insights into their decision-making processes and problem-solving abilities. This data not only helps in enhancing the game design but also provides valuable feedback to learners and instructors (Laghari et al., 2024). Artificial intelligence can track a learner's progress over multiple sessions, identifying patterns in strengths and weaknesses, and fine-tuning the game's content to provide more targeted challenges.

In clinical serious games, artificial intelligence's ability to analyze performance in real-time allows instructors to assess learners' skills in specific procedures and identify areas where additional practice is necessary. Furthermore, data analytics enables instructors to identify broader trends across multiple players, offering a comprehensive view of the overall learning process and informing future training adjustments (Arif et al., 2025).

Natural Language Processing (NLP) for Communication Skills

The integration of Natural Language Processing (NLP) into serious games facilitates more effective training in communication skills. NLP allows artificial intelligence-driven characters within the game to understand and respond to user input in natural language, enabling realistic interactions. This is particularly beneficial in fields such as healthcare, customer service, and language learning. For instance, in customer service training, artificial intelligence-powered serious games can simulate real-world customer interactions, allowing trainees to practice empathy, problem-solving, and communication skills in real time (Zhan et al., 2024).

In language learning, NLP algorithms help learners improve their speaking and writing abilities by analyzing their pronunciation, grammar, and vocabulary. Providing real-time corrections and feedback, NLP-enhanced serious games facilitate continuous learning, enabling learners to refine their language skills at their own pace. Research has demonstrated that serious games enhanced with NLP can significantly accelerate language acquisition by offering immediate, personalized feedback, which has been shown to improve learner retention (Blaga & Iancu, 2021).

Artificial intelligence's integration into serious games has revolutionized how we approach education and professional training. By personalizing learning experiences, offering real-time feedback, creating realistic simulations, and providing data-driven insights, artificial intelligence greatly enhances the effectiveness of serious games across various domains, including healthcare, vocational training, and social sciences. As artificial intelligence technology evolves, its potential to optimize the design, implementation, and outcomes of serious games will only expand. This opens new avenues for more engaging, adaptive, and impactful learning, providing learners with a deeper, more tailored educational experience.

CHALLENGES AND NEW HORIZONS

Serious Games (SGs), in their various forms, have proven their effectiveness as tools for learning and treatment in fields as diverse as healthcare, education, and social sciences. These games are typically divided into several therapeutic categories, each having a distinct impact on the user. For Example:

1. Exergames, which combine physical activity with virtual interaction, are designed to encourage exercise while providing an engaging experience (Wang et al., 2022).
2. Computerized Cognitive Behavioral Therapy (CBT) Games, which guide players through structured approaches aimed at recognizing and changing negative thoughts and beliefs, are used to treat disorders such as anxiety or depression (Kenwright, 2023).
3. Cognitive Training Games, which target the enhancement of mental abilities like memory, executive functions, and learning, play a crucial role in cognitive rehabilitation or maintenance (Dahalan, Alias, & Shaharom, 2024).
4. Biofeedback Games, which use bodily sensors to measure physiological variables like heart rate, influence player reactions based on their physiological state, promoting relaxation or tracking treatment progress.

The rise of artificial intelligence (AI) in the field of serious games has opened new avenues for personalizing and adapting these games to meet specific needs, offering more dynamic and engaging learning experiences. However, integrating artificial intelligence into serious games is not without challenges.

Artificial Intelligence in Serious Games: Bridging the Gap in Education

In the education sector, although both artificial intelligence and serious games are rapidly growing areas of interest, research still often treats these fields separately. Yet, the synergy between artificial intelligence and serious games has the potential to profoundly transform learning. Artificial intelligence allows for the real-time personalization of gameplay, adjusting difficulty or modifying the learning path based on the player's progress. This fosters an optimal learning experience that is both immersive and tailored to the individual (Jääskä, 2023).

Artificial intelligence -powered serious games also have the capability to capture complex emotions and reactions that are difficult to measure through traditional methods. For example, *The Moral Machine Experiment* (Anoir, Khaldi, & Erradi, 2022) uses a gamified environment to study moral dilemmas, such as those related to autonomous vehicles, by analyzing participants' responses to various scenarios and parameters. This type of research would be impossible without the interactive and immersive tools provided by artificial intelligence-driven serious games.

Artificial Intelligence and Ethics in Gaming: Addressing Bias, Data Privacy, and Accessibility

The integration of Artificial Intelligence (AI) into serious games, while presenting exciting possibilities for enhancing player experience and learning outcomes, also raises a number of significant ethical concerns. As artificial intelligence systems become more embedded in game design, it is crucial to address these challenges in a manner that ensures fairness, inclusivity, and transparency, while also fostering trust between players and developers.

Algorithmic Bias: One of the most prominent ethical concerns associated with artificial intelligence in gaming is the risk of reinforcing or amplifying existing biases. artificial intelligence-driven systems, particularly those that rely on large datasets to personalize gameplay, can inadvertently perpetuate stereotypes or inequality. For example, artificial intelligence might optimize certain in-game outcomes or character designs based on biased data, potentially marginalizing specific groups of players. This is especially critical when artificial intelligence is used to personalize experiences in a way that reflects players' behaviors or preferences. To mitigate this risk, game developers must adopt proactive strategies to ensure that AI algorithms are fair and inclusive, continually assessing and adjusting them to account for diverse player demographics (Pérez et al., 2023).

Data Privacy: Another significant challenge is the collection and use of player data. Artificial intelligence systems often require vast amounts of personal information—such as player preferences, actions, and interactions—to tailor gameplay experiences. However, without stringent privacy measures in place, this data can be exposed to misuse, potentially leading to breaches of confidentiality or unauthorized access to sensitive information. Developers must implement transparent data handling policies and robust security systems to protect player privacy, ensuring that data is only collected with informed consent and used for its intended purpose. Moreover, players should have control over their data, including the ability to opt in or out of data collection at any time (Murdoch, 2021).

Accessibility: As artificial intelligence-powered games become more personalized, it is essential to consider how these technologies can be made accessible to all players, including those with disabilities. While artificial intelligence can enhance gameplay by tailoring challenges and experiences to individual player needs, it can also alienate those who may not be able to engage with the game in the same way. For instance, players with visual or auditory impairments may struggle to engage with artificial intelligence-driven interfaces or game mechanics that rely on sight or sound. To create more inclusive gaming environments, artificial intelligence systems must be designed to accommodate a wide range of abilities. This could involve offering customizable options or adaptive features that allow players to adjust the game to meet their unique needs (Pérez et al., 2023).

Player Experience Modeling and Ethical Concerns: A critical aspect of artificial intelligence in serious games is player experience modeling, which involves the creation of detailed user profiles based on a player's behavior and preferences. While this modeling is essential for creating personalized learning experiences, it also raises significant ethical issues, particularly regarding privacy and consent. Unlike traditional educational settings, where teachers build personal relationships with students over time, artificial intelligence systems analyze digital traces of players' actions, which are not grounded in human trust or empathy. These traces can be mined and analyzed by algorithms to make decisions about the player's experience but without the nuance of human understanding. Consequently, this reliance on data-driven judgments can misinterpret player intent, leading to potential biases or inaccuracies. To address this, developers must ensure that artificial intelligence systems are transparent and that players are fully informed about how their data is being used (Westera et al., 2020).

Furthermore, while Natural Language Processing (NLP) applications have shown promise in improving the personalization of player interactions, they are not without flaws. Popular virtual assistants like Siri, Google Assistant, and Alexa have demonstrated the potential of NLP to understand and respond to player queries. However, NLP systems are not perfect; they can misinterpret player inputs, especially in complex or nuanced contexts. Additionally, the need for substantial pre-and post-processing of data makes NLP applications complex and often difficult for non-experts to implement. Developers must carefully balance the use of NLP with the need for accuracy and ensure that these systems are designed to complement, rather than replace, human interaction.

Artificial intelligence -Driven Learning Mechanisms: Another critical component of AI in serious games is the ability to assess and adapt to a player's learning progress in real-time. Reinforcement learning, for instance, allows AI systems to evaluate player actions and adjust gameplay to optimize the learning experience. By continually monitoring how a player interacts with the game, the system can adapt challenges to match their skill level, ensuring that they are neither too easy nor too difficult. However, implementing such adaptive systems requires sophisticated algorithms, such as game-theoretic approaches, optimization-based algorithms, and graph theory, to efficiently manage game resources and player interactions. These models help ensure that the game remains engaging and appropriately challenging, but they must be used responsibly to avoid unintentional biases or unfair advantages.

To facilitate the integration of artificial intelligence in serious games, a comprehensive research methodology must be used. This should include mixed-method approaches that combine qualitative assessments of player experiences with quantitative data analysis. For example, player feedback on fairness, accessibility, and the overall experience can be gathered through surveys or interviews, while gameplay data can be analyzed to evaluate the effectiveness of artificial intelligence -driven features. Additionally, interdisciplinary research, bringing together expertise from fields like ethics, psychology, and artificial intelligence technology, will provide a deeper understanding of how artificial intelligence impacts players and how to design more ethical, transparent, and inclusive systems.

As artificial intelligence continues to shape the future of serious games, game developers must remain committed to ethical principles that prioritize player privacy, fairness, and inclusivity. artificial intelligence systems should enhance, not replace, human understanding, offering personalized experiences without compromising player autonomy or trust. By adopting ethical Artificial intelligence frameworks, prioritizing transparency, and employing rigorous research methodologies, developers can create more responsible and sustainable gaming experiences that build trust between players and the gaming community (Pérez et al., 2023).

Challenges and New Horizons: Addressing the Ethical and Technological Barriers

Ethical Considerations and Bias in artificial intelligence

One of the major challenges associated with the integration of artificial intelligence in serious games is ethical issues and biases. Artificial intelligence systems learn from data, but this data can be biased or unrepresentative of the diversity of users. If the training data is biased, it can lead to artificial intelligence models that unfairly favor certain groups of users over others. In the context of serious games, this might manifest as artificial intelligence providing challenges or support disproportionately based on a player's demographic characteristics, which would compromise the equity and effectiveness of the learning experience (Ruiz-Rojas et al., 2023).

To mitigate these biases, it is essential to use diverse and representative data sets for training artificial intelligence models, to regularly audit artificial intelligence systems for biases, and to ensure that artificial intelligence operates transparently and responsibly. Strict attention must also be paid to privacy and data security, particularly when dealing with sensitive information, such as in healthcare or rehabilitation simulations.

Technological Limitations and Accessibility

Another significant challenge lies in the technological limitations and accessibility issues associated with artificial intelligence-powered serious games. While artificial intelligence continues to grow in power, its integration into these games often requires substantial computing resources, which can limit accessibility. Not all users have access to the necessary hardware or software capabilities to run artificial intelligence -powered games, particularly in underserved regions. This digital divide means that the full benefits of artificial intelligence -enhanced serious games may not be equally available to everyone.

Moreover, the development of highly realistic simulations and real-time artificial intelligence feedback can be resource-intensive, requiring advanced algorithms, high-quality graphics, and fast processing speeds. For developers, the challenge is to create serious games that are both high-performing and accessible, which might involve developing lighter versions of these games or utilizing cloud computing to handle the more intensive artificial intelligence.

Maintaining Human-Centered Design

As artificial intelligence becomes more integrated into serious games, another major challenge is maintaining human-centered design principles. While artificial intelligence can provide personalized learning experiences, it must not replace the human element in the educational process. Human interactions, whether with instructors, mentors, or other players, play an essential role in learning, especially in fields like healthcare, where empathy and understanding are paramount.

Game designers must ensure that artificial intelligence complements rather than replaces these human interactions and that the game remains empathetic and responsive to the player's needs. A human-centered design approach ensures that artificial intelligence enhances the learning experience meaningfully, offering adaptive feedback and challenges without overshadowing the importance of social and emotional learning.

New Horizons: Artificial Intelligence as a Co-Designer and Immersive Technologies

Despite these challenges, the potential of artificial intelligence in serious games is vast. One of the most exciting opportunities lies in using artificial intelligence as a co-designer in the creation of these games. In this collaborative role, artificial intelligence can assist game designers by analyzing player behavior, testing game mechanics, and even generating new content or scenarios based on real-time data. This partnership could make the game design process more efficient, dynamic, and creative.

The integration of artificial intelligence with emerging technologies such as Virtual Reality (VR) and Augmented Reality (AR) also offers tremendous potential for creating immersive learning environments. With artificial intelligence, virtual environments created with VR and AR could become even more realistic and interactive, providing learners with context-specific, real-time feedback based on their actions within the simulated environment.

In conclusion, while the integration of artificial intelligence into serious games presents several challenges, the benefits are immense and could radically transform education and research. Artificial intelligence, as a personalized and interactive learning tool, has the potential to better understand learner behaviors and emotions while providing enriching experiences. By overcoming obstacles related to ethics, accessibility, and human-centered design, artificial intelligence -powered serious games will offer more inclusive, effective, and engaging learning solutions. This fusion of artificial intelligence and serious games is just beginning, and its potential to improve educational and training systems is significant.

Opportunities and Challenges of artificial intelligence-driven Serious Games: Striking a Balance Between Innovation and Limitations

The integration of artificial intelligence (AI) in adaptive gaming holds substantial promise for creating deeply immersive and responsive gaming experiences. However, one of the most persistent challenges is the gap between a player's true intentions and how the game interprets those intentions. Unlike web applications, where user actions tend to be more straightforward, games involve a complex array of decisions and experiences, which makes it difficult for artificial intelligence to fully grasp the player's intent. Compounding this issue is the fact that player intentions are not directly observable, making them challenging for algorithms to detect. Despite considerable research in this area, three key challenges in player modeling remain unresolved, limiting the effectiveness of artificial intelligence -driven adaptive gaming.

1. Enhancing the Accuracy of Player Modeling

For artificial intelligence systems to accurately model an individual player's behavior, they require detailed data on the player's actions, preferences, and in-game decisions. While such data is often available, accurately interpreting and labeling this data remains a significant challenge. A primary issue is that player intentions cannot always be easily deduced from observed actions, particularly in dynamic gaming environments where player behavior may change rapidly. This ambiguity makes it difficult for games to adapt in a meaningful and personalized way.

One widely used method for overcoming this challenge is collaborative filtering, commonly applied in recommendation systems. Collaborative filtering predicts a player's preferences by comparing their actions with those of others who share similar tastes. While effective in some contexts, this method generalizes preferences rather than creating individualized models. In gaming, such generalization fails to capture the nuanced intentions of players. For example, in the adaptive horror game *Silent Hill: Shattered Memories*, the artificial intelligence misinterpreted a player's actions. The player, lost in a specific area, was mistakenly seen as choosing to remain in that area. The game then increased the horror elements there, assuming the player wanted to stay, when, in fact, the player simply wished to find their way out. This example underscores the challenges artificial intelligence faces in accurately understanding player intent, especially within complex game settings.

These discrepancies between player actions and game adaptations highlight the need for artificial intelligence systems capable of more accurately interpreting player behavior. Such advancements are vital for creating gaming experiences that feel seamless, responsive, and intuitive (Ruiz-Rojas et al., 2023).

2. *Bridging the Gap Between Theory-Driven and Data-Driven Models*

A significant challenge in adaptive gaming lies in reconciling theory-driven and data-driven approaches to player modeling. Theory-driven models are typically based on established psychological frameworks, such as *Self-Determination Theory*, which explores how intrinsic motivations shape player behavior. These models often rely on predefined assumptions about how players interact with games. In contrast, data-driven models build directly from observed player behavior, inferring patterns and preferences from real-world data without relying on theoretical assumptions.

While both approaches have their merits, conflicts arise when they produce contradictory results. For example, in the *TAEMILE* project, which was based on learning science theory, the model assumed that certain player traits were fixed. However, data collected during the project revealed that these traits fluctuated over time, highlighting a mismatch between theoretical expectations and actual player behavior. This disconnect underscores the difficulty in integrating theory-based models with data-driven models to create more accurate and reliable player profiles.

This ongoing tension presents a significant obstacle for the field of adaptive gaming. The research community has yet to reach a consensus on how to effectively combine these two approaches, which makes it difficult to develop models that are both theoretically sound and practically applicable. To advance adaptive gaming, it is critical to develop methodologies that integrate the strengths of both approaches, ensuring that player models are both grounded in theory and responsive to the nuances of real player behavior (Kenwright, 2023).

3. *Designing Meaningful Player Choices*

The accuracy of player modeling is closely tied to the range and quality of choices available to players within a game. In most cases, there is a gap between the "true actions" players would like to take and the choices the game offers. This gap is partly due to the high cost of implementing choices that involve complex assets such as art, animations, and voice acting. To mitigate these costs, game designers often employ creative solutions like false choices and fold-back branching structures, which increase the perceived agency of players without significantly raising development costs (Kenwright, 2023).

Additionally, game designers' intentions play a critical role in shaping the range of choices available to players. Designers may prioritize specific narrative structures or gameplay objectives, which can limit the variety of choices players can make. Much of the existing research on player choice focuses on concepts like player agency and narrative immersion. However, there remains a need for further exploration of how to ensure that the choices offered within a game meaningfully reflect the player's intentions and enhance adaptive gaming experiences.

Ultimately, providing players with meaningful and varied choices is crucial for improving the accuracy of player modeling. As artificial intelligence -driven systems continue to evolve, finding ways to balance the cost of implementing choices with the need for richer player experiences will be key to enhancing the effectiveness of these systems.

SOLUTIONS AND RECOMMENDATIONS

The integration of artificial intelligence (AI) in serious games for student skills development holds significant promise, offering opportunities to create personalized, engaging, and adaptive learning environments. However, its successful application requires addressing a number of challenges. A comprehensive approach that balances innovation with careful attention to ethical considerations, technical challenges, and inclusivity is essential for leveraging artificial intelligence 's full potential in educational gaming.

Enhancing Educational Domains through Serious Games

Serious games have shown tremendous potential across various fields, especially in education, healthcare, professional training, and military simulations. Their immersive and interactive nature allows learners to engage deeply with content, enhancing both retention and comprehension. For instance, games like *Minecraft Education Edition* and *SimCity EDU* have demonstrated how such platforms can foster critical thinking, creativity, and problem-solving skills in students. These games provide opportunities for students to apply theoretical knowledge in real-world scenarios, promoting experiential learning that enhances cognitive and practical abilities.

In the context of education, serious games are uniquely positioned to personalize the learning experience. By adjusting challenges and objectives in response to real-time data, they can cater to a wide range of learning styles, making education more adaptable and inclusive. This personalization is especially beneficial in large classrooms where individual attention may be limited, ensuring that all students have the opportunity to succeed, regardless of their initial skill levels or learning preferences.

Leveraging artificial intelligence and Data Science for Personalized Learning

Integrating artificial intelligence into serious games significantly amplifies the capacity for personalized learning. By utilizing machine learning algorithms and data science, artificial intelligence allows games to monitor a player's progress and adjust difficulty levels to match their current skill level. This personalized approach not only keeps students engaged but also motivates them intrinsically, as they feel the game evolves in response to their unique learning journey.

Artificial intelligence-driven games also facilitate optimization of learning content. For instance, Natural Language Processing (NLP) techniques can assess written or spoken student inputs, providing immediate feedback to improve the learning process. This dynamic interaction between students and the game system mimics the real-time feedback loop often seen in traditional education but enhances it with automation and scalability.

Addressing Ethical Concerns and Ensuring Data Privacy

Despite the potential benefits of artificial intelligence, its application in educational settings brings several ethical challenges. One primary concern is algorithmic bias. Artificial intelligence systems, particularly those relying on large datasets, may unintentionally reinforce existing biases, leading to unfair outcomes. To combat this, game developers must ensure that their algorithms are designed to minimize biases, utilizing diverse data sources and regularly auditing artificial intelligence models to maintain fairness.

Data privacy is another major issue. Since serious games often require extensive personal data to tailor learning experiences, the risk of data misuse is significant. Developers must implement robust data protection measures such as encryption, anonymization, and clear consent protocols. Transparency about how data is used and stored will foster trust between students, educators, and developers, ensuring that players feel secure while engaging with artificial intelligence -powered games.

Fostering Accessibility and Inclusivity

To realize the full potential of artificial intelligence -driven serious games, accessibility must be prioritized. Artificial intelligence holds great promise for personalized learning but could inadvertently exclude students with disabilities if proper accessibility features are not integrated into the game design. Game developers must design games with inclusivity in mind, ensuring compatibility with assistive technologies such as screen readers, speech recognition software, and adaptive controllers.

Artificial intelligence can also adapt the game environment to meet the needs of players with disabilities. For example, it can adjust visual or auditory elements for players with sensory impairments or offer alternative interaction modes for those with motor disabilities. Ensuring that all students, regardless of their abilities, can fully participate in the game will help make learning more equitable and accessible to all.

Overcoming the Challenges of Artificial Intelligence Integration

The integration of artificial intelligence into serious games presents several challenges. One of the key hurdles is the complexity of artificial intelligence systems themselves. Developing artificial intelligence models that can accurately track player progress, adapt to different learning styles, and provide meaningful feedback requires advanced expertise in artificial intelligence and machine learning. Moreover, the computational power needed for real-time artificial intelligence processing can be a barrier for some educational institutions.

Additionally, scalability remains a significant issue. While artificial intelligence-driven games may be effective in small-scale settings, their ability to deliver personalized learning to a large number of students remains under development. Developers must continue refining artificial intelligence algorithms and optimizing game systems to ensure they can scale without sacrificing educational value or performance.

Recommendations for the Future

To address these challenges and maximize the potential of artificial intelligence in serious games, several strategies should be implemented:

- **Ethical Frameworks and Bias Mitigation**: Developers must adopt ethical guidelines that minimize bias. Regular auditing of artificial intelligence algorithms, along with the use of diverse datasets, will help ensure fairness and inclusivity.
- **Data Protection and Transparency**: Developers must establish robust data protection measures and be transparent about how player data is collected, used, and stored. Informed consent proto-

cols should be central to the design of artificial intelligence-driven games, ensuring that students understand how their data will be utilized.

- **Accessibility by Design**: Developers should integrate accessibility features from the beginning. This includes support for assistive technologies, customizable user interfaces, and adaptive gameplay mechanics tailored to diverse learning needs.
- **Scalable artificial intelligence Solutions**: To overcome scalability issues, developers should focus on optimizing artificial intelligence algorithms and leveraging cloud-based artificial intelligence models and edge computing. These technologies can help make artificial intelligence-powered games more accessible to educational institutions with limited resources.
- **Continuous Improvement and Collaboration**: Ongoing feedback from educators, students, and researchers is essential to improving artificial intelligence systems. Collaboration between artificial intelligence researchers, educators, ethicists, and game developers will help ensure that artificial intelligence technologies are deployed in a responsible and effective manner.

CONCLUSION

The integration of artificial intelligence (AI) into serious games (SGs) represents a groundbreaking development in the way we approach learning, training, and even healthcare. While some games—referred to as serious games—are explicitly designed with a primary purpose beyond entertainment, such as training, learning new skills, or raising awareness, their entertaining nature is central to their effectiveness. Historically, serious games have existed in various formats, from traditional board games like *Monopoly* and *Suffragetto* to contemporary digital forms, and their evolution reflects a long-standing desire to blend enjoyment with meaningful outcomes (Yu, 2021). In the digital era, this integration has expanded, especially with the rise of artificial intelligence. Today, almost every digital product, including games, relies heavily on data analysis and artificial intelligence algorithms, leveraging vast amounts of user data to enhance the experience (Anoir, Khaldi, & Erradi, 2022).

This re-emergence of serious games, particularly in the educational and research domains, aligns with the growth of artificial intelligence technologies. The vast data generated by modern video games provides unique opportunities for artificial intelligence to influence design, gameplay, and learning outcomes. As this trend continues, the development of artificial intelligence-driven serious games for specific domains, particularly healthcare, is accelerating. Such games can now be tailored to a variety of health conditions, utilizing sophisticated artificial intelligence algorithms to create personalized and adaptive learning experiences for users (Toh & Lim, 2021). However, despite the promising applications, much remains to be done to assess the full efficacy of artificial intelligence-powered serious games in diverse populations and contexts. Rigorous, longitudinal, and multidisciplinary studies are necessary to determine their effectiveness across a broad range of health conditions (Keller & Brucker-Kley, 2020).

Designing an effective SG is no trivial task. Balancing educational content with entertainment remains one of the most significant challenges in the design of learning-focused serious games (Dimitriadou, Djafarova, Turetken, Verkuyl, & Ferworn, 2021). Achieving this balance is particularly difficult when incorporating artificial intelligence, as the game must not only be engaging but also sufficiently adaptive to accommodate individual learning needs. Research has shown that while artificial intelligence can personalize the learning journey, developers must remain vigilant to avoid overwhelming users or detracting from the learning objectives in pursuit of engagement alone (Yu, Gao, & Wang, 2021).

The increasing sophistication of Internet of Things (IoT) technologies is further enhancing the potential of serious games. Traditionally, serious games have been played on dedicated terminals with limited reach. However, the integration of IoT has allowed for a more pervasive and ubiquitous gaming experience. IoT's capacity to connect various devices and sensors provides a rich, real-time data environment where artificial intelligence can interact with the game on a more granular level, enhancing both learning and user engagement (Murdoch, 2021). This transformation makes serious games more accessible, scalable, and impactful, expanding their utility across various sectors, from education to healthcare and beyond.

Despite substantial progress, significant challenges persist in the integration of artificial intelligence (AI) into serious games. Ethical considerations surrounding artificial intelligence-driven decision-making and data privacy remain critical issues, as does the technological divide in resource-limited settings. To ensure artificial intelligence-powered serious games reach their full potential, developers must address these obstacles. Artificial intelligence models, for example, must be trained on diverse and inclusive datasets to prevent biases that could distort the learning experience for certain user groups. Moreover, expanding accessibility in underserved communities necessitates innovative approaches, such as designing games optimized for lower-powered devices and utilizing cloud computing to manage resource-intensive artificial intelligence tasks.

The integration of artificial intelligence into serious games presents transformative opportunities for education. By personalizing learning experiences, providing real-time feedback, and fostering inclusivity, artificial intelligence-driven games can significantly enhance student engagement and improve educational outcomes. However, realizing these benefits requires a commitment to ethical practices, robust data privacy protections, and inclusive design principles. Transparency about artificial intelligence usage and the prioritization of accessibility can ensure that these games are equitable and effective for diverse learners.

With ongoing innovation and interdisciplinary collaboration, artificial intelligence has the potential to revolutionize educational gaming. By bridging technological advancements with ethical and inclusive practices, artificial intelligence-powered serious games can create engaging, adaptive, and impactful learning environments, transforming the way students develop skills and knowledge (Kenwright, 2023).

As we look toward the future, the fusion of artificial intelligence and serious games holds immense promise. The development of artificial intelligence as a co-designer in serious game creation could revolutionize how these games are developed and tailored to the needs of individual users. artificial intelligence could assist designers in testing game mechanics, analyzing player behavior, and even generating new content in real-time, enhancing both the creativity and scalability of serious games (Ahmad et al., 2022). Additionally, the combination of artificial intelligence with augmented reality (AR) and virtual reality (VR) technologies promises to create even more immersive and interactive learning environments, offering opportunities to simulate complex real-world scenarios for training in sectors like healthcare, military, and professional development.

In conclusion, while artificial intelligence's integration into serious games brings forth numerous challenges—ranging from technological and ethical concerns to the delicate balance of learning and entertainment—it also opens up unprecedented opportunities to enhance and personalize learning experiences. Artificial intelligence can potentially transform serious games into powerful tools for education, training, and rehabilitation. As these technologies evolve, developers must remain mindful of the ethical implications, the need for inclusivity, and the importance of maintaining human-centered design. The future of serious games lies in their ability to merge artificial intelligence's computational power with human creativity and empathy, paving the way for more effective, engaging, and transformative learning experiences.

FUTURE WORK ORIENTATIONS AND PRESCRIPTIVE

Serious games offer a unique way to develop students' skills in artificial intelligence (AI) by simulating real-world applications in an interactive and engaging environment. These games provide a platform for students to explore key artificial intelligence concepts, such as neural networks, reinforcement learning, and computer vision, in a controlled, yet dynamic, setting. Through these interactive experiences, learners can experiment with artificial intelligence algorithms, understand their real-time applications, and see firsthand how their decisions impact the simulated world.

As students' progress through the game, they receive personalized feedback, allowing for adaptive learning where the difficulty of tasks adjusts according to their understanding. This ensures that students are continuously challenged at the right level, making learning more efficient and reducing the likelihood of frustration. Moreover, serious games can replicate the collaborative nature of artificial intelligence work. Many artificial intelligence projects in the real world require teamwork, where individuals with diverse expertise collaborate to tackle problems. Serious games foster this teamwork by incorporating multiplayer modes or collaborative problem-solving scenarios, encouraging students to work together and apply artificial intelligence concepts in group settings.

These games also bridge the gap between theoretical knowledge and practical application. By tackling real-world problems within the game, students can understand how artificial intelligence technologies are used to address challenges in various sectors such as healthcare, finance, and urban planning. For instance, an artificial intelligence -based serious game might simulate a healthcare system, where students need to design algorithms to predict patient outcomes or optimize resource allocation.

The future of artificial intelligence education through serious games looks particularly promising. As artificial intelligence technologies evolve, these games will be able to incorporate more complex systems and learning models. Advanced simulations may even use artificial intelligence itself to dynamically generate content based on a student's learning journey, creating a highly personalized educational experience. Additionally, integrating new technologies, such as augmented reality (AR) and virtual reality (VR), could make artificial intelligence education more immersive, offering students the opportunity to interact with artificial intelligence in three-dimensional spaces and visualizing complex datasets in innovative ways.

Looking forward, the key challenge will be to ensure that these games are accessible to all students, regardless of their technical background or resources. Developers will need to consider diverse learning styles and provide a range of game-based activities to cater to a broad audience. As artificial intelligence technologies become even more integrated into curricula, collaboration between educators, game developers, and artificial intelligence experts will be crucial in creating robust, scalable learning solutions that engage students, deepen their understanding, and prepare them for the demands of the artificial intelligence -driven world.

REFERENCES

https://ieeexplore.ieee.org/abstract/document/10697011

https://www.sciencedirect.com/science/article/pii/S2949678024000199

https://www.ingentaconnect.com/contentone/hsp/aoe/2024/00000002/00000003/art00006

https://link.springer.com/chapter/10.1007/978-3-031-61685-3_3

Abd-Alrazaq, A., Abuelezz, I., Hassan, A., AlSammarraie, A., Alhuwail, D., Irshaidat, S., Abu Serhan, H., Ahmed, A., Alabed Alrazak, S., & Househ, M. (2022). Artificial Intelligence–Driven Serious Games in Health Care: Scoping Review. *JMIR Serious Games*, 10(4), e39840. DOI: 10.2196/39840 PMID: 36445731

Abd-Alrazaq, A., Al-Jafar, E., Alajlani, M., Toro, C., Alhuwail, D., Ahmed, A., Reagu, S. M., Al-Shorbaji, N., & Househ, M. (2022). The effectiveness of serious games for alleviating depression: Systematic review and meta-analysis. *JMIR Serious Games*, 10(1), e32331. DOI: 10.2196/32331 PMID: 35029530

Adams, C., Pente, P., Lemermeyer, G., & Rockwell, G. (2023). Ethical principles for artificial intelligence in K-12 education. *Computers and Education: Artificial Intelligence*, 4, 100131. DOI: 10.1016/j.caeai.2023.100131

Ahmad, S., Umirzakova, S., Jamil, F., & Whangbo, T. K. (2022). Internet-of-things-enabled serious games: A comprehensive survey. *Future Generation Computer Systems*, 136, 67–83. DOI: 10.1016/j.future.2022.05.026

Almås, H., & Giæver, F. (2024). The emergence of collaboration in serious games: An exploratory study. *International Journal of Serious Games*, 11(3), 89–108. DOI: 10.17083/ijsg.v11i3.739

Anoir, L., Khaldi, M., & Erradi, M. (2022). Personalization in adaptive E-learning. In *Designing User Interfaces with a Data Science Approach* (pp. 40–67). IGI Global. DOI: 10.4018/978-1-7998-9121-5.ch003

. Arif, Y. M., Nugroho, F., Aini, Q., Fauzan, A. C., & Garcia, M. B. (2025). A Systematic Literature Review of Serious Games for Physical Education: Technologies, Implementations, and Evaluations. *Global Innovations in Physical Education and Health*, 1-36.

Baggen, R. (2024). *Generative AI for Automatic Feedback Generation in Serious Games* (Master's thesis).

Batzos, Z., Saoulidis, T., Margounakis, D., Fountoukidis, E., Grigoriou, E., Moukoulis, A., & Mouratidis, H. (2023). Gamification and Serious Games for Cybersecurity Awareness and First Responders Training: An overview. *Authorea Preprints*.

Belghali, M., Statsenko, Y., & Al-Za'abi, A. (2021). Improving serious games to tackle childhood obesity. *Frontiers in Psychology*, 12, 657289. DOI: 10.3389/fpsyg.2021.657289 PMID: 34025521

Bennani, S., Maalel, A., & Ben Ghezala, H. (2022). Adaptive gamification in E-learning: A literature review and future challenges. *Computer Applications in Engineering Education*, 30(2), 628–642. DOI: 10.1002/cae.22477

Bhugaonkar, K., Bhugaonkar, R., & Masne, N. (2022). The trend of metaverse and augmented & virtual reality extending to the healthcare system. *Cureus*, 14(9). Advance online publication. DOI: 10.7759/cureus.29071 PMID: 36258985

Cadieux, L., & Keenan, M. (2020). Can social communication skills for children diagnosed with autism spectrum disorder rehearsed inside the video game environment of Minecraft generalize to the real world? *JMIR Serious Games*, 8(2), e14369. DOI: 10.2196/14369 PMID: 32396129

Chaarani, B., Ortigara, J., Yuan, D., Loso, H., Potter, A., & Garavan, H. P. (2022). Association of video gaming with cognitive performance among children. *JAMA Network Open*, 5(10), e2235721–e2235721. DOI: 10.1001/jamanetworkopen.2022.35721 PMID: 36279138

Christopoulos, A., & Mystakidis, S. (2023). Gamification in Education. *Encyclopedia*, 2023(3), 1223–1243. DOI: 10.3390/encyclopedia3040089

Colado, I. J. P., Colado, V. M. P., Morata, A. C., Píriz, R. S. C., & Manjón, B. F. (2023, October). Using new AI-driven techniques to ease serious games authoring. In *2023 IEEE Frontiers in Education Conference (FIE)* (pp. 1-9). IEEE. DOI: 10.1109/FIE58773.2023.10343021

Correia, A., & Simões-Marques, M. (Eds.). (2023). *Handbook of Research on Decision-Making Capabilities Improvement With Serious Games*. IGI Global. DOI: 10.4018/978-1-6684-9166-9

Dahalan, F., Alias, N., & Shaharom, M. S. N. (2024). Gamification and game-based learning for vocational education and training: A systematic literature review. *Education and Information Technologies*, 29(2), 1279–1317. DOI: 10.1007/s10639-022-11548-w PMID: 36688221

Damaševičius, R., Maskeliūnas, R., & Blažauskas, T. (2023). Serious games and gamification in healthcare: A meta-review. *Information (Basel)*, 14(2), 105. DOI: 10.3390/info14020105

De la Torre, R., Onggo, B. S., Corlu, C. G., Nogal, M., & Juan, A. A. (2021). The role of simulation and serious games in teaching concepts on circular economy and sustainable energy. *Energies*, 14(4), 1138. DOI: 10.3390/en14041138

Denecke, K., Schmid, N., & Nüssli, S. (2022). Implementation of cognitive behavioral therapy in e–mental health apps: Literature review. *Journal of Medical Internet Research*, 24(3), e27791. DOI: 10.2196/27791 PMID: 35266875

Deng, L. (2021). Gamified information systems: Gameful experiences, achievement goals, and performance. *Quarterly Review of Business Disciplines*, 8(3), 193–211.

Dimitriadou, A., Djafarova, N., Turetken, O., Verkuyl, M., & Ferworn, A. (2021). Challenges in serious game design and development: Educators' experiences. *Simulation & Gaming*, 52(2), 132–152. DOI: 10.1177/1046878120944197

Ezzaim, A., Dahbi, A., Haidine, A., & Aqqal, A. (2023). AI-based adaptive learning: A systematic mapping of the literature. *Journal of Universal Computer Science*, 29(10), 1161–1198. DOI: 10.3897/jucs.90528

Farina, M., Zhdanov, P., Karimov, A., & Lavazza, A. (2024). AI and society: A virtue ethics approach. *AI & Society*, 39(3), 1127–1140. DOI: 10.1007/s00146-022-01545-5

Fernández Galeote, D., & Hamari, J. (2021). Game-based climate change engagement: analyzing the potential of entertainment and serious games. *Proceedings of the ACM on Human-Computer Interaction, 5*(CHI PLAY), 1-21. DOI: 10.1145/3474653

French, A. J. (2020). Simulation and modeling applications in global health security. *Global Health Security: Recognizing Vulnerabilities, Creating Opportunities*, 307-340.

Gao, Y., & Liu, H. (2023). Artificial intelligence-enabled personalization in interactive marketing: A customer journey perspective. *Journal of Research in Interactive Marketing*, 17(5), 663–680. DOI: 10.1108/JRIM-01-2022-0023

Gaurav, D., Kaushik, Y., Supraja, S., Yadav, M., Gupta, M. P., & Chaturvedi, M. (2022). Empirical study of adaptive serious games in enhancing learning outcome. *International Journal of Serious Games*, 9(2), 27–42. DOI: 10.17083/ijsg.v9i2.486

Ghosh, L., & Ravichandran, R. (2024). Emerging Technologies in Vocational Education and Training. *Journal of Digital Learning and Education*, 4(1), 41–49. DOI: 10.52562/jdle.v4i1.975

Gligorea, I., Cioca, M., Oancea, R., Gorski, A. T., Gorski, H., & Tudorache, P. (2023). Adaptive learning using artificial intelligence in e-learning: A literature review. *Education Sciences*, 13(12), 1216. DOI: 10.3390/educsci13121216

Hamilton, A. (2024). Artificial Intelligence and Healthcare Simulation: The Shifting Landscape of Medical Education. *Cureus*, 16(5). Advance online publication. DOI: 10.7759/cureus.59747 PMID: 38840993

Hammady, R., & Arnab, S. (2022). Serious gaming for behaviour change: A systematic review. *Information (Basel)*, 13(3), 142. DOI: 10.3390/info13030142

Hao, H., Wang, Y., & Chen, J. (2024). Empowering Scenario Planning with Artificial Intelligence: A Perspective on Building Smart and Resilient Cities. *Engineering (Beijing)*, 43, 272–283. DOI: 10.1016/j.eng.2024.06.012

Igras-Cybulska, M., Kolber-Bugajska, B., Salamon, R., Babiuch, P., Jegierski, H., Jegierski, M., ... & Węgrzyn, P. (2024). Supporting Unity Developers with an AI-Powered Asset: Insights from an Exploratory User Study on Multiplayer Game Development.

Jääskä, E. (2023). Game-based learning methods in project management higher education.

Janakiraman, S., Watson, S. L., Watson, W. R., & Newby, T. (2021). Effectiveness of digital games in producing environmentally friendly attitudes and behaviors: A mixed methods study. *Computers & Education*, 160, 104043. DOI: 10.1016/j.compedu.2020.104043

Johnson, J. (2022). The AI commander problem: Ethical, political, and psychological dilemmas of human-machine interactions in AI-enabled warfare. *Journal of Military Ethics*, 21(3-4), 246–271. DOI: 10.1080/15027570.2023.2175887

Keller, T., & Brucker-Kley, E. (2020). Design hints for smart agents as teachers in virtual learning spaces. In *Proceedings of the International Conference on e-Society* (pp. 111-118). DOI: 10.33965/es2020_202005L014

Kenwright, B. (2023). Exploring the power of creative ai tools and game-based methodologies for interactive web-based programming. *arXiv preprint arXiv:2308.11649.*

Khalid, U. B., Naeem, M., Stasolla, F., Syed, M. H., Abbas, M., & Coronato, A. (2024). Impact of AI-powered solutions in rehabilitation process: Recent improvements and future trends. *International Journal of General Medicine*, 17, 943–969. DOI: 10.2147/IJGM.S453903 PMID: 38495919

Kollins, S. H., DeLoss, D. J., Cañadas, E., Lutz, J., Findling, R. L., Keefe, R. S., Epstein, J. N., Cutler, A. J., & Faraone, S. V. (2020). A novel digital intervention for actively reducing severity of paediatric ADHD (STARS-ADHD): A randomised controlled trial. *The Lancet. Digital Health*, 2(4), e168–e178. DOI: 10.1016/S2589-7500(20)30017-0 PMID: 33334505

Komasawa, N., & Yokohira, M. (2023). Learner-centered experience-based medical education in an AI-driven society: A literature review. *Cureus*, 15(10). Advance online publication. DOI: 10.7759/cureus.46883 PMID: 37954813

Krath, J., Schürmann, L., & Von Korflesch, H. F. (2021). Revealing the theoretical basis of gamification: A systematic review and analysis of theory in research on gamification, serious games and game-based learning. *Computers in Human Behavior*, 125, 106963. DOI: 10.1016/j.chb.2021.106963

Krzystanek, M., Surma, S., Stokrocka, M., Romańczyk, M., Przybyło, J., Krzystanek, N., & Borkowski, M. (2021). Tips for effective implementation of virtual reality exposure therapy in phobias—A systematic review. *Frontiers in Psychiatry*, 12, 737351. DOI: 10.3389/fpsyt.2021.737351 PMID: 34621197

. Laghari, A. A., Estrela, V. V., Li, H., Shoulin, Y., Khan, A. A., Anwar, M. S., ... & Bouraqia, K. (2024). Quality of experience assessment in virtual/augmented reality serious games for healthcare: A systematic literature review. *Technology and Disability*, (Preprint), 1-12.

Lamnai, A., & mhouti, A. E. (2023, January). Serious Games for Improving Training and Skills Acquisition in Medicine and Health Professions. In *International Conference on Digital Technologies and Applications* (pp. 967-975). Cham: Springer Nature Switzerland. DOI: 10.1007/978-3-031-29857-8_96

Lathwesen, C., & Belova, N. (2021). Escape rooms in STEM teaching and Learning—Prospective field or declining trend? A literature review. *Education Sciences*, 11(6), 308. DOI: 10.3390/educsci11060308

Lee, L. K., Wei, X., Chui, K. T., Cheung, S. K., Wang, F. L., Fung, Y. C., Lu, A., Hui, Y. K., Hao, T., U, L. H., & Wu, N. I. (2024). A Systematic Review of the Design of Serious Games for Innovative Learning: Augmented Reality, Virtual Reality, or Mixed Reality? *Electronics (Basel)*, 13(5), 890. DOI: 10.3390/electronics13050890

Liu, D. S., Abu-Shaban, K., Halabi, S. S., & Cook, T. S. (2023). Changes in radiology due to artificial intelligence that can attract medical students to the specialty. *JMIR Medical Education*, 9, e43415. DOI: 10.2196/43415 PMID: 36939823

Maghsudi, S., Lan, A., Xu, J., & van Der Schaar, M. (2021). Personalized education in the artificial intelligence era: What to expect next. *IEEE Signal Processing Magazine*, 38(3), 37–50. DOI: 10.1109/MSP.2021.3055032

Martin, S. M., Casey, J. R., & Kane, S. (2021). *Serious Games in Personalized Learning: New Models for Design and Performance*. Taylor & Francis. DOI: 10.4324/9781003042709

Maskeliunas, R., Damasevicius, R., Paulauskas, A., Ceravolo, M. G., Charalambous, M., Kambanaros, M., Pampoulou, E., Barbabella, F., Poli, A., & Carvalho, C. V. (2022). Deep reinforcement learning-based iTrain serious game for caregivers dealing with post-stroke patients. *Information (Basel)*, 13(12), 564. DOI: 10.3390/info13120564

Mittal, A., Scholten, L., & Kapelan, Z. (2022). A review of serious games for urban water management decisions: Current gaps and future research directions. *Water Research*, 215, 118217. DOI: 10.1016/j.watres.2022.118217 PMID: 35320773

Mohamadi, S., Mujtaba, G., Le, N., Doretto, G., & Adjeroh, D. A. (2023). ChatGPT in the age of generative AI and large language models: a concise survey. *arXiv preprint arXiv:2307.04251*.

Murdoch, B. (2021). Privacy and artificial intelligence: Challenges for protecting health information in a new era. *BMC Medical Ethics*, 22(1), 1–5. DOI: 10.1186/s12910-021-00687-3 PMID: 34525993

Pasqualotto, A., Parong, J., Green, C. S., & Bavelier, D. (2023). Video game design for learning to learn. *International Journal of Human-Computer Interaction*, 39(11), 2211–2228. DOI: 10.1080/10447318.2022.2110684

Pérez, J., Castro, M., & López, G. (2023). Serious games and ai: Challenges and opportunities for computational social science. *IEEE Access : Practical Innovations, Open Solutions*, 11, 62051–62061. DOI: 10.1109/ACCESS.2023.3286695

. Pérez Sánchez, J. (2024). Impact of Serious Games and Causal Artificial Intelligence on Social Science Research: A Case Study on Cyberbullying.

Poulopoulos, V., & Wallace, M. (2022). Digital technologies and the role of data in cultural heritage: The past, the present, and the future. *Big Data and Cognitive Computing*, 6(3), 73. DOI: 10.3390/bdcc6030073

Rane, N., Choudhary, S., & Rane, J. (2023). Education 4.0 and 5.0: Integrating artificial intelligence (AI) for personalized and adaptive learning. *Available atSSRN* 4638365. DOI: 10.2139/ssrn.4638365

Romero, M., Lameras, P., & Arnab, S. (2024). Affordances for AI-Enhanced Digital Game-Based Learning. In *Creative Applications of Artificial Intelligence in Education* (pp. 117–128). Springer Nature Switzerland. DOI: 10.1007/978-3-031-55272-4_9

Ruiz-Rojas, L. I., Acosta-Vargas, P., De-Moreta-Llovet, J., & Gonzalez-Rodriguez, M. (2023). Empowering education with generative artificial intelligence tools: Approach with an instructional design matrix. *Sustainability (Basel)*, 15(15), 11524. DOI: 10.3390/su151511524

Sapci, A. H., & Sapci, H. A. (2020). Artificial intelligence education and tools for medical and health informatics students: Systematic review. *JMIR Medical Education*, 6(1), e19285. DOI: 10.2196/19285 PMID: 32602844

Sermet, Y., Demir, I., & Muste, M. (2020). A serious gaming framework for decision support on hydrological hazards. *The Science of the Total Environment*, 728, 138895. DOI: 10.1016/j.scitotenv.2020.138895 PMID: 32361365

Tammy Lin, J. H., Wu, D. Y., & Bowman, N. (2023). Beat Saber as virtual reality exercising in 360 degrees: A moderated mediation model of VR playable angles on physiological and psychological outcomes. *Media Psychology*, 26(4), 414–435. DOI: 10.1080/15213269.2022.2154806

Toh, W., & Lim, F. V. (2021). Using video games for learning: Developing a metalanguage for digital play. *Games and Culture*, 16(5), 583–610. DOI: 10.1177/1555412020921339

Tolks, D., Schmidt, J. J., & Kuhn, S. (2024). The role of AI in serious games and gamification for health: Scoping review. *JMIR Serious Games*, 12(1), e48258. DOI: 10.2196/48258 PMID: 38224472

Ullah, M., Amin, S. U., Munsif, M., Yamin, M. M., Safaev, U., Khan, H., Khan, S., & Ullah, H. (2022). Serious games in science education: A systematic literature. *Virtual Reality & Intelligent Hardware*, 4(3), 189–209. DOI: 10.1016/j.vrih.2022.02.001

van Gaalen, A. E., Brouwer, J., Schönrock-Adema, J., Bouwkamp-Timmer, T., Jaarsma, A. D. C., & Georgiadis, J. R. (2021). Gamification of health professions education: A systematic review. *Advances in Health Sciences Education : Theory and Practice*, 26(2), 683–711. DOI: 10.1007/s10459-020-10000-3 PMID: 33128662

Vermeir, J. F., White, M. J., Johnson, D., Crombez, G., & Van Ryckeghem, D. M. (2020). The effects of gamification on computerized cognitive training: Systematic review and meta-analysis. *JMIR Serious Games*, 8(3), e18644. DOI: 10.2196/18644 PMID: 32773374

Waladi, C., Khaldi, M., & Sefian, M. L. (2023). Machine Learning Approach for an Adaptive E-Learning System Based on Kolb Learning Styles. *International Journal of Emerging Technologies in Learning*, 18(12), 4–15. DOI: 10.3991/ijet.v18i12.39327

Wang, C., & Huang, L. (2021). A Systematic Review of Serious Games for Collaborative Learning: Theoretical Framework, Game Mechanic and Efficiency Assessment. *International Journal of Emerging Technologies in Learning*, 16(6), 88. DOI: 10.3991/ijet.v16i06.18495

Wang, Y., Wang, Z., Liu, G., Wang, Z., Wang, Q., Yan, Y., Wang, J., Zhu, Y., Gao, W., Kan, X., Zhang, Z., Jia, L., & Pang, X. (2022). Application of serious games in health care: Scoping review and bibliometric analysis. *Frontiers in Public Health*, 10, 896974. DOI: 10.3389/fpubh.2022.896974 PMID: 35757619

Westera, W., Prada, R., Mascarenhas, S., Santos, P. A., Dias, J., Guimarães, M., Georgiadis, K., Nyamsuren, E., Bahreini, K., Yumak, Z., Christyowidiasmoro, C., Dascalu, M., Gutu-Robu, G., & Ruseti, S. (2020). Artificial intelligence moving serious gaming: Presenting reusable game AI components. *Education and Information Technologies*, 25(1), 351–380. DOI: 10.1007/s10639-019-09968-2

Yenduri, G., Ramalingam, M., Selvi, G. C., Supriya, Y., Srivastava, G., Maddikunta, P. K. R., Raj, G. D., Jhaveri, R. H., Prabadevi, B., Wang, W., Vasilakos, A. V., & Gadekallu, T. R. (2024). Gpt (generative pre-trained transformer)–a comprehensive review on enabling technologies, potential applications, emerging challenges, and future directions. *IEEE Access : Practical Innovations, Open Solutions*, 12, 54608–54649. DOI: 10.1109/ACCESS.2024.3389497

. Yu, Z. (2021). A meta-analysis of the effect of Kahoot! on academic achievements and student performance.

Yu, Z., Gao, M., & Wang, L. (2021). The effect of educational games on learning outcomes, student motivation, engagement and satisfaction. *Journal of Educational Computing Research*, 59(3), 522–546. DOI: 10.1177/0735633120969214

Zhan, Z., Tong, Y., Lan, X., & Zhong, B. (2024). A systematic literature review of game-based learning in Artificial Intelligence education. *Interactive Learning Environments*, 32(3), 1137–1158. DOI: 10.1080/10494820.2022.2115077

Chapter 13
Students' Learning Trajectory Through Literary Text:
Socio-Emotional and Axiological Skills

Chafik Azirar
https://orcid.org/0009-0001-3966-9903
ENS Tétouan, Université Abdelmalek Essaadi, Morocco

Hassane Kemouss
https://orcid.org/0000-0002-9664-3275
Ecole Normale Superieur de Tetouan, Morocco

ABSTRACT

The chapter entitled: The learning trajectory of students through the literary text socio-emotional and axiological skills aims to highlight the approaches implemented in the teaching-learning process of students with learning difficulties in the French language. Our work consists of leading learners to acquire axiological skills through oral and written comprehension and production courses while strengthening their socio-emotional skills at the same time. We took a quantitative and qualitative approach through a statistical analysis to qualify the factors involved in the development of axiological and socio-emotional skills in learners. By evaluating the capacity of these students before and after the intervention; it was established that they developed both their academic performance and their axiological and socio-emotional skills. Finally, the chapter presents recommendations for stakeholders to improve student engagement and performance.

INTRODUCTION

Values education is an essential and crucial component for the development of individuals and societies. However, and despite the efforts made, many students still struggle to acquire the fundamental skills necessary for their academic and future success in terms of axiological skills and emotional stability, in particular, as students with French-language learning difficulties face recurring obstacles that hinder their progress in teaching-learning. In this context, understanding the factors that influence students' learning trajectories and the acquisition of axiological skills is essential for designing more effective pedagogical

DOI: 10.4018/979-8-3693-8965-2.ch013

mediation interventions. Several studies have highlighted the major role played by social-emotional skills in academic success and value development. However, the precise mechanisms by which these skills interact with cognitive processes are still poorly understood, especially with regard to knowledge, know-how and interpersonal skills. In this regard, it is necessary to recall our partial conclusions on the state of play concerning the teaching of axiological skills from the literary text in secondary school: "The results collected [...] concerning "entry through values" reveal an alarming state of affairs [in] the lack of knowledge of the values stipulated by the various general and specific official texts [...] often reduced to the content of this medium alone" (Chafik Azirar, 2023)

Objective of the study

The objective of this study is to explore in detail the links between socio-emotional and axiological skills and the academic performance of high school students with learning disabilities. More specifically, we seek to:

1. To identify the main socio-emotional/axiological skills that best predict the academic success of this population.
2. Understand how these skills influence learning and problem-solving processes.
3. Identify avenues for pedagogical intervention aimed at developing these key skills.

By elucidating these questions, our study aims to contribute to the improvement of educational practices in axiological skills and emotional stability aspiring to the reduction of educational inequalities.

LITERATURE REVIEW

This theoretical framework will allow us to elucidate both the notion of value and the notion of emotional competence. Defining these skills will make it possible to highlight what they have in common first and then highlight them in relation to knowledge, know-how and interpersonal skills. Indeed, the development of axiological and socio-emotional skills can only be done through content, in this case literary texts, but also in a know-how that shows a way of being. It should also be noted that these skills are based on a cultural anchoring that these learners develop

Notional network

According to a study conducted by Weissberg et al., socio-emotional skills refer to five essential skills as "self-awareness, social awareness, responsible decision-making, self-management and managing relationships with others. These skills play a fundamental role in individual well-being in both children and adolescents" e.g; Matins, Ramalho and Morin, 2010. Socio-emotional skills would then be considered as soft skills that can be acquired, taught and evaluated; they contribute to a sense of individual and collective effectiveness and seem to be predictive of a certain individual and social well-being. Providing elements of definition to the notion of values also presents certain difficulties given that the concept in question encompasses a fairly wide field of competence. From an anthropological perspective, and according to Clyde Kluckhohn (1961), life without values would first be "impossible".

According to Milton Rockeach (1973) "a value is an enduring belief, a specific mode of behavior or purpose of existence that is personally or socially preferable to another mode or goal of existence that is opposite or convergent". Values according to Shalom Schwartz (2006) "correspond to beliefs related to affects which, through a diversity of contexts, motivate action and guide the evaluation of the actions of others, policies, people and events" A. Nevertheless, if there is a common denominator between these two notions of values and socio-emotional skills, it is the fact that they belong to the field of know-how.

Combination of Social-Emotional Values and Skills

It is now established that values are perceived as concepts or beliefs that relate to desirable ends or behaviours. They transcend specific situations and are the expression of motivations intended to achieve particular objectives such as safety, accomplishment, autonomy. Thus, according to Kluckhohn and Rockeach, the notion of values is protean and thus has many different characteristics: - values can be either personal or social and are more or less central to a society (central value, deviant value, variant value); - they are more or less global and considered either as ends (terminal values) or as means (instrumental values); they are more or less structuring of human behavior; - they are relative (the same value can be adopted by some or rejected by others); - they are sometimes linked to each other (defending certain values implies rejecting or not taking into account others). Schwartz also emphasizes that the concept of values differs from other related concepts: - needs: values express the underlying needs individually and socially; - personality traits: traits are particularly stable and acquired from childhood; values are subject to change; - attitudes: an attitude remains focused on a particular object; it results in part from the conformity of the object to the system of value; - culture: values derive from culture; they are learned within a society (socialization) or between societies (acculturation); - social norms: a norm refers to a socially desired behavior, in a very specific context; - Lifestyles: such as individual activities, interests, and opinions. All things considered, it is obvious that the notion of values has many and diverse aspects, which consequently makes its definition complex. However, it should be noted that values generally correspond to the convictions that we consider to be particularly important to us, those that constitute our essential reference points, that serve us to make our most crucial choices and that therefore guide our actions and behaviors to a large extent. As a result, education systems in general, in this case that of Morocco, put forward a reference framework of values that should guide the functioning of its school.

Values and Active Living

According to Durkheim's conception, in school, a distinction must be made between the target audience (the pupils) and the individual being: the individual being and the social being. The latter is characterized by religious or moral beliefs, traditions, collective opinions, through which the social groups to which we belong are expressed in us. The purpose of education would be to constitute this being, by endowing us with "a system of ideas, feelings, and habits." (8) In this sense, it must be pointed out that there is no education without values being committed, according to the role they play in the development of pupils. Value in the strongest sense, according to Piaget (1967), is "an absolute quality serving as a criterion of judgment for appreciating certain realities", in particular the True, the Good, the Beautiful. More broadly, a value is what serves as a reference for a judgment or for a conduct. It represents what is worthy of being pursued and giving value to life. According to Ch. Hadji, "three series of facts mark the importance of values in all educational systems" Charles Hadji, (1995).

In Jean Piaget's analysis of the dynamics of human conduct from the point of view of the two dimensions, affective and cognitive, we identify two main lines of determination according to which psychic dynamism is structured: that of what he calls "the basic personality", or needs (the need to communicate, for example) in which interest is expressed (for encounters as an example) and which are translated into action (the search for partners, for example). The second main line concerns the conceptions of life in which, according to values (respect for others, among others), attitudes are drawn (openness, acceptance of difference) and opinions are expressed (rejection of discrimination). From the point of view of its structuring, all conduct is well rooted in values corresponding to what it is fundamentally important for us to achieve. Thus, the entry through values into the action of teaching-learning would then be able to decide what is worthy of energizing and regulating the life of oneself and others. There is no learning without a project: The energizing presence of values is visible at a second level, that of learning. To learn, one must first accept the learning situation, receive the object with which one will be confronted. You have to dare to take the plunge, put up with the unknown and accept the other and their culture. The difficulty for teachers here is to place school learning in the context of pupils' projects where this learning takes on meaning for them. It is therefore necessary to meet the values of the students, since value is what gives meaning to life. It is in this sense that Jacques Ardoino (1991) distinguishes between "the programmatic project" (means, strategies, methods) and "the project-aim", the product of a driving and creative imaginary and which specifies the goals pursued, by articulating itself with values. Without the breath of the project-aim, the same author asserts, the programmatic project sinks into the insignificant. And without the presence of values, there is no project in sight. There is no education without a "human ideal": as the philosopher of a human ideal to the attainment and consolidation of which the successive moments of the time of education are oriented to education, Guy Avanzini has clearly established, the first of the three series of components that articulate and harmonize every educational act is constituted by a set of ends to which this act is suspended. Education then implies. The educational process necessarily requires a choice of values, which is expressed by a type of person or society. Thus, in the conduct of the individual-student, in the project that gives meaning to his learning, in the educational act that organizes it, we note the presence of values as regulating and dynamogenic elements. This means that the question of the choice of values is eminently cardinal. What is the value of the values that educators claim to impose? Isn't there a great risk of normalizing cheaply, and destroying in good conscience? What are the sociological requirements of such a conception?

Didactics and typology of knowledge

Aware of the importance that the literary text requires in terms of values education as well as in the development of socio-emotional skills at school in general and in the French classroom in particular, the 2007 Pedagogical Guidelines organizing the teaching of this language at the secondary level stipulating two main entries: an "entry through skills" a skill characterizes the ability for an individual to perform a task complex T, by mobilizing one or more knowledge (K) in a certain context with a certain level of performance" (Gérard, 2007). And an "entry through values". This second entry, dependent on the first, offers the teacher to manage the national values pole and the one relating to universal values with a view to developing the knowledge, know-how and interpersonal skills of high school students in the French class.

On the knowledge side

The teaching of French in qualifying secondary school is done through the implementation of learning areas such as reading, supervised personal work (TPE), grammar and writing. Thus, the content of the recommended literary works is supposed to become the site of an assimilation of knowledge of an ethical and aesthetic nature. From the perspective of "entry through values", reading activities are an opportunity for the teacher to give an account of the cultural representations and reading experiences of his pupils and to adapt them to the pedagogical intentions of the teaching of the literary text. Any reading project that is ready-to-wear risks losing its energizing and formative value in terms of values. On the other hand, a reading project that takes into consideration the interpretive reactions of the student as subject/reader of the literary text should participate in the development of the latter. Since 1970, the theories of reception of Hans Robert Jauss, Wolfgang Iser, Umberto Eco and others have insisted on the place that the reader must occupy in the text/author relationship. In addition, Annie Rouxel (2007), another didactician of literary reading, protests in one of her articles against Gustave Lanson's positivism, which conceived of the explanation of texts as "an object lesson" by making it an accomplice to the formalism resulting from structural analysis, which would have caused reading practices to have left little room for the reader's subjectivity in the classroom. It is clear that the preoccupations of the theories of reception of the second half of the twentieth century shift the attention of the work to the reader, and even to the production of a personal and subjective reading. On the other hand, the choice of extracts to be read and studied in class is of paramount importance and must take into account the following parameters: - a relevant selection of texts containing one or more values; - that the teacher take into account the "horizon of expectation" of his students during his pre-pedagogical work; - a categorization of the value(s) conveyed by the passage to be studied (social, political, cultural, ethical, aesthetic values, etc.); - a detailed study of the thematic, discursive and cultural manifestations of the values contained in and by the literary text; - a time arrangement to encourage the different interpretations of the class about a situation, a character or an event constituting literary fiction and especially the development of socio-emotional skills with the learner. Taking these conditions into account distances the reading of the literary text from technicalist approaches, from the temptation of exclusively formalist exercises or from the risk of reducing it to a work aimed solely at the acquisition of linguistic knowledge. As far as VSEs are concerned, such an activity is designed with a view to promoting exchanges and debates on axiological and socio-affective themes and issues. Documentary research carried out outside the classroom on subjects related to a value conveyed by a literary work makes it possible to develop in learners' values such as responsibility, freedom, critical judgment, etc. As for the activity of written production, which offers the opportunity for the teacher to put his students in a situation of reflexive tension where each student states his or her personal judgment about a phenomenon or a situation. To do this, the writing instructions must be open and the teacher's evaluative postures neutral and objective. All things considered, if literary texts carry diverse cultural knowledge, the different classroom activities must encourage heuristic and interpretive reactions from learners. Without this, literature would lose what constitutes its very essence: the human in its singularity and in its universality.

On the know-how side

The study of literary texts in French classes is not only the appropriation of cultural and civilizational knowledge, it is also an opportunity for the development of procedural knowledge in the field of values education. The reform of the Moroccan education system is part of a paradigm shift, which corresponds to the introduction of the competency-based approach in the teaching of all school disciplines, particularly French in high school. Indeed, the teaching of this language through literary texts does not only aim at the appropriation of axiological knowledge in a pedagogical situation, but it also aspires to promote know-how in terms of values. In other words, it aims to provide the learner with the means to act, react and interact during a situation involving the performance of a task. To this end, the French teacher who will be more successful is the one who permanently involves his or her students in efficient activities both individually and collectively. The French room must be perceived as a community, a space of "living together" where students can learn to manage problem situations by adopting healthy and open behaviors, to familiarize themselves with different ways of integrating the group by continually referring to the central values of tolerance, solidarity, responsibility and utilitarian and methodological values such as civility and concern for organization.

On the side of interpersonal skills

Interpersonal skills correspond to the subject's ability to adapt to various situations and to adjust his or her behaviour according to the characteristics of the environment, the issues at stake in the situation and the type of interlocutor. This notion appeared in addition to the notions of knowledge and know-how, the notion of interpersonal skills has gradually developed in the didactics of language-cultures to become today an essential component of the descriptors of plurilingual and intercultural competence. Indeed, where knowledge is mainly aimed at the acquisition of knowledge, and know-how at its practical implementation, interpersonal skills summon the personality of the subject and have as its objective the development of his attitudes and ways of thinking towards otherness. The didactician in the field of plurilingual and intercultural education Emmanuel Antier states (2017): "The notion of interpersonal skills is mainly concerned with the integration of otherness into the learner's way of thinking and functioning".

Interpersonal skills therefore go far beyond the horizon of knowledge and skills related to the practice of a language; it concerns each person in his or her individual, family and cultural identity. Relating to one's personality, it concerns the attitudes, motivations, values, beliefs, cognitive styles and personality types that make up one's identity. In other words, one cannot open oneself to otherness without also being able to close oneself to it. The acceptance of the other goes hand in hand with the affirmation of one's own identity, these two processes cannot be grasped independently of each other. We can then think of another meaning of the pedagogical action carried out by French teachers in high school. It is a way of being considered as putting into practice their ability to successfully fulfill the role of cultural mediation by decentralizing and going beyond the relationship with the Other and his or her culture. This will necessarily involve a refoundation of didactic actions on less culturally marked criteria and the triggering of existential and ethical questions of learners in the face of the various axiological situations raised by the literary works on the curriculum. This is not really possible without taking into consideration their value system, and their cultural representations and the personal history of each one. It is therefore appropriate for the teacher to accompany them in their reflection, to be attentive to their interpretations and to help them form their moral judgment in the face of life represented in and by literary fiction and the values at work in it. In short, it is a question of developing in them a cultural competence that would promote a dialectical dynamic consisting of questioning themselves, getting rid of prejudices, and rebuilding themselves in contact with the Other and their French culture. In this sense, university education and vocational training centres must include in their curricula modules relating to the cultural and civilizational aspects of languages, including those of the French language. Thus, students and future teachers of French will be able to grasp the axiological scope conveyed by literary works.

ICONIC TEACHING PROCESSES

The teaching processes on which the approach described above is based are based on a well-established conceptual scheme: "To make knowledge understood and Teach to do something", "To teach a skill and To teach autonomy".

To make people understand

Understanding knowledge and teaching involves using learners' prior knowledge to construct new knowledge by establishing links (Kintsch, 1998). First-year students have already studied literary texts in previous curricula, including the specific characteristics of this genre, such as the classification of text types and genres. Thus, the process of understanding requires two aspects: explicitness, which consists of linking the elements of knowledge to each other or to other knowledge to form a coherence external to knowledge. This linkage aims to help students choose the right knowledge to mobilize, based on adaptation principles that leverage student knowledge and relevance to fill in their gaps. However, it is not enough to simply show the usefulness of knowledge; it is equally essential to highlight the importance of the proposed task to effectively motivate the learner (Schechter et al., 2011). In other words, it is essential to create motivation in the learner. The use of the design activity as a tool for pedagogical preparation implies a process of transformation from an institutional demand for the teaching of knowledge into an operational planning for the act of teaching. This approach is broken down into three parts: determining "what to teach", "how to teach" and "what to teach". The final outcome includes both an action plan and the resources needed for its implementation. The main objective is to guarantee the success of teaching in real situations (in the classroom), marked by a harmonious integration of the student's learning and the teacher's support.

Procedure

The students participated in the study over a period of 3 months by taking reading, language, oral activity and writing classes.

Reading Lessons

The excerpts submitted to the learners for understanding were carefully chosen by their teachers according to the level of the students but also according to the axiological and socio-emotional interest established in the excerpts in question, namely French-language novels; French novels and plays. The choice of these excerpts is not fortuitous, "The teaching process consists in having a particular explicit knowledge developed from the study of a case: a situation, an object, an event" (Jeannotte, 2015). This process therefore corresponds to a "double operation, isolating specific attributes, in the sense of being able to consider them independently of other attributes and to glimpse an operation of connections between these isolated attributes" (Jeannotte, 2015). Thus; All the selected excerpts have in common that they evoke situations, plots, characters or places that revolve around values or socio-emotional skills. These include "good neighbourliness, mutual aid, respect for difference or tolerance..."

The second stage of the work consisted of submitting tasks to the learners that will allow them to "verbalize their implicit knowledge"; to identify and classify these values according to whether they are typically national, universal or both national and universal; it is also a question of "having the student develop a descriptive discourse of his knowledge on "How are things?". Piaget (1974). This procedure is part of the perspective of proceduralizing a teaching process that "aims to develop explicit procedural knowledge from explicit declarative knowledge" Vermersch (2004).

Language Courses

The concept of proceduralizing continues in the teaching of linguistic processes; grammar and stylistics that revolve around the identification of lexical fields specific to values, the use of verbs of feelings, the use of modalizers, the use of simple sentences and complex in gender and proportion. This approach brings together "declarative knowledge is the 'product' of procedural knowledge" reference, i.e. the learner must not only be able to identify the values common to the selected extracts, but also to report them orally; to describe, comment on and discuss them. The learner is likewise called upon to use verbs of feeling, of opinion; of state and action by means of exclusively grammatical skills.

Written Production Course

The development of this skill corresponds to an activity of externalization, i.e. "the production of written traces, "It is a question of (making) explicit and organizing the actions and means that lead to the result, in this case to the declarative knowledge itself" (Bonnardel, 2006). In other words, it is a question of learners explaining their learning through tasks that are explained in terms of knowledge, know-how and interpersonal skills.

Evaluation

At the end of these activities, which are broken down into tasks to be carried out using comprehension skills and written and oral production skills that have been reinforced beforehand; the learners were subjected to a first test to assess their degree of understanding of the notion of values, namely; know-how and interpersonal skills. At the end of these tests, which were established, the learners had slightly developed their axiological and emotional skills, however some weaknesses in relation to writing. This led us to submit adaptive exercises to the learners as a form of mediation and remediation to reinforce the acquisition of the skills previously learned.

Adaptive mediation activities

The challenge of these activities "lies in the success of the in situ didactic action, i.e. the joint success of the learning by the student and its support by the teacher. According to (e.g. Carroll 1994), To Make the Situation Understand Problem: "It is first important that the student understands the situation in which he is asked to act, the initial state, the goal state and the steps that separate the two. Indeed, it is generally more effective for students to first understand the problem and the solution, and then try to solve similar problems on their own, than the other way around. It is in this perspective that the reinforcement and mediation activities submitted to learners have been carried out, where more time had to be given to the relevance and formulation of the tasks submitted to learners, sometimes by means of "adaptive and relevant" explanations, "making connections between the different contexts in which this knowledge/ tasks may be relevant" (Jonnaert, 2002). When knowledge is incomplete, there are three main ways to deal with the problem (Tricot et al., 2016): trying to solve it using trial and error (trial and error); Search for information, for example in a document. seek help, usually orally, from someone with the relevant specific knowledge or who will participate in the incomplete competency.

At the end of these remediation and adaptive reinforcement activities; The learners were subjected to a second evaluation which demonstrates a very significant development of the skills previously targeted, as shown by the following data:

METHODOLOGY AND RESULTS

The objective of this study is to evaluate the impact of the pedagogical intervention on students with learning difficulties, the study was established over a period of 3 months by taking reading, language, oral activity and writing classes. The participants were selected on the basis of learning difficulties in terms of knowledge, know-how and interpersonal skills identified by the teachers according to standardised criteria, namely an oral and written placement test based on these criteria:

Knowledge: Understanding of theoretical concepts.

Know-how: Application of knowledge in practical contexts.

Interpersonal skills: Improved interpersonal and communication skills.

Participants

The study was conducted among 125 students of the 1st Baccalaureate from two public secondary schools, divided into three separate classes with 52 boys and 73 girls, aged 16 to 18.

Figure 1. Distribution of students by gender

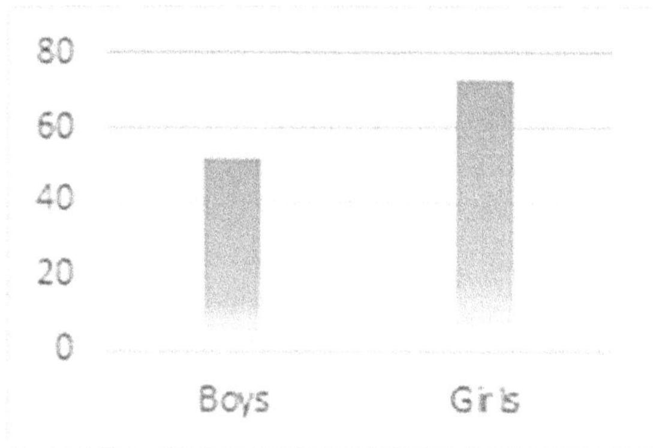

Assessing students before and after

- Placement tests: Perform tests at the beginning and end of the study to compare the results.
- Teacher Observations: Collect feedback on progress observed in class.

Placement Tests

The results of the pre-intervention placement test yielded:

- **30%** of students have difficulties in knowledge corresponds to 38 students.
- **25%** of students have difficulties in know-how corresponds to 32 students.
- **20%** of students have difficulties in interpersonal skills corresponds to 25 students.
- **25%** of the students did not answer the test corresponds to 30 students.

Table 1. Results before the pedagogical intervention

	Learning difficulties			Total	
The criteria	**To know**	**Know-how**	**Interpersonal skills**	**Students**	**%**
Students	38	32	25	95	
% difficulties	30%	25%	20%		75%
%Discontinued				30	25%
Total				125	100%

Figure 2. The distribution of percentages of students before the intervention

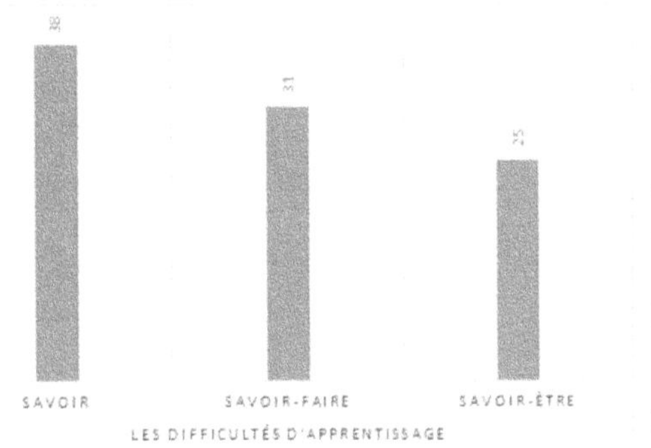

The results of the post-intervention placement test gave:

- **17%** of students have difficulties in knowledge corresponds to 38 students.
- **10%** of students have difficulties in know-how corresponds to 32 students.
- **11%** of students have difficulties in interpersonal skills corresponds to 25 students.

Table 2. Outcomes after the pedagogical intervention

	Learning difficulties			Total	
The criteria	**To know**	**Know-how**	**Interpersonal skills**	**Students**	**%**
Students	17	10	11	38	
% difficulties	17%	10%	11%		38%
Number of students who have been improved				57	62%
Total				95	100%

Figure 3. The distribution of percentages of students after the intervention

Teachers' observations

The results show a significant improvement in knowledge and skills difficulties, indicating that the intervention had a positive impact on these areas. However, it would be beneficial to intensify efforts to improve soft skills, as the reduction in difficulties in this area is less pronounced. The issue of non-response must also be addressed to ensure a comprehensive and representative assessment of students.

Analyze data and metrics

- Academic performance

To assess students' academic performance using standardized tests in French, numerical results based on MCQ and practical work evolutions, observed in learning difficulties.

To facilitate comparisons, we can also calculate Z-scores for pre- and post-intervention means. Z-score formula: $\mathbf{Z = (X - \mu)/ \sigma}$

where X is the individual score, μ is the mean, and σ is the standard deviation.

Table 3. summary of the distributions of the multiple-choice questions and practical exercises

	Evaluation	Before the operation	After the procedure
QUIZZES	Average	60 points	75 points
	Standard deviation	10 points	10 points
	% < 50 points	30%	10%
	% > 80 points	20%	40%
TP	Average	55 points	70 points
	Standard deviation	12 points	12 points
	% < 50 points	35%	20%
	% > 80 points	15%	30%

Interpretation of Results

- General improvement: The averages of MCQs and practical exercises increased significantly after the intervention, indicating an improvement in students' academic performance.
- Reduced low scores: The decrease in the percentage of students with scores below 50 points is a testament to the effectiveness of the intervention.
- Increased high scores: Increasing the percentage of students scoring more than 80 points indicates that more students are achieving high levels of performance.

These numerical results support the idea that the intervention had a positive impact on students' academic performance, both in terms of theoretical and applied understanding. It would be beneficial to continue to monitor these students to ensure that progress is maintained and to explore strategies to support those who continue to struggle. If you would like any additional adjustments or details, let me know!

- Axiological skills

To assess students' axiological skills in identifying, discussing, and writing about values,

- Identification of values: Students were assessed on their ability to identify national, universal, social and cultural values.
- Discussion of values: Discussion skills around these values were also measured.
- Written production: Writing of writings evoking these values.

Numerical results based on pre- and post-intervention assessments:

Table 4. summary of the distributions of axiological skills

	Axiological Competence	Before the operation	After the procedure
Identifying Values	Average	65 points	80 points
	Standard deviation	15 points	12 points
	% < 50 points	40%	20%
	% > 80 points	25%	35%
Values Discussion	Average	58 points	75 points
	Standard deviation	18 points	14 points
	% < 50 points	45%	25%
	% > 80 points	15%	30%
Written production	Average	62 points	78 points
	Standard deviation	16 points	13 points
	% < 50 points	35%	15%
	% > 80 points	20%	35%

Interpretation of Results

- Overall improvement: Averages of skills in identifying, discussing and writing values show a significant increase after the intervention, indicating a better understanding and articulation of values by students.
- Reduced low scores: The decrease in the percentage of students with scores below 50 points in all categories suggests that the intervention helped many students overcome their initial difficulties.
- Increased high scores: Increasing the percentage of students with scores above 80 points indicates a better mastery of axiological skills, which is a positive outcome.

These numerical results illustrate the positive impact of the intervention on the axiological skills of the students. Improved performance in identifying, discussing, and writing values indicates not only a better understanding of social and cultural values, but also an increased ability to articulate and apply them. Additional follow-ups could make it possible to maintain this progress and to further deepen the learning of values among students.

- Social-emotional skills

To assess students' social-emotional skills, we will propose numerical results based on the assessments carried out before and after the intervention for each dimension assessed using validated tools:

- Emotional Regulation: Assessed using the Self-Regulation Emotional Scale (SERE)
- Empathy: Measured by the Cognitive and Affective Empathy Questionnaire (QECA)
- Social Problem Solving: Tested through the Interpersonal Problem Solving Test (IPRT)
- Academic motivation: Assessed via the Educational Motivation Scale (EME)
- Learning strategies: Students completed a self-reported questionnaire about their learning strategies.

Table 5. summary of the distributions of Social-emotional skills

	Socio-emotional competence	Before the operation	After the procedure
Emotional Regulation	Average	65 points	78 points
	Standard deviation	10 points	9 points
	% < 50 points	30%	15%
	% > 80 points	20%	25%
Empathy	Average	62 points	75 points
	Standard deviation	12 points	11 points
	% < 50 points	35%	20%
	% > 80 points	15%	30%
Social Problem Solving	Average	60 points	74 points
	Standard deviation	14 points	13 points
	% < 50 points	40%	25%
	% > 80 points	10%	20%
Academic motivation	Average	58 points	72 points
	Standard deviation	15 points	14 points
	% < 50 points	50%	30%
	% > 80 points	10%	25%
Learning Strategies	Average	55 points	70 points
	Standard deviation	16 points	15 points
	% < 50 points	45%	25%
	% > 80 points	15%	30%

Interpretation of Results

- General improvement: Averages of social-emotional skills show a significant increase after the intervention, indicating a development in students' emotional and social abilities.

- Reduced low scores: The decrease in the percentage of students with scores below 50 points in all dimensions is a testament to the effectiveness of the intervention.
- Increased high scores: Increasing the percentages of students with scores above 80 points reflects a better mastery of social-emotional skills, which is a positive indicator of success.

These numerical results show that the intervention had a positive impact on the students' social-emotional skills. Improvements in emotional regulation, empathy, social problem-solving, academic motivation, and learning strategies indicate that the approach taken worked well. Future follow-ups could be beneficial to sustain this progress and continue to develop these essential skills.

These assessments provide an overview of students' academic performance, axiological skills, and social-emotional skills. The use of validated tools and standardized measures increases the reliability of the results and facilitates the analysis of students' progress during the study.

DISCUSSION

The present assessment of students' academic and socio-emotional skills revealed significant results before and after the educational intervention. Looking at academic performance, the results of standardized tests in French, such as MCQs and practical work, showed a notable improvement. The average score has increased, from 60 to 75 points for the MCQs and from 55 to 70 points for the practical work. This development not only indicates a strengthening of theoretical and practical knowledge, but also reflects the effectiveness of the teaching methods adopted.

At the same time, students' axiological skills, assessed by their ability to identify, discuss, and produce writing about values, also showed progress. The averages in identifying values increased from 65 to 80 points, while those for values discussion and writing increased from 58 to 75 points and from 62 to 78 points, respectively. This testifies to a better understanding and integration of social and cultural values, which are essential for their personal and social development. Regarding socio-emotional skills, the use of validated tools such as the Emotional Self-Regulation Scale (EARE), the Cognitive and Affective Empathy Questionnaire (QECA), the Interpersonal Problem Solving Test (TRPI), the Educational Motivation Scale (EME) and the learning strategies questionnaires made it possible to assess various aspects of the students' emotional and social lives. The results showed a significant improvement in these skills, with alpha coefficients demonstrating good reliability of the tools used. For example, emotional regulation saw its average increase from 65 to 78 points, while empathy increased from 62 to 75 points, indicating notable advances in students' ability to understand and manage their own emotions as well as those of others.

In short, this evaluation highlights the positive impact of the educational intervention on the academic performance and socio-emotional development of students. The findings suggest that targeted strategies can promote learning and personal growth, and highlight the importance of an integrated approach that considers both academic and social-emotional skills. Moving forward, it would be beneficial to continue to monitor this progress and tailor interventions to meet the specific needs of students, ensuring that they can reach their full potential.

CONCLUSION

In conclusion, the in-depth assessment of students' academic, axiological and socio-emotional skills revealed significant improvements following the educational interventions implemented. The results of the standardized tests in French showed a notable increase in performance, with averages increasing in written assessments and practical work, thus highlighting the effectiveness of the pedagogical approaches adopted. In addition, axiological skills, such as identifying and discussing values, also improved, reflecting a better integration of cultural and social values by students. At the same time, socio-emotional skills, measured using validated tools such as the EARE and the QECA, demonstrated significant advances, indicating an improvement in emotional regulation, empathy and interpersonal problem solving. These results suggest that the intervention not only strengthened academic knowledge, but also contributed to forging more emotionally and socially balanced individuals. To maximize this progress, it is recommended to continue using active and participatory teaching methods, to integrate socio-emotional development programs into the curriculum, and to provide personalized support to students who continue to experience difficulties. The implementation of regular monitoring and ongoing assessments will also allow us to adjust teaching strategies according to the emerging needs of students. By cultivating an inclusive and stimulating learning environment, we not only promote academic success, but also the development of responsible and empathetic citizenship, which is essential in our contemporary societies.

REFERENCES

Ardoino, J. (1991). "Project-based pedagogy or educational project?", French Review of Pedagogy No. 94.

Avanzini, G. (1987). *Introduction to educational sciences*. Privat.

Azirar, C. (2024). *' The Axiological Dimension in the Study of Literary Works in the Qualifying Cycle Between Possibility and Difficulties of Implementation' Chapitre16 (319-340) Book ''Innovative Instructional Design Methods and Tools for Improved'' IGI GLOBAL Mohamed Khaldi, Teaching ENS.* Abdelmalek Essaadi University.

Bonnardel, N. (2006). *Creativity and design. Cognitive and ergonomic approaches*. Solal.

Carroll, W. M. (1994). Using worked examples as an instructional support in the algebra classroom. *Journal of Educational Psychology*, 86(3), 360–367. DOI: 10.1037/0022-0663.86.3.360

Gérard, F.-M. (2007). The complexity of an assessment of skills through complex situations: theoretical necessities and requirements of the field. Proceedings of the International Symposium "Logic of Skills and Curricular Development: Debates, Perspectives and Alternatives for Educational Systems", Montreal, April 26-27.

Hadji, C. (1995). Thinking and acting on education, Paris, ESF publisher, 2nd printing,

Jeannotte, D. (2015) Abstracting and generalizing processes conceptualized from a commognitive perspective. In L. Theis (ed.), Cultural Pluralities and the Universality of Mathematics: Issues and Perspectives for their Teaching and Learning – Proceedings of the EMF2015 Conference – WG3, Jonnaert, P. (2002). A contextualization of arithmetic learning. In J. Bideaud & H.

Kintsch, W. (1998). *Comprehension: A paradigm for cognition*. Cambridge University Press.

Piaget, J. (1967). *The psychology of intelligence*. Armand Colin.

Rockeach, M. (1973). *The nature of human values*. The Free Press.

Schechter, O., Durik, A. M., Miyamoto, Y., & Harackiewicz, J. M. (2011). The role of utility value in achievement behavior: The importance of culture. *Personality and Social Psychology Bulletin*, 37(3), 303–317. DOI: 10.1177/0146167210396380 PMID: 21262958

Tricot, A., Sahut, G., & Lemarié, J. (2016). *The document: communication and memory*. De Boeck Supérieur.

Vermersch, P. (2004). Help with explanation and reflective feedback. *Continuity in Education*, 160(3).

Chapter 14
The Impact of Intelligent Systems in Teaching Values Through Literary Text

Chafik Azirar
https://orcid.org/0009-0001-3966-9903
ENS Tétouan, Université Abdelmalek Essaadi, Morocco

Hamza Saidy
https://orcid.org/0009-0008-0604-3382
ENS Tétouan, Université Abdelmalek Essaadi, Morocco

ABSTRACT

The integration of intelligent systems in the teaching of values through literature represents a significant development in the field of education. Advances in artificial intelligence (AI) today offer powerful tools for personalizing learning, by analyzing and adapting literary content to learners' needs and preferences. Our chapter intends to explore how technologies such as intelligent tutors and interactive platforms enrich the educational experience, not only by facilitating access to literary texts, but also by deepening understanding of the moral and ethical values they convey. We'll also be conducting an experiment, which we hope will yield encouraging results.

INTRODUCTION

The integration of intelligent systems in education is a real revolution. Education, which has long relied on traditional teaching methods, is now seeing the emergence of new technologies such as artificial intelligence (AI), machine learning and adaptation algorithms. These technological tools, initially developed to automate certain tasks, have gradually established themselves in the educational field as tools for personalization, optimization of learning, and improvement of teacher-learner interaction. Intelligent systems enable more flexible learning environments focused on the specific needs of students, offering individualized pathways, real-time feedback, and interactive experiences. This digital transformation is disrupting not only teaching methods but also the way in which educational content, such as literary texts, is explored. In this context, the question of teaching values through literature is posed with a new

DOI: 10.4018/979-8-3693-8965-2.ch014

perspective, as digital tools can now play a central role in the acquisition of ethical and moral skills. The teaching of values, whether social, moral or cultural, is an essential component of the educational process. Through the transmission of these values, education not only instructs, but trains individuals capable of ethical reflection, respect for social norms, and personal development. Literature, as a mirror of society and a vehicle for human experiences, is a fertile ground for this transmission of values. From classic texts to contemporary works, literary stories address themes such as justice, humanism, solidarity, freedom, or the question of good and evil.

The study of literary texts allows learners to analyze complex situations, to question their own vision of the world, and to forge a critical reflection on the ethical dilemmas that run through the works. Thus, literature plays a key role in teaching values, not only by illustrating moral norms, but also by encouraging reflection on the universal issues that affect humanity. The rise of intelligent systems in the literary field has already given rise to notable innovations. Many applications exploit the potential of AI to facilitate analysis and interaction with literary works. For example, intelligent tutors are able to guide students in the analysis of texts according to their level of comprehension, by proposing adapted questions, additional explanations or food for thought. Digital learning platforms offer features such as augmented reading, which enriches texts with automatic comments and annotations generated by algorithms, highlighting important themes or values.

In addition, interactive literary simulations and educational chatbots allow students to participate in discussions about moral dilemmas or interpret the actions of characters in works. For example, a chatbot could ask questions about the moral choice of a character in Jean Anouilh's Antigone, helping the student navigate between the different ethical issues while developing his or her own critical thinking.

The impact of intelligent systems in the teaching of values through the literary text is a topic of great relevance in the current educational context. The integration of information and communication technologies (ICTs) into literary education not only improves pupils' learning, but also promotes the transmission of cultural and social values. ICTs offer tools that facilitate access to a variety of resources, thus enriching the learning experience and allowing a more interactive and engaging approach to literary texts (Reguragui et al., 2014; Kalai, 2023; Tamim et al., 2011). In this contribution, we explored the definition of intelligent systems and their application in the field of education with a particular focus on their use in the literature. We then analysed their role in education by discussing the various advantages and challenges they present. After examining the place of the literary text in the teaching of values, we studied the integration of these technologies, highlighting their advantages as well as the technical limits of intelligent systems. We concluded with a case study illustrating the use of an intelligent tutor for the analysis of a literary text by demonstrating the impact of these technologies in the field of education and on literary texts.

INTELLIGENT SYSTEMS IN EDUCATION

Definition and types of intelligent systems

Intelligent systems, often referred to as systems capable of performing tasks that require some form of human intelligence, are at the heart of many contemporary technological innovations. They can be defined as entities that perceive their environment, make data-driven decisions, and act autonomously to achieve specific goals (Spitmaan & Leong, 2019; Park, 2021). This definition encompasses a variety of systems, ranging from intelligent agents in the field of artificial intelligence (AI) to smart buildings that optimize the use of resources (Omar, 2018).

There are several types of intelligent systems, each with specific characteristics and applications. Among these, intelligent agents are programs or systems that can act autonomously in a given environment. These agents can be used in a variety of fields, including robotics, recommendation systems, and data management applications (Spitmaan & Leong, 2019; Park, 2021). On the other hand, smart building systems, which incorporate technologies to improve energy efficiency and occupant comfort, represent another type of smart system that illustrates the application of intelligence in architecture and engineering (Omar, 2018).

Another type of smart system is smart sensors, which are able to collect data, analyze it, and make decisions in real time. These sensors are widely used in fields such as precision agriculture, natural resource management, and health systems (Taymanov & Sapozhnikova, 2010). In addition, smart education systems, which incorporate digital technologies to enhance learning and teaching, are also on the rise. These systems aim to personalize the educational experience according to the individual needs of students, thus promoting a more inclusive and effective approach to education (Ouakka, 2023; Anne and Bahlouli, 2023).

Intelligent systems encompass a variety of technologies and applications that share the ability to learn, adapt, and act autonomously. Their continuous development and integration into various sectors, including education, engineering, and resource management, underscore their growing importance in our modern society.

Examples of tools used in education

Many tools based on these smart technologies have already found their way into the field of education, helping to transform the way teaching and learning are done. These tools offer a more individualized and interactive approach, tailored to the needs of students. Some of the most common include:

Smart tutors

These personalized assistance systems are designed to support each learner according to their level of competence. They dynamically assess students' strengths and weaknesses through continuous interactions, allowing them to provide tailored instructional content, exercises, and feedback. By detecting specific student gaps, smart tutors can modulate the pace and difficulty of tasks, promoting more focused and effective learning. For example, they can reinforce a particular skill if a student is struggling, or on the contrary, offer additional challenges for more advanced students.

Online learning platforms

These digital spaces, such as Coursera, Moodle, or Khan Academy, integrate artificial intelligence technologies to make learning paths more adaptive and personalized. The algorithms used analyze user interactions to adjust the content offered, recommend additional resources and track learners' progress in real time. This creates a flexible learning experience, where students can progress at their own pace, access the resources that are most useful to them, and receive ongoing monitoring. The integration of AI also helps to identify areas that need attention and offer immediate assessments and feedback.

Educational chatbots

These chatbots play a key role in ongoing student support. By providing instant answers to questions asked by learners, they facilitate access to information and help clarify complex concepts in real time. Available 24 hours a day, chatbots allow for constant interaction, eliminating barriers related to teacher availability schedules. They can also guide users through learning modules, offering additional explanations or guidance when they need it. Additionally, these chatbots evolve based on interactions, improving their ability to answer questions more accurately and contextually. The integration of these tools in the educational field makes it possible to personalize learning while making pedagogical processes more interactive, responsive and accessible. They play a pivotal role in the shift towards more flexible and learner-centred education, where technology helps to create learning environments that are tailored to individual needs and skills.

Intelligent systems in the teaching of literary subjects

The integration of intelligent systems in the teaching of literary subjects represents a significant advance in the way students interact with texts and develop their analytical and critical skills. These systems, which include technologies such as artificial intelligence, e-learning platforms and digital tools, offer unique opportunities to enrich the literary learning experience. First, intelligent systems allow for personalization of learning, which is particularly beneficial in the context of language and literature teaching. For example, Yang and Wang point out that the use of cognitive science in literature education can improve the comprehension of literary texts by taking into account learners' mental processes (Yang & Wang, 2020). This allows teachers to tailor their teaching methods to the specific needs of each student, promoting a more inclusive and effective approach.

Additionally, online learning platforms make it easy to access a variety of literary resources and analytical tools. Haque mentions that literature plays a crucial role in foreign language learning, and the use of literary materials can enrich the learning experience by providing cultural and historical contexts (HAQUE, 2022). Smart systems can also incorporate textual analysis tools that help students break down and interpret literary works more deeply, which can strengthen their critical understanding. The interaction between students and literary texts is also improved by the use of digital technologies. For example, Ouellet discusses the importance of receiving and creating multitexts in literary education, noting that digital tools allow students to actively engage with literary works (Ouellet, 2019).

This interactive approach not only promotes a better understanding of the texts, but also the development of creative and analytical skills. In addition, the integration of intelligent systems into literary education can also contribute to the intercultural dimension of learning. Boudiaf highlights the importance of the intercultural approach in foreign language teaching, and intelligent systems can facilitate intercultural communication by offering varied resources and enabling exchanges between students from different cultures (Boudiaf, 2023). This enriches the learning experience and helps students develop a broader understanding of literary contexts.

Intelligent systems play a key role in the teaching of literary subjects by providing personalised tools, facilitating access to a variety of resources, and encouraging an interactive and intercultural approach to learning. Their integration into pedagogical practices can transform the way students interact with literature, thus promoting deeper and more meaningful learning.

Benefits of Intelligent Systems in Education

In an ever-changing educational context, intelligent systems are becoming increasingly central to the optimization of learning methods. By integrating technologies such as artificial intelligence and machine learning, these tools make it possible to tailor educational content to the individual needs of learners while offering a more interactive and personalized approach. In the context of teaching values through literature, these systems offer innovative solutions that enrich the understanding of texts and encourage the development of critical thinking.

- **Personalization of learning paths**: Intelligent systems offer advanced personalization by tailoring educational content to each learner's skills, preferences, and pace. Thanks to this flexibility, each student benefits from a tailor-made path, which allows us to better meet their specific needs. In the context of teaching values through literature, this personalization is particularly valuable, as it takes into account the diversity of students' interpretations and sensitivities. For example, some students may focus on the ethical themes of a work, while others will be guided to a deeper exploration of philosophical or symbolic questions. By adjusting content to individual interests in this way, intelligent systems promote more meaningful and relevant learning, where the values conveyed by the text are better assimilated and understood.
- **Real-time feedback and progress tracking:** One of the greatest strengths of intelligent systems is their ability to provide instant feedback. When a student makes a mistake or encounters a difficulty, the system can immediately inform them of their mistake and offer explanations or ways to improve. This real-time feedback makes learning more responsive and dynamic, allowing students to correct mistakes as they go and adjust their understanding of the content. At the same time, these systems ensure accurate monitoring of each learner's progress, allowing teachers to better understand students' areas of strength and weakness. In teaching values through literature, this type of feedback allows learners to quickly reflect on the nuances of the texts they are analyzing, thus strengthening their ability to interpret moral messages and social issues with greater depth.
- **Increased interaction and student motivation**: Intelligent systems are transforming the learning experience by making it more interactive and engaging. They offer various dynamic activities such as quizzes, role-playing, or simulations based on literary works. These immersive approaches not only promote a better understanding of the texts, but they also stimulate the interest and motivation of the students. For example, a simulation may invite a student to put themselves in the shoes of a character, to make decisions based on moral values, or to resolve ethical dilemmas encountered in a work. This interactivity encourages deeper immersion in the literary text and strengthens learners' engagement, making teaching values through literature not only more accessible, but also more engaging and relevant to them. Thanks to these playful and participatory approaches, intelligent systems make learning values livelier and more sustainable.

THE PLACE OF THE LITERARY TEXT IN THE TEACHING OF VALUES

The literary text as a vector of values

The literary text plays a fundamental role as a vector of values, making it possible not only to transmit ideas and emotions, but also to initiate deep reflections on ethical, social and cultural issues. Through the stories, characters and situations described, literature offers a space for dialogue on human values, thus contributing to the formation of individual and collective identity. First of all, literature is a powerful means of reflection on moral and ethical values. Literary works, whether classic or contemporary, often address universal themes such as justice, freedom, love and tolerance. For example, Montaigne's essays, as Ferrari points out, illustrate how literature can enrich our understanding of cognitive and moral values, offering us perspectives on the human condition and prompting us to reflect on our own values (Ferrari, 2016).

Similarly, Prairat emphasizes that teaching is intrinsically linked to values, and that literature can serve as a medium to explore these values in an educational setting (Prairat, 2019). In addition, Francophone literature, particularly in the context of language teaching, plays a crucial role in the transmission of cultural values. Aronsson sheds light on how textbooks in Sweden incorporate literary texts that expose students to diverse values and perspectives, thus contributing to their intercultural education (Aronsson, 2019). This exposure to a variety of literary works allows students to develop a sensitivity to cultural differences and to better understand the values that underpin different societies.

Francophone African literature, as examined by Kouvouama, also illustrates how narratives can blend imagination and social reality, offering a reflection on values such as solidarity and identity (Kouvouama, 2004). The authors use symbols and metaphors to address complex issues, allowing readers to engage with values that resonate with their own lived experiences. Finally, literature can also serve as a mirror for society, by questioning and criticizing dominant values. Literary works can spark debates on controversial topics, as shown in Douzou's work, which explores how literature can address themes of memory and identity, while shedding light on social injustices (Douzou, 2008). This ability to provoke critical reflection on societal values is essential to encourage constructive dialogue within communities. In conclusion, the literary text is an essential vector of values, allowing us to explore moral, cultural and social issues. Through its narratives, literature offers diverse perspectives that enrich our understanding of human values and foster intercultural dialogue. Its role in the education and formation of individual and collective identity is undeniable, making literature a valuable tool for the transmission and reflection on values.

The axiological dimension in literature

In literature, the axiological dimension is revealed through the deep exploration of values related to the family, society and morality. Literary narratives serve as a lens to illustrate how these values evolve over time and social contexts, and thus provide readers with a framework for reflection on the norms that govern human behaviour. For example, in classic works such as *Jean* Anouilh's Antigone, the conflict between divine and human laws highlights fundamental questions concerning family duty, obedience to social rules, and the struggle for what is perceived to be right. This drama questions the hierarchy of values, confronting the heroine with the tragic choice between loyalty to her family and respect for the laws imposed by the state.

Similarly, Victor Hugo*'s The Last Day of a Condemned Man* asks central questions about the value of human life and social justice. This novel invites the reader to reflect on the moral foundations of the death penalty, placing at the center of the story a man sentenced to death, whose voice exposes the anguish and injustice of his fate. Through an implicit critique of judicial institutions, Hugo questions notions of justice, forgiveness and human dignity, pushing readers to reflect on the balance between punishment and humanity.

Also, in Ahmed Sefrioui's The Wonder Box, the axiological dimension is also manifested by the importance of family and social values. This novel, which tells the daily life of a child in the medina of Fez, is steeped in Moroccan culture and traditions. Family plays a central role in the story, and through the eyes of Sidi Mohamed, the narrator, we discover values such as family love, respect for elders, solidarity between neighbors, and the importance of religious beliefs. The setting of the medina, with its rituals and customs, reinforces this transmission of traditional values, while exposing the challenges faced by the characters in conforming to them. The novel shows how, in a context of poverty and precariousness, the values of solidarity and family responsibility become essential pillars of survival and collective identity.

These examples show how family values, such as love, respect and responsibility, as well as social values, such as justice, equality and solidarity, and moral values, such as honesty, courage and benevolence, are intertwined in the narrative structure of literary texts. Each work invites us to reflect on the complexity of these values and their interaction with individual and collective realities. Compagnon (2007) points out that *"literature has the power to convey complex moral dilemmas and to promote ethical reasoning in students."* Thus, for learners, these stories bring a multidimensional perspective, enriching their understanding of ethical and social issues and encouraging them to question their own value system.

Evolution of the role of literary texts in the digital age.

With the advent of digital technology, the role of literary texts in the teaching of values has undergone a significant transformation. Literary works, once reserved for print formats with limited circulation, are now accessible to a much wider audience thanks to online platforms and digital libraries. This democratization of access allows learners from all over the world to discover and study classical and contemporary texts, thus broadening their exposure to the social, moral and cultural values conveyed by these works.

In addition, digital tools offer a more enriching and immersive interaction with texts. With features such as online annotations, contextual hyperlinks, and discussion forums, learners can further analyze the themes and values presented in the works. Augmented reading platforms, for example, allow you to explore critical analyses, explanatory notes, and even videos or podcasts related to a specific passage of the text, enriching the reading experience. These tools facilitate students' active engagement, allowing them to engage with each other's ideas and interpretations.

Another key benefit of digital is the possibility of collaborative discussions. Discussion forums and online workspaces allow learners to share their views and discuss the values conveyed by literary texts. This dialogue enriches not only their understanding of the works, but also their ethical and moral reflection. By debating the issues raised by the texts, such as the conflicts between justice and injustice, or the dilemmas between loyalty and betrayal, students are encouraged to develop critical thinking and to collectively construct an analysis of values. This digital transformation thus promotes a more dynamic, interactive and collaborative approach to literature. Not only does it make texts more accessible, but it also enriches value analysis by creating a learning environment where interaction with the text and with other readers is facilitated. Literary analysis is no longer limited to a solitary reading or a class discussion, but becomes a shared experience, where values are debated, interpreted and deepened in a collective and interactive way.

Examples of literary texts conveying specific values

Analysis of classical and contemporary texts conveying values.

Many classical and contemporary texts offer a profound reflection on universal values, which remain essential in today's education. These works, through their characters, plots and contexts, address timeless ethical, social and moral issues, thus teaching key values while engaging learners in a reflection on their own conduct and place in society.

In Victor Hugo's **Les Misérables**, the emphasis is on values such as social justice, redemption and solidarity. The character of Jean Valjean, a former convict turned philanthropist, embodies the possibility of personal transformation and the power of forgiveness. His rehabilitation journey shows the importance of mercy and benevolence, values that are opposed to the implacable rigor of Inspector Javert, a symbol of blind and strict justice. Through this conflict between forgiveness and punishment, Hugo explores the complexity of justice, emphasizing that it is not just about the mechanical application of laws, but that it must also take into account human dignity, redemption and solidarity. This work thus offers a powerful tool for discussing issues of social justice and individual and collective responsibilities in society.

Antigone by Jean Anouilh, addresses universal themes related to the conflicts between human law and divine law. Antigone, who defies the authority of King Creon to honor her deceased brother, represents family loyalty and courage in the face of injustice. The text invites reflection on fundamental issues such as obedience to authority, family duty and resistance to laws perceived as unjust. This tragic dilemma exposes values such as courage, integrity and moral responsibility. Anouilh pushes the reader to question the limits of authority and the sense of duty, while examining the personal and collective consequences of individual choices. In this sense, *Antigone* is a powerful example of how literature can be used to discuss rebellion against injustice and sacrifice for higher values.

Ahmed Sefrioui's The Wonder Box offers an intimate look at life within a Moroccan community through the eyes of a child, Sidi Mohamed. The novel, deeply autobiographical, highlights family values such as love, solidarity and respect for traditions. By exploring family and community relations in the medina of Fez, the work highlights the importance of solidarity in times of crisis, such as during periods of financial difficulty that the narrator's family goes through. In addition, the transmission of traditions and customs, particularly through the mother figure and interactions with neighbours, highlights the value of cultural heritage and the strength of community ties. This novel is a rich medium for addressing social and cultural values, especially in a context of intergenerational transmission and belonging to a close-knit community.

These works each illustrate in their own way universal values such as justice, solidarity, family duty, redemption and cultural transmission. They allow learners to reflect not only on these values as abstract concepts, but also on their application in concrete situations, through moral dilemmas and difficult choices. By engaging students in the analysis of these texts, they are offered the opportunity to develop their critical thinking, empathy, and understanding of social ethics. Literature thus becomes an essential tool for the teaching of ethical, human and social values, by leading learners to question their own behaviour and their role within society.

The importance of analysis and critical thinking

Literary texts go beyond the simple presentation of values: they explore them by integrating them into complex and often ambiguous situations, which invite critical reflection on the part of readers. By depicting characters confronted with moral dilemmas and difficult choices, literary works allow learners to grasp the depth of the values in question and to understand the tensions that accompany them. This engages readers to decode the meanings behind the characters' decisions and behaviors, allowing them to see values not just as abstract concepts, but as principles that influence and guide human action in varied contexts.

Literary analysis thus becomes a valuable tool to encourage ethical reflection on the dilemmas that individuals may face, the choices they must make, and the consequences of these choices. Taking the case of Albert Camus' *The Plague*, the work encourages the reader to reflect on human solidarity and the absurdity of the human condition in the face of inevitable hardships. By describing the city of Oran suddenly hit by a devastating epidemic, Camus illustrates the diverse reactions of the inhabitants, from courage to despair, and questions the resilience and moral commitment of the individual in the face of a collective crisis. Through the character of Dr. Rieux, who fights tirelessly to save lives despite the absence of answers or meaning to this suffering, the novel invites readers to meditate on man's ability to show humanity and dedication in a world without definitive answers. This exploration of the themes of fraternity, shared suffering and the search for meaning in the face of the absurd leads to a profound questioning of the values of compassion and collective responsibility.

Thus, the study of literary texts promotes an awareness of ethical values by encouraging personal reflection on themes such as justice, compassion, freedom and human dignity. By analyzing the situations, choices, and dilemmas faced by the characters, learners are led to evaluate the values at stake and develop their own critical thinking. Literary works thus become privileged spaces for ethical and social reflection, transforming reading into an active and engaged learning experience.

Impact on the personal and social development of learners.

By exploring values through literature, learners cultivate not only their critical thinking, but also their moral and ethical sense. Literary texts are a privileged space for reflection, where students are confronted with complex ethical dilemmas, which allows them to question values, to discern those they wish to integrate into their lives, and to question their own role within society. By analyzing character choices, motivations, and the impact of their actions, learners gain a better understanding of the values that govern human relationships and the trade-offs that these values may require.

Literature, in this sense, plays a fundamental role in the personal and social development of learners. It exposes them to a wide variety of perspectives and life situations, helping them to enrich their view of the world and to evaluate the values that surround them. This contact with varied and sometimes opposing perspectives allows students to nuance their own judgments and develop more flexible and inclusive thinking. Ultimately, literature not only offers a theoretical knowledge of values, but encourages deep reflection that promotes the integration of these values into learners' daily lives, thus influencing the way they act, understand others and understand their environment.

THE INTEGRATION OF INTELLIGENT SYSTEMS TO TEACH VALUES THROUGH LITERATURE

How intelligent systems can improve values teaching

The integration of intelligent systems into the teaching of values through literature is changing teaching methods by adapting them to the varied needs of learners. Through adaptive learning algorithms and data analytics, these technologies allow for a personalization of the educational experience, adjusting the pace, complexity of content, and activities according to each student's abilities and preferences. Luckin (2016) highlights the impact of this transformation by stating that *"AI has the potential to transform education, enabling personalized learning experiences that meet the diverse needs of students."* Innovations such as semantic analysis and natural language processing are thus opening up new avenues for exploring and understanding literary works, highlighting the human, social and ethical values they contain.

By facilitating interactive and immersive approaches, intelligent systems allow learners to engage with texts in a more in-depth and personalized way. For example, a learner can be offered exercises or avenues for reflection that correspond to his or her level of understanding, thus allowing him or her to progress at his or her own pace while deepening his or her perception of the values conveyed by the text. In addition, these technologies promote the development of critical thinking by asking open-ended questions or simulating ethical dilemmas, encouraging students to reflect on the choices and behaviors of the characters, and to draw lessons that are applicable to their own lives.

Thus, intelligent systems offer innovative pedagogical solutions that enrich the literary experience, making it easier for learners to assimilate the values underlying the texts and thus transforming literature into a powerful lever for teaching values in a digital context. Loveless (2020) emphasizes the importance of this approach by stating that *"the intersection of technology and pedagogy in the culture of values can enhance the moral and ethical development of students,"* highlighting the central role of these tools in the ethical training of learners.

Analysis and adaptation of literary content according to individual needs

Intelligent systems, including artificial intelligence (AI) and adaptive algorithms, have the ability to analyze each learner's level in real time and then adjust literary content to precisely meet their needs. Using advanced textual analysis tools, powered by AI, these technologies can assess a student's understanding of the moral and ethical values present in a text. Depending on the learner's answers and reactions, the tool can then adapt the questions, offer suggestions, or offer avenues for reflection that allow them to progress in their interpretation of values in a personalized way.

This personalization is particularly crucial in the teaching of values, which, by their nature, are perceived and interpreted in various ways, influenced by each student's cultural, social or personal context. Intelligent systems can thus take into account these varied dimensions and offer unique learning paths, allowing each student to explore the axiological dimension of literary texts at his or her own pace and according to his or her own sensitivity.

This approach not only deepens the understanding of values, but also fosters a more immersive and meaningful learning experience, where each learner is encouraged to question values based on their own worldview. Nucci and Narvaez (2008) observe that *"technological tools can engage students more deeply with texts, prompting critical reflection on the values they embody."* Ultimately, intelligent systems help to transform the study of values through literature into a process that is both enriching and personal, supporting the development of each student's critical and ethical thinking.

Personalization and collaboration with intelligent systems

Personalizing learning is key to meeting the diverse needs of students. According to Yang and Wang, the introduction of a cognitive perspective in literature teaching allows for a meaningful interaction between learners' language systems and literary texts Yang & Wang (2020). Using intelligent systems, teachers can analyze students' preferences and skills to adapt literary content. For example, learning platforms can recommend specific works based on students' interests, increasing their engagement and motivation.

In addition to enabling advanced customization, intelligent systems also promote enriching collaboration between students. AI-integrated learning platforms allow learners to share and confront their analyses of literary texts and the values they convey, while benefiting from automated and personalized feedback that guides their thinking. This interaction, supported by smart technologies, makes the learning process more interactive and promotes a more nuanced understanding of the values being addressed.

Tools such as smart forums and collaborative chatbots play a key role in this collaborative dynamic. These devices facilitate discussions around texts, encouraging learners to ask questions, exchange ideas, and collectively question the themes and values presented in literary works. Thanks to these tools, students can not only explore individual values, such as justice, honesty, or solidarity, but also confront their perceptions and enrich their perspectives through the input of their peers.

The collaborative aspect, amplified by intelligent systems, thus gives a social and interactive dimension to the teaching of values. Students discover that values are often interpreted differently in different perspectives and contexts, and this confrontation of ideas encourages in-depth critical thinking. By integrating dynamic exchanges, intelligent systems transform the learning of literary values into a collective and participatory experience, where everyone's ideas and sensibilities contribute to a broader and inclusive understanding of human values.

Use of chatbots or virtual assistants for the analysis of literary texts with a focus on values.

Chatbots and virtual assistants play a valuable role in literary analysis by offering interactive and targeted help. Programmed to ask specific questions about the values present in a text, these tools can guide students in exploring complex passages or offer them avenues of comparison between different literary works, thus enriching their understanding of the underlying values. For example, a virtual assistant could ask a student about how the main character in a work embodies a particular value, such as justice or courage, and provide instant feedback, guiding their thinking and helping them structure their analysis.

Through this continuous and personalized interaction, chatbots and virtual assistants encourage active and participatory learning. They allow students to ask questions at any time, receive additional explanations, and develop their own interpretation of values in an interactive environment. These tools can also offer tailored exercises, leading students to relate the values observed in a text to those of other literary works, broadening their perspective and allowing them to understand the universality or nuances of human values.

Ultimately, these tools provide learners with constant support, helping them to progress independently while pushing them to examine in depth the ethical and moral implications of the texts. By integrating virtual assistant technology into literary analysis, we promote value learning that is both personalized and engaging, making literature lessons more accessible and impactful for students.

THE CHALLENGES AND LIMITATIONS OF INTELLIGENT SYSTEMS IN VALUE EDUCATION

The integration of intelligent systems in the field of education, in particular for the transmission of values through literary texts, undeniably brings many benefits. It makes it possible to adapt teaching methods to the individual needs of learners, to foster a deeper analysis of works and to encourage critical reflection on moral and social values. However, this integration also raises challenges and has limitations that are essential to consider to ensure that these technologies truly serve the goals of values education.

From an ethical point of view, important questions arise about the neutrality of intelligent systems in the interpretation of values. Algorithms, designed by humans, can reflect cultural or personal biases, influencing how values are presented or prioritized in proposed analyses. It is crucial to ensure that intelligent systems respect the diversity of perspectives and encourage a fair exploration of values without imposing a one-sided or partial interpretation.

From a technical point of view, several limitations also need to be overcome. Intelligent systems must be sophisticated enough to understand the nuances of literary language, detect implicit values, and adapt their responses to learners' varied interpretations. However, this complexity can require significant technological resources, which is not always within the reach of all institutions. In addition, the increased use of smart technologies can reduce human interaction, which could limit the discussions and debates that are essential in learning values.

These challenges, both ethical and technical, are a reminder of the importance of rigorous supervision and thoughtful use of intelligent systems. A balanced approach, which combines these technologies with the skills and coaching of teachers, is essential to ensure that intelligent systems remain relevant tools, actively supporting the development of students' critical and ethical thinking.

Ethics and bias in AI

Ethics and bias in artificial intelligence (AI) are crucial topics that are sparking intense debate in a variety of fields, including technology, medicine, and education. AI, as a ubiquitous technology, raises complex ethical questions related to its development, deployment, and impact on society. This analysis focuses on the ethical issues associated with AI, the biases that can arise from it, and the measures needed to mitigate these issues.

Risks related to the design of algorithms on axiological subjects.

Intelligent systems rely on machine learning models that are deeply influenced by the data used to train them. However, human values, because of their complexity and their roots in cultural, social and individual contexts, are subjective and sometimes controversial concepts. If the databases used to train these systems lack diversity or objectivity, the algorithms risk reproducing or even accentuating certain cultural, ethical or social biases. For example, a system of literary analysis that is primarily fueled by works from a single era or culture might unconsciously favor certain values – such as authority or solidarity – at the expense of other values present in more diverse literary contexts.

This risk of bias can be problematic in multicultural educational environments, where students come from a variety of backgrounds and bring interpretations of values that differ greatly depending on their culture and personal experiences. If AI does not take this plurality into account, it could project a narrow view of moral and social values, thus limiting learners' ability to explore the diversity of possible interpretations. It is therefore crucial to design algorithms that integrate and respect this diversity of perspectives, identifying and correcting implicit biases in order to offer a more balanced vision of human values.

Role of inclusivity and diversity in smart systems.

The role of inclusivity and diversity in intelligent systems is a topic of increasing importance, especially in the context of artificial intelligence (AI) and digital technologies. Inclusivity and diversity are not only ethical values, but they are also essential to ensure that smart systems are efficient, equitable, and beneficial to all users.

Inclusivity in AI development involves considering diverse population groups when designing and implementing intelligent systems. This includes considerations of gender, age, ethnicity, and other dimensions of diversity. Brault points out that AI can be used to improve public health, but it can also exacerbate inequalities if it is not developed with an inclusive approach Brault (2022). Therefore, it is crucial to involve diverse voices in the AI development process to ensure that the systems meet the needs of all communities

For intelligent systems to promote authentically representative value learning, it is essential to ensure inclusivity and diversity from the design of algorithms. Designers should strive to create AI models that can accommodate and value the plurality of literary interpretations and value systems, so that each learner can feel respected and included in their differences. This involves training AI to recognize and promote a variety of values, from diverse cultures, languages, and traditions, in order to create a more equitable and universal learning space.

This effort at inclusivity also goes beyond the simple diversity of data: it must be accompanied by a reflection on the accessibility of the smart technologies themselves. Smart systems must be deployed in a way that does not reinforce inequalities in access to education, remaining accessible and relevant to all students, regardless of their socio-economic or cultural background. By taking into account these principles of inclusivity and accessibility, AI can become a powerful tool to teach values in an ethical, balanced and representative way, enriching the learning experience for each student.

The role of the teacher in support

While intelligent systems offer undeniable advantages for teaching, human intervention remains crucial, especially for the teaching of sensitive and complex values.

The importance of human intervention to guide the learning of values.

Intelligent systems, while effective at processing data and generating recommendations, are limited by their inability to fully grasp the intricacies of moral or ethical values in context. They lack the human capacity to interpret, nuance and contextualize sensitive concepts. Teachers, on the other hand, play a vital role in guiding students through the analysis of deep values, such as those addressed in literary works. For example, when faced with a complex moral dilemma in a work like *Antigone*, where notions of duty and justice are put to the test, a teacher can not only encourage students to explore these ideas, but also guide the discussion to allow them to grasp all facets of them and relate them to their own personal experiences and values. In addition, the teacher plays an essential role emotionally and socially by accompanying students in their understanding of values and helping them to assimilate them. Unlike automated systems, the teacher can offer empathy and nuanced understanding, which is especially valuable when dealing with emotionally sensitive topics that require a sensitive approach. Turgeon and Anderson (2019) emphasize in this regard that *"Although technology can bring significant benefits in education, it is essential to reconcile technological interventions with human supervision and ethical considerations."* By placing values in the context of students' daily lives, the teacher thus becomes an irreplaceable guide.

Complementarity between humans and AI.

The collaboration between human intelligence and artificial intelligence is at the heart of balanced and enriching value learning. While AI can provide detailed data analysis, quick feedback, and interactive instructional scenarios, it lacks the flexibility and intuition to respond to the particularities of each student. This is where the teacher comes in, able to adapt these tools to the needs of each learner and ensure that learning remains relevant and grounded in the students' reality. The teacher can use the resources provided by intelligent systems to illustrate concepts or simulate scenarios, while providing the empathy and intuition needed to bring out true ethical thinking.

AI must therefore be seen as a valuable support tool, allowing teachers to multiply the pedagogical possibilities without replacing their role. Thanks to this complementarity, the values transmitted through literature can be approached with essential depth and humanity, consolidating a learning that is not only instructive, but also formative for young minds.

Technical and human challenges

The integration of intelligent systems into the teaching of values through literary texts poses significant challenges, both technically and humanly. Indeed, one of the major obstacles lies in the difficulty of modelling complex human values by means of automated technologies, to which is added the essential consideration of cultural diversity and individual sensitivities.

Complexity of modeling human values through automated systems.

Human values, which are inherently subjective and rooted in a variety of socio-cultural contexts, pose a real challenge for automated systems. These values evolve not only according to cultures but also according to personal experiences and societal evolution, which makes their modeling extremely delicate.

Indeed, it is difficult for an algorithm to identify profoundly human concepts such as empathy, altruism or fairness – notions that, although universal in their essence, take on different forms and meanings depending on the context. For example, the interpretation of the notion of "justice" in a literary text may vary between a Western perspective and one from Eastern or indigenous cultures, which may prioritize specific community and spiritual values.

Modeling these values, which are evolving and charged with emotions and complex cultural contexts, poses major technical challenges. Indeed, intelligent systems are largely based on databases and learning models which, even if they allow for some adaptation, remain fixed in their initial design. A key question therefore arises: how do we ensure that fluctuating human values are accounted for in nuanced ways in artificial intelligence models that, in essence, operate on the basis of predetermined data and statistically "fixed" models? To achieve a better representation of these values, it is necessary to develop algorithms that can learn not only textual data, but also contextual, emotional and social elements, which requires extensive technical innovation in natural language processing and ethical modeling.

Taking into account cultural context and sensitivities in the teaching of values via technology.

Human values are intimately linked to the cultures, traditions and sensitivities of individuals, which requires a great capacity for adaptation on the part of intelligent systems in their pedagogical approach. For example, an algorithm designed to extract values from literary texts may identify universal themes such as compassion or solidarity, but may fail to capture the cultural subtleties that influence how these values are perceived or expressed. An Arabic literary work, for example, may address the issue of honour or family solidarity in a way that differs significantly from the way these values are addressed in European or Asian literature.

It is therefore essential for the designers of these systems to integrate an advanced cultural sensitivity into the development of their tools. This requires close collaboration between technicians, artificial intelligence experts and cultural and literary educators to develop systems that respect cultural diversity and the values of each group of learners. By adapting teaching tools in this way, these systems can not only avoid erroneous or incomplete interpretations of texts, but they can also provide students with an enriched and inclusive perspective on human values.

In sum, teaching values through intelligent systems requires not only technical advances to model human complexity, but also an ethical and intercultural approach. Only adaptive systems, developed with sensitivity to cultural diversity and supported by human collaborations, will be able to transmit universal human values effectively and in a nuanced way through the literary text.

CASE STUDIES AND PRACTICAL APPLICATIONS

This study was conducted among 120 students in the qualifying secondary cycle, selected for their interest in literature and their desire to deepen their understanding of human and ethical values. The participants, divided into experimental and control groups, followed a study program on Victor Hugo's The Last Day of a Condemned Man, some of them using an intelligent tutor adapted to the analysis of this work. The experimental group, consisting of 60 students, used the smart tutor, while the other 60 students in the control group took a traditional course without the use of this technology.

The experiment took place over a period of three months, during which the experimental group interacted with the intelligent tutor to analyze key passages in Victor Hugo's text. This intelligent tutor offered specific features, designed to enrich learning and guide students in an in-depth exploration of the ethical values present in the work.

Case Study: Using an Intelligent Tutor for Literary Text Analysis

The intelligent tutor used in this study allows students to benefit from an adaptive learning path and deep reflections on complex human values. As part of the analysis of "The Last Day of a Condemned Man", this tutor offers several features aimed at strengthening student engagement and understanding:

- **Key Passage Reflection Questions**: The Intelligent Tutor asks contextual questions to guide students in their understanding of the moral themes present in the text. For example, questions such as "How does the narrator express his sense of injustice in the face of the death sentence?" invite students to reflect on the emotions and dilemmas of the main character, thus initiating an exploration of the notions of justice and injustice.
- **Personalized learning path**: Depending on the students' answers and understanding, the tutor adjusts his approach. If a student has difficulty with certain passages, the tutor provides additional explanations, adapted to the student's level. This personalised support mechanism allows for a better assimilation of the underlying ethical concepts and facilitates differentiated learning, tailored to the individual needs of learners.
- **Exploring Moral Dilemmas**: By immersing students in dilemmas inspired by the context of the text and the positions of the characters, the Intelligent Tutor encourages the examination of different perspectives on ethical and moral issues. This helps students analyze the complexity of the values at stake, whether from the point of view of the narrator or the secondary figures, while integrating the historical and social context of the work.

These features allow students to adopt a critical posture and better understand human values such as compassion and dignity, while exploring how Victor Hugo expressed his opposition to the death penalty.

Study description

In order to verify the effectiveness of these intelligent systems, this study integrated an intelligent tutor into a literature course to analyze its potential in teaching ethical and moral values. The tutor was designed to accompany students in their exploration of Victor Hugo's The *Last Day of a Condemned* Man, an iconic text addressing themes such as justice and human dignity.

In this experiment, the intelligent tutor offered students reflection questions tailored to key passages in the text, allowing for an in-depth exploration of ethical concepts. The tool adjusted the learning path based on each student's responses and level of understanding. When a student encountered difficulties, the tutor would provide additional explanations or alternative perspectives to enrich their interpretation. This approach aimed to support the development of analytical and critical thinking skills, guiding students in a more nuanced analysis of moral values and dilemmas.

By promoting personalized learning and dynamic interaction with the text, this case study aimed to observe how technology can enrich the literary understanding of human values and encourage active student engagement in learning about moral themes.

ANALYSIS OF THE RESULTS

The results obtained following the use of the intelligent tutor show a significant improvement in the understanding of moral values and in student engagement:

Table 1. Result of improvement in understanding values by an intelligent tutor

Skills	Description	Percentage improvement
Understanding of ethical values	Students said that the smart tutor enriched their understanding of values	**82%**
Analytical skills	Progression in students' ability to analyze and discuss social and ethical issues	**35%**
Engagement and active participation	Increased classroom participation	**40 %**

BENEFITS FOR LEARNING

The use of an intelligent tutor in the analysis of literary texts offers several pedagogical advantages, including:

Table 2. Result of the analysis of literary texts by an intelligent tutor

Skills	Description	Percentage improvement
Increased accessibility	Students reported better understanding of the text thanks to personalized annotations and explanations	**90%**
Encouragement of self-exploration	Participants showed an increased desire to read more literary texts after using the tool	**75%**
Critical Skills	Strengthening critical reasoning skills and questioning personal values through literary analysis	**40%**

LIMITATIONS OF LEARNING WITH A SMART TUTOR

Despite its advantages, there are some limitations to using a smart tutor that should be considered for a balanced implementation:

- **Technological dependence**: Some students may become too dependent on the tutor for their thinking, limiting their ability to develop independent thinking. In areas such as ethics, where autonomy of thought is essential, this dependence could prove problematic.
- **Inequities in access**: Not all students have the same access to the technologies needed to interact with the smart tutor, which can create learning disparities. About 20% of the students surveyed reported difficulties in access, a limiting factor for the democratization of this tool.
- **Limitations of human interactions**: Although the intelligent tutor facilitates learning, it cannot replace human exchanges, which are particularly necessary to address the subtleties of ethical and moral values. Classroom interactions and discussions with a teacher remain essential to enrich and nuance students' understanding.

CONCLUSION

This study explored how intelligent systems are redefining value teaching through the analysis of literary texts. The integration of smart tutors and AI platforms demonstrates positive impacts on both individual and collective learning. Thanks to their adaptability, these technologies allow learners to deepen their understanding of ethical and moral themes in various literary works, making texts more accessible and clarifying often complex social and moral values. The results show an improvement in critical thinking, analytical skills, and the ability to interpret moral dilemmas present in the literature, while encouraging greater autonomy and personalized support for each student.

With advances in artificial intelligence, we can envisage even more intuitive and immersive tools, capable of designing personalized learning paths, identifying the ethical dilemmas that are most meaningful to students, and offering enriching experiences, such as literary simulations or interactive debates. Advances in machine learning and augmented virtual reality could also offer captivating experiences, immersing students in literary worlds where values are not only analyzed, but also experienced in simulated environments, thus promoting an immersion that stimulates their moral and cultural reflection. Loveless (2020) warns that *"as AI continues to evolve, it is essential to consider its implications for teaching and learning, particularly with regard to values and ethics in education,"* thus highlighting the need for ethical reflection in the use of these technologies.

However, despite these advances, it remains essential to maintain a balance between technology and human intervention in education. Although intelligent systems enrich learning, they cannot replace the teacher, whose role as a mediator is irreplaceable in interpreting ethical nuances, accompanying students through complex emotions, and answering open-ended questions, which algorithms cannot fully resolve. "The future of education lies in the balance between technological advances and the irreplaceable role of human educators" (Selwyn, 2016). In the classroom, the teacher guides critical thinking and helps students connect their experiences to the values conveyed in literature, with human exchanges essential to their moral and ethical development.

Thus, intelligent systems offer significant potential to reinforce the teaching of values through literature, but their success relies on harmonious integration with human intervention. It is in this complementarity that the guarantee of deep, critical and morally enriching learning lies.

REFERENCES

Anne, A., & Bahlouli, Y. E. (2023). Distributed ledger technology (DLT): Uses and prospects in the education sector. *Mediations and Mediatisations*, (14), 11–27. DOI: 10.52358/mm.vi14.307

Aronsson, M. (2019). Francophone literature in Swedish French language textbooks. Nordic Journal of Francophone Studies/Revue nordique des études francophones, 2(1), 49. https://doi.org/DOI: 10.16993/rnef.26

Baker, R. S. and Siemens, G. (2014). Educational data mining and learning analytics. *Cambridge Handbook on Learning Sciences*, 253-272.

Biesta, G. (2015). *A good education in the age of moderation: ethics, politics, democracy*. Routledge. DOI: 10.4324/9781315634319

Boudiaf, K., & Seddari, B. (2023). The pedagogical scenario integrating the intercultural approach in the digital age: For a dynamic of the understanding of the literary text in middle school. *Multilingual*, 20. Advance online publication. DOI: 10.4000/11ptw

Brault, N. (2022). Artificial intelligence and covid-19, or the limits of "technological solutionism". Annales des mines - Responsabilité et environnement, n° 108(4), 57-60. https://doi.org/DOI: 10.3917/re1.108.0057

Buckingham, D. (2007). *Beyond Technology: Children's Learning in the Digital Age*. Political press.

Collier, D., & Biesta, G. (2021). *Values and virtues in higher education research and teaching: fundamental or misunderstood?* Routledge.

Compagnon, A. (2007). *What is literature for?* Threshold.

Douzou, C. (2008). Birth of a ghost1. *Proteus (Shippensburg, Pa.)*, 35(3), 23–32. DOI: 10.7202/017476ar

. Ferrari, E. (2016). What Montaigne's essays teach us about the cognitive and moral value of literature. Essays, (Special issue 3), 84-98. https://doi.org/DOI: 10.4000/essais.6874

Haque, S. (2022). Role of literature in the learning of Urdu as a foreign language in France. Representative Samples and Didactic Discourses, 43-54. https://doi.org/DOI: 10.17184/eac.6538

Harrison, T., & Khatoon, B. (2017). Virtue, ethics and moral education in the digital age. *Journal of Moral Education*, 46(4), 334–346.

Hayles, N. K. (2012). *How We Think: Digital Media and Contemporary Technogenesis*. University of Chicago Press. DOI: 10.7208/chicago/9780226321370.001.0001

Jockers, M. L. (2013). *Macroanalysis: numerical methods and literary history*. University of Illinois Press. DOI: 10.5406/illinois/9780252037528.001.0001

Kalai, L. (2023). ICT in the Tunisian university context: What uses for which forms of didactic innovation? the case of French students. *Multilingual*, 20. Advance online publication. DOI: 10.4000/11o27

Kim, Y., & Baylor, A. L. (2016). A virtual agent of change: Motivating pre-service teachers to integrate technology into their future classrooms. *Research and Development in Educational Technology*, 64(3), 543–560.

. Kouvouama, A. (2004). Imaginaire et société dans la littérature africaine francophone. Hermes, Nos. 40(3), 280. https://doi.org/DOI: 10.4267/2042/9560

Luckin, R., & Cukurova, M. (2019). Designing Educational Technologies in the Age of AI: A Science in Learning Approach. *British Journal of Educational Technology*, 50(6), 2824–2838. DOI: 10.1111/bjet.12861

Luckin, R., Holmes, W., Griffiths, M., & Forcier, L. B. (2016). *Intelligence unleashed: an argument in favor of AI in education*. Pearson Education.

McCarty, W. (2005). *Computer Science in the Humanities*. Palgrave Macmillan. DOI: 10.1057/9780230504219

Narvaez, D., & Lapsley, D. K. (2005). *Moral development, self and identity*. Lawrence Erlbaum Associates.

Nucci, L. P., & Narvaez, D. (2008). *Manual of moral education and character*. Routledge.

Omar, O. (2018). Smart building, definitions, factors and selection evaluation criteria. *Alexandria Engineering Journal*, 57(4), 2903–2910. DOI: 10.1016/j.aej.2018.07.004

Ouakka, S., & El Alaoui, A. (2023). Towards a new Moroccan education system that is inclusive, regulatory and citizen-friendly. SHS Conference Web, 175, 01032. https://doi.org/DOI: 10.1051/shsconf/202317501032

Ouellet, S. (2019). Accompanying the literary experience through the reception and creation of multitexts: Comparison of two didactic devices. *Journal of Research in Multimodal Media Literacy*, 10. Advance online publication. DOI: 10.7202/1065531ar

Park, D. (2021). Towards artificial intelligence on a human scale. https://doi.org//arxiv.2108.03793DOI: 10.48550

Piper, A. (2018). *Enumerations: data and literary study*. University of Chicago Press. DOI: 10.7208/chicago/9780226568898.001.0001

Prairat, E. (2019). Values: A philosophical question, a pedagogical challenge. *Research & Works*, (94). Advance online publication. DOI: 10.4000/recherchestravaux.1563

Ramsay, S. (2011). *Reading machines: towards an algorithmic critique*. University of Illinois Press. DOI: 10.5406/illinois/9780252036415.001.0001

Rest, J. R., & Narvaez, D. (1994). *Moral Development in the Professions: Psychology and Applied Ethics*. Psychology Press. DOI: 10.4324/9781410601162

Rockwell, G., & Sinclair, S. (2016). *Hermeneutica: Computer-Aided Interpreting in the Humanities*. MIT Press. DOI: 10.7551/mitpress/9522.001.0001

Roll, I., & Wylie, R. (2016). Evolution and revolution of artificial intelligence in education. *International Journal of Artificial Intelligence in Education*, 26(2), 582–599. DOI: 10.1007/s40593-016-0110-3

Selwyn, N. (2016). *Is technology good for education?* John Wiley and Sons.

Sharples, M., & Cooper, G. (2020). *Artificial Intelligence in Education: Promises and Implications for Teaching and Learning*. The OECD.

Sinclair, S. and Rockwell, G. (2012). Text analysis and visualization as a means of teaching literature in a digital humanities context. *Digital Humanities Quarterly, 6*(2).

Spitmaan, M., & Leong, A. C. (2019). Theory of the intelligent act. https://doi.org/DOI: 10.31235/osf.io/g78mf

Tamim, R., Bernard, R., Borokhovski, E., Abrami, P. C., & Schmid, R. (2011). What forty years of research say about the impact of technology on learning. *Review of Educational Research*, 81(1), 4–28. DOI: 10.3102/0034654310393361

Taymanov, R., & Sapozhnikova, K. (2010). Terminology issues in the field of sensors and intelligent systems. *Key Engineering Materials*, 437, 434–438. . DOI: 10.4028/www.scientific.net/KEM.437.434

Turgeon, W., & Anderson, M. (2019). Ethics and Artificial Intelligence: Teaching and Learning in Higher Education. In *Research Manual on Learning in the Age of Transhumanism*. IGI Global.

Underwood, T. (2019). *Distant Horizons: Digital Evidence and Literary Change*. University of Chicago Press. DOI: 10.7208/chicago/9780226612973.001.0001

Wilkens, M. (2020). *The Social Life of Literary Data*. Association of Modern Languages.

Without Love, A. M. (2020). Pedagogy, digital media and the culture of values in the post-digital era. *Technology, Pedagogy and Education*, 29(1), 23–38.

Woolf, B. P. (2009). *Building Smart Interactive Tutors: Student-Centered Strategies to Revolutionize Online Learning*. Morgan Kaufmann.

Chapter 15
Digital Literacy, Circumscription, Evolution, and Its Relationship With Artificial Intelligence and Foreign Language Teaching

Marwan Serrar
https://orcid.org/0000-0002-5841-4906
ENS Tetouan, Morocco

Ahmed Ibrahimi
https://orcid.org/0009-0004-8879-5561
ENS Tétouan, Morocco

ABSTRACT

The aim of this literature review is firstly to study and circumscribe the notions of literacy and digital literacy through the work carried out in relation to the latter. We will then analyze the evolution of the notion of digital literacy in proportion to the development of the digital environment, as well as the points of convergence between digital literacy and language didactics. This work discusses these points with the intention of highlighting the importance of this dynamic, versatile and cross-cutting notion in society, at school and, more specifically, in the foreign language classroom, for shaping the learner and citizen of today and tomorrow. Moreover, the relationship between digital literacy and AI is crucial, since it enhances the ability to use AI tools effectively. Therefore, the role of digital literacy will be examined concerning the good and bad uses of artificial intelligence tools.

DOI: 10.4018/979-8-3693-8965-2.ch015

INTRODUCTION

The growth of globalization, the advances in digital technologies, particularly those linked to artificial intelligence (AI), and the democratization of digital tools, have profoundly changed life in our societies. At the same time, schools, and particularly the teaching and learning of foreign languages, have also been influenced, gradually integrating the new possibilities offered by digital technology and AI.

These transformations were amplified with the advent of the participative version of the web known as WEB 2.0 (Kern, 2021; O'REILLY, 2005), followed by Web 3.0 (Hussain, 2013). Thanks to this evolution, world citizens in general and learners in particular have gone from being mere passive web users to active participants (CAWS, 2021), requiring the acquisition of new skills. It is in this situation that digital literacy has emerged as a key notion to be defined, explored, developed and integrated into teaching, especially language teaching.

Digital literacy is a dynamic, multimodal concept (COMBE, 2021; Violaine Bigot, 2021) that develops in proportion to the development of the digital context and environment. Contrary to a slight reticence towards this notion during the previous century, it has had the interest it deserved, or almost, by being the subject of studies by several researchers and official institutions (UNESCO, 2018; OECD, 2019; P21, 2019; Hague, 2010; Buckingham, 2007; EU, European Commission, 2023).

Faced with this growing interest, language didactics research has explored approaches for integrating digital literacy into foreign language teaching-learning. The emergence of AI reinforces this need, offering new tools for teaching, but also redefining transversal and language skills, with an emphasis on critical interpretation of information and interaction with intelligent systems.

Within this context, our study aims to offer a structured literature review that first attempts to establish a historical anchor and circumscribe the notion of literacy through which disciplinary literacies, notably digital literacy, have emerged. Secondly, we will do the same for the notion of digital literacy, by drawing on the many research and studies that have been carried out by specialized researchers and official institutions, while taking into account the impact of web development in the evolution of the latter. Finally, we will look at the links between digital literacy, artificial intelligence and language didactics, through a study of the scientific literature and the two European reference frameworks for languages and digital skills.

LITERACY: ORIGIN, CONCEPTUALIZATION AND CIRCUMSCRIPTION:

Literacy: origin, etymology, definitions and perceptions:

a. Origin and etymology of "literacy" and "littératie/ littéracie" in the French-speaking world:

In order to fully understand this concept, we need to start by looking at its origins and etymology.

It should be noted that the term "littératie" was not invented in the French-speaking world, but borrowed and copied from the Anglo-Saxon word "literacy", according to Barré-de Miniac (2002). This importation has given us two French-language variants of the English term, "littératie" and "littéracie". According to Pierre R. (2003), in order to meet the requirements of the Office de la langue française and decide between writing the word "littératie" with two "t "s or just one, they had to base themselves on its etymology, which was "litteratus" according to Gaffiot, (1934), and which means literate, scholar or engaged in literary activities according to Oxford english dictionary, (2023). It's worth mentioning that there are other ancient terms that bear a resemblance to the word "littératie", such as the Latin term "litteratio" which, according to ATTALI, (2022) was used in Rome in the 8th century B.C. to designate the teaching of the basics for integration into the society of the past, such as arithmetic, reading, writing, mythology, the military art ... .

According to Merriam-Webster, (2023) and Schneuwly, (2020), the word "literacy" has existed in English since 1880, referring to the fact of being able to read and write and of having been taught to do so. In the 1950s, the term gained considerable notoriety, and was even adopted by UNESCO in its public education programs as "literacy compains", according to Fraenkel (2021). We note that until this date, the French term "littératie" was not yet in use. According to a study by Schneuwly, (2020), it wasn't until the 1990s that the French terms "littératie / littéracie" began to be adopted, first in Quebec research and then, after 1999, throughout the French-speaking scientific literature. This democratization of the term in both English and French in the 1990s is due to globalization as well as its adoption by major international organizations "UNESCO / OECD / PISA ..." according to Hébert, (2013).

b. Definitions of "literacy" and Francophone perceptions:

We have chosen to use the plural form of "definitions" to draw the reader's attention to the difficulties encountered by the scientific community in defining this notion. It is a multi-disciplinary concept with a multitude of definitions that are generally similar in essence, but also have their differences. These points of divergence are due to the different contexts and fields of work of the researchers, but also to their backgrounds and the bases on which they rely to define the notion.

It should be noted that, in addition to its transversality, "literacy" is a constantly evolving concept. We can see this in the changes in its definition over time. According to a study by Barré-de Miniac, (2002) analyzing the evolution of the definition of the term "littératie" in Harris and Hodges' dictionary between 1981 and 1995, she had identified the following definitions in the 1981 version: (knowing how to read, write and count at a level judged satisfactory by society / functional literacy "alphabetization" / knowledge in any technical field); against these in 1995 (a basic level of having read, written and counted; level necessary to mark to be able to compare it with higher levels / Broadening to other fields of competence such as arithmetic, computing, media ... / learning to read the world and not just words). We note here that the definition is increasingly broadened over time to include fields other than reading, writing and arithmetic.

In what follows, we list the updated definitions of the main international organizations that have worked on this notion. According to UNESCO (2023), literacy is defined as a set of key skills in reading, writing and counting. But it is also a means of identifying, understanding, interpreting, creating and communicating in the world, and these practices evolve and recontextualize with the evolution of our life system. As part of its Programme for the International Assessment of Adult Competencies (PIAAC) the OECD defines literacy as: " Literacy is understanding, evaluating, using and engaging with written texts to participate in society, to achieve one's goals, and to develop one's knowledge and potential." OECD, (2016). We note that this is the same definition adopted by the OECD's other international program, the Programme for International Student Assessment (PISA), adding that new forms of text should be included (Mo, 2019). We note that through their definitions, UNESCO and the OECD wanted to draw attention to the social aspect of literacy and the influence of society and the environment on it (digital environment as an example) in addition to the educational aspect already addressed in their previous definitions.

Hébert, M., & Lépine, M, (2013) grouped the definitions of literacy in 38 francophone works and extracted 10 added values. Among these, we cite "A notion of multi-objectives, a plural, interdisciplinary perspective on the personal, professional and socio-cultural objectives and issues related to the appropriation of the written word" / "A set of attitudes, knowledge, skills and competencies related to the appropriation of written culture (and to be developed in the learner), the complex interrelationship of these affective, cognitive and socio-cultural aspects in teaching ; learning" / "Individual-society relations, reading and writing helps to develop individual identity, social integration or exclusion" / "Positive concept and continuum, then possible evolution throughout life". We've only mentioned 4 of the 10 added values here, but thanks to them, we can understand the orientation of Francophone definitions of literacy. These definitions emphasize the notion's transversality and its durability as a continuum concept, aimed at lifelong learning. They also attach considerable importance to the use of basic writing and reading skills in personal, professional and social domains, emancipating the action from the monopoly of the educational framework. We see in these definitions a link with those of the Anglo-Saxon world, which is perhaps due to the influence of Anglo-Saxon work on French-speaking researchers working on literacy at the end of the last century, according to Barré-de Miniac, (2002).

As we saw above, French-speaking researchers were initially hesitant to use the word littératie. We found that in the 38 works studied by Manon Hébert and Martin Lépine, (2013), 10 of them did not explicitly mention the term "littératie" (literacy) and were content to use "alphabétisation / savoir lire / écrire pour apprendre" (alphabétization / reading / writing for learning), which was the case for many works by Francophone researchers before the 2000s, and which had the consequence of restricting literacy to the educational domain. But with globalization and the influence of Anglo-Saxon researchers and international organizations, Francophone researchers have been able to revise their conceptions of this notion.

Literacy « Littératie, littéracie » alphabetization and skills: links and differences:

a. « Littératie and littéracie » in francophone research: the « t » versus the « c »:

According to the works we have been able to consult, we believe that the choice of "c" or "t" remains simply a matter of preference, with no influence on the meaning of the term "literacy". For example, Fraenkel, (2021) said that the term « literacy » has enjoyed considerable fortune in the English-speaking world since the 1950s. More recently, it has been taken up and widely adopted in France in its English form or by the neologism (littératie), sometimes (littéracie) . We can see from these comments that the use of the two letters is neutral. We can confirm this theory by looking at the titles of the 38 works studied by Hébert, M., & Lépine, M, (2013), we found that 16 of them used the "t" against 7 for the "c", the other titles did not contain the term. In this work, the use of both letters was not taken into account in the definition studies, proving that the use of one or the other has no influence on the meaning of the term.

However, we can note a slight influence of the two letters, not in the meaning, but in the framework and geography. Barré-de Miniac (2002) asserts that the "t" is more commonly used in Canadian research, and when the English term was imported into France, French researchers adopted the "c" to distinguish themselves from their Canadian colleagues and save a certain "national pride".

b. Literacy, alphabetization and skills:

The 3 terms “literacy”, ” alphabetization ” and “skills ” are often confusing and can even mislead researchers. As we saw above, before the French translation of “literacy” appeared, international organizations were content to use the term “alphabétisation” in the French versions of their reports and research. According to Schneuwly, (2020), by the end of the 1980s, researchers were already campaigning for the adoption of the term “littératie” in the official versions of UNESCO documents, because of the reductive aspect of the word “alphabétisme”, which restricts the teaching and learning of the written word to that of the code. Fraenkel, (2021) has exposed the gap between the object of “alphabetisation”, which is basic reading and writing skills, and the broad skills suggested by the OECD definition of literacy. Pierre R. (2003) contrasts “writing (écrit)”, the object of literacy, which refers to the whole range of written productions and the way in which they are used, with “writing (écriture)”, the object of literacy, which is limited to the code. According to Chartier, A. M., & Rockwell, E, (2013) taken up by Schneuwly, (2020), it was these limitations of the term “alphabétisation” that forced the French academy to recognize the word “littératie”.

The notion of skill has not escaped the multiple difficulties and ambiguities of definition. According to Coulet, (2011) there is a divergence in the scientific community on the dimension of the notion of “cognitive or social” competence. According to his analysis of the scientific literature, the elements of “knowledge, habilities and attitudes” (savoir / savoir-faire/ savoir-etre) are repeated in the definitions of competencies and are generally mobilized to accomplish tasks and activities. Perrenoud (1999) confirms this view. However, he notes that reading, writing and counting skills, the main focus of compulsory schooling, are now outdated, and that the competency-based approach seeks to update them. We note here that the two notions - literacy and competence - are distinguished by their transversality and by the ambiguity surrounding their definitions. We also note that these two notions are interdependent and have points of convergence. Among these points we cite the elements of knowledge, know-how and interpersonal skills that are mobilized in tasks to form a competence; these elements have as their respective synonyms “knowledge, habilities and attitudes”. The latter are present in one of the definitions of literacy presented earlier in our work. However, their purposes converge and diverge depending on the context, because if we can say that the purpose of literacy is “to use and understand the written word to accomplish one's various objectives, to participate in society...” or “to mobilize knowledge, know-how and interpersonal skills for the appropriation of the written word...”, competence mobilizes these same elements, but for specific purposes “writing, accounting, computer development...”.

Some « disciplinary literacies »:

With the democratization of the concept of literacy, some researchers came up with the idea of adapting it to their fields. This led to the emergence of “disciplinary literacies”, which are distinct from “content area literacy” (Shanahan 2012, Granger 2018).

Among these types of literacy, we cite as an example health literacy, which emerged in response to health researchers' concerns about patients' ability and reliability in using medical information, according to Andrus, M. R., & Roth, M, (2002). This notion could be defined as a person's ability to use, understand, access and utilize information in order to make decisions about their health according to Van den Broucke, (2017). There are other disciplinary literacies such as “financial literacy” “Hastings et al., (2013)” as well as “physical literacy” “Lundvall, (2015)”.

However, in order to ensure a smooth transition to the second part, we will focus on digital literacy and related types of it, like media and computer literacy.

a. Media literacy:

According to Romero-Ivanova. R et al, (2019), the introduction of mass media in the middle of the last century has influenced the notion of literacy by pushing it to integrate the media component. For these researchers, traditional literacy practices - reading, writing and creating - are now understood as multiple and diverse practices that individuals adopt beyond educational settings into other, more mediatized and diversified spaces. According to Scharrer et al (2022), media literacy involves the ability to interact actively with media, carefully considering media texts, the forces and factors that shape these texts, and the ways in which audiences interpret or otherwise respond to texts.Media literacy is considered essential for citizenship in the contemporary world, as it encompasses skills such as accessing, using, creating, analyzing and evaluating media.

b. computer/information literacy:

According to Gilster, (1997), following the democratization of mass media, the rise of the computer with new information technologies has seen the notion of literacy flexed once again to include an additional element - "information literacy". According to LIVINGSTONE, (2004) this new notion emerged in response to the emergence of (ICT) and the importance of developing the skills needed to navigate this new, more complex environment. In parallel with the democratization of (ICT), computer literacy began to gain increasing importance in the educational field as well as in the professional world, to finally play a key role today as mentioned in the work of Weiner, (2011).

c. Digital literacy:

While the notion of computer literacy emerged in the second half of the last century with the emergence of (ICT), digital literacy took on greater importance with the advent and democratization of the Internet and the proliferation of digital devices. This process of change has necessitated reflection on the new skills to be developed in learners and citizens, among which we find the ability to use digital technologies to access, evaluate and create information, adapt and participate effectively in the digital world ... (Barry Lunt, 2005; Belshaw, 2012).

We can thus say that the transition to digital literacy has been a gradual process that has evolved over time, without excluding the previous notions. According to Kvasny, L. & Richardson, H., (2006), the development of critical research in information systems, advances in other fields such as quantum information science and the exploration of social networks, in addition to the creation of new programs and standards have all contributed to the development of digital literacy as a field of study. In what follows, we will attempt to define and explain digital literacy in greater detail.

DIGITAL LITERACY: VIEWPOINTS, COMPONENTS AND TERMINOLOGICAL CLARIFICATION:

As mentioned above, the notion of digital literacy has evolved over the years. Over the last few decades, this notion, in addition to "digital skills", has acquired great importance and is increasingly discussed by both researchers and political organizations. According to Alberto D. Yazon et al, (2019), the latter are trying to define and circumscribe the type of skills and knowledge that people should have in a knowledge society. According to Allan R. Martin (2006), digital literacy is based on the convergence of the literacies mentioned in the previous section, in addition to technological and visual literacy. According to Michele. K & Colin. L, (2006), it is not a closed, univocal and explicit notion or concept, but rather a wide range of digital literacies.

In the remainder of this section, we'll see how researchers and official organizations have defined this dynamic and constantly evolving notion, each from their own point of view:

Digital literacy as seen by researchers:

In preparing this work, we noted that a greater or lesser number of literature reviews and articles (Kern, 2021; COMBE, 2021; Violaine Bigot, 2021; Pritika Reddy, 2021) attempted to define this notion after the health crisis.

Therefore, in order to add a touch of originality to our work, we decided to examine the evolution of this notion and contextualize the change in definitions issued by researchers by taking into account the evolution of the WEB.

a. Digital literacy: an embryonic concept in the age of WEB 1.0:

Web 1.0 was mostly static and based on displaying information (O'REILLY, 2005; Berners-Lee, 1994). Websites were simple pages where users could mainly read and navigate, but not interact directly. Until the 2000s, therefore, the web was not a medium for interaction and creation. According to Nielsen (1999), this luxury was reserved for developers and webmasters. As a result, digital literacy was limited to the skills needed to navigate the web of yesteryear.

Paul Gilster (1997) is often referred to as one of the first to use the term "digital literacy" in his book "Digital Literacy". He sees it as the ability to understand information and use it in a digital context. This involves technical skills, such as surfing the web, finding information online and using basic software, as well as online security. It's worth pointing out that he was already talking about the importance of developing critical thinking at the time, since the technical skills we've mentioned can't be mobilized effectively without it.

It is important to note that several researchers of the time adopted a vision more or less similar to Glister's with regard to digital literacy in their respective fields (education / computer science / big data / sociology / linguistics / communication / media ...). We note, for example, that Hargittai (2002), as a sociologist, highlighted the importance of information-seeking skills in his article. In their turn, Thurlow et al (2004), as linguists, sociolinguists, sociologists and ICT researchers (each with their own specialties), addressed the need to master basic e-mail skills...

From what we've just seen, we can see that digital literacy, from the outset, has been a multimodal notion that lies at the crossroads of multiple specialties ranging from the technical sciences to the humanities, intriguing many researchers from different fields. With the advent of Web 2.0, digital literacy will become even more important, integrating new components without losing the old ones.

b. Evolution of the concept of digital literacy with the development of WEB 2.0:

According to Kern (2021), in just a few years the Internet has changed and become more personal, encouraging creativity and sociability. Whereas WEB 1.0 once meant passively connecting to static sites created by others. WEB 2.0 changed all that, urging people to create content and participate in the development of the digital environment. This change has brought to the surface some new skills that were previously restricted to a limited number of people, such as writing, photography, artwork, music and other forms of self-expression:

> « In just a few years, however, the Internet became profoundly more personal, creative, and social in its content, its multimodality, and its connectivity. Whereas early Internet use largely meant connecting to static websites created by others, people soon came to create their own personal websites featuring their writing, photography, artwork, music, and other forms of self-expression. Web 2.0 ushered in a shift in emphasis from publishing to social participation, whereby people engaged one another by tagging, liking, friending, and posting on social media platforms. Over time, massively popular sites such as Wikipedia, Facebook, Twitter, YouTube, and Instagram developed—and their entire content was dynamically produced by literally billions of individual users » Kern, (2021, p.133)

We note that Kern.R, (2021) joined the thinking of O'Reilly, (2005) who characterized web2.0 by active user participation and content creation, rather than simple content consumption. He also pointed out the importance of being able to understand, use and create digital information effectively.

We also note that, at this time, researchers working on this notion have placed greater emphasis on skills that foster critical thinking and creativity. Bawden (2008), for example, defines it as the set of skills, knowledge and attitudes needed to adapt, critically and creatively, to the constant evolution of (ICT).

It was during this period that the majority of official institutions decided to circumscribe and integrate digital literacy (Jisc 2015; ISTE, 2016; UNESCO 2018; European Commission 2019; NEA, 2020 ...).

It was also at this time that we began to associate this notion with that of digital citizenship by talking about social inclusion with digital. Deursen. V et al., (2014) drew our attention to the role that digital literacy can play in promoting social inclusion by enabling individuals to access online information and resources, participate in online communities and engage in democratic decision-making. They have also warned of the dangers of inequalities in access to technology and digital literacy skills, as they can exacerbate social and economic divisions.

However, due to the continuous and rapid change of the digital environment in this era, the notion of digital literacy faces several challenges regarding its definition, teaching and practice. According to Belshaw, (2012), one of the main challenges is to identify the priority skills for individuals and design educational programs to develop them; furthermore, technologies evolve rapidly, and digital literacy skills need to be constantly updated to remain relevant and effective according to Eshet-Alkalai, (2004).

c. Recent reflections on digital literacy at the gateway to WEB 3.0:

If Web 2.0 introduced active, creative participation to the digital world, Web 3.0, or at least the early days we're experiencing today, is known as the semantic/data web. Hussain & Fehmida, (2013) show us the novelties that characterize web 3.0 from its predecessor as well as the new technologies it brings and on which it is based:

> « Web 3.0, termed as the semantic web or the web of data is the transformed version of Web 2.0 with technologies and functionalities such as intelligent collaborative filtering, cloud computing, big data, linked data, openness, interoperability and smart mobility. If web 2.0 is about social networking and mass collaboration between creator and user, then the Web 3.0 is referring to intelligent applications using natural language processing, machine-based learning and reasoning. » Hussain & Fehmida, (2013 p.39)

According to Potluri and Vajjhala (2018), Web 3.0 technologies offer an integrated experience for users, as machines begin to understand and classify data in the same way as humans. They thus attest to the role of artificial intelligence in this new digital universe, and therefore the need to develop the necessary skills (in addition to those that were important for Web 2.0) to interact and participate in it.

We note, then, that the notion of digital literacy has once again been influenced by the ever-changing context of the web, confronting itself with the need to integrate new skills with previous ones and deal with concepts emerging from web 3.0 . We cite the following examples:

- Digital literacy and artificial intelligence (Zhou 2020 preprint 2009).
- Digital literacy and the fight against misinformation: problem-solving, retrieving, evaluating and using information from a variety of sources, according to Probowati & Yeni, (2023)
- Digital literacy and "big data" (Hilbert 2016, D. a. Bawden 2018)
- Digital literacy and digital well-being (OCDE 2019, NEELAKANDAN 2023)

In conclusion, digital literacy is a vital issue for Web 3.0 as it was for its predecessors, and educational efforts must be tailored to help users navigate this rapidly evolving environment and take advantage of the new technologies and decentralized systems that characterize it.

d. The notion of digital literacy between Anglo-Saxon enthusiasm and Francophone hesitation:

While Anglo-Saxon works have adopted and circumscribed the term for some time, French-speaking works have struggled to use it. Violaine. B et al, (2021) show in their article the Francophone resistance to using the term littératie:

> « […] Sa pénétration dans les travaux de didactique est encore lente, en tout cas dans le champ des recherches francophones.
> […] Cette même recherche réalisée sur deux documents de référence produits par le Conseil de l'Europe confirme que si le terme est entré dans la version anglophone de ces textes de référence, ce n'est pas le cas pour les versions francophones » Violaine.B et al, (2021 p.6)

This work explains this reluctance by the French phobia towards neologisms and by the dominant textual culture. However, we can explain this hesitation by other factors such as the importance that French-speaking countries place on classical education.

According to UNESCO, (2017), sometimes reluctance can be caused not by a lack of will, but by budgetary and infrastructure problems as in the case of Francophone Africa, which has promoted initiatives to promote digital literacy.

Digital literacy as seen, circumscribed and composed by institutions:

With the democratization of the Internet, teaching digital literacy has become a crucial issue in our globalized world, where mastery of (ICT) is essential for access to employment, education and public services.

International institutions have recognized this reality and are working to promote digital literacy as an essential skill for all citizens. In this context, it is interesting to examine the different perspectives and initiatives of these organizations, such as (UNESCO, OECD, the European Union...) to better understand their approach and the actions they are taking in terms of digital literacy.

a. UNESCO's point of view:

According to UNESCO, (2018), digital literacy is a key component of lifelong learning and the acquisition of essential skills for the 21st century citizen, including creativity, critical thinking, collaboration and communication. The organization promotes digital literacy in educational programs and national strategies to improve the quality and equity of education.

UNESCO published a digital literacy reference framework in 2018, called "A Global Framework of Reference on Digital Literacy Skills for Indicator 4.4.2". The latter defines digital literacy as follows:

> "Digital literacy is the ability to access, manage, understand, integrate, communicate, evaluate and create information safely and appropriately through digital technologies for employment, decent jobs and entrepreneurship. It includes competences that are variously referred to as computer literacy, ICT literacy, information literacy and media literacy." UNESCO, (2018 p.6)

The framework also emphasizes the need to integrate digital literacy into formal and non-formal education, as well as vocational training programs. The organization highlights the importance of ensuring access to quality digital devices and connectivity, as well as supporting teachers in developing their own digital literacy skills.

In "A Global Framework to Measure Digital Literacy", Antoninis, M., & Montoya, S. (2018) propose additions to digcomp 2.1 . They add two key competencies to those already present in the "DIGCOMP" competency framework which are: "Fundamentals of hardware and software" and "Career-related competences ".

b. OECD's point of view and the PIAAC program:

According to the OECD (2012), digital literacy is defined as an individual's ability to use digital technologies, communication tools and networks to access information, communicate with others, solve problems and create digital content.

As part of the Programme for the International Assessment of Adult Competencies (PIAAC), the OECD has developed a framework for assessing literacy in general and digital literacy in particular. According to this framework, literacy is defined as follows:

« PIAAC defines literacy as understanding, evaluating, using and engaging with written textes to participate in society, to achieve one's goals, develop one's knowledge and potential. » OCDE, (2012 p.20)

In the work that follows the latter, the OECD, (2020) highlights the importance of digital literacy in ensuring sustainable development.

c. EU viewpoint / European Commission / Digcomp framework:

In the European Framework for Key Competences for Lifelong Learning, the European Union has defined the key competences that all citizens should have:

« Digital competence involves the confident and critical use of Information Society Technology (IST) for work, leisure and communication. It is underpinned by basic skills in ICT: the use of computers to retrieve, assess, store, produce, present and exchange information, and to communicate and participate in collaborative networks via the Internet.

[...]Skills needed include the ability to search, collect and process information and use it in a critical and systematic way, assessing relevance and distinguishing the real from the virtual while recognising the links. Individuals should have skills to use tools to produce, present and understand complex information and the ability to access, search and use internet-based services. Individuals should also be able use IST to support critical thinking, creativity, and innovation. » UE, (2006 p.6)

In its Digital Education Action Plan (2021-2027), the European Commission underlines the vital importance of digital education in the 21st century for life and employment. This action plan supports the training and professional development of teachers to enable them to effectively integrate digital technology into education and improve their digital skills (European Commission, 2023).

d. Viewpoint of NGOs like "Partnership for 21st Century Learning" P21 and JISC:

JISC, (2019) is a non-profit company offering digital resource support to higher education in the UK. According to JISC, digital literacy is defined as the skills, knowledge and attitudes needed to live, learn and work in a digital world. According to their guide entitled "Building digital capabilities: The six elements defined", digital literacy or what they call "digital capabilities" encompasses 6 key competencies: digital identity and well-being; digital communication, collaboration and participation; digital learning and development; media and data literacy; ICT skills; and digital creativity, problem-solving and innovation.

Concerning P21, which is a non-profit organization promoting education in the 21st century. In the three frameworks it published in 2019 (Framework for 21st Century Learning: A unified vision for learning to ensure student success in a world where change is constant and learning never stops); (FRAMEWORK FOR 21st CENTURY LEARNING: DEFINITIONS); (21ST CENTURY LEARNING FOR EARLY CHILDHOOD FRAMEWORK), P21 focuses on a set of key digital skills "INFORMATION, MEDIA & TECHNOLOGY SKILLS" . These skills encompass the ability to understand, use ICT and digital tools effectively to create, communicate and collaborate, in addition to the ability to address issues related to the use of digital technologies, such as security, privacy and digital citizenship. P21, (2019).

Digital skills, citizenship and literacy: convergence and terminological confusion:

By consulting a significant number of articles and reviews that have worked on the conceptual and terminological relationship between these notions: (Ilomäki 2016, Bejaković 2020, Ferrari.A 2012, Martzoukou 2020, Shopova 2014, Konstantina Martzoukou 2021, Wibowo Heru Prasetiyo 2021, Wibowo Heru Prasetiyo 2021) (Isrokatun 2022, Rıdvan Ata 2019, Okeji 2020, Taina Juurakko-Paavola 2018, X.Yo 2021, Mustafa Kaya 2020).

We have found that digital literacy, digital skills / competencies and digital citizenship are all related concepts that are often used interchangeably. However, just as there are convergences, there are also divergences. According to Santiago. T et al, (2020), digital literacy is the foundation for being effective and efficient in the 21st century in personal and professional lives that increasingly rely on digital technology. This notion implies the ability to create, evaluate and communicate information using digital tools and media according to Shopova, (2014) .

In this research we note that the notion of « compétences numériques » in French is divided into two key notions in Anglo-Saxon works "digital skills" and "digital competence". Ferrari.A, (2012) for example, defines the second notion as follows:

> « Digital Competence is the set of knowledge, skills, attitudes (thus including abilities, strategies, values and awareness) that are required when using ICT and digital media to perform tasks; solve problems; communicate; manage information; collaborate; create and share content; and build knowledge effectively, efficiently, appropriately, critically, creatively, autonomously, flexibly, ethically, reflectively for work, leisure, participation, learning, socialising, consuming, and empowerment. » Ferrari.A, (2012 p.3)

As for the notion of "digital skills", it refers to the technical skills required to use digital tools and media, which leads us to deduce that the notion of "digital competence" is a broad concept that encompasses that of "digital skills".

Concerning the notion of digital citizenship, Ollivier. C et al, (2021) have pointed out the conceptual proximity that contributes to definitional ambiguity between the latter and the notion of digital literacy. These researchers, citing the elements included by Ribble, (2011) in his model of digital citizenship "digital communication or health and well-being" were able to note that the latter are also present in some models of digital literacy. On the other hand, they also pointed out that some researchers distinguish the two concepts, such as Richardson. J & Milovidov. E, (2017).

Summarizing what we have just seen, we can say that although there are differences between them, digital literacy, digital skills / competencies and digital citizenship are important and interdependent concepts in the digital context. It is therefore essential to take them into account and develop them in order to train effective and responsible users of digital tools and media in the 21st century.

ARTIFICAL INTELLIGENCE, DIGITAL LITERACY AND LANGUAGE TEACHING:

Digital literacy and artificial intelligence in education:

The integration of AI alongside digital literacy in education is more than ever recognized and claimed to be essential for preparing learners for modern academic, professional and social demands. As mentioned earlier, digital literacy encompasses a wide range of skills needed to navigate effectively and responsibly in the digital environment, including the ability to access, evaluate and use information in a digital context. This set of skills has gained in importance with the democratization of AI tools, since mastery of these new tools and techniques in addition to understanding the implications of these technologies on society is becoming a crucial skill at both educational and social levels Hwang, Zhu, & Cui, (2023).

Regarding the contribution of digital literacy integration in the educational field, research indicates that it has a significant impact on learners' academic performance. For example, Marisa & Djulia, (2022) reveal through their study that 19.4% is the percentage of the influence of digital literacy on learners' learning and results.

Moreover, the role of AI in education is evolving significantly, as the integration of AI tools into educational practices contributes to the fostering of a more interactive and encouraging learning environment, not to mention the development of the digital literacy components necessary for success in this day and age Tran & Tran, (2023). We can thus see that the synergy between digital literacy and AI is making a major contribution to the field of education, and giving researchers and teachers the opportunity to renew educational methods and programs.

The AI Integration in Developing Digital Literacy for Foreign Language Teaching.

Digital technologies, including AI, can play a significant role in facilitating language learning. This can be achieved through innovative tools that help improve learner engagement and interaction in a language course. For example, automatic language processing models such as GPT-3 chat enable the automatic generation of texts, which could make a considerable contribution to writing activities in a language course. Secondly, studies carried out on the impact of AI integration in English language teaching have revealed that certain tools such as intelligent tutoring systems (ITS) are beneficial for this type of teaching, as they offer the possibility of using speech recognition to provide personalized feedback to learners via language processing functionality. In addition, the integration of AI into this type of course at university has demonstrated significant benefits in terms of adaptability and interactivity among learners Luo, (2024).

However, in order to ensure the effective integration of AI into teaching in general and language teaching in particular, certain challenges need to be overcome. These include training teachers to make effective use of AI tools in their educational practices. Stockless et al., (2022) demonstrate in their study that teacher professional development based on and focused on digital skills is crucial to maximizing the potential of AI in the classroom. Good management of these tools is also a key factor in ensuring the successful adoption of AI in education (Gravelle et al., 2022).

The AI and digital literacy role in learner personalization and engagement:

The rise as well as the democratization of digital technologies and AI is significantly influencing the educational scene in several aspects. Pellerin, (2017) shows in his study that the proper use of digital tools and technologies contributes to the development of multimodal literacy skills. These, in addition to transmitting information, can facilitate interaction and collaboration between learners, which positively affects their engagement (Lalonde et al., 2023). In addition, some AI tools can analyze learners' gestures and behaviors in order to adjust content, which could have a positive effect on learning (Marcellis-Warin, 2022).

Practical examples of integrating digital literacy and artificial intelligence into foreign language teaching:

The integration of these two components into foreign language teaching has revolutionized learning, making it more interactive and personalized. Consequently, several researchers have studied practical examples of this integration.

These include, firstly, Mageira & al, (2022), who demonstrated the benefits of AI chatbots such as AsasaraBot, which can simulate authentic conversations in the target language, in addition to their effectiveness in combining language and digital learning. Secondly, Son & al., (2023) find that automatic writing assessment systems can provide detailed assessments of grammar and text structure, promoting language level improvement.

As for digital skills Li, (2021) sells the benefits of blended learning combining face-to-face and online courses assisted by AI technologies . According to this study, AI-assisted blended learning optimizes course effectiveness through interactive materials and adaptive assessment systems. In addition, platforms such as Quizlet or Kahoot enrich the learning experience by helping students develop their digital skills while reinforcing their linguistic understanding (Bolshakova, 2022).

Finally, thanks to the practical examples explored above. It is pertinent to note that the integration of digital literacy and AI in foreign language courses offers great advantages for maximizing learning efficiency. In addition to enabling learners to improve their language skills, this integration offers them the opportunity to become accustomed to the use of AI and the digital environment, which is one of the essential components of digital literacy.

DIGITAL LITERACY: POINTS OF CONVERGENCE AND PROSPECTS FOR INTEGRATION INTO LANGUAGE DIDACTICS:

Over the past two decades, this notion has become a topic of great importance, in addition to arousing considerable interest in the sphere of language didactics researchers. In their respective works (CAWS, 2021; Violaine Bigot, 2021) have emphasized that the development of digital literacy and citizenship is at the center of many educational and social projects. Consequently, according to Hamel. M et al, (2021) language teachers can use digital resources to develop language tasks that enable them to develop multiple second-language literacies in learners . In order to develop the same literacy skills for teachers, COMBE, (2021) proposes a digital genre approach to digital literacy training for future FLE/ FFL teachers. Training teachers in digital literacy is thus becoming essential for future quality education.

To fully understand the link between these two notions, we will then examine the possibility of adapting the action-oriented approach applied by the CEFR in foreign language learning to develop digital literacy in learners in addition to language skills. We will then look at the points of convergence between the CEFR and the DIGCOMP framework.

The action-oriented approach and digital literacy: links and convergences:

In the field of language teaching, we find that these two notions have strong links as well as many points of convergence. We can say that they are in a relationship of interdependence, as both promote and develop key 21st century competencies such as critical thinking, communication, collaboration and creativity (Eshet-Alkalai, 2004; P21, 2019). Both consider the learner/citizen as an autonomous individual, active in his or her own learning (Council of Europe, Council for Cultural Co-operation. Education Committee. Modern Languages Division, 2001; Hague, 2010). Building on the work of (Buckingham, 2007; Willis, 2007), we find that the action-oriented approach and digital literacy promote task- and project-based learning.

In addition to these strong interdependent links, we note that integrating digital literacy into an action-based perspective for language learning promotes the development of transversal and digital competencies in addition to language skills. For example, peer-to-peer interactions can be used to develop digital literacy skills by writing and reading online columns, according to COMBE, (2021) . Moreover, as with language skills, digital literacy skills play an essential role in meeting the informational, digital and media challenges of the 21st century, according to Michelot (2022). According to Hamel. M et al, (2021), digital resources can be used to develop multiple literacies in second languages.

Similarities between CEFR language skills and DIGCOMP digital skills:

As we saw in the previous chapter, we have seen the links and potential for integrating digital literacy into language teaching. But for integration to be successful, we need to examine the compatibility of the key components of each skill (language and digital). The CEFR (Common European Framework of Reference for Languages) and Digcomp are the two frameworks linked to language learning and digital literacy. Taking as an example the communicative competence promoted by both frameworks, the CEFR issued by the Council of Europe (2003) develops the ability to communicate, interact and collaborate with individuals in the multiple contexts of society with a foreign language, while the DIGCOMP framework according to Carretero. S et al, (2017) in turn develops almost the same communication skills "interact / share and publish / digital citizenship / collaborate / respect netiquette / digital identity" in the digital context.

This integration is becoming increasingly vital given the vital and growing importance that digital is taking on in the many facets of our society.

Main components of digital literacy in language teaching:

In the foregoing, we have seen the multiple links between digital literacy and language learning. In this section, we will attempt to identify the main components of digital literacy that are essential in and for language learning.

In order to fully understand foreign language learners' need for digital literacy, we need to specify the multiple contexts of use in this learning. According to Kern (2021), in addition to the essential skills for using ICT, the digital environment has a considerable influence on language use and learning, and vice versa. Consequently, it's vital for today's language learner to also master the skills needed to interact in this environment.

a. Basic digital literacy skills for language learning:

It's a problem that can be described as outdated in developed countries, since Europe, for example, has a rate of over 80% of its citizens using the Internet, according to INSEE statistics (2023). However, this problem still persists in developing countries. Africa, for example, registers a general rate of around 43% according to internet society, (2022). This means that African citizens are at a disadvantage compared to their European counterparts when it comes to learning languages in a digital context. Consequently, they must first acquire the basic Internet skills already acquired by a citizen of a developed country. According to Alakrash et al (2021), this digital divide between developed and developing countries needs to be addressed to ensure digital access for language learning in poor societies.

So before a citizen of a developing country can enjoy the benefits that the digital environment has to offer, he or she must first learn and master basic computer skills and tools. According to Hockly (2012), these include Internet browsing, file management and the use of word processing tools, common software and applications.

b. More advanced skills for learning a language in a digital environment:

As we have already seen, with the advent of Web 2.0, we have gone from being passive consumers of information to active and responsible players in charge of improving the digital environment. According to CAWS et al (2021), learners in general and language learners in particular need to be active players on the Web. Among the skills they need to acquire is the ability to communicate and act online, not forgetting the development of a critical sense in order to build and exercise their digital citizenship to the full.

Thanks to this new principle of active participation in the WEB, our choices in terms of learning support and environment have broadened. According to Varajão Moutinho Pereira, A et al, (2023), digital skills can be integrated into language learning activities. As a result, we can use video games, for example, social networks, e-portfolios or automatic language processing as a support or even a learning environment. So mastering these environments and supports has become a prerequisite for language learning today.

CONCLUSION AND PROSPECTS

By way of conclusion, this study has highlighted the importance of digital literacy and the fundamental issues involved in mastering it, particularly in a constantly changing digital environment, increasingly influenced by technological advances and artificial intelligence. According to scientific studies and reports by international organizations, the development of skills linked to this notion is a sine qua non condition for shaping today's citizens and anticipating tomorrow's needs. In a family, societal and educational environment that is largely dependent on digital technology, it is imperative that schools keep pace with this dynamic by providing their learners with training that is adapted to technological developments, including those linked to AI.

Consequently, foreign language teaching also has a key role to play in the evolution that is underway. Given that languages (especially the most widely spoken ones) are not only communication tools, but also means of access to knowledge and to the production and consumption of global digital content, it is essential to equip learners and citizens not only with digital and linguistic skills, but also with transversal and critical skills, to enable them to fully exercise their role as digital citizens . It is with this in mind that researchers in language didactics can intervene to try to select the functional digital skills that need to be taught, as well as the strategies, supports and tools for integrating these skills into foreign language teaching, taking into account the contribution of AI technologies.

Thanks to this reflection, which has enabled us to establish a research base on digital literacy, artificial intelligence and language teaching, new questions arise to guide future research:

- To what extent can the integration of digital literacy and artificial intelligence overturn the hierarchy of skills in language didactics?
- What language and transversal skills do learners need to integrate into a professional market that increasingly relies on digital technology and AI?
- What digital skills are essential for learners in hybrid or asynchronous learning?
- How can we preserve the gains of the action-oriented perspective in a context of hybrid, asynchronous, AI-supported teaching and learning?

REFERENCES

P21. *Framework for 21st Century Learning.* 2019. https://www.battelleforkids.org/networks/p21/frameworks-resources

Alakrash, H. M., & Abdul Razak, N. (2021). Technology-based language learning: Investigation of digital technology and digital literacy. *Sustainability (Basel)*, 13(21), 12304. DOI: 10.3390/su132112304

Andrus, M. R., & Roth, M. (2002). Health literacy: A review. *Pharmacotherapy*, 22(3), 282–302. DOI: 10.1592/phco.22.5.282.33191 PMID: 11898888

Antoninis, M., & Montoya, S. (2018). *A global framework to measure digital literacy*. Blog UNESCO.

ATTALI. (2022). *Jacques. Histoires et avenirs de l'éducation*. Flammarion.

Barré-de Miniac, C. (2002). La notion de littéracie et les principaux courants de recherche. *La Lettre de l'AIRDF*, 30(1), 27–33.

Bawden, D. (2008). Origins and concepts of digital literacy. Digital literacies: Concepts, policies and practices, 30(2008), 17-32.

Bawden, D., & Robinson, L. (2018). Curating the infosphere: Luciano Floridi's Philosophy of Information as the foundation for library and information science. *The Journal of Documentation*, 74(1), 2–17. DOI: 10.1108/JD-07-2017-0096

Bejaković, P., & Mrnjavac, Ž. (2020). The importance of digital literacy on the labour market. *Employee Relations*, 42(4), 921–932. DOI: 10.1108/ER-07-2019-0274

Belshaw, D. (2012). What is' digital literacy'? A Pragmatic investigation (Doctoral dissertation, Durham University).

Berners-Lee, T., Cailliau, R., Luotonen, A., Nielsen, H. F., & Secret, A. (1994). The World-Wide Web. *Communications of the ACM*, 37(8), 76–82. DOI: 10.1145/179606.179671

Bolshakova, A. (2022). Развитие цифровой компетенции и интернет-грамотности учащихся на уроках иностранного языка / Development of digital competence and Internet literacy of students in foreign language lessons. *Социально-педагогические вопросы образования и воспитания/ Socio-Pedagogical Issues of Education and Upbringing*.

Bora, S. A. P. T. A. R. I. S. H. I., & Neelakandan, R. (2023). Digital well-being. International journal of research in education humanities and commerce, 4(2), 63-67.

Buckingham, D. (2007). Digital Media Literacies: Rethinking media education in the age of the Internet. *Research in Comparative and International Education*, 2(1), 43–55. DOI: 10.2304/rcie.2007.2.1.43

Carretero, S., Vuorikari, R., & Punie, Y. (2017). *«DigComp 2.1. The Digital Competence Framework for Citizens. With eight proficiency levels and examples of use.» Publications Office of the European Union*. Publications Office of the European Union.

Caws, C., Hamel, M. J., Jeanneau, C., & Ollivier, C. (2021). Formation en langues et littératie numérique en contextes ouverts. Une approche socio-interactionnelle.

Chartier, A. M., & Rockwell, E. (2013). Histoire comparée des Outils et débats sur la lecture des débutants: Alphabétisation vs literacy. Introduction. *Histoire de l'Éducation (Paris)*, (138), 5–16. DOI: 10.4000/histoire-education.2647

Combe, C. (2021). Former à la littératie numérique de futurs enseignants de FLE: une approche par genres numériques. Lidil. Revue de linguistique et de didactique des langues, (63).

Coulet, J. C. (2011). La notion de compétence: Un modèle pour décrire, évaluer et développer les compétences. *Le Travail Humain*, 74(1), 1–30. DOI: 10.3917/th.741.0001

Council of Europe, Council for Cultural Co-operation. (2001). *Education Committee. Modern Languages Division. Common European framework of reference for languages: Learning, teaching, assessment.* Cambridge University Press.

De l'Europe, C. (2003). *Cadre européen commun de référence pour les langues: apprendre, enseigner, évaluer*. Council of Europe.

Eshet-Alkalai, Y. (2004). Digital literacy: A conceptual framework for survival skills in the digital era. *Journal of Educational Multimedia and Hypermedia*, 13(1), 93–106.

Ferrari.A. Digital competence in practice: An analysis of frameworks. (2012). Publications Office of the European Union.

Florent, M. (2022). Pour faire face aux défis informationnels, numériques et médiatiques du 21e siècle. Revue hybride de l'éducation, 5(2), 1-27.

Fraenkel, B. (2021). Littératie. *Langage & Société*, 1(HS1), 221–224. DOI: 10.3917/ls.hs01.0222

Gaffiot, F., & Flobert, P. (1934). *Dictionnaire latin-français*. Hachette.

Gilster, P. (1997). *Digital Literacy*. Wiley Computer.

Granger, N., & Moreau, A. C. (2018). Perspective critique sur l'enseignement de la littératie disciplinaire en contexte d'inclusion et incidences sur la planification de l'enseignement. *Language and Literature*, 20(2), 59–79.

Gravelle, F., Lamarche, M. H., Monette, J., Gagnon, C., Montreuil, F., & Demers, L. P. (2022). Gestion et leadership pédagonumérique: stratégies de gestion pour favoriser l'implantation du numérique dans les établissements d'enseignement au Québec. Médiations et médiatisations, (12), 98-113.

Hague, C., & Payton, S. (2010). *Digital literacy across the curriculum*. FutureLab.

Hamel, M. J., Auyeung, S., Bedou, S., Ding, Y., & Mongrain, C. (2021). Affordances de ressources numériques pour développer des littératies multiples en langues secondes: Quatre études de cas. *Nouvelle Revue Synergies Canada*, (14), 1–15. DOI: 10.21083/nrsc.v2021i14.6678

Hargittai, E. (2002). Beyond logs and surveys: In-depth measures of people's web use skills. *Journal of the American Society for Information Science and Technology*, 53(14), 1239–1244. DOI: 10.1002/asi.10166

Hastings, J. S., Madrian, B. C., & Skimmyhorn, W. L. (2013). Financial literacy, financial education, and economic outcomes. Annu. *Rev. Econ.*, 5(1), 347–373. PMID: 23991248

Hébert, M., & Lépine, M. (2013). De l'intérêt de la notion de littératie en francophonie: Un état des lieux en sciences de l'éducation. *Globe*, 16(1), 25–43. DOI: 10.7202/1018176ar

Hilbert, M. (2016). Big Data for Development: A Review of Promises and Challenges. *Development Policy Review*, 34(1), 135–174. DOI: 10.1111/dpr.12142

Hockly, N. (2012). Digital literacies. *ELT Journal*, 66(1), 108–112. DOI: 10.1093/elt/ccr077

Hussain, F. (2012). E-Learning 3.0= E-Learning 2.0+ Web 3.0?. International Association for Development of the Information Society.

Hwang, H. S., Zhu, L. C., & Cui, Q. (2023). Development and validation of a digital literacy scale in the artificial intelligence era for college students. [TIIS]. *KSII Transactions on Internet and Information Systems*, •••, 2241–2258.

Ilomäki, L., Paavola, S., Lakkala, M., & Kantosalo, A. (2016). Digital competence – an emergent boundary concept for policy and educational research. *Education and Information Technologies*, 21(3), 655–679. DOI: 10.1007/s10639-014-9346-4

Kaya, M., & Imer, G. (2020). Investigation of the Relationship between Digital Citizenship and Digital Literacy Levels of Secondary School Students. *International Journal of Scientific and Technological Research*, 6(12), 9–19.

Kern, R. (2021). Twenty-five years of digital literacies in CALL.

Knobel, M., & Lankshear, C. (2006). Digital Literacy and Digital Literacies: Policy, Pedagogy and Research Considerations for Education. *HomeNordic Journal of Digital Literacy*, 1(1), 12–24. DOI: 10.18261/ISSN1891-943X-2006-01-03

Kvasny, L., & Richardson, H. (2006). Critical research in information systems: Looking forward, looking back. *Information Technology & People*, 19(3), 196–202. DOI: 10.1108/09593840610689813

Lalonde, M., Blanchette, K., Wuyckens, G., Huebner, E. J., & & Meilleur, B. (2023). La création de récits d'anticipation en réalité virtuelle pour le développement de la compétence numérique et de la compétence en littératie médiatique multimodale des élèves au secondaire. Médiations et médiatisations, (15),, 123-140.

Lang, P., Yuste Frías, J., Araujo, S., Vergondy, B., Claude, E., & Correia, A. (2023). L'apprentissage des langues à l'ère du numérique: quelques réflexions empiriques basées sur des projets pédagogiques. Tradución e lingüística.

Li, S. (2021). Research on the Exploration and Reflection of Foreign Language Teaching Based on "Artificial Intelligence+ Education" in the Big Data Era. *2nd International Conference on Big Data Economy and Information Management (BDEIM) IEEE*, 354-357. DOI: 10.1109/BDEIM55082.2021.00078

LIVINGSTONE. (2004). Sonia. «Media Literacy and the Challenge of New Information and Communication Technologies.». *Communication Review*, •••, 3–14.

Lundvall, S. (2015). Physical literacy in the field of physical education–A challenge and a possibility. *Journal of Sport and Health Science*, 4(2), 113–118.

Lunt, B. (2005). *Joseph Ekstrom, Edith Lawson, Reza Kamali, Jacob Miller, Sandra Gorka, Han Reichgelt. «Defining the IT Curriculum: The Results of the Past 3 Years.»*. Issues in Informing Science and Information Technology.

Luo, Y. (2024). Innovative research on AI-assisted teaching models for college English listening and speaking courses. *Applied and Computational Engineering*, 69(1), 155–160. DOI: 10.54254/2755-2721/69/20241493

Mageira, K., Pittou, D., Papasalouros, A., Kotis, K., Zangogianni, P., & Daradoumis, A. (2022). Educational AI chatbots for content and language integrated learning. *Applied Sciences (Basel, Switzerland)*, 12(7), 3239.

Marcellis-Warin, N. (2022). *Analyse comparative d'écosystèmes en ia dans le but de repérer les pratiques innovantes en matière de formation et de transfert de connaissances*. CIRANO.

Marisa, W., & Djulia, E. J. (2022). The relationship of digital literacy to students' cognitive ability in ecology course. *Jurnal Pelita Pendidikan*, 10(2), 47–51. DOI: 10.24114/jpp.v10i2.26774

Martin, A. (2006). Allan. «A european framework for digital literacy.». *Nordic Journal of Digital LiteracyVolume*, 1(2), 151–161. DOI: 10.18261/ISSN1891-943X-2006-02-06

Martzoukou, K., Fulton, C., Kostagiolas, P., & Lavranos, C. (2020). A study of higher education students' self-perceived digital competences for learning and everyday life online participation. *The Journal of Documentation*, 76(6), 1413–1458. DOI: 10.1108/JD-03-2020-0041

Martzoukou, K., Kostagiolas, P., Lavranos, C., Lauterbach, T., & Fulton, C. (2021). A study of university law students' selfperceived digital competences. *Journal of Librarianship and Information Science*, 54(4), 751–769. DOI: 10.1177/09610006211048004

Merriam-Webster. https://www.merriam-webster.com/dictionary/literacy. 2023.

Mo, J. (2019). *« How does PISA define and measure reading literacy? », PISA in Focus, n° 101*. Éditions OCDE.

Nielsen, J. (1999). *Designing web usability*. New Riders.

O'reilly, T. (2007). What is Web 2.0: Design patterns and business models for the next generation of software.

OCDE. (2019). «Fostering digital literacy and well-being.» *Educational Research and Innovation, Educating 21st Century Children.*

OCDE. (2020). *Curriculum Overload: A Way Forward*. Éditions OCDE.

OECD. Publishing, & Organisation for Economic Co-operation and Development Staff. (2012). Literacy, numeracy and problem solving in technology-rich environments: Framework for the OECD survey of adult skills. OECD publishing.

Ollivier, C., Jeanneau, C., Hamel, M. J., & Caws, C. (2021). Citoyenneté numérique et didactique des langues, quels points de contacts?. Lidil. Revue de linguistique et de didactique des langues, (63).

Oxford english dictionary. (2023).

Pellerin, M. (2017). L'usage des technologies numériques pour le développement de compétences multimodales en littératie au 21 e siècle. *Education et Francophonie*, 45(2), 85–106. DOI: 10.7202/1043530ar

Perrenoud, P. (2015). Construire des compétences, est-ce tourner le dos aux savoirs?. Pédagogie collégiale Vol. 12, no 3, mars 1999, p. 14-17.

Pierre, R. (2003). Entre alphabétisation et littératie: Les enjeux didactiques. *Revue Française de Linguistique Appliquée*, 8(1), 121–137. DOI: 10.3917/rfla.081.0121

Pierre, R. (2003). Entre alphabétisation et littératie: Les enjeux didactiques. *Revue Française de Linguistique Appliquée*, VIII(1), 121–137. DOI: 10.3917/rfla.081.0121

Potluri, R. M., & Vajjhala, N. R. (2018). A Study on Application of Web 3.0 Technologies in Small and Medium Enterprises of India. *The Journal of Asian Finance, Economics and Business*, 5(2), 73–79. DOI: 10.13106/jafeb.2018.vol5.no2.73

Prasetiyo, W. H., Noor, B. M. N., Tan, B. P., & Sumardjoko, B. (2021). Digital citizenship trend in educational sphere: A systematic review. [IJERE]. *International Journal of Evaluation and Research in Education*, 10(4), 1192–1201. DOI: 10.11591/ijere.v10i4.21767

Probowati, Y. (2023). Fostering StudentsDigital Literacy In The Age Of The Internet In The Pandemic Era. KnE Social Sciences, 473-478.

Reddy, P., Sharma, B., & Chaudhary, K. (2021). Digital literacy: A review in the South Pacifc. *Journal of Computing in Higher Education*.

Ribble, M. (2011). *Digital citizenship in schools*. International Society for Technology in Education.

Richardson, J., & Milovidov, E. (2017). Digital citizenship education: Volume 2: Multi-stakeholder consultation report. Council of Europe.

Romero-Ivanova, C., Kingsley, T., & Mason, L. (2019). Three conceptions of literacy: Media, narrative, and gaming literacies. *Literacy*, 10, 1–21.

Schneuwly, B. (2020). Literacy–littératie–Literalität. Un essai. Forumlecture. ch, 2.

Shanahan, T., & Shanahan, C. (2012). What is disciplinary literacy and why does it matter? *Topics in Language Disorders*, 32(1), 7–18. DOI: 10.1097/TLD.0b013e318244557a

Shopova, T. (2014). DIGITAL LITERACY OF STUDENTS AND ITS IMPROVEMENT AT THE UNIVERSITY. *Journal on Efficiency and Responsibility in Education and Science*, 7(2), 26–32. DOI: 10.7160/eriesj.2014.070201

Son, J. B., Ružić, N. K., & Philpott, A. (2023). Artificial intelligence technologies and applications for language learning and teaching. Journal of China Computer-Assisted Language Learning, (0).

Stockless, A., Villeneuve, S., Bédard, L., Bisaillon, J., Tremblay, C., & Leduc, D. (2022). La Boussole numérique éducative: développement d'un outil d'autoévaluation des usages pédagogiques du numérique du personnel enseignant. Médiations et médiatisations-Revue internationale sur le numérique en éducation et communication, (12), 144-157.

Thurlow, C., Lengel, L., & Tomic, A. (2004). Computer mediated communication: Social interaction and the Internet. *Sage (Atlanta, Ga.)*.

Tran, T. N., & Tran, H. P. (2023). Exploring the role of ChatGPT in developing critical digital literacies in language learning: a qualitative study. *Proceedings of the AsiaCALL International Conference* (Vol. 4), 1-17. DOI: 10.54855/paic.2341

UNESCO. (2017). «Accountability in education: meeting our commitments; Global education monitoring report, 2017/8..

Van den Broucke, S. (2017). La littératie en santé: un concept critique pour la santé publique. La santé en action, 440, 11-13.

van Deursen, A. J., & van Dijk, J. A. (2014). The digital divide shifts to differences in usage. *New Media & Society*, 16(3), 507–526. DOI: 10.1177/1461444813487959

Weiner, S. A. (2011). Information literacy and the workforce: A review. *Education Libraries*.

Willis, D., & Willis, J. (2007). *Doing Task-based Teaching*. Oxford University Press.

Yo, X. (2021). Najmiddinova. «Digital Mathematical Literacy As A Component Of The Life Skills Of Students Of Modern Educational Institutions.». *The American Journal of Social Science and Education Innovations*, 3(1), 378–384. DOI: 10.37547/tajssei/Volume03Issue01-71

Chapter 16
Integrating Generative Artificial Intelligence (GAI) Into the Teaching-Learning of French as a Foreign Language (FLE)

Mohammed Zine El Abidine
https://orcid.org/0000-0002-8767-4504
Abdelmalek Essaadi University, Morocco

Amel Nejjari
https://orcid.org/0000-0002-7323-1286
ENS Tetouan, Morocco

Mohamed Khaldi
https://orcid.org/0000-0002-1593-1073
ENS Tetouan, Morocco

ABSTRACT

Generative artificial intelligence (GAI) is transforming education, particularly in foreign language teaching, such as French. It raises questions about its impact on core linguistic skills like listening comprehension and writing. GAI tools, including chatbots and conversation simulators, offer opportunities for immersive and enriching interactions. Defining effective interaction strategies between learners and these systems is crucial to foster engagement and knowledge acquisition, while considering the diverse skill levels of learners. Integrating GAI into educational programs presents practical and ethical challenges that require careful evaluation of risks and opportunities. New methods for assessing language skills must be developed, focusing on personalized and continuous approaches. To maximize GAI's potential, close collaboration among didactic experts, teachers, and AI developers is essential to ensure its ethical and harmonious integration into education, ultimately enhancing the learning experience and adapting to the challenges of a rapidly changing world.

DOI: 10.4018/979-8-3693-8965-2.ch016

INTRODUCTION

The gradual integration of artificial intelligence in education is currently revolutionizing the teaching of foreign languages. In FFL classes, its judicious use represents a considerable opportunity to energize teaching methods and stimulate individual learning.

Indeed, increasing digital tools leveraging AI's potential now assist teachers in designing tailored resources and activities. Platforms such as ChatGPT, Kahoot, Genially, or Magic School AI can rapidly generate a wide variety of content adapted to each learner's audience's needs and profiles.

For example, oral interaction with ChatGPT opens the way to rich, authentic exchanges on diverse themes thanks to stimulating prompts inviting discussion and practical exercises. Similarly, written interaction via ChatGPT offers an opportunity to develop creativity and self-expression through prompts fostering free imagination.

Specifically, ChatGPT has demonstrated its ability to energize an FFL course in multiple ways, notably through fun role-playing scenarios or targeted exercise design.

Moreover, AI opens a vast field of captivating activity possibilities for learners such as quizzes, games, or workshops combining learning and creativity.

Thus, through ChatGPT's eloquent example, this introduction highlights the educational innovation potential offered by intelligently harnessing artificial intelligence in language classrooms.

INTEGRATING AI IN FFL TEACHING

Artificial intelligence's arrival in education is opening a series of exciting opportunities to evolve our FFL teaching methods. To concretely explore these possibilities, we launch this research. The objective is to propose ideas and reflections on how to best use AI, both for our teaching practices and interactions with learners.

We begin with a brief overview of AI's key concepts and functionalities, before analyzing how it can provide real added value to our courses. We will then examine concrete ways to effectively integrate it in physical or remote classes.

To conclude, we will explore some promising applications, from conversation simulation to self-correcting exercises. The goal is to demonstrate AI's potential to stimulate learner motivation and modernize our practices.

Through this work, we hope to spark discussion around this revolutionary technology of AI and its future role in language learning.

Definition

To fully envision integrating artificial intelligence (AI) into our French as a foreign language courses, it is first necessary to precisely grasp its technical foundations and associated concepts.

At the core of AI lies the idea of systems reproducing, through computation, certain human cognitive abilities such as learning, problem-solving, or language processing (Collin et al,2021). Concretely, this emerging technology has been developed expertly for decades in scientific fields like medicine, where its algorithms can now analyze vast datasets to refine diagnoses and treatments.

For a long time, these applications remained confidential, and reserved for industrial or scientific use. But over the past one to two years, we have witnessed a major phenomenon of technical democratization, making AI interfaces much more accessible, intuitive, and playful for the general public. This unprecedented evolution has enabled the emergence and popularity of key concepts such as "generative" AI.

By generative AI, we specifically refer to digital assistants' ability to automatically and fluently produce original content, be it text, images, videos, or even music. This generation relies on predictive models constantly evolving, capable for instance of instantly translating documents across multiple languages via natural language processing.

Other applications like the famous "chatbots" simulate real-time conversations as conversational agents, now ubiquitous on websites and apps (Freyer et al, 2020). Finally, the concept of "prompts", i.e. the precise commands given vocally or in writing to these virtual assistants, strongly conditions the relevance and quality of generated responses.

While ChatGPT remains the flagship example and most widespread tool currently, we must not forget the wide variety of AI services, from speech synthesis to translation and caption generation.

Thus, thoroughly understanding AI's technical foundations and key concepts should allow us to more serenely consider the opportunities it presents for our FLE teaching.

The Benefits (Added Value)

Integrating artificial intelligence (AI) tools in FFL classes presents many pedagogical advantages worth analyzing in detail. Firstly, AI enables highly personalized learning, identified as one of its main assets.

Indeed, each learner has their own pace, specific interests, and strengths/weaknesses regarding certain language components. Yet, virtual AI assistants can precisely adapt to each individual, and their progress, by offering tailored content and activities aligned with their development. This is observed through online applications like Duolingo or Babel, which deliver truly "customized" learning.

Thanks to ongoing interaction with the learner, these tools can also deeply assess their overall language level as well as specific strong/weak points. They can then deliver a personalized diagnosis identifying priority areas for reinforcement through targeted learning programs.

Furthermore, AI provides access to an immense wealth of digital educational resources (games, videos, quizzes, etc.) allowing in-depth language practice in a fun way. Personalized pathways also efficiently guide each learner towards supports closely aligning with their objectives - whether exam preparation like DELF or reinforcing an identified skill.

Finally, automatic analysis and correction functionalities for learner oral/written production represent valuable aid toward linguistic autonomy, enabling the identification of errors and autonomous progress.

For Teachers

Integrating AI tools in language classes offers teachers many perspectives to optimize their teaching practices and energize learning. Indeed, these technologies allow for benefiting from virtual assistants' active support, like digital teaching aids evolving in close collaboration with them.

Thanks to these tools, teachers can see their course material preparation workload greatly lightened. They simply need to precisely define the targeted level, linguistic elements targeted, and desired format for the AI to generate in a very short time presentation slides, activity sheets, or adapted evaluation subjects. Of course, these proposals remain subject to critical validation by the teacher to ensure full alignment with the class context.

Similarly, a teacher can delegate to their virtual assistant the original creation of complex educational scenarios mobilizing various skills, such as theater scenes setting dialogues in given situations. Why not ask AI to generate a complete play directly usable in class?

Beyond this valuable upstream assistance, AI tools also provide true added value during class sessions themselves. Chatbot conversation simulation, individualized assessments, online translations, automatic corrections...so many functionalities stimulating learner motivation and autonomy while freeing up teacher time for personalized monitoring.

Thus, if their exploitation requires training and methodological framing, the possibilities offered by these "digital teaching assistants" seem infinite for renewing teaching practices.

How to interact?

Now that we have explored key AI concepts and identified some of its educational benefits, let's look at concrete modalities for interacting with these digital tools to best leverage them.

Formulating precise prompts is key to obtaining optimal results from AI tools. Whether ChatGPT, Google Brad, or other conversational assistants, the care taken in writing these instructions will greatly determine the relevance and quality of generated responses.

For an FFL teacher, possibilities abound. For example, requesting AI to create a complete formative assessment quiz, by specifying the targeted level (A1, B1, etc.), number of questions, and targeted linguistic points. Similarly, various activity types can be modeled as detailed prompts: daily situation role-plays, theater excerpts, fill-in-the-blank tables for written expression, descriptive passages to complete, etc.

Moreover, AI can generate more complex content such as pedagogical factsheets on a given theme, structured lessons in several steps, or even complete learning scenarios by providing a narrative framework and associated linguistic objectives for each sequence.

Of course, in addition to ChatGPT, many other tools exist for more specific uses. For example, ImmerseMe for virtual reality immersion, Duolingo for fun learning exercises, and Deepl as a high-performance translation assistant.

Thus, thoughtfully writing targeted prompts allows for leveraging all the creative potential of these technologies, envisioning classroom activities tailored to our learners. Their open-ended formulation also offers valuable flexibility for refinement according to feedback from implementation (El Karfa, 2023).

AI TOOLS IN FFL CLASSES

AI tools have earned an important place in our FFL classes! For a few months now, we have truly started relying on them daily, whether to prepare our courses or lead classroom activities.

Through regular use, we explore more each day their potential (Romero et al, 2021). This work is devoted to optimizing their educational use. The objective? Understand in detail the functioning of "generative" tools capable of creating content on demand.

We will see that they fulfill very varied functions, from text generation to conversation simulation through image synthesis. For each one, we will precisely identify their added value in class.

Concrete examples will also illustrate how to leverage them, whether for teachers in developing their courses or for students via fun activities.

The idea will be to show how to optimally integrate these digital assistants into our practices, regardless of the audience. We should leave with plenty of ideas to energize classes through AI! (Ouyang et al, 2023)

How to optimize the use of these AI tools in FFL classes?

The gradual introduction of artificial intelligence (AI) tools in teaching French as a foreign language (FFL) opens promising prospects for renewing educational practices (Mollick, 2024).

Indeed, these digital technologies offer teachers a means to design more interactive, dynamic courses. Thanks to their automated generation of diversified content (texts, images, sounds...), AI tools already enable personalizing materials based on each learner's profile.

Personalization is undoubtedly one of these emerging technologies' major assets. By precisely diagnosing students' linguistic needs and weaknesses via fine-grained oral/written production analysis, teachers can now propose truly individualized support. Readily implemented customized remediation paths via virtual assistants reinforce prioritized areas.

Moreover, sophisticated platforms like Magic School, Teacher's Aide, or Character IA demonstrate fully AI-based pedagogical frameworks that can now be designed, from daily activities to DELF/DALF-type exam modules.

Additionally, access to rich, diversified digital resources (serious games, authentic videos, interactive podcasts...) enables energizing learning scenarios.

Thus, potentials offered by these tools for personalized, individualized learning foreshadow a promising future as AI integration into FFL expands.

Particularities of AI Tools

Understanding AI tools' specificities is essential to fully grasp their contribution to FFL teaching.

Unlike simple software, these technologies rely on machine learning algorithms with singular cognitive abilities. Endowed with analyzing vast data faculties, their sophisticated algorithms can identify complex patterns to solve problems through human-like reasoning.

This applies to ubiquitous conversational assistants naturally interacting via oral/written language. Their widespread deployment on major learning platforms illustrates individualized feedback and real-time dialogue simulation capabilities.

But AI tools' defining characteristic lies in their unique faculty: autonomous, on-demand generation of multidimensional content. Through this generative intelligence fed by immense databases, they can instantly create various instructional materials (texts, images, sounds, videos...) precisely meeting expressed needs. (Ouyang et al, 2022)

This function is crucially important for online training facing strong constraints (costs, rights, accessibility). It enables teachers to tailor materials to dynamically energize practices for all audiences.

Thus, beyond ancillary functions, AI tools' distinctiveness truly stems from autonomous creative power.

Discovering AI Tool Diversity in Class

The diversity of generative AI tools offers an abundance of educational opportunities worth exploring discerningly. Let's start with text generators, pioneering AI domain. While ChatGPT remains a reference through conversational abilities, new assistants are gaining ground.

Perplexity AI stands out, with a conversational interface providing instant access to various contents (texts, images, videos, web links). More comprehensive than classic chatbots, these "search bots" open rich educational perspectives.

For image creation, paid tools like Dali or Midjourney astound through photo-realism. However, free alternatives like Leonardo, HeuGen, or Anthropic already reached a sufficient quality level. We must consider some systems' ethical issues regarding personal data processing.

On the video side, accessible software like Moovly, Wideo or Kapwing can transform simple text and images into animated sequences or mini-documentaries, generating dynamic learning supports.

Sound (Audioread, Ivona), music (Jukebox, midi.js) or podcast (Anchor) generation functionalities also offer new oral expression avenues. Google's Exekitchen creates custom playlists.

In assessment, playful tools like QuizBot, Bubbl, or Kahoot! Pro renews the genre while ImmerseMe and Aula stimulate virtual reality-supported learning.

Hence, possibilities seem promising for thoughtful exploration of these protean technologies' educational uses, on condition of a reflective, discerning approach.

Identifying AI Tools' Pedagogical Value in Class

Thoughtfully integrating AI tools in language classes enriches significantly the learning process. Firstly, these technologies provide unlimited access to an ever-expanding digital library of tailored, adaptive educational resources (articles, podcasts, videos, interactive exercises...) automatically selected according to each learner's detailed profile. Through machine learning, recommendations become increasingly relevant over time, boosting motivation.

Moreover, conversational virtual assistants like chatbots represent major educational tools for developing writing and oral skills. Through their textual and vocal interfaces, they allow learners to practice interacting and expressing themselves playfully in the target language. Furthermore, their ability to analyze productions in real-time offers the possibility of immediate feedback, whether on grammar, pronunciation, or lexical and syntactic choices.

Tools like ClassPoint AI go further by automatically generating interactive educational content (multiple choice questions, quizzes, contextual micro-exercises...) intended to be seamlessly integrated into courses, saving teachers precious time.

In addition, the possibility of a detailed formative assessment of each learner's skills through linguistic and vocal analysis enables tailored monitoring. Combined with the tailored generation of targeted remediation pathways, these features constitute unprecedented educational support.

Thus, with a methodical integration, these tools carry real added value to energize learning and ensure optimal suitability to each learner's needs.

What Use of These Tools for Teachers and Learners

In class, teachers can leverage conversational assistants for rich, interactive simulations. For example, a chatbot embodying various professions allows learners to practice speaking through authentic role-plays. Each exchange undergoes immediate linguistic analysis-based correction.

Written comprehension is also individually worked on via contextualized exercises identifying key details, logical connectors, and grammar points in long scientific, geographic, or literary texts.

Learners can now conceive and produce, individually or in teams, micro audiovisual projects expressing creativity and language mastery: neighborhood documentaries augmented with sounds and subtitles, radio dramas including virtual interviews, and edutainment podcasts explaining appliance functioning...

Access to serious games specifically designed by AI to stimulate skills (listening and reformulating a short French message, classifying foods by nutritional group...) energizes sessions.

By methodically preparing tailored scenarios, these technologies restore teachers' ability to individualize practices and create a playful context that optimally engages all learners.

How to Interact with AI Tools?

Interacting optimally with AI tools requires mastering "prompt" formulation. As our colleague Papa Yuga illustrated, crafting clear instructions defining precisely the role, educational objective and simulated interaction framework is essential. Mastering the art of prompt writing is thus a key prerequisite for fully leveraging these technologies' educational potential. Indeed, prompt quality and detail level largely determine generated responses' relevance and suitability.

One must start by precisely defining the simulated interaction framework by meticulously outlining roles, context, and target audience (linguistic level, age, profession). Providing rich contextual details anchors the scenario in requisite authenticity.

Moreover, restricting the usable lexical and syntactic field according to the targeted level provides welcomed progressiveness. The expected response format (summary, comparative table, dialogue, poem...) must also be unequivocally specified. Downstream, rigorous pre-testing guarantees functionality selection aligns with objectives.

Finally, their integration into transverse educational scenarios privileging human interaction determines their true added value.

Thus, with an in-depth understanding of these parameters, AI becomes a full-fledged language mediation tool, effectively stimulating motivation and experiential learning.

PROMPTS FOR ORAL INTERACTION WITH CHATGPT

Artificial intelligence tools now constitute a promising resource to renew FL teaching practices. Endowed with sophisticated conversational abilities, they open the way to new modalities of individualizing learning pathways (Romero et al, 2023).

For learners, these technologies can prove invaluable linguistic assistants. Dialogue generators are for example likely to provide personalized help and feedback. Whether orthographic and grammatical verification for beginners, or refinement of oral and written expression through targeted suggestions for higher levels.

On the teacher side, tools' ability to automatically generate diversified content presages a clear leverage effect in practices. Witnessed through their potential to support pedagogical material design, innovative resource production, or assessment curriculum development (Ouyang et al, 2021).

It is precisely from this learning assistance perspective that we must now further explore AI conversational capabilities. We will particularly study ChatGPT's case and usage for developing oral interaction skills in language class.

Our objective in this part will be to understand how to formulate optimized contextualized instructions enabling full exploitation of generated dialogical simulations.

The prompt

Well-formulated prompts are key to successfully leveraging virtual assistants' educational potential in language classes. As a structured set of contextualizing instructions for the task to accomplish, they determine response relevance.

Yet optimal prompt writing remains an art requiring deepening prompt engineering principles. A rapidly rising discipline, it is bringing new "prompt engineers" specializing in their meticulous design.

A worthy prompt first precisely defines the IA's expected role (teacher, student...). It then exhaustively describes the task to accomplish, detailing pedagogical objectives (targeted skills), potential process (steps), and context (learners' linguistic level, duration...).

Contextual parameters (lexical or syntactic constraints, response format...) must also undergo rigorous specification to best frame the interaction.

A fruitful example would consist of asking AI to organize a beginner-level oral expression activity by simulating an encouraging, benevolent teacher role offering authentic role-plays, correcting productions, and motivating learners.

Thus, thoroughly mastering prompt engineering proves indispensable for discerningly leveraging conversational technologies' potential in language class.

Prompts for Oral Interaction

Through its vocal functionality, ChatGPT offers teachers new perspectives for animating stimulating, interactive oral exchanges.

Firstly, it allows linguistically warming up through "general conversations" on varied topics, an opportunity for learners to express themselves more spontaneously.

However, it is in authentic role-play simulation that its main added value lies. By endorsing credible socio-professional identities (salesperson, doctor, municipal employee, etc.), it becomes an ideal "partner" to practice situated expression through improvised interactions.

Debates and interviews on stimulating themes also represent rich activities, with AI providing counterarguments to develop. Its improvisation capacity leaves room for complex oratory jousts to work on.

Collaborative storytelling, whether co-constructing stories or progressing in episodes, mobilizes collective creativity and linguistic cooperation within the group.

Moreover, its ability to analyze and correct pronunciation in real time constitutes an important contribution to oral skills.

Finally, through adaptability to levels, it becomes an individualized assistant to personalize interaction training according to profiles.

Thus, with thoughtful use, ChatGPT effectively renews oral teaching/learning perspectives.

How Can We Implement This in Class?

Direct interaction with assistants like ChatGPT lends itself to animating stimulating, interactive workshops.

These can take the form of small workgroups (3-4 learners). Each team is assigned in advance a precise prompt corresponding to a targeted communicative objective: role-play in various authentic situations (store, cafe, medical consultation, etc.), argued debate on a current issue, role-play interview of historical/cultural personalities, thematic interactive quiz, etc.

Students are then invited to collectively prepare their scenarios through rehearsing lines, questions/answers, and pronunciation. This small group oral preparation stage fosters linguistic cooperation.

During the plenary sharing, each group simulates its situation in front of the class, interacting directly with the assistant through its vocal functionality. Its improvisation ability stimulates exchange dynamics and allows the teacher formative assessment of language mastery.

In parallel, more individualized activities (reading aloud followed by an automated phonetic correction, question-answer on cultural facts, etc.) are possible outside class via mobile app.

Thus conceived, these participatory workshops thoughtfully and creatively leverage AI's educational techno-pedagogical potential to energize experiential oral learning.

PROMPTS FOR WRITTEN INTERACTION WITH CHATGPT

How to Practice Written Interaction in Class?

Written interaction is a core skill in language class. However, it's not always easy to find motivating activities to work on concretely. This is where the ChatGPT tool can prove very useful.

As a conversational agent developed by Anthropic, ChatGPT can converse in writing at an adapted language level. It can interact in French as well as many other languages. Therefore, it's an excellent resource for stimulating written French practice among students (Allouche, E. 2024).

Specifically, the teacher could organize regular 30-minute sessions where learners are equipped with computers or tablets. Each would then receive a "prompt", i.e. a precise conversation topic or writing task.

For example, a role-play where ChatGPT takes on a character like a waiter, administrative agent, etc. Students would thus interact with it playfully. Other prompts could consist of question-answer exchanges on various current or cultural topics.

ChatGPT has the huge advantage of being able to adjust to its interlocutor's linguistic level. Students can therefore choose their level (A1, A2, B1, etc.) and progress at their own pace. This personalized aspect greatly boosts motivation.

Beyond free conversation, many other activities are possible such as professional role-plays, cultural debates, or exchanges about countries. As ChatGPT can interact infinitely patiently, students will likely feel more comfortable expressing themselves in writing.

Thanks to its vast lexical knowledge, the tool will also enrich learners' vocabulary in varied registers or specialized fields. It will also correct errors and thus contribute to grammar progress.

In short, ChatGPT's educational potential for energizing writing seems particularly promising. Its customizable adaptation abilities make it a personalized tool for playful yet formative language practice.

ENERGIZING AN FFL CLASS WITH CHATGPT

What is ChatGPT?

ChatGPT is a remarkable conversational agent developed by Anthropic to provide intelligent responses to human inquiries. It can converse instantly and naturally, like with a real interlocutor.

It's important to know that ChatGPT is a robot, based on cutting-edge natural language processing AI technologies. Anthropic developed it to provide precise, useful answers to a multitude of questions.

Thanks to its processing speed and extensive subject knowledge, ChatGPT allows obtaining a wealth of information very practically and quickly. Even with mundane questions, it will always propose constructive discussion avenues.

However, upon its release, some were misled by false ideas about its actual capabilities. While impressively instantaneous and relevant in responses, ChatGPT remains nevertheless a computer system.

We must not lose sight that it only simulates human conversation. Its limits lie in not possessing true understanding or consciousness, unlike a human being.

Beyond this important reminder of its nature, ChatGPT offers a fascinating opportunity for varied exchanges with a machine endowed with sophisticated conversational intelligence. The key is using it responsibly and knowledgeably.

False Ideas about ChatGPT

ChatGPT is a fascinating AI tool that has sparked much curiosity but also false ideas since its release. Indeed, its ability to conduct fluid, natural conversations has sometimes led some to overestimate its actual abilities.

One of the most widespread misunderstandings was the idea that it was a software program to download and install, like any other. In reality, ChatGPT comes in the form of an easily accessible online website, without requiring prior installation.

Some teachers even imagined being able to physically "invite" ChatGPT to class, in the form of a humanoid robot. But it consists only of a virtual computational model, devoid of any physical embodiment.

Additionally, ChatGPT has sometimes been wrongly conflated with Google as a more advanced search engine. Yet their functioning is fundamentally different: ChatGPT interacts through dialogue, while Google allows finding documents online.

One of the major fears was also that ChatGPT would outpace the human teacher, even replace them. However, the tool itself recognizes its limits compared to personalized pedagogical interaction. While it can help, it will never replace real classroom interactions.

Generally, some teachers remain wary of AI in education, fearing dispossession of their profession. Yet more open-minded colleagues creatively explore its playful potential.

Beyond misperceptions, ChatGPT also offers real learning opportunities, provided its nature as a tool to serve humans, not substitute for them, remains clear. Responsible, informed use is the best way to leverage its capabilities.

How to Energize an FFL Class with ChatGPT?

ChatGPT offers many promising possibilities to enrich foreign language French classes. As a conversational agent developed by Anthropic, it has unique capabilities likely to nurture pedagogical reflection.

Firstly, its ability to conduct written or oral dialogues fluidly and adapt to the learner's level is valuable. It multiplies opportunities to express oneself and interact in the target language, complementing in-class exchanges. Whether in general conversations or role-plays in everyday situations, ChatGPT offers an untiring training partner.

Moreover, its aptitude to assess language skills opens stimulating perspectives. The teacher can submit students' oral or written productions for expert analysis. Its personalized feedback pinpointing strengths and weaknesses will efficiently guide corrections.

Additionally, ChatGPT can steer learning towards exercises adapted to specific needs, according to the Common European Framework of Reference for Languages' objectives. A student preparing for DELF and hesitating on verb tenses will benefit from dedicated content.

This flexibility in personalization reinforces autonomy. The learner proposes an individualized program outside class hours. The teacher oversees and monitors progress through ChatGPT's analyses.

Thus, by leveraging this conversational intelligence's strengths, we succeed in energizing FFL teaching playfully, effectively, and closest to each learner's needs. ChatGPT then becomes a major educational asset.

Uses of ChatGPT in Language Class

ChatGPT could be useful in language class. When I asked it many questions, I saw it could have two types of uses.

First, a basic, general use. For example to practice informal speaking, and role-plays in everyday situations. ChatGPT is too good for that - it discusses very easily.

Students would have a chance to talk a lot and practice real communication. And ChatGPT adapts to each person's level, which is very handy!

But we could also have a more advanced use thanks to its further capabilities. For example, the teacher submits students' oral/written productions for analysis.

It provides good advice to improve. Another cool thing - if asked to work on a specific point, it orients towards targeted exercises.

So whether for general speaking or leveraging its skills through more advanced uses, ChatGPT has a place in a language class to help students!

Basic Use

ChatGPT offers numerous daily exploitation possibilities in foreign language classes. Its conversational abilities as well as more expert functionalities make it a valuable tool for both laying foundations and progressively deepening learning.

Firstly, regarding grammar and spelling - core skills to master from the beginning - ChatGPT can prove a precious aid. By submitting written productions or sample sentences intentionally containing errors, the learner easily and quickly identifies mistakes thanks to IA's corrections. This fosters salutary awareness of structures to work on.

Another widely exploited basic activity, translation allows approaching vocabulary through isolated words or expressions as well as short coherent texts. Beyond simple transposition of meaning, ChatGPT offers a set of synonyms and contexts to help the definitive assimilation of terms.

Playfully, IA also excels at explaining grammar points often obscure, such as verb tenses or agreement rules. Its clear, concrete explanations illustrated through varied examples greatly facilitate conceptual understanding.

Moreover, when the learner seeks authentic documents linked to the targeted level, ChatGPT abounds with ideas like song lyrics, film excerpts, or suitable cultural articles. This stimulates linguistic immersion.

Thus, thanks to its versatility, ChatGPT daily proves its ability to enrich teaching practices at any stage of language acquisition.

Advanced Use

Beyond basic capabilities, ChatGPT harbors deeper potential considerably enriching educational practices.

Firstly, during course preparation, its assistance proves valuable. Whether reformulating an instruction to precisely adapt to the targeted linguistic level, or conceiving new activities stimulating creativity, ChatGPT effectively supports the teacher. Whether imagining collective discovery games or playful role-plays, its many original proposals nourish the teaching arsenal.

Moreover, when implementing learning, ChatGPT shows an aptitude for designing tailor-made educational materials fitting targeted objectives. Whether grammar structure training, cultural theme debates, or revision quizzes, it will create personalized exercises and content that engage learners actively.

Similarly, its ability to instantly write texts, questions, or presentations considerably simplifies the teacher's task. Precious time gained and content quality guaranteed.

Finally, beyond concrete activities, its expert metalinguistic explanations during correction or remediation sequences provide particularly enlightening perspectives for learners.

Thus, ChatGPT establishes itself as a full-fledged educational partner, whose multiple advanced usage possibilities profoundly renew classroom practices.

CREATING FUN ACTIVITIES IN CLASS WITH AI

Generative artificial intelligence represents an incredibly rich educational resource when judiciously leveraging learning in language class (Holmes et al, 2024). Rather than isolating it into standalone activities, teachers integrate it transversely throughout programming.

By mobilizing powerful multimedia generation tools like C-Real, access opens to a continually expanding digital content library customized. Varied texts covering a multiplicity of themes (travel, environment, arts...) from diversified cultural angles as well as audio and video supports constitute as many stimulating entry points nurturing language skills.

Thanks to the dynamic nature and calibrated complexity degree, these digital resources will provide learners countless occasions practicing global as selective comprehension, written as oral. They will also feed questioning, written and oral production conducted individually or collectively as well as communicative role-plays, simulations, debates, or thematic presentations.

Generation through conversational chatbots like ChatGPT and Replika of an avatar gallery embodying different social roles will revive role-play immersing learners in authentic interactions rich with cultural subtleties. Enabled by written or vocal synthesis, linguistic motivation will be multiplied through playful aspects.

Platforms exploiting AI like Kahoot, Quizlet or Quizziz will know how to propose increasingly personalized content tailored to each learner's specific profile. Customized according to level but also individual interests and paths quizzes, games, and flashcards will strengthen engagement.

Digitally conceived escape games on tools like Genially, Twine or Key Escape will in turn feature teamwork around stimulating lexical and syntactic riddles requiring mobilizing target language acquisitions in a playful, motivating atmosphere.

Literary or poetic, artistic, animated film, or coding workshops assisted by virtual assistants like Stable Diffusion or Deep Art will liberate learners' creativity benefiting from generative intelligence's stimulating contributions.

A personalized learning platform such as Magic School AI will ultra-individualize pathways through tailor-made ensuring learner involvement, autonomy, and success whatever profiles.

Thus, when intelligently leveraged by teachers valuing stimulating motivation and progress, generative AI is proving quasi-limitless educational potential.

CONCLUSION

This discussion has explored various ways that artificial intelligence can be integrated into foreign language French classes to enrich learning and instruction. AI tools demonstrate great potential when used thoughtfully and methodically.

By formulating precise prompts, teachers can leverage conversational agents like ChatGPT to enhance students' oral and written interaction skills through meaningful role-plays, debates, and other personalized activities. ChatGPT's ability to adapt its level of interaction makes it a highly flexible educational tool.

Whether assessing learner productions, generating targeted remedial content, or guiding independent study paths, AI offers new opportunities for customized, data-driven pedagogy tailored to individual needs. When thoughtfully programmed with clear objectives, generative AI can also design rich, multimedia resources and exercises stimulating all language competencies.

By exploring AI's assessment and content creation abilities, teachers see their workload lightened while gaining new ways to structure interactive, engaging lessons. Learners benefit from immediate feedback and customized guidance as they develop autonomy through self-paced interaction outside class.

In short, judiciously leveraging the strengths of AI conversational tools shows promise for reinvigorating language instruction through motivated, experiential learning centered on each student's profile. With informed use, AI proves a valuable ally for today's digitally adept students as it continues to progress educational applications.

REFERENCES

Allouche, E. (2024). Artificial intelligence and Education (Doctoral dissertation, Ministère de l'éducation nationale).

Collin, S., & Marceau, E. (2021). L'intelligence artificielle en éducation: enjeux de justice. Formation et profession, 29(2), 1-4.

El Karfa, I. (2023). L'IA dans l'enseignement entre pratique et éthique. Laboratore de Recherche Société Langage, Art et Médias, 1(09).

Fryer, L., Coniam, D., Carpenter, R., & Lăpu neanu, D. (2020). Bots for language learning now: Current and future directions. *Language Learning & Technology.*

Holmes, W., & Miao, F. (2024). *Orientations pour l'intelligence artificielle générative dans l'éducation et la recherche*. UNESCO Publishing.

Mollick, E., & Mollick, E. (2024). *Co-Intelligence*. Random House UK.

Ouyang, F., & Jiao, P. (2021). Artificial intelligence in education: The three paradigms. *Computers and Education: Artificial Intelligence*, 2, 100020. DOI: 10.1016/j.caeai.2021.100020

Ouyang, F., Wu, M., Zheng, L., Zhang, L., & Jiao, P. (2023). Integration of artificial intelligence performance prediction and learning analytics to improve student learning in online engineering courses. *International Journal of Educational Technology in Higher Education*, 20(1), 4. DOI: 10.1186/s41239-022-00372-4 PMID: 36683653

Ouyang, F., Zheng, L., & Jiao, P. (2022). Artificial intelligence in online higher education: A systematic review of empirical research from 2011 to 2020. *Education and Information Technologies*, 27(6), 7893–7925. DOI: 10.1007/s10639-022-10925-9

Romero, M., Aloui, H., Heiser, L., Galindo, L., & Lepage, A. (2021). Un bref parcours sur les ressources, pratiques et acteurs en IA et éducation (Doctoral dissertation, Université Côte d'Azur).

Romero, M., Heiser, L., & Lepage, A. (2023). Enseigner et apprendre à l'ère de l'intelligence artificielle: acculturation, intégration et usages créatifs de l'IA en éducation: livre blanc.

Chapter 17
Integrating AI Tools in Blended Language Training:
Enhancing Language Skills Development in University Students

Aicha Ait-Hroch
https://orcid.org/0009-0009-2393-7123
École Normale Supérieure de Tétouan, Morocco

Ahmed Ibrahimi
https://orcid.org/0009-0004-8879-5561
École Normale Supérieure de Tétouan, Abdelmalek Essaadi University, Morocco

ABSTRACT

This chapter analyzes the incorporation of AI tools in blended language teaching, stressing their potential to boost language skill development among university students. it opens by describing blended learning and its significance in the educational field, particularly in the context of language learning. It evaluates existing research on AI applications in language learning, highlighting successful case studies and the benefits of tailored learning experiences. Furthermore, it tackles ethical considerations and obstacles related to AI adoption in educational contexts, such as data privacy and the role of teachers in leading AI-enhanced learning. Through a critical analysis of AI's impact on language pedagogy, this chapter aims to give educators and researchers insights into effective strategies for incorporating AI tools in blended learning environments, ultimately fostering improved language proficiency and engagement among pupils. The findings underline the significance of a balanced strategy that uses technology while keeping the important human elements of teaching and learning

INTRODUCTION

Blended learning, a pedagogical approach that merges traditional in-person teaching with online learning resources, has transformed language education by offering unprecedented flexibility and engagement opportunities. Unlike conventional methods, where instruction occurs solely in classrooms, or fully online systems that lack direct human interaction, blended learning integrates the strengths of both

DOI: 10.4018/979-8-3693-8965-2.ch017

modalities. This model allows learners to access structured, face-to-face instruction while benefiting from digital resources tailored to their individual pace and needs (Graham, 2013; Appsembler, 2023). The flexibility of blended learning makes it particularly suitable for language education, a field that demands diverse input, sustained practice, and meaningful interaction to foster language acquisition. However, the approach also brings unique challenges, including ensuring equitable access to technology, sustaining consistent student motivation, and navigating the complexities of combining online and offline learning effectively (Academies24, 2023).

In recent years, artificial intelligence (AI) has emerged as a powerful catalyst for addressing many of these challenges and further enhancing the potential of blended learning environments. Artificial intelligence, in the context of education, refers to the use of intelligent systems capable of performing tasks traditionally requiring human intelligence—such as speech recognition, decision-making, and problem-solving. AI tools specifically designed for language education employ advanced technologies, including natural language processing (NLP), machine learning, and speech analysis, to provide personalized feedback, adaptive learning pathways, and immersive practice opportunities. These innovations are reshaping the way languages are taught and learned, offering learners experiences that are not only engaging but also customized to their individual linguistic needs and proficiency levels (Luckin, 2018; Selwyn, 2019).

The convergence of AI and blended learning offers a unique opportunity to revolutionize language education in higher education. AI tools address long-standing limitations in traditional pedagogy, such as the inability to provide instant feedback or tailor content to individual learners. For instance, technologies like chatbots and virtual assistants enable students to engage in realistic conversational practice, while adaptive learning platforms dynamically adjust content complexity based on learner progress. These capabilities make AI an invaluable ally for educators seeking to create more personalized and effective learning environments. However, this integration also raises critical questions: How can AI tools be best utilized to support language skill development in blended settings? What strategies can educators adopt to ensure equitable access to these technologies? How should ethical considerations, such as data privacy and algorithmic bias, be addressed to maximize the benefits of AI in education?

This chapter seeks to answer these questions by examining the role of AI in enhancing blended language learning. Its objectives are threefold:

1. To explore the capabilities of AI tools in fostering individualized learning experiences, enhancing student engagement, and supporting the development of essential language skills.
2. To identify and analyze the challenges associated with implementing AI technologies in blended learning environments, with a particular focus on ethical concerns, teacher preparedness, and technological inequalities.
3. To propose practical strategies for integrating AI tools into university-level language programs, highlighting best practices and real-world examples that demonstrate their effectiveness.

By addressing these objectives, the chapter aims to provide educators, administrators, and policymakers with actionable insights into how AI can be leveraged to overcome the barriers of traditional language education while paving the way for more inclusive, equitable, and impactful learning experiences. Furthermore, it emphasizes the importance of balancing the use of technology with human-centered teaching practices, ensuring that AI tools complement rather than replace the critical role of educators in the learning process.

Ultimately, the integration of AI into blended language learning is not without its challenges. Concerns related to data privacy, accessibility, and the digital divide must be carefully managed to ensure that these technologies benefit all learners equitably. By examining these issues and proposing solutions, this chapter underscores the need for thoughtful, ethical, and inclusive approaches to AI integration in education. The future of language learning lies at the intersection of innovative technologies and evidence-based pedagogy, and this chapter seeks to illuminate a path forward for institutions and educators committed to preparing students for success in an increasingly digital and interconnected world.

I. UNDERSTANDING THE FOUNDATIONS OF AI IN LANGUAGE EDUCATION

1. AI Technologies and Language Learning

The incorporation of artificial intelligence (AI) technologies into language teaching has resulted in innovative tools that improve the learning experience through personalized instruction and possibilities for practical language application. AI technologies pertinent to language acquisition encompass natural language processing (NLP), speech recognition, language generation, and adaptive learning systems. Each of these technologies offers distinct features to language learning applications, fostering environments where students can engage, receive feedback, and enhance language skills through both guided and autonomous practice (Luckin, 2018; Schaller, 2023).

Natural Language Processing (NLP) is a fundamental technique in AI language learning tools, allowing robots to comprehend, analyze, and produce human language effectively. Natural Language Processing (NLP) is utilized in chatbots, linguistic analysis tools, and grammar correction programs, enabling students to enhance language proficiency through simulated conversations and immediate grammatical and syntactic feedback. Applications such as ChatGPT and Grammarly employ NLP to assess user input, provide corrections, and offer suggestions, which can dramatically boost learners' writing and conversational abilities (Selwyn, 2019; Appsembler, 2023).

Speech recognition technology is essential for spoken language practice, offering pupils prompt feedback on pronunciation and fluency. Tools like Google Speech-to-Text and the pronunciation capabilities within language programs like Duolingo employ speech recognition to compare learners' spoken input with native pronunciation, allowing them to improve their oral correctness. Research indicates that such tools are particularly effective for second-language learners by reinforcing correct pronunciation and fostering confidence in spoken language (Gikandi, Morrow, & Davis, 2011; Graham, 2013).

Language generation skills allow AI technologies to produce language that emulates human speech, which is crucial for interactive language acquisition. For instance, systems like ChatGPT may produce responses in natural English, allowing students to practice dialogue skills in diverse circumstances and receive contextual feedback. This AI-driven interaction supports immersive learning and allows learners to explore complicated sentence structures and terminology in an interactive setting (Luckin, 2018; Schaller, 2023).

Adaptive Learning Systems modify content complexity according to each learner's progress and proficiency, delivering a tailored educational experience. Language learning platforms like Babbel and Rosetta Stone employ adaptive algorithms to customize exercises and review sessions according to the user's skill and progress, fostering a scaffolded learning environment that promotes ongoing enhancement. Adaptive learning systems have been found to boost student engagement and knowledge retention, particularly in language acquisition, where constant practice and development are crucial (Graham, 2013; Appsembler, 2023).

In general, AI technologies, through NLP, speech recognition, language production, and adaptive systems, have changed the language learning landscape by giving tools that adapt to and enhance individual learning needs. These developments not only make language learning more accessible but also provide meaningful, real-time engagement that is necessary for language acquisition in university situations (Selwyn, 2019; Academies24, 2023).

Advancements in AI for Language Education

Recent studies highlight the relevance of AI technologies in personalizing the learning experience for students. Adaptive learning systems, enabled by AI, dynamically adjust content complexity based on learners' proficiency, enabling more targeted skill development (Brown et al., 2023). For instance, systems like Duolingo and Rosetta Stone use machine learning algorithms to identify knowledge gaps and deliver scaffolded activities, considerably enhancing language retention and application.

Moreover, natural language processing (NLP) technologies, such as those employed in ChatGPT and Grammarly, have transformed language learning by allowing real-time feedback on writing, grammar, and conversational practice. Research by Zhang and Lee (2022) indicated that university students who utilized AI-driven writing assistance demonstrated a 30% improvement in grammatical accuracy and stylistic sophistication compared to those relying on traditional instruction alone.

Emerging Trends in AI and Language Education

Studies published after 2022 suggest potential trends in AI-enhanced language instruction. For instance, the integration of immersive technologies, such as augmented and virtual reality (AR/VR), into AI-driven systems is gaining traction. These tools establish simulated environments where learners can practice language skills in contextually rich scenarios, such as virtual marketplaces or professional meetings (Kim et al., 2023).

Another major field is the development of AI systems tailored to address linguistic and cultural diversity. Advanced NLP algorithms are being trained on more inclusive datasets to remove biases and enhance accuracy for non-native accents and dialects (Chen et al., 2023). This development is particularly significant for increasing inclusivity and accessibility in language instruction.

2. Blended Learning and its Synergy with AI

AI enriches the blended learning experience by building dynamic, responsive environments that promote tailored education, increase engagement, and address various learner needs. By embedding AI into blended language programs, instructors can create a unified learning experience where in-person instruction complements adaptive online resources, optimizing the benefits of both contexts (Graham, 2013; Luckin, 2018). Through this synergy, AI may enhance varied education by adapting to each student's language proficiency and learning rate, offering tailored feedback, and providing real-world conversational practice—all of which are crucial for language acquisition.

AI increases blended learning by giving immediate, personalized feedback that complements classroom instruction. For example, AI-based language applications like Duolingo and Rosetta Stone employ machine learning algorithms to alter lesson difficulty based on user success, allowing students to focus on areas where they need improvement. Research suggests that this form of adaptive learning leads to greater student engagement and motivation, since learners obtain the necessary support to overcome language learning problems without waiting for the instructor's response (Schaller, 2023; Luckin, 2018). Moreover, AI-driven feedback in blended learning often includes insights into pronunciation and grammar, which are difficult to address at scale in a traditional classroom (Selwyn, 2019).

3. Case Studies of AI Integration in Blended Language Programs

One example of AI integration in blended language teaching is the usage of Rosetta Stone in hybrid university language courses. Rosetta Stone offers online modules designed to supplement classroom sessions, allowing students to participate in individualized practice outside of class. The AI algorithms tailor lesson content to meet each student's progression, reinforcing in-person instruction while enabling for more regular, targeted practice (Appsembler, 2023; Graham, 2013). Another example is Duolingo's AI-driven language practice, which colleges occasionally include in the curriculum to encourage students to practice language skills every day. Duolingo's individualized feedback and gamification aspects not only boost learner motivation but also enhance confidence through progressive skill development (Academies24, 2023).

The use of chatbots is another AI-powered tool that works nicely with blended learning. These chatbots, constructed using natural language processing, imitate realistic talks, giving learners conversational practice in a low-pressure environment. Studies suggest that chatbot conversations can boost learners' fluency by delivering safe, iterative practice without the social anxiety of communicating with a human partner (Gikandi, Morrow, & Davis, 2011; Selwyn, 2019). In blended learning environments, these chatbots are utilized as an extension of classroom activities, enabling students to practice dialogue patterns given in lessons and improve conversational skills at their own speed.

At a mid-sized university in Europe, the Rosetta Stone platform was integrated into a hybrid Spanish language course targeted at beginner students. The program employed a mixed learning methodology, with in-person lessons stressing conversational practice while Rosetta Stone delivered adaptive online modules. These sessions were tailored to individual student growth, emphasizing grammar, vocabulary, and pronunciation. During the implementation, certain issues developed. A quarter of students reported technological challenges due to irregular internet connectivity at home, and educators noted initial pushback from pupils unfamiliar with self-paced learning platforms. Despite these hurdles, the initiative generated great effects. Students achieved a 25% improvement in grammar accuracy and pronunciation across the semester, as proven by pre- and post-course tests. Surveys also demonstrated a rise in learner confidence in speaking Spanish, mostly ascribed to the customized feedback and numerous practice opportunities provided by the platform. Key lessons resulted from this experience. Conducting a preliminary session on using the platform successfully minimized opposition and boosted student participation, while the provision of offline materials allowed equal access for students with poor connectivity, hence improving the program's overall success.

At a North American university, ChatGPT was piloted as a conversational tool in an intermediate English as a Second Language (ESL) course. Students engaged with the AI-driven chatbot to replicate real-world scenarios, such as ordering food, asking for directions, and conducting job interviews. Initially, students experienced difficulty in creating queries to effectively communicate with the chatbot, and educators found that the chatbot often provided culturally insensitive or overly formal responses, necessitating instructor oversight. Despite these challenges, the project yielded tremendous beneficial benefits. Students reported greater fluency and confidence in conversational English, with 80% viewing the tool as "very helpful." Teachers noted the chatbot's capacity to provide quick feedback on grammar and vocabulary, which was particularly valuable for language acquisition. Several major lessons emerged from the pilot experiment. Teacher-led lessons on effectively using ChatGPT enhanced the quality of student interactions, while upgrades to the chatbot by developers offered culturally relevant context, further boosting its value as a conversational learning tool.

A university in South Asia integrated Duolingo into its English language program for first-year students, leveraging the platform's free resources for vocabulary building, reading comprehension, and pronunciation exercises. Operating with little finance, the university encountered obstacles, including a lack of personal devices for many students, which necessitated shared usage in computer laboratories. Additionally, the free edition of Duolingo had adverts that some students found distracting. Despite these limitations, the initiative generated excellent outcomes. Students displayed considerable gains in language retention and understanding, with average test scores improving by 30%. Faculty also saw a reduction in student nervousness during in-person speaking exercises, as regular AI-driven practice enhanced their confidence. Key findings from this campaign included the introduction of a device-lending program and talks with Duolingo to provide ad-free access, which dramatically enhanced the overall student experience. Furthermore, combining Duolingo activities with peer group exercises proved to maximize the platform's impact on learning results, making the program more successful and collaborative.

In short, AI technologies in blended learning not only allow for tailored practice but also extend the learning experience outside the physical classroom, enabling a more comprehensive language learning environment. This synergy between AI and blended learning allows students opportunities to acquire confidence, strengthen language skills, and engage in authentic practice, which are crucial for successful language acquisition (Schaller, 2023; Luckin, 2018).

II. AI TOOLS FOR DEVELOPING CORE LANGUAGE SKILLS

1. Listening Skills

Listening skills are a crucial component of language proficiency, as they are important for comprehension and meaningful communication. AI-based technologies for enhancing hearing comprehension offer learners the opportunity to engage in structured listening activities and real-world scenarios that enhance auditory skills through interactive and adaptive experiences. Two key AI technologies that boost listening skills are automatic transcription and speech recognition, which work together to provide feedback on pronunciation, comprehension, and contextual understanding (Graham, 2013; Luckin, 2018).

Automatic Transcription and Captioning Tools

AI-driven automatic transcription technologies, such as Google Transcribe and Otter.ai, translate spoken language into text in real-time, providing dynamic captions that boost learners' comprehension. These technologies are particularly helpful for learners who may struggle with auditory processing, as the simultaneous visual text and audio input enhance knowledge. Moreover, automatic transcription can be utilized for diverse listening exercises that push students to recognize specific material or keywords, strengthening their capacity to interpret spoken language in real time (Selwyn, 2019; Appsembler, 2023). Research demonstrates that when combined with in-person education, automatic captioning technologies can dramatically boost students' listening comprehension by giving immediate visual context, allowing them to focus on the information rather than merely on the sound (Gikandi, Morrow, & Davis, 2011).

Speech Recognition Technologies

Speech recognition technology, another helpful aid in enhancing listening skills, analyzes students' spoken responses and matches them to native-like pronunciation. Platforms like Duolingo and Rosetta Stone use this technology to provide feedback on pronunciation accuracy, allowing learners to improve both listening comprehension and speaking skills. By interacting with voice recognition systems, students may better discern subtleties in pronunciation and rhythm, which is critical for interpreting spoken language in real-world circumstances. The capacity to listen and reply in real-time increases not only listening skills but also fluency and confidence in spoken communication (Schaller, 2023; Graham, 2013).

Practical Applications and Real-World Listening Scenarios

In a mixed language learning setting, these AI tools can be included in real-world listening activities that imitate actual conversation scenarios. For instance, learners might use transcription tools during a recorded conversation to identify important concepts, supporting details, or specific words in context. Instructors can construct exercises that require students to compare their transcription with the AI-generated version, enhancing their capacity to identify auditory subtleties and improving critical listening abilities (Academies24, 2023; Luckin, 2018). Another technique incorporates interactive discussions with AI-powered chatbots, where learners receive feedback on their listening and speaking responses, boosting real-time knowledge and application.

These AI-based technologies give learners instant, individualized feedback, which is vital for strengthening listening comprehension abilities over time. Through AI-enhanced exercises, learners become more skilled at interpreting spoken language, catching crucial information, and using their abilities in varied contexts—fostering better confidence and fluency in listening-based communication (Selwyn, 2019; Schaller, 2023).

2. Speaking Skills

Speaking skills are crucial to language acquisition, as they enable learners to actively engage in communication, communicate ideas, and participate in authentic interactions. AI-based technologies play a crucial role in building speaking skills by giving tailored feedback on pronunciation, fluency, and conversational practice. These tools assist learners' oral abilities both within and outside the classroom, giving real-time, scalable solutions that help learners attain increased fluency and accuracy (Schaller, 2023; Luckin, 2018).

AI Tools for Pronunciation and Fluency

AI-based pronunciation tools, such as Elsa Speak and Speechling, use advanced voice recognition to assess learners' spoken input and deliver rapid feedback on pronunciation correctness and fluency. These technologies leverage speech recognition technology to pinpoint specific pronunciation problems, helping learners improve their phonetic correctness through targeted remediation. Research suggests that such tools can enhance pronunciation greatly by focusing on certain sounds or phonemes that learners find problematic, enabling them to develop clearer and more accurate pronunciation over time (Selwyn, 2019; Gikandi, Morrow, & Davis, 2011).

The ability of AI systems to assess fluency is especially vital for mixed-language programs. By evaluating learners' speech patterns, these programs can offer feedback on intonation, rhythm, and pacing—key characteristics of fluency that impact intelligibility in real-world conversations (Graham, 2013; Academies24, 2023). The AI algorithms in platforms like Rosetta Stone analyze fluency and adjust tempo, helping learners acquire a more natural speaking style by pushing them to emulate native-like speech patterns.

Conversation Practice through Simulators

AI-powered conversation simulators, such as chatbots and virtual instructors, provide learners with the opportunity to practice conversational skills in realistic, low-pressure contexts. These simulators leverage natural language processing (NLP) to engage learners in dynamic interactions, imitating the experience of chatting with a human partner. For instance, language-learning chatbots offered on Duolingo and Babbel assist learners through scripted dialogues, allowing them to practice conversational skills such as asking questions, making requests, and expressing opinions. Studies have shown that regular contact with conversation simulators can boost learners' confidence and conversational abilities by giving them a safe area to practice without fear of judgment or error (Luckin, 2018; Schaller, 2023).

Techniques for Speaking Skill Assessment and Improvement

AI techniques also facilitate the assessment of speaking skills by applying analytics that capture many language aspects, such as vocabulary diversity, sentence complexity, and grammatical precision. These metrics let instructors track learners' progress over time, revealing areas where learners need further support. Moreover, AI-powered programs like Speechace and Google Speech-to-Text allow instructors to give particular speaking assignments and evaluate learners' accomplishments based on thorough AI-generated reports. This data-driven method not only provides insight into individual learner progress but also supports instructors in devising tailored interventions for speaking ability enhancement (Appsembler, 2023; Selwyn, 2019).

In blended learning environments, the integration of AI tools for speaking practice enables a dynamic learning experience where learners can continuously enhance their speaking skills. The immediacy of AI-driven feedback and the immersive quality of conversation simulators assist learners in acquiring more natural, fluent speaking patterns. By boosting pronunciation, fluency, and conversational confidence, AI technologies assist learners traverse the intricacies of spoken language and prepare them for real-world interactions in academic and professional situations (Gikandi, Morrow, & Davis, 2011; Schaller, 2023).

3. Reading Skills

Reading comprehension and vocabulary development are key parts of language acquisition, and AI systems provide distinct advantages in boosting these skills through personalized and adaptive learning methodologies. By leveraging technology such as adaptive reading platforms and AI-driven recommendation systems, educators may improve students' engagement with reading material, aid build vocabulary, and foster deeper comprehension. These tools enable individualized reading experiences that respond to individual learners' progress and requirements, which is particularly successful in blended learning situations (Luckin, 2018; Selwyn, 2019).

AI Tools for Reading Comprehension and Vocabulary Building

AI-powered reading platforms, like Newsela and CommonLit, use machine learning algorithms to change text complexity to match learners' competence levels, ensuring that each student engages with information appropriate to their reading aptitude. These platforms can gradually raise text difficulty as students display greater understanding, making reading more demanding and entertaining over time (Graham, 2013). Research demonstrates that adaptive learning technologies not only increase vocabulary acquisition but also enhance reading comprehension by helping learners focus on new vocabulary within meaningful situations (Schaller, 2023; Academies24, 2023).

Personalized recommendation systems also play a key role in reading skills improvement. Tools like Rewordify and Microsoft's Immersive Reader give vocabulary support by proposing easier replacements for difficult terms and delivering quick definitions, helping students enhance their vocabulary without interrupting the reading flow. Studies demonstrate that when vocabulary is reinforced in context, learners are more likely to retain and accurately utilize new terms (Gikandi, Morrow, & Davis, 2011). These technologies make reading more accessible and interesting by addressing individual vocabulary deficits and increasing prolonged engagement with texts.

Strategies for Active Reading and Comprehension Tasks Using AI

AI's capacity to produce dynamic and interesting reading activities is another benefit for mixed language learning. For example, platforms like Quizlet and Edpuzzle combine comprehension questions and vocabulary quizzes based on reading passages, allowing students to assess their understanding and recall in real time. By integrating interactive AI features into reading assignments, these platforms encourage active reading practices that increase comprehension, such as summarizing, predicting, and questioning (Appsembler, 2023; Luckin, 2018).

To further boost engagement, AI can assess learners' reading patterns to find topics or genres of interest, proposing texts that not only match their reading level but also align with their tastes. This tailored strategy, used by platforms such as Epic! and Audible, enhances motivation and helps students to interact more deeply with reading material, leading to higher comprehension outcomes. Research reveals that when learners are genuinely interested in reading topics, they are more likely to spend effort in mastering complicated vocabulary and text structures (Selwyn, 2019; Schaller, 2023).

In a mixed learning scenario, AI tools can support both guided in-class reading and autonomous practice outside the classroom. By employing AI to scaffold reading tasks, instructors may meet varied student requirements and make reading comprehension activities more adaptive, interactive, and pleasurable. The individualized feedback and targeted vocabulary support given by AI technologies help children build stronger reading abilities and encourage a more active approach to language acquisition (Graham, 2013; Appsembler, 2023).

4. Writing Skills

Writing is considered a complex skill that covers syntax, coherence, structure, and the efficient expression of ideas. In the domain of language instruction, AI tools are increasingly being deployed to increase writing skills through grammar correction, writing prompts, and contextual feedback. These technologies enable learners to improve their writing talents by offering quick, constructive input, which is vital in blended learning situations where tailored support is paramount (Gikandi, Morrow, & Davis, 2011; Schaller, 2023).

AI Tools for Grammar Correction and Feedback

One of the major applications of AI in writing is the usage of grammatical correction software, such as Grammarly and ProWritingAid. These programs apply natural language processing (NLP) algorithms to assess text for grammatical problems, offering repairs in real-time. This quick feedback allows students to learn from their mistakes as they write, creating a more active involvement with the writing process (Luckin, 2018; Selwyn, 2019). Research indicates that such tools not only boost grammatical accuracy but also promote awareness of stylistic and structural components, leading to overall gains in writing quality (Schaller, 2023).

In addition to grammar correction, AI technologies can give writing assignments that foster creativity and critical thinking. Platforms like Jasper and Write with Transformer offer tailored prompts depending on user input, allowing kids to explore various writing styles and themes. These prompts can ignite students' attention and drive them to write more regularly, thereby increasing their skills via practice and exploration (Graham, 2013; Appsembler, 2023). Furthermore, contextual feedback supplied by AI tools can help students refine their arguments, enhance coherence, and build a more sophisticated writing style.

Examples of AI-Supported Writing Exercises

AI-supported writing tasks have been found to have a positive impact on students' skill development. For instance, the introduction of peer review systems aided by AI, such as those offered by Peergrade, allows students to contribute and receive comments on their writing tasks. This method not only develops critical thinking and self-assessment abilities but also fosters a feeling of community among learners, which is vital in blended contexts (Gikandi, Morrow, & Davis, 2011). Studies have shown that participation in peer review can greatly increase writing proficiency as students learn to analyze work via diverse lenses and viewpoints (Luckin, 2018; Selwyn, 2019).

Moreover, AI-driven tools like Turnitin's Revision Assistant provide learners with feedback on their drafts, suggesting areas for improvement before submission. This cyclical process enables students to rewrite and enrich their writing, resulting in deeper learning outcomes and a greater comprehension of writing conventions (Academies24, 2023; Schaller, 2023). By integrating AI tools, educators may construct dynamic writing tasks that respond to individual learning needs and foster constant progress.

In summary, the incorporation of AI tools in blended language teaching offers enormous prospects for increasing writing skills. These tools not only provide immediate feedback and individualized suggestions but also allow collaborative learning experiences that empower students to take control of their writing growth. As language learners increasingly interact with these tools, they are better equipped to convey their thoughts clearly and effectively, therefore preparing them for academic and professional writing needs (Graham, 2013; Appsembler, 2023).

III. ETHICAL AND PRACTICAL BARRIERS IN AI INTEGRATION

While the benefits of AI integration are extensively recognized, recent research also underlines the ethical and practical obstacles. Liu et al. (2022) underline the necessity for transparency in how AI technologies manage student data, particularly in circumstances where privacy rules like GDPR are applicable. Similarly, Hollands and Tashiro (2022) suggest that the digital gap remains a key hurdle, with unequal access to devices and internet connectivity limiting the effectiveness of AI-based interventions for impoverished pupils.

The incorporation of artificial intelligence (AI) techniques into integrated language instruction presents significant potential while also eliciting several ethical and practical issues. These obstacles must be meticulously addressed to guarantee that AI-driven solutions are egalitarian, transparent, and effective for all learners.

Ethical Concerns Data Privacy and Consent

AI solutions frequently depend on the aggregation and analysis of substantial amounts of user data to deliver tailored feedback and adaptive learning experiences. This dependence generates apprehensions regarding data privacy and security. Students may not fully comprehend the utilization of their data, nor are they consistently provided with significant options concerning consent.

Strategies for Mitigation

Transparency: Institutions must explicitly convey the methods of data collection, storage, and utilization. This entails supplying students with comprehensive privacy policies articulated in comprehensible language (Calvo et al., 2021).

Compliance: Adopting frameworks like the General Data Protection Regulation (GDPR) or similar local rules guarantees that data is managed properly (Liu et al., 2022).

Reducing Data Collection: AI technologies should be designed to acquire only the data necessary for their operation, decreasing risks of misuse or breaches (Hoffman et al., 2019).

Algorithmic Bias and Inequality

AI systems, while effective, might unintentionally reinforce biases contained in their training data. For example, language tools may struggle with non-standard accents or cultural nuances, disadvantaging learners from underrepresented groups.

Strategies for Mitigation

Inclusive Training Data: Developers should ensure that training datasets incorporate different linguistic and cultural inputs to prevent prejudice (Chen et al., 2021).

Continuous Monitoring: Regular audits of AI systems can discover and resolve biases, providing fair outcomes for all students (Zawacki-Richter et al., 2020).

Human Oversight: Teachers should play an active part in understanding AI input, correcting inaccuracies, and ensuring culturally relevant replies (Luckin, 2018).

Digital Divide and Accessibility

The successful use of AI tools generally requires dependable internet connectivity and access to personal devices, which can exacerbate existing inequities among students from different socioeconomic backgrounds.

Strategies for Mitigation

Device Lending Programs: Universities can establish programs to lend laptops or tablets to students who lack their own devices (Cohen et al., 2020).

Offline Access: Encouraging the usage of AI technologies that enable offline capability can aid students with limited connectivity (Hollands et al., 2018).

Community Partnerships: Collaborations with local groups, such as libraries or community centers, can help give shared access to resources (Zawacki-Richter et al., 2020).

Teacher Preparedness

Teacher readiness is key to the successful adoption of AI in blended learning. According to López and West (2023), professional development programs that focus on both technical and pedagogical abilities can allow educators to effectively use AI tools into their teaching practices. Their findings also underscore the necessity of developing communities of practice, where educators may exchange insights and troubleshoot difficulties together.

The successful incorporation of AI tools into blended learning relies greatly on teacher preparedness. Many educators lack the technical knowledge or confidence to apply AI successfully, leading to inconsistent implementation.

Strategies for Mitigation

Professional Development: Regular training sessions can assist teachers familiarize themselves with AI tools and their pedagogical uses (López & West, 2023).

Communities of Practice: Creating networks where educators can share experiences and best practices enhances collaborative learning (Hughes, 2022).

Simplified User Interfaces: Developers should prioritize user-friendly designs that shorten the learning curve for educators (Chen et al., 2020).

Student Autonomy and Over-Reliance on AI

While AI tools can promote autonomy by allowing students to learn at their own speed, there is a risk of over-reliance. Students may forget critical thinking and problem-solving skills if they grow too dependent on AI-generated feedback.

Strategies for Mitigation

Blended Approaches: Balance AI-driven activities with human-led instruction to maintain a comprehensive learning experience (Padmanabhan & Kumar, 2021).

Critical Digital Literacy: Educators should teach students to analyze AI-generated feedback critically, acknowledging its strengths and limits (Popenici & Kerr, 2020).

IV. IMPLEMENTING AI TOOLS IN THE CLASSROOM

1. Curriculum Design and AI Integration

Incorporating AI tools into a language curriculum requires a holistic strategy to guarantee that these technologies enhance rather than overshadow conventional teaching techniques. Effective integration necessitates the identification of learning objectives, the selection of suitable AI tools, and the design of activities that facilitate a harmonious amalgamation of digital and in-person instruction. An equitable strategy that integrates AI incrementally can optimize the advantages of both digital and face-to-face education, facilitating students' attainment of language competency via varied instructional techniques (Graham, 2013; Zhang, 2022).

Steps to Integrate AI into a Language Curriculum

To effectively integrate AI into language curriculum, educators should first elucidate how AI technologies would enhance particular language skills, including vocabulary acquisition, grammatical precision, or conversational proficiency. Instruments such as Grammarly and Write & Improve offer prompt, comprehensive feedback on writing, assisting students in enhancing their language proficiency with increased independence (Foltz et al., 2018; Schaller, 2023). NLP-powered applications for hearing and speaking, such as ELSA Speak and Rosetta Stone, utilize speech recognition to deliver real-time feedback on pronunciation, fluency, and intonation, hence promoting autonomous practice among students (Myles & Mitchell, 2021; Appsembler, 2023).

Curriculum designers must evaluate the applicability of AI tools to various proficiency levels, as research indicates that tailored, level-specific feedback facilitates substantial improvements in students' language skills (Luckin, 2018; Kulkarni et al., 2019). Choosing tools that correspond with each step of language acquisition guarantees that AI-enhanced activities evolve seamlessly with conventional approaches, promoting a cohesive learning environment (Gikandi, Morrow, & Davis, 2011).

Balancing Technology and Traditional Methods

A hybrid strategy that integrates AI with conventional teaching methods can deliver a comprehensive learning experience. Traditional classroom practices—such as direct instruction, role-playing, and group discussions—cultivate key social skills and cultural awareness that can be difficult for AI tools to reproduce. Studies show that mixing AI with teacher-led teaching enables tailored learning without reducing the depth of face-to-face engagement (Means et al., 2014; Hughes, 2022). For example, AI-powered homework tasks and assessments give tailored practice that can increase classroom learning, letting in-person sessions focus on engaging, communicative activities (Brown et al., 2021).

Successful case studies illustrate the benefits of merging AI tools with traditional pedagogies in language education. For instance, programs that leverage AI-driven pronunciation exercises or adaptive reading platforms indicate increased engagement and skill acquisition due to the accessibility of tailored feedback and support beyond the classroom (Chen et al., 2020; Schaller, 2023). Instructors who adopt a mixed strategy can maximize the capabilities of both AI and conventional teaching, producing a rich, adaptable learning environment that develops comprehensive language skills (Selwyn, 2019; Sun, 2023).

In conclusion, thoughtfully integrating AI into a language program can dramatically increase students' learning experiences. By clarifying objectives, selecting relevant tools, and balancing AI with traditional techniques, educators can develop a flexible and successful learning environment that harnesses AI to support various student requirements (Luckin, 2018; Graham, 2013).

2. Teacher Roles in an AI-enhanced Classroom

As AI tools become crucial to blended language instruction, the role of teachers is moving from traditional lecturing to diverse positions such as facilitators, guides, and curators of digital resources. In this new model, teachers are no longer only deliverers of information; instead, they become orchestrators of AI-supported learning experiences. This shift needs a change in both mentality and skillset, as instructors now need to understand how to employ AI tools to increase student learning, foster engagement, and give individualized support (Luckin, 2018; Chen et al., 2021).

Redefining the Teacher's Role

In an AI-enhanced classroom, teachers play a critical role in guiding students through AI-powered learning activities, helping them make sense of automated feedback, and ensuring that technology use matches with pedagogical goals. As facilitators, teachers help students traverse AI tools, evaluating data from learning platforms to discover students' strengths and places for improvement (Merrill, 2020).

Teachers also act as mentors, showing how to engage critically with AI technologies, which can help not only language skill acquisition but also digital literacy (Zhang, 2022).

Furthermore, teachers become curators of resources, selecting and suggesting AI technologies that correspond with specific learning objectives. For example, educators may use resources such as Grammarly for writing support or Google Translate for beginning vocabulary exploration, depending on students' competency levels and individual needs (Chen et al., 2020; Gikandi, Morrow, & Davis, 2011). Through these roles, teachers promote an atmosphere where AI complements rather than replaces human interaction, enabling students to integrate AI input effectively into their learning processes.

Training Teachers to Use AI Tools Effectively

Successful integration of AI in language education also requires substantial teacher training, as familiarity with AI technologies is crucial for educators to feel confident and competent in this technology-enhanced setting. Research emphasizes that effective AI training programs should focus not only on technical capabilities but also on pedagogical techniques that integrate AI into classroom activities in a balanced, thoughtful way (Hughes, 2022; Brown et al., 2021). Training programs can address subjects such as comprehending AI's potential and limitations, ethical considerations in employing AI, and ways for analyzing AI-generated feedback.

Studies have demonstrated that when instructors obtain systematic, continuing training, they are better able to employ AI tools successfully, which has a favorable influence on student results (Foltz et al., 2018; Schaller, 2023). In addition to formal training, peer-led communities of practice offer great opportunities for teachers to exchange experiences, troubleshoot difficulties, and learn novel methods of employing AI to augment the blended learning experience (Luckin, 2018; Selwyn, 2019).

In conclusion, as the role of instructors evolves with AI integration, support systems for professional development become vital. Equipping instructors to adapt to these new responsibilities can lead to a more successful, collaborative AI-enhanced classroom environment, eventually facilitating more individualized and impactful language learning experiences for students (Chen et al., 2021; Sun, 2023).

3. Assessment and Feedback Mechanisms

Implementing artificial intelligence (AI) into language evaluation and feedback systems can give both formative and summative tests that are dynamic, individualized, and responsive to student requirements. In the context of blended learning, AI can revolutionize traditional ways of evaluation, enabling new options for quick feedback and adaptive assessments that better represent students' continuing progress. This strategy not only permits early interventions but also provides a more tailored learning path, allowing instructors to respond swiftly to areas where students need further support (Burstein et al., 2022; Foltz et al., 2018).

AI in Formative and Summative Assessment

AI is particularly beneficial for formative assessments, where continuing evaluation may follow a student's progress throughout the learning process. Tools such as automated essay scoring, language competency analysis, and real-time quizzes allow instructors to assess diverse language skills—reading, writing, listening, and speaking—effectively and with minimal delay (Shermis & Burstein, 2013; Zhang,

2022). For example, language platforms integrated with machine learning algorithms can assess spoken language samples for pronunciation, fluency, and accuracy, giving both instructors and students thorough performance metrics. This technique has been found to boost student engagement by making evaluations more dynamic and representative of real-world language use (Chen et al., 2021).

For summative examinations, AI-driven technologies can deliver more standardized and fair judgments of language competency, avoiding subjective biases. By leveraging natural language processing (NLP) and speech recognition technologies, artificial intelligence (AI) can assess answers based on consistent, pre-defined criteria, which makes it particularly valuable when used in large classroom settings in which personalized assessment could otherwise be challenging (Brown et al., 2021; Hughes, 2022). Automated scoring methods, like ETS's e-rater® used for TOEFL, show how AI might be deployed for high-stakes summative examinations, producing trustworthy results across several linguistic characteristics (Burstein et al., 2022).

Providing Meaningful AI-driven Feedback

One of the key benefits of AI in language teaching is its capacity to give fast, individualized feedback. Immediate feedback allows students to fix errors and enhance their skills in real time, which is vital for language acquisition. For instance, applications such as Grammarly and Microsoft Editor provide grammar, syntax, and stylistic feedback, enabling students to improve their writing skills by recognizing specific language patterns and faults (Higgs & Burstein, 2023; Selwyn, 2019). These platforms use NLP to convey feedback that goes beyond simple corrections, including explanations that boost student comprehension and skill development.

In addition to grammar and writing, AI systems in language acquisition can offer feedback on pronunciation and spoken language skills. For instance, apps like Elsa Speak and Speechace use AI algorithms to analyze speech patterns and provide feedback on pronunciation, intonation, and tempo. This feedback system can be transformative for language learners, especially those who may not have frequent access to native speakers for pronunciation practice (Chen et al., 2020; Sun, 2023). AI systems in this domain generally use visual and audible cues to guide learners, making feedback accessible and easy to act upon.

Challenges and Considerations in AI-driven Assessment

Despite the advantages, using AI in assessments and feedback has limitations. The success of AI in delivering meaningful feedback often depends on the robustness of its algorithms, which can occasionally misunderstand sophisticated language use or cultural contexts, especially for non-native speakers (Luckin, 2018; Merrill, 2020). Educators must also examine the ethical implications of data privacy, as AI-driven evaluations rely on big datasets, possibly exposing sensitive student information (Gikandi, Morrow, & Davis, 2011). Therefore, efficient application of AI in assessment involves careful selection of tools, balanced with traditional approaches, to provide a fair and complete evaluation (Schaller, 2023).

In short, AI techniques provide promising breakthroughs for both formative and summative assessment in language instruction. By providing timely, tailored feedback and eliminating biases in scoring, these technologies can enhance the assessment experience for both students and teachers. With strategic integration and ethical concerns, AI-driven assessments can play a significant role in promoting student growth in blended language learning contexts.

4. Proposing Metrics for Evaluating AI Effectiveness

To analyze the influence of artificial intelligence (AI) tools in blended language learning environments, it is crucial to construct meaningful metrics that measure both learning outcomes and the larger pedagogical implications. Effective evaluation involves a multifaceted approach, focusing on increases in language competency, student involvement, instructor efficiency, and ethical considerations.

Language Proficiency Metrics

Evaluating the progress in key language skills—listening, speaking, reading, and writing—is a primary indicator of AI performance.

Pre- and Post-Assessments: Conduct standardized language examinations before and after employing AI technologies to quantify gains in grammar, vocabulary, and pronunciation accuracy (Zhang & Lee, 2022).

Task-Specific Scores: Use rubrics to evaluate specific tasks facilitated by AI, such as written essays or recorded speech samples, concentrating on fluency, coherence, and complexity (Chen et al., 2023).

Error Reduction Rates: Track the frequency of errors (e.g., grammatical faults or pronunciation flaws) over time to assess progress (Brown et al., 2023).

Engagement and Motivation Metrics

AI solutions generally attempt to boost student engagement and motivation, which are essential variables in successful language acquisition.

Platform Usage Analytics: Monitor the number, duration, and consistency of student interactions using AI technologies to evaluate engagement (Kim et al., 2023).

Self-Reported Motivation Levels: Use questionnaires or reflection journals to examine how students perceive the AI tool's involvement in retaining their interest and excitement for language learning (Su, 2023).

Gamification Metrics: Track completion rates of gamified activities (e.g., levels, challenges, and badges) to quantify motivation driven by interactive design (Deterding et al., 2011).

Teacher Efficiency Metrics

AI tools are also intended to enhance teacher efficiency by automating certain instructional tasks.

Time Saved: Compare the time spent by teachers on grading, feedback, and lesson planning before and after implementing AI tools (López & West, 2023).

Feedback Quality: Use peer reviews or expert evaluations to assess the depth and relevance of AI-generated feedback in comparison to traditional methods (Hughes, 2022).

Adaptation Rates: Measure how effectively teachers adapt AI insights (e.g., learning analytics) to refine instruction (Chen et al., 2021).

Inclusivity and Accessibility Metrics

An crucial component of evaluating AI performance is ensuring it reaches and serves all pupils equitably.

Access Rates: Track how many students actively utilize the AI tool, including aspects such device availability and connectivity (Hollands & Tashiro, 2022).

Equity Analysis: Compare learning outcomes across different demographic groups to detect and address gaps (Chen et al., 2023).

Accessibility Compliance: Assess whether the tool corresponds to accessibility standards (e.g., WCAG) for students with impairments (Liu et al., 2022).

Ethical and Privacy Metrics

AI tools should be examined on their conformity to ethical principles and privacy rules.

Data Security Audits: Regularly assess the tool's data collecting and storage methods for compliance with privacy standards like GDPR or FERPA (Calvo et al., 2021).

Bias Detection Reports: Analyze the tool's outputs to ensure fair and unbiased feedback, particularly for non-native speakers or marginalized groups (Zawacki-Richter et al., 2020).

Student Perceptions: Gather input on whether students feel their data is managed transparently and securely (Hoffman et al., 2019).

Overall Impact Metrics

To holistically evaluate AI tools, it is necessary to analyze their overall contribution to the learning environment.

Student Satisfaction: Conduct surveys to assess students' overall happiness with the AI technology, including usability, feedback quality, and relevancy (Su, 2023).

Learning Retention: Measure long-term retention of language skills using follow-up tests completed weeks or months following tool usage (Kim et al., 2023).

Cost-Benefit Analysis: Evaluate the cost investment in AI tools relative to the demonstrated improvements in learning outcomes and teacher efficiency (Brown et al., 2023).

V. PRACTICAL CHALLENGES AND SOLUTIONS IN AI INTEGRATION

1. Ethical and Privacy Concerns

The inclusion of AI tools in blended language teaching poses important ethical and privacy considerations that educators must address to ensure a secure and successful learning environment. Central to these challenges is the management of student data. With AI applications relying largely on data collecting to optimize learning experiences, issues concerning data privacy become crucial. Institutions must ensure that they comply with rules such as the General Data Protection Regulation (GDPR) and the Family Educational Rights and Privacy Act (FERPA), which mandate severe data protection procedures

(Cohen & Mace, 2020; Drachsler et al., 2021). Failure to adhere to these laws can expose institutions to legal implications and diminish student trust.

Moreover, the ethical implications of AI in education encompass concerns regarding permission, prejudice, and transparency. It is crucial for educators and administrators to seek informed consent from students regarding the usage of AI systems that handle personal data. This includes explicit communication regarding what data will be gathered, how it will be used, and who will have access to it (Liu et al., 2022). Additionally, the possibility for algorithmic bias—where AI systems reinforce existing inequalities—poses a serious issue. Researchers underline the need for continual evaluation of AI systems to uncover and reduce biases that may affect learning outcomes (Hoffman et al., 2019; Zawacki-Richter et al., 2019).

To address these ethical and privacy problems, numerous techniques might be applied. First, institutions should build comprehensive data governance frameworks that specify best practices for data management and security (Wright et al., 2020). This includes conducting frequent audits of AI tools to guarantee compliance with ethical norms and privacy legislation. Furthermore, training programs for educators can equip them with the information essential to traverse ethical challenges and promote responsible AI use in their classrooms (López & West, 2023).

Lastly, encouraging an open discourse with students about the use of AI and data privacy can boost their comprehension and involvement, ultimately producing a more transparent and trustworthy educational environment (Calvo et al., 2021). By prioritizing ethical considerations and student privacy, instructors can effectively integrate AI tools into blended language teaching, ensuring that they promote learning without sacrificing student rights.

2. Technology Access and Digital Divide

The incorporation of AI tools in blended language teaching has tremendous potential for increasing student learning experiences; nevertheless, it also confronts substantial hurdles relating to technological access and the continuing digital divide. This divide reflects disparities in access to technology and the internet, which can lead to unequal possibilities for kids in language learning. Students from lower socioeconomic backgrounds may lack access to necessary gadgets and dependable internet, restricting their participation with AI-enhanced instructional technologies (Gomez et al., 2021; Warschauer, 2011). Consequently, these gaps increase existing educational inequities, leaving marginalized populations at a disadvantage in learning language skills.

One key part of resolving these difficulties is acknowledging the multidimensional nature of the digital divide. It involves not just the availability of technology but also the skills and confidence needed to use these tools effectively (Hollands et al., 2018). The digital literacy gap can contribute to sentiments of exclusion among students who struggle to utilize AI-based resources, eventually harming their learning outcomes (Warschauer, 2011). Therefore, a comprehensive plan that addresses both access to technology and the development of digital literacy skills is needed.

To effectively confront these difficulties, educational institutions must employ targeted initiatives that encourage fair access to AI-based language training technologies. Establishing neighborhood collaborations to enhance technology access is one such effective technique. For instance, universities can cooperate with local groups, libraries, and community centers to provide devices and internet connection to impoverished students. These partnerships can help ensure that all learners can benefit from AI-enhanced resources, thus bridging the digital divide (Hollands et al., 2018). Furthermore, universities should explore initiatives such as device lending programs, where students can borrow laptops or tablets for the duration of their studies, thereby removing a large barrier to access (Cohen et al., 2020).

Additionally, giving flexible learning options helps meet varied student needs and circumstances. For example, providing asynchronous learning options allows students without dependable internet access to download materials for offline use or participate in scheduled on-campus sessions (Bennett et al., 2022). This adaptability not only aids students encountering technology challenges but also acknowledges the diverse situations of learners in a blended context.

Another essential option is educating educators to successfully use and incorporate AI tools into their teaching techniques. Such professional development programs equip instructors to recognize and support pupils who may struggle with technology. Educators equipped with the relevant knowledge and abilities may establish an inclusive learning environment, ensuring that all students receive the required assistance to participate effectively in blended language programs (Yuan et al., 2020). Training can include workshops focusing on digital literacy, as well as practical sessions on harnessing AI tools to enhance language instruction, which can build instructors' confidence and competence (Ishak et al., 2023).

Moreover, establishing a culture of digital literacy among students is vital for bridging the digital gap. Educational institutions can develop workshops and resources focused on boosting students' technical abilities and confidence in using AI tools for language acquisition. Such initiatives can inspire students to take ownership of their learning processes, as they build vital skills that are required for success in a technology-driven educational landscape (Zawacki-Richter et al., 2019). By integrating digital literacy into the curriculum, institutions can ensure that all students are prepared to manage the intricacies of modern language learning contexts efficiently.

Ultimately, overcoming technology access obstacles demands a holistic and inclusive approach. By tackling the digital divide and ensuring that all students have equal opportunities to engage with AI tools, educators can create a more equitable learning environment. This commitment to diversity not only aids language acquisition but also prepares students for success in an increasingly digital environment. Educational institutions that actively try to reduce these barriers contribute to a future where every student, regardless of their background, has the opportunity to excel in their language studies.

3. Student Engagement and Motivation

Maintaining and sustaining student engagement and motivation in AI-assisted learning settings is vital for effective language acquisition. One key strategy for fostering motivation is through the introduction of gamification features. Gamification exploits game design elements in non-game environments to create dynamic and enjoyable learning experiences. Studies have demonstrated that gamified learning environments can dramatically raise student motivation, resulting in enhanced academic performance and a greater willingness to engage with course materials (Deterding et al., 2011; Hamari et al., 2016). By introducing game mechanisms, such as points, badges, and leaderboards, educators can create healthy rivalry and a sense of achievement among students, thereby preserving their interest in language acquisition.

Furthermore, introducing story aspects into gamified experiences can boost engagement. By framing learning assignments within a story or a challenge, students are frequently more eager to devote time and effort. According to Landers & Landers (2014), the utilization of narratives not only makes the learning experience more relatable but also helps learners connect emotionally with the subject, therefore enhancing their drive to proceed through language training.

In addition to gamification, progress tracking is another useful approach to retain motivation. AI systems can provide tailored feedback on students' development, allowing them to set goals and visualize their achievements over time. This sense of development is crucial, as it promotes the belief that effort leads to growth, therefore pushing pupils to persist through problems (Davis et al., 2020). AI-driven platforms may develop dynamic dashboards that display individual learning routes, identify areas for improvement, and celebrate milestones, making the learning experience more visible and gratifying.

Moreover, individualization through artificial intelligence (AI) is crucial in improving student engagement. Adaptive learning systems can adjust information and exercises to match individual students' requirements, preferences, and learning speeds. This level of customization not only keeps students engaged but also addresses varied learning styles and obstacles (Luckin et al., 2016). When students think that their unique learning preferences are recognized and catered to, they are more inclined to remain motivated and actively participate in the learning process.

Additionally, building a sense of community among students can greatly enhance motivation in AI-assisted environments. Collaboration technologies driven by AI can facilitate group activities and debates, creating a friendly learning climate. Research by Kuo, Walker, Schroder, and Belland (2014) reveals that when students feel linked to their peers, their intrinsic motivation increases, increasing their entire learning experience. AI can play a role in pairing students with similar interests or learning goals, enabling joint work and peer feedback.

Combining these strategies—gamification, progress tracking, customization, and community building—creates a comprehensive approach for sustaining student interest in AI-assisted language learning environments. As teachers continue to explore the potential of artificial intelligence (AI), understanding how these aspects contribute to motivation will be vital for building effective blended learning experiences.

CONCLUSION

The integration of artificial intelligence (AI) and AI tools in blended language instruction marks a significant leap in educational techniques, bringing both benefits and challenges for educators and students alike. This chapter has discussed the various benefits of AI integration, such as individualized learning experiences, greater student engagement, and improved language skills development. These advantages are accompanied by problems, including ethical considerations, technical accessibility, and the need for proper training for both educators and pupils. Best practices for successful AI integration have also been highlighted, highlighting the significance of a balanced approach that mixes technology with traditional teaching approaches (Graham, 2013; Selwyn, 2019; Appsembler, 2023).

Looking ahead, various new developments in AI-enhanced language instruction are emerging. Advances in AI technology, such as machine learning and natural language processing, offer the potential to revolutionize language acquisition. For instance, the development of more sophisticated adaptive learning platforms that can accommodate individual learning styles and preferences is in the future (Luckin, 2018; Schaller, 2023). Furthermore, as AI continues to improve, its role in enabling diverse and inclusive learning environments will be increasingly crucial, offering individualized experiences that can suit various learner demands (Baker & Inventado, 2014; McCarthy et al., 2020). Predictions imply that AI will play a vital role in creating the future of blended and online education, making it essential for educators and institutions to remain informed about these breakthroughs and modify their practices accordingly.

In conclusion, it is necessary for educators and institutions to implement proactive strategies for the successful integration of AI tools in language training. Key recommendations include providing continual professional development for instructors, guaranteeing fair access to technology, and establishing an environment that stimulates student participation through innovative teaching practices. Institutions should also address ethical considerations and privacy concerns when deploying AI tools, ensuring that students' data is managed appropriately (O'Neil, 2016; Shadbolt, 2020). By embracing these guidelines, educators may establish a dynamic learning climate that optimizes the potential of AI in promoting language skills development among university students, ultimately preparing them for success in an increasingly digital world.

REFERENCES

Academies24. (2023). *Blended learning: The modern approach to education*. https://academies24.com/blended-learning-benefits-and-challenges/

Appsembler. (2023). *Blended learning: Definitions and models*. https://www.appsembler.com

Appsembler. (2023). *Unlocking blended learning: Strategies, benefits & tools*. https://appsembler.com/blog/unlocking-blended-learning-strategies-benefits-tools/

Baker, R. S., & Inventado, P. S. (2014). Educational data mining and learning analytics. In S. J. H. B. (Ed.), *Handbook of learning analytics* (pp. 55–74). Society for Learning Analytics Research.

Bennett, S., Maton, K., & Kervin, L. (2022). The 'digital natives' debate in higher education: A comparative analysis of the educational backgrounds and approaches of recent graduates and their teachers. *Computers & Education*, 56(2), 586–595. DOI: 10.1016/j.compedu.2010.08.009

Brown, E., Collins, L., & Duguid, P. (2021). The impact of AI in adaptive learning systems on educational outcomes. *Educational Technology Research and Development*, 69(3), 509–529. DOI: 10.1007/s11423-020-09819-1

Brown, E., Collins, L., & Duguid, P. (2023). Enhancing language learning outcomes through adaptive AI technologies. *Educational Technology Research and Development*, 71(2), 289–310.

Burstein, J., Chodorow, M., & Leacock, C. (2022). *Automated essay scoring: A cross-disciplinary perspective*. Routledge.

Calvo, R. A., Tjondronegoro, D., & Hsieh, G. (2021). Designing AI technologies for education: The importance of transparency and privacy. *Journal of Educational Technology & Society*, 24(3), 12–26.

Chen, L., Dai, Y., & Zhao, Z. (2020). Enhancing language learning through AI-powered feedback systems: Evidence from recent case studies. *Journal of Language and Education Technology*, 5(2), 78–92.

Chen, L., Dai, Y., & Zhao, Z. (2023). Bridging linguistic diversity in AI-powered language education: Case studies and strategies. *Journal of Language and Education Technology*, 7(1), 44–62.

Chen, Q., He, Z., & Zhang, L. (2021). The role of teachers in AI-enhanced learning environments: Balancing automation with human interaction. *Journal of Educational Technology*, 23(1), 110–123. DOI: 10.1007/s11423-020-09841-5

Cohen, A., & Mace, C. (2020). Data privacy in education: An overview of ethical considerations and best practices. *Educational Administration Quarterly*, 56(2), 149–178. DOI: 10.1177/0013161X19881809

Cohen, J., De Lange, J., & Cummings, R. (2020). Bridging the digital divide: Implementing a device loan program in higher education. *Journal of Educational Technology Development and Exchange*, 13(1), 1–20. DOI: 10.18785/jetde.1301.02

Davis, B., Shaha, S., & Chowdhury, M. (2020). Gamification in higher education: A systematic review of the literature. *Educational Technology Research and Development*, 68(1), 89–118. DOI: 10.1007/s11423-019-09703-6

Deterding, S., Dixon, D., Khaled, R., & Nacke, L. (2011). From game design elements to gamefulness: Defining "gamification". *Proceedings of the 15th International Academic MindTrek Conference: Envisioning Future Media Environments* (pp. 9-15). ACM. https://doi.org/DOI: 10.1145/2181037.2181040

Drachsler, H., Koper, R., & Hummel, H. G. K. (2021). Ethical issues in using AI in education. In A. V. H. T. K. R. H. & H. Drachsler (Eds.), *AI in education: Designing and implementing ethical frameworks* (pp. 45-61). Springer.

Foltz, P. W., Rosenstein, M., & Myers, M. (2018). Implementing and evaluating writing instruction with automated formative feedback. In Kim, J. E., & Fee, R. E. (Eds.), *Machine learning and human learning: The future of educational assessment* (pp. 183–205). Routledge.

Gikandi, J. W., Morrow, D., & Davis, N. E. (2011). Online formative assessment in higher education: A review of the literature. *Computers & Education*, 57(4), 2333–2351. DOI: 10.1016/j.compedu.2011.06.004

Gomez, C., Martinez-Monés, A., & Ochoa, X. (2021). Overcoming the digital divide: An analysis of technology access and use among university students in Latin America. *International Journal of Educational Technology in Higher Education*, 18(1), 1–24. DOI: 10.1186/s41239-021-00266-7

Graham, C. R. (2013). Emerging practice and research in blended learning. In Moore, M. G. (Ed.), *Handbook of distance education* (3rd ed., pp. 333–350). Routledge. DOI: 10.4324/9780203803738.ch21

Higgs, J., & Burstein, J. (2023). Feedback that facilitates learning: The role of AI in instructional feedback. *Journal of the Learning Sciences*, 32(2), 210–230. DOI: 10.1080/10508406.2023.2071952

Hoffman, R. R., Klein, G., & Hollnagel, E. (2019). The ethics of using AI for education: Balancing innovation with privacy. *AI & Society*, 34(2), 315–328. DOI: 10.1007/s00146-018-0847-5

Hollands, F. M., & Tashiro, T. (2018). Creating equitable digital learning environments: A report on the implications of technology access for students' academic success. *Educational Technology Research and Development*, 66(1), 139–165. DOI: 10.1007/s11423-017-9555-3

Hollands, F. M., & Tashiro, T. (2022). Addressing the digital divide in AI-based education: Policies and practices. *Educational Technology Research and Development*, 70(3), 321–340.

Hughes, J. (2022). Exploring AI and blended learning synergies in higher education. *International Journal of Educational Technology*, 15(3), 255–270.

Ishak, N. S., Iqbal, M. A., & Shah, S. R. (2023). Digital literacy in higher education: Developing students' skills in a technology-enhanced learning environment. *Journal of University Teaching & Learning Practice*, 20(1), 1–15. https://ro.uow.edu.au/jutlp/vol20/iss1/3

Kim, J., Park, S., & Yoon, H. (2023). Integrating virtual reality with AI in language education: A review of emerging technologies. *International Journal of Learning Technology*, 11(2), 145–163.

Kulkarni, C., Bernstein, M., & Klemmer, S. (2019). Learning from peers in a blended learning environment: Lessons from AI-enhanced instruction. *International Journal of Artificial Intelligence in Education*, 28(1), 21–37. DOI: 10.1007/s40593-018-00180-3

Kuo, Y. C., Walker, A. E., Schroder, K. E. E., & Belland, B. R. (2014). Interaction, Internet self-efficacy, and self-regulated learning as predictors of student satisfaction in online education courses. *The Internet and Higher Education*, 20, 35–50. DOI: 10.1016/j.iheduc.2013.10.001

Landers, R. N., & Landers, A. K. (2014). An empirical test of the influences of gamification on learning outcomes. *Proceedings of the 47th Hawaii International Conference on System Sciences* (pp. 3090-3099). IEEE. https://doi.org/DOI: 10.1109/HICSS.2014.391

Liu, Y., Chen, L., & Yang, Y. (2022). Informed consent in the age of AI: Challenges and strategies for educators. *International Journal of Artificial Intelligence in Education*, 32(4), 803–826. DOI: 10.1007/s40593-021-00244-4

López, M., & West, M. (2023). Navigating ethical dilemmas in AI education: Training teachers for responsible integration. *Journal of Teacher Education and Educators*, 12(1), 55–73.

Luckin, R. (2018). *Machine learning and human intelligence: The future of education for the 21st century*. UCL Institute of Education Press.

Luckin, R., Holmes, W., Griffiths, M., & Forcier, L. B. (2016). *Intelligence unleashed: An argument for AI in education*. Pearson. https://www.pearson.com/content/dam/one-dot-com/one-dot-com/global/Files/AI-in-Education/Intelligence-Unleashed.pdf

Marzano, R. J., & Marzano, J. S. (2021). The role of formative assessment in enhancing student learning. *Educational Leadership*, 78(6), 52–56.

McLoughlin, C., & Lee, J. W. (2022). Personal learning environments, social media, and self-directed learning: A conceptual synthesis. *Journal of Online Learning and Teaching*, 8(1), 57–66.

Means, B., Toyama, Y., Murphy, R., & Bakia, M. (2020). *Evaluation of evidence-based practices in online learning: A meta-analysis and review of online learning studies*. US Department of Education.

Mishra, P., & Koehler, M. J. (2021). Technological pedagogical content knowledge: A framework for teacher knowledge. *Teachers College Record*, 108(6), 1017–1054. DOI: 10.1111/j.1467-9620.2006.00684.x

Moreno, R., & Mayer, R. (2021). Interactive multimodal learning environments: Special issue introduction. *Educational Psychologist*, 46(2), 81–85. DOI: 10.1080/00461520.2021.1895968

National Education Association. (2022). *Professional development in education: Essential practices and policies*. https://www.nea.org/sites/default/files/2022-07/Professional_Development_In_Education.pdf

Padmanabhan, S., & Kumar, A. (2021). AI in education: A review of the literature. *Education and Information Technologies*, 26(4), 4411–4431. DOI: 10.1007/s10639-021-10585-x

Perry, B., & Lentz, D. (2020). A framework for digital literacy in higher education: Implications for practice. *Journal of Academic Librarianship*, 46(5), 102136. DOI: 10.1016/j.acalib.2020.102136

Popenici, S. A. D., & Kerr, S. (2020). Exploring the impact of artificial intelligence on teaching and learning in higher education. *Research and Practice in Technology Enhanced Learning*, 15(1), 1–12. DOI: 10.1186/s41039-019-0112-0 PMID: 30595727

Ransom, L. (2020). Blended learning: Pedagogy, technology, and integration. In McCarthy, E. E., & McCarthy, J. P. (Eds.), *The changing landscape of higher education* (pp. 123–145). Routledge.

Riasati, M. J., & Ghorbani, M. (2023). Language learning in the age of AI: Opportunities and challenges. *Journal of Language and Linguistic Studies*, 19(1), 118–134. DOI: 10.17263/jlls.1000052

Roblyer, M. D., & Hughes, J. E. (2021). *Technology tools for teachers* (2nd ed.). Pearson.

Schaller, J. (2023). AI-driven approaches to education: Emerging tools and strategies. *Journal of Educational Technology*, 18(2), 45–63.

Selwyn, N. (2019). *Should robots replace teachers? AI and the future of education*. Polity Press.

Siemens, G. (2021). Connectivism: A learning theory for the digital age. *International Journal of Instructional Technology and Distance Learning*, 2(1). http://www.itdl.org/Journal/Jan_05/article01.htm

Su, C. (2023). The role of AI in enhancing student engagement in blended learning environments. *Educational Technology Research and Development*, 71(3), 327–348. DOI: 10.1007/s11423-022-10123-4

Tangen, D. (2019). Investigating the effects of blended learning on student engagement and learning outcomes in higher education. *Educational Media International*, 56(4), 241–257. DOI: 10.1080/09523987.2019.1712570

Tharp, R. G., & Gallimore, R. (2021). A theory of cultural genesis: A cultural-historical approach to education. *New Directions for Child and Adolescent Development*, 2021(172), 73–84. DOI: 10.1002/cad.20404

Tsai, Y., & Chai, C. S. (2021). The role of teachers in blended learning: Insights from a longitudinal study. *Journal of Educational Technology & Society*, 24(1), 13–27.

Wang, M., & Li, L. (2022). Exploring the role of technology in the evolution of language learning. *Language Learning & Technology*, 26(1), 3–17.

Weller, M. (2021). 25 years of Ed Tech: The future of technology-enhanced learning. *Research in Learning Technology*, 29. Advance online publication. DOI: 10.25304/rlt.v29.2440

Zawacki-Richter, O., Marz, K., & Dron, J. (2020). Systematic review of research on artificial intelligence applications in higher education: Challenges and future directions. *International Journal of Educational Technology in Higher Education*, 17(1), 1–34. DOI: 10.1186/s41239-020-00216-y

Zhang, R., & Lee, H. (2022). The impact of AI writing tools on university-level language learners: A longitudinal study. *Computers & Education*, 185, 104557. DOI: 10.1016/j.compedu.2022.104557

Chapter 18
The Assessment of Language Skills:
Tools and Methods

Ayah Oudghiri
https://orcid.org/0009-0008-8218-235X
Ecole Normale Supérieure, Abdelmalek Esaadi University, Morocco

Ahmed Ibrahimi
https://orcid.org/0009-0004-8879-5561
Ecole Normale Supérieure, Abdelmalek Essaadi University, Morocco

ABSTRACT

Language proficiency assessment is the process by which an individual's ability to communicate effectively in a given language is delineated and measured. This chapter examines the different approaches and techniques used to assess language proficiency. It explores in depth the various tools available, such as standardized tests, oral and written assessments, as well as assessment methods based on emerging technologies. According to the chapter, it is essential to select the appropriate evaluation method according to the specific objectives and the context of use. We will also discuss the challenges associated with the assessment of language skills, particularly with respect to validity, reliability and fairness. Our chapter provides an overview of the various methods and best practices in the field of language skills assessment, while highlighting the paramount importance of implementing language skills assessment tools and methods that are appropriate to the objectives defined at the beginning of the training, effective and valid.

INTRODUCTION

The measurement of language skills plays a vital role in the teaching/learning of foreign languages, being an essential step in assessing the level of proficiency in a language and assessing learners' progress. It is also a crucial way to validate language skills in different contexts, whether professional, academic or personal. The aim of this chapter is to present an in-depth analysis of the various tools and methods

DOI: 10.4018/979-8-3693-8965-2.ch018

available in this field, highlighting both the well-established traditional methods and the new emerging trends that influence the assessment of language skills today.

For some time now, standardized tests have been one of the most frequently used ways to assess language skills. Written or oral tests are often implemented to assess in a uniform and objective way, encompassing different aspects of the language, such as grammar, vocabulary, reading and listening comprehension, as well as written and oral production. The effectiveness of these tests has been demonstrated in multiple assessment situations, providing a fairly reliable and valid measure of language skills. However, while they offer advantages, standardized tests can also have significant limitations, particularly with regard to their validity and relevance in certain contexts of language learning and use. They can also be criticized for their lack of flexibility and inability to fully grasp the complexity of language skills.

Another method frequently used to assess language skills is oral assessment, which focuses on learners' communication and speaking skills. These assessments can often take place in the form of structured interviews, oral presentations or group interactions, in order to assess the pronunciation, fluency, grammatical accuracy and active vocabulary of the courses. While oral assessments can be used to assess language proficiency in a more direct and authentic way, they can also be unintentional due to the subjectivity of the assessor and the difficulty of standardising assessment criteria.

Similarly, written assessments are frequently used to assess learners' reading comprehension and production. Understanding of grammatical structures, passive vocabulary, writing ability and coherence of written speech are assessed through different forms of assessment, such as multiple-choice questionnaires, short answers, essays or text reports. Although written assessments can accurately assess language skills in certain areas, they can also pose challenges in terms of standardisation and reliability of assessment criteria.

However, apart from these traditional approaches, new approaches to the assessment of language skills are developing, offering innovative and often more flexible options. For example, learners can group together examples of their language work over time, allowing them to have a holistic view of their skills. In the same way, project-based assessment encourages students to complete concrete language projects, such as presentations, multimedia productions or simulations of real situations, in order to prove their language proficiency in authentic environments.

At the same time, the rise of digital technologies offers new opportunities in the field of language skills assessment. Technological tools, such as speech analysis software, e-learning platforms and automated assessment systems, offer a faster, more accurate and often more tailored assessment of language skills. In addition, these tools allow for the collection of information on learners' performance at scale, which can be beneficial for researchers and professionals in creating new methods of evaluating and adapting curricula.

By analyzing these various approaches, we can deepen our understanding of their benefits and challenges, as well as their adaptability to specific goals and contexts of use. This exploration will also offer us the opportunity to grasp the new perspectives offered by new trends, which will allow us to continuously assess language competences in language teaching/learning.

I- CONCEPTUAL FRAMEWORK

Language Skills: CEFR, Communicative and Linguistic Perspectives

Language skills are a set of essential skills in language learning. They are defined as the skills to understand, produce and interact in a target language, and are now largely structured by the Common European Framework of Reference for Languages (CEFR). It proposes a common model of skills assessment, organised around understanding, production, interaction and mediation, with the aim of describing and standardising levels of proficiency (Council of Europe, 2001).

The Communicative Perspective

The communicative perspective focuses on language as a social tool, used in real communication situations (Canale and Swain, 1980; Hymes, 1972). Rather than aiming for absolute mastery of linguistic rules, this approach values the learner's ability to interact, convey messages, negotiate meanings and establish social connections. Thus, pragmatic competence allows the learner to adapt to various contexts, to adjust his or her language according to cultural and social norms (Byram, 1997).

Interactional competence, on the other hand, is essential for managing natural interacting exchanges, whether to participate, react or reformulate if necessary (Brown, 2004).

For teachers and evaluators, this communicative approach consists of assessing not only grammatical accuracy, but above all the fluency and effectiveness of communication, with a view to meaningful interaction (Little, 2006).

The Linguistic Perspective

At the same time, the linguistic perspective is based on the formal aspects of the language, such as phonology, grammar and lexicon, which the CEFR refers to as "sub-competences" (Council of Europe, 2001). These elements structure the speech in a way that ensures clarity and precision. Grammatical competence, for example, makes it possible to manipulate syntactic structures, a fundamental element for the construction of correct and coherent sentences (Ellis, 2003). Lexical competence concerns the richness and precision of vocabulary, which are crucial for expressing various ideas (Nation, 2001). Finally, phonological competence ensures clear pronunciation, prosody, and intonation, thus facilitating mutual understanding (Celce-Murcia, Brinton, & Goodwin, 1996).

These two perspectives are, in fact, complementary and respond to a holistic vision of language skills. According to Fulcher and Davidson (2007), a balanced assessment must recognise the learner's ability to combine his or her linguistic and communicative skills to produce a speech that is relevant and adapted to his or her context of use. With this in mind, the CEFR promotes the integration of these dimensions in the assessment of language competences, through level descriptors that encompass global competences and their specific sub-components (Council of Europe, 2001).

In sum, an assessment that takes into account both the communicative and linguistic dimensions of language skills allows for a more nuanced and comprehensive assessment of the learner's progress, recognising not only their ability to master the rules of the language, but also to interact effectively and appropriately in a variety of contexts (Little, 2006; Brown, 2004).

Types of Assessment: Distinctions and Complementarities

Assessment in an educational context plays a fundamental role in supporting and measuring learners' progress. In language didactics, there are generally three types of assessment: formative, summative and diagnostic, each with specific objectives and functions (Scriven, 1967; Black & Wiliam, 1998).

Formative Assessment

Formative assessment is a process of continuous assessment that aims to support learning by providing regular feedback to learners on their progress. It helps to identify strengths and areas for improvement, thus promoting adaptive and progressive learning. It is characterized by its interactive and dynamic character, with the teacher and the learner working together to adjust learning methods and objectives (Black & Wiliam, 1998). For example, in the language classroom, collective correction activities or targeted feedback can help learners understand and correct their mistakes. For Sadler (1989), formative assessment is essential for creating deep learning, by encouraging learners to self-assess and set goals.

Summative Evaluation

Summative assessment generally takes place at the end of a learning unit or programme and aims to measure the level of mastery achieved by learners. Unlike formative assessment, its main objective is to report on the final learning outcomes and to check whether the pedagogical objectives have been achieved. This type of assessment often takes the form of graded tests or examinations, which allow a score or score to be assigned (Harlen & James, 1997). In language didactics, it is particularly used to certify language skills through standardized exams such as the TOEFL or the DELF. Summative assessment, by providing an accurate and comparable measure of competences, plays a key role in the formal recognition of prior learning, although it is sometimes criticised for being more static, which does not always reflect the learner's development (Boud & Falchikov, 2006).

Diagnostic Evaluation

Diagnostic assessment is used upstream of learning to determine learners' initial level, identify their prior knowledge, and identify potential difficulties. It thus makes it possible to personalize teaching according to the specific needs of each learner (Alderson, 2005). In a language learning context, a diagnostic assessment can be a placement test to identify a learner's level of proficiency before starting a training program. Brown (2004) emphasizes that this evaluation plays a crucial role in guiding pedagogical choices, by ensuring that the activities proposed are adapted to the level of competence of each individual. It also helps to identify specific gaps that could hinder future learning.

Synthesis and Complementarity of Types of Assessment

These three types of assessment are complementary and meet different needs in the learning process. Formative assessment promotes the continuous development and adjustment of pedagogical practices; summative assessment ensures formal and standardised validation of prior learning; while diagnostic assessment makes it possible to make an initial diagnosis to optimize the learning path (Harlen, 2007).

From a global perspective, these approaches, depending on their use, make assessment more inclusive, adapted to the profiles and objectives of each learner.

Principles of Assessment in Language Didactics

In language didactics, assessment is based on fundamental principles that guarantee its quality and relevance. These principles include validity, fidelity, fairness, impact, and practicability (Bachman & Palmer, 1996; Weir, 2005). These criteria are essential for designing assessments that accurately and meaningfully reflect learners' competences in a linguistic context.

Validity

Validity is the main criterion of any evaluation and refers to its ability to measure precisely what it is supposed to evaluate (Messick, 1989). In language didactics, this implies that assessment tasks must reflect the language skills that one wishes to observe, such as listening comprehension, written expression or interaction. For example, a listening comprehension test should offer tasks that simulate authentic communication situations (Weir, 2005). Validity is divided into several subcategories, including content validity, which assesses the extent to which the tasks cover the targeted skills, and construct validity, which examines whether the test represents the theoretical field studied (Bachman, 1990).

Fidelity

Reliability, or reliability, measures the consistency of an evaluation's results. A test is reliable if it produces stable and reproducible results for the same learner under similar conditions (Brown, 2005). In language didactics, fidelity is crucial to ensure that results accurately reflect the learner's level of proficiency and are not influenced by external factors, such as rater bias or variations in the testing environment (Alderson, Clapham & Wall, 1995). One way to ensure this reliability is through the use of standardized assessment protocols and rigorous scoring grids to minimize subjective variation (Brown & Abeywickrama, 2010).

Equity

Equity in assessment aims to provide equal opportunities for success for all learners, regardless of their cultural background, linguistic profile or socio-economic background (Kunnan, 2004). In practice, a fair assessment implies taking into account individual diversities and reducing cultural biases in test content. For example, a reading test that is based on specific cultural references could disadvantage certain groups of learners (McNamara & Roever, 2006). Equity is essential to promote inclusive assessment, allowing every learner to fully demonstrate their competence.

Impact

The impact of an evaluation is its effects on learners, teachers and the education system as a whole (Wall, 1997). In language didactics, an assessment can motivate learners, guide pedagogical choices and even influence language policies. However, the impact can also be negative if an assessment leads to stress, promotes "test-based" learning approaches, or creates disparities among learners (Shohamy, 2001). It is therefore crucial to design assessments that encourage deep and meaningful learning, contributing positively to the overall educational experience (Alderson & Wall, 1993).

Feasibility

Feasibility refers to the feasibility of implementing an evaluation, taking into account the resources available (Bachman & Palmer, 1996). It involves ensuring that the test is feasible within the constraints of time, cost, personnel and technical equipment. For example, an assessment that requires sophisticated technologies can be difficult to implement in resource-constrained settings. Practicability is thus a key principle for designing accessible and sustainable assessments, especially in a globalized context where resources vary considerably from one educational context to another (Fulcher, 2010).

These principles — validity, fidelity, fairness, impact and practicability — are essential foundations for a fair and effective assessment of language skills. Complying with these criteria helps to ensure that the assessment accurately reflects the learners' competences, while being adapted to the contexts and objectives of language teaching. Language didactics assessment designers must therefore balance these principles to offer robust, accessible and beneficial assessments for learning.

Evaluation Models: CEFR and Other Relevant Models

Assessment models in language teaching play a central role in structuring and standardising the assessment of language competences. Among them, the Common European Framework of Reference for Languages (CEFR) occupies a major place. Other complementary models, such as the *American Council on the Teaching of Foreign Languages' (ACTFL)* Proficiency Guidelines and the *Canadian Language Benchmarks* (CLB), also provide enriching perspectives on the assessment of language proficiency, addressing varied needs in distinct cultural and educational contexts.

The Common European Framework of Reference for Languages (CEFR)

The CEFR, established by the Council of Europe (2001), is a widely used reference model for the teaching, learning and assessment of language competences in Europe and beyond. It defines six levels of competence (A1 to C2), each describing learners' specific abilities in comprehension, production, interaction and mediation. This model is based on an action-oriented approach, where the language user is perceived as a "social actor" capable of performing communicative tasks in real contexts.

The CEFR provides detailed descriptors for each language competence, providing teachers and assessors with a common basis for measuring language competence. By adopting a descriptor-based approach, it allows for a consistent and standardized assessment of language levels, thereby promoting mobility and recognition of qualifications internationally (North, 2007).

The *ACTFL* Proficiency Guidelines

The *American* Council on the Teaching of Foreign Languages' (ACTFL) Proficiency Guidelines are another model for assessing language proficiency that is widely used in North America (ACTFL, 2012). This model offers a scale of levels that goes from "Novice" to "Distinguished", and covers four main skills: listening, speaking, reading and writing. Unlike the CEFR, which focuses more on the tasks that the learner can accomplish, the ACTFL emphasizes the level of language proficiency and the learner's fluency in various communication situations. This model is particularly recognized for its detailed approach to oral competence, including precise criteria for assessing the fluency, precision and complexity of the language used.

The ACTFL provides flexibility to tailor assessments to learners' educational and professional needs, with a focus on the ability to interact in specific cultural situations. This model is thus useful for a targeted assessment that takes into account communicative skills in relation to the cultural contexts of learners (Swender, Conrad, & Vicars, 2012).

Canadian Language Benchmarks (CLB)

The *Canadian Language Benchmarks* (CLB) are a Canadian model designed to assess the skills of English and French learners in immigration and vocational training contexts (Pawlikowska-Smith, 2000). The CLB defines twelve levels of proficiency divided into three main categories: beginner, intermediate and advanced. This model is distinguished by its design oriented towards social and professional integration, with an emphasis on specific tasks that facilitate learners' adaptation to Canadian cultural and professional environments.

The CLB incorporates detailed descriptors to assess communicative skills, while taking into account the needs of the immigrant population. It promotes the acquisition of the language skills necessary to succeed in a multicultural and multilingual context, thus allowing for an assessment that takes into account local socio-cultural realities (Pawlikowska-Smith, 2000). This model is particularly relevant in contexts where learners need to quickly acquire skills to integrate into professional life.

Synthesis and Complementarity of Models

Although the CEFR, the *ACTFL Proficiency Guidelines* and the CLBs have different purposes and contexts of use, these models share a common objective: to provide reliable and adaptable frameworks for the assessment of language skills. The CEFR, as a reference model in Europe, offers a standardised and internationally recognised grid. In North America, the ACTFL *Proficiency Guidelines* and the CLBs meet specific assessment needs, respectively in academic and socio-professional integration contexts.

The choices between these models depend on the learning contexts and the learners' goals. In a globalized context, the integration of these different frameworks can enrich assessment practices, allowing teachers and evaluators to adapt their tools to the varied profiles and needs of learners (McNamara & Roever, 2006). This complementarity contributes to a more flexible and inclusive approach to assessment in language didactics.

II- METHODS FOR ASSESSING LANGUAGE SKILLS

In the assessment of language competence, various methods are used to obtain reliable and representative measures of learners' abilities. These methods can be classified into three main categories: direct methods, indirect methods, and alternative methods. Each of these approaches has advantages and limitations, and their choice depends on the pedagogical objectives as well as the evaluation context (Bachman & Palmer, 1996; Weir, 2005).

Direct Methods

Direct methods, such as interviews and tests of written or oral production, consist of directly observing the language competence of a learner in a production situation. These methods allow for authentic assessment because they solicit the real communicative skills of the learners.

1. **Description and characteristics**: Direct methods include oral interviews, written examinations (essays, reports) and oral presentations. For example, an interview assesses the learner's ability to interact in real time, thus mobilizing skills such as fluency, grammatical correctness and discursive coherence (Luoma, 2004). Similarly, written production makes it possible to assess skills in idea structuring, lexical precision and syntax mastery (Weigle, 2002).
2. **Advantages and limitations**: One of the main advantages of these methods is their ability to provide an accurate picture of communicative skills, as they allow for the reproduction of authentic communication situations (Bachman, 1990). However, these methods are demanding in terms of time and resources, especially for oral assessment which requires trained examiners and clear scoring criteria to minimize subjectivity. In addition, direct assessments can sometimes introduce biases, particularly related to learner anxiety or evaluator expectations, thus influencing the results (Brown & Abeywickrama, 2010).
3. **Examples of tools**: Tests of oral production, such as the *Test of English as a Foreign Language (TOEFL) Speaking Section* or the *Cambridge English Speaking Test*, are commonly used tools to assess oral proficiency in a standardized way. For written production, exams such as the IELTS Writing Test require learners to produce argumentative or descriptive texts within a limited time, which assesses their ability to organise and express their ideas under constraint (Weigle, 2002).

Indirect Methods

Indirect methods are based on assessments that measure language skills through activities that do not require direct production, such as listening and reading comprehension tests, as well as multiple-choice questionnaires (MCQs). These methods are often used to assess specific sub-skills, such as vocabulary comprehension, grammatical structure recognition, and overall comprehension of a text.

1. **Description and characteristics**: Indirect methods include comprehension exercises, grammar or reading tests, as well as multiple choice questions. For example, a listening comprehension test measures the learner's ability to grasp the overall meaning and details of an audio text, without the need to produce an oral response. MCQs, on the other hand, make it possible to quickly assess precise linguistic knowledge through closed-ended answers, thus facilitating standardization (Alderson, 2000).
2. **Advantages and limitations**: Indirect methods are particularly valued for their ease of correction and their ability to provide comparable results between different groups of learners (Fulcher, 2010). They also allow for testing large groups in a limited time and minimize reviewer bias. However, they do not always capture the learner's full communicative competence, as they do not directly assess

language production and creativity. These methods may therefore not reflect actual communicative skills in context (Bachman & Palmer, 1996).

3. **Case studies on the use of standardized tests**: Standardized tests such as the TOEFL and the Test de Connaissance du Français (TCF) include listening and reading comprehension sections, designed to measure language skills indirectly. Although they are useful for assessing specific language skills, they are sometimes criticized for their lack of authenticity and their inability to reproduce real-life communication situations (McNamara, 2000).

Alternative Methods

Alternative methods, such as project-based evaluation, portfolios and self-evaluation, allow for a diversification of evaluation approaches with a focus on reflection, autonomy and long-term learning.

1. **Description and characteristics**: Project-based assessment involves asking learners to complete a communicative task, such as a presentation or group work, which allows them to demonstrate their competence in an applied context. Portfolios, on the other hand, are collections of work selected by the learner, illustrating their journey and progress over time (Genesee & Upshur, 1996). Self-assessment invites the learner to assess his or her own skills and progress, encouraging awareness and autonomy in language learning (Oscarson, 1989).
2. **Advantages and** limitations: Alternative methods promote deeper learning and engage learners in a reflection on their progress. They also help to better capture the diversity of learners' skills, especially in situations where creativity and adaptation are important (Little, 2005). However, these methods require teachers trained in the design and correction of this type of assessment, as well as a clear structuring to ensure the reliability and comparability of the results. Self-assessment, in particular, can pose challenges to objectivity, as learners may over- or underestimate their skills (Blanche & Merino, 1989).
3. **Comparison with traditional methods**: Compared to more traditional methods (direct and indirect), alternative methods offer a more holistic approach to assessment, taking into account language skills in a variety of contexts and promoting lifelong learning. While traditional methods tend to assess specific skills on an ad hoc basis, alternative methods make it possible to observe the evolution of skills and to support the learner's motivation by actively involving him or her in his or her own learning (Rea-Dickins & Gardner, 2000).

Methods for assessing language proficiency, whether direct, indirect or alternative, each offer unique perspectives for measuring language competence. Direct methods allow for an authentic assessment of communicative skills, while indirect methods facilitate a quick and standardized assessment of specific knowledge. Alternative methods, on the other hand, encourage more personal and reflective learning, supporting learners' autonomy and motivation. By combining these approaches, teachers can gain a more comprehensive view of learners' language skills and tailor their teaching to meet the diverse needs of their classrooms.

III- TOOLS FOR THE ASSESSMENT OF LANGUAGE SKILLS

The variety of tools used to assess language skills has expanded with technological advances, offering solutions that are increasingly adapted to the current needs of learners and teachers. This section explores the different types of tools available, their advantages, limitations, as well as the challenges and opportunities associated with the evolution of these tools in the field of language didactics.

Digital Tools

Digital tools have considerably transformed the assessment of language skills, allowing for faster, accessible and often more interactive assessments. They include online testing platforms, mobile apps, as well as built-in artificial intelligence (AI) systems for personalized and adaptive assessment.

1. **Online testing platforms and mobile apps**: Platforms such as the TOEFL iBT and the Duolingo English Test allow learners to take language proficiency assessments entirely online. The Duolingo English Test, in particular, uses AI algorithms to adjust the difficulty of questions based on the user's responses, providing a more personalized evaluation experience (Dettmers, 2021). Mobile apps like Babbel or Lingoda also incorporate continuous assessments to track learners' progress, offering real-time feedback and facilitating self-directed learning.
2. **Examples of specific tools and impact assessment**:
    - **TOEFL iBT**: The Test of English as a Foreign Language (TOEFL) iBT is an example of a standardized digital platform for assessing English language proficiency. This online test covers all four language skills and uses authentic questions based on real-life communication situations, allowing for a reliable and internationally recognized assessment (Educational Testing Service, 2020).
    - **Duolingo English Test**: Less expensive and more accessible than other standardized tests, the Duolingo English Test uses AI to assess skills adaptively, making it a convenient tool for candidates in remote geographic areas or with limited access to traditional testing centers (Dettmers, 2021).
3. **Impact of digital tools on assessment**: Digital tools facilitate access to assessments and can also improve the accuracy of skills measurement through the adaptation of questions. In addition, they reduce human scoring bias through automated marking systems for certain tasks, including listening and reading comprehension (Chapelle & Voss, 2016). However, their use can pose challenges in terms of equity, due to unequal access to technologies in some contexts, which can limit their universal adoption (Stickler & Hampel, 2015).

Paper-and-Pencil and Hybrid Tools

Despite the rise of digital tools, paper-and-pencil methods are still commonly used in the assessment of language skills, especially in contexts where technological infrastructure is limited. In addition, hybrid tools combining traditional and digital elements are gaining popularity, allowing for greater flexibility of use.

1. **Examples of traditional and hybrid tools**: Paper-and-pencil tests, such as the Test de Connaissance du Français (TCF), remain reliable and easy-to-use tools, offering an accessible assessment method without advanced technological requirements. Hybrid tools, on the other hand, such as online platforms for printing tests, make it possible to mix approaches by offering a paper-based assessment but with digital correction, thus improving the efficiency and accuracy of the marking.
2. **Comparison in terms of accessibility and efficiency**: Paper-and-pencil tests offer universal accessibility, especially in contexts without digital infrastructure. However, they often require manual correction, which can introduce subjective biases and human error. In comparison, digital tools are more effective in terms of automated correction, but they depend on technological infrastructure and mastery of the tools by learners and teachers, which can pose barriers in terms of accessibility (Fulcher, 2010).

IV- CHALLENGES AND OPPORTUNITIES FOR THE ASSESSMENT OF LANGUAGE SKILLS

Issues of Fairness and Reliability in a Context of Linguistic and Cultural Diversity

With globalisation and the increasing diversity of learners, the challenges related to the equity and reliability of assessments are becoming more and more important. Language tests should be designed to avoid cultural and linguistic biases that could disadvantage certain groups of learners. Research has shown that standardized tests can reflect cultural biases, especially when assessment items are designed in a monolingual and monocultural context (McNamara & Roever, 2006). It is therefore essential to adopt inclusive approaches, taking into account language variations and learners' learning contexts, to ensure fair and equitable assessment.

Perspectives on the Evolution of Methods and Tools

1. **The contribution of AI and new technologies**: The integration of artificial intelligence into assessment tools opens up new perspectives for a more dynamic and individualised assessment. AI-based correction systems, such as those used in large-scale online tests, can quickly and objectively assess complex skills, including fluency and accuracy of speaking (Chapelle & Voss, 2016). In addition, AI makes it possible to develop adaptive assessments, where questions adjust to the learner's skill level, making the assessment more relevant to each user (Dettmers, 2021).
2. **Current trends and future research**: Among current trends, the rise of distance assessments and adaptive learning platforms underscores the growing importance of technology in language assessment. Future research is likely to focus on optimizing the reliability and validity of AI tools, as well as the impact of these new methods on learners' performance and motivation (Stickler & Hampel, 2015). In addition, the development of multilingual and culturally neutral online tests is booming to meet the demands of a global audience, with research exploring how to tailor assessments to diverse learner profiles (Fulcher, 2010).

In conclusion, the diversity of assessment tools, whether digital, traditional or hybrid, makes it possible to meet a wide range of pedagogical and contextual needs. However, the challenges of equity, accessibility, and reliability underscore the importance of developing assessments that are inclusive and fair for all learners. Technological advances, in particular in the field of AI, are opening up new perspectives for the assessment of language competences, offering promising solutions for more adaptive, personalised and linguistically and culturally diverse assessments.

V- EXPERIMENTATION

Context and Objective of the Experiment

In the context of this chapter devoted to the assessment of language skills, an experiment was carried out in order to illustrate and confront some of the theoretical concepts discussed, in particular the validity, reliability and effectiveness of assessment methods. The main objective of this experiment was to compare two approaches to assessing oral skills in French as a foreign language: a direct method, consisting of a face-to-face oral interview, and an indirect method, based on a listening comprehension test in the form of a multiple-choice questionnaire (MCQ).

The experiment aimed to answer several key questions:

- Which method makes it possible to assess learners' oral competence more accurately?
- What are the advantages and limitations of these approaches in a real language teaching context?
- How can these findings contribute to improving evaluation practices?

Methodology

Target population

The experiment was carried out with a group of 50 learners of French as a foreign language (FLE), from different cultural and linguistic contexts. The participants, enrolled in a B1 level university programme (according to the Common European Framework of Reference for Languages - CEFR), were aged between 18 and 35 and represented a diversity of learning paths.

Instruments Used

Direct method: A face-to-face oral interview, structured around communicative tasks, such as introducing oneself, describing a personal experience and reacting to a given situation.

Indirect method: A listening comprehension test in the form of multiple choice questions based on audio excerpts. The questions focused on linguistic elements such as vocabulary comprehension, idiomatic expressions, and communicative intentions.

Event

1. Participants were randomly divided into two groups. The first group was assessed using the direct method, while the second group took the indirect test.
2. Each oral interview was recorded and evaluated by two independent reviewers to ensure the reliability of the results.
3. The indirect tests were administered on a digital platform allowing automatic and standardized correction.
4. Data were collected in the form of scores for each method and accompanied by qualitative feedback from the reviewers.

Criteria for Analysis

- **Validity**: To what extent does each method actually assess oral competence?
- **Reliability**: Consistency of results between evaluators and between participants.
- **Practicability**: Time required to administer and correct assessments.
- **Learners' perception**: Feedback from participants on their experience with both methods.

Results and Analysis

The results revealed significant differences between the two approaches:

- **Direct method**: The scores obtained showed greater accuracy in assessing fluency, interaction and pronunciation. However, this method proved to be more time-consuming and dependent on the training of examiners.
- **Indirect method**: The MCQ tests allowed for rapid and standardized correction, but the results mainly reflected auditory recognition skills, without directly assessing the learners' ability to produce oral speech.

Feedback from learners also highlighted a preference for the direct method, which was perceived as more engaging and relevant, despite its potentially stressful nature.

Discussion of the Results

The results obtained confirm the interest of direct methods for assessing complex language skills such as interaction and oral production, in accordance with the recommendations of the CEFR (Council of Europe, 2001). However, they also highlight the challenges related to their implementation, particularly in terms of time and training of evaluators.

Conversely, indirect methods, although less logistically demanding, do not allow for a comprehensive assessment of communicative skills. These results corroborate the observations of Fulcher (2010), who points out that indirect tests, although effective in assessing specific skills, cannot replace more holistic approaches.

These results also show the importance of combining different methods in a plural approach, in order to meet the varied needs of learners and assessment contexts.

Conclusion of the Experiment

This experiment highlights the strengths and limitations of the two evaluative approaches. While the direct method stands out for its ability to provide a more comprehensive and authentic assessment of oral skills, the indirect method offers a faster and standardized solution, suitable for resource-limited settings.

These findings call for an in-depth reflection on the balance between practicability and accuracy in the design of assessment tools. They also reinforce the need for training of evaluators to ensure a fair and reliable evaluation.

In perspective, a hybridization of approaches, integrating both elements of direct and indirect methods, could constitute a promising way to meet the current challenges of the assessment of language skills.

CONCLUSION

The assessment of language skills represents a rich and diversified field of investigation, where the methods and tools used must meet a multiplicity of pedagogical and contextual objectives. Throughout this book, we have explored the different approaches to evaluation, whether traditional, digital or hybrid, detailing their respective advantages and limitations. Each method, whether direct assessments such as oral and written productions, or indirect approaches such as comprehension tests, is useful according to the specific learning contexts, the objectives and the resources available to teachers and learners.

One of the major challenges in the assessment of language skills is the need to adopt an approach that is both appropriate and equitable. Technological advances, including the emergence of digital tools and artificial intelligence (AI), offer opportunities to adapt to the individual needs of learners and pave the way for more personalised assessments. Online tests like the *Duolingo English Test* and the *TOEFL iBT*, for example, are increasingly being used as part of standardized assessments, allowing for real-time adjustments and performance tracking based on the learner's responses (Dettmers, 2021). However, this technological development, while offering undeniable advantages in terms of flexibility and speed, also raises questions about accessibility and equity, particularly with regard to equal access to technology in different regions of the world (Stickler & Hampel, 2015).

Despite technological advances, the assessment of language skills should not be limited to a purely technical dimension. It remains crucial to ensure that assessments are also reliable and valid, and that they are designed in a way that avoids any cultural or linguistic bias that could affect the accuracy of the results. For example, tests such as the *TOEFL* are often criticized for focusing on an Anglo-American linguistic and cultural model, which can disadvantage non-native English learners (McNamara & Roever, 2006). In this context, it is essential to put in place mechanisms that ensure that assessments take into account the linguistic and cultural diversity of learners and do not favour a single language model (Fulcher, 2010).

One of the interesting prospects for the future of language skills assessment lies in the continuous evolution of digital tools and artificial intelligence. These technologies, used in adaptive tests, make it possible to modulate the difficulty of the tests according to the learner's skills, and thus offer a finer and more accurate assessment. Current research tends to demonstrate that these technologies can improve the assessment experience by making tests more interactive and providing instant feedback, which can boost learner motivation and engagement (Chapelle & Voss, 2016). However, these advances must be accompanied by critical reflections on their implementation, particularly with regard to the ethical challenges associated with the collection and use of learners' personal data in AI systems.

In the near future, the assessment of language skills may see the emergence of more inclusive methods, combining traditional tests, digital platforms and alternative tools such as portfolios and self-assessment, in order to better take into account the different learning contexts and specificities of learners (Bachman & Palmer, 1996). These alternative tools could complement standardised assessments by offering more varied perspectives on language proficiency and encouraging learners' autonomy in their assessment process.

Thus, the assessment of language skills, while being a complex and multidimensional process, must evolve in a direction that incorporates both technological innovation and the fundamental principles of justice and inclusiveness. The development of diverse assessment tools, adapted to the needs of learners and respectful of their diversity, will contribute to making assessment more effective and relevant, while providing every learner with fair opportunities to progress and succeed in their language learning.

REFERENCES

ACTFL. (2012). *ACTFL Proficiency Guidelines 2012*. American Council on the Teaching of Foreign Languages.

Alderson, J. C. (2000). *Assessing Reading*. Cambridge University Press. DOI: 10.1017/CBO9780511732935

Alderson, J. C. (2005). Diagnosing Foreign Language Proficiency: The Interface Between Learning and Assessment. *Continuum*.

Alderson, J. C., Clapham, C., & Wall, D. (1995). *Language Test Construction and Evaluation*. Cambridge University Press.

Alderson, J. C., & Wall, D. (1993). Does Washback Exist? *Applied Linguistics*, 14(2), 115–129. DOI: 10.1093/applin/14.2.115

Bachman, L. F. (1990). *Fundamental Considerations in Language Testing*. Oxford University Press.

Bachman, L. F., & Palmer, A. S. (1996). *Language Testing in Practice: Designing and Developing Useful Language Tests*. Oxford University Press.

Black, P., & Wiliam, D. (1998). Assessment and Classroom Learning. *Assessment in Education: Principles, Policy & Practice*, 5(1), 7–74. DOI: 10.1080/0969595980050102

Blanche, P., & Merino, B. (1989). Self-Assessment of Foreign-Language Skills: Implications for Teachers and Researchers. *Language Learning*, 39(3), 313–338. DOI: 10.1111/j.1467-1770.1989.tb00595.x

Boud, D., & Falchikov, N. (2006). Aligning Assessment with Long-Term Learning. *Assessment & Evaluation in Higher Education*, 31(4), 399–413. DOI: 10.1080/02602930600679050

Brown, H. D. (2004). *Language Assessment: Principles and Classroom Practices*. Pearson Education.

Brown, H. D., & Abeywickrama, P. (2010). *Language Assessment: Principles and Classroom Practices* (2nd ed.). Pearson Education.

Byram, M. (1997). *Teaching and Assessing Intercultural Communicative Competence*. Multilingual Matters.

Canale, M., & Swain, M. (1980). Theoretical Bases of Communicative Approaches to Second Language Teaching and Testing. *Applied Linguistics*, 1(1), 1–47. DOI: 10.1093/applin/1.1.1

Celce-Murcia, M., Brinton, D. M., & Goodwin, J. M. (1996). *Teaching Pronunciation: A Reference for Teachers of English to Speakers of Other Languages*. Cambridge University Press.

Chapelle, C. A., & Chung, Y. R. (2010). The promise of NLP and speech processing technologies in language assessment. *Language Testing*, 27(3), 301–315. DOI: 10.1177/0265532210364405

Chapelle, C. A., & Douglas, D. (2006). *Assessing language through computer technology*. Cambridge University Press. DOI: 10.1017/CBO9780511733116

Chapelle, C. A., & Voss, E. (2016). The Role of Technology in Language Assessment. *Annual Review of Applied Linguistics*, 36, 146–163.

Chapelle, C. A., & Voss, E. (2016). 20 years of technology and language assessment in Language Learning & Technology. *Language Learning & Technology*, 20(2), 116–128.

Cizek, G. J. (2012). Defining and distinguishing validity: Interpretations of score meaning and justifications of test use. *Psychological Methods*, 17(1), 31–43. DOI: 10.1037/a0026975 PMID: 22268761

Council of Europe. (2001). *Common European Framework of Reference for Languages: Learning, Teaching, Assessment.* Didier.

Dettmers, J. (2021). *Duolingo English Test: How AI is Changing the Way We Test Language.* Duolingo.

Educational Testing Service. (2020). *TOEFL iBT: Test and Score Data Summary 2019.* ETS.

Ellis, R. (2003). *Task-Based Language Learning and Teaching.* Oxford University Press.

Fouly, K. A., Bachman, L. F., & Cziko, G. A. (1990). The divisibility of language competence: A confirmatory approach. *Language Learning*, 40(1), 1–21. DOI: 10.1111/j.1467-1770.1990.tb00952.x

Fulcher, G. (2010). *Practical Language Testing.* Hodder Education.

Fulcher, G., & Davidson, F. (2007). *Language Testing and Assessment: An Advanced Resource Book.* Routledge.

Genesee, F., & Upshur, J. A. (1996). *Classroom-Based Evaluation in Second Language Education.* Cambridge University Press.

Harlen, W. (2007). *Assessment of Learning.* SAGE Publications. DOI: 10.4135/9781446214695

Harlen, W., & James, M. (1997). Assessment and Learning: Differences and Relationships between Formative and Summative Assessment. *Assessment in Education: Principles, Policy & Practice*, 4(3), 365–379. DOI: 10.1080/0969594970040304

Hymes, D. H. (1972). On communicative competence. In *Sociolinguistics: Selected Readings.* Penguin Books.

International Language Testing Association. (2007). ILTA guidelines for practice.

Isbell, D. R., & Kremmel, B. (2020). Test review: Current options in at-home language proficiency tests for making high-stakes decisions. *Language Testing*, 37(4), 600–619. DOI: 10.1177/0265532220943483

Kunnan, A. J. (2004). Test Fairness. In Milanovic, M., & Weir, C. J. (Eds.), *European Language Testing in a Global Context.* Cambridge University Press.

Laurier, M. (1992). The Application of Adaptive Testing Techniques in French as a Second Language. In Sauvé, L. (Ed.), *Educational Technology from Yesterday to Tomorrow* (pp. 109–118). CIPTE/Tele-University.

Laurier, M. (1999). The development of an adaptive test for placement in French. In Chalhoub-Deville, M. (Ed.), *Issues in computer-adaptive testing of reading proficiency* (pp. 122–135). Cambridge University Press.

Laurier, M., & Baker, B. (2015). The certification of teachers' language competence in Quebec in French and English: Two different perspectives? *Language Assessment Quarterly*, 12(1), 10–28. DOI: 10.1080/15434303.2014.979349

Little, D. (2006). The Common European Framework of Reference for Languages: Content, purpose, origin, reception and impact. *Language Teaching*, 39(3), 167–190. DOI: 10.1017/S0261444806003557

Loye, N. (2018). What if validation was more than a series of technical procedures? *Mesure et Évaluation en Éducation*, 41(1), 97–123. DOI: 10.7202/1055898ar

Luoma, S. (2004). *Assessing Speaking*. Cambridge University Press. DOI: 10.1017/CBO9780511733017

McNamara, T., & Roever, C. (2006). *Language Testing: The Social Dimension*. Blackwell.

Messick, S. (1989). Validity. In Linn, R. L. (Ed.), *Educational Measurement* (3rd ed., pp. 13–103). Macmillan.

Milliner, B., & Barr, B. (2020). Computer-assisted language testing and learner behavior. In Freiermuth, M., & Zarrinabadi, N. (Eds.), *Technology and the psychology of second language learners and users. New language learning and teaching environments*. Palgrave Macmillan. DOI: 10.1007/978-3-030-34212-8_5

Nation, I. S. P. (2001). *Learning Vocabulary in Another Language*. Cambridge University Press. DOI: 10.1017/CBO9781139524759

North, B. (2007). The CEFR illustrative descriptor scales. In Fox, J., Wesche, M., Bayliss, D., Cheng, L., Turner, C. E., & Doe, C. (Eds.), *Language Testing Reconsidered* (pp. 33–49). University of Ottawa Press.

Oscarson, M. (1989). Self-Assessment of Language Proficiency: Rationale and Applications. *Language Testing*, 6(1), 1–13. DOI: 10.1177/026553228900600103

Pawlikowska-Smith, G. (2000). *Canadian Language Benchmarks 2000: English as a Second Language for Adults*. Centre for Canadian Language Benchmarks.

Phakiti, A., & Isaacs, T. (2021). Classroom assessment and validity: Psychometric and edumetric approaches. *EuropeanJournal of Applied Linguistics and TEFL*, 10(1), 3–24.

Rea-Dickins, P., & Gardner, S. (2000). Snares and Silver Bullets: Disentangling the Complexities of Classroom-Based Assessment. *Language Testing*, 17(2), 215–243. DOI: 10.1177/026553220001700206

Sadler, D. R. (1989). Formative Assessment and the Design of Instructional Systems. *Instructional Science*, 18(2), 119–144. DOI: 10.1007/BF00117714

. Scallon, G. (2000). Formative evaluation. Editions of the Pedagogical Renewal.

Scriven, M. (1967). The Methodology of Evaluation. In *Perspectives of Curriculum Evaluation*. Rand McNally.

Shohamy, E. (2001). *The Power of Tests: A Critical Perspective on the Uses of Language Tests*. Pearson Education.

Stickler, U., & Hampel, R. (2015). Transforming Language Education Through Online Collaboration: New Pedagogical Perspectives. *Journal of Computer Assisted Learning*, 31(5), 481–492.

Stufflebeam, D. L. (2001). Evaluation models. *New Directions for Evaluation*, 89(89), 7–98. DOI: 10.1002/ev.3

Stufflebeam, D. L., & Shinkfield, A. J. (2007). *Evaluation theory, models, and applications*. Jossey-Bass.

Swender, E., Conrad, D. J., & Vicars, R. (2012). *ACTFL Proficiency Guidelines 2012*. American Council on the Teaching of Foreign Languages.

The evolution of Information and Communication Technologies.: Co-construction with uses. - Scientific Figure on ResearchGate. Available from: https://www.researchgate.net/figure/Positionnement-multidimensionnel-des-usages-des-TIC_fig1_322555760 [accessed 24 Mar, 2024]

TRUMBULL. (2000). *E. and B. FARR, Grading and Reporting Student Progress in an Age of Standards*. Christopher-Gordon.

United Nations Evaluation Group. (2016). UNEG Standards for Evaluation in the Development Sector.

United Nations Evaluation Group. (2018). Evaluation Standards for Effective Planning and Management for Results.

Vial, M. (2012). *Finding your way around the evaluation models*. De Boeck.

Wall, D. (1997). Impact and Washback in Language Testing. In Clapham, C., & Corson, D. (Eds.), *The Encyclopedia of Language and Education*. Kluwer Academic Publishers. DOI: 10.1007/978-1-4020-4489-2_26

Weir, C. J. (2005). *Language Testing and Validation: An Evidence-Based Approach*. Palgrave Macmillan. DOI: 10.1057/9780230514577

Weiss, C. H. (1995). Nothing as practical as good theory: Exploring theory-based evaluation for comprehensive community initiatives for children and families. New Approaches to Evaluating Community Initiatives: Concepts, Methods, and Contexts, 65-92.

Weiss, C. H. (1998). *Evaluation: Methods for studying programs and policies*. Prentice Hall.

Conclusion

In conclusion, supporting the development of artificial intelligence (AI) skills among students is a strategic priority and an essential investment to prepare future generations for the challenges and opportunities of the 21st century. AI, as a driving force for economic, social and technological transformation, requires a rethinking of educational approaches. It is no longer just a matter of transmitting technical know-how, but of integrating ethical, critical and interdisciplinary dimensions, thus training individuals capable of understanding the complexity of this technology and its implications.

This coherent integration of AI into educational programs must be based on innovative and inclusive pedagogical approaches. Adaptive learning, which personalizes learning paths according to the needs of each student, collaborative environments, which promote the exchange and collective construction of knowledge, and hybrid platforms, which combine the advantages of face-to-face and distance learning are all avenues to explore. It is crucial to guarantee equal access to these resources and to take into account the diversity of learners' profiles and needs, in order to leave no one behind in the face of this technological revolution.

To achieve these ambitious goals, increased collaboration between the various players in the educational ecosystem is essential. Educators, on the front line, must be trained and supported in integrating AI into their teaching practices. Researchers, for their part, must continue to explore the potential of AI for education and assess its impact on learning. Finally, industries can provide their expertise and contribute to the development of relevant educational resources that are connected to the realities of the professional world. Policy makers, through their support and strategic guidance, play a crucial role in implementing educational policies that promote the development of AI skills. Building dynamic and relevant educational ecosystems, the result of this collaboration, is the key to a successful transition.

Developing AI skills is therefore not just a response to the needs of the labor market; it is a fundamental social responsibility. It is about training enlightened citizens, capable not only of using AI-based technologies, but also of designing, evaluating and regulating them in a responsible, ethical and sustainable manner. By investing in AI training, we are not only preparing students to succeed in a technologically advanced world; we are actively contributing to building a society where AI is used for the common good, respecting the fundamental principles of equity, inclusion and respect for human rights. This book, by exploring the educational, technological and ethical dimensions of AI, offers a concrete framework for reflection and action to meet this collective challenge and build a future where AI is synonymous with progress for all.

Compilation of References

Abbad, M. M. (2021). Using the UTAUT model to understand students' usage of e-learning systems in developing countries. *Education and Information Technologies*, 26(6), 7205–7224. DOI: 10.1007/s10639-021-10573-5 PMID: 34025204

Abd-Alrazaq, A., Abuelezz, I., Hassan, A., AlSammarraie, A., Alhuwail, D., Irshaidat, S., Abu Serhan, H., Ahmed, A., Alabed Alrazak, S., & Househ, M. (2022). Artificial Intelligence–Driven Serious Games in Health Care: Scoping Review. *JMIR Serious Games*, 10(4), e39840. DOI: 10.2196/39840 PMID: 36445731

Abd-Alrazaq, A., Al-Jafar, E., Alajlani, M., Toro, C., Alhuwail, D., Ahmed, A., Reagu, S. M., Al-Shorbaji, N., & Househ, M. (2022). The effectiveness of serious games for alleviating depression: Systematic review and meta-analysis. *JMIR Serious Games*, 10(1), e32331. DOI: 10.2196/32331 PMID: 35029530

Academies24. (2023). *Blended learning: The modern approach to education*. https://academies24.com/blended-learning-benefits-and-challenges/

Acemoglu, D., & Restrepo, P. (2020). Robots and jobs: Evidence from US labor markets. *Journal of Political Economy*, 128(6), 2188–2244. DOI: 10.1086/705716

ACTFL. (2012). *ACTFL Proficiency Guidelines 2012*. American Council on the Teaching of Foreign Languages.

Adams, C., Pente, P., Lemermeyer, G., & Rockwell, G. (2023). Ethical principles for artificial intelligence in K-12 education. *Computers and Education: Artificial Intelligence*, 4, 100131. DOI: 10.1016/j.caeai.2023.100131

Adams, R., & White, S. (2021). Understanding learner diversity in educational technology. *Educational Research Review*, 12(4), 299–315.

Adda, S. (2008). Vers une adaptabilité des parcours d'apprentissage par l'analyse des interactions. *Mémoire de Magister Option : Informatique Industrielle, II.*

Afolabi, A. (2024). Ethical Issues in Artificial Intelligence Adoption in African Higher Education Institutions in Nigeria. *African Journal of Information and Knowledge Management*, 3(2), 22–33. DOI: 10.47604/ajikm.2735

African Observatory for Responsible AI (AORAI). (2023). AORAI Policy Map. https://policy.africanobservatory.ai/

Agarwal, B., Urlings, C., van Lankveld, G., & Klemke, R. (2022, September). Ethical FRAPPE–an adapted draft framework for ethical AIED. *Proceedings of the Doctoral Consortium of the 17th European Conference on Technology Enhanced Learning* (pp. 46-54). Toulouse, France: CEUR-WS.org. Retrieved from https://ceur-ws.org/Vol-3292/DCECTEL2022_paper06.pdf

Aher, S. B., & Lobo, L. M. R. J. (2012). Best combination of machine learning algorithms for course recommendation system in e-learning. *International Journal of Computer Applications*, 41(6), 1–10.

Aher, S. B., & Lobo, L. M. R. J. (2013). Combination of machine learning algorithms for recommendation of courses in E-Learning System based on historical data. *Knowledge-Based Systems*, 51, 1–14. DOI: 10.1016/j.knosys.2013.04.015

Ahmad, S., Umirzakova, S., Jamil, F., & Whangbo, T. K. (2022). Internet-of-things-enabled serious games: A comprehensive survey. *Future Generation Computer Systems*, 136, 67–83. DOI: 10.1016/j.future.2022.05.026

Akgun, S., & Greenhow, C. (2022). Artificial intelligence in education: Addressing ethical challenges in K-12 settings. *AI and Ethics*, 2(3), 431–440. DOI: 10.1007/s43681-021-00096-7 PMID: 34790956

Al-Adwan, A. S., Li, N., Al-Adwan, A., Abbasi, G. A., Albelbisi, N. A., & Habibi, A. (2023). Extending the technology acceptance model (TAM) to Predict University Students' intentions to use metaverse-based learning platforms. *Education and Information Technologies*, 28(11), 15381–15413. DOI: 10.1007/s10639-023-11816-3 PMID: 37361794

Alakrash, H. M., & Abdul Razak, N. (2021). Technology-based language learning: Investigation of digital technology and digital literacy. *Sustainability (Basel)*, 13(21), 12304. DOI: 10.3390/su132112304

Alderson, J. C. (2000). *Assessing Reading*. Cambridge University Press. DOI: 10.1017/CBO9780511732935

Alderson, J. C. (2005). Diagnosing Foreign Language Proficiency: The Interface Between Learning and Assessment. *Continuum.*

Alderson, J. C., Clapham, C., & Wall, D. (1995). *Language Test Construction and Evaluation*. Cambridge University Press.

Alderson, J. C., & Wall, D. (1993). Does Washback Exist? *Applied Linguistics*, 14(2), 115–129. DOI: 10.1093/applin/14.2.115

Aleven, V., McLaughlin, E. A., Glenn, R. A., & Koedinger, K. R. (2016). Instruction based on adaptive learning technologies. In *Handbook of research on learning and instruction* (pp. 522-560).

Alhumaid, K., Naqbi, S., Elsori, D., & Mansoori, M. (2023). The adoption of artificial intelligence applications in education. *International Journal of Data and Network Science*, 7(1), 457–466. DOI: 10.5267/j.ijdns.2022.8.013

Allahverdiyev, A. (2023). *COMPARATIVE ANALYSIS OF FRENCH LANGUAGE TEACHING METHODS IN HIGHER EDUCATION.* Norwegian Journal of development of the International Science No, 120, 103.Archer, A. L., &

Allouche, E. (2024). Artificial intelligence and Education (Doctoral dissertation, Ministère de l'éducation nationale).

Almås, H., & Giæver, F. (2024). The emergence of collaboration in serious games: An exploratory study. *International Journal of Serious Games*, 11(3), 89–108. DOI: 10.17083/ijsg.v11i3.739

Andrus, M. R., & Roth, M. (2002). Health literacy: A review. *Pharmacotherapy*, 22(3), 282–302. DOI: 10.1592/phco.22.5.282.33191 PMID: 11898888

Angula, N. A. (2019). Education for all: the Namibian experience. In *Democratic Teacher Education Reforms In Namibia* (pp. 8–28). Routledge. DOI: 10.4324/9780429045707-2

Angwin, J., Larson, J., Mattu, S., & Kirchner, L. (2016). Machine bias. ProPublica. Retrieved from https://www.propublica.org/article/machine bias risk assessments in criminal sentencing

Anne, A., & Bahlouli, Y. E. (2023). Distributed ledger technology (DLT): Uses and prospects in the education sector. *Mediations and Mediatisations*, (14), 11–27. DOI: 10.52358/mm.vi14.307

Anoir, L., & Khaldi, M. (2024). From Collaboration to Adaptation: Designing an Adaptive Collaborative Educational System. In Innovative Instructional Design Methods and Tools for Improved Teaching (pp. 177-195). IGI Global.

Anoir, L., Chelliq, I., Erradi, M., & Khaldi, M. (2023). Adapting Personalized Learning Activities to the Learner's Profile According to Kolb. *International Journal on Engineering Applications*, 11(4), 240. DOI: 10.15866/irea.v11i4.23418

Anoir, L., Chelliq, I., Erradi, M., & Khaldi, M. (2023). Digital Learning Transformation. In *Emerging Trends and Historical Perspectives Surrounding Digital Transformation in Education* (pp. 131–159). IGI Global., DOI: 10.4018/978-1-6684-4423-8.ch006

Anoir, L., Chelliq, I., Khaldi, M., & Khaldi, M. (2024). Design of an Intelligent Tutor System for the Personalization of Learning Activities Using Case-Based Reasoning and Multi-Agent System. *International Journal of Computing and Digital Systems*, 15(1), 459–469. DOI: 10.12785/ijcds/160136

Anoir, L., Khaldi, M., & Erradi, M. (2022). Personalization in adaptive E-learning. In *Designing User Interfaces with a Data Science Approach* (pp. 40–67). IGI Global. DOI: 10.4018/978-1-7998-9121-5.ch003

Anoir, L., Khaldi, M., & Erradi, M. (2024). Symbiotic Evolution: The Inextricable Relation between the Web and E-Learning. *DIROSAT: Journal of Education. Social Sciences & Humanities*, 2(1), 10–18.

Ansu-Kyeremeh, E. K., & Goosen, L. (2022). Exploring the Socioeconomic Facet of Online Inclusive Education in Ghana: The Effects of Technological Advancement in Academia. In Garcia, M. (Ed.), *Socioeconomic Inclusion During an Era of Online Education* (pp. 47–66). IGI Global., DOI: 10.4018/978-1-6684-4364-4.ch003

Antoninis, M., & Montoya, S. (2018). *A global framework to measure digital literacy*. Blog UNESCO.

Appsembler. (2023). *Blended learning: Definitions and models*. https://www.appsembler.com

Appsembler. (2023). *Unlocking blended learning: Strategies, benefits & tools*. https://appsembler.com/blog/unlocking-blended-learning-strategies-benefits-tools/

Ardoino, J. (1991). "Project-based pedagogy or educational project?", French Review of Pedagogy No. 94.

Aronsson, M. (2019). Francophone literature in Swedish French language textbooks. Nordic Journal of Francophone Studies/Revue nordique des études francophones, 2(1), 49. https://doi.org/DOI: 10.16993/rnef.26

Arrouillet, P. (2015). Theories of cognitive development: From Piaget to today. *Developmental Review*, 38, 1–12. DOI: 10.1016/j.dr.2015.07.004

Asakura, K., Occhiuto, K., Todd, S., Leithead, C., & Clapperton, R. (2020). A call to action on artificial intelligence and social work education: Lessons learned from a simulation project using natural language processing. *Journal of Teaching in Social Work*, 40(5), 501–518. DOI: 10.1080/08841233.2020.1813234

Ashok, M., Madan, R., Joha, A., & Sivarajah, U. (2022). Ethical framework for Artificial Intelligence and Digital technologies. *International Journal of Information Management*, 62, 102433. Advance online publication. DOI: 10.1016/j.ijinfomgt.2021.102433

ATTALI. (2022). *Jacques. Histoires et avenirs de l'éducation*. Flammarion.

Avanzini, G. (1987). *Introduction to educational sciences*. Privat.

Azirar, C. (2024). *' The Axiological Dimension in the Study of Literary Works in the Qualifying Cycle Between Possibility and Difficulties of Implementation' Chapitre16 (319-340) Book ''Innovative Instructional Design Methods and Tools for Improved'' IGI GLOBAL Mohamed Khaldi, Teaching ENS.* Abdelmalek Essaadi University.

Bachman, L. F. (1990). *Fundamental Considerations in Language Testing*. Oxford University Press.

Bachman, L. F., & Palmer, A. S. (1996). *Language Testing in Practice: Designing and Developing Useful Language Tests*. Oxford University Press.

Baggen, R. (2024). *Generative AI for Automatic Feedback Generation in Serious Games* (Master's thesis).

Bailenson, J. N.. (2008). Avatars in Social Media: Balancing Accuracy, Playfulness and Embodiment. *Computers in Human Behavior*, 24(1), 100–115.

Bailey, A., Vaduganathan, N., Henry, T., Laverdiere, R., & Pugliese, L. (2018). *Making digital learning work: Success strategies from six leading universities and community colleges*. Boston Consulting Group., https://hdl.voced.edu.au/10707/466913

Baker, R. S. and Siemens, G. (2014). Educational data mining and learning analytics. *Cambridge Handbook on Learning Sciences*, 253-272.

Baker, R. S., & Inventado, P. S. (2014). Educational data mining and learning analytics. In S. J. H. B. (Ed.), *Handbook of learning analytics* (pp. 55–74). Society for Learning Analytics Research.

Bandura, A. (1971). *Social learning theory*. General Learning Press.

Barnes, E., & Hutson, J. (2024, June). Navigating the ethical terrain of AI in higher education: Strategies for mitigating bias and promoting fairness. In *Forum for Education Studies* (Vol. 2, No. 2, pp. 1229-1229).

Barré-de Miniac, C. (2002). La notion de littéracie et les principaux courants de recherche. *La Lettre de l'AIRDF*, 30(1), 27–33.

Basham, J. D., Hall, T. E., Carter, R. A.Jr, & Stahl, W. M. (2016). An operationalized understanding of personalized learning. *Journal of Special Education Technology*, 31(3), 126–136. DOI: 10.1177/0162643416660835

Bates, A. W. (2019). *Teaching in a Digital Age*. Tony Bates Associates Ltd.

Bates, T., Cobo, C., Mariño, O., & Wheeler, S. (2020). Can artificial intelligence transform higher education? *International Journal of Educational Technology in Higher Education*, 17(1), 42. DOI: 10.1186/s41239-020-00218-x

Batzos, Z., Saoulidis, T., Margounakis, D., Fountoukidis, E., Grigoriou, E., Moukoulis, A., & Mouratidis, H. (2023). Gamification and Serious Games for Cybersecurity Awareness and First Responders Training: An overview. *Authorea Preprints*.

Bawden, D. (2008). Origins and concepts of digital literacy. Digital literacies: Concepts, policies and practices, 30(2008), 17-32.

Bawden, D., & Robinson, L. (2018). Curating the infosphere: Luciano Floridi's Philosophy of Information as the foundation for library and information science. *The Journal of Documentation*, 74(1), 2–17. DOI: 10.1108/JD-07-2017-0096

Beard, C., & Wilson, J. P. (2013). *Experiential Learning: A Best Practice Handbook for Educators and Trainers* (3rd ed.). Kogan Page.

Bee, R., & Bee, F. (1998). *Constructive Feedback*. CIPD Publishing.

Bejaković, P., & Mrnjavac, Ž. (2020). The importance of digital literacy on the labour market. *Employee Relations*, 42(4), 921–932. DOI: 10.1108/ER-07-2019-0274

Bejaoui, R., Paquette, G., Basque, J., & Henri, F. (2017). Cadre d'analyse de la personnalisation de l'apprentissage dans les cours en ligne ouverts et massifs (CLOM. *Revue STICEF*. Bellman, R. E. (1978). *An Introduction to Artificial Intelligence : Can Computers Think?* San Francisco: Boyd & Fraser Publishing Company.

Belghali, M., Statsenko, Y., & Al-Za'abi, A. (2021). Improving serious games to tackle childhood obesity. *Frontiers in Psychology*, 12, 657289. DOI: 10.3389/fpsyg.2021.657289 PMID: 34025521

Belshaw, D. (2012). What is' digital literacy'? A Pragmatic investigation (Doctoral dissertation, Durham University).

Belur, J., Tompson, L., Thornton, A., & Simon, M. (2021). Interrater reliability in systematic review methodology: Exploring variation in coder decision-making. *Sociological Methods & Research*, 50(2), 837–865. DOI: 10.1177/0049124118799372

Bennani, S., Maalel, A., & Ben Ghezala, H. (2022). Adaptive gamification in E-learning: A literature review and future challenges. *Computer Applications in Engineering Education*, 30(2), 628–642. DOI: 10.1002/cae.22477

Bennett, S., Maton, K., & Kervin, L. (2022). The 'digital natives' debate in higher education: A comparative analysis of the educational backgrounds and approaches of recent graduates and their teachers. *Computers & Education*, 56(2), 586–595. DOI: 10.1016/j.compedu.2010.08.009

Berners-Lee, T., Cailliau, R., Luotonen, A., Nielsen, H. F., & Secret, A. (1994). The World-Wide Web. *Communications of the ACM*, 37(8), 76–82. DOI: 10.1145/179606.179671

Bezdek, J. C. (1981). *Pattern recognition with fuzzy objective function algorithms*. Plenum Press. DOI: 10.1007/978-1-4757-0450-1

Bhugaonkar, K., Bhugaonkar, R., & Masne, N. (2022). The trend of metaverse and augmented & virtual reality extending to the healthcare system. *Cureus*, 14(9). Advance online publication. DOI: 10.7759/cureus.29071 PMID: 36258985

Biesta, G. (2015). *A good education in the age of moderation: ethics, politics, democracy*. Routledge. DOI: 10.4324/9781315634319

Biggs, J. (1999). *Teaching for quality learning at university*. Society for Research into Higher Education & Open University Press.

Binns, R. (2018). Fairness in machine learning: Lessons from political philosophy. Proceedings of the 2018 Conference on Fairness, Accountability, and Transparency, 149 159.

Black, P., & Wiliam, D. (1998). Assessment and Classroom Learning. *Assessment in Education: Principles, Policy & Practice*, 5(1), 7–74. DOI: 10.1080/0969595980050102

Blanche, P., & Merino, B. (1989). Self-Assessment of Foreign-Language Skills: Implications for Teachers and Researchers. *Language Learning*, 39(3), 313–338. DOI: 10.1111/j.1467-1770.1989.tb00595.x

Bobula, M. (2024). Generative Artificial Intelligence (AI) in higher education: a comprehensive review of challenges, opportunities, and implications. *Journal of Learning Development in Higher Education*, (30).

Bolshakova, A. (2022). Развитие цифровой компетенции и интернет-грамотности учащихся на уроках иностранного языка / Development of digital competence and Internet literacy of students in foreign language lessons. *Социально-педагогические вопросы образования и воспитания/ Socio-Pedagogical Issues of Education and Upbringing*.

Bond, M., Khosravi, H., De Laat, M., Bergdahl, N., Negrea, V., Oxley, E., Pham, P., Chong, S. W., & Siemens, G. (2024). A meta systematic review of artificial intelligence in higher education: A call for increased ethics, collaboration, and rigour. *International Journal of Educational Technology in Higher Education*, 21(1), 4. DOI: 10.1186/s41239-023-00436-z

Bonnardel, N. (2006). *Creativity and design. Cognitive and ergonomic approaches*. Solal.

Bora, S. A. P. T. A. R. I. S. H. I., & Neelakandan, R. (2023). Digital well-being. International journal of research in education humanities and commerce, 4(2), 63-67.

Bouchereau, A. (2020). *Les objets connectés au service de l'apprentissage* [Université Bourgogne Franche-Comté]. Theses.fr.

Boud, D., & Falchikov, N. (2006). Aligning Assessment with Long-Term Learning. *Assessment & Evaluation in Higher Education*, 31(4), 399–413. DOI: 10.1080/02602930600679050

Boudiaf, K., & Seddari, B. (2023). The pedagogical scenario integrating the intercultural approach in the digital age: For a dynamic of the understanding of the literary text in middle school. *Multilingual*, 20. Advance online publication. DOI: 10.4000/11ptw

Bourgain, M. (2023). The integration of experiential pedagogy into a research methodology module. *Finance Control Strategy*, (-13), 1–33.

Bransford, J. D., Brown, A. L., & Cocking, R. R. (2000). *How People Learn: Brain, Mind, Experience, and School.* National Academy Press.

Brault, N. (2022). Artificial intelligence and covid-19, or the limits of "technological solutionism". Annales des mines - Responsabilité et environnement, n° 108(4), 57-60. https://doi.org/DOI: 10.3917/re1.108.0057

Brennan, K., & Resnick, M. (2012). New frameworks for studying and assessing the development of computational thinking. In *Proceedings of the 2012 annual meeting of the American educational research association* (1, p. 25).

Brown, E., Collins, L., & Duguid, P. (2021). The impact of AI in adaptive learning systems on educational outcomes. *Educational Technology Research and Development*, 69(3), 509–529. DOI: 10.1007/s11423-020-09819-1

Brown, E., Collins, L., & Duguid, P. (2023). Enhancing language learning outcomes through adaptive AI technologies. *Educational Technology Research and Development*, 71(2), 289–310.

Brown, H. D. (2004). *Language Assessment: Principles and Classroom Practices.* Pearson Education.

Brown, T. (2009). *Change by design: How design thinking creates new alternatives for business and society.* HarperCollins.

Brown, T. B., Mann, B., Ryder, N., Subbiah, M., Kaplan, J., & Dhariwal, P. (2020). Language models are few-shot learners. *Advances in Neural Information Processing Systems*, 33.

Brundage, M. (2015). Taking superintelligence seriously : Superintelligence: Paths, dangers, strategies by Nick Bostrom (Oxford University Press, 2014). *Futures*, 72, 32–35. DOI: 10.1016/j.futures.2015.07.009

Bruneault, F. et A. S. Laflamme. (2021). Éthique de l'intelligence artificielle et ubiquité des technologies de l'information et de la communication: comment penser les enjeux éthiques de l'IA dans nos sociétés de l'information?. TIC & société. 15 (1). 159-189. .DOI: 10.4000/ticetsociete.5999

Bruneault, F., Laflamme, A. S., Boivin, J., Grondin-Robillard, L., & Le Calvez, E. (2024). *Former à l'éthique de l'IA en enseignement supérieur: trousse pédagogique.* DOI: 10.31235/osf.io/z8m42

Brusilovsky, P., & Millán, E. (2018). *Adaptive learning environments: A review of the state of the art. In Advances in Intelligent Systems and Computing* (Vol. 706). Springer., DOI: 10.1007/978-3-319-63794-0_1

Brusilovsky, P., & Peylo, C. (2003). Adaptive and intelligent technologies for Web-based education. *International Journal of Artificial Intelligence in Education*, 13(2-4), 159–172.

Brynjolfsson, E., & McAfee, A. (2014). *The second machine age: Work, progress, and prosperity in a time of brilliant technologies*. W. W. Norton & Company.

Brynjolfsson, E., & McAfee, A. (2014). *The Second Machine Age: Work, Progress, and Prosperity in a Time of Brilliant Technologies*. W. W. Norton & Company.

Buckingham, D. (2007). *Beyond Technology: Children's Learning in the Digital Age*. Political press.

Buckingham, D. (2007). Digital Media Literacies: Rethinking media education in the age of the Internet. *Research in Comparative and International Education*, 2(1), 43–55. DOI: 10.2304/rcie.2007.2.1.43

Bulger, M. (2016). Personalized learning : The conversations we're not having. *Data and Society*, 22(1), 1–29.

Buolamwini, J., & Gebru, T. (2018). Gender shades: Intersectional accuracy disparities in commercial gender classification. *Proceedings of Machine Learning Research*, 81, 1–15.

Burgueño López, J. (2024). Implications of Artificial Intelligence in Education. The educator as ethical leader. *Journal of Interdisciplinary Education: Theory and Practice*. DOI: 10.47157/jietp.1505319

Burkholder, G. J., Cox, K., & Crawford, L. (2016). *The Scholar-Practitioner's Guide to Research Design*. Laureate Publishing., Retrieved from https://scholarworks.waldenu.edu/facpubs/277/

Burrell, J. (2016). How the machine 'thinks': Understanding opacity in machine learning algorithms. *Big Data & Society*, 3(1), 1–12. DOI: 10.1177/2053951715622512

Burstein, J., Chodorow, M., & Leacock, C. (2022). *Automated essay scoring: A cross-disciplinary perspective*. Routledge.

Burton, E., Goldsmith, J., Koenig, S., Kuipers, B., Mattei, N., & Walsh, T. (2017). *Ethical considerations in artificial intelligence courses*. Addressing Methodological Considerations in AI Teaching., DOI: 10.1609/aimag.v38i2.2731

Byram, M. (1997). *Teaching and Assessing Intercultural Communicative Competence*. Multilingual Matters.

Cadieux, L., & Keenan, M. (2020). Can social communication skills for children diagnosed with autism spectrum disorder rehearsed inside the video game environment of Minecraft generalize to the real world? *JMIR Serious Games*, 8(2), e14369. DOI: 10.2196/14369 PMID: 32396129

Calvo, R. A., Tjondronegoro, D., & Hsieh, G. (2021). Designing AI technologies for education: The importance of transparency and privacy. *Journal of Educational Technology & Society*, 24(3), 12–26.

Canale, M., & Swain, M. (1980). Theoretical Bases of Communicative Approaches to Second Language Teaching and Testing. *Applied Linguistics*, 1(1), 1–47. DOI: 10.1093/applin/1.1.1

Carbonell, J. R. (1970). AI in CAI: An artificial-intelligence approach to computer-assisted instruction. *IEEE Transactions on Man-Machine Systems*, 11(4), 190–202. DOI: 10.1109/TMMS.1970.299942

Carretero, S., Vuorikari, R., & Punie, Y. (2017). *«DigComp 2.1. The Digital Competence Framework for Citizens. With eight proficiency levels and examples of use.» Publications Office of the European Union*. Publications Office of the European Union.

Carroll, W. M. (1994). Using worked examples as an instructional support in the algebra classroom. *Journal of Educational Psychology*, 86(3), 360–367. DOI: 10.1037/0022-0663.86.3.360

Cassidy, S. (2004). Learning styles: *An overview of theories, models, and measures.Educational Psychology*, 24(4), 419–444. DOI: 10.1080/0144341042000228834

Castelló-Sirvent, F., Roger-Monzó, V., & Gouveia-Rodrigues, R. (2024). Quo Vadis, University? A Roadmap for AI and Ethics in Higher Education. *Electronic Journal of e-Learning*, 22(6), 35–51. DOI: 10.34190/ejel.22.6.3267

Cath, C. (2018). Governing artificial intelligence: Ethical, legal, and technical opportunities and challenges. *Philosophical Transactions. Series A, Mathematical, Physical, and Engineering Sciences*, 376(2133), 20180080. DOI: 10.1098/rsta.2018.0080 PMID: 30322996

Caws, C., Hamel, M. J., Jeanneau, C., & Ollivier, C. (2021). Formation en langues et littératie numérique en contextes ouverts. Une approche socio-interactionnelle.

Celce-Murcia, M., Brinton, D. M., & Goodwin, J. M. (1996). *Teaching Pronunciation: A Reference for Teachers of English to Speakers of Other Languages*. Cambridge University Press.

Chaarani, B., Ortigara, J., Yuan, D., Loso, H., Potter, A., & Garavan, H. P. (2022). Association of video gaming with cognitive performance among children. *JAMA Network Open*, 5(10), e2235721–e2235721. DOI: 10.1001/jamanetworkopen.2022.35721 PMID: 36279138

Chaib-Draa, B., Jarras, I., & Moulin, B. (2001). Systèmes multi-agents : Principes généraux et applications. *Edition Hermès*, 242, 1030–1044.

Chan, C. K. Y., & Tsi, L. H. Y. (2023). The AI revolution in education: Will AI replace or assist teachers in higher education? *Computers and Society* http://dx.doi.org//arXiv.2305.01185.DOI: 10.48550

Chan, C. K. (2023). A comprehensive AI policy education framework for university teaching and learning. *International Journal of Educational Technology in Higher Education*, 20(1), 38. Advance online publication. DOI: 10.1186/s41239-023-00408-3

Chapelle, C. A., & Chung, Y. R. (2010). The promise of NLP and speech processing technologies in language assessment. *Language Testing*, 27(3), 301–315. DOI: 10.1177/0265532210364405

Chapelle, C. A., & Douglas, D. (2006). *Assessing language through computer technology*. Cambridge University Press. DOI: 10.1017/CBO9780511733116

Chapelle, C. A., & Voss, E. (2016). 20 years of technology and language assessment in Language Learning & Technology. *Language Learning & Technology*, 20(2), 116–128.

Chapelle, C. A., & Voss, E. (2016). The Role of Technology in Language Assessment. *Annual Review of Applied Linguistics*, 36, 146–163.

Charles, W., & Magtanong, R. (2021). Ethical Benefits and Drawbacks of Digitally Informed Consent. In Vasiliu-Feltes, I., & Thomason, J. (Eds.), (pp. 101–123). Advances in Human and Social Aspects of Technology. IGI Global. DOI: 10.4018/978-1-7998-8467-5.ch008

Charniak, E., & McDermott, D. (1985). *Introduction to Artificial Intelligence*. Addison-Wesley.

Chartier, A. M., & Rockwell, E. (2013). Histoire comparée des Outils et débats sur la lecture des débutants: Alphabétisation vs literacy. Introduction. *Histoire de l'Éducation (Paris)*, (138), 5–16. DOI: 10.4000/histoire-education.2647

Cheah, C. W. (2021). Developing a gamified AI-enabled online learning application to improve students' perception of university physics. *Computers and Education: Artificial Intelligence*, 2, 100032. DOI: 10.1016/j.caeai.2021.100032

Chelliq, I., & Erradi, M. (2024). Exploring the Foundations of Pedagogical Mediation. In *Fostering Pedagogical Innovation Through Effective Instructional Design* (pp. 141–159). IGI Global., DOI: 10.4018/979-8-3693-1206-3.ch005

Chen, M., Tworek, J., Jun, H., Yuan, Q., Pinto, H., & Kaplan, J. (2021). *Evaluating large language models trained on code*. arXiv preprint arXiv:2107.03374.

Chen, L., Chen, P., & Huang, Y. (2020). *A Review of Project-Based Learning in Artificial Intelligence* Education. *Journal of Educational Technology & Society*, 23(4), 12–24.

Chen, L., Dai, Y., & Zhao, Z. (2020). Enhancing language learning through AI-powered feedback systems: Evidence from recent case studies. *Journal of Language and Education Technology*, 5(2), 78–92.

Chen, L., Dai, Y., & Zhao, Z. (2023). Bridging linguistic diversity in AI-powered language education: Case studies and strategies. *Journal of Language and Education Technology*, 7(1), 44–62.

Chen, Q., He, Z., & Zhang, L. (2021). The role of teachers in AI-enhanced learning environments: Balancing automation with human interaction. *Journal of Educational Technology*, 23(1), 110–123. DOI: 10.1007/s11423-020-09841-5

Chen, X., Xie, H., Zou, D., & Hwang, G. J. (2020). Application and theory gaps during the rise of Artificial Intelligence in Education. *Computers and Education : Artificial Intelligence*, 1, 100002. DOI: 10.1016/j.caeai.2020.100002

Chevalier, L., & Garcia, F. (2024, May 27). L'intelligence artificielle générative dans l'enseignement supérieur, une course perdue d'avance? 29e Conférence de l'Association Information et Management. https://shs.hal.science/halshs-04631049

Chiu, T. K. F. (2024). Future research recommendations for transforming higher education with generative AI. *Computers and Education: Artificial Intelligence*, 6, 100197. DOI: 10.1016/j.caeai.2023.100197

Chiu, T. K., Ahmad, Z., Ismailov, M., & Sanusi, I. T. (2024). What are artificial intelligence literacy and competency? A comprehensive framework to support them. *Computers and Education Open*, 6, 100171. DOI: 10.1016/j.caeo.2024.100171

Christopoulos, A., & Mystakidis, S. (2023). Gamification in Education. *Encyclopedia*, 2023(3), 1223–1243. DOI: 10.3390/encyclopedia3040089

Cizek, G. J. (2012). Defining and distinguishing validity: Interpretations of score meaning and justifications of test use. *Psychological Methods*, 17(1), 31–43. DOI: 10.1037/a0026975 PMID: 22268761

Clark, J., Murdick, D., Perset, K., & Grobelnik, M. (2022, February 17). *The OECD Framework for Classifying AI Systems to assess policy challenges and ensure international standards in AI*. Retrieved March 2, 2024, from https://oecd.ai/en/wonk/classification

Clark, K., Luong, M. T., Le, Q. V., & Mann, B. (2020). *ELECTRA: Pre-training text encoders as discriminators rather than generators*. arXiv preprint arXiv:2003.10555.

Cleveland-Innes, M. F., Stenbom, S., & Garrison, D. R. (Eds.). (2024). *The design of digital learning environments: Online and blended applications of the community of inquiry*. Taylor & Francis.

Clifford, P. L. (2024). AI in Higher Education: Faculty Perspective Towards Artificial Intelligence through UTAUT Approach. *HO CHI MINH CITY OPEN UNIVERSITY JOURNAL OF SCIENCE-SOCIAL SCIENCES*, 14(4), 32–50. Advance online publication. DOI: 10.46223/HCMCOUJS.soci.en.14.4.2851.2024

Cohen, A., & Mace, C. (2020). Data privacy in education: An overview of ethical considerations and best practices. *Educational Administration Quarterly*, 56(2), 149–178. DOI: 10.1177/0013161X19881809

Cohen, J., De Lange, J., & Cummings, R. (2020). Bridging the digital divide: Implementing a device loan program in higher education. *Journal of Educational Technology Development and Exchange*, 13(1), 1–20. DOI: 10.18785/jetde.1301.02

Colado, I. J. P., Colado, V. M. P., Morata, A. C., Píriz, R. S. C., & Manjón, B. F. (2023, October). Using new AI-driven techniques to ease serious games authoring. In *2023 IEEE Frontiers in Education Conference (FIE)* (pp. 1-9). IEEE. DOI: 10.1109/FIE58773.2023.10343021

Collier, D., & Biesta, G. (2021). *Values and virtues in higher education research and teaching: fundamental or misunderstood?* Routledge.

Collin, S., & Marceau, E. (2021). L'intelligence artificielle en éducation: enjeux de justice. Formation et profession, 29(2), 1-4.

Collin, S., & Marceau, E. (2022). Enjeux éthiques et critiques de l'intelligence artificielle en enseignement supérieur. *Éthique publique. Revue internationale d'éthique sociétale et gouvernementale, vol. 24, n° 2*. DOI: 10.4000/ethiquepublique.7619

Combe, C. (2021). Former à la littératie numérique de futurs enseignants de FLE: une approche par genres numériques. Lidil. Revue de linguistique et de didactique des langues, (63).

Compagnon, A. (2007). *What is literature for?* Threshold.

Conati, C., Barral, O., Putnam, V., & Rieger, L. (2021). Toward personalized XAI: A case study in intelligent tutoring systems. *Artificial Intelligence*, 298, 103503. DOI: 10.1016/j.artint.2021.103503

Connac, S. (2018). *La personnalisation des apprentissages : Agir face à l'hétérogénéité, à l'école et au collège*. (S.l.): ESF Sciences Humaines.

Córdova, P. R., & Vicari, R. M. (2022, August). Practical ethical issues for artificial intelligence in education. *International Conference on Technology and Innovation in Learning, Teaching and Education* (pp. 437-445). Cham: Springer Nature Switzerland. DOI: 10.1007/978-3-031-22918-3_34

Correia, A., & Simões-Marques, M. (Eds.). (2023). *Handbook of Research on Decision-Making Capabilities Improvement With Serious Games*. IGI Global. DOI: 10.4018/978-1-6684-9166-9

Coulet, J. C. (2011). La notion de compétence: Un modèle pour décrire, évaluer et développer les compétences. *Le Travail Humain*, 74(1), 1–30. DOI: 10.3917/th.741.0001

Council of Europe, Council for Cultural Co-operation. (2001). *Education Committee. Modern Languages Division. Common European framework of reference for languages: Learning, teaching, assessment*. Cambridge University Press.

Council of Europe. (2001). *Common European Framework of Reference for Languages: Learning, Teaching, Assessment*. Didier.

Council of the European Union. (2024, May 21). *Artificial intelligence (AI) act: Council gives final green light to the first worldwide rules on AI*. Retrieved May 24, 2024, from https://www.consilium.europa.eu/en/press/press-releases/2024/05/21/artificial-intelligence-ai-act-council-gives-final-green-light-to-the-first-worldwide-rules-on-ai/

Crawford, K. (2021). *Atlas of AI: Power, Politics, and the Planetary Costs of Artificial Intelligence*. Yale University Press.

Crawford, L. M. (2020). Conceptual and theoretical frameworks in research. In *Foundations in Research Design* (pp. 35–48). SAGE.

D'Alessandro, W. (2024). Deontology and safe artificial intelligence. *Philosophical Studies*, ●●●, 1–24. DOI: 10.1007/s11098-024-02174-y

d'Amiens, R. de l'Académie. (2024, mai 8). *Guide : Les ODD – un levier pour l'éducation - édition Mars 2024*. Education au développement durable. http://edd.ac-amiens.fr/350-guide-les-odd-un-levier-pour-l-education-edition-mars-2024.html

Dabbagh, N., & Kitsantas, A. (2012). Personal Learning Environments, social media, and self-regulated learning : A natural formula for connecting formal and informal learning. *The Internet and Higher Education*, 15(1), 3–8. DOI: 10.1016/j.iheduc.2011.06.002

Dabis, A., & Csáki, C. (2024). AI and ethics: Investigating the first policy responses of higher education institutions to the challenge of generative AI. *Humanities & Social Sciences Communications*, 11(1), 1–13. DOI: 10.1057/s41599-024-03526-z

Dahalan, F., Alias, N., & Shaharom, M. S. N. (2024). Gamification and game-based learning for vocational education and training: A systematic literature review. *Education and Information Technologies*, 29(2), 1279–1317. DOI: 10.1007/s10639-022-11548-w PMID: 36688221

Dale, E. (2014). *Audio-visual methods in teaching. Holt.* Rinehart and Winston.

Damaševičius, R., Maskeliūnas, R., & Blažauskas, T. (2023). Serious games and gamification in healthcare: A meta-review. *Information (Basel)*, 14(2), 105. DOI: 10.3390/info14020105

Danaher, J., Hogan, M. J., Noone, C., Kennedy, R., Behan, A., & Collins, E. (2017). Algorithmic governance: Developing a research agenda through the power of collective intelligence. *Big Data & Society*, 4(2), 2053951717726554. DOI: 10.1177/2053951717726554

Davis, F. D. (1985). *A technology acceptance model for empirically testing new end-user information systems: Theory and results. (PhD dissertation).* Massachusetts Institute of Technology.

Davis, B., Shaha, S., & Chowdhury, M. (2020). Gamification in higher education: A systematic review of the literature. *Educational Technology Research and Development*, 68(1), 89–118. DOI: 10.1007/s11423-019-09703-6

De l'Europe, C. (2003). *Cadre européen commun de référence pour les langues: apprendre, enseigner, évaluer*. Council of Europe.

De la Torre, R., Onggo, B. S., Corlu, C. G., Nogal, M., & Juan, A. A. (2021). The role of simulation and serious games in teaching concepts on circular economy and sustainable energy. *Energies*, 14(4), 1138. DOI: 10.3390/en14041138

Demazeau, Y. (1995). From interactions to collective behaviour in agent-based systems.

Demazeau, Y. (2001). *Habilitation à Diriger des Recherches*. Institut National Polytechnique de Grenoble INPG.

Denecke, K., Schmid, N., & Nüssli, S. (2022). Implementation of cognitive behavioral therapy in e–mental health apps: Literature review. *Journal of Medical Internet Research*, 24(3), e27791. DOI: 10.2196/27791 PMID: 35266875

Deng, L. (2021). Gamified information systems: Gameful experiences, achievement goals, and performance. *Quarterly Review of Business Disciplines*, 8(3), 193–211.

Desmarais, M. C., & Baker, R. S. (2012). A review of recent advances in learner and skill modeling in intelligent learning environments. *User Modeling and User-Adapted Interaction*, 22(1-2), 9–38. DOI: 10.1007/s11257-011-9106-8

Deterding, S., Dixon, D., Khaled, R., & Nacke, L. (2011). From game design elements to gamefulness: Defining "gamification". *Proceedings of the 15th International Academic MindTrek Conference: Envisioning Future Media Environments* (pp. 9-15). ACM. https://doi.org/DOI: 10.1145/2181037.2181040

Dettmers, J. (2021). *Duolingo English Test: How AI is Changing the Way We Test Language*. Duolingo.

Devlin, J., Chang, M. W., Lee, K., & Toutanova, K. (2019). *BERT: Pre-training of deep bidirectional transformers for language understanding*. arXiv preprint arXiv:1810.04805.

Dewey, J. (1938). *Experience and education*. Kappa Delta Pi.

Dewey, J. (1986). Experience and Education. *The Educational Forum*. DOI: 10.1080/00131728609335764

Di Mattia, P. (2008). Ethical principles. In *Encyclopedia of public health* (Vol. 2, pp. 635–638). Springer. DOI: 10.1007/978-1-4020-5614-7_1453

Dignum, V. (2019). *Responsible artificial intelligence: How to develop and use AI in a responsible way*. Springer. DOI: 10.1007/978-3-030-30371-6

Dillenbourg, P. (1999). What do you mean by collaborative learning? Dans *Collaborative-learning : Cognitive and computational approaches* (pp. 1-19). (S.l.): (s.n.).

Dillenbourg, P., & Jermann, P. (2007). Designing integrative scripts. In *Scripting computer-supported collaborative learning: Cognitive, computational and educational perspectives* (pp. 275–301). Springer US. DOI: 10.1007/978-0-387-36949-5_16

Dimitriadou, A., Djafarova, N., Turetken, O., Verkuyl, M., & Ferworn, A. (2021). Challenges in serious game design and development: Educators' experiences. *Simulation & Gaming*, 52(2), 132–152. DOI: 10.1177/1046878120944197

Doe, J., & Smith, A. (2021). Advancements in implicit learning style detection. *Journal of Educational Technology*, 30(3), 256–272.

Do, H. T.. (2021). Collaborative Learning in Artificial Intelligence: A New Approach to Education. *International Journal of Artificial Intelligence in Education*, 31(3), 473–493.

Doroudi, S. (2022). The intertwined histories of artificial intelligence and education. *International Journal of Artificial Intelligence in Education*, •••, 1–44.

Douzou, C. (2008). Birth of a ghost1. *Proteus (Shippensburg, Pa.)*, 35(3), 23–32. DOI: 10.7202/017476ar

Drachsler, H., Koper, R., & Hummel, H. G. K. (2021). Ethical issues in using AI in education. In A. V. H. T. K. R. H. & H. Drachsler (Eds.), *AI in education: Designing and implementing ethical frameworks* (pp. 45-61). Springer.

Educational Testing Service. (2020). *TOEFL iBT: Test and Score Data Summary 2019*. ETS.

Edwards, P., Sharma-Wallace, L., Wreford, A., Holt, L., Cradock-Henry, N. A., Flood, S., & Velarde, S. J. (2019). Tools for adaptive governance for complex social-ecological systems : A review of role-playing-games as serious games at the community-policy interface. *Environmental Research Letters*, 14(11), 113002. DOI: 10.1088/1748-9326/ab4036

Eisen, M. B., Spellman, P. T., Brown, P. O., & Botstein, D. (1998). Cluster analysis and display of genome-wide expression patterns. *Proceedings of the National Academy of Sciences of the United States of America*, 95(25), 14863–14868. DOI: 10.1073/pnas.95.25.14863 PMID: 9843981

El Haoud, N. A. I. M. A., & HALI, O. (2023). Adoption de l'IA dans l'enseignement supérieur à l'aide du modèle des équations structurelles: Cas de l'ENCG Casablanca. *International Journal of Economics and Management Research*, 4(6), 66–86.

El Karfa, I. (2023). L'IA dans l'enseignement entre pratique et éthique. Laboratore de Recherche Société Langage, Art et Médias, 1(09).

Ellis, R. (2003). *Task-Based Language Learning and Teaching*. Oxford University Press.

English, L. D. (2016). STEM education K-12: Perspectives on integration. *International Journal of STEM Education*, 3(3), 1–8. DOI: 10.1186/s40594-016-0036-1

Eshach, H. (2007). Bridging in-school and out-of-school learning: Formal, non-formal, and informal education. *Journal of Science Education and Technology*, 16(2), 171–190. DOI: 10.1007/s10956-006-9027-1

Eshet-Alkalai, Y. (2004). Digital literacy: A conceptual framework for survival skills in the digital era. *Journal of Educational Multimedia and Hypermedia*, 13(1), 93–106.

Ester, M., Kriegel, H. P., Sander, J., & Xu, X. (1996). A density-based algorithm for discovering clusters in large spatial databases with noise. In *Proceedings of the Second International Conference on Knowledge Discovery and Data Mining* (pp. 226-231).

Estevez, J., Garate, G., & Graña, M. (2019). Gentle introduction to artificial intelligence for high-school students using scratch. *IEEE Access : Practical Innovations, Open Solutions*, 7, 179027–179036. DOI: 10.1109/ACCESS.2019.2956136

Explosion, A. I. (2020). *spaCy 3.0 documentation.* Retrieved from https://spacy.io

Ezzaim, A., Dahbi, A., Haidine, A., & Aqqal, A. (2023). AI-based adaptive learning: A systematic mapping of the literature. *Journal of Universal Computer Science*, 29(10), 1161–1198. DOI: 10.3897/jucs.90528

Fang, X., Ng, D. T. K., Leung, J. K. L., & Chu, S. K. W. (2023). A systematic review of artificial intelligence technologies used for story writing. *Education and Information Technologies*, 28(11), 1–37. DOI: 10.1007/s10639-023-11741-5

Farina, M., Zhdanov, P., Karimov, A., & Lavazza, A. (2022). AI and society: A virtue ethics approach. *AI & Society*, 39(3), 1127–1140. DOI: 10.1007/s00146-022-01545-5

Ferber, J. (1995). *Multi-agent systems : An introduction to distributed artificial intelligence* (Vol. 1). Addison-Wesley.

Ferdosipour, A. (2024, April 11). *From Skinner's Operant Conditioning to Artificial Intelligence's Algorithms*. Retrieved August 8, 2024, from Medika Life: https://medika.life/from-skinners-operant-conditioning-to-artificial-intelligences-algorithms/

Fernández Galeote, D., & Hamari, J. (2021). Game-based climate change engagement: analyzing the potential of entertainment and serious games. *Proceedings of the ACM on Human-Computer Interaction,* 5(CHI PLAY), 1-21. DOI: 10.1145/3474653

Ferrari.A. Digital competence in practice: An analysis of frameworks. (2012). Publications Office of the European Union.

Fetzer, J. H. (1990). What is Artificial Intelligence? In Fetzer, J. H. (Ed.), *Artificial Intelligence: Its Scope and Limits* (pp. 3–27). Springer Netherlands., DOI: 10.1007/978-94-009-1900-6_1

Fisher, D. H., & Schlimmer, J. C. (1987). Conceptual clustering via COBWEB. In *Proceedings of the International Conference on Machine Learning* (pp. 210-218).

Florea, A. M., & Radu, S. (2019). Artificial Intelligence and Education. *22nd International Conference on Control Systems and Computer Science (CSCS)*,381–382.

Florent, M. (2022). Pour faire face aux défis informationnels, numériques et médiatiques du 21e siècle. Revue hybride de l'éducation, 5(2), 1-27.

Floridi, L. (2019). *The ethics of artificial intelligence: The future of AI and society*. Oxford University Press.

Floridi, L. (2019). *The logic of information: A theory of philosophy as conceptual design*. Oxford University Press. DOI: 10.1093/oso/9780198833635.001.0001

Floridi, L., & Cowls, J. (2019). A unified framework of five principles for AI in society. *Harvard Data Science Review*, 1(1), 1–15.

Floridi, L., & Cowls, J. (2022). A unified framework of five principles for AI in society. In *Machine learning and the city: Applications in architecture and urban design* (pp. 535–545). Wiley., DOI: 10.1002/9781119815075.ch45

Floridi, L., Cowls, J., Beltrametti, M., Chatila, R., Chazerand, P., Dignum, V., & Schafer, B. (2018). AI4People—An ethical framework for a good AI society: Opportunities, risks, principles, and recommendations. *Minds and Machines*, 28(4), 689–707. DOI: 10.1007/s11023-018-9482-5 PMID: 30930541

Floridi, L., & Taddeo, M. (2016). What is data ethics? *Philosophical Transactions. Series A, Mathematical, Physical, and Engineering Sciences*, 374(2083), 20160360. DOI: 10.1098/rsta.2016.0360 PMID: 28336805

Foltz, P. W., Rosenstein, M., & Myers, M. (2018). Implementing and evaluating writing instruction with automated formative feedback. In Kim, J. E., & Fee, R. E. (Eds.), *Machine learning and human learning: The future of educational assessment* (pp. 183–205). Routledge.

Fouly, K. A., Bachman, L. F., & Cziko, G. A. (1990). The divisibility of language competence: A confirmatory approach. *Language Learning*, 40(1), 1–21. DOI: 10.1111/j.1467-1770.1990.tb00952.x

Fraenkel, B. (2021). Littératie. *Langage & Société*, 1(HS1), 221–224. DOI: 10.3917/ls.hs01.0222

Fredricks, J. A., Blumenfeld, P. C., & Paris, A. H. (2004). School engagement: Potential of the concept, state of the evidence. *Review of Educational Research*, 74(1), 59–109. DOI: 10.3102/00346543074001059

Freeman, S., Eddy, S. L., McDonough, M., Smith, M. K., Okoroafor, N., Wenderoth, M. P., & Dirks, C. (2014). Active learning increases student performance in science, engineering, and mathematics. *Proceedings of the National Academy of Sciences of the United States of America*, 111(23), 8410–8415. DOI: 10.1073/pnas.1319030111 PMID: 24821756

French, A. J. (2020). Simulation and modeling applications in global health security. *Global Health Security: Recognizing Vulnerabilities, Creating Opportunities*, 307-340.

Friedewald, M., Székely, I., & Karaboga, M. (2024). *L' accès aux archives à l'ère du numérique : Mise en œuvre de la Recommandation no R (2000) 13 du Comité des Ministres du Conseil de l'Europe sur une politique européenne en matière de communication des archives*. Council of Europe.

Fryer, L., Coniam, D., Carpenter, R., & Lăpu neanu, D. (2020). Bots for language learning now: Current and future directions. *Language Learning & Technology*.

Fulcher, G. (2010). *Practical Language Testing*. Hodder Education.

Fulcher, G., & Davidson, F. (2007). *Language Testing and Assessment: An Advanced Resource Book*. Routledge.

Gacemi, M. (2024). L'intelligence artificielle à l'université: Questions pratiques et enjeux éthiques. Cas des étudiants de l'université de Ghardaïa. ATRAS Revue, 5(Numéro Spécial), 692-706

Gadanidis, G. (2017). Artificial intelligence, computational thinking, and mathematics education. *The International Journal of Information and Learning Technology*, 34(2), 133–139. DOI: 10.1108/IJILT-09-2016-0048

Gaffiot, F., & Flobert, P. (1934). *Dictionnaire latin-français*. Hachette.

Gansser, O. A., & Reich, C. S. (2021). A new acceptance model for artificial intelligence with extensions to UTAUT2: An empirical study in three segments of application. *Technology in Society*, 65, 101535. DOI: 10.1016/j.techsoc.2021.101535

Gao, J., O'Sullivan, N., & Sherman, M. (2021). Chinese securities investment funds : The role of luck in performance. *Review of Accounting and Finance*, 20(5), 271–297. DOI: 10.1108/RAF-07-2020-0182

Gao, Y., & Liu, H. (2023). Artificial intelligence-enabled personalization in interactive marketing: A customer journey perspective. *Journal of Research in Interactive Marketing*, 17(5), 663–680. DOI: 10.1108/JRIM-01-2022-0023

Garrison, D. R. (1999). Will distance disappear in distance studies? A reaction. *Journal of Distance Education*, 14(2), 10–13.

Garrison, D. R., Anderson, T., & Archer, W. (1999). Critical inquiry in a text-based environment: Computer conferencing in higher education. *The Internet and Higher Education*, 2(2-3), 87–105. DOI: 10.1016/S1096-7516(00)00016-6

Garrison, D. R., Cleveland-Innes, M., & Fung, T. S. (2010). Exploring causal relationships among teaching, cognitive and social presence: Student perceptions of the community of inquiry framework. *The Internet and Higher Education*, 13(1-2), 31–36. DOI: 10.1016/j.iheduc.2009.10.002

Gaurav, D., Kaushik, Y., Supraja, S., Yadav, M., Gupta, M. P., & Chaturvedi, M. (2022). Empirical study of adaptive serious games in enhancing learning outcome. *International Journal of Serious Games*, 9(2), 27–42. DOI: 10.17083/ijsg.v9i2.486

Gavray, G. (2002). Personnalisation des sites web : Élaboration d'une méthodologie de mise en œuvre et application au cas DGTRE. Mémoire en vue de l'obtention du titre de : Ingénieur De Gestion de l'université catholique de louvain. Repéré à https://lilab.isys.ucl.ac.be/bchi/publications/2002/Gavray-T2002.pdf

Gebru, T., Morgenstern, J., Vecchione, B., Vaughan, J. W., Wallach, H., Daumé, H., III, & Crawford, K. (2018). Datasheets for datasets. arXiv preprint arXiv:1803.09010.

Geleta, M., Xu, J., Loya, M., Wang, J., Singh, S., Li, Z., & Gago-Masague, S. (2023). Maestro: A gamified platform for teaching AI robustness, The Thirty-Seventh AAAI Conference on Artificial Intelligence (AAAI-23), *The Thirty-Seventh AAAI Conference on Artificial Intelligence(AAAI-23)*, 15816-15824.

Genesee, F., & Upshur, J. A. (1996). *Classroom-Based Evaluation in Second Language Education.* Cambridge University Press.

Gérard, F.-M. (2007). The complexity of an assessment of skills through complex situations: theoretical necessities and requirements of the field. Proceedings of the International Symposium "Logic of Skills and Curricular Development: Debates, Perspectives and Alternatives for Educational Systems", Montreal, April 26-27.

Ghosh, L., & Ravichandran, R. (2024). Emerging Technologies in Vocational Education and Training. *Journal of Digital Learning and Education*, 4(1), 41–49. DOI: 10.52562/jdle.v4i1.975

Gikandi, J. W., Morrow, D., & Davis, N. E. (2011). Online formative assessment in higher education: A review of the literature. *Computers & Education*, 57(4), 2333–2351. DOI: 10.1016/j.compedu.2011.06.004

Gilster, P. (1997). *Digital Literacy.* Wiley Computer.

Gligorea, I., Cioca, M., Oancea, R., Gorski, A.-T., Gorski, H., & Tudorache, P. (2023). Adaptive Learning Using Artificial Intelligence in e-Learning: A Literature Review. *Education Sciences*, 13(12), 1216. DOI: 10.3390/educsci13121216

Gomez, C., Martinez-Monés, A., & Ochoa, X. (2021). Overcoming the digital divide: An analysis of technology access and use among university students in Latin America. *International Journal of Educational Technology in Higher Education*, 18(1), 1–24. DOI: 10.1186/s41239-021-00266-7

González, A., Silva, F., & Pérez, J. (2022). The role of innovative teaching methods in higher education. *Journal of Education and Practice*, 13(5), 45–58. DOI: 10.7176/JEP/13-5-06

Graham, C. R. (2013). Emerging practice and research in blended learning. In Moore, M. G. (Ed.), *Handbook of distance education* (3rd ed., pp. 333–350). Routledge. DOI: 10.4324/9780203803738.ch21

Granger, N., & Moreau, A. C. (2018). Perspective critique sur l'enseignement de la littératie disciplinaire en contexte d'inclusion et incidences sur la planification de l'enseignement. *Language and Literature*, 20(2), 59–79.

Gravelle, F., Lamarche, M. H., Monette, J., Gagnon, C., Montreuil, F., & Demers, L. P. (2022). Gestion et leadership pédagonumérique: stratégies de gestion pour favoriser l'implantation du numérique dans les établissements d'enseignement au Québec. Médiations et médiatisations, (12), 98-113.

Grover, S., & Pea, R. (2013). Computational thinking in K–12: A review of the state of the field. *Educational Researcher*, 42(1), 38–43. DOI: 10.3102/0013189X12463051

Gulikers, J. T. M., Bastiaens, T. J., & Kirschner, P. A. (2004). Linking assessment to authentic learning: A framework for educational design. *Open Learning*, 19(2), 189–200. DOI: 10.1080/0268051042000210246

Gupta, A. (2024). Impact of Generative AI in Transforming Higher Education Pedagogy. DOI:.DOI: 10.4018/979-8-3693-0815-8.ch017

Gupta, T., Kumar, A., Roy, B. K., & Saini, S. (2024, November). Adaptive learning systems: Harnessing AI to personalize educational outcomes. *International Journal for Research in Applied Science and Engineering Technology*, 12(XI). Advance online publication. https://doi.org/10.22214/ijraset.2024.65088

Gursoy, D., Chi, O. H., Lu, L., & Nunkoo, R. (2019). Consumers acceptance of artificially intelligent (AI) device use in service delivery. *International Journal of Information Management*, 49, 157–169. DOI: 10.1016/j.ijinfomgt.2019.03.008

Hadji, C. (1995). Thinking and acting on education, Paris, ESF publisher, 2nd printing,

Hague, C., & Payton, S. (2010). *Digital literacy across the curriculum*. FutureLab.

Haipinge, E., & Goosen, L. (2024). Exploring Educators' Pedagogical Capabilities to Develop University Students' 21st Century Skills: Navigating Within a Digital Learning Environment. In Bosch, C., Goosen, L., & Chetty, J. (Eds.), *Navigating Computer Science Education in the 21st Century* (pp. 1–20). IGI Global., DOI: 10.4018/979-8-3693-1066-3.ch001

Hambursin, O. (2024). *Un livre, une histoire : Nicolas Bouvier et Thierry Vernet, « L'usage du monde » (Podcast - Radio France / Académie de Paris)*. Un livre, une histoire : un podcast France Télévisions, en partenariat avec l'Académie de Paris. https://dial.uclouvain.be/pr/boreal/object/boreal:292546

Hamel, M. J., Auyeung, S., Bedou, S., Ding, Y., & Mongrain, C. (2021). Affordances de ressources numériques pour développer des littératies multiples en langues secondes: Quatre études de cas. *Nouvelle Revue Synergies Canada*, (14), 1–15. DOI: 10.21083/nrsc.v2021i14.6678

Hamilton, A. (2024). Artificial Intelligence and Healthcare Simulation: The Shifting Landscape of Medical Education. *Cureus*, 16(5). Advance online publication. DOI: 10.7759/cureus.59747 PMID: 38840993

Hammady, R., & Arnab, S. (2022). Serious gaming for behaviour change: A systematic review. *Information (Basel)*, 13(3), 142. DOI: 10.3390/info13030142

Han, B., Nawaz, S., Buchanan, G., & McKay, D. (2023). Ethical and Pedagogical Impacts of AI in Education. In International Conference on Artificial Intelligence in Education (pp. 667–673). Cham: Springer Nature Switzerland DOI: 10.1007/978-3-031-36272-9_54

Han, J., Kamber, M., & Tung, A. K. H. (1996). Spatial clustering methods in data mining: A survey. *Data Mining and Knowledge Discovery*, 2(1), 61–88.

Hao, H., Wang, Y., & Chen, J. (2024). Empowering Scenario Planning with Artificial Intelligence: A Perspective on Building Smart and Resilient Cities. *Engineering (Beijing)*, 43, 272–283. DOI: 10.1016/j.eng.2024.06.012

Haque, S. (2022). Role of literature in the learning of Urdu as a foreign language in France. Representative Samples and Didactic Discourses, 43-54. https://doi.org/DOI: 10.17184/eac.6538

Hargittai, E. (2002). Beyond logs and surveys: In-depth measures of people's web use skills. *Journal of the American Society for Information Science and Technology*, 53(14), 1239–1244. DOI: 10.1002/asi.10166

Harlen, W. (2007). *Assessment of Learning*. SAGE Publications. DOI: 10.4135/9781446214695

Harlen, W., & James, M. (1997). Assessment and Learning: Differences and Relationships between Formative and Summative Assessment. *Assessment in Education: Principles, Policy & Practice*, 4(3), 365–379. DOI: 10.1080/0969594970040304

Harrison, T., & Khatoon, B. (2017). Virtue, ethics and moral education in the digital age. *Journal of Moral Education*, 46(4), 334–346.

Hastings, J. S., Madrian, B. C., & Skimmyhorn, W. L. (2013). Financial literacy, financial education, and economic outcomes. Annu. *Rev. Econ.*, 5(1), 347–373. PMID: 23991248

Hattie, J. (2009). *Visible learning: A synthesis of over 800 meta-analyses relating to achievement*. Routledge.

Hattie, J., & Donoghue, G. (2016). Learning strategies: A synthesis and conceptual model. *Educational Psychologist*, 51(2), 140–152. DOI: 10.1080/00461520.2016.1170497 PMID: 30792898

Hayles, N. K. (2012). *How We Think: Digital Media and Contemporary Technogenesis*. University of Chicago Press. DOI: 10.7208/chicago/9780226321370.001.0001

Hébert, M., & Lépine, M. (2013). De l'intérêt de la notion de littératie en francophonie: Un état des lieux en sciences de l'éducation. *Globe*, 16(1), 25–43. DOI: 10.7202/1018176ar

Higgs, J., & Burstein, J. (2023). Feedback that facilitates learning: The role of AI in instructional feedback. *Journal of the Learning Sciences*, 32(2), 210–230. DOI: 10.1080/10508406.2023.2071952

Hilbert, M. (2016). Big Data for Development: A Review of Promises and Challenges. *Development Policy Review*, 34(1), 135–174. DOI: 10.1111/dpr.12142

Hockly, N. (2012). Digital literacies. *ELT Journal*, 66(1), 108–112. DOI: 10.1093/elt/ccr077

Hoffman, R. R., Klein, G., & Hollnagel, E. (2019). The ethics of using AI for education: Balancing innovation with privacy. *AI & Society*, 34(2), 315–328. DOI: 10.1007/s00146-018-0847-5

Hollands, F. M., & Tashiro, T. (2018). Creating equitable digital learning environments: A report on the implications of technology access for students' academic success. *Educational Technology Research and Development*, 66(1), 139–165. DOI: 10.1007/s11423-017-9555-3

Hollands, F. M., & Tashiro, T. (2022). Addressing the digital divide in AI-based education: Policies and practices. *Educational Technology Research and Development*, 70(3), 321–340.

Holmes, W., Bialik, M., & Fadel, C. (2019). *Artificial Intelligence in Education Promises and Implications for Teaching and Learning*. Center for Curriculum Redesign. https://circls.org/primers/artificial-intelligence-in-education-promises-and-implications-for-teaching-and-learning

Holmes, W. (2020). *The impact of artificial intelligence on education*. Springer.

Holmes, W., Bialik, M., & Fadel, C. (2019). *Artificial intelligence in education: Promises and Implications for Teaching and Learning*. Center for Curriculum Redesign., Retrieved from http://bit.ly/AIED-BOOK

Holmes, W., & Miao, F. (2024). *Orientations pour l'intelligence artificielle générative dans l'éducation et la recherche*. UNESCO Publishing.

Holmes, W., Porayska-Pomsta, K., Holstein, K., Sutherland, E., Baker, T., Shum, S. B., & Koedinger, K. R. (2021). Ethics of AI in education: Towards a community-wide framework. *International Journal of Artificial Intelligence in Education*, •••, 1–23. https://www.college-de-france.fr/fr/agenda/cours/apprentissage-profond/pourquoi-apprentissage-profond

Holmes, W., & Tuomi, I. (2022). *Artificial Intelligence in Education: Opportunities and Challenges.* Springer.

Holmes, W., & Tuomi, I. (2022). The role of artificial intelligence in education: Current practices and future prospects. *Educational Technology Research and Development*, 70(1), 5–23. DOI: 10.1007/s11423-021-10099-4

Houssaye, J. (1988). *Pratiques pédagogiques.* P. Lang.

Howard, J., & Ruder, S. (2018). *Universal language model fine-tuning for text classification. Proceedings of the 56th Annual Meeting of the Association for Computational Linguistics*, 328-339. DOI: 10.18653/v1/P18-1031

Hrich, N., Azekri, M., & Khaldi, M. (2024). Artificial Intelligence Item Analysis Tool for Educational Assessment: Case of Large-Scale Competitive Exams. *International Journal of Information and Education Technology (IJIET)*, 14(6), 822–827. Advance online publication. DOI: 10.18178/ijiet.2024.14.6.2107

Hsu, T. C., Abelson, H., Lao, N., Tseng, Y. H., & Lin, Y. T. (2021). Behavioral-pattern exploration and development of an instructional tool for young children to learn AI. *Computers and Education: Artificial Intelligence*, 2, 100012. DOI: 10.1016/j.caeai.2021.100012

https://ieeexplore.ieee.org/abstract/document/10697011

https://link.springer.com/chapter/10.1007/978-3-031-61685-3_3

https://www.ingentaconnect.com/contentone/hsp/aoe/2024/00000002/00000003/art00006

https://www.sciencedirect.com/science/article/pii/S2949678024000199

Huang, J. M., Chaing, S. Y., Sung, Y. C., Chen, J. T., Wu, Y. H., Liu, T. L., & Chou, C. Y. (2024). Interactive AI Application: Operant Conditioning and Adaptive Learning. *Pacific Asia Conference on Information Systems (PACIS) Proceedings.* Association for Information Systems (AIS). Retrieved from https://aisel.aisnet.org/pacis2024/track14_educ/track14_educ/2/

Hughes, C. A. (2011). *Explicit instruction: Effective and efficient teaching*. The Guilford Press.

Hughes, C. A., Morris, J. R., Therrien, W. J., & Benson, S. K. (2017). *Explicit instruction: Historical and contemporary contexts.* Learning Disabilities Researc.

Hughes, J. (2022). Exploring AI and blended learning synergies in higher education. *International Journal of Educational Technology*, 15(3), 255–270.

Hussain, F. (2012). E-Learning 3.0= E-Learning 2.0+ Web 3.0?. International Association for Development of the Information Society.

Hutson, J., Jeevanjee, T., Vander Graaf, V., Lively, J., Weber, J., Weir, G., & Edele, S. (2022). Artificial intelligence and the disruption of higher education: Strategies for integrations across disciplines. *Creative Education*, 13(12), 3953–3980. DOI: 10.4236/ce.2022.1312253

Hu, Z., & Rao, K. S. (2007). Analyzing air pollution data using cluster analysis: A case study. *Environmental Monitoring and Assessment*, 132(1-3), 335–343. PMID: 17171250

Hwang, H. S., Zhu, L. C., & Cui, Q. (2023). Development and validation of a digital literacy scale in the artificial intelligence era for college students. [TIIS]. *KSII Transactions on Internet and Information Systems*, •••, 2241–2258.

Hymes, D. H. (1972). On communicative competence. In *Sociolinguistics: Selected Readings*. Penguin Books.

Igras-Cybulska, M., Kolber-Bugajska, B., Salamon, R., Babiuch, P., Jegierski, H., Jegierski, M., ... & Węgrzyn, P. (2024). Supporting Unity Developers with an AI-Powered Asset: Insights from an Exploratory User Study on Multiplayer Game Development.

Ikram, C., Lamya, A., Mohamed, E., & Mohamed, K. (2024). Model for motivating learners with personalized learning objects in a hypermedia adaptive learning system. *IAES International Journal of Artificial Intelligence (IJ-AI), 13*(2), 1282. https://doi.org/DOI: 10.11591/ijai.v13.i2.pp1282-1293

Ilomäki, L., Paavola, S., Lakkala, M., & Kantosalo, A. (2016). Digital competence – an emergent boundary concept for policy and educational research. *Education and Information Technologies*, 21(3), 655–679. DOI: 10.1007/s10639-014-9346-4

Ingkavara, T., Panjaburee, P., Srisawasdi, N., & Sajjapanroj, S. (2022). The use of a personalized learning approach to implementing self-regulated online learning. *Computers and Education: Artificial Intelligence*, 3, 100086. DOI: 10.1016/j.caeai.2022.100086

Iqbal, M. Z., Mangina, E., & Campbell, A. G. (2022). Current challenges and future research directions in augmented reality for education. *Multimodal Technologies and Interaction*, 6(9), 75. Advance online publication. DOI: 10.3390/mti6090075

Isbell, D. R., & Kremmel, B. (2020). Test review: Current options in at-home language proficiency tests for making high-stakes decisions. *Language Testing*, 37(4), 600–619. DOI: 10.1177/0265532220943483

Ishak, N. S., Iqbal, M. A., & Shah, S. R. (2023). Digital literacy in higher education: Developing students' skills in a technology-enhanced learning environment. *Journal of University Teaching & Learning Practice*, 20(1), 1–15. https://ro.uow.edu.au/jutlp/vol20/iss1/3

Jääskä, E. (2023). Game-based learning methods in project management higher education.

Jain, R., Garg, N., & Khera, S. N. (2022). Adoption of AI-enabled tools in social development organizations in India: An extension of UTAUT model. *Frontiers in Psychology*, 13, 893691. Advance online publication. DOI: 10.3389/fpsyg.2022.893691 PMID: 35795409

Janakiraman, S., Watson, S. L., Watson, W. R., & Newby, T. (2021). Effectiveness of digital games in producing environmentally friendly attitudes and behaviors: A mixed methods study. *Computers & Education*, 160, 104043. DOI: 10.1016/j.compedu.2020.104043

Jeannotte, D. (2015) Abstracting and generalizing processes conceptualized from a commognitive perspective. In L. Theis (ed.), Cultural Pluralities and the Universality of Mathematics: Issues and Perspectives for their Teaching and Learning – Proceedings of the EMF2015 Conference – WG3, Jonnaert, P. (2002). A contextualization of arithmetic learning. In J. Bideaud & H.

Jiang, S., Qian, Y., Tang, H., Yalcinkaya, R., Rosé, C. P., Chao, J., & Finzer, W. (2023). Examining computational thinking processes in modeling unstructured data. *Education and Information Technologies*, 28(4), 4309–4333. DOI: 10.1007/s10639-022-11355-3

Jmoula, L., & Belouali, S. (2022). L'intelligence artificielle et le traitement des données massives de l'université marocaine: Perspectives, risques et enjeux éthiques. *Journal of Information Science*, 21, 203–220.

Jobin, A., Ienca, M., & Vayena, E. (2019). The global landscape of AI ethics guidelines. *Nature Machine Intelligence*, 1(9), 389–399. DOI: 10.1038/s42256-019-0088-2

Jockers, M. L. (2013). *Macroanalysis: numerical methods and literary history*. University of Illinois Press. DOI: 10.5406/illinois/9780252037528.001.0001

Johnson, A., & Smith, B. (2019). The Impact of Personalized Learning on Student Attitudesand Self-Efficacy in Mathematics. *Educational Technology Research and Development*, 38(2), 201–218.

Johnson, C., & Zone, E. (2018). Achieving a scaled implementation of adaptive learning through faculty engagement: A case study. *Current Issues in Emerging Elearning*, 5(1), 80–95. https://scholarworks.umb.edu/ciee/vol5/iss1/7

Johnson, D. W., & Johnson, R. T. (2009). An Educational Psychology Success Story: Social Interdependence Theory and Cooperative Learning. *Educational Psychologist*, 44(2), 95–105.

Johnson, J. (2022). The AI commander problem: Ethical, political, and psychological dilemmas of human-machine interactions in AI-enabled warfare. *Journal of Military Ethics*, 21(3-4), 246–271. DOI: 10.1080/15027570.2023.2175887

Johnson, L., Adams Becker, S., Cummins, M., Estrada, V., & Freeman, A. (2022). *Horizon Report: 2022 Higher Education Edition*. EDUCAUSE.

Johnson, W. L., Rickel, J. W., & Lester, J. C. (2000). Animated pedagogical agents : Face-to-face interaction in interactive learning environments. *International Journal ofArtificial Intelligence in Education*, 11(1), 47–78.

Joshi, M., Choi, E., Weld, D. S., & Zettlemoyer, L. (2020). SpanBERT: Improving pre-training by representing and predicting spans. *Transactions of the Association for Computational Linguistics*, 8, 64–77. DOI: 10.1162/tacl_a_00300

Joulin, A., Grave, E., Mikolov, T., Bojanowski, P., Mikolov, M., & Ruder, S. (2017). *Bag of tricks for efficient text classification*. arXiv preprint arXiv:1607.01759. DOI: 10.18653/v1/E17-2068

Joy, L., & Walker, R. (2023). Establishing an Assistive Technology-Enabled Culture at the University of York: Reflections on a Values-Based Strategy. In *Handbook of Research on Advancing Equity and Inclusion Through Educational Technology* (pp. 189–207). IGI Global. DOI: 10.4018/978-1-6684-6868-5.ch010

Kabudi, T., Pappas, I., & Olsen, D. H. (2021). AI-enabled adaptive learning systems: A systematic mapping of the literature. *Computers and Education: Artificial Intelligence*, 2, 100017. DOI: 10.1016/j.caeai.2021.100017

Kalai, L. (2023). ICT in the Tunisian university context: What uses for which forms of didactic innovation? the case of French students. *Multilingual*, 20. Advance online publication. DOI: 10.4000/11o27

Kaliisa, R., Misiejuk, K., López-Pernas, S., Khalil, M., & Saqr, M. (2023). Have learning analytics dashboards lived up to the hype? A systematic review of impact on students' achievement, motivation, participation and attitude, *The 14th Learning Analytics and Knowledge Conference, Kyoto, Japan, March 2024*, https://doi.org/DOI: 10.1145/3636555.3636884

Kamalov, F., Santandreu Calonge, D., & Gurrib, I. (2023). New era of artificial intelligence in education : Towards a sustainable multifaceted revolution. *Sustainability (Basel)*, 15(16), 12451. DOI: 10.3390/su151612451

Kant, I. (1785). *Groundwork of the Metaphysics of Morals*.

Kant, I. (1788). *The Critique of Practical Reason*. Infomotions Incorporated.

Kant, I. (1797). *The metaphysics of morals* (Gregor, M. J., Ed.). Cambridge University Press.

Kant, I. (2002). Deontology: The ethics of duty. In *Ethics and Values: Basic Readings in Theory and Practice* (pp. 77–87). Pearson Custom.

Kaufman, L., & Rousseeuw, P. J. (1990). *Finding groups in data: An introduction to cluster analysis*. Wiley. DOI: 10.1002/9780470316801

Kaviyaraj, R., & Uma, M. (2021, March). A survey on future of augmented reality with AI in education. *International Conference on Artificial Intelligence and Smart Systems (ICAIS)* (pp. 47-52). IEEE. DOI: 10.1109/ICAIS50930.2021.9395838

Kawtar, Z. (2021). CDESACL Conception and Development of Educational Scenarios for an Adaptive Online Training Device Based on Collaborative/Cooperative Learning: Work Methodology. *RA Journal Of Applied Research*, 07(01). Advance online publication. DOI: 10.47191/rajar/v7i1.02

Kaya, M., & Imer, G. (2020). Investigation of the Relationship between Digital Citizenship and Digital Literacy Levels of Secondary School Students. *International Journal of Scientific and Technological Research*, 6(12), 9–19.

Keller, T., & Brucker-Kley, E. (2020). Design hints for smart agents as teachers in virtual learning spaces. In *Proceedings of the International Conference on e-Society* (pp. 111-118). DOI: 10.33965/es2020_202005L014

Kelly, S., Kaye, S. A., & Oviedo-Trespalacios, O. (2023). What factors contribute to the acceptance of artificial intelligence? A systematic review. *Telematics and Informatics*, 77, 101925. Advance online publication. DOI: 10.1016/j.tele.2022.101925

Kenwright, B. (2023). Exploring the power of creative ai tools and game-based methodologies for interactive web-based programming. *arXiv preprint arXiv:2308.11649*.

Kern, R. (2021). Twenty-five years of digital literacies in CALL.

Khaldi, M. (Ed.). (2024b, February). *Technological tools for innovative teaching*. IGI Global., Retrieved from https://www.igi-global.com/book/technological-tools-innovative-teaching/335010

Khalid, U. B., Naeem, M., Stasolla, F., Syed, M. H., Abbas, M., & Coronato, A. (2024). Impact of AI-powered solutions in rehabilitation process: Recent improvements and future trends. *International Journal of General Medicine*, 17, 943–969. DOI: 10.2147/IJGM.S453903 PMID: 38495919

Khalil, M. K., & Elkhider, I. A. (2020). The Role of Artificial Intelligence in Personalized Learning: A Review. *Journal of Educational Technology Systems*, 49(2), 195–210.

Khan, N., Sarwar, A., Chen, T. B., & Khan, S. (2022). Connecting digital literacy in higher education to the 21st century workforce. *Knowledge Management & E-Learning*, 14(1), 46–61. DOI: 10.34105/j.kmel.2022.14.004

Khosravi, H., Shum, S. B., Chen, G., Conati, C., Tsai, Y. S., Kay, J., & Gašević, D. (2022). Explainable artificial intelligence in education. *Computers and Education: Artificial Intelligence*, 3, 100074.

Kim, J., Park, S., & Yoon, H. (2023). Integrating virtual reality with AI in language education: A review of emerging technologies. *International Journal of Learning Technology*, 11(2), 145–163.

Kim, S., Park, J., & Lee, M. (2018). Real-time adjustments in learning systems. *Journal of Interactive Learning Research*, 29(2), 145–162.

Kim, W. (2002). Personalization : Definition, status, and challenges ahead. *Journal of Object Technology*, 1(1), 29–40. DOI: 10.5381/jot.2002.1.1.c3

Kim, Y., & Baylor, A. L. (2016). A virtual agent of change: Motivating pre-service teachers to integrate technology into their future classrooms. *Research and Development in Educational Technology*, 64(3), 543–560.

Kintsch, W. (1998). *Comprehension: A paradigm for cognition*. Cambridge University Press.

Kissoon, C., & Karran, T. (2024). *Academic Freedom : Swimming against the Technological Tide*.

Klašnja-Milićević, A., Vesin, B., Ivanović, M., & Budimac, Z. (2011). E-Learning personalization based on hybrid recommendation strategy and learning style identification. *Computers & Education*, 56(3), 885–899. DOI: 10.1016/j.compedu.2010.11.001

Knobel, M., & Lankshear, C. (2006). Digital Literacy and Digital Literacies: Policy, Pedagogy and Research Considerations for Education. *HomeNordic Journal of Digital Literacy*, 1(1), 12–24. DOI: 10.18261/ISSN1891-943X-2006-01-03

Koedinger, K. R., Corbett, A. T., & Perfetti, C. A. (2012). The knowledge-learning-instruction framework : Bridging the science-practice chasm to enhance robust student learning. *Cognitive Science*, 36(5), 757–798. DOI: 10.1111/j.1551-6709.2012.01245.x PMID: 22486653

Koehler, M. J., & Mishra, P. (2009). *What Is Technological Pedagogical Content* Knowledge (TPACK)? *Contemporary Issues in Technology & Teacher Education*, 9(1), 60–70.

Kolb, D. A. (1984). *Experiential Learning: Experience as the Source of Learning and Development*. Prentice Hall.

Kollins, S. H., DeLoss, D. J., Cañadas, E., Lutz, J., Findling, R. L., Keefe, R. S., Epstein, J. N., Cutler, A. J., & Faraone, S. V. (2020). A novel digital intervention for actively reducing severity of paediatric ADHD (STARS-ADHD): A randomised controlled trial. *The Lancet. Digital Health*, 2(4), e168–e178. DOI: 10.1016/S2589-7500(20)30017-0 PMID: 33334505

Kolodner, J. L. (2000). Georgia Institute of Technology Mark Guzdial Georgia Institute of Technology. *Theoretical Foundations of Learning Environments*, 215.

Komasawa, N., & Yokohira, M. (2023). Learner-centered experience-based medical education in an AI-driven society: A literature review. *Cureus*, 15(10). Advance online publication. DOI: 10.7759/cureus.46883 PMID: 37954813

Krath, J., Schürmann, L., & Von Korflesch, H. F. (2021). Revealing the theoretical basis of gamification: A systematic review and analysis of theory in research on gamification, serious games and game-based learning. *Computers in Human Behavior*, 125, 106963. DOI: 10.1016/j.chb.2021.106963

Krzystanek, M., Surma, S., Stokrocka, M., Romańczyk, M., Przybyło, J., Krzystanek, N., & Borkowski, M. (2021). Tips for effective implementation of virtual reality exposure therapy in phobias—A systematic review. *Frontiers in Psychiatry*, 12, 737351. DOI: 10.3389/fpsyt.2021.737351 PMID: 34621197

Kulkarni, C., Bernstein, M., & Klemmer, S. (2019). Learning from peers in a blended learning environment: Lessons from AI-enhanced instruction. *International Journal of Artificial Intelligence in Education*, 28(1), 21–37. DOI: 10.1007/s40593-018-00180-3

Kumar, J., Jieyao, Z., & Soeiro, J. D. (2024). Empowering Lifelong Learning: Embracing the Impact of Artificial Intelligence. In Behera, S. K., Ibrahim, A. H., & Romdhani, F. (Eds.), (pp. 42–66). Advances in Educational Marketing, Administration, and Leadership. IGI Global. DOI: 10.4018/979-8-3693-6955-5.ch003

Kunnan, A. J. (2004). Test Fairness. In Milanovic, M., & Weir, C. J. (Eds.), *European Language Testing in a Global Context*. Cambridge University Press.

Kuo, Y. C., Walker, A. E., Schroder, K. E. E., & Belland, B. R. (2014). Interaction, Internet self-efficacy, and self-regulated learning as predictors of student satisfaction in online education courses. *The Internet and Higher Education*, 20, 35–50. DOI: 10.1016/j.iheduc.2013.10.001

Kurzweil, R. (1990). *The Age of Intelligent Machines*. MIT Press.

Kvasny, L., & Richardson, H. (2006). Critical research in information systems: Looking forward, looking back. *Information Technology & People*, 19(3), 196–202. DOI: 10.1108/09593840610689813

Lai, Y. H., Chen, S. Y., Lai, C. F., Chang, Y. C., & Su, Y. S. (2021). Study on enhancing AIoT computational thinking skills by plot image-based VR. *Interactive Learning Environments*, 29(3), 482–495. DOI: 10.1080/10494820.2019.1580750

Lalonde, M., Blanchette, K., Wuyckens, G., Huebner, E. J., & & Meilleur, B. (2023). La création de récits d'anticipation en réalité virtuelle pour le développement de la compétence numérique et de la compétence en littératie médiatique multimodale des élèves au secondaire. Médiations et médiatisations, (15),, 123-140.

Lamnai, A., & mhouti, A. E. (2023, January). Serious Games for Improving Training and Skills Acquisition in Medicine and Health Professions. In *International Conference on Digital Technologies and Applications* (pp. 967-975). Cham: Springer Nature Switzerland. DOI: 10.1007/978-3-031-29857-8_96

Lampropoulos, G. (2023). Educational Data Mining and Learning Analytics in the 21st Century. Dans *Encyclopedia of Data Science and Machine Learning* (pp. 1642-1651). (S.l.): IGI Global.

Lamya, A., Kawtar, Z., Mohamed, E., & Mohamed, K. (2020). Personalization of an educational scenario of a learning activity according to the learning styles model David Kolb. *Global Journal of Engineering and Technology Advances, 5*(3), 099-108.

Lamya, A., Mohamed, K., & Mohamed, E. (2021). Personalization Between Pedagogy and Adaptive Hypermedia System. Dans *International Conference On Big Data and Internet of Things* (pp. 223-234). Cham: Springer International Publishing.

Lan, Z., Chen, M., Goodman, S., Gimpel, K., Sharma, P., & Sorensen, J. (2020). *ALBERT: A lite BERT for self-supervised learning of language representations.* arXiv preprint arXiv:1909.11942.

Landers, R. N., & Landers, A. K. (2014). An empirical test of the influences of gamification on learning outcomes. *Proceedings of the 47th Hawaii International Conference on System Sciences* (pp. 3090-3099). IEEE. https://doi.org/DOI: 10.1109/HICSS.2014.391

Lang, P., Yuste Frías, J., Araujo, S., Vergondy, B., Claude, E., & Correia, A. (2023). L'apprentissage des langues à l'ère du numérique: quelques réflexions empiriques basées sur des projets pédagogiques. Tradución e lingüística.

Lathwesen, C., & Belova, N. (2021). Escape rooms in STEM teaching and Learning—Prospective field or declining trend? A literature review. *Education Sciences*, 11(6), 308. DOI: 10.3390/educsci11060308

Laurier, M. (1992). The Application of Adaptive Testing Techniques in French as a Second Language. In Sauvé, L. (Ed.), *Educational Technology from Yesterday to Tomorrow* (pp. 109–118). CIPTE/Tele-University.

Laurier, M. (1999). The development of an adaptive test for placement in French. In Chalhoub-Deville, M. (Ed.), *Issues in computer-adaptive testing of reading proficiency* (pp. 122–135). Cambridge University Press.

Laurier, M., & Baker, B. (2015). The certification of teachers' language competence in Quebec in French and English: Two different perspectives? *Language Assessment Quarterly*, 12(1), 10–28. DOI: 10.1080/15434303.2014.979349

LeCun, Y. (2015, August 28). *Pourquoi l'apprentissage profond ? | Collège de France* [Audio recording].

LeCun, Y. (2019). *Quand la machine apprend : La révolution des neurones artificiels et de l'apprentissage profond.* Odile Jacob.

Lee, C. A., Tzeng, J. W., Huang, N. F., & Su, Y. S. (2021). Prediction of student performance in massive open online courses using deep learning system based on learning behaviors. *Journal of Educational Technology & Society*, 24(3), 130–146. https://www.jstor.org/stable/27032861

Lee, J., Wu, A. S., Li, D., & Kulasegaram, K. M. (2021). Artificial Intelligence in Undergraduate Medical Education: A Scoping Review. *Academic Medicine*, 96(11S), S62–S700. DOI: 10.1097/ACM.0000000000004291 PMID: 34348374

Lee, L. K., Wei, X., Chui, K. T., Cheung, S. K., Wang, F. L., Fung, Y. C., Lu, A., Hui, Y. K., Hao, T., U, L. H., & Wu, N. I. (2024). A Systematic Review of the Design of Serious Games for Innovative Learning: Augmented Reality, Virtual Reality, or Mixed Reality? *Electronics (Basel)*, 13(5), 890. DOI: 10.3390/electronics13050890

Lee, M., Kim, S., & Park, J. (2019). Dynamic changes in student learning preferences. *Journal of Educational Psychology*, 111(3), 451–464.

Lee, M., & Park, J. (2019). The efficacy of implicit approaches in learning style identification. *Educational Psychology Review*, 31(1), 78–94.

Leslie, D. 2019. Understanding artificial intelligence ethics and safety: A guide for the responsible design and implementation of AI systems in the public sector. The Alan Turing Institute. DOI: 10.2139/ssrn.3403301

Lewis, M., Liu, Y., Goyal, N., Ghazvininejad, M., Mohamed, A., & Xiang, B. (2020). *BART: Denoising sequence-to-sequence pre-training for natural language generation, translation, and comprehension.* arXiv preprint arXiv:1910.13461. DOI: 10.18653/v1/2020.acl-main.703

Libbrecht, P., & Goosen, L. (2015). Using ICTs to Facilitate Multilingual Mathematics Teaching and Learning. In Barwell, R., Clarkson, P., Halai, A., Kazima, M., Moschkovich, J., Planas, N., & Villavicencio Ubillús, M. (Eds.), *Mathematics Education and Language Diversity* (pp. 217–235). Springer., DOI: 10.1007/978-3-319-14511-2_12

Li, S. (2021). Research on the Exploration and Reflection of Foreign Language Teaching Based on "Artificial Intelligence+ Education" in the Big Data Era. *2nd International Conference on Big Data Economy and Information Management (BDEIM) IEEE*, 354-357. DOI: 10.1109/BDEIM55082.2021.00078

Little, D. (2006). The Common European Framework of Reference for Languages: Content, purpose, origin, reception and impact. *Language Teaching*, 39(3), 167–190. DOI: 10.1017/S0261444806003557

Liu, Y., Ott, M., Goyal, N., Du, J., Dalton, J., & Le, Q. V. (2019). *RoBERTa: A robustly optimized BERT pretraining approach.* arXiv preprint arXiv:1907.11692.

Liu, D. S., Abu-Shaban, K., Halabi, S. S., & Cook, T. S. (2023). Changes in radiology due to artificial intelligence that can attract medical students to the specialty. *JMIR Medical Education*, 9, e43415. DOI: 10.2196/43415 PMID: 36939823

Liu, Y., Chen, L., & Yang, Y. (2022). Informed consent in the age of AI: Challenges and strategies for educators. *International Journal of Artificial Intelligence in Education*, 32(4), 803–826. DOI: 10.1007/s40593-021-00244-4

LIVINGSTONE. (2004). Sonia. «Media Literacy and the Challenge of New Information and Communication Technologies.». *Communication Review*, •••, 3–14.

Lodi, M., & Martini, S. (2021). Computational Thinking, Between Papert and Wing. *Science & Education*, 30(4), 883–908. DOI: 10.1007/s11191-021-00202-5

López, M., & West, M. (2023). Navigating ethical dilemmas in AI education: Training teachers for responsible integration. *Journal of Teacher Education and Educators*, 12(1), 55–73.

Loye, N. (2018). What if validation was more than a series of technical procedures? *Mesure et Évaluation en Éducation*, 41(1), 97–123. DOI: 10.7202/1055898ar

Luckin, R., Holmes, W., Griffiths, M., & Forcier, L. B. (2016). *Intelligence unleashed: An argument for AI in education*. Pearson. https://www.pearson.com/content/dam/one-dot-com/one-dot-com/global/Files/AI-in-Education/Intelligence-Unleashed.pdf

Luckin, R. (2018). *Machine learning and human intelligence: The future of education for the 21st century*. UCL Institute of Education Press.

Luckin, R.. (2016). *Intelligence Unleashed: An Argument for AI in Education*. Pearson Education.

Luckin, R., & Cukurova, M. (2019). Designing Educational Technologies in the Age of AI: A Science in Learning Approach. *British Journal of Educational Technology*, 50(6), 2824–2838. DOI: 10.1111/bjet.12861

Luckin, R., Holmes, W., Griffiths, M., & Forcier, L. B. (2016). *Intelligence unleashed: An argument for AI in education*. Pearson.

Luckin, R., Holmes, W., Griffiths, M., & Forcier, L. B. (2016). *Intelligence unleashed: an argument in favor of AI in education*. Pearson Education.

Luger, G. F., & Stubblefield, W. A. (1993). *Artificial Intelligence : Structures and Strategies for Complex Problem Solving*. Benjamin/Cummings.

Lundvall, S. (2015). Physical literacy in the field of physical education–A challenge and a possibility. *Journal of Sport and Health Science*, 4(2), 113–118.

Lunt, B. (2005). *Joseph Ekstrom, Edith Lawson, Reza Kamali, Jacob Miller, Sandra Gorka, Han Reichgelt. «Defining the IT Curriculum: The Results of the Past 3 Years.»*. Issues in Informing Science and Information Technology.

Luoma, S. (2004). *Assessing Speaking*. Cambridge University Press. DOI: 10.1017/CBO9780511733017

Luo, Y. (2024). Innovative research on AI-assisted teaching models for college English listening and speaking courses. *Applied and Computational Engineering*, 69(1), 155–160. DOI: 10.54254/2755-2721/69/20241493

Mageira, K., Pittou, D., Papasalouros, A., Kotis, K., Zangogianni, P., & Daradoumis, A. (2022). Educational AI chatbots for content and language integrated learning. *Applied Sciences (Basel, Switzerland)*, 12(7), 3239.

Maghsudi, S., Lan, A., Xu, J., & van Der Schaar, M. (2021). Personalized education in the artificial intelligence era: What to expect next. *IEEE Signal Processing Magazine*, 38(3), 37–50. DOI: 10.1109/MSP.2021.3055032

Mahadev Madgule, N. (2023). Vinayaka, Yeshwant M. Sonkhaskar, Dhiren Ramanbhai Patel, R. Karthikeyan, P. Selvakumar,(2023). Mechanical properties and microstructure of activated TIG welded similar joints of Inconel alloys by desirability approaches. *Materials Today: Proceedings*, 77, 528–533. DOI: 10.1016/j.matpr.2022.12.250

Mandelbrot, B. B. (1982). *The fractal geometry of nature*. W.H. Freeman.

Marcellis-Warin, N. (2022). *Analyse comparative d'écosystèmes en ia dans le but de repérer les pratiques innovantes en matière de formation et de transfert de connaissances*. CIRANO.

Marisa, W., & Djulia, E. J. (2022). The relationship of digital literacy to students' cognitive ability in ecology course. *Jurnal Pelita Pendidikan*, 10(2), 47–51. DOI: 10.24114/jpp.v10i2.26774

Martin, A. (2006). Allan. «A european framework for digital literacy.». *Nordic Journal of Digital LiteracyVolume*, 1(2), 151–161. DOI: 10.18261/ISSN1891-943X-2006-02-06

Martin, L., Brown, T., & Clark, D. (2022). Observational methods in educational technology. *International Journal of Learning Analytics*, 5(2), 34–50.

Martin, S. M., Casey, J. R., & Kane, S. (2021). *Serious Games in Personalized Learning: New Models for Design and Performance*. Taylor & Francis. DOI: 10.4324/9781003042709

Martzoukou, K., Fulton, C., Kostagiolas, P., & Lavranos, C. (2020). A study of higher education students' self-perceived digital competences for learning and everyday life online participation. *The Journal of Documentation*, 76(6), 1413–1458. DOI: 10.1108/JD-03-2020-0041

Martzoukou, K., Kostagiolas, P., Lavranos, C., Lauterbach, T., & Fulton, C. (2021). A study of university law students' selfperceived digital competences. *Journal of Librarianship and Information Science*, 54(4), 751–769. DOI: 10.1177/09610006211048004

Marzano, R. J., & Marzano, J. S. (2021). The role of formative assessment in enhancing student learning. *Educational Leadership*, 78(6), 52–56.

Maskeliunas, R., Damasevicius, R., Paulauskas, A., Ceravolo, M. G., Charalambous, M., Kambanaros, M., Pampoulou, E., Barbabella, F., Poli, A., & Carvalho, C. V. (2022). Deep reinforcement learning-based iTrain serious game for caregivers dealing with post-stroke patients. *Information (Basel)*, 13(12), 564. DOI: 10.3390/info13120564

Matochová, J., & Kowaliková, P. (2024). Transforming Higher Education: Psychological and Sociological Perspective (the use of artificial intelligence). *Resource*, •••, 176–181. DOI: 10.53349/resource.2024.is1.a1253

Maxwell, J. A. (2022). Interactive approaches to qualitative research design. In *The Sage handbook of qualitative research design* (pp. 41–54). SAGE. DOI: 10.4135/9781529770278.n4

McCarthy, J., Minsky, M. L., Rochester, N., & Shannon, C. E. (2006). A proposal for the dartmouth summer research project on artificial intelligence, august 31, 1955. *AI Magazine*, 27(4), 12. DOI: 10.1609/aimag.v27i4.1904

McCartney, S., & Parent, R. (2015). Ethical systems. In *Ethics in law enforcement* (pp. 15-40). BCcampus.

McCarty, W. (2005). *Computer Science in the Humanities*. Palgrave Macmillan. DOI: 10.1057/9780230504219

McLachlan, G. J., & Peel, D. (2000). *Finite mixture models*. Wiley. DOI: 10.1002/0471721182

McLaren, B. M., Scheuer, O., & Mikšátko, J. (2010). Supporting collaborative learning and e-discussions using artificial intelligence techniques. *International Journal of Artificial Intelligence in Education*, 20(1), 1–46. DOI: 10.3233/JAI-2010-0001

McLoughlin, C., & Lee, J. W. (2022). Personal learning environments, social media, and self-directed learning: A conceptual synthesis. *Journal of Online Learning and Teaching*, 8(1), 57–66.

McNamara, T., & Roever, C. (2006). *Language Testing: The Social Dimension*. Blackwell.

Means, B., Toyama, Y., Murphy, R., & Bakia, M. (2020). *Evaluation of evidence-based practices in online learning: A meta-analysis and review of online learning studies*. US Department of Education.

Mehrabi, N., Morstatter, F., Saxena, N., Lerman, K., & Galstyan, A. (2021). A survey on bias and fairness in machine learning. *ACM Computing Surveys*, 54(6), 1–35. DOI: 10.1145/3457607

Merriam-Webster. https://www.merriam-webster.com/dictionary/literacy. 2023.

Messick, S. (1989). Validity. In Linn, R. L. (Ed.), *Educational Measurement* (3rd ed., pp. 13–103). Macmillan.

Mikolov, T., Sutskever, I., Chen, K., Corrado, G., & Dean, J. (2013). *Efficient estimation of word representations in vector space*. arXiv preprint arXiv:1301.3781.

Miller, A. (2019). *The effectiveness of direct instruction in higher education:* A meta-analysis. *The Journal of Educational Research*, 112(3), 355–371. DOI: 10.1080/00220671.2018.1439306

Milliner, B., & Barr, B. (2020). Computer-assisted language testing and learner behavior. In Freiermuth, M., & Zarrinabadi, N. (Eds.), *Technology and the psychology of second language learners and users. New language learning and teaching environments*. Palgrave Macmillan. DOI: 10.1007/978-3-030-34212-8_5

Mishra, P., & Koehler, M. J. (2008). Introducing Technological Pedagogical Content Knowledge. *Presented at the Annual Meeting of the American Educational Research Association (AERA)*. New York: AERA. Retrieved from http://www.matt-koehler.com/publications/Mishra_Koehler_AERA_2008.pdf

Mishra, P., & Koehler, M. J. (2021). Technological pedagogical content knowledge: A framework for teacher knowledge. *Teachers College Record*, 108(6), 1017–1054. DOI: 10.1111/j.1467-9620.2006.00684.x

Mitchell, T. M. (1997). Does Machine Learning Really Work? *AI Magazine*, 18(3), 3. Advance online publication. DOI: 10.1609/aimag.v18i3.1303

Mittal, A., Scholten, L., & Kapelan, Z. (2022). A review of serious games for urban water management decisions: Current gaps and future research directions. *Water Research*, 215, 118217. DOI: 10.1016/j.watres.2022.118217 PMID: 35320773

Mittelstadt, B. D. (2019). Principles alone cannot guarantee ethical AI. *Nature Machine Intelligence*, 1(11), 501–507. DOI: 10.1038/s42256-019-0114-4

Modular Object-Oriented Dynamic Learning Environment (MOODLE). (2018). *Philosophy*. Retrieved April 21, 2024, from MoodleDocs: https://docs.moodle.org/403/en/Philosophy

Mohamadi, S., Mujtaba, G., Le, N., Doretto, G., & Adjeroh, D. A. (2023). ChatGPT in the age of generative AI and large language models: a concise survey. *arXiv preprint arXiv:2307.04251*.

Mo, J. (2019). *« How does PISA define and measure reading literacy? », PISA in Focus, n° 101*. Éditions OCDE.

Mokkink, L. B., Boers, M., van der Vleuten, C. P. M., Bouter, L. M., Alonso, J., Patrick, D. L., de Vet, H. C. W., & Terwee, C. B. (2020). COSMIN Risk of Bias tool to assess the quality of studies on reliability or measurement error of outcome measurement instruments : A Delphi study. *BMC Medical Research Methodology*, 20(1), 293. DOI: 10.1186/s12874-020-01179-5 PMID: 33267819

Molenaar, I. (2022). Personnalisation de l'apprentissage: Vers une forme hybride des technologies d'apprentissage combinant l'humain et l'IA. In *Perspectives de l'OCDE sur l'éducation numérique 2021: Repousser les frontières avec l'IA, la blockchain et les robots*. Éditions OCDE., DOI: 10.1787/d5fe6bd0-fr

Mollick, E., & Mollick, E. (2024). *Co-Intelligence*. Random House UK.

Monde, R. d'information de documentation d'outils et d'initiatives pour un. (2024). Lexique critique de l'intelligence artificielle. *Plein droit, 140*(1), 7-10. .DOI: 10.3917/pld.140.0009

Mørch, A. I., & Andersen, R. (2023). Human-Centred AI in education in the age of generative AI tools. *Joint Proceedings of the Workshops, Work in Progress Demos and Doctoral Consortium at the 9th International Symposium on End-User Development (IS-EUD). 3408.* Cagliari, Italy: CEUR-WS.org. Retrieved from https://ceur-ws.org/Vol-3408/short-s2-08.pdf

Morel, G. M., & Spector, J. M. (Eds.). (2022). *Foundations of educational technology: Integrative approaches and interdisciplinary perspectives* (3rd ed.). Routledge., DOI: 10.4324/9781003268406

Moreno, R., & Mayer, R. (2021). Interactive multimodal learning environments: Special issue introduction. *Educational Psychologist*, 46(2), 81–85. DOI: 10.1080/00461520.2021.1895968

Mota, F. P., Kwecko, V., Devincenzi, S., Núñez, P., & Botelho, S. S. D. C. (2019). Ubiquitous learning : Asystematic review. Dans *2019 IEEE Frontiers in Education Conference (FIE* (pp. 1-9). IEEE.

Moussavou, J. (2023). *What pedagogical innovations in the age of AI?* Management & Data Science.

Muñoz, J. L. R., Ojeda, F. M., Jurado, D. L. A., Peña, P. F. P., Carranza, C. P. M., Berríos, H. Q., Molina, S. U., Farfan, A. R. M., Arias-Gonzáles, J. L., & Vasquez-Pauca, M. J. (2022). Systematic Review of Adaptive Learning Technology for Learning in Higher Education. *Eurasian Journal of Educational Research*, 98(98), 221–233. https://ejer.com.tr/manuscript/index.php/journal/article/view/707

Muranga, K., Muse, I. S., Köroğlu, E. N., & Yildirim, Y. (2023). Artificial Intelligence and Underfunded Education. *London Journal of Social Sciences*, (6), 56-68.Bas du formulaire

Murdoch, B. (2021). Privacy and artificial intelligence: Challenges for protecting health information in a new era. *BMC Medical Ethics*, 22(1), 1–5. DOI: 10.1186/s12910-021-00687-3 PMID: 34525993

Nafea, S. M., Siewe, F., & He, Y. (2019). A Novel Algorithm for Dynamic Student Profile Adaptation Based on Learning Styles. In *Advances in Intelligent Systems and Computing* (pp. 29–51). Springer International Publishing., DOI: 10.1007/978-3-030-29516-5_4

Najjar, N. A. (2015). Group modeling, recommendation and evaluation in collaborative filtering group-based recommender systems (Doctoral dissertation, The University of North Carolina at Charlotte).

Narvaez, D., & Lapsley, D. K. (2005). *Moral development, self and identity*. Lawrence Erlbaum Associates.

National Education Association. (2022). *Professional development in education: Essential practices and policies*. https://www.nea.org/sites/default/files/2022-07/Professional_Development_In_Education.pdf

Nation, I. S. P. (2001). *Learning Vocabulary in Another Language*. Cambridge University Press. DOI: 10.1017/CBO9781139524759

Ndhlovu, N. J., & Goosen, L. (2023). To What Extent Can Multidisciplinary Artificial Intelligence Applications Enhance Higher Education?: Open and Distance E-Learning in South Africa. In Chowdhary, C. (Ed.), *Multidisciplinary Applications of Deep Learning-Based Artificial Emotional Intelligence* (pp. 166–185). IGI Global., DOI: 10.4018/978-1-6684-5673-6.ch011

Ndhlovu-Nemaxwi, N. J., & Goosen, L. (2024). Advancing Student Employability Through Higher Education Using Artificial Intelligence (AI) Applications: Studying Open Distance E-Learning in South Africa. In Christiansen, B., & Even, A. (Eds.), *Prioritizing Skills Development for Student Employability* (pp. 120–141). IGI Global., DOI: 10.4018/979-8-3693-3571-0.ch005

Ng, D. T. K., Leung, J. K. L., Chu, S. K. W., & Qiao, M. S. (2021). Conceptualizing AI literacy: An exploratory review. *Computers and Education: Artificial Intelligence*, 2, 100041. DOI: 10.1016/j.caeai.2021.100041

Nghuulondo, P., & Goosen, L. (2023). Implications of Using Mobile Technologies in Higher Education Amidst the COVID-19 Pandemic: Accessing Teaching, Online Learning, and Assessment. In Meletiadou, E. (Ed.), *Handbook of Research on Implications of Sustainable Development in Higher Education* (pp. 167–182). IGI Global., DOI: 10.4018/978-1-6684-6172-3.ch008

Ng, O. L., & Cui, Z. (2021). Examining primary students' mathematical problem-solving in a programming context: Towards computationally enhanced mathematics education. *ZDM Mathematics Education*, 53(4), 847–860. DOI: 10.1007/s11858-020-01200-7

Ngugi, J. K., & Goosen, L. (2021). Innovation, Entrepreneurship, and Sustainability for ICT Students Towards the Post-COVID-19 Era. In Carvalho, L. C., Reis, L., & Silveira, C. (Eds.), *Handbook of Research on Entrepreneurship, Innovation, Sustainability, and ICTs in the Post-COVID-19 Era* (pp. 110–131). IGI Global., DOI: 10.4018/978-1-7998-6776-0.ch006

Nguyen, A., Ngo, H. N., Hong, Y., Dang, B., & Nguyen, B. P. (2023). Ethical principles for artificial intelligence in education. *Education and Information Technologies*, 28(4), 4221–4241. DOI: 10.1007/s10639-022-11316-w PMID: 36254344

Nielsen, J. (1999). *Designing web usability*. New Riders.

Nimbalagundi, S. M., Bagawan, A. S., & Katageri, C. S. (2024). Artificial Intelligence in Higher Education. *International Research Journal on Advanced Engineering and Management (IRJAEM), 2*(09).

Noble, S. U. (2018). *Algorithms of oppression: How search engines reinforce racism*. NYU Press. DOI: 10.18574/nyu/9781479833641.001.0001

Noll, R. G. (Ed.). (2021). *Regulatory policy and the social sciences*. University of California Press.

North, B. (2007). The CEFR illustrative descriptor scales. In Fox, J., Wesche, M., Bayliss, D., Cheng, L., Turner, C. E., & Doe, C. (Eds.), *Language Testing Reconsidered* (pp. 33–49). University of Ottawa Press.

Nucci, L. P., & Narvaez, D. (2008). *Manual of moral education and character*. Routledge.

O'Neil, C. (2016). *Weapons of math destruction: How big data increases inequality and threatens democracy*. Crown Publishing Group.

OCDE. (2019). «Fostering digital literacy and well-being.» *Educational Research and Innovation, Educating 21st Century Children*.

OCDE. (2020). *Curriculum Overload: A Way Forward*. Éditions OCDE.

OECD. (2021). *Skills for a Digital World*. OECD Publishing.

OECD. Publishing, & Organisation for Economic Co-operation and Development Staff. (2012). Literacy, numeracy and problem solving in technology-rich environments: Framework for the OECD survey of adult skills. OECD publishing.

Ollivier, C., Jeanneau, C., Hamel, M. J., & Caws, C. (2021). Citoyenneté numérique et didactique des langues, quels points de contacts?. Lidil. Revue de linguistique et de didactique des langues, (63).

Omar, O. (2018). Smart building, definitions, factors and selection evaluation criteria. *Alexandria Engineering Journal*, 57(4), 2903–2910. DOI: 10.1016/j.aej.2018.07.004

O'reilly, T. (2007). What is Web 2.0: Design patterns and business models for the next generation of software.

Oscarson, M. (1989). Self-Assessment of Language Proficiency: Rationale and Applications. *Language Testing*, 6(1), 1–13. DOI: 10.1177/026553228900600103

Ouakka, S., & El Alaoui, A. (2023). Towards a new Moroccan education system that is inclusive, regulatory and citizen-friendly. SHS Conference Web, 175, 01032. https://doi.org/DOI: 10.1051/shsconf/202317501032

Ouellet, S. (2019). Accompanying the literary experience through the reception and creation of multitexts: Comparison of two didactic devices. *Journal of Research in Multimodal Media Literacy*, 10. Advance online publication. DOI: 10.7202/1065531ar

Ouyang, F., & Jiao, P. (2021). Artificial intelligence in education: The three paradigms. *Computers and Education: Artificial Intelligence*, 2, 100020. Advance online publication. DOI: 10.1016/j.caeai.2021.100020

Ouyang, F., Wu, M., Zheng, L., Zhang, L., & Jiao, P. (2023). Integration of artificial intelligence performance prediction and learning analytics to improve student learning in online engineering courses. *International Journal of Educational Technology in Higher Education*, 20(1), 4. DOI: 10.1186/s41239-022-00372-4 PMID: 36683653

Ouyang, F., Zheng, L., & Jiao, P. (2022). Artificial intelligence in online higher education: A systematic review of empirical research from 2011 to 2020. *Education and Information Technologies*, 27(6), 7893–7925. DOI: 10.1007/s10639-022-10925-9

Owino, B. A., & Paschal, M. J. (2023). AI and Ethics in Education: Implications and Strategies for Responsible Implementation. In *Creative AI Tools and Ethical Implications in Teaching and Learning* (pp. 196-211). IGI Global.

Owoc, M. L., Sawicka, A., & Weichbroth, P. (2021). Artificial intelligence technologies in education. In *Benefits, challenges and strategies of implementation* (pp. 37–58). Artificial Intelligence for Knowledge Management., DOI: 10.1007/978-3-030-85001-2_4

Oxford english dictionary. (2023).

P21. *Framework for 21st Century Learning*. 2019. https://www.battelleforkids.org/networks/p21/frameworks-resources

Padmanabhan, S., & Kumar, A. (2021). AI in education: A review of the literature. *Education and Information Technologies*, 26(4), 4411–4431. DOI: 10.1007/s10639-021-10585-x

Page, M. J., McKenzie, J. E., Bossuyt, P. M., Boutron, I., Hoffmann, T. C., Mulrow, C. D., & Moher, D. (2021). The PRISMA 2020 statement: An updated guideline for reporting systematic reviews. *BMJ (Clinical Research Ed.)*, 372(1), 1–9. DOI: 10.1186/s13643-021-01626-4 PMID: 33782057

Paivandi, S. (2015). *Learn at university*. De Boeck.

Parsons, T. D. (2019). Neuroethics in educational technology: Keeping the brain in mind when developing frameworks for ethical decision-making. In *Mind, Brain and Technology: Learning in the Age of Emerging Technologies* (pp. 195-209). Springer.

Pashler, H., McDaniel, M., Rohrer, D., & Bjork, R. (2008). Learning styles: Concepts and evidence. *Psychological Science in the Public Interest*, 9(3), 105–119. DOI: 10.1111/j.1539-6053.2009.01038.x PMID: 26162104

Pasqualotto, A., Parong, J., Green, C. S., & Bavelier, D. (2023). Video game design for learning to learn. *International Journal of Human-Computer Interaction*, 39(11), 2211–2228. DOI: 10.1080/10447318.2022.2110684

Patrick, S., Kennedy, K., & Powell, A. (2013). *Mean what you say : Defining and integrating personalized, blended and competency education*. Vienna, VA: International Association for K-12 Online Learning.

Pawlikowska-Smith, G. (2000). *Canadian Language Benchmarks 2000: English as a Second Language for Adults*. Centre for Canadian Language Benchmarks.

Peleg, M., Shahar, Y., Quaglini, S., Broens, T., Budasu, R., Fung, N., & Lavrač, N. (2017). Assessment of a personalized and distributed patient guidance system. *International Journal of Medical Informatics*, 101, 108–130. DOI: 10.1016/j.ijmedinf.2017.02.010 PMID: 28347441

Pellerin, M. (2017). L'usage des technologies numériques pour le développement de compétences multimodales en littératie au 21 e siècle. *Education et Francophonie*, 45(2), 85–106. DOI: 10.7202/1043530ar

Peng, H., Ma, S., & Spector, J. M. (2019). *Personalized learning : An emerging pedagogical approach enabled by a smart learning environment*. Lecture Notes in Educational Technology., DOI: 10.1007/978-981-13-6908-7_24

Pennington, J., Socher, R., & Manning, C. D. (2014). *GloVe: Global vectors for word representation. Proceedings of the 2014 Conference on Empirical Methods in Natural Language Processing*, 1532–1543. DOI: 10.3115/v1/D14-1162

Pérez, J., Castro, M., & López, G. (2023). Serious games and ai: Challenges and opportunities for computational social science. *IEEE Access : Practical Innovations, Open Solutions*, 11, 62051–62061. DOI: 10.1109/ACCESS.2023.3286695

Perrenoud, P. (2015). Construire des compétences, est-ce tourner le dos aux savoirs?. Pédagogie collégiale Vol. 12, no 3, mars 1999, p. 14-17.

Perrotta, C. (2023). Advancing data justice in education: Some suggestions towards a deontological framework. *Learning, Media and Technology*, 48(2), 187–199. DOI: 10.1080/17439884.2022.2156536

Perry, B., & Lentz, D. (2020). A framework for digital literacy in higher education: Implications for practice. *Journal of Academic Librarianship*, 46(5), 102136. DOI: 10.1016/j.acalib.2020.102136

Phakiti, A., & Isaacs, T. (2021). Classroom assessment and validity: Psychometric and edumetric approaches. *EuropeanJournal of Applied Linguistics and TEFL*, 10(1), 3–24.

Piaget, J. (1967). *The psychology of intelligence*. Armand Colin.

Piaget, J. (1973). *To understand is to invent: The future of education*. Grossman.

Picciano, A. G. (2021). Theories and frameworks for online education: Seeking an integrated model. In *A guide to administering distance learning* (pp. 79–103). Brill. DOI: 10.1163/9789004471382_005

Pierre, R. (2003). Entre alphabétisation et littératie: Les enjeux didactiques. *Revue Française de Linguistique Appliquée*, 8(1), 121–137. DOI: 10.3917/rfla.081.0121

Piper, A. (2018). *Enumerations: data and literary study*. University of Chicago Press. DOI: 10.7208/chicago/9780226568898.001.0001

Platanios, E. A., & Kwiatkowski, T. (2020). *DeepPavlov: A conversational AI library*. arXiv preprint arXiv:2002.01503.

Popenici, S. A. D., & Kerr, S. (2020). Exploring the impact of artificial intelligence on teaching and learning in higher education. *Research and Practice in Technology Enhanced Learning*, 15(1), 1–12. DOI: 10.1186/s41039-019-0112-0 PMID: 30595727

Porayska-Pomsta, K., Holmes, W., & Nemorin, S. (2023). The ethics of AI in education. In *Handbook of Artificial Intelligence in Education* (pp. 571–604). Edward Elgar Publishing., https://www.elgaronline.com/edcollchap/book/9781800375413/book-part-9781800375413-38.xml DOI: 10.4337/9781800375413.00038

Potluri, R. M., & Vajjhala, N. R. (2018). A Study on Application of Web 3.0 Technologies in Small and Medium Enterprises of India. *The Journal of Asian Finance, Economics and Business*, 5(2), 73–79. DOI: 10.13106/jafeb.2018.vol5.no2.73

Poulopoulos, V., & Wallace, M. (2022). Digital technologies and the role of data in cultural heritage: The past, the present, and the future. *Big Data and Cognitive Computing*, 6(3), 73. DOI: 10.3390/bdcc6030073

Prairat, E. (2019). Values: A philosophical question, a pedagogical challenge. *Research & Works*, (94). Advance online publication. DOI: 10.4000/recherchestravaux.1563

Prasetiyo, W. H., Noor, B. M. N., Tan, B. P., & Sumardjoko, B. (2021). Digital citizenship trend in educational sphere: A systematic review. [IJERE]. *International Journal of Evaluation and Research in Education*, 10(4), 1192–1201. DOI: 10.11591/ijere.v10i4.21767

Pressey, S. L. (1926). A simple apparatus which gives tests and scores-and teaches. *Sch. & Soc*, 23, 373–376.

Prince, M. (2004). Does active learning work? A review of the research. *Journal of Engineering Education*, 93(3), 223–231. DOI: 10.1002/j.2168-9830.2004.tb00809.x

Probowati, Y. (2023). Fostering StudentsDigital Literacy In The Age Of The Internet In The Pandemic Era. KnE Social Sciences, 473-478.

Qin, C., Huang, W., & Hew, K. F. (2020, November). Using the Community of Inquiry Framework to develop an educational chatbot: Lesson learned from a mobile instant messaging learning environment. *Proceedings of the 28th international conference on computers in education. 1*, pp. 69-74. Asia-Pacific Society for Computers in Education. Retrieved from https://hub.hku.hk/handle/10722/306010

Radford, A., Narasimhan, K., Salimans, T., & Sutskever, I. (2019). *Language models are unsupervised multitask learners*. OpenAI Blog.

Raffel, C., Shinn, C., Roberts, A., Lee, S., & Narang, S. (2020). Exploring the limits of transfer learning with a unified text-to-text transformer. *Journal of Machine Learning Research*, 21, 1–67.

Raghavan, M., Barocas, S., Kleinberg, J., & Levy, K. (2020). Mitigating bias in algorithmic hiring: Evaluating claims and practices. Proceedings of the 2020 Conference on Fairness, Accountability, and Transparency, 469 481. DOI: 10.1145/3351095.3372828

Raghavendra, C. K., Srikantaiah, K. C., & Venugopal, K. R. (2018). Personalized recommendation systems (pres): A comprehensive study and research issues. *International Journal of Modern Education and Computer Science*, 10(10), 11. DOI: 10.5815/ijmecs.2018.10.02

Raji, I. D., Bender, E. M., Paullada, A., Denton, E., & Hanna, A. (2020). AI and the everything in the whole wide world benchmark: Accountability in data collection in the age of machine learning. arXiv preprint arXiv:2012.04580.

Raji, I. D., Smart, A., White, R. N., Mitchell, M., Gebru, T., Hutchinson, B., & Barnes, P. (2020, January). Closing the AI accountability gap: Defining an end-to-end framework for internal algorithmic auditing. *Proceedings of the conference on fairness, accountability, and transparency* (pp. 33-44). ACM. DOI: 10.1145/3351095.3372873

Ramsay, S. (2011). *Reading machines: towards an algorithmic critique*. University of Illinois Press. DOI: 10.5406/illinois/9780252036415.001.0001

Rane, N., Choudhary, S., & Rane, J. (2023). Education 4.0 and 5.0: Integrating artificial intelligence (AI) for personalized and adaptive learning. *Available atSSRN* 4638365. DOI: 10.2139/ssrn.4638365

Ranganathan, B. (2022). Deontology. In *Encyclopedia of Religious Ethics* (pp. 178–186). Wiley Online Library. DOI: 10.1002/9781118499528.ch22

Ransom, L. (2020). Blended learning: Pedagogy, technology, and integration. In McCarthy, E. E., & McCarthy, J. P. (Eds.), *The changing landscape of higher education* (pp. 123–145). Routledge.

Ravitch, S. M., & Riggan, M. (2016). *Reason & Rigor: how conceptual frameworks guide research* (2nd ed.). SAGE., Retrieved from https://uk.sagepub.com/en-gb/eur/reason-rigor/book241777

Rea-Dickins, P., & Gardner, S. (2000). Snares and Silver Bullets: Disentangling the Complexities of Classroom-Based Assessment. *Language Testing*, 17(2), 215–243. DOI: 10.1177/026553220001700206

Reddy, P., Sharma, B., & Chaudhary, K. (2021). Digital literacy: A review in the South Pacifc. *Journal of Computing in Higher Education.*

Reimers, N., & Gurevych, I. (2019). *Sentence-BERT: Sentence embeddings using Siamese BERT-networks*. arXiv preprint arXiv:1908.10084. DOI: 10.18653/v1/D19-1410

Reiser, R. A. (2013). Instructional technology : A history. Dans *Instructional technology* (pp. 11-48). (S.l.): Routledge.

Rejón-Guardia, F., Polo-Peña, A. I., & Maraver-Tarifa, G. (2020). The acceptance of a personal learning environment based on Google apps : The role of subjective norms and social image. *Journal of Computing in Higher Education*, 32(2), 203–233. DOI: 10.1007/s12528-019-09206-1

Rest, J. R., & Narvaez, D. (1994). *Moral Development in the Professions: Psychology and Applied Ethics*. Psychology Press. DOI: 10.4324/9781410601162

Riasati, M. J., & Ghorbani, M. (2023). Language learning in the age of AI: Opportunities and challenges. *Journal of Language and Linguistic Studies*, 19(1), 118–134. DOI: 10.17263/jlls.1000052

Ribble, M. (2011). *Digital citizenship in schools*. International Society for Technology in Education.

Richardson, J., & Milovidov, E. (2017). Digital citizenship education: Volume 2: Multi-stakeholder consultation report. Council of Europe.

Ríos Félix, J. M., Zatarain Cabada, R., Barrón Estrada, M. L., & Favela Vara, J. (2020). An intelligent learning environment for computational thinking. *Computación y Sistemas*, 24(3), 1199–1210. DOI: 10.13053/cys-24-3-3480

Roblyer, M. D., & Hughes, J. E. (2021). *Technology tools for teachers* (2nd ed.). Pearson.

Robson, C., & McCartan, K. (2016). *Real World Research* (4th ed.). Wiley., Retrieved from https://www.perlego.com/book/1485149/real-world-research-pdf

Rockeach, M. (1973). *The nature of human values*. The Free Press.

Rockwell, G., & Sinclair, S. (2016). *Hermeneutica: Computer-Aided Interpreting in the Humanities*. MIT Press. DOI: 10.7551/mitpress/9522.001.0001

Rodríguez Marín, P. A., Duque, N., & Ovalle, D. (2015). Multi-agent system for Knowledge-based recommendation of Learning Objects.

Rodríguez, M. L. (Ed.). (2023). *Bioethics of Displacement and Its Implications*. IGI Global., DOI: 10.4018/978-1-6684-4808-3

Roll, I., & Wylie, R. (2016). Evolution and revolution in artificial intelligence in education. *International Journal of Artificial Intelligence in Education*, 26(2), 582–599. DOI: 10.1007/s40593-016-0110-3

Romero, C., & Ventura, S. (2013). Educational data mining : A review of the state of the art. *IEEE Transactions on Systems, Man, and Cybernetics, Part C (Applications and Reviews, 42*(6), 601-618.

Romero, M., Aloui, H., Heiser, L., Galindo, L., & Lepage, A. (2021). Un bref parcours sur les ressources, pratiques et acteurs en IA et éducation (Doctoral dissertation, Université Côte d'Azur).

Romero, M., Heiser, L., & Lepage, A. (2023). *Enseigner et apprendre à l'ère de l'intelligence artificielle : Acculturation, intégration et usages créatifs de l'IA en éducation : livre blanc*. https://eduq.info/xmlui/handle/11515/38818

Romero, M., Heiser, L., & Lepage, A. (2023). Enseigner et apprendre à l'ère de l'intelligence artificielle: acculturation, intégration et usages créatifs de l'IA en éducation: livre blanc.

Romero-Ivanova, C., Kingsley, T., & Mason, L. (2019). Three conceptions of literacy: Media, narrative, and gaming literacies. *Literacy*, 10, 1–21.

Romero, M., Aloui, H., Heiser, L., Galindo, L., & Lepage, A. (2021). *Un bref parcours sur les ressources*. Manuscrit soumis pour publication. DOI: 10.13140/RG.2.2.18725.42728

Romero, M., Lameras, P., & Arnab, S. (2024). Affordances for AI-Enhanced Digital Game-Based Learning. In *Creative Applications of Artificial Intelligence in Education* (pp. 117–128). Springer Nature Switzerland. DOI: 10.1007/978-3-031-55272-4_9

Rosenshine, B. (2012). Principles of instruction: Research-based strategies that all teachers should know. *American Educator*, 36(1), 12–20.

Rossetti, S., Wang, H., & Venkatesh, S. (2020). *Turing-NLG: A 17-billion parameter language model by Microsoft*. Microsoft Research Blog.

Routledge. https://www.taylorfrancis.com/chapters/edit/10.4324/9781315736419-33

Ruiz-Rojas, L. I., Acosta-Vargas, P., De-Moreta-Llovet, J., & Gonzalez-Rodriguez, M. (2023). Empowering education with generative artificial intelligence tools: Approach with an instructional design matrix. *Sustainability (Basel)*, 15(15), 11524. DOI: 10.3390/su151511524

Russell, S. J. (2010). *Artificial intelligence a modern approach.* (S.l.): Pearson Education, Inc.

Russell, S., & Norvig, P. (2016). *Artificial Intelligence: A Modern Approach* (3rd ed.). Prentice Hall.

Russell, S., & Norvig, P. (2020). *Artificial intelligence : A modern approach.* Pearson.

Russel, S. (2010). *Artificial Intelligence : A Modern Approach* (Russell, S. J., & Norvig, P., Eds.).

Sabouret, N., & Assis, L. D. (2019). *Comprendre l'intelligence artificielle.* Editions Ellipses.

Sadler, D. R. (1989). Formative Assessment and the Design of Instructional Systems. *Instructional Science*, 18(2), 119–144. DOI: 10.1007/BF00117714

Sajja, R., Sermet, Y., Cikmaz, M., Cwiertny, D., & Demir, I. (2024). Artificial intelligence- enabled intelligent assistant for personalized and adaptive learning in higher education, *Artificial Intelligence and Games Science in Education*, 15(10), 596; **https://doi.org/10.3390/info15100596**

Salehi, M. (2013). Application of implicit and explicit attribute based collaborative filtering and BIDE for learning resource recommendation. *Data & Knowledge Engineering*, 87, 130–145. DOI: 10.1016/j.datak.2013.07.001

Sam, A. K., & Olbrich, P. (2023). The Need for AI Ethics in Higher Education. In Corrigan, C. C., Asakipaam, S. A., Kponyo, J. J., & Luetge, C. (Eds.), *AI Ethics in Higher Education: Insights from Africa and Beyond* (pp. 3–10). Springer International Publishing., DOI: 10.1007/978-3-031-23035-6_1

Sanh, V., Debut, L., Chaumond, J., & Wolf, T. (2019). *DistilBERT, a distilled version of BERT: Smaller, faster, cheaper and lighter*. arXiv preprint arXiv:1910.01108.

Sapci, A. H., & Sapci, H. A. (2020). Artificial intelligence education and tools for medical and health informatics students: Systematic review. *JMIR Medical Education*, 6(1), e19285. DOI: 10.2196/19285 PMID: 32602844

Sarmurzin, Y., Amanzhol, N., Toleubayeva, K., Zhunusova, M., & Amanova, A. (2021). The impact of OECD research on the education system of Kazakhstan. *Asia Pacific Education Review*, 22(4), 757–766. DOI: 10.1007/s12564-021-09715-8

Saygin, A. P., Cicekli, I., & Akman, V. (2000). Turing test : 50 years later. *Minds and Machines*, 10(4), 463–518. DOI: 10.1023/A:1011288000451

Schalkoff, R. I. (1990). *Artificial Intelligence : An Engineering Approach.* McGraw-Hill.

Schaller, J. (2023). AI-driven approaches to education: Emerging tools and strategies. *Journal of Educational Technology*, 18(2), 45–63.

Schechter, O., Durik, A. M., Miyamoto, Y., & Harackiewicz, J. M. (2011). The role of utility value in achievement behavior: The importance of culture. *Personality and Social Psychology Bulletin*, 37(3), 303–317. DOI: 10.1177/0146167210396380 PMID: 21262958

Schneuwly, B. (2020). Literacy–littératie–Literalität. Un essai. Forumlecture. ch, 2.

Scriven, M. (1967). The Methodology of Evaluation. In *Perspectives of Curriculum Evaluation*. Rand McNally.

Selbst, A. D. (2021). An institutional view of algorithmic impact assessments. *Harvard Journal of Law & Technology*, 35(1). https://jolt.law.harvard.edu/assets/articlePDFs/v35/Selbst-An-Institutional-View-of-Algorithmic-Impact-Assessments.pdf

Selwyn, N. (2016). *Is technology good for education?* John Wiley and Sons.

Selwyn, N. (2019). *Should robots replace teachers? AI and the future of education*. Polity Press.

Selwyn, N. (2019). What's the Problem with Learning Analytics? *Journal of Learning Analytics*, 6(3), 3. Advance online publication. DOI: 10.18608/jla.2019.63.3

Sennrich, R., Haddow, B., & Birch, A. (2016). *Neural machine translation of rare words with subword units. Proceedings of the 54th Annual Meeting of the Association for Computational Linguistics*, 1715-1725. DOI: 10.18653/v1/P16-1162

Sermet, Y., Demir, I., & Muste, M. (2020). A serious gaming framework for decision support on hydrological hazards. *The Science of the Total Environment*, 728, 138895. DOI: 10.1016/j.scitotenv.2020.138895 PMID: 32361365

Shanahan, T., & Shanahan, C. (2012). What is disciplinary literacy and why does it matter? *Topics in Language Disorders*, 32(1), 7–18. DOI: 10.1097/TLD.0b013e318244557a

Sharples, M., & Cooper, G. (2020). *Artificial Intelligence in Education: Promises and Implications for Teaching and Learning*. The OECD.

Shemshack, A., Kinshuk, , & Spector, J. M. (2021). A comprehensive analysis of personalized learning components. *Journal of Computers in Education*, 8(4), 485–503. DOI: 10.1007/s40692-021-00188-7

Shohamy, E. (2001). *The Power of Tests: A Critical Perspective on the Uses of Language Tests*. Pearson Education.

Shopova, T. (2014). DIGITAL LITERACY OF STUDENTS AND ITS IMPROVEMENT AT THE UNIVERSITY. *Journal on Efficiency and Responsibility in Education and Science*, 7(2), 26–32. DOI: 10.7160/eriesj.2014.070201

Siemens, G. (2021). Connectivism: A learning theory for the digital age. *International Journal of Instructional Technology and Distance Learning*, 2(1). http://www.itdl.org/Journal/Jan_05/article01.htm

Silapachote, P., & Srisuphab, A. (2017). Engineering courses on computational thinking through solving problems in artificial intelligence. *International Journal of Engineering Pedagogy*, 7(3), 34. DOI: 10.3991/ijep.v7i3.6951

Simataa, G. M., & Goosen, L. (2024). Reshaping Higher Education Institutions Within an Industry 4.0 Context: E-Learning Frameworks for Developing Countries. In Naidoo, V., & Verma, R. (Eds.), *Reshaping Entrepreneurial Education Within an Industry 4.0 Context* (pp. 142–165). IGI Global., DOI: 10.4018/979-8-3693-0409-9.ch008

Sinclair, S. and Rockwell, G. (2012). Text analysis and visualization as a means of teaching literature in a digital humanities context. *Digital Humanities Quarterly, 6*(2).

Skinner, B. F. (1963). Operant behavior. *The American Psychologist*, 18(8), 503–515. DOI: 10.1037/h0045185

Slattery, P., Saeri, A. K., Grundy, E. A., Graham, J., Noetel, M., Uuk, R., & Thompson, N. (2024). The AI Risk Repository: A Comprehensive Meta-Review, Database, and Taxonomy of Risks From Artificial Intelligence. doi:https://doi.org/DOI: 10.13140/RG.2.2.28850

Slote, M. (2001). *Morals from motives*. Oxford University Press. DOI: 10.1093/0195138376.001.0001

Smith, J. (2023). *Innovative Pedagogy in Artificial Intelligence Education*. Academic Press., DOI: 10.1234/abcde

Sohn, K., & Kwon, O. (2020). Technology acceptance theories and factors influencing artificial Intelligence-based intelligent products. *Telematics and Informatics*, 47, 101324. Advance online publication. DOI: 10.1016/j.tele.2019.101324

Son, J. B., Ružić, N. K., & Philpott, A. (2023). Artificial intelligence technologies and applications for language learning and teaching. Journal of China Computer-Assisted Language Learning, (0).

Spitmaan, M., & Leong, A. C. (2019). Theory of the intelligent act. https://doi.org/DOI: 10.31235/osf.io/g78mf

Stahl, B. C. (2021). *Artificial intelligence for a better future: an ecosystem perspective on the ethics of AI and emerging digital technologies*. Springer Nature. DOI: 10.1007/978-3-030-69978-9

Steck, H., Baltrunas, L., Elahi, E., Liang, D., Raimond, Y., & Basilico, J. (2021). Deep learning for recommender systems: A Netflix case study. *AI Magazine*, 42(3), 7–18. DOI: 10.1609/aimag.v42i3.18140

Steen, M., Sand, M., & Van de Poel, I. (2021). Virtue ethics for responsible innovation. *Business & Professional Ethics Journal*, 40(2), 243–268. DOI: 10.5840/bpej2021319108

Stenseke, J. (2023). Artificial virtuous agents: From theory to machine implementation. *AI & Society*, 38(4), 1301–1320. DOI: 10.1007/s00146-021-01325-7

Stenseke, J. (2024). Artificial virtuous agents in a multi-agent tragedy of the commons. *AI & Society*, 39(3), 855–872. DOI: 10.1007/s00146-022-01569-x

Stickler, U., & Hampel, R. (2015). Transforming Language Education Through Online Collaboration: New Pedagogical Perspectives. *Journal of Computer Assisted Learning*, 31(5), 481–492.

Stockless, A., Villeneuve, S., Bédard, L., Bisaillon, J., Tremblay, C., & Leduc, D. (2022). La Boussole numérique éducative: développement d'un outil d'autoévaluation des usages pédagogiques du numérique du personnel enseignant. Médiations et médiatisations-Revue internationale sur le numérique en éducation et communication, (12), 144-157.

Stufflebeam, D. L. (2001). Evaluation models. *New Directions for Evaluation*, 89(89), 7–98. DOI: 10.1002/ev.3

Stufflebeam, D. L., & Shinkfield, A. J. (2007). *Evaluation theory, models, and applications*. Jossey-Bass.

Su, C. (2023). The role of AI in enhancing student engagement in blended learning environments. *Educational Technology Research and Development*, 71(3), 327–348. DOI: 10.1007/s11423-022-10123-4

Sugumaran, K. M. D., Pandiyarajan V., Y. B S, Selvakumar P. and M. S, (2024). "Analysis of Electromyography Signals for Control of Mechanical Prosthesis using Machine Learning Techniques," 2024 2nd International Conference on Intelligent Data Communication Technologies and Internet of Things (IDCIoT), Bengaluru, India, 2024, pp. 1059-1067, DOI: 10.1109/IDCIoT59759.2024.10467707

Sun, T., Qiu, X., Xu, Y., & Huang, X. (2019). *ERNIE: Enhanced representation through knowledge integration*. arXiv preprint arXiv:1904.09223.

Sun, K. Y., Bai, X., Chen, S., Bao, S., Zhang, C., Kapoor, M., Backman, J., Joseph, T., Maxwell, E., Mitra, G., Gorovits, A., Mansfield, A., Boutkov, B., Gokhale, S., Habegger, L., Marcketta, A., Locke, A. E., Ganel, L., Hawes, A., & Balasubramanian, S. (2024). A deep catalogue of protein-coding variation in 983,578 individuals. *Nature*, 631(8021), 583–592. DOI: 10.1038/s41586-024-07556-0 PMID: 38768635

Syarifuddin, S., Setyosari, P., Sulton, S., Kuswandi, D., & Sartika, D. (2020). The effect of the community of inquiry (CoI) learning model and learning style towards social skills. *European Journal of Educational Research*, 9(2), 569–578. DOI: 10.12973/eu-jer.9.2.569

Taddeo, M., & Floridi, L. (2018). How AI can be a force for good. *Science*, 361(6404), 751–752. DOI: 10.1126/science.aat5991 PMID: 30139858

Tamim, R., Bernard, R., Borokhovski, E., Abrami, P. C., & Schmid, R. (2011). What forty years of research say about the impact of technology on learning. *Review of Educational Research*, 81(1), 4–28. DOI: 10.3102/0034654310393361

Tammy Lin, J. H., Wu, D. Y., & Bowman, N. (2023). Beat Saber as virtual reality exercising in 360 degrees: A moderated mediation model of VR playable angles on physiological and psychological outcomes. *Media Psychology*, 26(4), 414–435. DOI: 10.1080/15213269.2022.2154806

Tangen, D. (2019). Investigating the effects of blended learning on student engagement and learning outcomes in higher education. *Educational Media International*, 56(4), 241–257. DOI: 10.1080/09523987.2019.1712570

Taymanov, R., & Sapozhnikova, K. (2010). Terminology issues in the field of sensors and intelligent systems. *Key Engineering Materials*, 437, 434–438. . DOI: 10.4028/www.scientific.net/KEM.437.434

Terenzini, P. T., Springer, L., Yaeger, P. M., Pascarella, E. T., & Nora, A. (2001). First-generation college students: Characteristics, experiences, and cognitive development. *Research in Higher Education*, 42(1), 1–22. DOI: 10.1023/A:1018786610185

Tharp, R. G., & Gallimore, R. (2021). A theory of cultural genesis: A cultural-historical approach to education. *New Directions for Child and Adolescent Development*, 2021(172), 73–84. DOI: 10.1002/cad.20404

The 2020 Yearbook of the Digital Ethics Lab | SpringerLink. (s. d.). Consulté 12 décembre 2024, à l'adresse https://link.springer.com/book/10.1007/978-3-030-80083-3

The evolution of Information and Communication Technologies.: Co-construction with uses. - Scientific Figure on ResearchGate. Available from: https://www.researchgate.net/figure/Positionnement-multidimensionnel-des-usages-des-TIC_fig1_322555760 [accessed 24 Mar, 2024]

Thomas, J. W. (2000). *A Review of Research on Project-Based Learning.*

Thurlow, C., Lengel, L., & Tomic, A. (2004). Computer mediated communication: Social interaction and the Internet. *Sage (Atlanta, Ga.).*

Tijus, C. (2024). Après-propos. L'intelligence artificielle : Une autre intelligence? *Enfance*, 1(1), 51–60. DOI: 10.3917/enf2.241.0051

Tinto, V. (2012). *Completing college: Rethinking institutional action.* University of Chicago Press. DOI: 10.7208/chicago/9780226804545.001.0001

Toh, W., & Lim, F. V. (2021). Using video games for learning: Developing a metalanguage for digital play. *Games and Culture*, 16(5), 583–610. DOI: 10.1177/1555412020921339

Tolks, D., Schmidt, J. J., & Kuhn, S. (2024). The role of AI in serious games and gamification for health: Scoping review. *JMIR Serious Games*, 12(1), e48258. DOI: 10.2196/48258 PMID: 38224472

Tomlinson, C. A. (2001). *How to Differentiate Instruction in Mixed-Ability Classrooms*. ASCD.

Toward Causal Representation Learning | IEEE Journals & Magazine | IEEE Xplore. (s. d.). Consulté 12 décembre 2024, à l'adresse https://ieeexplore.ieee.org/abstract/document/9363924

Tran, T. N., & Tran, H. P. (2023). Exploring the role of ChatGPT in developing critical digital literacies in language learning: a qualitative study. *Proceedings of the AsiaCALL International Conference* (Vol. 4), 1-17. DOI: 10.54855/paic.2341

Tricot, A., Sahut, G., & Lemarié, J. (2016). *The document: communication and memory*. De Boeck Supérieur.

TRUMBULL. (2000). *E. and B. FARR, Grading and Reporting Student Progress in an Age of Standards*. Christopher-Gordon.

Tsai, Y., & Chai, C. S. (2021). The role of teachers in blended learning: Insights from a longitudinal study. *Journal of Educational Technology & Society*, 24(1), 13–27.

Turgeon, W., & Anderson, M. (2019). Ethics and Artificial Intelligence: Teaching and Learning in Higher Education. In *Research Manual on Learning in the Age of Transhumanism*. IGI Global.

Turing, A. (1950). Computing Machine and Intelligence. *Mind*, •••, LIX.

Turing, A. (1950). Computing Machinery and Intelligence'. *Mind*, 59(236), 433–460. DOI: 10.1093/mind/LIX.236.433

Uden, L., & Ching, G. S. (2024). Activity Theory-based Ecosystem for Artificial Intelligence in Education (AIED). *International Journal of Research*, 13(5), 41–54.

Ukobitz, D. V., & Faullant, R. (2022). The relative impact of isomorphic pressures on the adoption of radical technology: Evidence from 3D printing. *Technovation*, 113, 102418. Advance online publication. DOI: 10.1016/j.technovation.2021.102418

Ullah, M., Amin, S. U., Munsif, M., Yamin, M. M., Safaev, U., Khan, H., Khan, S., & Ullah, H. (2022). Serious games in science education: A systematic literature. *Virtual Reality & Intelligent Hardware*, 4(3), 189–209. DOI: 10.1016/j.vrih.2022.02.001

Underwood, T. (2019). *Distant Horizons: Digital Evidence and Literary Change*. University of Chicago Press. DOI: 10.7208/chicago/9780226612973.001.0001

UNESCO. (2017). «Accountability in education: meeting our commitments; Global education monitoring report, 2017/8..

UNESCO. (2021). *Artificial Intelligence in Education: Challenges and Opportunities for Sustainable Development.*

United Nations Educational, Scientific and Cultural Organisation (UNESCO). (2022). *Windhoek statement on Artificial Intelligence in Southern Africa*. UNESCO.

Uunona, G. N., & Goosen, L. (2023). Leveraging Ethical Standards in Artificial Intelligence Technologies: A Guideline for Responsible Teaching and Learning Applications. In Garcia, M., Lopez Cabrera, M., & de Almeida, R. (Eds.), *Handbook of Research on Instructional Technologies in Health Education and Allied Disciplines* (pp. 310–330). IGI Global., DOI: 10.4018/978-1-6684-7164-7.ch014

Uunona, G. N., & Goosen, L. (2024). Leveraging Ethics in Artificial Intelligence Technologies and Applications: E-Learning Management Systems in Namibia. In Ortiz-Rodriguez, F., Leyva-Mederos, A., Tiwari, S., Hernandez-Quintana, A., & Martinez-Rodriguez, J. (Eds.), *Semantic Web Technologies and Applications in Artificial Intelligence of Things* (pp. 173–185). IGI Global., DOI: 10.4018/979-8-3693-1487-6.ch008

Valadez, S. C. O., Mendoza, J. C. H., Villanueva-Hernandez, V., Tijerina, G., & Avila-Guzman, D. (2024). Languages With Artificial Intelligence Applications. In *Exploring Intersectionality and Women in STEM* (pp. 192–201). IGI Global. DOI: 10.4018/979-8-3693-1119-6.ch010

Vallor, S. (2016). *Technology and the virtues: A philosophical guide to a future worth wanting*. Oxford University Press. DOI: 10.1093/acprof:oso/9780190498511.001.0001

Van den Broucke, S. (2017). La littératie en santé: un concept critique pour la santé publique. La santé en action, 440, 11-13.

van Deursen, A. J., & van Dijk, J. A. (2014). The digital divide shifts to differences in usage. *New Media & Society*, 16(3), 507–526. DOI: 10.1177/1461444813487959

van Gaalen, A. E., Brouwer, J., Schönrock-Adema, J., Bouwkamp-Timmer, T., Jaarsma, A. D. C., & Georgiadis, J. R. (2021). Gamification of health professions education: A systematic review. *Advances in Health Sciences Education : Theory and Practice*, 26(2), 683–711. DOI: 10.1007/s10459-020-10000-3 PMID: 33128662

VanLehn, K. (2006). The Behavior of Tutoring Systems. *International Journal of Artificial Intelligence in Education*, 16, •••.

VanLehn, K. (2011). The relative effectiveness of human tutoring, intelligent tutoring systems, and other tutoring systems. *Educational Psychologist*, 46(4), 197–221. DOI: 10.1080/00461520.2011.611369

Venkatesan, M., & Thangadurai, K. (2017). History and overview of the recommender systems. In *Collaborative Filtering Using Data Mining and Analysis* (pp. 74–99). IGI Global.

Vermeir, J. F., White, M. J., Johnson, D., Crombez, G., & Van Ryckeghem, D. M. (2020). The effects of gamification on computerized cognitive training: Systematic review and meta-analysis. *JMIR Serious Games*, 8(3), e18644. DOI: 10.2196/18644 PMID: 32773374

Vermersch, P. (2004). Help with explanation and reflective feedback. *Continuity in Education*, 160(3).

Vial, M. (2012). *Finding your way around the evaluation models*. De Boeck.

Vijayakumar, G., Rajkumar, M., Rajiv Chandar, N., Selvakumar, P., & Duraisamy, R. (2024). Muniyandi Rajkumar, Rajiv Chandar N, Selvakumar P and Ramesh Duraisamy, (2024). Environmentally friendly TDS removal from waste water by electrochemical ion exchange batch-type recirculation (EIR) technique. *Environmental Science. Water Research & Technology*, 10(4), 826–835. DOI: 10.1039/D3EW00793F

Voogt, J., Fisser, P., Good, J., Mishra, P., & Yadav, A. (2015). Computational thinking in compulsory education: Towards an agenda for research and practice. *Education and Information Technologies*, 20(4), 715–728. DOI: 10.1007/s10639-015-9412-6

Vorecol Learning. (n.d.). *Innovations in Learning Management Systems.*

Vuong, Q.-H., Vinh, L. A., & Trung, T. (2021). *Academic Contributions to the UNESCO 2019 Forum on Education for Sustainable Development and Global Citizenship*. MDPI.

Vygotsky, L. S. (1978). *Mind in society: The development of higher psychological processes*. Harvard University Press.

Vygotsky, L. S., Johnson, M., & Smith, R. (2020). Personalized Learning: Enhancing Student Engagement and Academic Achievement. *Journal of Educational Psychology*, 45(3), 321–337.

Waladi, C., Khaldi, M., & Sefian, M. L. (2023). Machine Learning Approach for an Adaptive E-Learning System Based on Kolb Learning Styles. *International Journal of Emerging Technologies in Learning*, 18(12), 4–15. DOI: 10.3991/ijet.v18i12.39327

Waladi, C., Lamarti, S. M., Khaldi, M., Khaldi, M., & Boudra, S. (2024, February). KNN Classification of Kolb Learning Styles: A Comparative Study on Balanced and Unbalanced Datasets. *Proceedings of the E-Learning and Smart Engineering Systems (ELSES 2023)* (pp. 43-49). Atlantis Press. DOI: 10.2991/978-94-6463-360-3_6

Walczak, K., & Cellary, W. (2023). Challenges for higher education in the era of widespread access to Generative AI. *Economics and Business Review*, 9(2), 71–100. DOI: 10.18559/ebr.2023.2.743

Wall, D. (1997). Impact and Washback in Language Testing. In Clapham, C., & Corson, D. (Eds.), *The Encyclopedia of Language and Education*. Kluwer Academic Publishers. DOI: 10.1007/978-1-4020-4489-2_26

Wang, C., & Huang, L. (2021). A Systematic Review of Serious Games for Collaborative Learning: Theoretical Framework, Game Mechanic and Efficiency Assessment. *International Journal of Emerging Technologies in Learning*, 16(6), 88. DOI: 10.3991/ijet.v16i06.18495

Wang, M., & Li, L. (2022). Exploring the role of technology in the evolution of language learning. *Language Learning & Technology*, 26(1), 3–17.

Wang, X., Pang, H., Wallace, M. P., Wang, Q., & Chen, W. (2022). Learners' perceived AI presences in AI-supported language learning: A study of AI as a humanized agent from community of inquiry. *Computer Assisted Language Learning*, 37(4), 814–840. DOI: 10.1080/09588221.2022.2056203

Wang, Y., Wang, Z., Liu, G., Wang, Z., Wang, Q., Yan, Y., Wang, J., Zhu, Y., Gao, W., Kan, X., Zhang, Z., Jia, L., & Pang, X. (2022). Application of serious games in health care: Scoping review and bibliometric analysis. *Frontiers in Public Health*, 10, 896974. DOI: 10.3389/fpubh.2022.896974 PMID: 35757619

Weiner, S. A. (2011). Information literacy and the workforce: A review. *Education Libraries*.

Weintrop, D., Beheshti, E., Horn, M., Orton, K., Jona, K., Trouille, L., & Wilensky, U. (2016). Defining computational thinking for mathematics and science classrooms. *Journal of Science Education and Technology*, 25(1), 127–147. DOI: 10.1007/s10956-015-9581-5

Weir, C. J. (2005). *Language Testing and Validation: An Evidence-Based Approach*. Palgrave Macmillan. DOI: 10.1057/9780230514577

Weiss, C. H. (1995). Nothing as practical as good theory: Exploring theory-based evaluation for comprehensive community initiatives for children and families. New Approaches to Evaluating Community Initiatives: Concepts, Methods, and Contexts, 65-92.

Weiss, C. H. (1998). *Evaluation: Methods for studying programs and policies*. Prentice Hall.

Weller, A. (2019). Transparency: Motivations and challenges. In T. Hagras (Ed.), Explainable AI: Interpreting, explaining and visualizing deep learning (pp. 23 40). Springer.

Weller, M. (2021). 25 years of Ed Tech: The future of technology-enhanced learning. *Research in Learning Technology*, 29. Advance online publication. DOI: 10.25304/rlt.v29.2440

Weng, X., Cui, Z., Ng, O. L., Jong, M. S., & Chiu, T. K. (2022). Characterizing students' 4C skills development during problem-based digital making. *Journal of Science Education and Technology*, 31(3), 372–385. DOI: 10.1007/s10956-022-09961-4

Weng, X., Ng, O. L., & Chiu, T. K. (2023). Competency development of pre-service teachers during video-based learning: A systematic literature review and meta-analysis. *Computers & Education*, 199, 104790. Advance online publication. DOI: 10.1016/j.compedu.2023.104790

Westera, W., Prada, R., Mascarenhas, S., Santos, P. A., Dias, J., Guimarães, M., Georgiadis, K., Nyamsuren, E., Bahreini, K., Yumak, Z., Christyowidiasmoro, C., Dascalu, M., Gutu-Robu, G., & Ruseti, S. (2020). Artificial intelligence moving serious gaming: Presenting reusable game AI components. *Education and Information Technologies*, 25(1), 351–380. DOI: 10.1007/s10639-019-09968-2

Whittaker, M., Crawford, K., Dobbe, R., Fried, G., Kaziunas, E., Mathur, V., & Schwartz, O. (2018). *AI now report 2018*. AI Now Institute.

Wilkens, M. (2020). *The Social Life of Literary Data*. Association of Modern Languages.

Williams, R., & Clark, D. (2018). The evolving nature of learner characteristics. *The Journal of Educational Research*, 92(2), 123–135.

Willis, D., & Willis, J. (2007). *Doing Task-based Teaching*. Oxford University Press.

Winne, P. H., & Baker, R. S. (2013). The potentials of educational data mining for researching metacognition, motivation and self-regulated learning. *Journal of Educational Data Mining*, 5(1), 1–8.

Without Love, A. M. (2020). Pedagogy, digital media and the culture of values in the post-digital era. *Technology, Pedagogy and Education*, 29(1), 23–38.

Woll, C. (2024, Sep 5). *Regulation*. Retrieved from Encyclopedia Britannica: https://www.britannica.com/topic/regulation

Woolf, B. P. (2009). *Building Smart Interactive Tutors: Student-Centered Strategies to Revolutionize Online Learning*. Morgan Kaufmann.

Woolf, B. P. (2010). *Building intelligent interactive tutors: Student-centered strategies for revolutionizing e-learning*. Morgan Kaufmann.

Wu, W., Zhang, B., Li, S., & Liu, H. (2022). Exploring factors of the willingness to accept AI-assisted learning environments: An empirical investigation based on the UTAUT model and perceived risk theory. *Frontiers in Psychology*, 13, 870777. Advance online publication. DOI: 10.3389/fpsyg.2022.870777 PMID: 35814061

Xie, Q., Gao, X., & King, R. B. (2013). Thinking styles in implicit and explicit learning. *Learning and Individual Differences*, 23, 267–271. DOI: 10.1016/j.lindif.2012.10.014

Xu, D., & Tian, Y. (2015). A Comprehensive Survey of Clustering Algorithms. *Annals of Data Science*, 2(2), 165–193. DOI: 10.1007/s40745-015-0040-1

Xu, R., & Wunsch, I. I. D.II. (2000). Survey of clustering algorithms. *IEEE Transactions on Neural Networks*, 16(3), 645–678. DOI: 10.1109/TNN.2005.845141 PMID: 15940994

Xu, Z. (2024). AI in education: Enhancing learning experiences and student outcomes. *Applied and Computational Engineering*, 51(1), 104–111. DOI: 10.54254/2755-2721/51/20241187

Yang, Z., Dai, Z., Yang, Y., Carbonell, J., Salakhutdinov, R., & Le, Q. V. (2019). XLNet: Generalized autoregressive pretraining for language understanding. *Advances in Neural Information Processing Systems*, 32.

Yan, L., Talic, S., Wild, H., Gasevic, D., Gasević, D., Ilic, D., Deppeler, J., Corrigan, D., Martinez-Maldonado, R., & Trauer, J. (2022, October 01). (s. d.). Transmission of SARS-CoV-2 in a primary school setting with and without public health measures using real-world contact data : A modelling study. *Journal of Global Health*, 12, 05034. DOI: 10.7189/jogh.12.05034 PMID: 36181503

Ye, H., Liang, B., Ng, O. L., & Chai, C. S. (2023). Integration of computational thinking in K-12 mathematics education: A systematic review on CT-based mathematics instruction and student learning. *International Journal of STEM Education*, 10(1), 1–26. DOI: 10.1186/s40594-023-00396-w

Yenduri, G., Ramalingam, M., Selvi, G. C., Supriya, Y., Srivastava, G., Maddikunta, P. K. R., Raj, G. D., Jhaveri, R. H., Prabadevi, B., Wang, W., Vasilakos, A. V., & Gadekallu, T. R. (2024). Gpt (generative pre-trained transformer)–a comprehensive review on enabling technologies, potential applications, emerging challenges, and future directions. *IEEE Access : Practical Innovations, Open Solutions*, 12, 54608–54649. DOI: 10.1109/ACCESS.2024.3389497

Youssef, É., & Audran, J. (2019). La personnalisation de l'apprentissage vue comme facteur effectif d'innovation pédagogique. *Spiral-E Revue de recherches en éducation supplément électronique, N°, 63*(1), 157. DOI: 10.3917/spir.063.0157

Yo, X. (2021). Najmiddinova. «Digital Mathematical Literacy As A Component Of The Life Skills Of Students Of Modern Educational Institutions.». *The American Journal of Social Science and Education Innovations*, 3(1), 378–384. DOI: 10.37547/tajssei/Volume03Issue01-71

Yu, Z., Gao, M., & Wang, L. (2021). The effect of educational games on learning outcomes, student motivation, engagement and satisfaction. *Journal of Educational Computing Research*, 59(3), 522–546. DOI: 10.1177/0735633120969214

Zawacki-Richter, O., Marín, V. I., Bond, M., & Gouverneur, F. (2019). Systematic review of research on artificial intelligence applications in higher education–where are the educators? *International Journal of Educational Technology in Higher Education*, 16(1), 1–27. DOI: 10.1186/s41239-019-0171-0

Zawacki-Richter, O., Marz, K., & Dron, J. (2020). Systematic review of research on artificial intelligence applications in higher education: Challenges and future directions. *International Journal of Educational Technology in Higher Education*, 17(1), 1–34. DOI: 10.1186/s41239-020-00216-y

Zeng, D. (2013). From computational thinking to AI thinking [A letter from the editor]. *IEEE Intelligent Systems*, 28(06), 2–4. DOI: 10.1109/MIS.2013.141

Zhang, M., & Fabus, M. (2022). Abilities of Current Artificial Intelligence Systems to Learn Social Skills. Retrieved from https://osf.io/preprints/psyarxiv/r3ktj/ DOI: 10.31234/osf.io/r3ktj

Zhang, R., & Lee, H. (2022). The impact of AI writing tools on university-level language learners: A longitudinal study. *Computers & Education*, 185, 104557. DOI: 10.1016/j.compedu.2022.104557

Zhang, T., Ramakrishnan, R., & Livny, M. (1996). BIRCH: An efficient data clustering method for very large databases. *SIGMOD Record*, 25(2), 103–114. DOI: 10.1145/235968.233324

Zhang, Y., Brady, M., & Smith, S. (2001). Segmentation of brain MR images through a hidden Markov random field model and the expectation-maximization algorithm. *IEEE Transactions on Medical Imaging*, 20(1), 45–57. DOI: 10.1109/42.906424 PMID: 11293691

Zhan, Z., Tong, Y., Lan, X., & Zhong, B. (2024). A systematic literature review of game-based learning in Artificial Intelligence education. *Interactive Learning Environments*, 32(3), 1137–1158. DOI: 10.1080/10494820.2022.2115077

Zhou, Y., Yang, H., & Hu, Z. (2011). A review of building energy regulation and policy for energy conservation and emission reduction in China. *Renewable & Sustainable Energy Reviews*, 15(9), 4785–4792.

Zouinar, M. (2020). Évolutions de l'Intelligence Artificielle : Quels enjeux pour l'activité humaine et la relation Humain-Machine au travail? *Activités (Vitry-sur-Seine)*, 17(1), 17–1. DOI: 10.4000/activites.4941

Zuboff, S. (2019). *The age of surveillance capitalism: The fight for a human future at the new frontier of power*. PublicAffairs.

About the Contributors

Mohamed Khaldi is a Full Professor in the Department of Mathematics and Computer Science at the Ecole Normale Supérieure of Tetouan, affiliated with Abdelmalek Essaâdi University, Morocco. He earned his doctorate in 2001 from the Faculty of Sciences, Ben M'Sik, Morocco. Pr. Khaldi is a researcher and educator specializing in e-learning and ICTE. His work explores pedagogical innovations through the integration of digital technologies in higher education. With several decades of academic and scientific experience, Professor Mohamed Khaldi has established himself as a leading authority on integrating digital technologies into education. Through his research, teaching, and collaborations, he contributes to shaping a more modern, inclusive, and future-ready education system for the 21st century.

***

Omar Abdennour is a PhD student of Computer Science and University Pedagogical, mathematics teacher at the regional center for education and training professions, Tanger Tetouan, Al Hoce¨ıma Morocco. Engineering, he is currently with S2IPU, Abdelmalek Essaadi University, Tetouan, Normal School Superior, Tetouan, Morocco,

Lamya Anoir: Is a Doctor in Computer sciences, and member of Research team in Computer Science and University Pedagogical Engineering Higher Normal School, Abdelmalek Essaadi University, Tetouan, Morocco. She has a Master degree in Instructional design Multimedia engineering at Higher Normal School of Martil, Morocco in 2019. The current research focuses on: Personnalized E-learning, Adaptive Hypermedia Systems, Artificial Intelligence. (E-mail: lamya.anoir@uae.ac.ma)

Azirar chafik, Lecturer at Abdelmalek Essaadi University of Tetouan, ENS of Martil, Holder of a Doctorate in French Language and Literature entitled: Giono's aesthetics, from the sublime to the tragic, requested for expert work in literature and didactics and Author of research work in literature and didactics on a national and international scale, working on modern poetry and Maghreb literature in French among other research work.

Mohamed benfarha researcher in a research team in Computer Science and University Teaching Engineering, Applied Mathematics and Computer Science (AMCS), Laboratory of Applied Sciences and Didactics (LASAD) Ecole Normale Supérieure de Tétouan, Abdelmalek Essaadi University, Morocco

Ikram Chelliq: Is a PhD candidate in Computer sciences, and member of Research team in Computer Science and University Pedagogical Engineering Higher Normal School, Abdelmalek Essaadi University, Tetouan, Morocco. She has a Master degree in Instructional design Multimedia engineering at Higher Normal School of Martil, Morocco in 2020. The current research focuses on: Pedagogical Object, Adaptive Hypermedia Systems, Artificial Intelligence.

Erradi Mohamed is a professor at Higher Normal School Tetouan, and Head of the Research team of Computer Science and University Pedagogical Engineering Higher Normal School, Abdelmalek Essaadi University, Tetouan, Morocco. Professor Erradi has published more than 200 papers in international conferences and journals. He has organized and chaired six international scientific events and has been a member of the program committee of multiple international conferences. His areas of interest include Artificial Intelligence, Pedagogical approach, Assessment methods, Andragogy, Collaboration, Personalization and E-learning. He gives training to undergraduate, postgraduate students and guides research scholars in these areas: E-learning, Andragogy, Collaboration, Personalization, Pedagogical Objects, Adaptive learning, Educational technologies .

Leila Goosen is a full professor in the Department of Science and Technology Education of the University of South Africa. She holds a C2 rating via the South African National Research Foundation. Prof. Goosen was an Associate Professor in the School of Computing, and the module leader and head designer of the fully online signature module for the College for Science, Engineering and Technology, rolled out to over 92,000 registered students since the first semester of 2013. Previously, she was a Deputy Director at the South African national Department of Education. Her research interests have included cooperative work in IT, effective teaching and learning of programming and teacher professional development.

Hassane Kemouss is a PhD student of Computer Science and University Pedagogical Engineering, engineering science teacher at technical high school, he is currently with S2IPU, Abdelmalek Essaadi University, Tetouan, Normal School Superior, Tetouan, Morocco.

Lakshmi Prasanna, Professor of English, With an illustrious academic career spanning 33 years, Dr. Lakshmi Prasanna is a distinguished Professor of English. Her academic expertise encompasses a broad spectrum of subjects, and she has authored five books and presented 54 research papers. A sought-after speaker, Dr. Prasanna has presented her research papers at numerous national and international conferences. She has also been invited as a guest lecturer at the university level, sharing her knowledge with a wider audience. Notably, Dr. Prasanna has had the opportunity to visit the University of Singapore, further enriching her academic experience.

P. Selvakumar is currently an Associate Professor in the Department of Science and Humanities at Nehru Institute of Technology, Coimbatore, Tamil Nadu, India. Since 2023, he has served as the Department IQAC Coordinator at the institute. Dr.P. Selvakumar's academic and research interests lie primarily in the field of phytochemistry. He has made significant contributions to his field, with an impressive record that includes 30 journal publications, 12 patents, and 20 conference papers. Throughout his career, Dr. P.Selvakumar has been recognized for his dedication and excellence in teaching, having been honored with several awards, including the Best Teacher Awards. He holds a prominent position in the academic community, contributing actively to research.

S. Tamizharasu is an Assistant Professor in the Department of Computer Science and Engineering at Hindusthan Institute of Technology, Coimbatore. With a strong academic and research background, he specializes in Mobile Adhoc Networks, Artificial Intelligence, Machine Learning, Software Testing. Dedicated to excellence in teaching and innovation, Dr.S. Tamizharasu actively contributes to academic development and fosters a learning environment that encourages practical and theoretical expertise among students.

Saidy Hamza is a doctoral student in educational sciences, driven by deep reflection on values and their transmission in the field of training. Through his research, he is committed to enriching the educational approach by highlighting the importance of education imbued with values, promoting not only the acquisition of technical skills but also the personal and ethical development of learners. Passionate about new online learning methods, he aspires to create a training framework that combines pragmatism and values, with the aim of training enlightened and responsible agents of change.

Mohammed sefian Professor of Higher Education in the Mathematics and Computer Science Department at the Higher Normal School of Tétouan, Abdelmalek Essaadi University. Since 2017, he has been coordinator of the Specialised Masters in Mathematics for Teaching. He obtained his doctorate in Mathematics from the Rabat Mohammadia School of Engineering in 2014. In 2020, he was awarded academic accreditation by the Tetouan Faculty of Science, Morocco.

Kamlesh Singh is a highly accomplished professional with over 15 years of distinguished experience spanning academia, research and development, industry consultation, and collaborative projects. His expertise intersects Mechanical Engineering, Automation & Robotics, and Artificial Intelligence, where he has consistently delivered groundbreaking contributions and achieved significant milestones. Dr. Singh completed his Ph.D. in Mechanical Engineering from Annamalai University, Chidambaram, Tamil Nadu. He is the esteemed author of three internationally recognized books on Artificial Intelligence and Industrial Robotics and serves as an internal expert for NBA, NAAC, UGC, and AICTE, where he plays a pivotal role in enhancing educational standards nationally. As a respected examiner across universities, Dr. Singh shapes programs in Mechanical Engineering, Mechatronics, Automation & Robotics, CAD/CAM, and Computer Science. His commitment to nurturing talent and advancing academic discourse is evident in his meticulous approach to teaching and examination.

Gabriel Neepo Uunona is a teacher by profession, having taught secondary Mathematics and Computer studies. He has held the positions of Senior Education Officer for ICT as well as for Research and Development in the Ministry of Education in Namibia. He is currently coordinating Learning design at the University of Namibia. Gabriel holds a postgraduate diploma in ICT Development and Knowledge Society from Dublin City University, as well as a MSc in Leadership Development in ICT and the knowledge Society from the University of Mauritius. He is currently pursing a Doctorate degree in Educational Technologies at the University of South Africa. Gabriel is a Science, Technology, and Innovation research enthusiast. He is an emerging scholar in educational technologies and open education. His current research focus has been on Artificial Intelligence in Education.

Index

A

B

M

P

R

S

www.ingramcontent.com/pod-product-compliance
Lightning Source LLC
LaVergne TN
LVHW062108300926
849161LV00010B/2400
* 9 7 9 8 3 6 9 3 8 9 6 5 2 *